THE ADMINISTRATION OF
BRITISH FOREIGN POLICY
1782–1846

THE ADMINISTRATION OF BRITISH FOREIGN POLICY 1782–1846

Charles Ronald Middleton

Duke University Press
Durham, N.C.
1977

© 1977, Charles Ronald Middleton
L.C.C. card no. 76–51017
I.S.B.N. 0–8223–0383–3
Printed in the United
States of America

Contents

Preface   vii

I. The Conduct of Foreign Policy: 1782–1846   3

II. The Cabinet and Foreign Policy   42

III. The Sovereign and Foreign Policy   66

IV. The Secretaries of State   96

V. The Undersecretaries of State   123

VI. The Foreign Office Establishment: 1782–1821   151

VII. The Foreign Office Establishment: 1821–1846   177

VIII. The Diplomatic Service: 1812–1850   214

IX. The Consular Service   244

X. Conclusion   254

Appendix I. The Personnel of the Foreign Office: 1782–1846   260

Appendix II. Office Divisions Directed by the Undersecretaries of State   321

Appendix III. ("Regulations for Agents . . .")   325

Appendix IV. ("Scale of the Establishment . . .")   326

Appendix V. The Emoluments of the Foreign Service   327

Appendix VI. List of His Majesty's Consuls General and Consuls, August, 1828   330

Appendix VII. Consuls Prohibited from Trading after 1832   332

Appendix VIII. The Foreign Secret Service   333

Select Bibliography   340

Index   354

83-5874

PREFACE

This is an administrative history in the broadest sense of the term. It deals with the institutions which at the turn of the nineteenth century and for nearly fifty years thereafter were in some way involved with the formulation and implementation of British foreign policy. The focus is on the operation and organization of these institutions in the realm of foreign affairs during the period between 1782 and 1846. It is concerned not so much with policy as such as it is with the manner in which policy was determined and implemented, and with the roles played by monarchs, ministers, and bureaucrats in this process. For this reason the reader who looks to find a history of the evolution of British foreign policy in this period will be disappointed. But for those concerned with the organization of the machinery of diplomacy and with the men who operated it the material will be grist in their mill.

The period after 1782 was replete with constitutional and political development. Changes in demography, the growth of industrialism, the wars with France, and Britain's emergence as an international power had profound repercussions on the decision-making process. The development of political parties and of the cabinet in a more modern form, and the creation of new loci of power in British society and politics required alterations in the nature and theory of government and of administration. In the area of foreign affairs administration all of these trends had an impact which lends unity to the apparent diversity of the institutions involved.

History is a process, albeit a disordered one. My first problem was to delineate the period to be investigated so that the changes which took place could be viewed with some perspective without distorting their significance to the period or to the process itself. After all, where one chooses to sample a stream may dramatically influence the analysis of its contents. The premise on which I tried always to rely was that in administrative and constitutional history institutions are continually changing in response both to the abilities and ideas of the men who operate them, and to the problems faced at a particular time. It seems to me that the history of the formulation and administration of British foreign policy between 1782 and 1846 marks a distinct period in the evolution of those institutions involved in these processes. The period under consideration begins in March 1782 when, as the result of various political and administrative changes on the accession of Rockingham's ministry, the foreign affairs of Great Britain were concentrated in the hands of a single secretary of state. I chose June 1846 to conclude my study for several reasons. First, I wished to avoid the question of the effects of the agitation for civil service reform on the Foreign Office since this subject appeared to be beyond the scope of my topic and because it is significant enough to warrant the separate and detailed study which it has already received. Second, the reforms in the Foreign Office between 1838 and 1841 had been in effect long enough by 1846 to assess their significance. Third, Queen Victoria had in June 1846 completed the first nine years of her reign and that seemed sufficient time to measure her immediate impact on the role of the sovereign in the conduct of foreign affairs. Finally, the defeat of Peel's government in June 1846 marked a convenient change in ministries. Russell's government, which succeeded Peel's, survived until 1852 and by that time the movement for civil service reform was well under way. Unquestionably many of the elements in the conduct of foreign affairs that I have discussed were either inherited from the days prior to 1782 or were conspicuous after 1846. Nevertheless there were significant changes during this period. Some elements of the machinery for the conduct of foreign policy in the eighteenth century became extinct. Other prominent features of the machinery after 1846 emerged. Why and how they did so is the subject of this investigation.

During the course of my research I have had the valuable assistance of too many people to mention them all separately. There are some, however, to whom I am especially grateful. The royal correspondence in the Palmerston Papers is quoted by the gracious permission of Her Majesty Queen Elizabeth II. The general correspondence in these papers is cited by permission of the Broadlands Trustees. His Grace, the Duke of Wellington generously permitted me to consult the Wellington Papers and to cite from them. I am particularly grateful to the present and past staff at the National Register of Archives for their assistance while I worked in these two collections, and especially to Miss Felicity Ranger, without whose

assistance I never could have read the hieroglyphics of Lords Melbourne and Grey.

I am indebted to the Right Honourable, the Earl of Harewood for
permission to read and quote from the Canning MSS at the Leeds
Public Library. I also wish to thank the Right Honourable, the Earl
of Harrowby for making the Harrowby MSS available to me, and
Miss Pauline Adams, his Lordship's former manuscript librarian,
for her hospitality and assistance to me and Mrs. Middleton while we
were at Sandon Hall. David Holland, Esq., was kind enough to make
the Holland (Perceval) Papers available. I am also grateful for the
permission of Col. A. C. Barnes to read the Barnes MSS and to him
and Lady Barnes for their hospitality while I was at Foxholme.
Papers in the Duke University Library are cited with permission of
Dr. B. E. Powell, University Librarian Emeritus.

Of innumerable archivists and librarians without whose assistance
I could not have completed this study Mr. William Erwin of the
Duke University Manuscripts Department deserves special mention. His efforts in compiling biographical information on the personnel of the Foreign Office provided me with more complete
sketches than I otherwise would have been able to give in so short a
time as I had to work on them.

I wish to thank the University of Colorado Council on Research
and Creative Work for a summer grant that enabled me to complete
my manuscript. I am especially indebted to the University of Colorado Committee on University Scholarly Publications for its financial generosity at a critical moment after the work was accepted for
publication.

The late William B. Hamilton kindly let me read his notes and
microfilm of the Grenville MSS. No tribute is adequate to express my
gratitude to him, both for his valuable encouragement and suggestions on earlier drafts of this work, and for his many personal and
professional contributions to my early career.

I am also indebted more than he would care to acknowledge to my
colleague James P. Jankowski for his diligence in preparing the final
copy of my manuscript while I was abroad and for his confidence in
both it and me at that critical period.

To my wife Sandy I dedicate the whole work.

C.R.M.

Boulder, Colorado
December 1976

THE ADMINISTRATION OF
BRITISH FOREIGN POLICY
1782–1846

Chapter I

THE CONDUCT OF FOREIGN POLICY:
1782–1846

For over a century after the creation of the Foreign Office in 1782 the conduct of foreign affairs remained a process in which the formulation and implementation of foreign policy were the responsibilities of two distinct groups. The cabinet and the sovereign were primarily concerned with stating policy while it was the duty of the establishments of the Foreign Office and of the diplomatic and consular services to implement the decisions of the king and his ministers. Rarely during this period were those who made policy, with the exception of the foreign secretary, concerned with the details of its execution. Nor did persons on the establishments in London and abroad have much influence over the formulation of policy in foreign affairs. Only at the end of the nineteenth century, as Zara Steiner has recently shown,[1] did the professionals at the Foreign Office and to a lesser extent the professionals abroad begin to participate with the politicians in the process of formulating policy. Much later, with the appearance of summit meetings in the midtwentieth century, the politicians in turn began to assume a role previously reserved—except in rare instances such as Disraeli's participation in the Berlin Congress of 1878—almost exclusively to professional diplomats.

Yet despite these generalizations the period between 1782 and 1846 witnessed some fundamental changes in the process of administering foreign policy. That these changes took place within the two groups involved in the process rather than between them should not mask their significance. The period was one of important economic and social changes wrought by Britain's growing industrialization. These changes were reflected in the political community

1. *The Foreign Office and Foreign Policy, 1898–1914* (Cambridge, 1969).

most obviously in the legislation passed in the 1830s, particularly in the Reform Act of 1832 and the Municipal Corporations Act of 1835. But they could be seen as well in the redefinition of royal power, in the emergence of political parties, and in the growing efficiency of the cabinet as an executive body able to manage British affairs. These processes, furthermore, stimulated reforms in the bureaucracy which affected to a certain extent administrative practices in the Foreign Office and the services overseas.

The importance of these developments within the two groups responsible for the administration of foreign policy at the turn of the nineteenth century will be developed fully in subsequent chapters. Here it is necessary only to undertake a general discussion of these changes and to emphasize that there was much continuity of practice during the period. This continuity was best seen in the fact that for all the differences that distinguished the conduct of foreign policy in Palmerston's time from the conduct of foreign policy in Fox's, the dual nature of the system remained intact. Cabinet development in the years 1783 to 1835 reflected the increasing importance of that institution as the principal governing body in British politics.[2] The cabinets of the 1830s and 1840s were more cohesive bodies than those of the late eighteenth century, though it would be unwise to draw this distinction too finely. In the area of foreign relations, however, the cabinets of the 1840s as well as those of the 1780s were primarily responsible for formulating the general outlines of foreign policy. Inevitably a small group of ministers was more interested in and informed about foreign affairs than their colleagues. The opinions of these men—the prime minister, the foreign secretary, and one or two others—carried more weight within the cabinet than the opinions of other ministers. Cabinet decisions frequently reflected the attitudes of these key individuals and the course of policy they wished to pursue. Collectively the members of the cabinet were concerned with the statement of policy guidelines and perhaps with the initial dispatch drawn up to implement a decision. The daily conduct of foreign affairs was not a cabinet concern except in times of crisis. The foreign secretary, of course, consulted particular ministers on problems relating to their departments. Palmerston, for example, occasionally discussed naval activities for the suppres-

2. Arthur Aspinall, "The Cabinet Council, 1783–1835," *Proceedings of the British Academy, London,* 38 (1952), 145–252.

sion of the slave trade in the 1830s with Sir James Graham, the first lord of the Admiralty.[3] Usually, however, most members of the cabinet were too occupied with their own responsibilities to take much notice of the day to day conduct of foreign affairs.

Throughout the period the sovereign shared with the cabinet the responsibility for the formation of foreign policy, but as the years passed and the personal monarchy of George III was transformed into the constitutional monarchy of Victoria the ability of the sovereign to play a positive role in the formulation of policy was circumscribed. The capacity of the sovereign to influence foreign policy, however, was always limited by personal and political considerations. This was as true of the personal monarchy as it was of the constitutional monarchy. In both cases influence depended to a degree on the idiosyncracies of the sovereigns and the balance of political forces in the country at any given moment. George III, like his predecessors,[4] played an active part in determining policy. Indolent as a youth, as king he proved to be an excellent man of business, and ministers implemented few important decisions without his prior approval. George IV, however, lacked his father's driving energy and paid less attention to business. His ministers, despairing of any quick decisions on his part, began to assume more responsibility for affairs and to secure his approval of policies, if they bothered to do so at all, only after the policies were being executed. William IV expressed his opinions on all matters and was nearly as attentive to business as his father had been. He was able, therefore, to recapture some of the direct and daily supervision of foreign policy that George IV had surrendered. Victoria's inexperience and her youth encouraged her ministers to return to a great extent to the practices their predecessors had employed in the reign of George IV.

Another and more significant factor in addition to personal ability and experience affected the changes in the sovereign's capacity to influence foreign policy decisions. Increasingly the difficulty of assuring parliamentary support for the ministries of the period provoked a reevaluation of the sovereign's role in politics. During these

3. Graham to Palmerston, Admiralty, 5 Feb. 1831, F.O. 84/124; Same to Same, Admiralty, Wednesday night, [Feb. 1832?], F.O. 84/132.

4. D. B. Horn, "The Machinery for the Conduct of British Foreign Policy in the Eighteenth Century," *Journal of the Society of Archivists*, 3 (July 8, 1966), 234.

years there were changes in the nature and extent of the influence of the crown over the selection and activities of members of the House of Commons. These changes have usually been attributed to specific measures such as Burke's economical reforms or the Reform Act of 1832. They were, however, more the result of a growing tendency during the period for men to give their principal political allegiance to others than the king. In the eighteenth century the crown had enjoyed considerable support in Parliament because of the numbers of independent country gentlemen who habitually voted with the king's ministers because they felt it their duty to support the king, the church, and the establishment. George III was instinctively attuned to the feelings, prejudices, and beliefs of these men, while they could count on him to share their attitudes and to promote their interests. So long as the ministers appeared to have the confidence of the king, and so long as there was no national disaster such as occurred in 1781 at Yorktown, these members were willing to give the government of the day their support. This attachment to the king and as a result to his ministers was translated easily into royal influence over policy. Ministers may have been responsible both to the king and to Parliament, but their principal responsibility lay to the king.

George's son and successor, George IV, however, forfeited much of the personal support his father had enjoyed because of his personality and his disreputable character.[5] But long before he became Regent traditional political loyalties were being eroded by the emergence of political parties. These initial efforts at party organization were aborted in the 1790s by the split of the Whig party over the war with France.[6] But the fact that ministers after 1782 tended to enter office and to retire together reinforced the inclination of politicians to regard politics in a new way: to identify with parties rather than with the crown or with factions in the British political community. By the 1820s, but particularly after 1832, politicians realized that electoral support could be maintained only by more careful attention to party organization. The expansion of the electorate, both because of the numbers of the newly enfranchised and the social, economic, and religious composition of these groups, created problems of electoral management which traditional electoral prac-

5. Roger Fulford, *George the Fourth* (London, 1935), passim.
6. Donald Ginter, *Whig Organization in the General Election of 1790* (Berkeley, 1967), pp. xi–lvii.

tices could not fully solve.[7] Enough of the unreformed system survived to assure that the traditional groups in society would retain considerable electoral power,[8] but William IV's action in sacking the Whigs in 1834 and their subsequent return to office in 1835[9] demonstrated clearly the changes in royal electoral influence brought about by the Act of 1832. Thereafter the ministers, less dependent on the king's support for political survival, naturally could defer less to royal judgment in all matters—including foreign affairs. The weakness of the Whig ministry after 1835 meant that William was able to maintain his influence over the conduct of foreign policy, but these political events and their implications were clearly reflected in the decreased importance and deference ministers were willing to attach to the opinions of Queen Victoria.[10] In foreign affairs as well as in other matters ministerial responsibility was by 1846 owed more to Parliament, and especially to the House of Commons, than had been the case in the eighteenth century.

Of the other institutions interested in foreign policy, Parliament and other government departments, Parliament as an institution exercised little positive influence over policy. Ministers, of course, were always aware of the attitudes of members. Before embarking on any policy that might lead to the expenditure of money or the employment of force they invariably were careful to test their support, at least quietly. Parliamentary support became increasingly important as the ability of the crown to influence elections declined, and parliamentary control of the purse always loomed as a potential check to too ambitious a foreign policy. Ministerial concern over Parliament's ability to intervene in foreign affairs in this way in part contributed to the fact that the amount of information presented to Parliament about foreign affairs rose sharply in the 1820s and afterwards; but the ability of the House of Commons to extract papers from ministers did not reflect any power to force the implementation of particular courses of policy. Parliament in the early

7. Norman Gash, *Politics in the Age of Peel* (London, 1953), pp. 393–427.

8. Ibid., pp. 105–392.

9. Abraham D. Kriegel, "The Politics of the Whigs in Opposition, 1834–1835," *Journal of British Studies*, 7 (May, 1968), 65–91.

10. Victoria was able in subsequent years to play a more influential role in foreign affairs as a result of her family ties with other sovereigns in Europe and because of her long experience. H. J. Hanham, *The Nineteenth-Century Constitution 1815–1914: Documents and Commentary* (Cambridge, 1969), pp. 28, 56–58.

nineteenth century was, therefore, only peripherally involved in the administration of foreign policy.

There was much interdepartmental correspondence between the Foreign Office and other branches of the government. Bureaucrats in other departments, however, could hardly be expected to exercise any influence over foreign policy when officials in the Foreign Office could not affect policy. It is true that the activities of other branches of the government impinged on the conduct of foreign relations. The Anglo-French rivalry in North Africa, for example, was as much a concern of the Admiralty and the Colonial Office as it was of the Foreign Office. Most interdepartmental correspondence, however, was concerned with administrative matters, such as seeking technical advice from the Admiralty on the rights of maritime law. Any question of policy was usually settled by the foreign secretary in private consultation with the heads of other interested departments. The result was that Britain's foreign policy reflected the opinions and decisions of a very restricted group of men, who, though they were not totally isolated from Parliament and the bureaucracy, were nonetheless independently taking their decisions in consultation privately with one another.

The concentration of all foreign business in the hands of one secretary of state in 1782 was a significant administrative change and one that perhaps has not been given the attention it deserves. The immediate result was to put an end to the backbiting of the secretaries and to their intriguing against one another with diplomatic personnel abroad. The secretaries in the eighteenth century had, in fact, little regard for the division of foreign responsibilities between the Southern and Northern Departments. They frequently encroached on the duties of their colleagues and usually the more influential of the two ran the affairs of both departments.[11] After 1782 there was no need for and no profit in continuing such activities.

A more long-term and more significant result of the reform of 1782 only gradually became apparent. With the increasing importance of Britain as an international power the foreign secretaryship

11. Basil Williams, "The Foreign Office Under the First Two Georges," *Blackwoods Magazine*, 181 (Jan., 1907), 92–95.

became one of the most sought after positions in the government. The secretaryships of the eighteenth century had been powerful positions and forceful men—such as the elder Pitt after 1756— could dominate the ministry from the office. But the division of responsibility served to make the influence of the positions dependent on the personality and ability of the men who served in them. The reform of 1782 meant that thereafter there was only one minister solely concerned with the conduct of foreign affairs and he was able to exert an authority which other ministers found it difficult to challenge, especially as the years passed. As the importance of foreign affairs in British politics increased, therefore, it was natural that the most talented, influential, and ambitious men in every ministry should seek the seals of the Foreign Office. Usually the foreign secretary, as the dominant secretary of state before 1782 had been, was among the two or three leading figures in the ministry. Palmerston was for a short time after his first appointment in 1830 an exception to this rule, but he had not been too long in office before he had moved into the front ranks of Grey's government.

The foreign secretary formed the only connection between the men who formulated and the establishments that implemented British foreign policy. He took a leading role in cabinet discussions of foreign affairs. He was also responsible for the day to day conduct of foreign business. He prepared the dispatches, supervised the personnel of the Foreign Office, and was responsible for the welfare of the establishments in London and abroad.

The foreign secretary was assisted by two undersecretaries of state. The duties of these officers were primarily administrative. They distributed the business of the office among the clerks, prepared reports and draft dispatches for their principal, and performed any other duty, official or unofficial, he assigned to them. By the 1830s one of these men had come to be considered a permanent official and he invariably remained in his position on a change of ministries. The records in the archives indicate that neither of the undersecretaries had much influence over policy. Doubtless they had numerous unrecorded conversations with their principals in which they discussed the affairs of the day and where their opinions probably had some weight with the secretary of state. But so long as the cabinet and the sovereign were actively involved in making every decision, no matter how trivial, there was little opportunity or need for the undersecretaries to take an active or official part in these discussions.

The creation of the Foreign Office has been called "the most important administrative change in the sphere of foreign policy during the eighteenth century. . . ."[12] Yet there is surprisingly little record of who was responsible for the change. Charles James Fox's dispatch announcing the concentration of foreign affairs in the hands of a single secretary is the only official record to survive.[13] The ministers probably recommended the reorganization as part of the arrangements which included the abolition of the secretaryship for America on the accession of Rockingham's ministry in March 1782. George III had long advocated such a measure[14] and almost certainly was pleased to sanction it. But it is not unlikely that the king insisted that the former American colonies be considered the responsibility of the home secretary. Once peace negotiations were underway he referred to the home secretaryship as the "secretary for the Home Department and British Settlements. . . ." He clearly appreciated the significance of disagreements among ministers that arose because of the dual negotiations proceeding in Paris.[15] The fact that the home secretary was responsible for negotiations with the representatives of the American states while the foreign secretary was concerned with negotiations with the continental powers eventually contributed to the resignation of Fox, the king's bête noire, and caused a good deal of dissatisfaction in the lower echelons of the Foreign Office.[16] The king might not have planned the reorganization but he certainly schemed to take advantage of its weaknesses and of its potential for creating conflicts among his ministers.

The principal administrative development in the years between 1780 and 1830 was the emergence of a constitutional bureaucracy out of the departmental service of the eighteenth century. A good deal will be said about this problem elsewhere. The process involved

12. D. B. Horn, *The British Diplomatic Service, 1689–1789* (Oxford, 1961), p. 1.

13. Fox to Sir Robert M. Keith, St. James's, 29 Mar. 1782, No. 1, Add. MS 35525 f. 39.

14. George III to Lord North, Queen's House, 46 Min. past 7 p.m., 13 Jan. 1771, Sir John William Fortescue (ed.), *The Correspondence of King George the Third, 1760–1783* (6 vols.; London, 1928), vol. 2, 205–6.

15. George III to Shelburne, Windsor, 21 min. past 7 a.m., 1 July 1782, ibid., vol. 6, 70.

16. George Aust to Earl of Hardwicke, Tuesday, 3 Sept. 1782, Add. MS 35619 f. 273. American affairs were transferred to the Foreign Office in April 1783. Lord Apsley to Keith, Apsley House, 11 Apr. 1783, Sir Robert Murray Keith, *Memoirs and Correspondence of Sir Robert Murray Keith* (2 vols.; London, 1849), vol. 2, 177–78.

the separation of politics and administration which was made possible by the gradual withdrawal of the crown from the political arena, so that "Constitutional bureaucracy was [to become] the counterpart of constitutional monarchy."[17]

But these changes were to take place slowly in the Foreign Office. Before 1782 the offices of state, like many other government departments in the eighteenth century, were personalized bureaus attached to their secretaries. As elsewhere in the bureaucracy there was no clear line distinguishing political and civil servants of the crown in these offices, at least at the higher ranks, and as a result politics and administration tended to become confused in the minds of contemporaries. On the surface some of the practices of the modern civil service seem to have prevailed in the offices of state. For instance, the clerks were relatively secure in their places. But they were often employed by the secretary in the Northern Department during one ministry and by the secretary in the Southern Department during the next, and they tended to regard themselves as clerks attached to a particular secretary more than as clerks serving in one department or the other. The establishment only gradually came to have a self-identity during the twenty years after the reorganization of 1782. Canning in 1808 marked the end of this period of transition by instituting the practice of placing "Foreign Office" at the head of all dispatches and papers prepared by the department. During the first forty years of the office's history there were some changes in its organization. The most important reforms were financial; the clerks received better salaries, other financial rewards were improved, and provisions were made for pensions. The reforms instituted after 1821 were more substantive. By 1846 the organization of the office was essentially that of the establishment down to the twentieth century. It was divided into political departments headed by senior division clerks and there were separate departments for consular and slave trade affairs. The office was a modern administrative department conforming to the requirements of constitutional bureaucracy with a hierarchy of positions, regular assignments for everyone on the establishment, and uniform rules with regard to personnel matters.[18]

17. Henry Parris, *Constitutional Bureaucracy* ("Minerva Series of Student Handbooks, Number 23"; London, 1969), p. 49.
18. Ibid., pp. 22–27.

There can be no doubt that the personnel of the Foreign Office thought that they were the hardest working and most efficient government department in the first half of the nineteenth century. The historian becomes involved in invidious comparisons of this sort only at great peril. Furthermore, there is no profitability in such a discussion. What can be determined is the efficiency of the office and people in it. Some of the regulations and methods of business, to be sure, appear antiquated when compared with the standards of the twentieth century. But it is difficult to discover any criticism of the office and its performance of required duties in the papers of the foreign secretaries of the period. Even Palmerston, the most exacting of these men, resented any imputation that clerks in the Foreign Office were "idle and inattentive,"[19] and no secretary was ever forced to postpone or delay any important business because of a lack of cooperation from the establishment. It is important to remember this tradition when considering the reluctance of the Foreign Office to adopt the administrative reforms of the second half of the nineteenth century.

One student of administrative history has defined the field broadly as the study of "institutions and their individual members considered in their social context."[20] The Foreign Office in the nineteenth century alone of all government departments resisted with moderate success the general administrative trends of the period. It was unaffected by them in part because some of the most important goals of the reform movement had long been the accepted standards of the office,[21] and in part because the office was seen to be the last administrative bastion of the traditional governing classes.[22] Partly for these reasons the Foreign Office of the early nineteenth century has escaped serious study. Resistance to change

19. Minute, Palmerston, 2 Nov. 1836, F.O. 96/18.
20. G. E. Aylmer, "Problems of Method in the Study of Administrative History," *Annali della Fondazione Italiana per la Storia Amministiva*, 1 (1958), 20.
21. The delightful sketches of the Department of Weights and Measures in Anthony Trollope, *The Three Clerks: A Novel* (London, 1858), bear little relation to the conditions in the Foreign Office, though there are resemblances between certain of the fictional senior clerks and the flesh and blood variety in Downing Street.
22. See appendix I for short biographical sketches of all personnel. The Treasury also appears to have been an elitist organization, but not until the last half of the nineteenth century did Treasury attitudes resemble those prevalent in the F.O. prior to 1850. Henry Roseveare, *The Treasury: The Evolution of a British Institution* (New York, 1970), pp. 152–82.

in the last half of the century has been taken to imply very little change in the first half when there were few if any outside pressures for reform being exerted on government departments.

There is, however, another consideration. Administrative history of the nineteenth century is concerned with more complex problems that that of the eighteenth century. The rapid growth of industrial, demographic, and agricultural problems is juxtaposed to the equally rapid proliferation of the means to combat these problems as a result of the increased medical and scientific research of the period. Bentham's ideas and those of his disciples have attracted the interest of most scholars whose work has been concerned largely with their effect on the establishing and functioning of new government de-partments. Little attention has been given to "the silent metamor-phosis taking place within" such "long-established arms of govern-ment"[23] as the Foreign Office. The impact of new ideas on new institutions dealing with social problems naturally has attracted the interest of historians of the period,[24] while the older departments, especially those of stature, seem at first glance pallid by comparison. Too, most of the ideas motivating the new departments are clearly of marginal application to many of the old. This would appear to be the case particularly with regard to the Foreign Office where not only does the business of the department have little to do with these new trends in British society, but where it has also long been known that since the business of foreign affairs could not safely be delayed, the establishment of the office was forced to be efficient and to complete their work before they left for home at night.[25] The changes which took place in the organization of the establishment between 1782 and 1846 were designed primarily to promote the efficient man-agement of business. These reforms were on balance successful.

23. O. O. G. M. MacDonagh, "The Nineteenth-Century Revolution in Government: A Reappraisal," *Historical Journal*, 1 (1958), 55. For a contrasting viewpoint on the revolution in government see Henry Parris, "The Nineteenth-Century Revolution in Government: A Reap-praisal Reappraised," ibid., 3 (1960), 17–37.

24. A useful survey of this and related literature is to be found in Gertrude Himmelfarb, "The Writing of Social History: Recent Studies of 19th Century England," *Journal of British Studies*, 11 (Nov. 1971), 148–70.

25. Harold Temperley, *The Foreign Policy of Canning 1822–1827* (2nd ed; London, 1966), p. 262 and n. 1 says that the clerks were "idle and troublesome." But this statement was based on the case of Edward Scheener, the most lazy and irresponsible clerk in the 1820s and in fact one of the few cases of complaint against any clerk on record; hardly sufficient evidence for such a sweeping generalization.

Their unforeseen result, however, was to contribute in the late nineteenth century to Foreign Office resistance to more fundamental reforms in the civil service. Largely because a tradition of efficiency had long been instilled in the clerks from the day of their appointment they found nothing new in the reformer's ideas. Because they were efficient there was little internal pressure for successive secretaries of state to make any more than the token changes in recruiting procedure and organization that occurred during the last half of the nineteenth century. The result was that the department became the principal "study in resistance" for this later period. In the process the fundamental changes which occurred earlier have been underestimated.[26]

It would be misleading, however, to ascribe the resistance to the civil service reforms solely to the efficiency of the office. Objections were made also because it was thought that the reforms would lead inevitably to the creation of a more catholic establishment: to the admittance of men socially and educationally inferior to the clerks already employed at the office. There is no way to measure the effect this argument had on successive secretaries of state, but given their own background it cannot have fallen totally on unsympathetic ground. Even before the challenge of the reformers the undersecretaries and clerks had striven to maintain the social purity of the establishment. Joseph Planta requested in 1823 that the replacement of Udney Passmore, a clerk being considered for a South American consulship, be a "real good *Gentleman. . . .*"[27] When Henry Unwin Addington, the second man to serve as permanent undersecretary, retired in 1854, he gave his blessing to the office: "Let it but continue what it is, an office of Gentlemen in feeling and spirit, and it must go on well. Esto Perpetua!"[28] The fact that this attitude prevailed from top to bottom of the office contributed decisively to the

26. See below, chapters 6–7. Valerie Cromwell and Zara S. Steiner, "The Foreign Office before 1914: a study in resistance," in *Studies in the Growth of Nineteenth-Century Government*, ed. Gillian Sutherland (Totowa, N.J., 1972), pp. 167–94; Ray Jones, *The Nineteenth-Century Foreign Office: An Administrative History* ("L.S.E. Research Monographs, 9"; London, 1971), pp. 41–64. The result of the failure to keep abreast with changes in procedure and recruitment in other departments made the F.O. less efficient than other offices by the 1890s. Steiner, *Foreign Office*, pp. 1–22.

27. To Canning, F.O., 23 Oct. 1823, *Secret and Confidential*, Canning MSS Bundle 136, Archives Department Leeds Public Libraries.

28. To E. Hammond, 78 Eaton Place, 10 Apr. 1854, Barnes MSS, Foxholme Surrey.

continuation of the social and educational elitism in the Foreign Office until well after the first world war.[29]

Most clerks at the Foreign Office were mere lads when they began their careers. Richard Wellesley, for example, was only seventeen when he first set foot in the office in 1839,[30] while Edward McMahon was a youth of fifteen on his appointment in 1818.[31] They were naturally inexperienced and naive and as they progressed through the ranks it is not surprising that their work at the Foreign Office often became their whole life. Many of them lived in the attic flats of the office, where they installed a piano, boxing gloves, and other items for their amusement. They frequently created such a commotion that their superiors called their residence "the Nursery."[32] The older resident clerks were responsible for receiving mails or messengers that arrived after hours. These men occupied more spacious accommodations on lower floors.[33]

The vast majority of clerks had no experience in government service before they were appointed, but there were exceptions. William Money, for example, had been employed in the diplomatic service[34] and Edmund Hammond was a clerk in the Council Office[35] before they went to the Foreign Office. But clerks with prior experience were rare. Nor were there any requirements or standards for a prospective clerk to meet. The seniors in the office expected to teach new appointees good habits of business and how to write in a legible manner, as well as the forms of diplomatic correspondence. Most clerks were familiar with French though they were not required to know any language. Some had special linguistic skills. James Manby could read Italian[36] and Aberdeen regularly employed Richard

29. See Robert T. Nightingale, "Personnel of the British Foreign Office and Diplomatic Service, 1851–1929," *American Political Science Review*, 24 (May, 1930), 310–31 for the social and educational backgrounds of senior personnel in the F.O.; also Steiner, *Foreign Office*, appendix 3.

30. Wellesley to H. D. Scott, Linden Lodge, Linden Grove, Bayswater, 20 Aug. 1860, F.O. 366/533.

31. Draft, Aberdeen to Treasury, F.O., 14 Jan. 1846, ibid.

32. Sir Edward Hertslet, *Recollections of the Old Foreign Office* (London, 1901), p. 23.

33. "A Return of all the Houses and Apartments. . . ," F.O., 23 Feb. 1831, F.O. 366/366 f. 161.

34. "The Case of Mr. Money late Secretary to the Earl of Buckinghamshire," [14 Apr. 1787], F.O. 366/313.

35. George Canning to George Hammond, F.O., 29 Apr. 1824, Private, Hammond Papers, M 581, British Library of Political and Economic Science, London.

36. Aust to Hardwicke, Tuesday, 9 Jan. 1781, Add. MS 35617 ff. 166–67.

Mellish to read to him the letters Prince Albert received from his relations and from other German princes.[37]

Clerks were secure in their positions so long as they performed their duties moderately well. There usually was little immediate reward for those clerks who showed extra zeal and some of the better clerks complained that they were not fully appreciated. Promotions were based on seniority, not merit, and this practice stifled initiative in the lower branches of the office.[38] Only one clerk was dismissed for incompetence,[39] though others were asked to resign for personal reasons.

Despite the secret nature of much of the work of the Foreign Office, there was no security clearance of clerks on their appointment. Had there been such investigations they probably would have been an insult to gentlemen. The clerks were nonetheless surprisingly trustworthy. Though ministers sometimes transacted the most secret and delicate business without letting it get into the office,[40] more often no attempt was made to conceal intelligence from the establishment. There were occasional leakages of information,[41] but these were as often as not the result of loose talk or ill-placed confidence at the Court.[42] There remains the indisputable fact that of all the delegations at the Congress of Vienna in 1815 only the British delegation, composed mainly of clerks, managed to thwart efforts of the Austrian secret police to secure state secrets.[43]

A few of the clerks were not quite so scrupulous in their dealings with opposition leaders. Stephen Rolleston, a senior clerk, Francis Moore, a junior clerk, and George Aust, a clerk turned undersecre-

37. Aberdeen to Prince Albert, F.O., 31 Oct. 1842, Copy, and Foreign Office, 25 Nov. 1842, Copy, Add. MS 43042 ff. 167, 224.

38. James Bandinel to Marian Hunter, Downing Street, 2 June 1812, Bandinel Family Papers, Duke University Library, saying "I shall no longer try to show myself more zealous than others if no good can arise from it."

39. John Henry Temple Browne. Draft to Browne, Foreign Office, 8 Apr. 1835, F.O. 84/184. Browne was re-employed in 1838 but proved to be as troublesome and as inattentive to business as he had been earlier. He resigned in 1841 when it became apparent that he was going to earn the distinction of being the only clerk ever to be dismissed not only once but twice. Browne to [Bandinel?], Foreign Office, 20 Oct. 1841, F.O. 84/389.

40. Grenville to George III, St. James's Square, 5 Oct. 1794, Copy, Great Britain, Historical Manuscripts Commission, *Report on the Manuscripts of J. B. Fortescue, Esq., Preserved at Dropmore* (10 vols.; London, 1892–1927), vol. 2, 637–38.

41. Same to Henry Dundas, Cleveland Row, 16 Aug. 1799, Copy, ibid., vol. 5, 284.

42. Arthur Aspinall, *Politics and the Press, c. 1780–1850* (London, 1949), pp. 192–93.

43. C. K. Webster. *The Foreign Policy of Castlereagh, 1812–1822* (2 vols.; London, 1931–1934), vol. 1, 331–32.

tary, conspired with the Duke of Leeds in his unsuccessful attempt in 1792 to forge an alliance with the Duke of Portland and Charles Fox in order to force a change in ministries.[44] Leeds and company were extremely well-informed of all activities of ministers, down to the exchange of letters between Grenville and Pitt.[45] These three men owed their situations to Leeds, but their gratitude ought not to have carried them to these extremes. It is surprising that ministers knew nothing of the extent of these communications, for if they had it is improbable that they would have let them continue unobstructed. There were in the nineteenth century no large-scale operations of this sort against any ministry, but some clerks were still not above secret partisan communications as late as the 1850s. John Bidwell, Jr., for example, forwarded to Disraeli in 1857 and 1858 for his use in attacking Palmerston's foreign policy a regular stream of information procured by Ralph Earle, an attaché at the embassy in Paris.[46]

The Foreign Office has been located in four places since 1782. From March 1782 to September 1786 it was in Cleveland Row in the same office occupied by the old Northern Department. During the years from 1786 to December 1793 business was conducted from the Cockpit in Whitehall. Thereafter, to 27 August 1861 when the present building was occupied, the office was located in Downing Street.[47] The offices in Downing Street were dismal and run-down. They consisted of one large and two small buildings divided into what one clerk called "small dark & inconvenient Rooms, some of which from their confined state are not healthy."[48] The floors sagged[49] and ministers complained of "all the dark passages."[50] There were at least two serious fires between 1793 and 1846. One occurred in 1836, the other in 1843, the latter so severe that Aberdeen surmised that had it happened at night "in all probability the build-

44. Francis Moore to [Leeds], Whitehall, 20 Nov. [1792], Add. MS 28067 ff. 83–84; Sir Ralph Woodward to Leeds, 17 Aug. 1792, ibid., ff. 55–56.
45. Stephen Rolleston to Aust, Dover, 19 Oct. 1792, *H.M.C. Fortescue*, vol. 3, 473–75, copy in Add. MS 28067 ff. 75–78.
46. Robert Blake, *Disraeli* (London, 1966), p. 370–71.
47. *The Records of the Foreign Office* ("Public Record Office Handbooks," No. 13; London, 1969), pp. 1–2.
48. Unsigned memorandum, George Lenox-Connyngham, n.d., F.O. 95/9.
49. Bandinel to John Backhouse, Slave Trade Dept., F.O., 12 Jan. 1835, Copy, F.O. 84/183; Same to Thomas Bidwell "or his deputy," Foreign Office, 21 Nov. 1838, Immediate, Copy, F.O. 84/265.
50. 26 Jan. 1829, Lord Colchester (ed.), *A Political Diary 1828–1830 by Edward Law, Lord Ellenborough* (2 vols.; London, 1881), vol. 1, 323.

ing would have been destroyed."[51] Small wonder that clerks cherished the six weeks annual leave of absence granted them as a means to escape these conditions into the outdoors.[52]

The diplomatic and consular services were distinct organizations throughout the nineteenth century. There was little interchange of personnel between them. Surprisingly, however, many on the establishment in London served abroad in some capacity at some time during their careers.[53] The diplomatic service was by far the more professional of the two foreign establishments. It had a regular hierarchy of positions ranging from unpaid attaché to ambassador. With the exception of the heads of embassies promotions were made from one rank to the next, though not always with a strict regard to seniority. A growing sense of professionalism was the most important feature of the diplomatic service. More men entered the service with the intention of making it a career and junior diplomatic personnel increasingly received promotions to responsible positions as heads of missions.

The consular service throughout the period remained the most insignificant of the establishments. Despite Britain's growing commerce ministers envisioned the consular service as little more than an organization for collecting data on the trade and industry of other powers. Consuls represented British commercial interests in their ports but they were clearly subordinate figures. Diplomatic personnel settled major disputes and negotiated all agreements affecting trade and commerce. The few reforms in the consular service improved the quality of the men who served as consuls, standardized the collection of fees, and provided for more close supervision and coordination of consular activities by the Foreign Office.

There were many changes in the machinery for the conduct of British foreign policy in the first half of the nineteenth century, but they did little to alter the fundamental division between the policy makers and the implementers of policy. The volume of business increased dramatically but it still remained possible for one individual to read every paper and to make all decisions at the Foreign

51. Frederick Byng to Lord Granville, 22 Jan. 1836, P.R.O. 30/29/7/13 ff. 1080–83; Aberdeen to Victoria, London, 2 Feb. 1843, Add. MS 43042 f. 277.
52. Draft, Lewis Hertslet to———Mann, Foreign Office, 20 Feb. 1843, F.O. 83/241.
53. See appendix I for the nature of these services.

Office. The influence of the Crown, though diminished, was still considerable and the sovereign always took a special interest in foreign affairs. These factors meant that there was really no need for ministers to rely on the establishments in London and abroad to recommend courses of policy. At the same time the growth in the volume of business provoked changes in the organization of the Foreign Office and in the diplomatic and consular services. These establishments were organized along more modern lines to enable them to cope with the increased volume of business. As a result, at least insofar as the establishment in London was concerned, once the number of dispatches and other papers had increased to such an extent that one individual could not digest everything, weigh every possible option, and make every decision no matter how insignificant, there were junior officials with the expertise to offer opinions on which course of policy should be pursued.

Any treatment of the institutions responsible for the administration of foreign policy cannot ignore the policy or policies formulated during the period discussed. It is impossible, however, and in fact unnecessary[54] to go into any great detail in this discussion. In the pages which follow two purposes will serve. First, it will be useful to trace the development of general policy attitudes through the eighteenth century into the nineteenth, making specific reference to the years 1782 to 1846. Second, British attitudes towards the various states or groups of states during this period will be briefly discussed in light of these prevalent attitudes.

Prior to 1701 English foreign policy had been royal foreign policy. The Stuarts were not particularly adept in foreign affairs and, except in extraordinary circumstances, England was regarded on the continent as a minor power in European politics.[55] The events of 1688–89, however, led to a greater role for Britain in continental affairs, while the Act of Settlement (1701) dramatically transformed the nature of foreign policy. By providing that Englishmen were not in the future to be obliged to go to war to defend the foreign territories of the sovereign, Parliament, conveniently ignoring the

54. The most recent and extensive accounts of foreign policy in the eighteenth and nineteenth centuries are David Bayne Horn, *Great Britain and Europe in the Eighteenth Century* (Oxford, 1967); and Kenneth Bourne, *The Foreign Policy of Victorian England 1830–1902* (London, 1970).

55. The European impact on British affairs, however, was considerable. J. R. Jones, *Britain and Europe in the Seventeenth Century* (New York, 1966).

fact that English interests were at stake in William's wars as well, by this single statute "marked the clear emergence of the idea of national as distinct from royal policy in foreign affairs."[56] But, though foreign affairs were to play an increasingly important role in British politics, particularly during the reign of Anne[57] and when the Stuart Pretenders threatened invasion,[58] most politicians looked on foreign affairs as clearly secondary to domestic considerations and "usually adopted a line in foreign policy which they hoped would fit in with, or at least cause as little disturbance and damage as possible to, what they regarded as the more important policies they were anxious to follow at home."[59]

The coming of war in 1793 transformed this situation. It was Britain which organized the coalitions against France, British gold that financed allied armies in the field.[60] By 1815 there could be no doubt that Great Britain was a European power and had a right to a voice in European affairs. Thus was inaugurated a period of what has been called British "pre-eminence"[61] in international affairs during the nineteenth century.

It is difficult to discern any single principle or set of principles on which British foreign policy was based prior to 1782. Initially Britain became involved in continental affairs for the purpose of self-defense and to secure the Protestant succession and the Revolution settlement.[62] At first glance this principle of self-defense, which motivated Englishmen off and on throughout the century,[63] appears remarkably similar to the prevalent notion in the nineteenth century that the foremost principle of foreign policy should be preventing the "consolidation of Europe under one potentially hostile regime. . . ."[64] Closer examination of the period reveals that this prospect was never a very serious one in the eighteenth century and

56. Horn, *Great Britain and Europe*, p. 2.

57. Geoffrey Holmes, *British Politics in the Age of Anne* (London, 1967), pp. 64–81.

58. Horn, *Great Britain and Europe*, p. 378.

59. Ibid., pp. 382–83.

60. This role is developed fully in John M. Sherwig, *Guineas and Gunpowder: British Foreign Aid in the Wars with France, 1793–1815* (Cambridge, Mass., 1969).

61. The term is that of C. J. Bartlett (ed.), *Britain Pre-Eminent: Studies of British World Influence in the Nineteenth Century* (London, 1969), pp. 1–6, though he uses it in a broader context to include more subtle influences than governmental; for instance, trade, parliamentary institutions, missionaries, and even (with reservation) culture.

62. Horn, *Great Britain and Europe*, p. 378.

63. Ibid., pp. 378–79.

64. Bourne, *Foreign Policy of Victorian England*, p. 7.

it was only Napoleon's successes which demonstrated to the British how "fatal to Britain's political, economic, and strategic security" such a situation would be.[65]

Commercial interests, particularly in the Mediterranean and the Baltic, increasingly were evident in discussions affecting foreign policy in the eighteenth century,[66] and it was these considerations which contributed to the principal change in foreign policy in this century—the additional importance attached to extra-European problems.[67] Furthermore, these interests after 1815 led to the expansion of the "informal empire," which meant "the expansion of trade and influence so far as possible without incurring the expense and responsibility of colonial sovereignty."[68] But commercial considerations should not be given too great a weight. The government rarely intervened in foreign states in behalf of traders except in those rare instances when legal rights had been violated.[69] And despite the concern with commercial expansion in the Americas, immediate political considerations in Europe were always sufficient to override these other interests.[70]

One of the basic principles of foreign policy in the nineteenth century, the balance of power in Europe, was only apparent in a rudimentary form in the preceding century. Horn argues that it is easy to demonstrate that the men of the eighteenth century did not regard this principle as central to foreign affairs. Too often the nearest thing to a dominant idea in foreign policy between 1701 and 1789—the hatred and suspicion of France—has been translated into a belief in a balance of power system,[71] when in fact the efforts to organize the petty German states into an effective anti-French league fell far short of a commitment to this policy.[72] Furthermore, such a system of balance as existed in the eighteenth century involved an "almost mechanical adjustment to every petty alteration in the *status quo*. . . ."[73] As such it was a phenomenon, not a policy.

65. Ibid.
66. Horn, *Great Britain and Europe*, pp. 378–79.
67. Ibid., p. 380.
68. Bourne, *Foreign Policy of Victorian England*, p. 5.
69. Ibid., p. 4.
70. A case in point was the diversion of a British army in 1808 from an expedition to South America to Spain to take advantage of the Spanish insurrection. John Lynch, "British Policy and Spanish America, 1783–1808," *Journal of Latin American Studies*, 1 (May, 1969), 1–30.
71. Horn, *Great Britain and Europe*, pp. 381–83.
72. Ibid., pp. 178–200.
73. Bourne, *Foreign Policy of Victorian England*, p. 10.

In the hands of nineteenth-century statesmen, however, the balance of power became a flexible and valuable policy. Rather than seeking allies in Europe and thereby attaching Britain to the policies of foreign states whether or not British statesmen approved of them, successive foreign secretaries beginning with Castlereagh sought to retain relative independence by holding aloof from entangling alliances.[74] Flexibility in international relations was the rationale behind the congress system established in 1815, and though the system broke down in the 1820s, the tradition of independence was to survive in Britain, and contributed to the remarkable success of British foreign policy to 1850 if not beyond.

Furthermore, conditions in Europe were favorable to British policies in the decades after the wars with France. The policies pursued by successive governments were designed to maintain the status quo in Europe and in overseas areas as well. The fact that foreign leaders of the period tended to be "cautious, defensively-minded statesmen" proved useful to securing this goal. It was, it has been aptly noted, "no coincidence that one of the great periods of British influence in Europe should approximate to the period of their rule."[75] Coupled with the effective use of the Royal Navy by both Conservative and Liberal foreign secretaries, whether in the Tagus, in the Eastern Mediterranean, or on the shores of America,[76] this inclination of foreign statesmen reinforced the main preoccupation of British foreign policy.

Moving to events that took place between 1782 and 1846 it is clear that these years were important in witnessing a dramatic alteration in the fortunes and the impact of British foreign policy. By the spring of 1782 the war against the American colonies was going very badly. Hopes for military victory had proven futile and the defeat of Cornwallis at Yorktown served to emphasize the necessity to bring the struggle to a conclusion. Furthermore, the policy of the government, which seemed to offer no chance for a quick termination of the struggle, coupled with the growing financial burden of the war, provoked dissatisfaction among the governing classes. The situation

74. Ibid., pp. 10–12.
75. C. J. Bartlett, "Statecraft, Power and Influence," in *Britain Pre-Eminent: Studies of British World Influence in the Nineteenth Century*, ed. C. J. Bartlett (London, 1969), p. 175.
76. Ibid., pp. 185–87.

with respect to the European powers was equally grim. On the continent Britain could count no effective ally. The powers were either openly belligerent, such as France and Spain, or hung off like Russia and the Baltic states in an inimical neutrality. A negotiated peace, though not essential, became an increasingly attractive solution to the war. Despite the objections of George III, therefore, Rockingham's ministry began negotiations for peace early in 1782. Eventually, in the autumn of 1783, Portland's ministry ratified the various peace treaties.

After the peace settlement Britain remained isolated in Europe and estranged from America. Pitt's government in the decade following 1783 concentrated its energies on repairing the country's finances and instituting domestic reforms such as the reduction of sinecures and places. The emphasis in British diplomacy was towards securing commercial treaties with as many of the continental states as possible.[77] Britain in these negotiations was in a strong position. Despite the strains the war placed on the finances of the country, its trading and commercial positions were more viable than those of many continental states. William Fraser, an undersecretary of state, expressed the basic soundness of the economy when he wrote that "though Millions & Millions have been shamefully lavished [during the war] we are still in a much better State than our neighbours on which Side soever you may please to look towards them. . . ."[78]

Though political affairs abroad during this decade rarely consumed much energy or attention of the government, there was some discussion among ministers about the possibility of forming alliances with various powers. The French remained the principal adversary, but neither the politicians nor the king wished to form alliances against the Bourbons unless English interests required them. Grantham best expressed the consensus of the politicians when he told Sir James Harris that "*Alliance really against the House of Bourbon is the most desirable connexion in the world,* but alliance to fight the battles of other

77. John Ehrman, *The British Government and Commercial Negotiations with Europe, 1783–1793* (Cambridge, 1962); John Ehrman, *The Younger Pitt: The Years of Acclaim* (London, 1969), especially pp. 467–574.

78. To Sir Robert M. Keith, St. James's, 7 Nov. 1783, Add. MS 35530 ff. 158–59.

powers . . . is not an eligible position."[79] The Baltic Powers, particularly the Danes and the Prussians, were regarded as the most desirable allies because of their strategic location astride the access routes to the naval stores so important to English naval power.[80] Despite temporary estrangement Carmarthen also hoped that Austria could be secured as the "*perpetual*, as it is the *natural* ally of England. . . ."[81] Not much was done, however, to give effect to these ideas.

Occasionally the ministers took an active interest in continental diplomacy as they did in 1787 when the spectre of French military intervention in Holland caused considerable alarm,[82] and as they did in the Russo-Turkish conflict in the Ochakov district in 1791. Yet despite their concern they hesitated to undertake any program that might require the employment of force or the expenditure of large sums of public money, and with the exception of these instances there is not much evidence to suggest that the continental powers actively consulted Britain on international developments not directly affecting her interests or security.

The wars with revolutionary and Napoleonic France were significant in the development of British influence in Europe because they not only brought the country out of its isolation but provided English statesmen the opportunity to assume the leadership of the states opposed to France. Alone among the great powers of Europe Britain struggled against French aggression from the commencement to the conclusion of the conflict. The ineffectual efforts to secure peace in 1796 and 1797, and the short-lived peace following the Treaty of Amiens (1802), should not hide the fact that for a generation Britain was almost continuously at war and that for most of that time the prospects of success were dim. Grenville characterized Britain's position in 1806, in terms that applied with equal force to most of the struggle, as that of "a great power, having weak allies, and not thinking it compatible with her honour, or even with

79. St. James's, 22 Feb. 1783, Third Earl of Malmesbury (ed.), *Diaries and Correspondence of James Harris, first Earl of Malmesbury* (4 vols.; London, 1844), vol. 2, 32–35. See also Carmarthen's memorandum, c. 1784, Oscar Browning (ed.), *The Political Memoranda of the Duke of Leeds* ("The Camden Society, new ser.," vol. 35; London, 1884), p. 101; and Pitt to Carmarthen, Downing Street, 24 June 1784, Private, Eg. MS 3498 Bundle 3.

80. Fox to Harris, St. James's, 11 Apr. 1783 and 27 July 1783, Malmesbury, *Diaries*, vol. 2, 39–40, 50–52; Carmarthen, mem., "Reasons for a Danish Alliance," c. 1784, Add. MS 28059 ff. 54–55.

81. To Harris, Tunbridge Wells, 24 July 1786, Malmesbury, *Diaries*, vol. 2, 211–12.

82. See Ehrman, *Pitt*, pp. 520 ff.

her interests, well understood, to abandon them."[83] At one time or another every continental power came under the influence of French hegemony. Only British naval power preserved the country from the same fate.

In the end the war and the role of the British army in it strengthened Britain's claim to a voice in European affairs. In the eighteenth century naval power had been the mainstay of Britain's military power. The wars with France enhanced the reputation of the British army and though it is often overlooked, even after 1815 Britain was "by no means a contemptible power on land," maintaining in peace time a moderately sized army.[84] The need for army reform was not to become evident until the disasters of the Crimean War. Until then Britain enjoyed a moderate reputation as a military power. In 1814 this military prowess was very evident to European statesmen and it was used to best advantage in European politics. What "an extraordinary display of power!" Castlereagh exclaimed when reporting that the effective contributions of British supplies and troops provided under the Treaty of Chaumont (1814) were beyond the effective contributions of any other power. "This, I trust, will put an end to any doubts as to the claim we have to an opinion on continental matters."[85]

British naval and military leadership in Europe during the war of itself insured British statesmen an influential voice in the peace settlement. But only the efforts of Viscount Castlereagh, foreign secretary from 1812 to 1822, secured this influence after the war. Castlereagh's genius and energy were directed towards securing an everlasting peace. To this end he argued that it was essential not to take "any step that might call our good faith in the course we are pursuing into question," for to do so "would weaken our *ground* abroad and at home, and essentially impair our influence with our Allies in pressing the necessity of adequate terms of peace."[86] Under his direction Britain assumed the role of mediator in the discussions

83. To Howick, Dropmore, 29 Sept. 1806, Secret, *H.M.C. Fortescue*, vol. 8, 367.

84. Bourne, *Foreign Policy of Victorian England*, p. 6.

85. To William Hamilton, Chaumont, 10 Mar. 1814, Charles William Stewart Vane, Marquess of Londonderry (ed.), *Correspondence, Despatches, and other Papers of Viscount Castlereagh* (12 vols.; London, 1848–1853), vol. 9, 335–36.

86. To Bathurst, Harwich, 30 Dec. [1818], 3 p.m., Private, Great Britain, Historical Manuscripts Commission, *Report on the Manuscripts of Earl Bathurst, Preserved at Cirencester Park* (London, 1923), pp. 250–51.

of the European settlement, a role that Canning had envisioned as early as 1807.[87]

As a result of Castlereagh's efforts Europe from 1814 to 1822 enjoyed a period of allied cooperation. Sometimes this cooperation was unsteady and there were instances when European statesmen harbored suspicions of one another. For the most part, however, the Congress system established in 1815 rested on the mutual consultation, respect, and cooperation of the European sovereigns and their ministers. Castlereagh was "quite convinced that past Habits, Common Glory, and these occasional Meetings, Displays, and Pledges are amongst the best Securities Europe now has for a durable Peace."[88]

> It really appears to me to be a new discovery in the Science of European Govt. at once extinguishing the Cobwebs, with which Diplomacy obscures the Horizon—bringing the whole bearing of the System into Its true light, and giving to the Councils of the Great Powers the Efficiency and almost the Simplicity of a single State.[89]

The close consultation of the allies and their meeting in periodic conferences to discuss international issues was undoubtedly Castlereagh's great contribution to the conduct of the international relations of the period.[90] Because of his activities during the peace conferences of 1814 and 1815 Castlereagh was known personally to the leading figures in continental politics. More important, they trusted him and felt him (often erroneously) to be at one with their ultraconservative views. He was able, therefore, to exercise an influence over international affairs seldom accorded any statesman. In allied conferences Castlereagh was Britain. His influence meant British influence, his voice a British voice.

The salient feature of the Treaty of Vienna was the interdependence of the European system it established. The territorial arrangements were inviolable. A threat to any aspect of the system, if not firmly repulsed, was seen inevitably to undermine every other feature of the settlement.[91] The Treaty of Vienna was unquestionably a conservative document and the system it established was de-

---

87. Canning to Granville, Foreign Office, 2 Oct. 1807, Private, P.R.O. 30/29/8/4 ff. 460–65.
88. To Liverpool, Aix, 4 Oct. 1818, Private & Confidential, Add. MS 38566 ff. 65–66.
89. Same to Same, 20 Oct. 1818, Private, ibid., ff. 67–68.
90. Webster, *For. Pol. Castlereagh.*
91. Ibid., vol. 2, 51.

signed primarily to preserve the status quo. The settlement was not as reactionary as it has often been portrayed, but the system it established was a static one in which the "dynamic forces of the age—liberalism and nationalism—too often found themselves thwarted or repressed and therefore sought fulfillment in more violent ways."[92] In reaction to this violence and perhaps inevitably the alliance became an agency for repression in the 1820s. Prince Metternich, Chancellor of Austria, with Russia and Prussia in tow and France acquiescing, skillfully interpreted the precepts of the alliance to justify allied intervention in the domestic affairs of any state. If the unity of the system were necessary to preserve European tranquility, Metternich reasoned, then any threat to an established government was a threat to the stability of established governments everywhere. Intervention, therefore, was justifiable whenever the status quo, domestic or international, was challenged. Every disturbance evoked a European interest and required European intervention if the established authorities failed to suppress it.

This interpretation of European affairs germinated and blossomed during the last years of Castlereagh's secretaryship. It was a system to which the British government, advocating the right of self-determination for all established states, could not adhere. Castlereagh himself was alarmed by this use of the Congress system,[93] but it was George Canning, his successor, who withdrew Britain from the alliance after the interventions of the continental states in Naples and Spain were undertaken without British concurrence and even despite her objections.[94] There were, as a consequence of Canning's decision, two important changes in British foreign policy in the 1820s.

First, nonintervention became the policy of the government. No effort was made to interfere actively either in the domestic affairs of other states or with the execution of allied programs.[95] Canning

92. Bourne, *Foreign Policy of Victorian England*, pp. 11–12.
93. William Ranulf Brock, *Lord Liverpool and Liberal Toryism, 1820–27* (London, 1967), pp. 232–33.
94. There is an interesting memorandum dated Gloucester Lodge, Sun. 12 Dec. 1824 in F.O. 27/326 in which Canning, reflecting on the accounts of Ireland in the French press, especially in *Etoile*, noted an "expression which is *identical* with that employed by the French Government to justify the Invasion & Conquest, & now the retention of Spain.
"Naples—Piedmont—Spain—Ireland!—who shall draw the line, if the principle of 'European question' be once admitted?"
95. Temperley, *For. Pol. Canning*.

simply stood aloof and observed events, except in the case of Latin America, where he made it clear that the British navy would intercept any troop convoys sent to subdue the emergent republics.[96] Eventually, of course, the whole congress system established after the wars, already shaken after British withdrawal, collapsed amidst national rivalries and hostilities, particularly over the question of Greek independence.

The second result of the change in the allied system was to reaffirm British suspicions of the extensive use of international congresses as a means of conducting diplomacy. Liverpool's cabinet as early as 1818 decided against establishing them at regular intervals because "tho' the mind might anticipate circumstances under which such meetings might be productive of many advantages, one may likewise contemplate those under which they might be likely to great Embarrassment."[97] The misuse of the congress system (as the British saw it in the early 1820s) confirmed this attitude and led later British statesmen to object even more strenuously at times to the idea of multilateral European congresses. This attitude was particularly evident in cases where political principles as opposed to the national interests of the great powers were the cause for calling a conference.[98] But even when the question of political ideology was not expressly stated British statesmen were still reluctant to participate in proposed congresses. Palmerston felt "we ought to prevent any more Congresses till we have another General war in Europe which I trust will not be in our Time,"[99] and even objected in 1838 to a general conference of maritime powers to discuss a uniform system of quarantine because he felt it "would somehow or other inevitably lead to making it an instrument for political intrigue."[100] He did participate nonetheless in the conferences on the Levant and on the slave trade in the 1830s, but only because they were called to deal with specific issues of great importance to the British government. Aberdeen, too, shared the general distrust of allied confer-

96. The best account of Anglo-American relations on the question is W. W. Kaufmann, *British Policy and the Independence of Latin America* ("Yale Historical Publications, Miscellany no. 52"; New Haven, 1951).

97. Liverpool to Castlereagh, F.O., 28 Oct. 1818, No. 3, Copy, Add. MS 38574 ff. 79–83.

98. Canning to Liverpool, Liverpool, 26 Aug. 1823, Secret, Copy, Canning MSS Bundle 70.

99. To Granville, Foreign Office, 31 May 1831, Private, P.R.O. 30/29/404.

100. Minute, Palmerston, 2 Aug. 1838, F.O. 27/571.

ences. He rejected an Austrian bid for a conference on the Levant in 1841 because he believed "it little calculated to preserve the desired union" of the powers on Middle Eastern affairs.[101] As a result of this general distrust the first major European congress after the London Conference on Belgium of 1830 did not assemble until 1856 when the combatants in the Crimean War met in Paris.

Palmerston's secretaryships in the 1830s in one sense marked another period of British involvement in international affairs. The Whigs on coming to office in 1830 reaffirmed the doctrine of nonintervention,[102] but Palmerston's interpretation of it was considerably more activist than Canning's had been. This change reflected one of the principal features of the State system in the nineteenth century. Throughout the nineteenth and into the twentieth century Britain was the leading liberal power.[103] Metternich's system was invariably employed to suppress not only the liberals but their allies in the continental states. Even after the dissolution of the alliance as it existed immediately following the wars with France, the Austrian, Prussian, and Russian governments remained inimical towards all reform movements. Palmerston, therefore, made it clear that active British support for liberal causes was inevitable if the conservative powers intervened in the domestic affairs of other states.[104]

Palmerston also believed that any decision to intervene in the affairs of other states was not always a matter of merely choosing between two alternative policies, intervention or nonintervention, each based on a principle with respect to the proper relation of one power to another. He felt that each case had to be considered in its own context. "It is, " he wrote, "one Thing to Interfere in the purely internal Concerns of a Country such as its Constitution &c, it is another to interfere in those matters which are common to it & its neighbours, and which it cannot itself decide without interfering in the affairs of those neighbours."[105] This policy of course allowed the

101. Aberdeen to Victoria, F.O., 28 Oct. 1841, Copy, Add. MS 43041 ff. 72–73.

102. Grey to Palmerston, The Hoo, 8 Sept. 1833, Palmerston Papers GC/GR/2249, National Register of Archives, London.

103. James Joll (ed.), *Britain and Europe Pitt to Churchill, 1793–1940* ("The British Political Tradition," eds. Alan Bullock and F. W. Deakin, Book 3; London, 1961), pp. 2–3.

104. Sir Charles K. Webster, *The Foreign Policy of Palmerston, 1830–1841* (2 vols.; London, 1951). He told Granville, for example, that "we cannot wish to see Austrian Bayonets putting down the germs of Liberty all over Italy. . . ." Stanhope Street, 13 Mar. 1831, P.R.O. 30/29/404.

105. To Granville, F.O., 31 Jan. 1831, ibid.

government to hedge a little when dealing with specific crises. Events in Spain and Portugal, for example, states which Palmerston hoped to bring into an alliance with Britain and France to form a liberal, western bloc opposed to the conservative, eastern powers, revealed his ideas in action. Palmerston regarded the "quadruple alliance" of 1834 "among the constitutional states of the west . . . as a powerful counterpoise to the Holy Alliance of the East."[106] He encouraged, therefore, the causes of the moderate parties in Iberia, and the conservative pretenders to the thrones were eventually removed from the countries with the aid of French and British arms.[107]

Between the electoral defeat of Melbourne's government in 1841 and the revolutions of 1848 Britain's relations with foreign powers were relatively unstrained. Not only were the central figures of European diplomacy at the Congress of Vienna, with the exception of Metternich and Wellington, no longer alive, but the disputes which bedevilled governments of the 1820s and 1830s—especially the crises in the Levant and in Iberia—had either been resolved or were quiescent. The major issues for Aberdeen and Peel involved the settlement of the American-Canadian boundary and the effectual suppression of the slave trade. Palmerston's precepts by 1840 were generally those of the Tory leadership, though they naturally disagreed on tactics in specific instances.[108] Furthermore, by the 1840s British influence in international affairs was well established. This is not to suggest that every initiative met with success. Aberdeen's difficulties with France over the suppression of the slave trade and with the United States on boundary questions were troublesome and time-consuming.[109] But these were minor issues compared with the problems faced by Aberdeen's predecessors and successors, and by the 1840s these more troublesome problems had been resolved,

106. Palmerston to Temple, Stanhope Street, 21 Apr. 1834, Evelyn Ashley, *The Life and Correspondence of Henry John Temple, Viscount Palmerston* (2 vols.; London, 1879), vol. 1, 297–300.
107. An earlier statement of this attitude may be found in Palmerston to Granville, Foreign Office, 28 Aug. 1832, P.R.O. 30/29/413 where the "Principles & Policy of England and France" are described as being "pitted against those of the absolutist Powers. . . ."
108. Peel to Aberdeen, Drayton Manor, 26 Nov. [1843], Add. MS 43063 ff. 80–86; Aberdeen, however, thought Palmerston's handling of the Levant crisis of 1839–40 to be essentially sound. To Peel, Haddo House, 11 Aug. 1840, Add. MS 40312 ff. 330–31.
109. Bourne, *Foreign Policy of Victorian England*, pp. 48–56.

at least for the time being, in a manner not unfavorable to British interests.

Turning finally to Britain's relations with individual states, considerations of strategy and security, with an occasional fleeting glance to trade and manufacturing interests when they did not conflict with these more important considerations,[110] were the principal factors influencing these relations. It is primarily for this reason that British policy seems at times so decidedly undoctrinaire, especially when compared to policies pursued by the other powers during this period. It is also possible for this reason to discern remarkable strains of continuity in the decisions of successive ministers throughout the first half of the nineteenth century and indeed beyond.[111] This truth was not lost on contemporaries, and it is fitting that it was Palmerston who best expressed it when he wrote his brother that "English interests continue the same let who will be in office, and that upon *leading principles and great measures* men of both sides, when they come to act dispassionately and with responsibility upon them, will be found acting very much alike."[112]

Although British interests came first in the calculations of the politicians, the broader interests of Europe were always of importance as well.[113] Even the promotion and protection of international trade in the nineteenth century was undertaken in part to benefit others.[114] In making their decisions, therefore, British politicians were usually suspicious of programs or policies that smacked of more esoteric considerations than security and strategy. Their attitude toward the Holy Alliance perhaps best reflects their general position on these questions. Castlereagh, describing the audience he

110. For example, G. Canning to S. Canning, F.O., 14 Feb. 1826, Private & Confl., F.O. 352/13 (Part I)/1 and minute, Palmerston, 2 Sept. 1834, F.O. 96/17.
111. By the late 1820s and the 1830s ministers also began at times, though not as a matter of course, consciously to investigate the policies of their predecessors. Wellington to Aberdeen, London, 8 July 1828, Add. MS 43056 ff. 82–85.
112. Foreign Office, 21 Apr. 1835, Ashley, *Life of Palmerston*, vol. 1, 318, italics mine.
113. See for examples Grenville to Pitt, Dropmore, 8 Oct. 1797, Copy, *H.M.C. Fortescue*, vol. 3, 378–80; Palmerston to William IV, Foreign Office, 5 Aug. 1832, draft, Palmerston Papers RC/AA/43/1–4; Grey to Palmerston, Howick, 9 Oct. 1833, Private, ibid., GC/GR/2259/1–2; Aberdeen to Prince Albert, F.O., 31 Oct. 1842, Copy, Add. MS 43042 ff. 167–68.
114. Bourne, *Foreign Policy of Victorian England*, p. 4.

and Wellington had with Emperor Alexander of Russia, told Liverpool that "it was not without difficulty that we went through the Interview with becoming gravity." The reason was "the awkwardness of this piece of Sublime mysticism and nonsense, especially to a British Sovereign . . . ," as a governing factor in foreign policy.[115] In dealing with each power, therefore, British statesmen looked to conflicts of national interests more than to ideological differences as sources of difficulty.

France, because of her geographical location and her military and political importance in Europe, was the power with which British governments were most concerned. The colonial rivalry of the eighteenth century and the continental expansion of the revolutionary and Napoleonic governments engaged the British in a military as well as a diplomatic struggle with the French. After 1815, but especially as time passed and British relations with Austria, Prussia, and Russia deteriorated, it became a leading principle of British foreign policy that an understanding with the French was essential to the maintenance of peace in Europe. On this point, at least, Canning, Wellington, Palmerston, and Peel all agreed,[116] though some, like Dudley, thought the French were still "our natural enemies."[117] An Anglo-French understanding became more feasible after 1830 when the July Monarchy was established in Paris. In the decade and a half that followed, though French activities were always regarded somewhat with suspicion,[118] the two powers worked fairly closely together. The fact that the Eastern powers regarded Louis Philippe's government as revolutionary, Aberdeen said, kept the French tied to an understanding with Britain "and was a better guarantee of peace than all our batteries and block ships."[119]

The most important area of Anglo-French conflict in Europe was in the Low Countries where both powers had a vital national interest in preventing the other from gaining an ascendancy. The French

115. Paris, 28 Sept. [1815], most Private, The Duke of Wellington (ed.), *Supplementary Despatches, Correspondence, and Memoranda of Field Marshal Arthur Duke of Wellington* (15 vols.; London, 1858–1872), vol. 11, 165.

116. Canning to Granville, Ickworth, 15 Nov. 1824, Private and Confidential, No. 1, P.R.O. 30/29/392; Wellington to Aberdeen, Woodford, 24 Oct. 1828, Add. MS 43056 ff. 341–44; Palmerston to Granville, F.O., 8 June 1838, P.R.O. 30/29/423; Peel to Aberdeen, Drayton Manor, 21 Aug. [1844], Add. MS 43063 ff. 324–32.

117. To Granville, Arlington Street, 8 May 1828, P.R.O. 30/29/14/4 ff. 153–54.

118. Palmerston to Granville, C.T., 16 Apr. 1840, P.R.O. 30/29/425.

119. To Peel, The Grove, 21 Oct. 1845, Add. MS 40455 ff. 230–33.

invasion of Holland was the *casus belli* for Britain in 1793, and Liverpool felt in 1814 that the "defence of Holland and the Low Countries is the only object on the Continent of Europe . . ." which would warrant a renewal of hostilities if the peace negotiations failed.[120] The object of British policy was to keep the French from gaining control of Antwerp and the Scheldt where they could establish a powerful naval and military base from which to strike to the north by sea into the Channel or to the south over land into central Europe.[121] This policy was promoted in the 1820s by maintaining a special relationship with the Dutch which included the maintenance of diplomatic relations at the ambassadorial level and the practice of sharing confidentially with the king of the Netherlands all that passed between Britain and the other powers.[122] There was, however, no real attachment to Holland and once it became clear after the revolution of 1830 that an independent and neutral Belgium would satisfactorily guarantee French exclusion from the Low Countries, Palmerston did not hesitate to support the dismemberment of The Netherlands.[123]

Prussia also initially figured in Castlereagh's plans for the defense of the Low Countries as a guarantor of Dutch independence from France, though he was concerned about "the tendency of their [the Prussian's] politics."[124] His fears were well-founded. Prussia, the least of the great powers after 1815, proved the most difficult for the British to understand and to work with. Though there was little conflict of interests between the two powers, British statesmen universally disliked the Prussians. Canning thought Berlin "the foolishest Court in Europe" "with no notion of politics but the drum-head & cat-o-nine tails,"[125] while Aberdeen, who was worried about Prus-

---

120. To Castlereagh, Fife House, 23 Dec. 1814, Most Secret and Confidential, Charles Duke Yonge, *Life and Administration of Robert Banks Jenkinson, 2d Earl of Liverpool* (3 vols.; London, 1868), vol. 2, 85–87.

121. Palmerston to William IV, F.O., 26 May 1834, Copy, Palmerston Papers RC/AA/112/1–3.

122. Wellington to Clancarty, Paris, 19 Dec. 1822, The Duke of Wellington (ed.), *Despatches, Correspondence, and Memoranda of Field Marshal Arthur Duke of Wellington 1819–1832* (8 vols.; London, 1867–1880), vol. 1, 662 (hereafter cited as *W.N.D.*); Canning to Granville, G. L., 9 Apr. 1824, Private and Confl., P.R.O. 30/29/389.

123. Palmerston to William IV, Foreign Office, 23 July 1832, Copy, Palmerston Papers RC/AA/38/1–5.

124. To George Rose, Bickling, 28 Dec. 1815, Londonderry, *Castlereagh Corresp.*, vol. 11, 105.

125. To Granville, Storrs, 13 Aug. 1825, Private, No. 72, P.R.O. 30/29/8/9 ff. 1035–40, and same to same, F.O., 8 Nov. 1825, Private Political, No. 88, P.R.O. 30/29/8/8 ff. 975–78.

sian designs on Hanover, thought it "the most rascally government in Europe; the most selfish and rapacious."[126] The Prussians were regarded, as a result, as being totally unreliable allies against either French or Russian aggression.

The other central European power, Austria, seemed only slightly more useful as a buffer to French and Russian expansion. During the struggles with France between 1793 and 1815 Austrian inconsistency and inefficiency perplexed and angered British statesmen.[127] After the war the Austrians became an even greater enigma. Austrian foreign policy was directed by Count Metternich, an able, shrewd diplomat who shared with Castlereagh a hope for a united Europe. But Metternich's foreign politics were ultra-conservative and his efforts to stamp out liberalism earned him few friends among the British. Canning, who survived Metternich's intrigues to have him removed, was most critical. He characterized Metternich as "the greatest rogue, & liar on the Continent, perhaps in the Civilized world,"[128] and told Liverpool that it was impossible to "enter into joint counsel with him, without the certainty of being betrayed."[129] Palmerston, too, did not much care for his politics, but admired his ability,[130] and felt, as did Aberdeen, that Metternich could be counted upon to join with the British in what Aberdeen called any "real emergency," particularly if it appeared likely that Austrian interests and prestige would be promoted as a result.[131]

The Central European powers, despite their ideological conservatism in foreign affairs, were for British statesmen "the great bulwark of Europe against future aggression, either from France or from Russia. . . ."[132] In the eighteenth century the Eastern Question, as Russian designs in the Middle East and Central Asia were euphemistically labeled, had not played a major role in British foreign policy. The events in the Ochakov district in 1791, however,

126. To Wellington, Foreign Office, 6 Nov. 1828, *W.N.D.*, vol. 5, 221–22.
127. Grenville to Dundas, Dropmore, 27 July 1799, Secret, Copy, *H. M. C. Fortescue*, vol. 5, 198–99.
128. To Granville, F.O., 11 Mar. 1825, Private & Confidential, No. 40, P.R.O. 30/29/8/7 f. 849.
129. Seaford, 25 Oct. 1825, Edward J. Stepleton (ed.), *Some Official Correspondence of George Canning* (2 vols.; London, 1887), vol. 1, 317.
130. To Granville, F.O., 6 Apr. 1832, P.R.O. 30/29/14/6 ff. 32–35.
131. Palmerston to Granville, F.O., 23 May 1834, P.R.O. 30/29/415; Aberdeen to Peel, Rosenau near Coberg, 28 Aug. 1845, Add. MS 40455 ff. 102–7.
132. Palmerston to William IV, Foreign Office, 29 Sept. 1833, Copy, Palmerston Papers RC/AA/88/1–3.

marked a break with this tradition of disinterest in or even sympathy with the Russians.[133] After 1815 the British increasingly regarded Russia as the principal threat to Britain's interests in this part of the world. This was a very serious conflict of interest because of the legitimate claims of both parties to influence in the region. The struggle with Russia for hegemony in Central Asia and the Middle East during the nineteenth century was among the most difficult problems faced by British statesmen, and the conflict was only barely papered over after 1907 despite the fear of both powers of Germany.[134] Prior to 1815 Anglo-Russian antagonism and competition had been primarily concentrated in the Baltic.[135] But increasingly at the end of the eighteenth century Russian designs in the Middle East attracted an equal share of British attention. Pitt as early as 1791 feared that Russian successes in the Levant would result in her emergence as a major naval power which would be able to challenge Britain both in the Mediterranean and in the Baltic.[136] Russian ambitions were clear to Castlereagh at Vienna[137] and contributed to the decision to keep the Ionian Islands for Britain in the peace settlement.[138] Suspicions of Russia were not limited to one party. Both Wellington and Palmerston thought Nicholas I devious and unfaithful.[139] Palmerston was anxious to work with the French in great part because he thought their common interest in checking the "Encroachments & aggressions of Russia" would overcome their rivalries in other parts of the world.[140]

British opposition to Russian expansion governed relations with the Baltic powers and the Ottoman Empire. Fear of Russian military power led Carmarthen to support an alliance with the Danes in the 1780s,[141] while during the wars with France Canning thought Sweden would serve as a useful check on Russia,[142] though he was careful to provide funds only for land forces lest the Swedes them-

133. Horn, *Great Britain and Europe*, p. 381.
134. Ira Klein, "The Anglo-Russian Convention and the Problem of Central Asia, 1907–1914," *Journal of British Studies*, 11 (Nov., 1971), 126–47.
135. Horn, *Great Britain and Europe*, pp. 201–35.
136. Unsigned memo by Pitt, "Notes, Russia, 1791," P.R.O. 30/8/195 ff. 49–54.
137. To Liverpool, Vienna, Nov. 1814, Yonge, *Liverpool*, vol. 2, 52–53.
138. Same, Vienna, 24 Dec. 1814, Private and Confidential, Add. MS 38566 ff. 31–35.
139. Wellington to Aberdeen, Walmer Castle, 14 July 1829, Add. MS 43057 ff. 177–80; Palmerston to Taylor, Stanhope St., 30 Oct. 1833, Copy, Palmerston Papers RC/CC/10/1–3.
140. Palmerston to Granville, Woburn, 26 Nov. 1833, P.R.O. 30/29/415.
141. To Pitt, 9 June 1784, Eg. MS 3498 Bundle 3.
142. To Pierrepont, Foreign Office, 10 Oct. 1807, Private, F.O. 334/9 ff. 595–601.

selves become too strong a naval power in the Baltic.[143] After 1815 little attention was given to the northern courts whose combined power was not a serious rival to Russian military might. But these old ideas of a Northern coalition did not disappear completely and they were revived in 1833 by Grey who sought to promote an alliance with Sweden.[144] Palmerston, who was not very receptive to the idea, was more interested in securing Danish neutrality in case of an Anglo-Russian war[145] and in preventing the French and the Swedes from engaging in quarrels that might endanger Britain's position in the Baltic.[146]

Because Russian expansion to the south and west directly affected British interests, it was in Turkey that Britain's main efforts to contain Russia were made. Primarily because of strategic interests Britain wished to avoid the dissolution of the Ottoman Empire. The Turks were not highly regarded either as allies or as a people. But the route to India through the Levant was thought secure only so long as a single power controlled the area. The opposition to Mehemet Ali in the 1830s, therefore, reflected British desires to prevent his success because Palmerston thought it would lead ultimately to the partition of the Ottoman Empire "into petty States, as a man cuts his meat into morcels in order to devour it the more Easily afterwards."[147]

In opposing Russian expansion into the Levant British statesmen of both parties regarded France as their principal ally in the task. The problems raised by the Greek revolution of the 1820s convinced Aberdeen that Russian influence with the Greeks could not be checked "unless France and England cordially unite to accomplish the business."[148] Wellington's government was not very successful in its Greek policy in part at least because of their inability to secure the close cooperation of the French. The Whigs, too, hoped to work with France in maintaining peace in the Levant,[149] but the Four Power Treaty of 1840 and France's exclusion from the discussion of the

143. Same to Same, Foreign Office, 31 May 1807, Private, ibid., ff. 545–50.
144. Grey to Palmerston, Howick, 5 Oct. 1833, Private; 10 Nov. 1833, Private; Downing Street, 13 Dec. 1833, Private, Palmerston Papers GC/GR/2257/1–2, GC/GR/2272, GC/GR/2282/1–2.
145. Palmerston to William IV, Broadlands, 1 Jan. 1834, Copy, ibid., RC/AA/99.
146. Same to Granville, F.O., 27 Nov. 1839, Private, P.R.O. 30/29/415.
147. To Granville, Panshanger, 13 Oct. 1834, P.R.O. 30/29/419/1.
148. To S. Canning, Foreign Office, 28 Oct. 1828, Private, F.O. 352/20 (Part 2)/9.
149. Palmerston to Granville, F.O., 7 Oct. 1834, P.R.O. 30/29/419/1.

question of Mehemet Ali's challenge to the Porte marked the failure of Palmerston's initial policy. He did, however, succeed in maintaining the territorial integrity of the Ottoman Empire. Not until the Crimean War did England and France cooperate together to a significant extent in the Levant.

The other states in Europe with which British diplomacy was concerned were the Iberian powers, Portugal and Spain. The Spanish Borbon monarchs in the eighteenth century were allied with their French cousins against the English in the American war of 1776–1782. After the revolution in France, however, Spain along with Portugal, which had always enjoyed something of a special relationship with Britain because of its position as a counterbalance to Spain in the region and the usefulness of Portuguese ports to the Royal Navy, became important as checks on French power and expansion. British military victories in Portugal and Spain after 1810 paved the way to Waterloo and the ultimate defeat of Napoleon. Successive ministries after 1815 were anxious to prevent too great a French influence from establishing itself in Spain,[150] and to keep the Spanish and the Portuguese on friendly terms with one another.[151] Palmerston also thought of the Iberian powers as part of a western European bloc opposed to the powers of the East.[152] British interests in Iberia were principally strategic and though Aberdeen spoke for others when he said Spain "may not be a very powerful or useful ally . . . ," he still regarded Spanish friendship as better than having none.[153]

Britain's commercial relations with Spain and Portugal were not regarded as significant factors in determining policy towards either power. Canning thought French jealousy about Portugal's relationship with England "excessively foolish" because the commercial treaties which cemented the alliance were "clogs upon us in our new course of extended & liberal commercial principles."[154] The turmoil of Iberian politics kept Spain and Portugal in a prominent position

150. Temperley, *For. Pol. Canning* and Webster, *For. Pol. Palmerston* deal extensively with this problem. See also Peel to Aberdeen, Whitehall, 17 Oct. [1841], Confidential, Add. MS 43061 ff. 289–90 where the "primary object" of British policy in Iberia is said to be "Resistance to the establishment of French Influence in Spain."

151. Palmerston to William IV, Foreign Office, 25 June 1832, Copy, Palmerston Papers RC/AA/33/1–3; Peel to Aberdeen, Whitehall, 9 Nov. 1841, Add. MS 43061 ff. 327–36.

152. See supra, pp. 29–30.

153. To Wellington, Foreign Office, 2 Sept. 1828, Copy, Add. MS 43056 ff. 222–25.

154. To Granville, F.O., 21 Jan. 1825, No. 20, Private Political, P.R.O. 30/29/8/6 ff. 773–76.

in Britain's foreign affairs, but Iberia was clearly a lesser concern than other areas of Europe.

Britain's relations with the states of the western hemisphere were not particularly good between 1782 and 1846, though relations with the United States did improve somewhat after the Webster-Ashburton Treaty (1842). For many years after 1783 the British had hopes of settling the American hinterland and of confining the United States to the eastern seaboard of the continent. These hopes eventually proved chimerical, although Aberdeen as late as 1845 considered the possibility of military action to preserve California for Mexico if the French government could be persuaded to join with Britain in the venture.[155] In the years after American independence the two countries fought one war and had numerous quarrels on nearly every issue imaginable. They bickered about trading privileges, especially in the West Indies. The pro-American sentiment in the maritime provinces of Canada was a source of concern to British statesmen because of the region's importance to British naval power.[156] There were numerous disputes over the suppression of the slave trade which involved emotional issues as well as commercial and shipping antagonisms. By the 1830s, however, it had become apparent that the commercial relations of the two powers were so extensive that "it would require a very Extraordinary State of Things to bring on actual war . . . ,"[157] and when the boundary question had been settled in 1842, thereby removing the most immediate cause of friction from Anglo-American relations, it became possible to work on solving other less contentious issues. Even so this task was formidable since "the misunderstandings of the period" left a "legacy of mutual suspicion" in Anglo-American relations[158] which did not entirely disappear until the twentieth century.

Relations with the United States were strained in part because of American resentment of British influence in Spanish America. Long before the end of the wars with France Britain had established a flourishing and profitable trade, both licensed and clandestine, with the area.[159] Britain's political interests in the region were to cultivate friendship with the states who might be effective allies against the

155. To Peel, Foreign Office, 23 Sept. 1845, Add. MS 40455 ff. 172–75.
156. Castlereagh to Bathurst, Vienna, 4 Oct. [1814], Private, B.M. Loan 57/8/819.
157. Palmerston to Granville, Stan. St., 29 Mar. 1839, P.R.O. 30/29/14/6 ff. 91–92.
158. Bourne, *Foreign Policy of Victorian England*, p. 17.
159. Lynch, "British Policy and Spanish America," pp. 24–30.

United States. One concern was American economic and territorial expansion,[160] but European interests were involved as well. There was for a good part of the nineteenth century considerable fear of an American naval alliance with France or with Russia, or even with both powers.[161]

Objectively, however, British diplomacy fared poorly in the southern hemisphere of America. After an initial burst of enthusiasm for the potential of the new Latin American states in the mid-1820s, ministers tended to ignore that region of the world so long as British interests there were safeguarded and it did not appear that any European power other than Spain or Portugal was becoming active in its affairs.[162] The only exception to this benign neglect was Mexico, which Palmerston and others "looked to as a Commercial & political ally of England to Counterbalance the Influence of the United States under any circumstances in which that Influence might by Possibility be adverse to us."[163] With this exception, however, British politicians regarded with despair the hopelessly tangled affairs of the former Spanish and Portuguese colonies, and generally felt there would be little progress in South America as long as these governments were continually locked in internecine strife.[164]

The effort to suppress the African slave trade after 1815 was one of the country's most noble ventures in the sphere of foreign policy. The program was one of considerable expense and frustration. Only the eastern powers, whose subjects had little interest in the trade, gave Britain no trouble over the question. The British had bitter quarrels, on the other hand, with all the western states, and none more so than those with France and the Iberian powers. The issue of the slave trade was unquestionably a divisive one between Britain and those states most likely to support her in a contest with the eastern powers. But the policy of suppressing the trade was pursued by every ministry because domestic political considerations after 1814 made it impossible for ministers to abandon it.[165] No one

160. Bartlett, "Statecraft, Power and Influence," p. 183.
161. Bourne, *Foreign Policy of Victorian England*, p. 14.
162. Wellington to Aberdeen, Walmer Castle, 19 July 1829, Add. MS 43057 ff. 185–86.
163. Palmerston to Granville, For. Off., 23 Dec. 1830, Private, P.R.O. 30/29/404.
164. Minutes, Palmerston, 11 and 12 Nov. 1835, F.O. 96/18.
165. Jerome Reich, "The Slave Trade at the Congress of Vienna—A Study of English Public Opinion," *Journal of Negro History*, 53 (Apr., 1968), 129–43.

had much faith in succeeding in the effort,[166] but despite the frustrations all were committed to seeing it through. The antislavery societies were regularly consulted about policy in this field,[167] and Palmerston even said that the British would have no objection to the establishment of French colonies on the west coast of Africa because "lawful Commerce would have a Tendency to turn the Habits of the Africans away from the Slave Trade."[168] Every conceivable program was tried, including the passage of parliamentary legislation designed to prohibit the trade in vessels and by nationals of those countries who refused to sign treaties to suppress it, though with only moderate success until the second half of the century.

British foreign policy in the first half of the nineteenth century was designed to promote the strategic interests of the country—both commercial and imperial—and to protect British security in Europe. It was, therefore, to Britain's advantage to remain as much as possible on good terms with all the powers, and to hold back from too close an attachment to any single state. Even in times of crisis British statesmen resisted the establishment of too close an alliance with any other power. This system has been usually referred to as maintaining the balance of power in Europe and was the principal factor in British foreign policy in the nineteenth century. Palmerston perhaps more accurately described it as a "System of Practical Mediation" where British interests were promoted by switching support from one camp in Europe to the other "according as the opposite Side may manifest a Spirit of Encroachment & Injustice."[169] In such a system British interests were best preserved by peace in Europe and it is not surprising, therefore, that despite Britain's growing commercial and industrial preeminence during the nineteenth century few decisions in foreign policy reflected merely trading interests. The government, in fact, made little direct attempt to influence the course of British trade at any time during the century. Though they tried to "maintain 'equal favour and open competition' for British finance and trade overseas," most ministers were too "limited by their aristocratic tastes and prejudices and by

166. Wellington to Aberdeen, S. Saye, 4 Sept. 1828, Add. MS 43056 ff. 230–33; Aberdeen to Peel, Foreign Office, 18 Oct. 1844, Add. MS 40454 ff. 282–83.
167. Minute, Bandinel, on Richo Allen to Aberdeen, Dublin, 25 June 1842, F.O. 84/447.
168. Minute, Palmerston, 22 Apr. 1840, F.O. 27/615.
169. To William IV, Foreign Office, 8 Oct. 1832, Copy, Palmerston Papers RC/AA/ 52/1–3.

the *laissez-faire*, Free Trade tradition of classical political economy" to propose or conceive of any coherent plan of action to promote commerce by direct political means. Trading and commercial considerations affected decisions, but usually only insofar as they contributed to or reflected other interests in foreign policy involving national security.[170]

170. D. C. M. Platt, *Finance, Trade, and Politics in British Foreign Policy, 1815–1914* (Oxford, 1968), pp. xxxix–xl, 353. This is the only good study of this important question. Much more work needs to be done on the relations between commercial interests and political decisions during the nineteenth century.

CHAPTER II

THE CABINET AND FOREIGN POLICY

The history of the emergence of the cabinet as a relatively efficient administrative institution is one of the most difficult problems in modern British historiography. Ian Christie has written recently that despite the fact that the cabinet is among the more thoroughly studied institutions, its history "is perhaps the most elusive and least clearly depicted facet of eighteenth-century government."[1] In this single institution, in fact, the problems of institutional history in the broader sense are clearly identified. The first of these difficulties is the fact that the men of the late eighteenth century themselves were not certain about the nature of the institution. This uncertainty was reflected in many ways, but was evident principally in the rather loose use of terms such as cabinet and council to identify the same or similar institutions at different times.[2] Related to this problem was the continuous and almost kaleidoscopic fluctuation in the composition and size of eighteenth-century advisory bodies of the crown. There were very good political reasons for these fluctuations but their effect was to leave the impression of institutional fluidity.[3]

More important stumbling blocks stand in the way of a more clearly depicted history of the cabinet. These difficulties are related to the scholars who have set themselves the task of investigating this problem. On the one hand there has been a tendency on the part of historians to find the origins of the cabinet in their own period. J. H. Plumb, for instance, argued on the basis of the material in Robert Harley's memoranda of "the *highest executive bodies* of the English government during the most vital years of the War of the Spanish Succession"[4] that "it is possible for the first time [1956] to establish

1. "The Cabinet in the Reign of George III, to 1790," in *Myth and Reality in Late Eighteenth-Century British Politics and other Papers*, by Ian Christie (Berkeley, 1970), p. 55.
2. Ibid., p. 59.
3. Ibid., pp. 56–58.
4. J. H. Plumb, "The Organization of the Cabinet in the Reign of Queen Anne," *Transactions of the Royal Historical Society*, 5th series, 7 (1957), 137. Italics mine.

with certainty the organization of cabinet government in the reign of Queen Anne."[5] This article was and remains a highly suggestive piece of historical writing, but "highest executive bodies" were not necessarily cabinets in the modern sense and even if they were one must really stretch the point to argue that "cabinet government" existed in the reign of Queen Anne.

On the other hand there has been a tendency to assume that the cabinets of the twentieth century conform to the ideals of the textbooks. Christie, for example, states that "Regularity and system are the hall-marks of healthy governmental institutions."[6] The assumption is that the institutions of the present are healthy, ergo they operate in a regular and systematic fashion, and that therefore in studying the same or similar institutions in the past the historian should look for the emergence of system and regularity. Christie is careful always to point out that every generalization has its exception,[7] but others have not been so careful.[8]

The discussion at hand is how the cabinet as an institution was involved in formulating foreign policy at the turn of the nineteenth century. Throughout the eighteenth century cabinets had spent a good deal of their time discussing foreign affairs and a considerable amount of business involving colonial and military problems was also related to some extent to foreign relations.[9] The crown's role in these discussions will be discussed more fully in the next chapter, but here it should be stated that the cabinet took the responsibility of deciding policy which was implemented only after the king had approved.[10] The reasons for this arrangement are obvious. Ministers were individually responsible both to the king and to Parliament, but their primary responsibility was to the king since administrations were formed by the active use of the prerogative. After 1783–84 this system began to break down and to be replaced by a new system of "joint Cabinet responsibility, which implies unanimity of political opinion, common responsibility to Parliament, and sub-

5. Ibid., 157.
6. Christie, "The Cabinet in the Reign of George III, to 1790," p. 66.
7. Ibid., pp. 69, 84.
8. Take, for instance, the forced symmetry in the statement that in the eighteenth century "Ministerial responsibility came to be owed politically to the Crown and legally to the Courts, especially to the House of Lords, for impeachment had not yet rusted into disuse." E. T. Williams, "The Cabinet in the Eighteenth Century," in *The Making of English History*, Robert Livingston Schuyler and Herman Ausubel, eds. (New York, 1952), p. 388.
9. Christie, "The Cabinet in the Reign of George III, to 1790," p. 73.
10. Ibid., pp. 84–108 passim.

mission to a Prime Minister who enjoys the largest share of the King's confidence and the greatest authority in the Council. . . ."[11] But the emergence of the new system was a tedious process that was by no means completed by 1850.

In foreign affairs this trend was more and more evident. Eighteenth-century cabinets collectively had deliberated and determined foreign policy. Increasingly after 1782 the number of active participants in these discussions declined. Only the prime minister and the foreign secretary were continuously involved in the determination of policy. There were always some other men among the ministers, such as Lord Harrowby in the 1820s, who participated more or less regularly in these discussions because of their experience abroad or in the Foreign Office at an earlier period. But except in times of crisis when there were lengthy discussions of individual dispatches the cabinet was increasingly concerned only with the principles on which policy administered by the secretary of state was based.

There were several reasons for this development. The most obvious was the growing size and hence cumbersome nature of the cabinet. The cabinet was never very large. Pitt's first cabinet, formed in 1783, had only eight ministers; Peel's in the 1840s numbered twelve. Yet ministers always found it difficult to reach a decision quickly on any issue brought before the whole cabinet. Newly-appointed ministers hesitated to make decisions without time to read the dispatches of their predecessors and in 1828 Wellington's ministry delayed all action on the Greek question for over a month after coming to office because they were unable "to read the correspondence, much less make up their mind upon a subject that presents so many difficulties," while they were settling in at their respective departments.[12] There was also the usual difficulty of securing agreement among a group of men who could be counted on to have strong opinions on any matter brought before them. Palmerston in 1836 told Granville, the ambassador at Paris, that if he took "'Twelve of the ablest men in England, & put them into a Room together to discuss a Great Question of State Policy, . . . the Chances are that you find upon an Equation that they will come out just equal

11. Arthur Aspinall, "The Cabinet Council, 1783–1835," *Proceedings of the British Academy, London*, 38 (1952), 214.
12. Dudley to Granville, F.O., 30 Jan. 1828, P.R.O. 30/29/14/4 ff. 105–06.

to *Shelley*.'"[13] The problem was made all the more difficult when a foreign secretary had to secure the approval of his colleagues for programs ironed out after hours of sitting in conferences with representatives of foreign powers in London. Palmerston spent an afternoon in August, 1831, arguing with the French, Austrian, Prussian, Belgian, and Dutch representatives over the sixth protocol on Belgian affairs; "then the Draft was debated in Cabinet last night from Ten till Two in the morning, & I afterwards had Some Difficulties about it with Grey [the prime minister] this morning, who being out of Town last night was not at the Cabinet."[14] Small wonder that Ellenborough said in 1828 that Dudley and Wellington could settle in half an hour's conversation what it would take five hours or more to decide in cabinet.[15]

Of course it was not necessary for many questions to be taken before a full cabinet. The secretaries of state in the eighteenth century had divided business into two categories. More important issues involving broader questions of policy required that the "sense of the Cabinet" be taken while issues that were administrative in nature were dealt with by the secretary in consultation with the king.[16] It is not surprising, therefore, that after 1782 every foreign secretary acted without prior consultation with his colleagues. Leeds in 1790 without the knowledge of even Pitt remonstrated against the Flanders government for seizing the house of the British consul at Ostend and for not recognizing the consul as an agent of the British government.[17] Fox frequently sent dispatches before anyone had read them,[18] and Canning angered his colleagus in 1823 by not consulting them before telling Sir William A'Court, the ambassador at Madrid, to follow the King of Spain if the Cortes removed him from his capital.[19] Aberdeen sent Peel in 1843 "my Instructions to Lyons, which I could have wished that you had seen before they

13. Palmerston to Granville, F.O., 9 Feb. 1836, Confidential, quoting Dudley, P.R.O. 30/29/421.

14. Palmerston to Granville, F.O., 7 Aug. 1831, Private, P.R.O. 30/29/404.

15. 19 May 1828, Colchester, *Ellenborough Diary*, vol. 1, 109–10.

16. Christie, "The Cabinet in the Reign of George III, to 1790," pp. 74–75.

17. Drafts to Francis Wilson, Whitehall, 8 and [18] June 1790, and Wilson to Burges, Brussels, 14 June 1790, No. 41, F.O. 26/15; Pitt to Leeds, Saturday Night, 19 June 1790, P.R.O. 30/8/102 ff. 172–73.

18. Fox to Grenville, 6 Mar. 1806, *H. M. C. Fortescue*, vol. 8, 49.

19. 27 Mar. 1823, Francis Bamford and the Duke of Wellington (eds.) *The Journal of Mrs. Arbuthnot, 1820–1832* (2 vols.; London, 1950), vol. 1, 220.

were sent off; but there was no time to send them to you."[20] There was a danger in a secretary's acting on his own authority since his initiatives could be repudiated by his successors. This was particularly so if there was no record of his transactions. Palmerston, for example, felt that "verbal assurances are good for the moment, but bind only the Minister who made them; and unless recorded are of little value when other Ministers succeed."[21] Only Shelburne's ministry, however, appears to have considered themselves unfettered by the action of "any one minister done without communication" with his colleagues.[22]

Because of the difficulty in making policy quickly in full cabinet meetings those who took a more active role in foreign affairs often determined policy among themselves before summoning their colleagues. The existence of an inner cabinet for foreign affairs[23] is a feature of nearly all the ministries of the period. It invariably consisted of the prime minister, the foreign secretary, and one or two other ministers whose concurrence was necessary before any decision was made. Once these men agreed on a policy it was difficult for their colleagues to alter it.[24] If they were divided, affairs were likely to drift.[25]

There were, in addition to the difficulty and loss of time in taking every aspect of foreign policy before a full cabinet, other incentives for a few ministers to manage Britain's foreign relations. Leeds in the early days of his secretaryship found it almost impossible to interest his colleagues in foreign affairs while Parliament was in session, though they were always willing to attend to his concerns

20. 27 Nov. 1843, Foreign Office, Add. MS 40454 ff. 24–25.

21. Minute, Palmerston, 12 Mar. 1840, on Melbourne to Palmerston, Downing Street, 11 Mar. 1840, Palmerston Papers GC/ME/359/1.

22. Shelburne to Grantham, Thursday 8 o'clock [Sept. 1782?], Lucas Collection L 30/14/306/9, Bedfordshire Record Office.

23. The small cabinets of the eighteenth century did not have inner cabinets, though for a time in the early 1760s there were "concentric circles of confidence" which disappeared by 1766 and were replaced by "a certain formal precedence . . . conceded to the head of the treasury and the secretaries of state." Christie, "The Cabinet in the Reign of George III, to 1790," pp. 61, 65. After 1783, however, there was invariably an inner cabinet composed of "a small group of men peculiarly in the Prime Minister's confidence." Aspinall, "The Cabinet Council," pp. 209–12.

24. They could, however, force a formal meeting to discuss questions about which they had doubts. Dundas to Grenville, Downing Street, 20 Mar. 1800, Private, H. M. C. Fortescue, vol. 6, 170.

25. Dundas's "Memorandum on the State of the Cabinet," 22 Sept. 1800, A Aspinall and E. Anthony Smith (eds.), English Historical Documents 1783–1832 (London, 1959), pp. 110–11.

during recesses.[26] After the peace with France in 1815 ministers faced the reverse of Leeds's problem. Liverpool told Wellington that

> As long as the war continued we were all constantly at our posts or within a few days' call. This is more than could reasonably be expected in time of peace; but I still think that we ought not to separate indefinitely as we have done; that we ought to reassemble at fixed and not very distant periods, and . . . I can by no means approve of the new practice of ministers passing a part of their holidays on the continent, though in some particular cases it might be attended with advantage.[27]

Dudley felt that the "dispersion of the Cabinet . . . is a great inconvenience—and a great evil. Those that have important publick duties to discharge, should be a little more ready to sacrifice their personal comforts and the charms of a country life."[28] Once a general outline of policy was decided in cabinet it was not necessary to reconvene the ministers so long as any action taken was designed only to implement their decision.[29] An important consideration in Palmerston's desire to keep as much of foreign affairs as possible in the hands of a select group of ministers was his belief that "there are very few public men in England who follow up Foreign affairs Sufficiently to foresee the Consequences of Events which have not happened."[30]

The first clearly distinguishable inner cabinet was composed of Pitt, Grenville, and Henry Dundas, home secretary (1791–1794) and secretary for war (1794–1801). These men frequently met together just prior to cabinet meetings so that they could present a united front to their colleagues on a given policy.[31] Grenville wrote Pitt in 1795, when the question of further subsidies to Prussia was under discussion, that "the worst thing that can happen is that you & Dundas should be *acting* on one line, & I on another; for this must

26. Diary, 1784, Browning, *Leeds Political Memoranda*, pp. 102–2.
27. Liverpool to Wellington, Walmer Castle, 15 Oct. 1826, *W.N.D.*, vol. 3, 422.
28. Dudley to Granville, Friday, 12 Oct. 1827, P.R.O. 30/29/14/4 ff. 53–54.
29. Grenville to Pitt, Dropmore, 5 Feb. 1797, P.R.O. 30/8/140 ff. 91–92.
30. Palmerston to Granville, F.O., 5 June 1838, P.R.O. 30/29/423, Palmerston was always projecting possible events out of present circumstances. Same to Same, Foreign Office, 21 Feb. 1832, P.R.O. 30/29/413; Palmerston to Russell, Stanhope Street, 7 Mar. 1836, Private, P.R.O. 30/22/2A ff. 274–77.
31. Pitt to Grenville, Downing Street, [20 Mar.], 1800, and Dundas to Grenville, Downing Street, 20 Mar. 1800, Private, *H. M. C. Fortescue*, vol. 6, 170.

defeat both chances. It would be very desirable that before we have another Cabinet on the subject we should have discussed this point a little amongst ourselves."[32]

When Castlereagh was foreign secretary (1812–1822) the inner cabinet initially was composed of him, Liverpool, and Bathurst, secretary for war and the colonies. Bathurst had served briefly as foreign secretary in 1809 and his responsibility for conducting the war made it necessary to consult him on all questions of foreign policy. After the war he maintained his position in the inner cabinet. With the exception of Castlereagh he possessed more breadth of vision in foreign affairs than any other minister and he shared at least in part Castlereagh's view of European politics.[33] Canning, however, seems to have consulted him less frequently than Castlereagh had,[34] and his importance declined after 1822.

When Canning joined Liverpool's ministry in 1817, Liverpool made certain that he was kept abreast of all affairs.[35] But Canning never really became part of the inner group before he resigned in 1820, probably because he wished to reduce British involvement in continental affairs as much as possible while his colleagues favored a policy of close cooperation with the allied powers.[36]

The Duke of Wellington joined the ministry and became part of the inner cabinet in 1816. His colleagues were anxious for the support his prestige and his international connections gave them, and he took advantage of their feeling to declare that he would follow the dictates of his own opinion on all matters of policy regardless of what the rest of the cabinet decided.[37] While Castlereagh was alive Wellington worked closely with him. Both men shared the experiences of the peace settlement and they viewed European politics in much the same manner. Castlereagh always sought Wellington's advice. Canning, however, assumed that Wellington would offer his opinion without being called upon for it. Certainly Canning rarely solicited it on the feeble though plausible pretext that "the current business of every day so fully occupies and overflows the

32. Monday, 4 o'clock, [23 Feb. 1795], marked "1794?", P.R.O. 30/8/140 ff. 75–76.
33. Webster, *For. Pol. Castlereagh*, vol. 1, 35.
34. 27 Mar. 1823, Bamford and Wellington, *Journal of Mrs. Arbuthnot*, vol. 1, 220.
35. Liverpool to Bathurst, Walmer Castle, 9 Oct. [1818?], 11 p.m., Private, *H. M. C. Bathurst*, p. 458.
36. Webster, *For. Pol. Castlereagh*, vol. 2, 19.
37. Ibid., 17.

day, that I have seldom a moment for *seeking* communication. . . ."[38] The duke at first felt abused but soon resumed his practice of writing voluminous memoranda on all aspects of policy. Occasionally he criticized Canning's dispatches paragraph by paragraph.[39] Partly because of his feelings of isolation and partly because of his disagreement with Canning on Britain's role in European politics, Wellington was in opposition to Canning's policies almost immediately after Canning's accession to the ministry in 1822. The duke's effectiveness, however, was blunted by his habit of corresponding frequently with the ministers of foreign sovereigns in London and by his telling them when he disagreed with the majority of the cabinet.[40] He was also a favorite at the Court and some ministers, particularly Harrowby and Sidmouth who otherwise might have supported him in cabinet, were "afraid of saying so lest they should be supposed to be giving support to the King's Favourite."[41]

Wellington was always a difficult colleague because he believed strongly that his opinions were the best policy. In the 1840s, when he was long past his prime, Aberdeen and Peel continued to consult him frequently, even when they knew he would disagree with the rest of the cabinet. Peel told Aberdeen after the duke had disapproved of Aberdeen's decision not to protest the French refusal to ratify the Five Power Slave Trade Treaty of 1841, that he was "sure whatever may be the inconvenience of such a communication from him, it is much less, than that which would arise from taking any step in a matter of so much importance without previous Concert with him—leaving him at Liberty not only to state his dissent from it but to state publicly that he was not even Consulted."[42]

Some members of every cabinet who were not part of the inner group nonetheless worked diligently over the foreign correspondence. Lord Harrowby, a former foreign secretary and from 1812 to 1827 lord president of the council, was one of the few ministers to read every paper and memorandum circulated.[43] Dud-

---

38. Canning to Wellington, Colchester, Tuesday, 11 Feb. 1823, *W.N.D.*, vol. 2, 33–34.
39. There are numerous examples in ibid., vols. 1–4, passim.
40. Brock, *Lord Liverpool and Liberal Toryism*, pp. 240–41.
41. Arbuthnot to Bathurst, Whitehall, 24 Mar. 1824, Private and most confidential, *H. M. C. Bathurst*, p. 565.
42. 30 Oct. 1842, Drayton Manor, Private, Add. MS 43062 ff. 168–69.
43. Canning to Liverpool, F.O., 11 June 1826, Stapleton, *Corresp. of Canning*, vol. 2, 58.

ley lamented his resignation in 1827 because though "Harrowby worried me a little, . . . still he understood and attended to foreign business—besides his authority, when he was satisfied, contributed to keep other people quiet."[44]

Harrowby was useful in his attendance to foreign affairs; more often ministers in his situation were nuisances. Lord Ellenborough, Lord Privy Seal and president of the Board of Control in Wellington's ministry, was openly contemptuous of both Dudley and Aberdeen. He hoped to succeed Dudley in May, 1828, but when Peel and Wellington preferred Aberdeen he resolved to "do as much of the business of the Foreign Office as I can."[45] Aberdeen occasionally requested Ellenborough to work over a draft dispatch,[46] but he and Wellington consulted regularly only Peel, the home secretary, when it was necessary to make decisions.[47]

Lord Holland, chancellor of the duchy of Lancaster in the ministries of Grey and Melbourne, took an active interest in foreign affairs. Holland, who was "as uncomfortable a colleague as a Foreign Minister could have," had inherited a slavish attachment to France from his connection with his uncle, Charles James Fox. Holland House, presided over by Lady Holland, an incorrigible gossip, was, however, the center of Whig social circles in London and Holland could not be ignored.[48] He expressed his opinion freely on any and every subject and dispatches frequently returned to the Foreign Office from Holland House accompanied by little scraps of paper on which he habitually wrote long unsigned and undated memoranda in a close illegible scrawl.[49] Sometimes his minutes were left with the dispatches, but Palmerston kept most of them. After Holland's death in 1840 Palmerston collected them together and pronounced his epitaph: "Ld. Holland carried into Government all the factious and wrong headed Feelings & opinions which he had taken up in

44. To Granville, 16 Arlington St., 21 Aug. 1827, P.R.O. 30/29/14/4 ff. 15–16.

45. 28 May 1828 and 3 June 1828, Colchester, *Ellenborough Diary*, vol. 1, 124–28, 135–36; Wellington to Peel, 16 Aug. 1828, *W.N.D.*, vol. 4, 615–17.

46. 4–5 Nov. 1829, Colchester, *Ellenborough Diary*, vol. 2, 126.

47. Wellington to Aberdeen, London, 18 June 1828, Add. MS 43056 ff. 60–61; same to same, Stratfield Saye, 22 Apr. 1829, Add. MS 43057 ff. 146–47.

48. Webster, *For. Pol. Palmerston*, vol. 1, 40.

49. For example, undated minutes in F.O. 78/309 in one of which he accused the author of a memorandum on Turkish affairs of being prejudiced against Russia for seeing "ambitious designs on Constantinople" in "so laudable and natural a project as . . . a railroad to facilitate the intercourse between Petersburgh, Odessa, & Moscow."

opposition. Luckily he was singularly Easy Tempered & this together with his Inferiority [in rank in the Cabinet] made him less troublesome than he otherwise would have been."[50]

Although cabinet decisions were most often made in formal meetings it was not always possible or even necessary to convene a cabinet to secure a decision. Pitt, for example, suggested to Grenville on one instance that no formal cabinet be called "as you will probably see most of our colleagues at the Queen's House tonight."[51] Dudley sent to Lord Lansdowne in the country a draft instruction on the blockade of Greece in 1827 with a note telling him "If you approve send us your proxy;—if you do not, come up immediately that we may confer."[52] Pitt in 1799 felt that if Grenville wished to avoid calling a cabinet he could send "instructions, and the despatches on which they are founded, to the reading-room, and . . . send a circular notice that you have done so, meaning to dispatch them without delay if no objection occurs."[53] This course of action had the merit of appearing to leave a question open for discussion while leaving it to the initiative of the other cabinet ministers to bring the matter before the whole cabinet. In January 1845 Aberdeen circulated a memorandum arguing for the renewal of negotiations with France over the suppression of the slave trade despite the fact that the cabinet was scheduled to meet within the week. Haste was necessary because the French ministry needed an answer when they met the Chambers, which were scheduled to convene before an answer could be received in Paris after the regular cabinet meeting in London.[54] Peel even urged Aberdeen to accept the French offer on his own initiative because "In my opinion you have a fair right to ask for Confidence in Your Judgment in a matter of such great and, in point of time, urgent importance. . . ."[55] Grey encouraged Palmerston in a similar situation in 1831 to sign the articles of the proposed treaty between Belgium and Holland without formally laying them before the cabinet, since "the urgency of proceeding as

50. Minute, Palmerston, "Notes by Ld. Holland on Some F. O. Despatches, 1843," Palmerston Papers, GC/HO/139–41.
51. 19 May 1800, Hollwood, *H. M. C. Fortescue*, vol. 6, 232.
52. 10 Oct. 1827, F.O., Copy, Add. MS 38751 ff. 173–75.
53. 22 Nov. 1799, Wimbledon, *H. M. C. Fortescue*, vol. 6, 36.
54. Memorandum, Aberdeen, Foreign Office, 5 Jan. 1845, Add. MS 43244 ff. 9–10; Aberdeen to Peel, Foreign Office, 3 Jan. 1845, Add. MS 40454 ff. 382–83.
55. Saturday, 4 Jan. [1845], Drayton Manor, Add. MS 43064 ff. 158–61.

expeditiously as possible, on account of the conclusion of the armistice, may I think justify the [need for their] immediate communication" to the two powers.[56]

Formal cabinet meetings usually met in the Cabinet Room at the Foreign Office.[57] In the eighteenth century dispatches or extracts were read at these meetings and drafts of replies were approved.[58] To a degree this practice continued after 1782, but in the first half of the nineteenth century circulation of dispatches before meetings was more common. In practice there was no acceptable method for keeping all ministers informed at any time during the period from 1782 to 1846, though various expedients were tried.

The foreign secretary and the prime minister read every dispatch, but the amount of information other ministers received, whether they were in Town or in the country, varied. There was no fixed regulation prior to 1831 that dispatches should go in circulation.[59] Grenville occasionally instructed his undersecretaries to circulate dispatches,[60] but even Dundas was not always kept abreast of affairs when he was out of London without express directions from Grenville that he be kept informed.[61] The system was so irregular that undersecretaries frequently asked ministers if they might be interested in seeing dispatches. Howard de Walden sent Huskisson dispatches in 1827 that Dudley did not think to put into circulation.[62] Planta in 1826 was willing to send dispatches to Peel, the home secretary, if he was "near enough to London to receive & return Boxes daily . . . ."[63] Canning agreed with Wellington in 1826 that the cabinet ought to adopt a regular procedure, "whether it be

56. 15 Oct. 1831, Palmerston Papers, GC/GR/2044.
57. Palmerston ordered in 1831 that "The books of Reference Such as Parliamentary Debates, Statutes &c. Should be put on Some Book Shelves & kept constantly arranged & put in order before & after Every Meeting of the Cabinet." Minute, 20 Oct. 1831, F.O. 83/205. Books relating to foreign affairs kept in the Cabinet Room included Pinkerton's *Geography*, Marten's *Recueil des Traites*, Crutwell's *Geographical Gazetteer*, papers presented to Parliament since 1800, Hertslet's *Commercial Treaties* and *British and Foreign State Papers*. "List of Books in the Cabinet Room," ibid.
58. Pares, *George III and Politicians*, p. 160; Mark Alméras Thomson, *The Secretaries of State, 1681–1782* (Oxford, 1932), p. 97.
59. Hamilton to Perceval, Foreign Office, 8 p.m., 1 July 1810, Add. MS 49185 ff. 69–70.
60. Aust to Grenville, 14 Sept. 1791, Grenville MSS, notes and microfilm in possession of W. B. Hamilton estate.
61. Dundas to Grenville, Horse Guards, 21 June 1800 [sic; 1795?], *H. M. C. Fortescue*, vol. 6, 253.
62. 8 Oct. 1827, F. O., private and most confidential, Add. MS 28751 ff. 148–53.
63. Planta to Peel, F.O., 11 Oct. 1826, Private, Add. MS 40389 ff. 141–42.

that of the reading-room or that of separate and successive communication. The mixture of both spoils both, and leaves the Foreign Office at a loss what to do."[64] Apparently they settled on depositing the dispatches in the Cabinet Room at the Foreign Office since Aberdeen referred to this procedure in 1828 as the "usual" practice and Ellenborough on occasion mentions in his diary going to the Foreign Office to read dispatches.[65]

The Whigs returned to the practice of circulating dispatches by messenger to all ministers in Town. The messengers were given a list of the ministers and carried the dispatches to their homes or offices, depending on the hour of the day, in the order their names appeared on the list. Dispatches were never left for ministers who could not be found at home or at their departments, but were carried on to the next minister on the list. Once a messenger had been to each of the ministers he started at the top of the list and took the dispatches back to those ministers he did not find the first time. He went through the list in this manner until every minister in Town had read the papers in circulation.[66] Despite these complicated regulations, however, ministers frequently failed to receive as much information as they felt they ought to be sent.[67]

Naturally with papers passing through so many hands they invariably became disorganized and misplaced. Ministers occasionally forgot to replace papers in the boxes when they finished reading them,[68] and undersecretaries sometimes received official papers from servants of ministers accompanied by apologetic notes, such as "Lord John Russell presents his compts to Mr. Backhouse, & by the desire of Lord Holland transmits to him a paper which was mislaid by accident in Ld. Holland's bedroom this morning, Jany 22."[69]

Palmerston also tried to insure that his colleagues in the country were kept abreast of affairs by sending them daily abstracts of

64. Wellington to Canning, Apethorpe, 13 Oct. 1826 and Canning to Wellington, Paris, 20 Oct. 1826, *W.N.D.*, vol. 3, 419–21, 431.
65. Aberdeen to Bathurst, Argyll House, 5 Aug. 1828, Private, *H. M. C. Bathurst*, pp. 654–55; 24 Oct. 1829, Colchester, *Ellenborough Diary*, vol. 2, 118.
66. Backhouse's and Shee's "Order to be observed by the Messengers in the delivery of Boxes sent in Circulation to the Members of the Cabinet," F.O., 8 Jan. 1831, F.O. 366/521.
67. Clarendon to Granville, London, 28 Aug. 1840, Private, P.R.O. 30/29/423; Granville to Holland, Paris, 16 Oct. 1840, Private, Add. MS 51608 f. 154.
68. Lansdowne to Backhouse, Lansdowne House, Monday Morning, n.d., Backhouse Papers, Duke University Library.
69. Ibid.

important dispatches.[70] This system was not always successful because the undersecretaries were frequently unaware of which cabinet ministers were in London and which were elsewhere.[71] The press of business also prevented the clerks from preparing these abstracts.[72] Naturally when there was nothing of importance to report no clerk thought to prepare abstracts saying so.[73] But Palmerston's colleagues complained when they heard nothing and in 1835 he ordered that "a Bulletin Should be Sent Every Day Even if it is to Say there is no news."[74] When Lansdowne, lord president of the council, was abroad in 1834, abstracts were prepared daily and sent to him twice a week.[75]

As long as there was no fixed procedure for circulating dispatches some ministers inevitably felt they were being deliberately excluded from a full share in affairs. Lord Thurlow, the Lord Chancellor in Pitt's ministry, for instance, complained to Lord Hawkesbury in 1791 that his opinion was worthless "considering that I am not in the full circulation. . . ."[76] Perhaps his complaint was just, but Pitt warned Grenville that in sending papers to Thurlow "you must . . . take care [not] to let him keep them a week."[77] No foreign secretary, in fact, systematically attempted to keep important dispatches from his colleagues, though much routine material was of course never circulated.

Occasionally the inner group of the cabinet did suppress information they deemed so sensitive that the fewer people who possessed it the better. Significantly in each of these instances they did so only with the full concurrence of the king. George III, in fact, insisted that Pitt and Mulgrave tell only Lord Granville, British minister at St. Petersburg, that the Russians suspected them of having "secret objects of Conquest and usurpation" in their efforts to forge a coalition against France in 1805. The "Source which leaves no doubt

70. There must have been hundreds of these abstracts prepared, yet Professor Webster said that he never saw one, *For. Pol. Palmerston*, vol. 1, 40 n. 3, and so far as I know there are only two extant: Abstract of Intelligence, Cabinet Circular, Foreign Office, 9 Dec. 1833, F.O. 366/280 ff. 93–95; Abstract of Intelligence, Cabinet Circular, Foreign Office, 24 Aug. 1838, P.R.O. 30/22/3B ff. 259–60.

71. Minute, Backhouse, 8 Dec. 1833, F.O. 96/17.

72. Minute, Backhouse, 7 Dec. 1833, ibid.

73. Minute, T. L. Ward, F.O., 1 Oct. 1835, F.O. 96/18.

74. Minute, Palmerston, 2 Oct. 1835, ibid.

75. Minute, Palmerston, 27 Oct. 1834, F.O. 96/17.

76. Docketed 10 Aug. 1791, Aspinall and Smith, *English Historical Documents*, p. 136.

77. 11 Jan. 1791, Burton Pynsent, 1½ p.m., *H. M. C. Fortescue*, vol. 2, 12.

of its authenticity" and which the king wished to protect[78] was perhaps the Hanoverian government. Grenville did not circulate to any of his colleagues except Pitt a memorandum that Henry Wellesley, one of Lord Malmesbury's staff in the negotiations with France at Lisle in 1797, wrote on his arrival in London about the secret approaches to Malmesbury by the moderate party in Paris asking him to delay breaking off negotiations to give them a chance to consolidate their power and to make genuine efforts to secure peace.[79] George III approved of Grenville's showing the paper to no one but Pitt, "as it can be of no use in forming any opinion, and the less papers not necessary towards effecting that [object] are circulated the better."[80] Canning, Liverpool, and Wellington, with the knowledge of only George IV, in 1826 approved the request of the Portuguese government that Lord Beresford be allowed to return to Lisbon to take command of the Portuguese army.[81]

In the eighteenth century dispatches were occasionally circulated to persons who were not members of the cabinet. William Grenville, joint paymaster of the forces, and Lord Hawkesbury, president of the Board of Trade, read the dispatches regularly in the 1780s.[82] The Duke of York while Commander-in-Chief of the Army also received dispatches in circulation.[83] This practice, however, was apparently never resorted to by the ministries of the early nineteenth century.

After important dispatches were circulated the cabinet convened. Formal cabinet meetings were usually attended only by cabinet ministers. On occasion, however, other persons were called in to give their advice on political or technical problems. Pitt and Dundas attended a cabinet meeting in Addington's ministry to give information about Danish relations with Sweden and Russia.[84] Admiral Sir George Cockburn, a junior lord of the Admiralty, convinced Goderich's cabinet in 1827 that they ought not to seize neutral

78. Mulgrave to Granville, Downing Street, 10 Apr. 1805, Private most Secret & Confidential, P. R. O. 30/29/384A.

79. Grenville to George III, Dropmore, 4 Aug. 1799, Copy, *H. M. C. Fortescue*, vol. 3, 343.

80. George III to Grenville, Weymouth, 5 Aug. 1799, ibid., 344.

81. The whole tale is told in letters among the parties involved dated 2–9 Oct. 1826, in Stapleton, *Corresp. of Canning*, vol. 2, 141–42, and *W.N.D.*, vol. 3, 408–13.

82. Pitt to Hawkesbury, Wimbledon, Thursday morning, 17 Aug. 1786, Add. MS 38566 f. 134; Fraser to Pitt, Whitehall, 24 Dec. 1787, ½ past Six p.m., P.R.O. 30/8/137 ff. 44–45.

83. Minute, Grenville, on Herbert Taylor to Brook [Taylor], Horse Guards, 31 Mar. 1799, F.O. 83/12.

84. Draft minute of Cabinet, n.d., Add. MS 38357 ff. 146–47.

transports under Turkish convoy in Greek waters by contending "that it would be impossible to discriminate whether neutrals were *under Convoy*, or only sailing *in Company*: and that we should be involved in endless disputes and difficulties, and have to pay large compensations."[85] Diplomatic personnel occasionally attended a cabinet meeting while they were home on leave. Lord Stewart, Castlereagh's brother, for example, was able to give the cabinet a more complete idea of Castlereagh's and Wellington's sentiments on the negotiations at Paris in 1815 than they could gather merely from reading the dispatches.[86]

Though cabinets were occasionally held in the absence of the foreign secretary, decisions on any major issue were frequently delayed until his return to London.[87] When decisions could not be delayed, the results of the cabinet's deliberations were transmitted to the foreign secretary in writing or in person by the prime minister or by another member of the inner cabinet.[88]

Once the cabinet decided to pursue a particular course of policy the secretary of state usually prepared an official cabinet minute. Until recently it was the generally accepted view that these minutes were actually declining in importance late in the eighteenth century.[89] It now seems clear that they were a new method of tendering advice. The papers of George III down to 1780 have few of these minutes in them, which suggests two things. First, that minutes of ministers during the 1760s and 1770s were working papers and personal records of cabinet decisions. Second, that "no regular practice of preparing a copy of a cabinet minute as a formal submission of advice to the king had yet been established."[90] Lord Stormont in 1782 was the first minister to send minutes to the king on a regular basis[91] and his successors institutionalized the practice. Grenville said in 1799 that

85. Huskisson to Howard de Walden, Eastham, 5 Oct. 1827, Private & Confidential, Copy, Add. MS 38751 ff. 124–25.

86. Liverpool to Castlereagh, Fife House, 28 Aug. 1815, Private and Confidential, Yonge, *Liverpool*, vol. 2, 217.

87. Melbourne to Palmerston, Downing Street, 30 May 1835, Palmerston Papers, GC/ME/29.

88. Pitt to Harrowby, Downing Street, Tuesday, 18 Sept. 1804, Harrowby MSS vol. 12 ff. 43–45, Sandon Hall, Staffordshire; Bathurst to Wellesley, Cabinet Room, 9 Jan. 1812, Add. MS 37296 ff. 171–72.

89. Pares, *George III and the Politicians*, p. 160.

90. Christie, "The Cabinet in the Reign of George III, to 1790," pp. 78–79, 81.

91. Ibid., pp. 82–83.

Sometimes, on points that have been considered as important in the conduct of foreign business, I have . . . made written minutes of the opinion then agreed to. These minutes have in that case invariably been read to the persons present, or afterwards transmitted to the King, but no office copy is ever kept of them.[92] Of these I have copies for my own satisfaction and private use, and I have always considered them as implying the consent or acquiescence of those persons only who were present, and who did not desire their dissent to be expressed.[93]

If a foreign secretary disagreed with the majority of the cabinet, as occasionally was the case, the premier usually prepared the minute.[94]

Cabinet minutes, however, were but one method by which the ministers tendered advice, though as time passed ministers came to rely on these other methods more frequently than they did on official minutes. On matters of grave concern, such as George IV's hesitation to accept cabinet advice to recognize the Spanish American republics of Mexico and Colombia in 1824, the prime minister and other ministers went to see the king personally.[95] More important, increasingly letters from the prime minister or the foreign secretary were used to inform the monarch of cabinet decisions. During the reigns of George IV, William IV, and in the early years of Queen Victoria, in fact, the foreign secretary usually preferred to write a private letter to the sovereign explaining what course of action the cabinet recommended. Palmerston, for example, used this form to tell William IV in 1834 that the cabinet wished to conclude a three-power treaty with Portugal and Spain to give Spanish troops the right to enter Portugal and to drive Don Carlos, the pretender to the Spanish throne, out of that country.[96] Private, informal letters proved to be so satisfactory that the cabinet sent an official minute only when the ministers recommended a major shift in policy, such as in 1824 when Liverpool's ministry decided to

92. Grenville was mistaken. There are copies of some of his cabinet minutes in F.O. 83/8.
93. Grenville to Wyndham, 26 Aug. 1799, Arthur Aspinall (ed.), *The Later Correspondence of George III* (5 vols.; Cambridge, 1962–1970), vol. 3, 183 n.1.
94. Pitt to George III, Downing Street, Thursday, 9 Apr. 1795, 12:10 p.m., and Cabinet minute, 8 Apr. 1795, written by Pitt, ibid., vol. 3, 330–31 and 330 n. 3.
95. Canning to Mrs. Canning, 19 Dec. 1824, Aspinall and Smith, *Eng. Historical Docs.*, vol. 11, 101–2.
96. Palmerston to William IV, F.O., 12 Apr. 1834, Private, Copy, Palmerston Papers, RC/AA/106/1–4.

extend diplomatic recognition to Mexico and Colombia,[97] and in 1840 when Melbourne's cabinet decided to sign a treaty with the Russians, Austrians, and Prussians—to the exclusion of the French—for pacifying the Levant.[98]

Cabinet minutes invariably had listed at their head all those who attended the meeting. Any minister who disagreed with the advice offered the sovereign by the minute could prepare a separate and dissenting opinion. Lord Holland in 1840 disapproved of abandoning the French in settling the affairs of the Levant and insisted on "recording that dissent in some manner or another that will relieve me from the responsibility of all advice which in my judgment has a direct tendency to involve us in unnecessary wars."[99] Grenville in 1797 reluctantly agreed to sign the instructions for Lord Malmesbury's guidance at Lisle, but he felt "it is my Duty to state without reserve to the King" that he felt peace was unattainable and unwise at that time.[100]

If no dissenting opinion was expressed the sovereign usually assumed unanimity in the cabinet. The secretary of state, therefore, had some responsibility to indicate dissent even if the dissenters acquiesced in the decision of the majority. In July, 1824, Canning's minute to George IV recommending that Britain negotiate a commercial treaty with Buenos Ayres clearly implied that the cabinet was undivided on the question.[101] The king so interpreted it and agreed, though reluctantly, to the proposal.[102] The Lord Chancellor, Wellington, Westmorland, and Sidmouth had opposed the decision, however, and Canning and Liverpool were able to prevent Sidmouth from telling the king the truth only by quoting the unwillingness of the other dissenters to bring the division before him.[103]

Once the cabinet had decided on a specific course of policy it could

97. Minute of Cabinet, 7 Dec. 1824, Augustus Granville Stapleton, *George Canning and His Times* (London, 1859), pp. 405–6.

98. Cabinet minute "at a meeting of your Majesty's Servants held at the Foreign Office on Wednesday the 8th of July," Palmerston Papers Cabinet 1840/1.

99. Minute, Holland, 8 July 1840, ibid., GC/HO/127/2.

100. Grenville to Pitt, Cleveland Row, 26 June 1797, P.R.O. 30/58/2 no. 12.

101. Cabinet minute, Foreign Office, 23 July 1824, Stapleton, *Canning and Times*, pp. 397–400.

102. 1 Aug. 1824, Arthur Aspinall (ed.), *The Diary of Henry Hobhouse, 1820–1827* (London, 1947), pp. 110–11.

103. Sidmouth to Canning, Early Court, 29 July 1824, Canning MSS Bundle 74a; Liverpool to Canning, 30 July 1824, Most Secret, ibid., Bundle 71; Sidmouth to Canning, Early Court, 31 July 1824, ibid., Bundle 49a.

reverse its decision only with difficulty. Between 1784 and 1846 there were two attempts to do so. One succeeded, the other failed; both created deep, though temporary, divisions in the cabinets involved. These occasions were important because they demonstrated the second major reason why certain individuals in the cabinet were able to control foreign policy effectively with only periodic references to the whole cabinet.

By 1783 it was "the generally accepted theory and the established practice that membership of the Cabinet should be confined to those Ministers holding the great offices of State, although, for very good reasons, rare exceptions were made to this rule."[104] By the turn of the nineteenth century these great offices—the first lord of the Treasury, the three secretaries of state, and increasingly the chancellor of the Exchequer—were reserved for the prominent members, peers and commoners alike, of the party with a majority in the House of Commons. Too much could be made of the significance of party leadership as an entree to office,[105] but certainly by the 1830s the important departmental offices in the cabinet were the exclusive preserve of these men. It would be stretching the point to say that Pitt in the 1790s presided over a political party. But the king's confidence in Pitt and the consequent support the ministry enjoyed from the majority of the members of the Commons gave him influence over policy which was not too different from Grey's influence in the 1830s or Peel's in the 1840s, based as it was in the latter cases on party leadership. In times of disagreement over policy the political influence of the great officers of the government, whether based on party leadership or royal favor, enabled them to dominate the decision-making process. This domination was best demonstrated on the two occasions already mentioned—occasions in which cabinet decisions were challenged by some of the lesser important political figures[106] in the cabinet—but it was clearly evident on every occasion.

The first instance of a cabinet's attempting to reverse a policy occurred in 1791 when Pitt's ministry, in response to Russian encroachment in the Ochakov district of the Ottoman Empire, decided

104. Aspinall, "The Cabinet Council," pp. 148–49.
105. Disraeli, Derby, and Gladstone were the first prime ministers whose position rested exclusively on party leadership. Hanham, *The Nineteenth-Century Constitution,* pp. 224–25.
106. The distinction is important since in 1791 though Leeds held the seals to the Foreign Office he was not among the more important politicians in the ministry. Ehrman, *Pitt,* p. 185.

to use military force in conjunction with the Prussians to make the Russian government negotiate with the sultan on the basis of the status quo.[107] The cabinet was not unanimous in the decision, but since Pitt and Leeds were among the majority, the decision appeared to be irrevocable. Leeds accordingly sent off a dispatch to request Prussian cooperation.[108] Influential supporters of the government such as the Duke of Grafton, however, expressed their doubts about the policy to Pitt, who began to wonder if the House of Commons would vote the necessary supplies to implement it.[109] The minority in the cabinet, Grenville, Stafford, and Richmond, thus encouraged, became more aggressive in presenting their objections and asked the majority to reconsider the decision, though it was already being implemented. In the discussions Richmond and the Lord Chancellor had one violent argument after a cabinet meeting on 31 March,[110] but it appeared that the majority could not be persuaded to alter the policy. When the Danish government, whose neutrality had been expected in the conflict, began to waver, however, Pitt decided to pursue the policy of military preparedness while seeking to negotiate on any other basis than the status quo except annexation, the policy advocated by the minority. Leeds refused to sign the dispatch altering the original decision when Pitt sent it to him and subsequently resigned.[111] Pitt's conversion to the minority viewpoint reflected the uncertainty of support from the country in case of armed conflict. Coupled with Leeds's political insignificance, the growing importance of Grenville, and the possibility of Danish opposition in the Baltic, Pitt's support enabled the minority to carry their point without forcing the breakup of the ministry.

The other attempt of a dissident minority to secure a reversal of policy in cabinet occurred in 1840 over the government's policy in

107. Memorandum, Pitt, "Copy sent to Mr. Whitworth," 27 Apr. [March?] 1791, F.O. 65/20.

108. Draft to Mr. Jackson, Whitehall, 27 Mar. 1791 (by Flint), F.O. 64/20.

109. Thursday, 31 Mar. 1791, Browning, *Leeds Political Memoranda*, pp. 154–58; Grenville to Joseph Ewart, Whitehall, 20 Apr. 1791, No. 1, F.O. 353/38.

110. Richmond to Pitt, Whitehall, Sunday night, 27 Mar. 1791, Philip Henry, 5th Earl Stanhope, *Life of the Right Honourable William Pitt* (4 vols.; London, 1861–1862), vol. 2, 112–13; Thursday, 31 Mar. 1791, Browning, *Leeds Political Memoranda*, pp. 154–58.

111. Francis Drake to Leeds, Copenhagen, 12 Mar. 1791, No. 25, F.O. 22/13 ff. 171–73; Leeds's "Copy of a Paper sent to Mr. Pitt, when I returned to him the Dt. of a Dispatch he had prepared for Berlin & Sent for my Perusal," 9 Apr. 1791, Eg. MS 3498 Bundle 10; Saturday, 16 Apr. 1791, Browning, *Leeds Political Memoranda*, pp. 164–68.

the Levant. The advance of Mehemet Ali's army on its conquest of the Ottoman Empire caused great excitement and concern in the European capitals. English interests seemed to require a single power in the area to act as a buffer state against Russian expansion to the south and west. The Porte, though not the most useful and attractive ally, nonetheless appeared to have a better chance to resist the Russians than any empire created by Mehemet Ali. When Palmerston failed to secure French cooperation in opposing Mehemet, he turned to Austria, Russia, and Prussia for assistance. These powers were anxious to separate England from France in European affairs and joined, therefore, with Britain in securing the integrity of the Ottoman Empire by signing the Quadruple Alliance of July 1840.

Palmerston secured cabinet approval of the alliance only by threatening to resign if his proposals were rejected and by securing the last minute support for the plan by Lord John Russell, the colonial secretary.[112] Only Lansdowne, the lord president of the council, and Holland, the chancellor of the duchy of Lancaster, opposed the treaty, but since neither of these men was in the interior councils of the ministry their opposition was not significant. Russell, however, remained hesitant about the policy. When an outcry arose in France about French isolation from the rest of the powers and the French press became belligerent he began to have second thoughts. Russell questioned the policy and sought to include the French in the alliance,[113] which surprised Melbourne, who for some reason "always understood John to agree strongly upon this Eastern question with Palmerston."[114] As time passed and the storm in the French press increased Russell began to see ominous signs of an Anglo-French war and thought of resigning if he could not secure some conciliatory gesture to the French government.[115] Melbourne seemed more concerned with whether the ministry would break up

112. Palmerston to Melbourne, Carleton Terrace, 5 July 1840, Ashley, *Life of Palmerston*, vol. 1, 370–73; Palmerston to William Temple, C.T., 27 July 1840, ibid., vol. 1, 375–76.

113. Russell to Melbourne, Naworth Castle, 24 Aug. 1840, Palmerston Papers, GC/ME/412/2.

114. Melbourne to Holland, Windsor Castle, 31 Aug. 1840, Add. MS 51559 ff. 68–69.

115. Russell to Holland, 15 Sept. 1840, G. P. Gooch (ed.), *The Latter Correspondence of Lord John Russell, 1840–1878* (2 vols.; London, 1925), vol. 1, 15; Russell to Melbourne, Woburn Abbey, 17 Sept. 1840, P.R.O. 30/22/3E ff. 16–17.

than with which policy prevailed and said he saw justice in both Russell's and Palmerston's positions.[116]

Palmerston's courage never failed in the face of Russell's opposition. Convinced that he had the support of the House of Commons[117] and that war was "out of the Question unless we draw it upon ourselves by mean Submission,"[118] he insisted "that when a Cabinet *has* agreed to a system of measures, they ought to give that system fair play, & not to raise impediments to its execution or the Detail of the measures by which it is to be effected. . . ."[119] Russell vacillated between opposition and lukewarm support of the alliance[120] until the fall of the fortress of Acre insured the success of Palmerston's policy.

Palmerston was successful for several reasons. His refusal to abandon his policy, his assurance of support from Peel, Aberdeen, Wellington, and a considerable number of backbenchers on both sides of the House of Commons, and Russell's indecision, which kept him from resigning or from forcing Palmerston to resign, contrasted sharply to the events of 1791. Furthermore, because Melbourne was unwilling to side firmly with either faction, thus not forcing either side to resign, the ministry was able to struggle on until events justified Palmerston's position. The events of 1791 and 1840 suggest the importance of agreement between the foreign secretary and the prime minister if cabinet decisions on policies for which there was not a unanimous support in the ministry were to be implemented without risk to the stability of the government. They also demonstrate the importance of politics and political influence—however maintained—to the ability of ministers to affect policy in any significant way. At the very least the premier had to be unwilling to side with either party in cabinet disputes if he hoped to avoid the resignation of some of his colleagues.

The cabinet had little to do with the daily conduct of foreign

116. Melbourne to Palmerston, Windsor Castle, 14 Sept. 1840, Palmerston Papers GC/ME/418; Melbourne to Russell, Windsor Castle, 19 Aug. 1840, Lloyd G. Sanders (ed.), *The Melbourne Papers* (London, 1889), pp. 460–61.

117. Palmerston to Holland, C.T., 19 Sept. 1840, Add. MS 51599 ff. 277–78.

118. Palmerston to Hobhouse, C.T., 29 Sept. 1840, Add. MS 46915 ff. 221–22.

119. Palmerston to Melbourne, C.T., 16 Sept. 1840, Copy, Palmerston Papers, GC/ME/540/1.

120. Clarendon to Holland, 9 Oct. 1840 Add. MS 51617 f. 63.

affairs. These duties were performed by the secretary of state consulting frequently with the prime minister, who read nearly as many of the dispatches as the secretary. Because both men were equally informed on foreign affairs they usually shared opinions on questions of policy. In cabinet meetings they could be a formidable pair since they were frequently better informed than their colleagues. Canning's success in securing cabinet approval for British recognition of the Latin American republics in 1824, for instance, reflected in great part Liverpool's perfect concurrence with him on the necessity of the measure. "It is incalculable," Canning said, "what an impediment & perplexity our strict union (L's and mine) upon the great subjects of foreign policy, is to the sighers after the Continental School."[121] Palmerston, despite the fact that he thought Grey was too easily persuaded by those "in whom he has Confidence,"[122] felt that "No two men . . . ever went on better together in office, and very few half as well. I never met with anybody with whom I found myself so constantly agreeing."[123]

Every prime minister made corrections in the drafts of dispatches written by secretaries of state. Wellesley was more displeased by alterations than most foreign secretaries and insisted that he approve every change made by Perceval before his dispatches went to the king.[124] Wellington wrote long memoranda as he read dispatches Aberdeen sent him[125] and if he disapproved of certain passages in any instruction that Aberdeen had already dispatched he ordered the alteration sent in pursuit of the original.[126] Grey usually limited his corrections to grammatical suggestions and attempted as a general rule to remove all unnecessary matter from Palmerston's dispatches. In 1831, for example, he wrote Palmerston that "I have ventured to make a good deal of alteration in the draft of your dispatch on the subject of Portugal, not in the substance or the reasoning but merely in the form and mode of expression, whether

121. Canning to Granville, Ch. Ch., 17 Jan. 1825, No. 20, Private, P.R.O. 30/29/8/6 ff. 765–72.
122. Palmerston to Granville, Stanhope Street, 3 Mar. 1831, P.R.O. 30/29/404.
123. Palmerston to William Temple, Foreign Office, 7 May 1833, Ashley, *Life of Palmerston*, vol. 1, 289.
124. Wellesley to Perceval, Apsley House, Sunday, 22 July 1810, Private, Copy, Add. MS 37295 ff. 336–37.
125. Memorandum, Wellington; 3 June [1828], at night, Add. MS 43056 ff. 41–53.
126. H. H. Parish to Stratford Canning, F.O., 20 Sept. 1828, Confidential, F.O. 352/22/2.

for better or not you will determine. The chief advantage is that of making the dispatch shorter."[127]

The concurrence of the prime minister and the foreign secretary was absolutely essential if any policy were to be decided upon and executed efficiently. The prime minister was invariably and properly the more important of the two men.[128] Melbourne, perhaps one of the least forceful of premiers during the period, prevented Palmerston in 1835 from sending a dispatch protesting a speech by the Emperor of Russia in Poland to Lord Durham, ambassador at St. Petersburg, because Palmerston's authority for what the emperor said was merely a newspaper account.[129] Aberdeen called Wellington the "sails and rudder" of the administration,[130] and told him that "it is impossible for me to dissent from any decision to which you may come *deliberately* and *dispassionately*."[131] Grey, not Palmerston, attempted to resign when they failed in 1834 to secure the unanimous approval of the cabinet for sending 5,000 troops to Portugal.[132]

When the secretary of state and the prime minister did not share the same view on a question of major importance, the secretary generally yielded his opinion to that of the premier. Grenville acquiesced in Pitt's and Dundas's decision to resume negotiations with France at Lisle in 1797, though "I shudder at what we are doing, and believe in my conscience that, if this country could be but brought to think so, it would be ten thousand times safer (and cheaper too, which they seem to consider above all other things) to face the storm, than to shrink from it."[133] Aberdeen in 1845 considered resigning before the subject of increasing British naval armaments in face of

127. Webster, *For. Pol. Palmerston*, vol. 1, 32–33; Grey to Palmerston, Downing Street, 2 Aug. 1831, Palmerston Papers, GC/GR/2011.

128. Foreign diplomats stationed in London appreciated the importance of the premier, but when they attempted to work on Grey and Melbourne behind Palmerston's back they received only soothing phrases and diplomatic platitudes in response to their questions. Palmerston to Melbourne, Stanhope Street, 24 May 1836, Copy, Palmerston Papers GC/ME/523/1–4.

129. Palmerston to Durham, F.O., Dec. 1835, Draft, and Melbourne to Palmerston, South Street, 14 Dec. 1835, Palmerston Papers, GC/ME/54/1–2.

130. Aberdeen to Wellington, Foreign Office, 4 Nov. 1828, *W.N.D.*, vol. 5, 212–13.

131. Italics mine. Aberdeen to Wellington, Foreign Office, 13 Oct. 1829, Copy, Add. MS 43058 ff. 28–29.

132. Palmerston to Sir Herbert Taylor, Stanhope Street, 15 Jan. 1834, Private and Confidential, Copy, Palmerston Papers RC/CC/11/1–2.

133. Grenville to Pitt, Dropmore, 8 Oct. 1797, Copy, *H. M. C. Fortescue*, vol. 3, 378–80. On other similar instances Grenville sent a dissenting opinion to the king. See supra p. 58.

the threat of an extensive French shipbuilding program came before the whole cabinet. Peel's decision to abandon the policy Aberdeen favored of a minimal armament program led Aberdeen to conclude that when the subject came before the cabinet he would be forced to resign amidst "unpleasant circumstances" in order to maintain "my own honour, conscience, and understanding. . . ."[134]

The formation of foreign policy in every ministry between 1782 and 1846 resided only nominally in the hands of the whole cabinet. Though this had not always been the case, drafts of important dispatches having been circulated during the eighteenth century before they were sent, in the course of Pitt's first ministry the practice did not continue to the same extent,[135] and by the nineteenth century it had nearly ceased altogether.[136] Though the cabinet ministers of lesser importance were involved in the decision-making process, a small coterie of senior cabinet officials, usually department heads, were responsible for the vast majority of the decisions taken by any cabinet. It was these men who studied the dispatches most carefully and who determined which of the options Britain had in any situation they would recommend that their colleagues and the sovereign adopt.

---

134. Aberdeen to Peel, Foreign Office, 18 Sept. 1845, Add. MS 40455 ff. 159–62.
135. Christie, "The Cabinet in the Reign of George III, to 1790," p. 78.
136. The circulation of dispatches was by this time for informational purposes. See supra, pp. 53–55.

CHAPTER III

THE SOVEREIGN AND FOREIGN POLICY

Sir Lewis Namier, in a now celebrated passage, described George III as "the *primus inter pares*, the first among the borough-mongering, electioneering gentlemen of England."[1] The implications of this statement are crucial to any evaluation of the ability of George III and to a lesser degree his successors to influence foreign policy decisions. Late in the eighteenth century the king was a personal participant in the political community, occupying a position on the national stage roughly analogous to that of the justices in the countryside. National politics centered around the king and the court[2] though to what extent George personally directed affairs has long been a subject of historical controversy.[3] By the accession of Queen Victoria in 1837 the political significance of the monarchy had been seriously, though not completely circumscribed. The growth of political parties in the 1830s and afterwards contributed to the increasing authority of the party leadership who collectively at first assumed the responsibilities of governing which the monarch had in the past enjoyed. Ultimately the party leader when prime minister was to wield this authority more strongly than even George III would have found possible.

These political changes had a significant impact on the sovereign's influence in the realm of foreign affairs. It has always been exceed-

---

1. *England in the Age of the American Revolution* (2d ed.; New York, 1961), p. 4.

2. The role of the court in politics and society has not yet been explored fully for the eighteenth century, but an excellent study does exist for the reign of George I. John M. Beattie, *The English Court in the Reign of George I* (New York, 1967).

3. Herbert Butterfield, *George III and the Historians* (London, 1957). Namier himself took a dim view of the influence of George III over government policy and argued that the king for the most part contented himself with approving his ministers' decisions. *Crossroads of Power: Essays on Eighteenth-Century England* (London, 1962), p. 137. Pares, on the other hand, argued that at least for that part of the reign prior to 1789, the king was in fact his own principal minister. *George III and the Politicians*, pp. 123–24. The insertion of "Other" before "Politicians" in the title would clearly delineate Pares's view.

ingly difficult to measure this influence after 1701. William III was the last king whose foreign policy can be directly attributed to the personal decision of the monarch.[4] Thereafter, to one degree or another, successive sovereigns had to share responsibility for determining policy with their ministers. The role of the cabinet in this process has already been examined from the point of view of purely cabinet activities. But the material in the preceding chapter lacks a significant dimension because there was no discussion on how the ministers coordinated their decisions with royal wishes. This discussion, therefore, will center around the crucial question of how the opinions of the sovereign from George III through the young Victoria modified or influenced the course of foreign affairs.

The problem of interpretation is compounded by the nature of the records. In the vast majority of decisions the monarch went along with the recommendations of the ministers, usually because he agreed with them, more infrequently because he did not think it worthwhile to argue against their policy. It was only on the occasional issue that conflict arose and it was only in a period of conflict that the relationship between the king and ministers on foreign policy questions was defined with any degree of precision, and then only because the people involved were more apt to express their ideas on this relationship than they were when all was peace and harmony. The result is that the historian must be very careful not to see the decision-making process as one of continuous contention, the ministers wanting to pursue one course of action, the sovereign another. The focus of the material is on these occasions, but on balance they were exceedingly few in number between 1782 and 1846.

Another difficulty arises from the fact that the record is comprised principally of letters from ministers to the king, with replies. In ministerial correspondence of the late eighteenth century the assumption was "that at the stage of referring a matter to the cabinet and at the stage of implementing its decision the approval of the sovereign was largely formal. However punctillious the care taken to obtain the royal pleasure—and it was punctillious—the king might be expected to follow the wishes or advice of his ministers."[5] Expected, but not required. Here lay the crucial distinction between

4. Horn, *Great Britain and Europe*, pp. 1–2.
5. Christie, "The Cabinet in the Reign of George III, to 1790," pp. 89–90.

the reigns of George III and Victoria. Based upon other records, such as notes in the press on ministerial visits to the royal presence, it is clear that many of the important decisions were made in informal talks between George III and his ministers; talks the substance of which there is no written record. This sort of consultation was more likely to occur when "major strokes of policy" were under consideration; that is, precisely on those issues which the king personally might be expected to take a greater interest in foreign affairs and wish to play an active role in the decision-making process. One of these occasions occurred in 1762 during the peace negotiations with France. There is no substantial written record of George's precise role in these discussions, but in all probability it was considerable.[6] These conferences were largely abandoned as the reign of George III drew to a close. They were not continued in the reigns of his successors, and as a result the influence of the crown was diminished to a degree. By way of generalization, therefore, it is arguable that the monarch had to take his chances along with all the other politicians. When there were difficulties, at times he could prevail, at times the policicians overrode his wishes, and on other occasions a compromise was struck.[7] Whatever the case, the crown was always part of a larger political community in which precise relationships on these issues were not yet settled at the turn of the nineteenth century.

In the material with which this chapter is concerned political changes in the broader community were crucial to the influence of the sovereign over policy. The years between 1782 and 1850 were years of profound political adjustment in British society. The most important change was the fact that the political community was extended as new groups were admitted to the franchise. The broader franchise required different types of electoral influence and the politicians began to be more concerned with issues than had been the case in the past. But these changes came only gradually. George III in selecting ministers was concerned with men, not measures,[8] and the principal asset to attaining cabinet office was "not so much ability as aristocratic connexions and a large landed prop-

6. Ibid., pp. 94–97.
7. Ibid., pp. 94–105.
8. Ibid., p. 84.

erty."[9] These generalizations held true in 1827[10] and it was not until the emergence of party organization in the 1830s that the pattern began to change.

George III was in fact at the center of politics and when he desired he could demand (1783)[11] or at least force (1807)[12] the resignation of ministers who still technically enjoyed the confidence of a majority of the House of Commons. To a degree the situation of the ministers of George IV and William IV was similar to that of their predecessors. The ability of the king to dismiss them continued as the Whigs discovered in November 1834,[13] though subsequent events proved he could not make his decision stick. This power, however, was always tempered by political considerations. By sacking one ministry and replacing it with another the king risked having his new ministers propose the same or similar policies as those advocated by their predecessors. Such changes in ministries, too, were unpleasant affairs and ones not to be undertaken lightly. It should be remembered that though George succeeded in 1783, the initial response of the politicians and members of Parliament (including the country gentlemen) was to continue their support of Pitt's and the king's opponents, an allegiance that was severed only gradually as Pitt stood firm in the House of Commons.[14] Also of importance, particularly during the reigns of George III and George IV, was the fact that the opposition was usually composed of those men the king disliked for personal or political reasons, or both. Therefore, though the ultimate weapon in the king's arsenal was his power to replace his ministers, it was a weapon to be used sparingly and only in the most extreme circumstances.

Ultimately the most important check on this aspect of the prerogative was the fact that during the reign of George IV and to a greater

9. Aspinall, "The Cabinet Council," p. 199.
10. Arthur Aspinall (ed.), *The Formation of Canning's Ministry, February to August, 1827* ("The Camden Society, 3d Series," vol. 59; London, 1937); Charles R. Middleton, "The Formation of Canning's Ministry and the Evolution of the British Cabinet, February to August 1827," *Canadian Journal of History*, 10 (April, 1975), 17–34.
11. Donald Grove Barnes, *George III and William Pitt, 1783–1806* (Reprint; New York, 1965), pp. 66–67.
12. W. B. Hamilton, "Constitutional and Political Reflections on the Dismissal of Lord Grenville's Ministry," *Report of the Annual Meeting of the Canadian Historical Association*, 49 (1964), 89–104.
13. Kriegel, "The Politics of the Whigs in Opposition," pp. 65–66.
14. Barnes, *George III and William Pitt*, chapter 3.

extent during William's reign the ministers increasingly were aware of the importance of parliamentary support to their survival. Royal support was a necessary ingredient in the stability of every ministry in the 1820s and the early 1830s, especially when the politicians were disorganized as they were in 1827 and after 1835.[15] But it was less important than it had been during the reign of George III, and by the accession of Queen Victoria, ministers were aware that their position rested primarily on their ability to command a parliamentary majority. Whatever the other consequences of the Reform Act of 1832 may have been, it is certain that the reformed House of Commons was not as tractable as its predecessors had been. Ministers soon discovered that they were responsible more to Parliament than to the sovereign for their activities. It was natural, therefore, even though they could not ignore the sovereign's opinions, that they should be less concerned with them than their predecessors had been.

There can be no doubt that Victoria had considerably less opportunity to influence foreign policy than her grandfather. George III frequently read dispatches before the ministers saw them and he was always aware of the intricate details of the course of events. He appears to have been the last sovereign to recommend, as he did on more than one occasion, that the ministers suggest courses of policy for his consideration.[16] His successors invariably reacted to ministerial proposals; they did not instigate them. Victoria, in fact, usually learned of decisions only as they were being implemented. She complained to Aberdeen in 1845 that she never saw dispatches until "they are already gone, so that if the Queen wished to make any observations or ask any explanations respecting them, it would be too late, which may be of serious inconvenience in particular instances."[17] Aberdeen's reply is instructive: The "practice has usually been to submit to Y.M. the Drafts of dispatches at the same time that they are sent from the office. Should Your Majesty then be pleased to make any remark or objection, it would be immediately attended to by Lord Aberdeen, who would forthwith either make the necessary

15. Aspinall, *Formation of Canning's Ministry*, passim; Middleton, "Formation of Canning's Ministry," pp. 28–30; Hanham, *The Nineteenth-Century Constitution*, p. 29.
16. George III to Fox, 15 June 1782, 55 min. past 7 a.m., Bonamy Dobreé (ed.), *The Letters of King George III* (London, 1935), p. 157; George III to Grenville, Weymouth, 5 Oct. 1798, 4 p.m., Aspinall, *Later Corresp. Geo. III*, vol. 3, 136.
17. 28 Oct. 1845, Windsor Castle, Add. MS 43045 ff. 220–21.

alteration, by additional instructions; or He would humbly represent to Your Majesty the reasons which induced him to think that the interest of Y.M. Services required an adherence to what had already been done."[18]

George III had reigned for nearly a quarter of a century when the Foreign Office was created in 1782. He was a man of immense experience and limited intellect. He was also a consummate politician and few of his ministers rivaled him in political skill. He had an "affection for details" that is unusual in any sovereign and he worked harder than many of his ministers.[19] He had great confidence in his knowledge of foreign affairs and as he became more experienced in foreign relations it became increasingly difficult for ministers to implement policies when they disagreed with his opinions. There can be no doubt that his personal authority increased with the passage of time. His influence was due in part to the fact that he understood that politics was the art of managing men.[20] More important was his character as monarch and the "respect in which he was held by his people."[21]

Personally the king was an austere individual who preferred reading, outdoor sports, informal card games, and music to ribaldry, a lively court, and ostentatious displays of wealth. He loved his family and was solicitous about the affairs of his fifteen children, most of whom at some time or other drove him to despair.[22] The key to his character was an intense "humility, based on a deep religious faith."[23] Partly as a result of this humility he was a very shy person who preferred the company of a close circle of friends to the acclaim of a large crowd.[24] It certainly was this humility which contributed to

18. 31 Oct. 1845, F.O., Copy, ibid., ff. 222–23.

19. George's indolence as a youth has long been a subject of historical discussion. The usual interpretation has been that his later energy and almost slavish attention to detail resulted from his desire to escape this natural tendency. A more plausible argument, however, has been recently advanced suggesting that the attention of the king to all the details of business later in his reign was the result principally of his increased experience and confidence which gives an "impression of greater activity" when in fact there was none. Christie, "The Cabinet in the Reign of George III, to 1790," p. 105. In fact the king, largely because of the influence of Bute, had overcome his early tendency to indolence by the beginning of the reign. The problem anyway was apparently "psychological not organic, the inability to concentrate on his work rather than inherent dullness or lack of intelligence." John Brooke, *King George III* (New York, 1972), p. 54.

20. A fact which his mentor, Bute, never learned. Brooke, *George III*, p. 64.

21. Ibid., p. 231.

22. Barnes, *George III and William Pitt*, pp. 27–40.

23. Brooke, *George III*, p. 90.

24. Ibid., p. 42.

his popularity as the reign progressed. Historians for too long forgot that he was exceptionally popular both as king and as gentleman, which he was first and last.[25] However one might assess him as king, it is difficult not to give him credit as a man for his generosity to others, "'those acts of benevolence,' as he described his charitable distributions, 'which alone make the station bearable.'"[26]

George III was better informed about foreign affairs than any of his successors. He habitually rose early in the morning when he read the dispatches that the undersecretaries sent him from London late the previous evening. This routine was interrupted only when papers of extreme importance arrived at Whitehall.[27] Even on these occasions, however, the routine dispatches were kept back and sent at the usual time.[28] The king was punctual in replying to any communication he received[29] which explains in great part the fact that so long as he remained sane[30] he had a decided influence on policy. Dispatches were frequently sent to him before they were circulated to the cabinet,[31] and if the secretary of state was in the country when dispatches arrived, the undersecretary invariably sent them to his principal only when they had returned from the king.[32] Occasionally, when the number of dispatches received was extraordinarily large, they were sent to the king in equal installments on successive days. He appreciated this kindness, as "I confess when the load is too great I find that I cannot retain in my mind any part of the contents. . . ."[33] Only after he began to lose his sight did the secretaries

25. Ibid., p. 316.

26. Ibid., pp. 211–15. The money came from the Privy Purse and totalled about half of his personal income per year.

27. Hammond to George III, Downing Street, 13 July [1798], 1 a.m., Aspinall, *Later Corresp. Geo. III*, vol. 3, 92; Grenville to George III, Cleveland Row, 30 Mar. 1797, 12:15 p.m., ibid., vol. 2, 557–58.

28. Grenville to George III, Cleveland Row, 27 Apr. [1798], 11:17 a.m., ibid., vol. 3, 52.

29. Envelope docketed by Fox "Original Draft. This Messenger is directed to be at Windsor tomorrow Morning by 6 o'clock," 25 Mar. [1806], with minute, George III, "m/30 pt 8 A.M.", Add. MS 51457 f. 23.

30. Recent medical research has argued plausibly that the king was suffering from a physical disease known as porphyria, the symptoms of which resemble insanity. Ida Macalpine and Richard Hunter, *George III and the Mad-Business* (New York, 1969). Whatever the cause of his incapacitation, however, contemporaries thought him to be mad and he was as incapable of exercising the responsibilities of kingship after 1811 as if he had been mentally deranged.

31. Grantham to Shelburne, ½ past 12, Sunday Morg., 3 Nov. 1782, Lucas L 30/14/306/46; Carmarthen to Pitt, St. James's, 8 Nov. 1784, Copy, Eg. MS 3498 Bundle 5.

32. Minute, Hammond, Downing Street, 13 Nov. [1804], 5 p.m., Harrowby MSS vol. 10 ff. 193–94.

33. George III to Grenville, Windsor, 5 Apr. 1796, *H. M. C. Fortescue*, vol. 3, 186.

of state simply make selections of the most important papers for his attention.[34]

George III was no less well-informed of every diplomatic action taken by his ministers. Cabinet minutes were sent to him when the ministers wished to recommend particular courses of policy. Ministers not infrequently sent drafts of these minutes to him for approval before submitting the formal minute.[35] Dispatches implementing the policy recommended by the cabinet invariably followed the minute within a few days.[36] The king made verbal corrections on many of these papers, though ministers frequently did not adopt his suggestions. Grenville, for example, referring to the proclamation to be made to the French on the commencement of hostilities in 1793, "ventured in one or two instances to depart from the precise words which your Majesty had the goodness to suggest, but he has altered the original passages in order to make the sense clearer than it was."[37]

George III's involvement in the determination of foreign policy was considerably more extensive than his making a few verbal alterations in state papers. On several occasions he disagreed seriously with his ministers over particular courses of policy. Most of these instances occurred after 1793 when ministers wished to seek peace with France. George continually opposed such overtures and told Grenville in 1796 that "I never would have entered into the war but in a fair supposition that we meant to go through with it."[38] The king's relations with his ministers on these occasions are instructive as to the roles of the sovereign and the ministers in determining policy during the reign.

As a matter of general policy the king was largely interested in "principles, not their translation into practice."[39] As he grew older

34. Harrowby to George III, [26 May 1804?], Copy, Harrowby MSS vol. 13 ff. 102–3.
35. Pitt to George III, Downing Street, Thursday, 9 Apr. 1795, 12:10 p.m., Aspinall, *Later Corresp. Geo. III*, vol. 2, 330; Fox to George III, Arlington Street, 12 Mar. 1806, Add. MS 51457 f. 6.
36. Fox to George III, St. James's, 18 Apr. 1783, 40 m. past 11 p.m., Lord John Russell (ed.), *Memorials and Correspondence of Charles James Fox* (4 vols.; London, 1853–1857), vol. 2, 124.
37. George III to Grenville, Kew, 27 Sept. 1793, *H. M. C. Fortescue*, vol. 2, 428; Grenville to George III, St. James's Square, 27 Sept. [1793], Aspinall, *Later Corresp. Geo. III*, vol. 2, 104–5. If a minister accepted the recommendation for alteration he returned the draft for final approval. Fox to George III, Downing Street, 25 Mar. [1806], Add. MS 51457 f. 21.
38. George III to Grenville, Queen's House, 9 Feb. 1796, *H. M. C. Fortescue*, vol. 3, 173.
39. Brooke, *George III*, p. 251.

and more experienced, however, he became more interested in discussing, if not personally directing the implementation of specific measures.[40] In February 1796 the ministers decided that in order to secure peace Austria would have to cede the Low Countries to Prussia in exchange for Prussian acquiescence in Austrian annexation of parts of Bavaria. The king objected to this proposal because he felt that "such a settlement would destroy every utility of Austria to Britain," and "what is much worse, be disposing of a country of a Prince [Bavaria] because [he was] less able to defend himself. This is so immoral and unjustifiable a proceeding that I cannot but in the outset protest against it. . . ." After stating his objections, however, the king concluded by agreeing to the proposition, though he told Grenville that "nothing but the opinions of my Ministers would have made me not reject the idea" out of hand.[41] Because of George's reluctant acquiescence Grenville delayed sending the dispatch and asked the king if he wished the cabinet to reconsider their decision.[42] The whole affair proceeded only after George assured Grenville that though he would not stand in the way of the implementation of the policy, "I should not have acted openly or honestly had I not expressed my own sentiments on the subject, and no reasoning of Lord Grenville on this subject would move me from what I think the Line of morality, though not perhaps of politics. I always choose to act on simple principles; Italian politics are too complicated paths for my understanding."[43]

It is clear from this and other similar incidents that ministers hesitated to act without the support of George III. Overcoming the king's objections was not always an easy task. When he disagreed with their advice he invariably stated "with frankness that [which] I think it right on all occasions ought to accompany the opinion of an honest man, my sentiments. . . ."[44] In July 1796 he summoned them to defend their written opinions in person when they proposed surrendering territory conquered by British arms to facilitate the proposed peace settlement with France.[45] The objections of the king were not insuperable. It was difficult for him to resist the unanimous

40. It is interesting to compare his role in the wars with France and his actions in the war with the American colonies nearly twenty years earlier. Ibid., p. 200.

41. George III to Grenville, Queen's House, 9 Feb. 1796, *H. M. C. Fortescue*, vol. 3, 173.

42. Grenville to George III, Downing Street, 9 Feb. 1796, Copy, ibid., 173–74.

43. George III to Grenville, Queen's House, 9 Feb. 1796, ibid., 174.

44. George III to Grenville, Windsor, 30 July 1796, ibid., 227–28.

45. George III to Grenville, Windsor, 31 July 1796, ibid., 230.

opinion of the cabinet and as long as the ministers believed firmly in their recommendations and were unwilling to alter their opinion the king was forced to acquiesce in their policy. One such instance occurred in 1783 on the question of seeking peace with the American colonies and their European allies. The king's objections on that occasion were overruled. In his anger and disgust he subsequently refused even to read the projects of the treaties of peace in protest of the ministry's policy.[46] A similar instance occurred in 1800 when the king strongly opposed a cabinet recommendation that some overture for peace be made to France.[47] The cabinet, however, sent a "Minute of the unanimous opinion of your Majesty's servants . . ." reaffirming their decision, and George merely replied that "I feel too much agitated to add more than that left alone in the opinion of prosecuting the war without continental assistance, I will not resist . . . the instructions being drawn up agreeable to the Minute of yesterday."[48]

Dispatches were sent from London usually only after the king had specifically approved them. Whenever an exception was made to this rule ministers notified the king when they sent him the drafts that the dispatches were already gone and why. Ministers acted without the king's immediate sanction only when immediate action was essential or in the belief that they were merely implementing "the general system which Your Majesty has been pleased to approve. . . ."[49] He never disapproved of their doing so.

Though George III was not a wise man, he was on occasion an astute observer of foreign affairs. As long as his emotions did not become involved in a policy or in opposition to a course of action, he was capable of making realistic and reasonable decisions. In the 1780s he strongly advocated a cautious line of policy with regard to the major powers "till we really see by the events which must occur in a few months what line we ought to pursue,"[50] and he encouraged Pitt's efforts to stabilize the country's finances instead of pursuing an

46. George III to Fox, Queen's House, 19 Apr. 1783, 25 m. pt. 9 a.m., Russell, *Memorials of Fox*, vol. 3, 125.

47. Grenville to George III, Cleveland Row, 27 June [1800], 11 p.m., and George III to Grenville, Windsor, 28 June [1800], 7:30 a.m., Aspinall, *Later Corresp. Geo. III*, vol. 3, 368.

48. Grenville to George III, 16 July 1800, 11 p.m., and George III to Grenville, Windsor, 17 July 1800, 6:41 a.m., ibid., 374–76.

49. Pitt to Harrowby, Downing Street, Tuesday, 18 Sept. 1804, Harrowby MSS vol. 12 ff. 43–45; Grenville to George III, Cleveland Row, 17 Nov. [1798], Aspinall, *Later Corresp. Geo. III*, vol. 3, 159.

50. George III to Fox, Windsor, 15 June 1783, Russell, *Memorials of Fox*, vol. 2, 130–31.

active foreign policy.[51] Once the war with France began he longed for an alliance of the states on the southern flanks of the enemy, but he despaired of any efficient aid and cooperation from the Austrians.[52] He was skeptical about peace negotiations with France and though he invariably acquiesced when ministers decided to attempt them, he warned Grenville on at least one occasion that treaties always fall "far short of the first project," which he felt should be drafted in as extreme a manner as the negotiators could imagine.[53]

George III had independent sources of information as Elector of Hanover.[54] In the 1780s ministers never were given information that the king received through the German Office in London.[55] Though the representatives of foreign powers in London were usually aware that the king kept "his English Ministers totally ignorant of the nature & extent of" his plans as Elector, they did not always choose to regard the affairs of the two countries as distinct.[56] After 1790, however, George apparently made more frequent disclosures of his Hanoverian intelligence than he had made in the previous decade.[57] Yet there was no regular system whereby English ministers read the intelligence reports and dispatches of the Hanoverian diplomatic corps and they in turn made little or no effort to interfere in the king's conduct of his German affairs.[58]

George III and his sons as electors (and later as kings) of Hanover had considerable independence in foreign affairs. George III corresponded freely with other German princes, and though he often gave ministers copies of some of his letters,[59] others must have been sent without their knowledge. His correspondence as king of England with other princes, in contrast to his Hanoverian business, was drafted by ministers and then written by his own hand.[60]

51. George III to Pitt, Kew, 6 o'clock p.m., 20 Oct. 1788, Dobree, *Letters of George III*, p. 199.

52. George III to Grenville, Queen's House, 18 Jan. 1795, *H. M. C. Fortescue*, vol. 3, 10.

53. 30 July 1796, Windsor, ibid., 227–28.

54. See Sir Adolphus William Ward, *Great Britain and Hanover* (Oxford, 1899), for the relations between England and Hanover in the reigns of George I and George II.

55. Fraser to Sir Robert M. Keith, St. James's, 10 Dec. 1784, Add. MS 35533 ff. 71–72.

56. Carmarthen to the Lord Chancellor, St. James's, 5 Aug. 1785, Copy, Eg. MS 3498 Bundle 10; Carmarthen to Pitt, St. James's, 28 Oct. 1785, Copy, ibid., Bundle 8.

57. George III to Grenville, Windsor, 24 Dec. 1797, *H. M. C. Fortescue*, vol. 3, 406–7; Mulgrave to Granville, Downing Street, 10 Apr. 1805, Private most Secret & Confidential, P.R.O. 30/29/384A.

58. Minute, Grenville, on W. Fawkener to Edward Fisher, Council Office, Whitehall, 29 Nov. 1800, F.O. 92/243.

59. George III to Grenville, Windsor, 10 Dec. 1797, *H. M. C. Fortescue*, vol. 3, 402–3.

60. Grenville to George III, St. James's Square, 16 July 1791, 2:30 p.m. and George III to Grenville, Windsor, 16 July 1791 [sic], 12:55 p.m., Aspinall, *Later Corresp. Geo. III*, vol. 1, 550.

As a master George III could be difficult. His personal feelings about foreign policies became at times inextricable from his attitude about the ministers who espoused them. Once a minister greatly displeased the king it was difficult for him to regain royal confidence. The king openly avowed his dislikes as Fox discovered to his dismay. In returning one set of dispatches in 1783 George remarked that the Dutch for a time would be outside the English sphere of influence even if "by subsequent kindness they may perhaps be regained, though in States as well as in Men, where dislike has once arose I never expect to see Cordiality."[61] Fox marked the passage, a sufficient caveat of the king's hostility. George III, however, once he had been brought to agree to a policy, was loyal to his ministers in the face of adversity. Lord Sidmouth, who attacked the burning of the Danish fleet in Copenhagen when he heard that the king had approved the expedition reluctantly, surprised many people, including Lord Malmesbury, who wrote that "Lord Sidmouth knew little of the King's character, if, after having consented, he ever would be pleased in having Ministers censured and condemned."[62]

George, Prince of Wales and after 1820 King George IV,[63] became Prince Regent in 1811 when his father became permanently incapacitated. George IV was anything but a model son. His morals were loose, his principles looser, and he courted and was courted by the opposition to his father's governments in true Hanoverian fashion. He was, however, more intelligent than his father or his brother, and he always was quick to see the merits of an argument and to grasp its significance. Even in the later years of his reign, when he had degenerated into a mass of flesh lying "day in day out, night in night out, propped on the pillows of his gilded bed at Windsor,"[64] his ministers appreciated the quickness of his intellect when he chose to exercise it.[65]

During the Regency (1811–1820) the prince took an active interest in all questions of foreign policy. Like his father he frequently

61. George III to Fox, Windsor, 7 Sept. 1783, 30 m. p. 7 a.m., Add. MS 47559 ff. 105–6.

62. Malmesbury, *Diaries*, vol. 4, 404.

63. The most complete studies of the king's life are Christopher Hibbert, *George IV, Prince of Wales, 1762–1811* (New York, 1972), and Christopher Hibbert, *George IV, Regent and King, 1811–1830* (London, 1973).

64. W. Gore Allen, *King William IV* (London, 1960), p. 5.

65. Wellington to Aberdeen, Apethrope, 1 Jan. 1830, Add. MS 43058 ff. 166–69: "The King understands every Subject perfectly. The Contents of the Paper will not enlighten His Mind. He will communicate it to others; and it will be made the groundwork of a justification of what we have reason to apprehend may pass."

received dispatches before they were circulated to the cabinet[66] and he read extensively enough to be well-informed on the major issues of peace and war. His support of Castlereagh's activities during the peace settlement and afterwards did much to keep opposition to Castlereagh's policies to a minimum.[67] Because Castlereagh's system sought peace based upon monarchical principles and allied cooperation, George accepted and subscribed to it freely and wholeheartedly. His support, as Sir Charles Webster has written, "was based on good Trade Union principles,"[68] and he saw any threat to "a monarchical aristocracy" by "The Jacobins of the world (now calling themselves the Liberals)" as a challenge to his throne and something to be resisted by every means in his power.[69]

George IV accepted the policies of Castlereagh out of conviction and he clearly adopted them as his own. This is the principal reason why he proved so intransigent when Canning began to shape British policy along other lines. In protesting against the decision of the cabinet to recognize certain Latin American states in 1824, George wrote that "The line of policy pursued by the King's Government under the King's direction at the close of the late war . . . was *unanimity* of co-operation with the great Continental Powers. . . ."[70] He clung to this system tenaciously, partly out of conviction and partly out of fear. He apparently equated a challenge to the system established by the postwar settlement with a challenge to the stability of his own throne and he made certain that ministers knew that he resented their forcing recognition on him. "When the Prince of Wales undertook the Regency of this Kingdom," he warned them,

> . . .the Prince abandoned all those friends, with whom he had lived in terms of the most unqualified friendship during the last years of his life; because the Prince, as Regent, thought their liberal and anti-Monarchical sentiments unfavorable to the good government of his father's dominions; but now the King finds, that the opinions of the Opposition & liberals are uni-

66. Castlereagh to Col. McMahon, St. James's Square, 10 Mar. [1812], Arthur Aspinall (ed.), *Letters of King George IV, 1812–1830* (3 vols.; London, 1938), vol. 1, 38.

67. Webster, *For. Pol. Castlereagh*, vol. 1, 28–29.

68. Ibid., vol. 2, 8–9.

69. Memorandum, George IV, Carleton House, 27 Jan. 1825, *W.N.D.*, vol. 2, 401–2.

70. George IV to Liverpool, [27 Jan. 1825], Aspinall, *Letters of George IV*, vol. 3, 98–100.

formly acted upon. The King cannot be supposed to be blind to this state of things.[71]

George IV was never an inconsiderable force in foreign affairs. As absolute ruler of Hanover he enjoyed an independence of action and had an independent source of information. He was initially as reserved as his father in sharing his Hanoverian intelligence with ministers, though he did order Wellesley in 1811 to meet with Count Münster, his Hanoverian adviser in London, to discuss the affairs of northern Europe.[72] Ministers reacted to the prince's secrecy by intercepting his Hanoverian correspondence much as they intercepted correspondence of representatives of other powers.[73] George Canning, however, was the first minister to receive copies of all the king's Hanoverian dispatches and papers,[74] though he received these communications not as a matter of right but as a mark of favor which could be discontinued on the slightest pretext.

Despite his independence George IV lost some of the initiative in foreign affairs that his father had possessed. His dilatory habits of business were the greatest single cause of this development. Canning sent dispatches to the king, "who will not speedily return them," only after they had been copied for the use of the cabinet.[75] Boxes piled up at Windsor and in 1826 Canning made a special trip down to the Castle "to point out to him among them those which it was most material for him to read, & to relieve him from the remainder."[76] When he delayed sending back important papers the Foreign Office dunned him for them, which annoyed him greatly.[77]

The shift in the method of transmitting papers to the king, however, was only gradual. When Canning went to the Foreign Office in 1822, he continued to submit drafts to the king and to wait for

71. George IV to the Cabinet, [July 1824], ibid., 97.
72. Wellesley to Perceval, Apsley House, Tuesday night [26 Nov. 1811], Private, Holland (Perceval) Papers Bundle I/36.
73. Liverpool to Bathurst, Bath, 16 Jan. 1815, *H. M. C. Bathurst*, p. 324.
74. Canning to Granville, Seaford, 13 Oct. 1825, No. 80, Private & Confidential, P.R.O. 39/29/8/8 ff. 995–98.
75. Canning to Liverpool, F.O., 1 Apr. 1828 [sic; 1823?], Stapleton, *Corresp. of Canning*, vol. 2, 26.
76. Canning to Liverpool, F.O., 1 Apr. 1826, Private & Confidential, Copy, Canning MSS Bundle 72.
77. George IV to Sir William Knighton, Rl. Lge., 20 Apr. 1826, Aspinall, *Letters of George IV*, vol. 3, 147.

approval before sending them abroad.[78] But Canning soon learned that George rarely read and returned papers quickly. It was impossible always to wait for his approval. Canning, in fact, eventually regarded the king's sanction of particular dispatches as something sought pro forma and frequently sent him drafts of dispatches that already were gone.[79] Wellington and Aberdeen, too, played this game. The dispatch to Lord Heytesbury instructing him to seek modifications in the Treaty of Adrianople, for example, was sent on 31 October, 1829. Aberdeen sent the draft, on which the date was entered only after the king returned it marked "Excellent & most highly app'd,"[80] down to Windsor for approval on 6 November.[81] Aberdeen obviously was relieved when the king did not object[82] and his reaction, coupled with the fact that the king was unaware that he was being by-passed, suggests that ministers feared the consequences of being discovered.

On really important questions it was as necessary for Liverpool's ministry to have the approval of George IV as it was for Pitt's to have George III's. The struggle within the cabinet over the diplomatic recognition of Colombia and Mexico in 1824 was carried on with the knowledge that the king opposed the majority who were for recognition. Wellington, who was in the minority, even suggested to Liverpool that the discussion be postponed since "Such measures are inconsistent with all his [the king's] opinions, and with everything which he feels a pride in having done since the establishment of the Regency. . . ."[83] The king protested the decision but acquiesced in a letter Liverpool termed "very foolish."[84] Canning and Liverpool were obliged, therefore, to travel to Windsor determined to extract a more graceful acquiescence from him or to resign. George finally consented with a better grace than at first, though he refused to concur in the necessity of the measure. Liverpool told Canning that this was sufficient since "when the King *did* what we desired, against

78. Canning to Wellington, Foreign Office, 8 and 11 Jan. 1823, *W.N.D.*, vol. 2, 11–12.
79. Canning to Granville, F.O., 8 July 1825, No. 65, Private Political, P.R.O. 30/29/8/8 ff. 941–44; 27 Mar. 1823, Bamford and Wellington, *Journal of Mrs. Arbuthnot*, vol. 1, 220.
80. Draft to Heytesbury, Foreign Office, 31 Oct. 1829, No. 22, with minute of the King, F.O. 65/178.
81. Aberdeen to George IV, Foreign Office, 6 Nov. 1829, Copy, Add. MS 43039 ff. 121–22.
82. Aberdeen to Wellington, Foreign Office, 7 Nov. 1829, Copy, Add. MS 43058 ff. 73–74. It is ironic that on this occasion the king returned the dispatch immediately after receiving it.
83. 7 Dec. 1824, London, *W.N.D.*, vol. 2, 364–66.
84. George IV to Liverpool, Royal Lodge, 17 Dec. 1824, ibid., 368; 18 Dec. 1824, Bamford and Wellington, *Journal of Mrs. Arbuthnot*, vol. 1, 368.

his opinions, we ought to let him grumble a little for consolation."[85]

When George IV opposed his ministers, they were, with the possible exception of Canning, usually tactful in their refusal to back down from their position. Handling the king was a very delicate operation at all times, but particularly on these occasions. He was sensitive to the fact that he could be overruled by his ministers if they remained undivided and occasionally he was petulant in exercising his prerogative. On 9 July, 1828, he kept Aberdeen at Windsor, despite Aberdeen's protests that he was to dine with the diplomatic corps that evening, so that "the Ambassadors should for once see that he was King of England."[86] He was also sensitive to the fact that many felt that he acted only on advice of royal favorites. In December 1827 he summoned Dudley to the Royal Lodge, as he told Sir William Knighton, keeper of his privy purse,

> in consequence of matter contain'd in the submitted draft of an intended dispatch to Lord Granville, relative to the Greek question, which would be not only most *imprudent* but *positive perdition* if allow'd to go. Perhaps it may be as well, that this should happen during your absence from this place, as the members of the Govt. will see, that I have *fix'd principles*, & that I *can*, & *that I do*, when it is *necessary act entirely from myself & by myself*.[87]

When ministers brought subjects to his attention that he did not wish discussed, he talked on and on about any other thing he could think to discuss until he wore himself out and they could return to the original topic.[88] Aberdeen made one trip to Windsor and Wellington took three journeys down to the Castle in 1830 before they could hold him to the point long enough to overcome his objections to their decision to support Prince Leopold as sovereign of the new Greek state.[89] Actions such as these emphasized the king's increasing inability to influence affairs as he wished.

George IV was perhaps the most indiscreet of British sovereigns.

85. Canning to Mrs. Canning, 19 Dec. 1824, Aspinall and Smith, *English Historical Documents*, pp. 101–2.
86. 10 July 1829, Lytton Strachey and Roger Fulford (eds.), *The Greville Memoirs, 1814–1860* (8 vols.; London, 1938), vol. 1, 330–1.
87. Suny. Nt., 9 Dec. 1827, Royal Lodge, Aspinall, *Letters of George IV*, vol. 3, 344.
88. 10 July 1829, Strachey and Fulford, *Greville Memoirs*, vol. 1, 301.
89. The king was ill and these audiences had to be terminated when he finished his ramblings and before Aberdeen and Wellington could review their arguments for Leopold's nomination. 13–19 Jan. 1830, Colchester, *Ellenborough Diary*, vol. 2, 167–74.

He was the last monarch to have private audiences with foreign ambassadors, a practice Castlereagh permitted despite the king's indiscretions[90] and one which Canning was eventually forced to terminate as being inconsistent with "the spirit, & practice too, of the British Constitution. . . ."[91] The king frequently and without reserve denounced his ministers, even to their undersecretaries and in the presence of representatives of foreign powers in London.[92] Bathurst was shocked when he learned that during dinner at the Royal Lodge in June 1826 George "made a violent declaration against the Greeks to Esterhazy [the Austrian ambassador], . . . by all accounts, much too strong for a Sovereign professing strict neutrality in the contest."[93]

The occasional indiscretions of the king were insignificant when compared with his treachery and love of intrigue. Without exception every minister who served him was aware of and deplored his duplicity. George's cleverness coupled with his perfidy made him a "dangerous opponent" for any minister since clever ministers can pit their wits against those of their sovereign but wise ministers dare not try to be more treacherous.[94] George's intrigues with the Austrian chancellor, Prince Metternich, with Princess Lieven, wife of the Russian ambassador in London, and with Prince Esterhazy, Austrian ambassador in London, in order to defeat Canning's policies threatened the stability of his throne more than Canning's policies did. For Canning, had he been defeated, would have resigned and revealed the intrigues to the House of Commons.[95] That George remained oblivious to this danger indicates the passion of his opposition to Canning, and his political imprudence.

Wellington and Aberdeen in 1829 also had to deal with intrigues at Court. They clashed with the king over the selection of a sovereign for Greece. The king's opposition to Prince Leopold, his son-in-law and the official British nominee, was decided. The other powers were not receptive to the prince but they were willing to accept him

---

90. Webster, *For. Pol. Castlereagh*, vol. 1, 28–29.

91. Canning to Granville, F.O., 4 Apr. 1825, No. 46, Private & Confidential, P.R.O. 30/29/8/7 ff. 868–71.

92. 11 May 1821, Bamford and Wellington, *Journal of Mrs. Arbuthnot*, vol. 1, 94; 26 Mar. 1824, ibid., vol. 1, 295.

93. Bathurst to Wellington, Wood End, 18 June 1826, *W.N.D.*, vol. 3, 340–41.

94. Temperley, *For. Pol. Canning*, p. 241.

95. Canning to Granville, F.O., 11 Mar. 1825, No. 40, Private & Confidential, P.R.O. 30/29/8/7 ff. 849–52.

as a compromise candidate. The King of Prussia, however, did not give up the hope that his choice, Prince Charles of Mecklenburgh, would be accepted by the allied powers. English opposition was the sole deterrent, in fact, to his nomination. The Grand Duke of Mecklenburgh-Strelitz approached the Duke of Cumberland, the king's ultra-conservative brother, on behalf of the King of Prussia. George was favorably disposed to Prince Charles and decided to write to the King of Prussia personally declaring his intention to support of Charles's nomination, despite the fact that his ministers were trying to persuade the allied conference to name Leopold. Aberdeen learned of this plan in a conversation he had with the king early in December.[96] The ministers were alarmed and Wellington urged Aberdeen "to strike at once at what is a gross unconstitutional irregularity, which may be followed by National Inconvenience Injury & Dishonour."[97] Aberdeen went to Windsor and persuaded the king, with some difficulty, to return only a civil reply to the effect that he was negotiating with his allies about the sovereignty of Greece.[98] Wellington subsequently drafted a dispatch to the British minister in Berlin placing the incident on record and stating that the king in making his decision to support a candidate would consider only "the Interests and feelings of those over whom he is to reign and of those of the Porte and of the Powers of the Mediterranean."[99] The ministers thereby retrieved the situation and returned affairs to their own hands. The surprising thing about this incident is not that the king gave way without much resistance. It is rather that he even seriously considered working at cross purposes with his ministers and that they did little more than admonish him for this action. George III would never have considered such a proposal. William IV and Victoria would have created a storm if they had.

George IV died in 1830 unmourned by his subjects and his ministers. He was succeeded by his brother, William, Duke of Clarence, whose accession created almost as little excitement as George's death evoked sorrow.[100] William IV was a man of simple tastes. He

96. Wellington to Peel, London, 10 Dec. 1829, *W.N.D.*, vol. 6, 319–20.

97. 8 Dec. 1829, Stowe, Add. MS 43058 ff. 110–15.

98. Wellington to Peel, London, 10 Dec. 1829, *W.N.D.*, vol. 6, 319.

99. Draft Dispatch to Sir George Rose, Winter, 1829, by Wellington, Add. MS 43058 ff. 122–25.

100. For the reaction of the English press to the accession of William IV see Kinglsey Martin, *The Crown and the Establishment* (London, 1962), p. 30.

was his brother's inferior in mental capacity but he compensated for his lack of imagination by working steadily and dutifully at being king.[101] He always tried to do his best even in difficult circumstances.[102] As the third son of George III he never expected to inherit the Crown and only after 1827 when the Duke of York died did he begin to work seriously to prepare for his responsibilities. His career prior to 1830 was in the navy, which always remained his first love. From the beginning of his reign he usually wore his naval uniform at audiences with foreign ministers, though he agreed on rare occasions to wear his military uniform.[103]

William took his responsibilities seriously. His principal interest and goal was to assure continuity in policy which he felt it was possible to achieve only through a stable executive.[104] He gave his unqualified support to his ministers except on those rare occasions when he seriously disagreed with them on some important question. He always expressed his opinions without reserve,[105] but he expected ministers on insignificant issues only to be aware of his opinion, not to alter their own. In 1830 he questioned the wisdom of two passages in a draft Aberdeen submitted to him without "any desire to object to Them, if His Confidential Servants should not Concur with Him."[106] By not insisting on this as well as on other occasions he usually had his way. This draft like numerous others was altered.[107]

101. The most recent account of William's life does much to dispel the image of the king as "a buffoon and lightweight incapable of forming a reasoned judgment on anything more complex than the most desirable colour for a naval uniform." Philip Ziegler, *King William the Fourth* (New York, 1973), p. 248 and passim. See also Webster, *For. Pol. Palmerston*, vol. 1, 24–25.

102. Allen, *William IV*, p. 227.

103. 7 July 1830, Colchester, *Ellenborough Diary*, vol. 2, 304.

104. Arthur Aspinall (ed.), *Three Early Nineteenth Century Diaries* (London, 1952), p. xv. Ministers appreciated the importance of this support and Palmerston took full advantage of it. In 1831 after the Whigs' defeat in the House of Commons over the Reform Bill he wrote to Granville to tell the French that the king's "having consented to dissolve Parliament is the Strongest Proof which he could have given of his approbation of his present Ministers, and of his Determination to give them Every Support which the Forms of the Constitution Enable him to afford them. This Event ought to add to our Influence abroad, by proving the Stability of the present administration." 21 Apr. 1831, Foreign Office, P.R.O. 30/29/404.

105. Curiously this practice annoyed Wellington much more than it did Palmerston or Grey. 8 Feb. 1835, Sunday, Strachey and Fulford, *Greville Memoirs*, vol. 3, 151.

106. William IV to Aberdeen, Windsor Castle, 29 Aug. 1830, Add. MS 43040 ff. 103–4.

107. Aberdeen to William IV, F.O., 30 Aug. 1830, Copy. Add MS 43040 ff. 106–7. In December 1830 the king objected to certain phrases in a dispatch Palmerston sent to the British Minister at Turin. Since the dispatch had already gone, a messenger was sent with another dispatch making the alterations the king suggested. William IV to Palmerston, Brighton, 19 Dec. 1830, Palmerston Papers, RC/A/4/1 and Draft, Mr. Foster, F.O., 24 Dec. 1830, Separate in Cypher, F.O. 67/81.

Unlike his brother, William always dealt fairly with his ministers on matters relating to foreign policy, except perhaps when he gave Wellington in 1835 copies of correspondence he and Palmerston had exchanged between 1830 and 1834.[108] He declared his intention at his first interview with the diplomatic corps of seeing no minister of a foreign power except in the presence of the secretary of state,[109] and he never abandoned his promise. When he gave a dinner for the diplomatic corps in 1832 while Palmerston was not in London, John Backhouse, the permanent undersecretary, was commanded to attend. "Of course," Backhouse reported, "there was not the most remote allusion to passing events."[110]

William's integrity and his attention to business gave him a greater influence in the conduct of foreign affairs than his brother had enjoyed in the latter years of his reign. William believed firmly that it was his duty to comment freely on questions of policy. He once told Grey that "there cannot be confidence where there is reserve."[111] When he felt that the "Character and Dignity" of his crown were involved in an issue he defended his opinions tenaciously and even entered on shaky constitutional grounds when justifying his opposition to ministerial policy. "Viscount Palmerston is doubtless responsible for the Advice he gives," William wrote near the end of his reign, "but there is no positive Obligation on the King to sanction that which He does not approve, and the very Process which is observed, of submitting Instructions for his Approval, establishes the necessity of such approval."[112] The king's power was indeed real and acted as a deterrent to some policies. In 1835 Palmerston refused even to consider a French proposal for a convention providing for joint military intervention in Spain because "I will lay my Life that to Such a Treaty The King would not consent and if he were to throw us over on that Point & call back the Tories It is probable that both Parlt. & the Country would Support him in his decision."[113]

Because William attended to business he received dispatches in circulation regularly. Palmerston's practice was to send incoming dispatches to the office when he had read them. The clerks then

108. Wellington to Peel, London, 5 Feb. 1835, Private, Add. MS 40310 ff. 52–53.
109. 7 July 1830, Colchester, *Ellenborough Diary*, vol. 2, 304.
110. Minute, Backhouse, 16 May 1832, Palmerston Papers GC/BA/2.
111. 17 Apr. 1832, 11 p.m., Windsor Castle, Henry, Earl Grey (ed.), *The Correspondence of the Late Earl Grey with His Majesty King William IV and with Sir Herbert Taylor from November 1830 to June 1832* (2 vols.; London, 1867), vol. 2, 366–70.
112. To Palmerston, Windsor Castle, 11 Sept. 1836, Palmerston Papers RC/A/493/1–3.
113. Palmerston to Granville, Stanhope Street, 2 June 1835, P.R.O. 30/29/421.

copied the dispatches, the originals going to the king, the copies to the prime minister. Wellington apparently sent dispatches to William and then to Peel after they had returned from Windsor. Palmerston quickly put a stop to this "idle innovation" because it was "preposterous that the First Lord of the Treasury Should be kept in Ignorance of Despatches till they have gone down to Windsor & have come back again."[114] William as a rule received dispatches a day or two after they arrived in London. When there was a delay he usually did not object, unless the dispatches held back were germane to policy being determined at the moment.[115] These instances, however, were rare.

Like his brother, William frequently did not see drafts of dispatches before they left London. Palmerston apparently had a regulation about which drafts had to have prior approval of the king and which were to be sent to him as a formality.[116] Doubtless the distinction was whether or not the subject was an issue of major importance. In 1833 Palmerston sent a draft dispatch to Paris to be shown to the French ministry before the king had approved it so that the French and British ministers in St. Petersburg would be able to protest simultaneously and in a similar manner against the Russo-Turkish Treaty of Unkiar Skelessi. "I authorize you to do so," he wrote, "under the peculiar Circumstances of the Case, *in the Strictest Confidence,* for the furtherance of our Common objects, but . . . the King would never forgive me if he knew that I have communicated to the minister of a foreign Power, the Draft of an Important Despatch before it had been approved by him."[117]

William naturally preferred to see every dispatch before it was sent to his representatives abroad because even when he agreed in principle with the measure he felt that there could be occasions when "expressions which might not accord with his view of the subject" would find their way into a dispatch.[118] Grey, to whom the king addressed his remarks, maintained that ministers always sub-

---

114. Minute, Backhouse, 28 Mar. 1833, F.O. 96/17; Minutes, Palmerston, 11 and 12 Oct. 1835, and minute, Edmund Hammond, [11 or 12 Oct. 1835], F.O. 96/18.
115. William IV to Palmerston, Brighton, 22 Nov. 1832, Palmerston Papers RC/A/174; Same to Same, Windsor Castle, 15 Oct. 1832, ibid., RC/A/161.
116. Minute, Backhouse, 9 Dec. 1836, F.O. 96/18.
117. To Aston, F.O., 6 Aug. 1833, Confidential, F.O. 355/6.
118. William IV to Grey, Windsor Castle, 19 Apr. 1832, Private, Grey, *Grey Corresp.,* vol. 2, 376–77.

mitted "instructions of any importance" and simply ignored the rest of William's complaint.[119] If William objected to certain passages in dispatches that had already left London, his alterations were merely sent to be inserted in the dispatch by the mission in question.[120]

William's objections to minor points were on occasion sufficient to cancel a dispatch. In 1836, for example, he returned a draft to George Villiers, British minister at Madrid, deprecating the inefficacy of the Spanish army in suppressing the Carlist forces.[121] Although his note gave no reason for his refusal to sanction the draft ("The King *cannot* approve of the Dispatch to Mr. Villiers and therefore returns it unsigned"),[122] Palmerston had the dispatch recalled rather than engaging in an argument with the king over an insignificant issue.[123]

On more important questions William's opposition was a serious matter. He refused to approve a draft dispatch to Villiers in September, 1836, pledging continued British support in suppressing the Carlists despite a coup d'état against the ministers who had signed the treaty providing for that support. He wished an amendment inserted in the dispatch stating that "He never will Consent to give his Countenance, direct or indirect, to the Revolutionary Proceedings of any Government . . . " forced on the Queen Regent of Spain.[124] Palmerston tried to secure his approval of the original draft by eliminating the passage which William's addition was designed to amend and by telling him that the proposed passage would be embarrassing to the government if produced in Parliament.[125] But William remained adamant,[126] and only the arrival of dispatches from Villiers which rendered the disputed dispatch unnecessary prevented a major confrontation.[127] Ministerial unanimity remained the only way to overcome the king's objections on these occasions. In 1832 Grey's ministry secured William's approval of

119. Grey to Taylor, Downing Street, 18 Apr. 1832, Private, ibid., 372–73.
120. Backhouse to Granville, Foreign Office, 31 Dec. 1836, Private, P.R.O. 30/29/14/3 ff. 121–25; Minutes, Backhouse and Palmerston, 21 Nov. 1836, F.O. 96/18.
121. Draft, Mr. Villiers, F.O., 30 June 1836, No. 55, Cancelled, Palmerston Papers RC/A/444/3–4.
122. William IV to Palmerston, 3 July 1836, ibid., RC/A/444/1.
123. Palmerston to Villiers, F.O., 14 July 1836, Private & Confidential, Copy, ibid., GC/CL/1270.
124. William IV to Palmerston, [Sept. 1836], ibid., RC/A/488/1.
125. Palmerston to William IV, Stanhope Street, 9 Sept. 1836, Copy, ibid., RC/A/490.
126. William IV to Palmerston, Windsor Castle, 10 Sept. 1836, ibid., RC/A/495.
127. Minute, Palmerston, Foreign Office, 12 Sept. 1836, ibid., RC/A/495.

joint Anglo-French naval and land operations against the Dutch only by having a second meeting on the subject and resubmitting their advice to him.[128] The king was not happy, but he acquiesced because he felt he could not "oppose the advice unanimously offered to him by his Cabinet, if after having considered his objection they persevere in it."[129]

William was able to get through his business in large part because he had the assistance of a private secretary. George III had been idefatigable and had written all his own notes to ministers. When he went blind Colonel Herbert Taylor served as his private secretary. George IV had a private secretary during the Regency but not after 1822.[130] William was the only sovereign before the twentieth century to have a private secretary for the duration of his reign.

William selected as his private secretary Sir Herbert Taylor, who served William as loyally from 1830 to 1837 as he had George III before he became incapacitated. Occasionally he disagreed with the king when he opposed his ministers. In these instances he told the king how he felt.[131] Generally, however, he agreed with William and was content to remain an observer of events. It is unlikely that he played any significant role in the formation of policy, but because the king rarely wrote his own letters and memoranda Taylor was able to influence the tone of royal correspondence. William and Taylor discussed what the king wished said in his letters to ministers and then Taylor drafted a letter which the king approved and Taylor wrote out for signature.[132] The few notes the king scribbled to his ministers were usually short and to the point.[133] If he wrote longer letters he was frequently obscure and ministers were forced to appeal to Taylor for an explanation.[134] Fortunately Taylor usually read William's lengthy memoranda and he frequently sent along

128. Palmerston to Granville, F.O., 16 Oct. 1832, Secret, P.R.O. 30/20/413.
129. Grey to Palmerston, E. Sheen, 16 Oct. 1832, Private, Palmerston Papers GC/GR/2157.
130. Aspinall, *Letters of George IV*, vol. 1, lix–lx. Sir William Knighton, keeper of the privy purse, continued to serve as George IV's secretary after 1822, but not in an official capacity.
131. Taylor to Palmerston, Windsor Castle, 20 Oct. 1833, Confidential, Palmerston Papers RC/C/113/102.
132. Taylor to Grey, Brighton, 23 Jan. 1831, Grey, *Grey Corresp.*, vol. 1, 79.
133. For example, "June 13, 1832. The Porte *must* be cultivated. William R." Palmerston Papers RC/A/97..
134. Palmerston to Taylor, Foreign Office, 20 Mar. 1832, Confidential, Copy, ibid., RC/CC/3.

covering explanatory letters without William's knowledge.[135] The ministers also approached the king through Taylor when they were too busy to send formal letters to Windsor.[136]

If William was very much unlike his brother in his work habits, he nonetheless shared George's political philosophy. He equated liberalism with revolution on more than one occasion and warned Palmerston that "The *Spirit of the Age* altho' it may be called *Liberal* is *Revolutionary* and its tendency is the overthrow of all that is established, whether good or bad."[137] Yer despite this peculiar view, at times he could be an extremely astute observer of political events. He worried about Russian encroachments in the Levant, ignored Russian claims of friendship ("attributable solely to the desire of gaining time and of passing over a Season which is unfavorable to display or Action"), and urged his ministers to take steps to prepare for meeting the threat.[138] He disapproved of Grey's and Palmerston's proposal to seek Austrian participation in an Anglo-French agreement for securing the integrity of the Turkish Empire because he felt that "the effect of such previous *Sounding* of Prince Metternich will be . . . the premature disclosure of the Arrangement to the Court of Petersburgh which would be fatal to the Policy & the Interest of this Country."[139]

Though William's dislikes were intense they were usually directed at foreign powers or personages instead of his own ministers. He complained "of the absurd, narrowminded, shuffling and impolitic Conduct of the King of the Netherlands" during the Belgian crisis of 1831.[140] Though he later became reconciled to working closely with the French in foreign affairs, he regarded France in the early years of his reign as "the natural and Constant Enemy of Great Britain,"[141] declared that he could "*never have any faith* in French diplomacy,"[142] and told Grey that Frenchmen would forever cherish "schemes of conquest and of extension of territory . . . by the propagation of

135. Taylor to Palmerston, Windsor Castle, 24 Aug., 1 and 18 Oct. 1833, Private, ibid., RC/C/92/1; RC/C/100; RC/C/111.
136. Grey to Taylor, Downing Street, 26 Aug. 1831, Grey, *Grey Corresp.*, vol. 1, 340.
137. 23 Mar. 1832, Windsor Castle, Palmerston Papers RC/A/85/1–3.
138. William IV to Palmerston, Brighton, 10 Apr. 1836, ibid., RC/A/434/1–3.
139. William IV to Palmerston, Brighton, 11 Feb. 1836, ibid., RC/A/422.
140. William IV to Palmerston, Windsor Castle, 25 Oct. 1831, ibid., RC/A/57/1.
141. William IV to Palmerston, Windsor Castle, July 1833, ibid., RC/A/255.
142. William IV to Palmerston, Brighton, 28 Jan. 1833, ibid., RC/A/217.

revolutionary doctrines and principles. . . ."[143] During his reign the Russians became increasingly unpopular at the Court and when Count Pozzo di Borgo, Russian ambassador at Paris, visited England in 1833 the king even "abstained from drinking the Emperor's Health after Dinner, though he delights in Toasting foreign Sovereigns when he has one of their Subjects at [the] Table."[144]

William was the last of the kings of England to be sovereign of Hanover as well. Unlike his brother and father, however, he was something of a constitutional ruler of his German dominions. He was kept fully informed about Hanoverian affairs, but his brother, the duke of Sussex, was regent and actually governed the small kingdom. William regularly communicated Hanoverian dispatches and interceptions to Palmerston and Wellington.[145] But he was tenacious in his belief that German affairs were not a primary concern of the English government, and he had one serious clash with Grey's ministry over his duties as King of Hanover and King of England.

Like many of the minor German princes William looked to Austria and Prussia to check "the *Liberal* or Revolutionary feeling, which has found its way into Germany. . . ."[146] He supported Metternich in the Zollverein Diet at Frankfort in 1832 when, in response to agitation by German liberals at Hanbach and elsewhere, the German princes unanimously approved six resolutions restricting the activities of the press and limiting suffrage in the South German States.[147] Palmerston's dispatch protesting the resolutions returned from Windsor unapproved. Among the things William protested[148] was being "called upon to condemn and repudiate" as King of England what he had approved as King of Hanover "on Principle and

143. 16 Apr. 1832, Windsor Castle, Grey, *Grey Corresp.* vol. 2, 351–55.
144. Palmerston to Granville, F.O., 15 Jan. 1833, P.R.O. 30/29/415.
145. Taylor to Palmerston, Windsor, 4 Mar. 1834, Palmerston Papers RC/C/134; Taylor to Wellington, Brighton, 23 Nov. 1834, Private, Wellington Papers, National Register of Archives, London.
146. William IV to Palmerston, Windsor Castle, 23 July 1832, Palmerston Papers RC/A/119/1–2.
147. Webster, *For. Pol. Palmerston*, vol. 1, 225–26.
148. He also disapproved of the dispatch going to Bavaria instead of to the Diet or to the leading German powers and he questioned Britain's right to interfere in the question. Grey found the first of these objections reasonable and copies were sent as the king wished. Palmerston dismissed the second objection by saying that the measure threatened the peace of the world in which Britain had an interest. Grey to Palmerston, E. Sheen, 3 Aug. 1832, Private, Palmerston Papers GC/GR/2131.

from a Conviction of the necessity of the Measure. . . ."[149] Palmerston felt "that if the Politics of the Two Countries are to be thus bound together, England being the most powerful and important is entitled to lead Hanover, and not Hanover to lead England."[150] More tactfully he told William that though both Hanover and England had the "Happiness to obey" the same sovereign no one in Europe believed that their foreign policies were one; that each of the kingdoms had to consult its own interests on every question and act accordingly; and that William's actions as king of Hanover were no bar to his pursuing a separate course of policy as King of England.[151] The cabinet assembled hastily and proved unanimous in opposing the king. William waived his objections to signing the dispatch and generously told Palmerston that he agreed with his reasoning on the question of his duties with respect to England and Hanover. He did not, however, surrender his opinion on the impropriety of British intervention in German affairs.[152]

William died in 1837 and was succeeded by his niece, the Princess Victoria.[153] The events of the first ten years of Queen Victoria's reign are scarcely sufficient to indicate her impact on the sovereign's role in the formation of foreign policy. Yet there was a decided difference in the role of the Crown during William's reign and at the beginning of Victoria's. The queen's letters to her foreign secretaries were rarely long and even more infrequently were they expositions of particular courses of policy. Aberdeen did not hesitate to tell her that dispatches were sent without her previous sanction.[154] Yet he and Palmerston never had the courage to tell George IV and William of the practice. Because Victoria generally agreed with Aberdeen's policies she did not object. But when Palmerston, who returned to office in 1846, resumed his secrecy and then pursued policies the queen did not approve, their conflict was inevitable. In 1840 Palmerston wrote for the guidance of his undersecretaries that

149. William IV to Palmerston, Windsor Castle, 3 Aug. 1832, ibid., RC/A/127/1–2.
150. Palmerston to Grey, Stanhope Street, 3 Aug. 1832, copy, ibid., GC/GR/2372.
151. 5 Aug. 1832, Foreign Office, draft, ibid., RC/AA/43/1–4.
152. William IV to Palmerston, Windsor Castle, 7 Aug. 1832, ibid., RC/A/129/1–2.
153. Of the innumerable studies of the queen that of Cecil Woodham-Smith, *Queen Victoria: Her Life and Times*, vol. 1, *1819–1861* (London, 1972), deserves separate mention.
154. Only select incoming dispatches were sent to her, apparently at the discretion of the undersecretaries. Aberdeen said in 1844 that he was "obliged to take for granted that all Papers are sent to the Queen which ought to be sent. . . ." To Peel, F.O., 24 Feb. 1844, Add. MS 40454 ff. 135–36.

"the *Rule* shd be to Send Her Drafts of important Dispatches before the Dispatches are Sent off. *The Execution* shd be the Sending off the Dispatches without Sending the Drafts to the Queen."[155] Eventually of course this policy let to unpleasant circumstances. In 1851 Palmerston sent a dispatch to Paris approving of Louis Napoleon's coup d'état without first securing the queen's approval. He probably would have survived her storm had he consulted Lord John Russell, the prime minister, before sending the dispatch. But Russell was as ignorant of the dispatch and as angry as the queen and forced Palmerston out of office. For a time thereafter the queen received all drafts before they were dispatched.[156] But Aberdeen and Clarendon in 1854 reinstated the former practice[157] and it seems unlikely that their successors abandoned it.

Victoria's inexperience accounts in part for the shift in the role of the sovereign in foreign affairs in the first years of her reign. During William's final illness Palmerston wrote that he hoped the king "Should wear the Crown Some Time, . . . for there would be no advantage in having a totally inexperienced Girl of 18 just out of a Strict Guardianship to govern an Empire. It would be well for her & for us that her ascent to the Throne Should be preceded by Some little Intercourse with the world."[158] Palmerston worked hard to overcome her initial uncertainties, spent hours with her going through dispatches,[159] and sent her letters of advice on what to say at audiences with foreign ministers.[160] Doubtless as her experience increased her opinions became more mature and her advice more valuable. Eventually her family ties with the courts of Europe gave her a voice abroad that none of her Hanoverian predecessors had enjoyed. But these were all later developments and the decided break in the sovereign's intense involvement in decisions on foreign affairs between William's and Victoria's reigns is unquestionable.

Nevertheless, the queen worked very hard at the dispatches. She

155. Minute, Palmerston, 21 Nov. 1840, F.O. 366/280 f. 44.
156. Minute, Malmesbury, [Feb. 1852], ibid., f. 39.
157. Victoria to Aberdeen, 27 Apr. and 13 May 1854, Lady Francis Balfour, *The Life of George, Fourth Earl of Aberdeen* (2 vols.; London, 1923), vol. 2, 219, 226.
158. To Granville, F.O., 26 May 1837, P.R.O. 30/29/423.
159. Victoria's Journal, n.d., Brian Connell (ed.), *Regina vs. Palmerston, The Correspondence Between Queen Victoria and Her Foreign and Prime Minister, 1837–1865* (London, 1962), p. 16.
160. Palmerston to Victoria, Stanhope Street, 22 July 1837, Arthur Christopher Benson and Viscount Esher (eds.), *The Letters of Queen Victoria, 1837–1861* (3 vols.; New York, 1907), vol. 1, 112.

was interested in foreign affairs and did not hesitate to tell Palmerston when she did not fully understand an issue.[161] In 1838 she requested a map of Asia so that she could see where the places mentioned in a draft dispatch were located.[162] She was shrewd enough to sense that she did not always receive everything she felt should have been sent to her, but though she mentioned the matter on several occasions she did not make a fuss about her suspicions.[163] Because she had no private secretary she often found it difficult to get through the dispatches sent for her to read, and she did not hesitate to tell Palmerston of her problems: "As the Queen has got a great many Foreign Dispatches which, from want of time she has been unable to read as yet, she requests Lord Palmerston not to send her any more until she has done with those which she already has with her. . . ."[164] Palmerston appreciated that she was a young girl and regulated the volume of business sent to her by the Foreign Office so that when she was engaged in other activities, such as attending the Ascot races, she would receive only what it was essential for her to read.[165]

Although Victoria rarely wrote long expositions on policy, when an issue roused her attention she did not hesitate to state her opinion. In 1840, for example, she was concerned lest the breach with France over the Eastern question should lead to hostilities between the two countries. "The Queen's *earnest* & *only* wish is Peace & a maintenance of friendly Relations with her Allies consistent with the honour & dignity of her Country," she wrote,[166] and throughout the crisis hers was a voice for a policy of Anglo-French conciliation. Her uncle, Leopold, was king of the Belgians and she always took an active interest in Belgian affairs.[167] She also was particularly concerned with conditions in Spain and Greece where events relating to the security of fellow monarchs held a peculiar fascination for

161. Victoria to Palmerston, Pavillion Brighton, 7 Oct. 1839, Palmerston Papers RC/F/131.
162. Melbourne to Palmerston, Windsor Castle, 1 Nov. 1838, ibid., GC/ME/252.
163. Melbourne to Palmerston, Brocket Hall, 14 Dec. 1840, Confidential, ibid., GC/ME/465; Victoria to Palmerston, [30] May 1841, Connell, *Regina vs. Palmerston*, p. 30; Victoria to Aberdeen, Claremont, 13 Jan. 1844, Add. MS 43043 f. 266.
164. Victoria to Palmerston, Buckingham Palace, 12 Aug. 1837, Palmerston Papers RC/F/15/1.
165 Minute, Palmerston, 10 June 1838, F.O. 96/19.
166 To Palmerston, Windsor Castle, 11 Nov. 1840, Palmerston Papers RC/F/212/1-3.
167 Melbourne to Palmerston, Downing Street, 31 Jan. 1839, ibid., GC/ME/270.

her.[168] Spanish affairs especially worried her and she shared her ministers' feeling "of what importance it is to England that Spain shd not become subject to French Interests, as it is evident France *wishes* to make it."[169]

After the queen's marriage to Prince Albert in 1840 the prince played an active role in the discussion of foreign affairs. When the queen was recovering from her first confinement boxes were sent to the prince who judged the best time to bring their contents to her attention.[170] His letters to ministers often were discussions of particular courses of policy[171] and occasionally he sent them memoranda on European politics in general.[172] The queen, of course, encouraged Albert's participation in affairs,[173] but ministers do not seem to have objected, and they occasionally even brought topics to the attention of the Court by conferring with the prince instead of the queen.[174]

The influence of the Crown in foreign affairs between 1782 and 1846 always reflected both the personality of the sovereign and the political organization of the country. None of the four monarchs who reigned during this period, therefore, exercised an influence over the conduct of foreign affairs in exactly the same manner as his predecessors or successors. Generally speaking, if a sovereign were to maintain a strict surveillance over the course of foreign affairs he had to work as hard as ministers. In this respect George III was an exceptional king. But it was unreasonable to suppose that his successors could or would be so diligent. George IV's habits of business, to be sure, forced more considerable alterations in the conduct of affairs than otherwise might have occurred during his reign. William, therefore, merely by dint of his attention to affairs and by his energy, was able to reassume some of the detailed supervision of foreign policy that his brother had surrendered.

168. Victoria to Aberdeen, Claremont, 10 Jan. 1844, Add. MS 43043 ff. 262–63; Same to Same, Windsor Castle, 9 Apr. 1844, Add. MS 43044 ff. 88–89.
169. Victoria to Aberdeen, Windsor Castle, 17 Oct. 1841, Add. MS 43041 ff. 56–59.
170. Melbourne to Palmerston, South Street, 22 Nov. 1840, Palmerston Papers GC/ME/454.
171. Prince Albert to Melbourne, Windsor, 9 Oct. 1840, ibid., RC/J/2/1; Prince Albert to Aberdeen, Blair Athol, 19 Sept. 1844; Add. MS 43044 ff. 354–55.
172. "Opinion on the interests of the 5 powers in the original question," by Prince Albert, 25 Aug. 1840, Palmerston Papers RC/J/4/1–3.
173. Victoria to Aberdeen, Windsor Castle, 14 Dec. 1841, Add. MS 43041 ff. 137–38.
174. Aberdeen to Prince Albert, F.O., 30 Jan. 1845, Add. 43045 f. 22.

A second factor was more responsible than the personal idiosyncracies of the monarchs for the shifting role of the sovereign in determining foreign policy. Changes in the body politic and the emergence of more or less disciplined parties in the House of Commons after 1832 undermined though they did not totally eliminate the importance of the support of the Crown as a factor in ministerial stability. These changes account for the ability and the willingness of ministers after 1832 to act more frequently without consulting the sovereign.

That is not to say, however, that William and Victoria were mere ciphers whose opinions counted for little or nothing. For if the trend was towards the exclusion of the Crown from the decision-making process, the progress towards this goal was painstakingly slow. No foreign secretary could ignore the opinion of the sovereign even had he wished to do so. But all agreed to consult the Crown only on issues of great national importance and to assume support for the daily conduct of affairs. It was a compromise solution to the problem of adjusting an existing institution to changing times, but it worked tolerably well and that was the most that could be expected.

CHAPTER IV

THE SECRETARIES OF STATE

The history of the secretaries of state prior to 1782 has been well explored.[1] The position was not in the seventeenth and early eighteenth centuries one of immense importance. Individual secretaries were frequently significant figures, but their influence, power, and prestige reflected personal ability and activity, not an inherent importance in the secretaryship. Nevertheless, the significance of the secretaries in ministerial affairs gradually increased during the eighteenth century. The secretaries by the second quarter of the nineteenth century ranked in importance second only to the premier, and Salisbury was in the last years of the century to combine the Foreign Office with the premiership. In the case of the foreign secretary the reasons for this expansion of official influence lay in the increased responsibility for the day to day administration of policy which devolved on his shouders. Of equal importance, however, was the fact that the succession of secretaries in the nineteenth century were on balance a remarkably able group of men. Whether the influence of these men over the course of foreign affairs was the result of institutional factors, of personal ability, or of a combination of the two is immaterial. By mid-century the foreign secretaryship was the key single position in the process of administering British foreign policy. That this situation did not occur immediately is self-evident, but its origins lay not in a single event such as the administrative reorganization of 1782. Rather they were to be found in the practices and abilities of individual secretaries, to a degree before 1782, but especially afterwards.

The division of the secretaryship of state (which is only one office) into departments has always been a matter of administrative convenience to the sovereign and the ministers.[2] Each secretary has the

---

1. Florence M. Grier Evans, *The Principal Secretary of State* ("Publications of the University of Manchester, Historical Series," vol. 43; Manchester, 1923); Thomson, *Secretaries of State.*
2. Pitt to Chatham, 12 July 1794, Aspinall, *Later Corresp. Geo. III*, vol. 2, 223 n.2.

authority to exercise the duties of any of his colleagues. In theory they are of equal rank and importance. Political and personal factors, however, have always made one secretary more influential than his colleagues. In 1794, for example, Pitt felt that it was absolutely impossible for the Duke of Portland to direct the War Department when he joined the ministry. The war with France enhanced the importance of the newest of the offices of state and though Pitt was willing to give the Foreign Office to Portland, who finally accepted the Home Office, he could not allow any but his closest associates to have direction of the department that was responsible for conducting the war.[3]

After the peace with France in 1815, however, preventing, not conducting, war became the primary responsibility of successive ministries. The importance of the foreign secretaryship was enhanced by the increased influence Britain had in continental affairs as a result first of her military and naval leadership in the struggle against Napoleon, and second because of Castlereagh's astute diplomacy in the postwar settlement. Lord Dudley regarded his as "the second political office in the state."[4] Viscount Palmerston refused to accept any other position in Melbourne's ministry formed in April 1835 because by so doing he felt, and Melbourne agreed, that he would be taking a demotion.[5]

With the increasing interest in and importance of British foreign relations, capable and influential men began to seek the foreign secretaryship. George Canning in 1822 gave up the prospect of considerable wealth and a peerage to take the position.[6] In 1834, when William IV sacked Melbourne's ministry, the Duke of Wellington temporarily, as Palmerston put it, "like an atlas Supports the whole weight [of government] on his shoulders: He is Treasy, Admty, 3 Secr of State, & Everything Else, Except ArchB of Canterbury."[7] But once Sir Robert Peel returned from abroad to head the

3. Pitt to Grenville, Downing Street, 5 July 1794, Private, *H. M. C. Fortescue*, vol. 2, 595–96.
4. Dudley to Aberdeen, Roehampton, 25 Aug. 1827, Add. MS 43231 ff. 267–68.
5. Palmerston to Melbourne, Stanhope Street, 14 Apr. 1835, Copy, Palmerston Papers GC/ME/27/3–4; Melbourne to Palmerston, South Street, 15 Apr., 1835, Private, ibid., GC/ME/28/1.
6. Arthur Aspinall, "Canning's Return to Office in September, 1822," *English Historical Review*, 78 (July, 1963), 532. The ministers did secure him a pension, however, as some security against his going out and as compensation for his sacrifices. 7 Feb. 1823, Bamford and Wellington, *Journal of Mrs. Arbuthnot*, vol. 1, 213.
7. Palmerston to Granville, Stanhope Street, 21 Nov. 1834, P.R.O. 30/29/419/1.

new ministry, Wellington willingly settled at the Foreign Office. The earl of Aberdeen, one of the least ambitious of politicians, said the Foreign Office was "the only office which at any time in my life was ever an object of desire."[8]

Nowhere can the importance of the foreign secretaryship to a career be better seen than in the case of Palmerston. When he joined Grey's government in 1830 he was by political connection a Canningite and by experience a second-rate politician. He had never been associated with the Whigs and he was not one of the leading lights of the cabinet at the time, though his interest in foreign affairs between 1828 and 1830 gained him considerable respect in Whig circles.[9] By 1835, however, Melbourne found it impossible to do without him on his own terms and in 1839–1840 he managed to carry his Eastern policy through a hostile and unsympathetic cabinet. Palmerston's abilities and energy explain in part his successes, but the fact that he was foreign secretary meant that his opinions carried that additional force necessary to give him considerable influence in cabinet and victory in the political crises caused by foreign affairs in the 1830s.

The Foreign Office was always headed by men of rank. For the most part they were also men of ability. With the exception of George Canning, all of the sixteen men who served as foreign secretary between 1782 and 1846 were peers or sons of peers. Eight of them at one time or other in their careers served as premier. Charles James Fox was the first secretary of state for foreign affairs. Although he held the seals three times, he served a total of only twenty-one months. Fox's administrative abilities and energy were appreciated by his subordinates as well as his political adversaries.[10] He initiated the practice of having conferences with foreign representatives in London every Thursday afternoon.[11] He gave more dinners to the diplomatic corps than any of his predecessors in the old Northern Department.[12] He took personal control over the machinery of the office during the early weeks of his third term in 1806 because his undersecretaries, both of whom had no acquain-

8. Aberdeen to Peel, F.O., 29 Sept. 1842, Add. MS 40453 ff. 171–72.
9. Herbert C. F. Bell, *Lord Palmerston* (2 vols.; London, 1936), vol. 1, 73–95.
10. Fraser to Sir Robert M. Keith, St. James's, 12 Oct. 1783, Add. MS 35530 f. 86; Grantham to Hardwicke, Whitehall, 22 July 1782, Add. MS 35619 ff. 214–15.
11. Aust to Hardwicke, Monday, 29 July 1782, Add. MS 35619 ff. 227–28.
12. Fraser to Keith, St. James's, 4 June 1782, Add. MS 35525 ff. 259–60.

tance with the Foreign Office, were too inexperienced at first to manage these affairs efficiently.[13]

But Fox's interests were wider than the affairs immediately under his own supervision, and he often neglected the Foreign Office to attend to other business. William Fraser, one of his undersecretaries and a man of considerable experience, was relieved in 1783 when the India Bill passed the House of Commons: "I shall hope our Times *here* will be less employed in what I call Domestick Concerns. They will . . . have their weight in the Scale with a Principal who takes so very large a Share in the Support of them—however he may wish to embrace both Objects."[14] Because George III objected to Fox on political and personal grounds and because of Fox's political opinions he spent most of his career in opposition. His administrative achievements were negligible and he is more remembered as the "patron saint" of successive generations of dissenters to British foreign policy[15] than as a creative political leader.

Thomas Robinson, second Baron Grantham, succeeded Fox in July, 1782. He was the least significant of all the foreign secretaries. He accepted office only on condition that he be adequately provided for when he retired.[16] After he had served his time he was given a pension of £2,000 and though Pitt offered the seals to him in December 1783, he declined.[17]

After a short interval during which Fox again was at the Foreign Office, Francis Godolphin Osborne, Marquess of Carmarthen and after 1789 fifth Duke of Leeds, held the seals. Leeds was a patrician. His social graces, his heritage, and his good looks made him one of the dandies of his age. He fussed over the foreign ministers, flat-

13. John Bernard Trotter, *Memoirs of the Latter Years of the Right Honourable Charles James Fox* (London, 1811), pp. 370–71. Trotter, Fox's secretary, is a highly unreliable source except for the most routine of details such as Fox's habits of business.

14. Fraser to Keith, St. James's, 28 Nov. 1783, Add. MS 35530 ff. 204–5.

15. Alan J. P. Taylor, *The Troublemakers: Dissent Over Foreign Policy, 1792–1939* (London, 1957), p. 25. Of the many studies of Fox the most apologetic is Edward Charles Ponsonby Lascelles, *The Life of Charles James Fox* (reprint; New York, 1970). Those who seek a more balanced assessment of his career should consult John W. Derry, *Charles James Fox* (New York, 1972).

16. Lady Grantham to Countess de Grey, Newby, Wednesday, 17 July 1782, Lucus L 30/11/240/23.

17. Henry Benjamin Wheatley (ed.), *The Historical and Posthumous Memoirs of Sir Nathanial Wraxall* (5 vols.; London, 1884), vol. 2, 26–27; Memorandum by Grantham, 21 Dec. 1783, Lucus L 30/14/308a/1.

tered them, and made them feel important.[18] Yet he "brought to the Government more of polish than weight."[19] He was inattentive to any business except his own, on occasion writing letters to his diplomatists "in the midst of the Cabinet."[20] He did not object, however, to others managing affairs directly involving his own department. Hawkesbury, Grenville, and Dundas, for example, conducted all the important commercial negotiations during his secretaryship (1784–1791) though they probably would have left them to him had he insisted, since James Bland Burges, his undersecretary, was able in 1789 to wrest the negotiation with the Two Sicilies from Hawkesbury without difficulty.[21] Leeds was such a political lightweight that the strength of the ministry was unimpaired when he resigned in 1791 over the decision to pursue a more conciliatory policy in response to Russian encroachments in the Oczakow district than ministers had first determined to follow.[22] Though he was a popular secretary in the office—the clerks presented the duchess with a portrait of him by Lawrence after he retired[23] —his colleagues scarcely missed him.

Leeds's influence was reduced by the fact that he served under William Pitt, whose abilities and personality enabled him to dominate almost all his colleagues. Besides Leeds, three men served as foreign secretary during Pitt's two premierships. Dudley Ryder, first Earl of Harrowby (1804–1805), and Henry Phipps, first Earl of Mulgrave (1805–1806), were little more than functionaries whose personal loyalty to Pitt was their outstanding characteristic. Harrowby, whose fretful nature was the source of much London gossip,[24] had little illusion about his or Mulgrave's importance. "Your first dispatches from my successor," he wrote Granville, "will have borne pretty decisively the stamp of Pitt."[25] Mulgrave seems to have immersed himself in minutiae. He ordered that no clerk leave the

18. Fraser to Keith, Whitehall, 9 May 1786, Add. MS 35536 ff. 266–67.

19. Stanhope, *Pitt*, vol. 1, 311.

20. Carmarthen to Sir James Harris, Whitehall, 14 Mar. 1788, Private, Copy, Add. MS 28063 ff. 91–92.

21. Ehrman, *Commercial Negotiations*, pp. 164–65, 187–91.

22. Leeds's diary, 4 Mar. 1791 to 20 Apr. 1791, Browning, *Leeds Political Memoranda*, pp. 148–73.

23. Algernon Cecil, "The Foreign Office," *Cambridge History of British Foreign Policy*, ed. Sir Adolphus Ward and G.P. Gooch (3 vols.; Cambridge, 1922–1923), vol. 3, 544.

24. George Jackson to his mother, 8 Jan. 1806, Lady Jackson (ed.), *The Diaries and Letters of Sir George Jackson* (2 vols.; London, 1872), vol. 1, 390.

25. 28 Mar. 1805, Bath, P.R.O. 30/29/384A.

office without obtaining permission from an undersecretary. This regulation offended the honor of the clerks who, "being too proud to ask leave to go to dinner, prefer to go without, and remain in the office till all the doors are closed, and they are almost turned out." These and other arrangements made Mulgrave one of the few secretaries who was "extremely unpopular" with his staff.[26]

The other foreign secretary to serve with Pitt was Leeds's successor, William Wyndham Grenville, first Baron Grenville. Grenville, who served from 1791 to 1801, was a man of ability, energy, and considerable imagination. Personally he was not a warm man but his subordinates and his colleagues respected him. He was conscientious and able. His French was excellent,[27] probably better than that of any British foreign secretary before or since. He took a good deal of interest in the daily routine of the office and on occasion performed some of the menial duties such as preparing ciphers.[28] He was an able if not eloquent speaker, and served as sole government spokesman in the House of Lords.[29] He was a supreme patriot and a man of principle and courage. He was, however, frequently rigid in his opinions and obstinate in defense of them. In 1795 he nearly resigned rather than to sign a dispatch offering a further subsidy to the Prussians to keep them in the war with France. Despite the fact that the rest of the cabinet and the king were opposed to him, Grenville persisted because he felt further subsidies were futile and a waste of money.[30] His greatest failings were his lack of a sense of humor to temper his stern character and his admitted inability to understand men and to manage them effectively.[31]

Unlike Leeds, Harrowby, and Mulgrave, Grenville enjoyed the fullest confidence of Pitt and worked closely with him on matters of policy. Burges found "these two friends ... so inseparably connected that there is but one sentiment between them."[32] There is

26. George Jackson to his mother, 23 July 1805, and diary, 29 Sept. 1805, Jackson, *Letters of G. Jackson*, vol. 1, 307, 329–30.

27. J. W. Fortescue, *British Statesmen of the Great War, 1793–1814* (Oxford, 1911), pp. 75–78.

28. Aust to Auckland, Whitehall, 23 Aug. 1791, Add. MS 34439 f. 254.

29. Burges to Auckland, White Hall, 10 July 1792, Private, Add. MS 34443 ff. 308–11.

30. He was right. "Minute of Lord Grenville on the Project of a New Convention between Great Britain and Prussia, January–March, 1795," *H. M. C. Fortescue*, vol. 3, 26–30; Grenville to Pitt, Dover Street, 2 Mar. 1795, Private, P.R.O. 30/8/140 ff. 85–86.

31. Stanhope, *Pitt*, vol. 2, 122.

32. Burges to Ewart, 7 July 1791, quoted in James Hutton (ed.), *Selections from the Letters of Sir James Bland Burges, Bart.* (London, 1885), pp. 174–75.

little doubt that Grenville initiated many policies.[33] Under his direction the commercial negotiations of the country were returned to the Foreign Office.[34] In the 1790s, however, the lines distinguishing the duties of the secretaries of state were imperfectly drawn. Grenville, Pitt, and Henry Dundas, secretary of state successively at the Home and War Offices during this decade, ran the war and governed the country. Whenever Grenville was out of town Dundas administered foreign affairs. Grenville took over Dundas's duties when he was in the country and Grenville was in London.[35] Dundas and Pitt occasionally had interviews with foreign ministers without the prior knowledge of Grenville.[36] Other factors often led to seemingly peculiar arrangements of business. Grenville, for example, felt it was natural for Dundas, the war secretary, to work closely with William Windham in 1796 when Windham was acting as liason between the royalists in France and the British government.[37] Apparently, however, War Office secret service funds were inadequate for Windham's needs and by 1798 Grenville, who of the three secretaries received the greatest amount of secret service money, was financing Windham's operations.[38] Yet Portland, the home secretary, used his secret service money to support French and Corsican emigrants in Portugal and Florence since he took a personal interest in their welfare.[39]

During Grenville's secretaryship there was a change in the mode of paying the secretaries. Viscount Stormont, the last of the northern secretaries of state, in 1780 received a salary of £1950 from the King's Civil List. In 1782 this sum was raised to £5680.[40] Fox and his successors received in addition to their salary, a £100 patent salary, £100 from the Irish Concordatum Fund, £26 from the East India

33. Ephraim Douglass Adams, *The Influence of Grenville on Pitt's Foreign Policy, 1787–1798* ("Carnegie Institute of Washington," no. 13; Washington, D.C., 1904), pp. 1–10.

34. Ehrman, *Commercial Negotiations*, p. 191.

35. Aust to Auckland, Whitehall, 11 Sept. 1792, Add. MS 34444 ff. 264–65; Grenville to George III, Whitehall, 24 Feb. 1793, 2:30 p.m., Aspinall, *Later Corresp. Geo. III*, vol. 2, 9.

36. Grenville to Pitt, Monday [23 Feb. 1795], 4 o'clock, marked "1794?", P.R.O. 30/8/140 ff. 75–76.

37. Grenville to Windham, Downing Street, 15 Apr. 1796, Private, Add. MS 37846 f. 40.

38. "Memorandum of Conversation between Mr. Pitt, Mr. Windham, and Lord Grenville," 19 Jan. 1798, in George Hammond's hand, ibid., f. 61.

39. Canning to Charles Long (Treasury), Downing Street, 13 Sept., 13 and 17 Nov. 1797, Copies, F.O. 366/427.

40. "Return . . . Of the amount of all Salaries . . . in the Year 1780. . . ," 19 Jan. 1831, F.O. 366/366 ff. 158–59.

Company, £6.16.6 from the Post Office, a percentage of the fees of the secretary's office, and a share in the profits of the *Gazette*.[41] They also received occasional gifts from foreign sovereigns on the ratification of treaties. From this revenue (except for the gifts) they paid taxes and fees on their salaries, all the tradesmen's bills for the office (for wax, coal, candles, and other supplies), and the salaries of everyone on the establishment except the undersecretaries and the chief clerk. Grenville calculated that these revenues in an average year netted between £5,000 and £5,600.

Because the secretaries of state shared the fees equally, the reform of 1795 may have been sparked by the creation of the third secretaryship. Grenville in 1793, the last year there were two secretaries, received £5,350 in fees and total net receipts of £8,400. In 1794 he calculated his net receipts at £5,300; his fees dropped to £2,600. In an effort to stabilize their revenue the secretaries decided that (retroactive to 12 January 1792 in the case of Grenville) their salaries would be £6,000 "clear of all Deductions, and in lieu of all former Salaries and Fees."[42] The land tax was in fact not abolished but paid out of the office fee fund, deficiencies of which were made up by the Treasury.[43] After 1795 the salaries and expenses of the establishment, which had been increasing slowly as Grenville needed and secured more assistance, also were paid from public revenues. The salary of the secretary was lowered to £5,000 in 1831 as part of Grey's program of economic retrenchment.[44] The secretaries retained, however, their right to "one Thousand ounces of White Plate, allowed at the price of Silver of the day, [plus] the Duty, and 2/6 pr. oz. for Fashion."[45] They also continued to pay a considerable amount in fees for having their appointment passed through the Patent Office, and for having the Signet, Privy, and Great Seals affixed to it. The

41. The figures on fees, salaries, and other incomes are from miscellaneous accounts Grenville had prepared in 1794 when he was trying to settle on a fair salary for the secretaryship. Grenville MSS, passim. The total fees of the Home Office and the Foreign Office were shared equally by the secretaries of state. The foreign secretary received 55 percent of his share of the fees. See also Ronald Roy Nelson, *The Home Office 1782–1801* (Durham, N.C., 1969), p. 23.

42. Order in Council, "For Regulating the Proper Establishment of the Foreign Office," St. James's, 27 Feb. 1795, F.O. 366/542.

43. Hammond and Bagot to George Harrison (Treasury), F.O., 14 Nov. 1808, Copy, F.O. 366/428.

44. Cecil, "The F.O.," p. 557 n. 4.

45. Thomas B. Mash (Lord Chamberlain's Department) to Palmerston, St. James's, 21 Feb. 1831, Palmerston Papers GC/MA/290.

Duke of Wellington in 1834, for example, paid £245.18.8 for these services.[46]

Grenville was the only secretary who did not receive the whole salary of the office. Because he held the place of Auditor of the Exchequer (salary £2,800), he and Pitt agreed that he would receive only enough of his Foreign Office salary to make his total salary £6,000.[47] This arrangement remained in effect until Grenville retired in 1801.

Robert Banks Jenkinson, Baron Hawkesbury and after 1808 the second Earl of Liverpool, succeeded Grenville in 1801. The transition from Grenville's to Hawkesbury's secretaryship set a pattern for changes later in the century, which were always at least outwardly cordial and cooperative. Grenville offered Hawkesbury his full cooperation and knowledge on any aspect of "those wretched things which are called governments on the Continent of Europe."[48] Their cooperation was so close, in fact, that for awhile at least Hawkesbury sent draft dispatches to Grenville to criticize "without mercy" and to alter in any way he thought proper.[49] Though no other transition was quite so cordial, outgoing secretaries often sent private letters and papers to their successors.[50] Aberdeen, in 1846, despite the fact that he had long regarded Palmerston's succeeding him with apprehension, spent two hours with Palmerston at the Foreign Office discussing foreign affairs.[51]

Hawkesbury was not a successful secretary of state. He lacked imagination and was of so nervous a temperament that Huskisson referred to him as "the grand figitatis."[52] He apparently made little impression on his subordinates at the Foreign Office, though he did

46. "Fees on the appointment of His Grace the Duke of Wellington—paid by the Chief Clerk," n.d., Wellington Papers.
47. Grenville to Pitt, St. James's Square, 24 Feb. 1794 [5?], P.R.O. 30/8/140 ff. 73–74; Same to Same, St. James's Square, 26 Feb. 1794 [5?], P.R.O. 30/58/1 no. 91.
48. Grenville to Hawkesbury, Cleveland Row, 11 Feb. 1801, Copy, H. M. C. Fortescue, vol. 6, 443–44.
49. Hawkesbury to Grenville, 26 Feb. 1801, Private, H. M. C. Fortescue, vol. 6, 445. This cooperation did not continue after Grenville's attack on the Treaty of Amiens (1802).
50. Canning to Bathurst, Gloucester Lodge, 12 Oct. 1809, Private, B.M. Loan 57/3/217; Aberdeen to Palmerston, Argyll House, 23 Nov. 1830, Copy, Add. MS 43235 ff. 314–15; Palmerston to Backhouse, Stanhope Street, 21 Mar. 1835, F.O. 84/183.
51. Aberdeen to Princess Lieven, Foreign Office, 2 Feb. 1844, E. Jones-Parry (ed.), The Correspondence of Lord Aberdeen and Princess Lieven, 1832–1854 (2 vols.; "The Camden Society, 3d Series," vols. 60, 62; London, 1938–1939), vol. 1, 244; 14 July 1846, Strachey and Fulford, Greville Memoirs, vol. 5, 334.
52. Quoted in Brock, Liverpool, pp. 32–33.

have the reputation among them of being extremely close-fisted with public money.[53] It was in his relations with representatives of foreign powers in London and with the king that his shortcomings proved most intolerable. The foreign ministers were unanimous in their dislike of him. George III said that he was "utterly unfit" for the foreign secretaryship and told George Rose that while foreign secretary he "always approached him with a vacant kind of grin, and had hardly ever anything business-like to say. . . ."[54] Because of these qualities and his inattention to business Pitt replaced him with Lord Harrowby in 1804.[55] Hawkesbury, however, remained in the ministry as home secretary. Subsequently there were some unkind words in the House of Commons about the switch and some expressions of doubt about his fitness for holding any public office. Hawkesbury immediately tendered his resignation but Pitt publicly denied the allegations and persuaded him to remain in office.[56]

Harrowby, Mulgrave, and Fox served between 1804 and September 1806 when Fox died and was succeeded by Charles Grey, Viscount Howick (afterwards second Earl Grey). Howick, in fact, directed at least some of the business of the Foreign Office during the last month's of Fox's illness.[57] His shift from the Admiralty relieved him from the detail of that office and gave him greater responsibility and authority in the government.[58] He was one of only four foreign secretaries between 1782 and 1846 to serve as leader of the House of Commons. His period of office, however, was so short that he made little impact on the Foreign Office, though his experience there proved valuable during his premiership in the 1830s.

George Canning's first secretaryship (1807–1809) followed Howick's. But Canning's significance and fame as foreign secretary re-

53. C. R. Broughton to Arthur Paget, Downing Street, 19 Jan. 1802, Sir Augustus B. Paget (ed.), The Paget Papers: Diplomatic and Other Correspondence of the Right Hon. Arthur Paget, G.C.B., 1794–1807 (2 vols.; London, 1896), vol. 2, 32–33.

54. Rose's diary, Sept. 1804, Rev. Leveson Vernon Harcourt (ed.), Diaries and Correspondence of George Rose (2 vols.; London, 1860), vol. 2, 157.

55. Lord Liverpool, Hawkesbury's father, said that although he would have preferred to remain at Foreign Office, "he suffers . . . from his supposed [lack of] abilities and attention to public business and is obliged to go into an office of more unpleasant detail. . . ." To the Archbishop of Dublin, 26 May 1804, Aspinall, Later Corresp. Geo. III, vol. 4, 162 n. 1.

56. Hawkesbury to Pitt, 20 June 1804, Copy, and Pitt to Hawkesbury, Downing Street, 24 June 1804, Private, Copy, Add. MS 38371 ff. 78–79; Sheridan and Pitt, speeches on 19 June 1804, Great Britain, 1 Hansard's Parliamentary Debates, vol. 2, 728–38, 747.

57. Grenville to Howick, Downing Street, 25 July 1806, Copy, H. M. C. Fortescue, vol. 8, 244.

58. George Maculay Trevelyan, Lord Grey of the Reform Bill (2d ed.; London, 1929), p. 149.

sulted from his second term in the office and in his role as successor
to Castlereagh. His first term was eventful, but his impact on the
secretaryship was negligible. It was during this term, in 1808, that
Canning instituted the practice of putting "Foreign Office" in place
of "Downing Street" at the head of all dispatches.

Canning left office in 1809 after his infamous duel with
Castlereagh. Henry Bathurst, third Earl Bathurst, succeeded him
on a temporary basis until the Marquess of Wellesley could return
from Spain to take the seals. It was unfortunate that Bathurst, a rigid
Tory but an able administrator, refused to remain at the Foreign
Office under any circumstances, despite pressure from the king to
do so.[59] For Wellesley, a man of genius and great ability,[60] was the
most lanquid of British foreign secretaries. He rarely corresponded
with a diplomatic corps that at that time always numbered fewer
than five.[61] He procrastinated in preparing dispatches until Spencer
Perceval, the prime minister, was forced to write him ultimatums to
send them immediately.[62] He filled the air with complaints about the
ability of his colleagues to manage the war, about Perceval's qualities
as head of the administration, and about the insufficient aid he felt
his brother was getting for his Peninsular campaigns. He resigned in
1812 amidst scenes of mutual recrimination. John Wilson Croker, a
shrewd judge of men, not unjustly called him the most brilliant
incapacity in England.[63]

Wellesley was succeeded by one of Britain's eminent foreign secretaries and statesmen, Robert Stewart, Viscount Castlereagh to
1821 when he became the second Marquess of Londonderry.
Castlereagh served ten years (1812–1822), the longest consecutive
service of any British foreign secretary.[64] A tall, handsome man,
Castlereagh was an unaffected aristocrat who enjoyed the sim-

59. Bathurst to Malmesbury, Wimbledon, Sunday Evening, 8 Oct. 1809, Third Earl of
Malmesbury (ed.), *A Series of Letters of the First Earl of Malmesbury* (2 vols.; London, 1870), vol. 2,
149; George III to Perceval, Windsor Castle, 5 Nov. 1809, Holland (Perceval) Papers, Bundle
III/9.

60. Sir Charles Webster (ed.), *Some Letters of the Duke of Wellington to his Brother William
Wellesley Pole* ("The Camden Society, 3d Series," vol. 79; London, 1948), p. 41.

61. Stratford Canning to Wellesley, 21 Apr. 1812, in cipher, Stanley Lane-Poole, *The Life of
the Right Honourable Stratford Canning, Viscount Stratford de Redcliffe* (2 vols.; London, 1888), vol.
1, 167.

62. Perceval to Wellesley, [1811?], Copy, Add. MS 37296 ff. 153–54.

63. To Lord Hertford, 18 Nov. [1830], Louis J. Jennings (ed.), *The Correspondence and
Diaries of John Wilson Croker* (2 vols.; London, 1884), vol. 2, 77.

64. Grenville served ten years less a few months from 1791–1801.

plicities of family life more than the splendors of the court. He was scrupulously honest, straight-forward in his relations with men, and unswerving in his loyalty to his country and its institutions.[65] To strangers and those who worked only occasionally near him he appeared aloof and stern, "like Mont Blanc, . . . a splendid summit of bright and polished frost which, like the travellers in Switzerland, we all admire; but no one could hope and few would wish to reach."[66] But he was always loyal both to his subordinates, who found him a "kind-hearted and considerate master,"[67] and to his close friends who knew of his "warm and gentle personality beneath the frigid exterior. . . ."[68] Stratford Canning, who served under almost every foreign secretary during the first half of the nineteenth century, recalled "that his practical abilities were decidedly superior to his education and also to his powers of oratory." Though his speech was involved, his composition clumsy, "a strong natural capacity and a clear judgment cropped out from under the rubbish."[69] His great strength lay in his power of persuasion in private conversation "where rhetoric was at a discount, and where patience, fact, logic and industry were decisive."[70] No one who dealt with him failed to appreciate his abilities and everyone admired him.

Perhaps more than any of his predecessors or successors Castlereagh personalized the conduct of British foreign policy. The paramount role he played in the peace settlement of 1814–1815 and his concept of a unified Europe meeting in periodic conferences to settle disputes peacefully and to encourage mutual cooperation and trust made him "the most European Foreign Minister" in British history.[71] He knew every sovereign and all the chief ministers of the continental powers. He appreciated their strengths and their weaknesses. He corresponded regularly with many of them. Most important, they trusted him and felt, often erroneously, that he shared their view of European politics. These personal contacts enhanced his importance and when he took his own life a measure of Britain's

65. Arthur Bryant, *The Age of Elegance, 1812–1822* (London, 1950), p. 195; Fortescue, *British Statesmen*, pp. 199–200; Webster, *For. Pol. Castlereagh*, passim.
66. Croker to Vesey Fitzgerald, 20 Dec. 1821, Extract, Jennings, *Croker Papers*, vol. 1, 219.
67. Nina L. Kay-Shuttleworth, *A Life of Sir Woodbine Parish* (London, 1910), p. 224.
68. C. J. Bartlett, *Castlereagh* (New York, 1966), pp. 1–2.
69. Memoirs, Lane-Poole, *Stratford Canning*, I, 213.
70. Bartlett, *Castlereagh*, p. 266.
71. Webster, *For. Pol. Castlereagh*, vol. 1, 3.

influence, regardless of who his successor might be, was inevitably lost.[72]

Castlereagh was a prodigious worker. He was not disposed to delegate authority or responsibility to others[73] and consequently wrote many dispatches by his own hand. At the office and elsewhere he worked long hours. He had great powers of concentration, frequently working on some aspect of policy during family parties at his country house at North Cray, just outside London. He preferred to conduct the business of the office personally and relied to a great extent on conversations with representatives of foreign powers in London, whom he often entertained at North Cray. His tactical skill in diplomatic negotiations was rivalled only by Metternich's and Talleyrand's.[74] His mind was strong, not subtle,[75] and he preferred these personal conversations to dealing through his own diplomatic agents, whom he often purposely kept uninformed.[76] A "due proportion of firmness and conciliation," he once told Liverpool, usually insured a quick and satisfactory termination of negotiations.[77]

Despite his failings as a public speaker, Castlereagh was a remarkably successful leader of the House of Commons. His speeches were usually sober and dispassionate, designed to persuade rather than to move.[78] He was the only member of Liverpool's ministry in the House who had any knowledge of foreign affairs and when he was not in London the ministry was constantly threatened with embarrassment in debates on foreign policy.[79] He was, furthermore, the only effective government spokesman in the Commons throughout most of his term at the Foreign Office. The demands this responsibility placed upon his time and energy, coupled with his role as a central figure in the administration which required that he be consulted on all matters of policy, inevitably placed great strain upon

72. His contemporaries realized the importance of his personal acquaintances; 20 Aug. 1822, Aspinall, *Diary of Hobhouse*, pp. 91–92.

73. Bartlett, *Castlereagh*, pp. 108, 266–67.

74. Cecil, "The F.O.," p. 554; Webster, *For. Pol. Castlereagh*, vol. 1, 49; vol. 2, 33.

75. Algernon Cecil, *British Foreign Secretaries, 1807–1916* (London, 1927), p. 19.

76. Webster, *For. Pol. Castlereagh*, vol. 2, 492; Castlereagh to Bathurst, Dover Castle, 2 Oct. 1813, Private & Secret, Copy, F.O. 72/155 ff. 54–55.

77. Castlereagh to Liverpool, Vienna, 3 Jan. [1815], Private and Most Secret, Add. MS 38191 ff. 45–46.

78. 13 Aug. 1822, Strachey and Fulford, *Greville Memoirs*, vol. 1, 127–28.

79. Liverpool to Castlereagh, Fife House, 29 Apr. 1814, Webster, *For. Pol. Castlereagh*, vol. 1, 539–40.

him.[80] His constant attention to government business of all sorts explains in part why, in comparison to other foreign secretaries, he carried on so little private correspondence with British diplomatists.[81]

Castlereagh spent more time abroad than any other foreign secretary. He attended allied conferences in 1814, 1815, and 1818, and was preparing to go to Verona when he committed suicide in 1822. He accompanied King George IV to Hanover in 1821. While he was abroad Bathurst, the war secretary, signed and received all dispatches. Liverpool superintended the daily work of the Foreign Office during Castlereagh's absences and made all the administrative decisions of the department.[82] Usually Castlereagh himself corresponded officially with Bathurst, though while accompanying the king in Hanover he corresponded with Lord Sidmouth, the home secretary.[83] Bathurst was so accustomed to directing the foreign correspondence in the absence of Castlereagh that one undersecretary, reporting Castlereagh's death, wrote that "Ld. Bathurst is named [successor] ad interim, according to custom."[84]

Powerful and influential men frequently leave an office or an institution more important than they found it. If they are succeeded by equally energetic and forceful men the significance of the office is assured. Such was the case when George Canning received the seals to the Foreign Office after Castlereagh's death in 1822. "They form, indeed, a pair of statesmen to whom there is no parallel in English foreign policy."[85]

George Canning was perhaps the cleverest of all the men who have served as foreign secretary. In energy and eloquence he was

80. Bartlett, *Castlereagh*, pp. 2, 179.
81. His correspondence was never voluminous, however, even when he was abroad and free of the daily pressures of business he faced in London. Castlereagh to Cathcart, Foreign Office, 8 Apr. 1813, Draft, Londonderry, *Castlereagh Correspondence*, vol. 8, 357; William Hamilton to Bathurst, Paris, 24 Aug. 1815, Private, *H. M. C. Bathurst*, pp. 373–75.
82. Castlereagh to the Prince Regent, The Hague, 8 Jan. 1814, Aspinall, *Letters of George IV*, vol. 1, 370–71; Minute, Liverpool, on T. H. Addington to Hamilton, Whitehall, 18 Oct. 1814, F.O. 27/108.
83. Castlereagh to Liverpool, Aix, 4 Oct. 1818, Private & confidential, Add. MS 38566 ff. 65–66; Londonderry to Sidmouth, Brussels, 28 Sept. 1821, No. 1, F.O. 92/46.
84. Clanwilliam to Sir William A'Court, [Aug. 1822], Add. MS 41541 f. 1.
85. Temperley, *For. Pol. Canning*, p. 448. Until recently there was no adequate biography of Canning. The best short study has been P. J. V. Rolo, *George Canning: Three Biographical Studies* (London, 1965), which suffers from compartmentalization. Wendy Hinde, *George Canning* (London, 1973), is the most complete account of his life.

unrivalled.[86] Whether standing by the ministerial box in the House of Commons, calling the new world into existence to redress the balance of the old, or writing in the solitude of his study, he had a flair for words. In 1814, for example, he wrote "'The festal blazes of the war at an end, the sun of Peace is scarcely yet above the horizon; we must take care that during the cold and cheerless twilight the spoiler and assassin don't break in.'"[87] Yet Canning was a man of passion and he roused the passions of other men. He was undoubtedly among the most self-seeking of all politicians during his lifetime. Loyal to his close personal friends such as Bagot and Granville to the extreme, he was treacherous in his dealings with most of his contemporaries and an implacable foe to his enemies. His cleverness served as a weapon with which to assail them, as in his memorable and devastating epigram comparing Addington to Paddington.

As foreign secretary Canning's energy and activity were extraordinary. He was the only secretary to live at the Foreign Office, which was a convenience for him, but which one undersecretary regarded as a "nuisance" and the other portrayed as the cause of the "great and incessant" labor he gave the establishment.[88] He was as exacting with his subordinates as Palmerston ever was and he never hesitated to rebuke anyone who displeased him.[89] Yet he took a special interest in their welfare and was not excessively harsh with them. Almost without exception his subordinates were personally attached to him. Lord Fitzharris, who served briefly as his undersecretary, has left the best vignette of him: "I found him a most kindhearted and agreeable man to act under, never saw him discomposed, and ever with astonishment viewed the labour he bestowed on his duties, and the rapidity with which he executed them."[90]

Canning like Castlereagh served as leader of the House of Commons as well as foreign secretary. Nightly attendance at the House seriously reduced the time he had for directing foreign affairs, while the volume of business conducted by the Foreign Office grew

86. Temperley, *For. Pol. Canning*, p. 237.
87. Quoted in Bryant, *Age of Elegance*, p. 351.
88. Howard de Walden to Granville, Foreign Office, 26 Mar. 1824, P.R.O. 30/29/6/7 ff. 1260–63; Planta to Stratford Canning, Foreign Office, 14 Feb. 1826, Private, F.O. 352/13 (Part 1)/1.
89. For example, Planta to James Henderson, Foreign Office, 31 Aug. 1824, F.O. 357/2.
90. Fitzharris' Journal, Extract, Malmesbury, *Series of Letters*, vol. 2, 25.

steadily.[91] Struggles over domestic affairs consumed his energy and sapped his strength. In 1826 he calculated that it would take two weeks after the end of the session "to work off my arrears of foreign correspondence."[92] To save time he refused all interviews except with foreign ministers and cabinet colleagues.[93] When ceremonial duties, such as attending the Recorder's Court, threatened to interfere with business, he took his business with him to these functions.[94] Occasionally dispatches waited a fortnight for him "to find a moment, to read them over, & put the last hand to them."[95] His energy and activity eventually killed him, but he left his mark on the office and by publishing diplomatic papers he began at least one practice in the conduct of foreign affairs that his successors could not ignore.

The question of the necessity and the propriety of publishing dispatches was a subject of intermittent debate in ministerial circles for many years prior to 1822. Pitt and Grenville preferred to lay as few documents as possible before the House of Commons, and when they did print papers they frequently let the writer of dispatches select those passages he wished omitted.[96] Canning, in his first term at the Foreign Office, was inclined to print much more than his predecessors. But even he produced very few documents after he and his undersecretaries finished editing the correspondence.[97] Only Wellesley urged "the most ample and complete disclosure of all the papers" as "our main advantage in the conflict with the opposition."[98]

The reason for any ministry's printing papers was to demonstrate to the satisfaction of the House of Commons that they had satisfactorily managed affairs. Parliament in the nineteenth century, even in those years in mid-century when there were a good many debates on

91. Canning to John Hookham Frere, Bath, 8 Jan. 1825, Gabrielle Festing, *John Hookham Frere and His Friends* (London, 1899), p. 264.

92. Canning to Granville, F.O., 9 May 1826, No. 26, Private, P.R.O. 30/29/8/10 ff. 1229–30; Same to Same, F.O., 12 May 1826, Private, ibid., ff. 1231–34.

93. Canning to J. Pattison, F.O., Thursday, 2 Mar. 1826, Stapleton, *Corresp. of Canning*, vol. 2, 182–83.

94. Canning to Liverpool, F.O., 17 Dec. 1826, Private, Copy, Canning MSS Bundle 72.

95. Canning to Granville, F.O., 22 Feb. 1825, No. 31, Private, P.R.O. 30/29/8/7 ff. 817–18.

96. Pitt to Grenville, [Downing Street, 23 Feb. 1794], and Grenville to Pitt, St. James's Square, 24 Feb. 1794, Copy, *H. M. C. Fortescue*, vol. 2, 512; Dundas to Grenville, Clarges Street, 28 Jan. 1801, F.O. 334/16 ff. 141–43.

97. Malmesbury, *Diaries*, vol. 4, 404.

98. To Perceval, Apsley House, Monday night, 12 Feb. 1810, Private & Confidential, Holland (Perceval) Papers Bundle I/16.

foreign affairs, had little influence over foreign policy.[99] What influence it did have was negative and involved only a few specific issues, such as the slave trade, which ministers were always careful to appear vigilant in their efforts to suppress.[100] Parliamentary support for any foreign policy could not be assumed,[101] but as long as ministerial policy reflected the interests and ideals of the classes represented in Parliament there was little doubt that ministers would be supported.[102] Moreover, while Britain was at war with France the Whig opposition in Parliament remained splintered and ineffective.[103] It was easy to refuse papers under these circumstances, and Castlereagh appears to have used great caution and even greater discretion in selecting papers to lay before the House.[104]

Canning's situation in the House of Commons was not too different from Castlereagh's. But the intrigues of the Austrian and Russian ambassadors at the Court, George IV's connivance with them and his hostility to Canning, and the unsteady support of some of the cabinet made it absolutely necessary for Canning to publish freely and frequently in an attempt to influence opinion and gain public support for his policies. By communicating decisions to the House of Commons Canning made it impossible for the continental powers to modify them later. "Publication served the double purpose of tying the hands of the Cabinet and of impressing foreigners."[105]

Canning's "Policy of Publicity" was remarkably effective in great part because of his sense of timing his announcements.[106] It also angered his opponents in the cabinet. Wellington complained, with some justification, that "the moment the government lay papers before Parliament on any political question, the decision is no longer

99. Valerie Cromwell, "The Private Member of the House of Commons and Foreign Policy in the Nineteenth Century," *Liber Memorialis Sir Maurice Powicke: Studies Presented to the International Commission for the History of Representative and Parliamentary Institutions*, 27 (Louvain, 1965), 196.

100. Henry Goulburn to Hamilton, Downing Street, 9 Oct. 1821, Private, F.O. 27/264.

101. Liverpool to Castlereagh, Walmer Castle, 23 Oct. 1818, Londonderry, *Castlereagh Corresp.*, vol. 12, 62.

102. Webster, *For. Pol. Castlereagh*, vol. 2, 21.

103. Michael Roberts, *The Whig Party, 1807–1812* (London, 1939), pp. 3–4, 106–7.

104. Harold W. V. Temperley and Lillian M. Penson, *A Century of Diplomatic Blue Books, 1814–1914* (Cambridge, 1938), p. 8.

105. Ibid., pp. 30–37; Temperley, *For. Pol. Canning*, pp. 310–11.

106. Temperley, *For. Pol. Canning*, p. 470.

practically in their hands."[107] But Liverpool refused to back Canning's opponents and as long as papers did not relate to a pending negotiation or refer to a private conversation with a foreign sovereign, they were printed.[108] Canning's was a conscious policy of demonstrating to the world that anything he said in private, if repeated in public, would be stated in precisely the same language.[109] His policy was very effective and probably explains his success in staying in office. Only after the crisis over the recognition of the Spanish American Republics in December 1824, however, was his position secured against the intrigues that marked the first two years of his secretaryship.[110]

When Canning became prime minister in 1827 he selected an old friend, John William Ward, ninth Baron Dudley and Ward,[111] as his foreign secretary. The foreign secretaryship was the only office Dudley ever held. Canning intended his appointment to be a temporary one, until Parliament was prorogued, a condition Dudley gladly accepted since "In three months I cannot do *much* harm to the public, nor to myself."[112] After the end of the session, however, he agreed to stay on[113] and he was in office when Canning died.

Indecision was Dudley's greatest failing. He was always in poor physical health and as he grew older the condition of his mind also deteriorated. He was oversensitive, highly nervous, and uncertain of his own opinions and abilities. All these factors made him extremely unfit for the responsibilities of high office.[114] While Canning was alive Dudley left all decisions to him.[115] After Canning's death he was initially energetic and attentive to business. He was a poor administrator who believed that "*He* ought never to hear of mechanical difficulties" and never showed "any feeling of considera-

107. To Liverpool, London, 5 Mar. 1824, *W.N.D.*, vol. 2, 228–29.
108. Liverpool to Wellington, London, Mar. 1824, and Bathurst to Wellington, Downing Street, 10 Apr. 1826, ibid., 242–43; vol. 3, 282–83.
109. Canning to C. R. Vaughan, F.O., 6 July 1826, Private, Copy, F.O. 360/4.
110. Planta to Stratford Canning, New Burlington Street, Saturday Night, 2 Apr. 1825, Private, F.O. 352/10 (Part 1)/3; Temperley, *For. Pol. Canning*, p. 229.
111. Created Earl Dudley in October, 1827.
112. Dudley to Aberdeen, Park Lane, 23 Apr. 1827, Add. MS 43231 ff. 228–29.
113. Planta to Stratford Canning, Treasury, 10 July 1827, Private, F.O. 352/17 (Part 1)/3.
114. Lord Brougham, quoted in S. H. Romilly, *Letters to "Ivy" From the First Earl of Dudley* (London, 1905), pp. 314–15.
115. Howard de Walden to A'Court, F.O., 18 June 1827, Most Confidential, Add. MS 41555 ff. 77–80.

tion for the office." Nevertheless he worked long and diligently over the dispatches.[116]

The disaster at Navarino Bay undermined Dudley's short-lived self-confidence. His indecisiveness returned and Lord Howard de Walden, his undersecretary, complained that on Greek affairs "He will not commit himself even to me previous to having heard the opinions of the different Cabinet Ministers upon which He will try whether he can adopt some one of his own. This is dreadful."[117] He remained at the Foreign Office during the first five months of Wellington's ministry, but he let the duke take a lead in all questions of foreign policy and when Wellington was overwhelmed with other affairs he complained in the cabinet that while his colleagues "talked of things of no real importance, . . . his concerns, which affected the peace of Europe, were left unsettled."[118]

Dudley resigned with the other Canningites in May, 1828, and was succeeded by the chancellor of the Duchy of Lancaster in Wellington's ministry, George Hamilton-Gordon, fourth Earl of Aberdeen. When he began his first secretaryship (1828–1830), Aberdeen was well-versed in foreign affairs, having served for five months as Dudley's "coadjutor *jure successionis.*"[119] Aberdeen was a quiet, serious Scot who loved his native country and tended his estates on the barren Aberdeenshire tundra with a devotion that at times seemed absurd.[120] He was a handsome aristocrat—Lady Granville said he was "beautiful"[121] —ever poised, charming, and sensitive. Tact and calmness were his greatest assets. He was a favorite at Court during his second term at the Foreign Office (1841–1846), and Queen Victoria preferred his company to that of the other secretaries when she travelled abroad.[122] Though he was not a reactionary, Aberdeen believed passionately in the right of his class to govern the country. He resented interference and criticism of his conduct of foreign

116. Same to Granville, F.O., 16 Nov. 1827, Most Private, P.R.O. 30/29/14/5 ff. 131–32; and 9 Oct. 1827, Most Private and Confidential, ibid., ff. 105–8.

117. Same to Same, F.O., 1 Dec. [1827], ibid., ff. 141–43.

118. Dudley to Granville, Easter Sunday, [6 Apr.] 1828, P.R.O. 30/29/14/4 ff. 135–36; 19 May 1828, Colchester, *Ellenborough Diary*, vol. 1, 109–10.

119. Dudley's phrase, quoted in Balfour, *Aberdeen*, vol. 1, 215.

120. In 1845, for example, he planned to travel nearly 500 miles to tend to estate matters for three or four days since that was all the time he could spare from his duties in London. Aberdeen to Peel, Foreign Office, 24 Oct. 1845, Add. MS 40455 ff. 243–44.

121. To Lady G. Morpeth, Sandon, 3 Jan. 1813, F. Leveson-Gower (ed.), *Letters of Harriet Countess Granville, 1810–1845* (2 vols.; London, 1894), vol. 1, 45.

122. Peel to Aberdeen, Windsor Castle, 27 Aug. [1843], Add. MS 43062 ff. 371–76.

affairs, whether it was by cabinet colleagues or by Parliament.[123] He also distrusted the ability of the uninitiated to deal with foreign problems. Sir Robert Peel, prime minister during his second term as foreign secretary, made him nervous when questions of foreign policy were raised in the House of Commons. Though Peel of necessity had to serve as government spokesman in these debates, Aberdeen felt that he too often said things which, had he been "in *the trade*," would never have transpired.[124]

Aberdeen's abilities were adequate. He was an uninspiring speaker, yet on occasion he could make a biting speech in the House of Lords.[125] He attended to his business regularly while he was in office, though he was not the taskmaster that Canning and Palmerston were. He disapproved of Palmerston's practice of having the clerks at the office writing all day and tried his best to discourage it.[126] Aberdeen inspired his subordinates by his example and by his kindness towards them,[127] and while he directed the Foreign Office the business was always completed in time to meet every deadline.

During Aberdeen's first year in office the question of the patronage of the secretaries of state became a source of contention between him and Peel, the home secretary. Aberdeen, like his predecessors, had absolute discretion in filling vacancies on his establishment in London. Subject to general political considerations, the same was true for appointments to the foreign service.[128] Every secretary was in fact as overwhelmed as Canning "with applications from the parents & friends of young men of the best education & connections, asking for appointments to the situation of Clerk at a Salary of £100 a year for the junior Clerks in my office." All undoubtedly kept lists of candidates for various positions at their disposal.[129]

123. 11 Oct. 1829, Colchester, *Ellenborough Diary*, vol. 2, 113; Aberdeen to Mr. Gurney, 14 Dec. 1833[4?], Balfour, *Aberdeen*, vol. 2, 11.

124. Peel to Lady Peel, Whitehall, 21 Aug. 1843, George Peel (ed.), *The Private Letters of Sir Robert Peel* (London, 1920), p. 244; 18 Mar. 1846 quoting Lord Clarendon, Strachey and Fulford, *Greville Memoirs*, vol. 5, 307.

125. 24 May 1830, Colchester, *Ellenborough Diary*, vol. 2, 255–56.

126. Aberdeen to Lieven, Foreign Office, 19 Oct. 1841, Parry, *Aberdeen-Lieven Correspondence*, vol. 1, 184.

127. John Backhouse, a retired undersecretary, referred to this characteristic as "the immense difference which is between working under Ld. Aberdeen and . . . Ld. P[almersto]n," minute on Sir George Shee to Backhouse, Stutgardt, 28 Mar. 1844, Backhouse MSS.

128. See below, chapter 8.

129. Canning to John Taylor, Gloucester Lodge, 6 May 1824, Private, Canning Papers, Duke University Library; Canning's patronage lists are in Canning MSS, Bundle 136 passim.

In filling vacancies secretaries often selected friends or sons of political allies.[130] Canning appointed Lord George Bentinck as his private secretary in an effort to gain the Duke of Portland's support for the ministry in 1822, though he vigorously denied that such was his motive in a letter to Portland.[131] Clerks in the office occasionally secured places for friends and relations. Grenville appointed John Bidwell, the nephew of Thomas Bidwell, chief clerk at the Foreign Office, to a junior clerkship in 1799 as partial compensation for losses the elder Bidwell suffered as a result of changes in the organization of the establishment.[132] Charles Pettingal, an assistant to James Bandinel, head of the slave trade department, owed his appointment to Bandinel's intercession with Canning on his behalf.[133] Occasionally persons of note used their influence to secure appointments from a secretary of state. Sir Walter Scott found a clerkship for his second son Charles by inducing George IV, who admired Scott's novels, to speak to Dudley about him.[134] Pledges of foreign secretaries were inevitably honored by their successors in the same ministry. Mulgrave agreed to Harrowby's appointments in 1805, and Howick sanctioned Fox's in 1807.[135]

The foreign secretary also shared with the home secretary the patronage of certain places that served both departments. Prior to 1824 they alternately appointed messengers.[136] After Canning reorganized the messengers corps into home and foreign services in 1824, the six home service messengers attached to each of the offices of state were appointed by the secretary of the office in which they worked. The eighteen foreign service messengers, however, were appointed in rotation by the three secretaries of state.[137] The patronage of these positions was insignificant when compared with the

130. Grantham to Earl of Chichester, Newby, 30 July 1782, Add. MS 33099 f. 402.

131. Canning to Liverpool, F.O., 28 Sept. 1822, Private, Copy, Canning MSS Bundle 70; Same to Portland, F.O., 23 Sept. 1822, ibid., Bundle 79.

132. Minutes, T. Bidwell, Downing Street, "1799," and 20 Aug. 1799, F.O. 95/9.

133. Minute, Bandinel, on Thomas Pettingal to Bandinel, Bagshot, 15 Nov. 1825, F.O. 84/46.

134. Fulford, George the Fourth, p. 256; W. Scott to Sir William Knighton, Abbotsford, Melrose, 20 July [1827?], and Edinburgh, 15 Nov. 1827, Lady D. Knighton, Memoirs of Sir William Knighton (2 vols.; London, 1838), vol. 1, 292–93, 387–89; Dudley to George IV, F.O., 21 Nov. 1827, Aspinall, Letters of George IV, vol. 3, 332.

135. Harrowby to Pitt, 10 Jan. 1805, P.R.O. 30/8/142 ff. 277–78; Howick to Grenville, Wimbledon, 21 Sept. 1806, H. M. C. Fortescue, vol. 8, 349.

136. Fraser to Keith, St. James's, 17 June 1783, Add. MS 35529 ff. 44–45.

137. "Plan agreed upon by the Under Secretaries, Messrs Hobhouse, Planta, & Wilmot Horton, at The Home Department, 3 Apr. 1824," F.O. 96/117.

patronage appointments of Gazette Writer, Gazette Printer, Collector and Transmitter of State Papers, and Keeper of State Papers, all of which were lucrative positions.

The death of Stephen Rolleston, Gazette Writer from 1802 to 1828, led to the dispute between Peel and Aberdeen over who should appoint his successor. The dispute centered on whether or not the principle of alternating patronage, which both men accepted, referred to each position or to all four places. If the former, since Rolleston had been a clerk in the Foreign Office and had been appointed by Hawkesbury, the patronage in 1828 belonged to Peel. If the latter, since Peel had filled the last vacancy by appointing Henry Hobhouse Keeper of State Papers in 1826, the patronage was Aberdeen's. Grenville and Dundas, who had originally made the appointments to three of the four offices, left no memoranda of the policy they expected their successors to adopt.[138] Subsequent appointments had failed to resolve the problem and every time the question was brought up, opinions varied as to the interpretation to be given to Grenville's and Dundas's decision.[139] Of course in 1828 the establishments of both departments, led by the suitors for the position, marshaled all the evidence they could to support one or the other interpretation.[140] Their arguments, most of them specious, so confused the issue that Aberdeen and Peel submitted the question to Henry Goulburn, the chancellor of the Exchequer, and Viscount Melville, the first lord of the Admiralty, who decided that since Hawkesbury had appointed Rolleston, Peel should appoint his successor.[141] Once this principle was clarified there were no further disputes over the question of joint patronage.

Aberdeen's successor in 1830 was John Henry Temple, third Viscount Palmerston. Palmerston has become the almost legendary figure in British history, "'the most English minister that ever governed England'. . . ."[142] An Irish peer, he moved in the best social

138. Peel to Aberdeen, Whitehall, 25 Nov. 1828, Private, F.O. 366/413.
139. Edmund Malone to William Windham, 15 Dec. [1802?], Lewis Saul Benjamin (ed.), *The Windham Papers* (2 vols.; London, 1913), vol. 2, 89–90; Liverpool to Canning, Charles Street, 27 Sept. 1809, Private, Copy, Add. MS 38321 ff. 142–43; Memorandum inclosed in Arbuthnot to Wellesley, Treasury Chambers, 13 Feb. 1810, Private, Add. MS 37309 ff. 337–40.
140. F.O. 366/413.
141. "Copy of a Memorandum of Mr. Goulburn and Lord Melville, on the subject of the disputed right of presentation to the office of Gazette Writer," 9 July 1829, F.O. 366/413.
142. Quoted from the *Daily Telegraph* obituary of Palmerston in Donald Southgate, *'The Most English Minister. . .': The Policies and Politics of Palmerston* (New York, 1966), p. xxviii. Palmerston's whole career has never received the full treatment it deserves. Even the most

circles while sitting always in the House of Commons where his energy and ability could best be turned to advantage. He was by temperament a man of the eighteenth century.[143] Long before he became foreign secretary he had a reputation of being "a gay and amusing London host and man of fashion, wit, a fine shot and fearless rider to hounds. . . ."[144] He had a special gift for the Romance languages and spoke French, Italian, Spanish, and Portuguese with ease.[145] He had an abiding faith in liberal institutions, which he told William IV made Britain "the most prosperous of Commercial, and the happiest of Constitutional States."[146] Few of his predecessors or successors at the Foreign Office possessed his energy; none the mastery of detail which enabled him to demolish the arguments of his opponents by marshaling his storehouse of knowledge against them.[147] At the Foreign Office he threw himself into his work with a passion and a concentration that left the clerks in the office in awe of his abilities. For the first three and a half years of his secretaryship he never quit London to return to his beautiful Georgian house and spacious estate of Broadlands in Hampshire.[148]

Palmerston had one great defect as an administrator: he ran the Foreign Office like a general commanding a division of élite troops. "I think," he once wrote, "that an office ought to be like a Regiment, one Body, the members of which Should in their respective grades be liable to perform any of the Duties for which the Body is Constituted, and to be Shifted from one Duty to another as occasion may require."[149] As the commander he expected to make all the decisions and said on more than one occasion that the foreign ministers in other states often got themselves into trouble by letting their clerks formulate policy.[150] Despite the fact that the volume of business doubled during the 1830s, he read every document that passed

---

recent biography, which is the most thorough to date, does not fill this need. See Jasper Ridley, *Lord Palmerston* (New York, 1971).

143. Philip Guedalla, *Palmerston* (New York, 1927), pp. 159–60.

144. Connell, *Regina vs. Palmerston*, pp. 5–6.

145. Webster, *For. Pol. Palmerston*, vol. 1, 7.

146. 21 July 1832, Foreign Office, Copy, Palmerston Papers RC/AA/37.

147. Webster, *For. Pol. Palmerston*, vol. 1, 31.

148. 17 Feb. 1835, Strachey and Fulford, *Greville Memoirs*, vol. 3, 157; Palmerston to Granville, F.O., 28 Mar. 1834, P.R.O. 30/29/415.

149. Minute, Palmerston, 6 May 1847, F.O. 366/313.

150. Palmerston to Queen Victoria, Stanhope Street, 25 Feb. 1838, Benson and Esher, *Q.V.L.*, vol. 1, 136–38; Palmerston to Granville, Windsor, 1 Oct. 1838, P.R.O. 30/29/423.

through the department.[151] He was demanding of his subordinates, though no more so than of himself. If they displeased him he could be extremely cruel in his criticism. He often overreacted to their errors, as in 1839 when he severely chastised Fox-Strangways, an undersecretary, for wasting "Thirty or Forty Pounds by sending me a Messenger down to Tiverton to bring what the Mail Coach could just as well have brought and as quickly; & that at a time when Constituents & Races, and ordinaries and Balls overfill Every minute of the Day & when I could not have read or written a line if you had sent me Twenty messengers."[152] He so terrified his subordinates that Backhouse, the permanent undersecretary, sent him minutes rather than going to see him when there was any business that had to be transacted between them.[153] He apparently never uttered a kind word to the clerks. When he retired briefly in 1834 they felt his letter of praise and thanks for their assistance and hard labors was an affront.[154] With few exceptions[155] they despised him and made no attempt to hide their feelings in London society.[156]

Palmerston dispensed his patronage much as his predecessors had. Perhaps because of his tenuous ties with the Whigs he was a bit more conscious than he otherwise might have been of appointing sons of Whig peers as his précis writers and private secretaries.[157] He also seems to have taken special care to appoint sons of his cabinet colleagues to these positions.[158] He was the first secretary to have advance notice of his leaving office because of a change in the majority party in the House of Commons. In 1841, after the election of that year, he took the opportunity to appoint six clerks (mostly to positions created by the reorganization of the establishment in

151. Speech, Palmerston, 8 Mar. 1842, Great Britain, 3 *Hansard's Parliamentary Debates*, vol. 61, 269–70.

152. Minute, Palmerston, Broadlands, 31 Aug. 1838, F.O. 366/521.

153. Leveson to Granville, London, 23 Mar. 1840, P.R.O. 30/29/6/4 ff. 713–14.

154. Palmerston to Fordwich, Stanhope Street, 19 Nov. 1834, Copy, Palmerston Papers GC/FO/26; Byng to Granville, 21 Nov. 1834, P.R.O. 30/29/7/13 ff. 994–99.

155. Edmund Hammond, for example, E. Hammond to G. Hammond, Therassia, 16 May 1832, No. 17, F.O. 391/28.

156. 29 Sept. 1841 and 11 Jan. 1842, Strachey and Fulford, *Greville Memoirs*, vol. 4, 418; vol. 5, 2.

157. Palmerston to William Temple, Foreign Office, 7 May 1833, Sir Henry Lytton, Lord Dalling and Bulwer, *The Life of John Henry Temple, Viscount Palmerston*, vol. 3 ed. by Evelyn Ashley (3 vols.; London, 1870–1874), vol. 2, 160–61.

158. Sir Henry G. Elliott, *Some Revolutions and other Diplomatic Experiences*, ed. by his daughter (London, 1922), pp. 3–4.

1839–1840), including the son of a loyal Whig MP, one of his Tiverton constituents, and the son of a cabinet colleague.[159]

Palmerston's blue book policy was the most liberal of any foreign secretary who served before 1846. In part his policy reflected his desire to enlighten the country. But the House of Commons after the Reform Act of 1832 was not the tractable body Canning swayed with his eloquence during the previous decade and the opposition to Grey's and Melbourne's governments was much better organized than any Canning faced. Palmerston was as a result rarely able to refuse papers, though he was very careful to edit correspondence well before he printed it.[160] The clerks assistant and the undersecretaries made the initial selection of papers, but Palmerston personally spent many hours "going carefully through" whole masses of them.[161]

Palmerston's relations with the newspaper press was one of the distinguishing features of his secretaryship. All foreign secretaries have to one degree or another dealt with the press.[162] In the eighteenth century, when certain newspapers were in the pay of the government, the undersecretaries usually instructed them.[163] The Foreign Office, like the War Office and the Admiralty, had a special relationship with several "ministerial" papers. An official Treasury memorandum in 1809 sharply scolded the delinquents, but Charles Arbuthnot, the secretary of the Treasury, was unsuccessful in his efforts to create a central source for all public news releases.[164] Aberdeen, in the 1840s, patronized *The Times*, despite its attacks on his colleagues, until Peel was forced to request that he sever the

159. Robert Bewick Seale, William F. Quick, and Spencer Cecil Brabazon Ponsonby. Sir John Seale to Palmerston, Mount Boone, 6 Aug. 1841, Private, Palmerston Papers PAT/S/29/1; Quick to [Spencer Cowper?], No. 2 Seymour Place, York Street, Walworth Road, 26 Aug. 1841, ibid., PAT/Q/7; Major General Sir John Ponsonby, *The Ponsonby Family* (London, 1929), pp. 159–63.

160. Webster, *For. Pol. Palmerston*, vol. 1, 60–63; Grey to William IV, Downing Street, 5 Aug. and 9 Aug. 1831, Grey, *Grey Corresp.*, vol. 1, 320, 324–25; Temperley and Penson, *Diplomatic Blue Books*, p. 56.

161. Minutes, Thomas Straveley and Backhouse, on William Thornton to Howick, Government House, Jersey, 26 May 1834, Copy, F.O. 97/182; Minute, Palmerston, 30 June 1837, F.O. 96/20.

162. Not until 1919, however, was there an official staff at the Foreign Office to deal with the press. Frank T. Ashton-Gwatkin, *The British Foreign Service* (Syracuse, N.Y., 1950), p. 15.

163. Aspinall, *Politics and Press*, pp. 200, 202.

164. Ibid., pp. 188–89, quoting letters to Bagot, 14 Apr. and 10 Aug. 1809; Treasury Memorandum, 11 Dec. 1809, F.O. 83/16.

connection between the Foreign Office and that "scandalous" paper.[165]

For twenty years before Palmerston became foreign secretary, ministers tried with varying degrees of success to influence the press, which by the nineteenth century was more independent than it had ever been. Liverpool acknowledged that "no paper that has any character, and consequently any established sale, will accept money from Government; and indeed their profits are so enormous in all critical times, when their support is the most necessary that no pecuniary assistance that Government could offer would really be worth their acceptance."[166] Palmerston continued the practice of his predecessors of supplying intelligence to those editors who gave general support to the government's foreign policy in their leading articles,[167] though he never hesitated to criticise them if he felt their editorials undermined the effectiveness of the government or its agents abroad.[168] But Palmerston also took a personal interest in the press. He reported to editors of friendly journals the effectiveness of their foreign correspondents.[169] Unlike his predecessors he personally wrote articles for insertion in the newspapers. In one of these articles intended for publication verbatim he called the government of Uruguay a bunch of "wiseacres" for declining to negotiate a treaty of friendship and commerce with Britain.[170] Though his colleagues never approved of this practice,[171] Palmerston enjoyed this aspect of his secretaryship and his successes proved that he was a competent journalist.

The Duke of Wellington served briefly as foreign secretary from November 1834 to April 1835. During this period because the stability of Peel's government was uncertain, Wellington was ex-

165. 15 Sept. 1843, Strachey and Fulford, *Greville Memoirs*, vol. 5, 132; Peel to Aberdeen, Whitehall, 6 July 1844, Private, Add. MS 43063 ff. 275–78.
166. To Castlereagh, Fife House, 15 Sept. 1815, Londonderry, *Castlereagh Corresp.*, vol. 11, 16–18.
167. Minutes, Palmerston, [1833?], F.O. 96/17; "Immediate," 10 Apr. 1839, F.O. 96/20; and 31 Mar. 1841 on Lord William Russell to Palmerston, Berlin 24/29 Mar. 1841, Palmerston Papers GC/RU/1475/1–3.
168. Palmerston to Sir John Easthope, Stanhope Street, 12 July 1838, Easthope Papers, Duke University Library.
169. Same to Same, Stanhope Street, 25 Oct. 1836, Private, ibid.
170. Minute, Palmerston, "For Globe *Today*," Saturday, 24 Oct. 1835, F.O. 96/18.
171. Melbourne to Queen Victoria, South Street, 17 Jan. 1842, Benson and Esher, *Q.V.L.*, vol. 1, 470–71.

tremely cautious in his activities. He therefore made little impact on the secretaryship.

Algernon Cecil, a pioneer in the study of the Foreign Office and the men who directed it, once wrote that "The Foreign Office is, at least, the equal in opportunity of any post that an Englishman can hold. . . ."[172] As Britain's role in European affairs expanded after 1782, the importance of the foreign secretary increased proportionately. Perhaps the foreign minister of any country will be a giant among his colleagues merely because his decisions may affect the peace and security of all his countrymen. Certainly in Britain between 1782 and 1846 when foreign affairs came to have an importance they never before enjoyed, the men who conducted them usually responded to challenges energetically and forcefully. They were not all equal in abilities, nor did they all share the same ideals and seek the same goals in their conduct of British foreign policy. But with few exceptions they all contributed to the importance of the foreign secretaryship and even the least among them did nothing to undermine this influence in the ministries in which they served.

172. *British Foreign Secretaries*, p. 5.

CHAPTER V

THE UNDERSECRETARIES
OF STATE

The office of undersecretary of state for foreign affairs was one of the most interesting and well-informed positions in the British government.[1] It could also be one of the most frustrating. The men who held the post were privy to some of the best kept and most important secrets of Britain and Europe. They watched the masters of European diplomacy—Castlereagh, Metternich, Talleyrand, Canning, and Palmerston—conduct the affairs of Europe in momentous times and through many difficult periods. Yet they rarely exercised a voice in questions of policy. They might have ventured opinions, but if they did they were careful to make them in the form of suggestions which their principals could accept or reject as out of hand.[2] Many of their ideas were probably expressed in conversations that never were recorded. They had no right to be consulted, no duty to offer advice.

The undersecretaryship was not a static institution, despite the limitations on the role of the undersecretaries in matters of foreign policy. In fact, because of this lack of official responsibility in the decision-making process, the power of the office was more susceptible to the personalities of the men who held it than it otherwise might have been. Energetic and capable men, such as Edward

1. William Lamb to John W. Ward, Panshanger, 28 Sept. 1822, and Ward to the Bishop of Llandaff, 9 New Street, Saturday, 12 Oct. 1822, Earl of Dudley, *Letters of the Earl of Dudley to the Bishop of Llandaff* (London, 1840), pp. 362–63.
2. James Bland Burges, after a long discourse on Austrian and Prussian affairs, told Grenville that it was better to err "by saying too much on matters which properly belong to your Lordship than by saying too little." 3 Sept. 1792, White Hall, Grenville MSS. When Sir George Shee urged Palmerston to take "a high & determined tone" to force the French to abandon the Belgian fortresses without destroying them in 1832, he also said: "I make no excuses my dear Palmerston for saying all this as you are well aware that be it sense or nonsense it can have but one *motive* & besides will give you no further trouble than that of reading it & throwing it into the fire." 19 Aug. 1931, 21 Hertford Street, Palmerston Papers, GC/SH/98/1–2.

Cooke, Joseph Planta, and (in a different way) John Backhouse, could and did expand the powers and authority not only of themselves but of their position. It was largely through the efforts of Planta and Backhouse that one undersecretary came to dominate the other in the one area where the undersecretaries could and did exercise initiative: the internal matters of the Foreign Office. Other considerations later in the nineteenth and early in the twentieth century eventually caused the permanent undersecretary to dominate his colleague in matters of foreign policy as well.[3]

Although there were usually two undersecretaries of state, on two occasions between 1782 and 1846 this general rule was not followed. The first exception was made by the Marquess of Carmarthen who appointed no second undersecretary when he became foreign secretary in 1783. Until William Fraser retired in 1789 he served as sole assistant to Carmarthen, George Aust, the first senior clerk, directing affairs when Fraser was not in London.[4] Carmarthen never appointed a colleague for him because "my regard for Fraser, & the advantage he derived from being sole under secretary was of such considerable importance to him & his family as to make me unwilling to make any change in his situation in the office."[5]

The second exception to the general rule occurred during two short periods in the 1820s when three undersecretaries served with Canning. The rapid expansion of the volume of business after 1815 convinced Canning that a third undersecretary was indispensable to the proper functioning of the Foreign Office. There was an uproar at the Treasury when he proposed the addition in 1824, however, and he was forced to adopt the expediency of dividing the salary as well as the responsibilities of one undersecretaryship.[6] Lord Francis Conyngham (who succeeded his brother to the courtesy title of Lord Mount Charles in 1824) and Lord Howard de Walden shared these

3. One of these considerations was the necessity for continuity in the office during changes of administrations. The permanent undersecretary, therefore, directed the most important political divisions. Evidence of Lord Wodehouse, Q. 879, 29 Apr. 1861, "Report from the Select Committee appointed to inquire . . . into the Diplomatic Service. . . ," Great Britain, *Parliamentary Papers, 1861*, vol. 6; Command 459, pp. 94–95; Mary Adeline Anderson, "Edmund Hammond, Permanent Under Secretary of State for Foreign Affairs, 1854–1873" (Ph.D. dissertation; University of London, 1955), pp. 259–63; Zara Steiner, "The Last Years of the Old Foreign Office, 1898–1905," *Historical Journal*, 11 (1963), 62–65, 87–88.

4. Aust to Thomas Steele (Treasury), Whitehall, 23 July 1789, Copy, F.O. 366/426 f. 177.

5. Leeds to Pitt, Whitehall, 27 July 1789, Private, Copy, Add. MS 28064 ff. 180–81.

6. See appendix II; Byng to Granville, London, 1 June 1824, P.R.O. 30/29/7/12 ff. 629–32a.

duties from July 1824, until Mount Charles retired in April 1825.[7] Howard carried on by himself for nine months but the recognition of the South American states so increased the business of the office that Canning again warned the Treasury in 1825 that he would soon seek permission to add a third undersecretary. In the meantime he again resorted to the expediency of dividing one of the places between Howard and a new appointee, the Marquess of Clanricarde.[8] It is impossible to say whether Canning, who went to the Treasury as First Lord in 1827, would ultimately have sanctioned a third undersecretaryship. After his death, however, Clanricarde resigned and for the remainder of the nineteenth century there were only two undersecretaries.[9]

With the exception of Canning and Carmarthen the secretaries of state had the assistance of only two men. One was always identified with the principal secretary and always left office with him except when Grenville retained James Bland Burges, Leeds's protégé, in 1791. Burges was inclined even on this occasion to resign, but Leeds, Pitt, and Grenville persuaded him to remain,[10] probably because he was not basically a political person. As has been demonstrated elsewhere,[11] the ability of undersecretaries of state as well as other subministers in the eighteenth century to survive changes in government was largely a matter of the individual, his career goals, and the department in which he served. Some of these undersecretaries were capable men. Burges (1789–1795), Edward Cooke (1812–1817), William Fox-Strangways (1835–1840), and Viscount Canning (1841–1846) all did their share of the work. Because of their close personal attachment to Castlereagh and Aberdeen, Cooke and Canning were accorded a voice in policy on several occasions. Many of these men, however, were impossible colleagues and failed to do any of the work that should have devolved on them. William Fraser,

7. These arrangements caused enemies of Canning and the Conynghams to spread vicious rumors that they were designed solely to insure Conyngham half of the salary without doing half of the work of one undersecretary. William Huskisson to Canning, Eastham, 3 Nov. 1824, Lewis Melville (ed.), *The Huskisson Papers* (London, 1931), pp. 178–80.

8. Draft, Canning to Treasury, F.O., 25 Nov. 1825, F.O. 366/386.

9. A third undersecretaryship was not added until 1917, though assistant undersecretaries were appointed in 1858, 1876, and 1898. *Records of the Foreign Office*, p. 6.

10. Diary of the Duke of Leeds, M[onday], 18 Apr. 1791, and T[uesday], 19 Apr. 1791, Browning, *Leeds Political Memoranda*, pp. 168–72.

11. Franklin B. Wickwire, "King's Friends, Civil Servants or Politicians," *The American Historical Review*, 71 (Oct., 1965), 18–42.

who served longer as undersecretary than anyone else and spoke with experience, did not expect much help from Fox's deputy, St. Andrew St. John. Nor did he get it: "I have not the least Assistance from my present Colleague. You will easily suppose my Situation is not the most comfortable."[12] Even under Canning, who worked his people as vigorously as he did himself, one of the undersecretaries managed to do so little that his colleague sighed after he had retired, "we certainly can go on better without than with Ulick John."[13]

The second undersecretary in the early eighteenth century had also frequently been a personal adherent of the principal secretary. Occasionally one of the clerks in the offices of state, however, had risen to be undersecretary.[14] These men usually served through several changes of ministries, though they often alternated between the Southern and the Northern Departments. William Fraser was one of them. He had been appointed a clerk in 1751 and in 1765 the Duke of Grafton appointed him undersecretary. He afterwards served in both departments of state,[15] but since he was working in the Northern Department in 1782 he became Fox's second assistant. Even Fraser, however, despite seventeen years experience, knew the tenuous nature of his appointment, though "I am very easy about it; as I think it impossible if I do not remain where I am, . . . [that] after so many years I shall [not] be properly provided for."[16] Apparently there was no concept of a permanent undersecretary of state in 1782.[17]

The next clerk to be appointed undersecretary was George Aust, "a good-natured man, with abilities equal to little more than the routine of the office."[18] Leeds appointed him in 1790 "*official or*

12. Fraser to Sir Robert M. Keith, St. James's, 1 Apr. 1783, Add. MS 35528 ff. 145–46; Same to Same, St. James's, 11 Sept. 1783, Add. MS 35530 f. 11.

13. Ulick John de Burgh, Marquess of Clanricarde. Howard de Walden to Granville, F.O., 29 Aug. [1827], Most Private, P.R.O. 30/29/14/5 ff. 61–64.

14. Thomson, *Secretaries of State*, pp. 130–31.

15. Grafton to Postmaster General, 23 July 1765, Great Britain, Public Record Office, *Calendar of Home Office Papers, George III* (4 vols.; London, 1878–1899), vol. 1, 579; for Fraser's movements between departments, ibid., vol. 2, passim, and Earl of Sandwich to Postmaster General, 21 Dec. 1770, ibid., vol. 3, 103.

16. Fraser to Keith, St. James's, 5 July 1782, Add. MS 35526 ff. 8–9.

17. In the twentieth century the title "permanent" undersecretary "emphasizes that this civil servant is distinguished from the political officers and is not affected by parliamentary changes." Donald G. Bishop, *The Administration of British Foreign Relations* (Syracuse, N.Y., 1961), p. 256 n. 6.

18. Sir Herbert Taylor's Memoirs, Ernest Taylor (ed.), *The Taylor Papers* (London, 1913), p. 17.

resident Under Secretary, an Appointment which he understood to be *comparatively* a permanent one, the Situation of his Colleague being declared by his Grace to be his *Confidential* Under Secretary."[19] The distinction of permanency in Aust's mind appears to have been more wishful thinking than anything else, though it enabled him to secure a comfortable retirement in 1796.

Usually after 1795 only one undersecretary of state was replaced on the change of a ministry. Only Fox in 1806 and Canning in 1807 brought in two new undersecretaries. Fox probably replaced George Hammond, who had served since 1795, because he was closely associated with Canning. Naturally one of Canning's first steps when he was appointed to replace Howick in 1807 was to return his friend to his former situation. Though Wellesley wished to bring two new assistants with him to the Foreign Office in 1809, he failed to overcome Perceval's, Harrowby's, and Bathurst's objections to his candidate and to his removing William Hamilton.[20] Wellesley's successors always retained one undersecretary without question. Even Backhouse, who was Canning's most conspicuous appointment in 1827, remained at his post after the Canningites retired in May 1828.

Based on this apparent continuity the editors of the *Foreign Office Lists* designated several of the early undersecretaries "permanent."[21] This designation was a valid one for one undersecretary when the *Lists* first were published in the middle of the nineteenth century. Sir Francis Vincent and Lord Clanwilliam, however, would have been surprised to find themselves in this category. Even Hammond, Hamilton, and Planta did not see themselves as permanent officials. Because they usually had served longer in the department than their colleague they regarded themselves merely as the senior undersecretary. Their colleagues were called the junior undersecretary even after the title of "permanent" undersecretary was well-established.[22]

19. Case of Mr. Aust, Delivered to Lord Grenville, 27 Mar. 1795, Eg. MS 3505 Bundle 4.
20. Lord Bathurst to Wellesley, Brighton, Dec. [1809], Private, Add. MS 37309 ff. 313–14; Charles Arbuthnot to Spencer Perceval, Sidmouth, 9 Jan. 1810, Private, Holland (Perceval) Papers Bundle XXI/24.
21. George Aust, George Hammond, Sir Francis Vincent, William Hamilton, Joseph Planta, Earl of Clanwilliam, John Backhouse, Henry Unwin Addington. Great Britain, Foreign Office, *Foreign Office List*, 1861, p. 6.
22. Minute, Backhouse to Palmerston, 28 June 1832, F.O. 366/313. There has been a tendency to call the junior undersecretary a "government" undersecretary. E. Jones-Parry, "Undersecretaries of State for Foreign Affairs, 1782–1855," *English Historical Review*, 44 (Apr.

Canning appears to have been the first secretary of state to regard one of his undersecretaries as a permanent official and to give him that title.[23] But Backhouse was the first man to call himself the permanent undersecretary, and to define the role of the position.[24]

That Backhouse, considering his political connections, should have become a senior or permanent undersecretary shows that the concept of a permanent undersecretary was only in its formative stages. The eldest son of a prominent Liverpool merchant, John Backhouse was born in 1784, as were both Aberdeen and Palmerston, his principals for most of his career. In 1812 when the electors of Liverpool first elected George Canning as their member of Parliament, they appointed Backhouse the first secretary for the Liverpool Office in London. There he acted as liason between Canning and his merchant constituents. Canning went to the Board of Control in 1816 and Backhouse became his private secretary at that time. Both men were bound for India when Castlereagh's suicide in 1822 placed Canning at the Foreign Office. Between September 1822 and January 1823 Backhouse served first as private secretary and then as undersecretary to Canning while Liverpool, fulfilling Canning's only stipulation for his friends, looked for a vacancy in "which the emoluments amount to, or exceed, £1,000 a year" and "which should not be liable to the vicissitudes of Ministerial arrangements." Backhouse served as commissioner of the excise from January 1823 until April 1827, when he succeeded Planta, who became secretary to the Treasury in Canning's ministry, at the Foreign Office.[25] No other person in office could be more closely identified with Canning than Backhouse was during the 1820s.

Backhouse was not replaced when Canning died in 1827, nor was he asked to leave when the Canningites resigned from Wellington's

1934), 312–13 and n. 3. The term was not used in the first part of the nineteenth century, and since it implies a necessary connection with a particular ministry which did not always exist (for example the case of Lord Dunglas, who served Canning, Dudley, and Aberdeen in various capacities) I have thought it best to stick with the terminology of contemporaries.

23. Canning to Lord George Bentinck, Foreign Office, 3 Apr. 1824, Draft, Canning MSS Bundle 179.

24. The details of this achievement are to be found in Charles R. Middleton, "John Backhouse and the Origins of the Permanent Undersecretaryship for Foreign Affairs: 1828–1842," *The Journal of British Studies*, 13 (May, 1974), 24–45.

25. Memorandum by Backhouse, Foreign Office, Nov. 1837; Backhouse to Rebecca Backhouse, Foreign Office, 11 Nov. 1822, fragment; undated biographical sketch, Backhouse Papers; *The Gentleman's Magazine* (1846), pt. 1, 95–97.

ministry in 1828. This was the type of permanency that undersecretaries later were to take for granted. Perhaps his survival of these
changes contributed to Backhouse's concept of the permanent undersecretaryship.

In 1838 the junior undersecretary, Strangways, suggested as
others had previously that the direction of all the consular business
be attached to his department as a method of relieving Backhouse of
some of his load, which was considerably greater than that of
Strangways. Backhouse refused to accept such an arrangement, "for
it has appeared to me that it would be inexpedient to leave the
permanent Under Secy without any current connection with the
practical course of Consular Concerns & Questions and consequently without the opportunity of contributing to preserve an
uniformity of rule & practice; & to maintain regulations of which
long experience alone may produce a sufficiently firm conviction of
the advantages."[26] This was the first statement of the theory that it
was the exclusive responsibility of the permanent undersecretary to
preserve the traditions of the Foreign Office. Thereafter the permanent official was responsible for maintaining continuity in the
routine functioning of the service. Later this official might become
the proponent of long-established policies as well.[27]

From 1782 the responsibilities of the undersecretaries were
clearly distinguished. Each man was responsible for superintending
the correspondence with select countries. The divisions they directed were not too different from the countries supervised by the
Northern and Southern Departments before 1782.[28] The countries
in each division, however, fluctuated greatly during the sixty-year
period following 1782. It is impossible after 1822 to find a strictly
geographical distribution in these divisions.[29] The political work of
the two undersecretaries was frequently carried on without much
intercommunication.[30] Sir Herbert Taylor recalled that when Aust

26. Minute, Backhouse, [1838], on minute, Strangways entitled "Remarks on general work
of the Under Secretaries," F.O. 366/386.
27. Minute, Lenox-Conyngham, F.O., 19 July 1842, F.O. 366/270 f. 151; Anderson,
"Edmund Hammond," p. 263.
28. See Thomson, *Secretaries of State*, pp. 2–3.
29. See appendix II.
30. There were, of course, times when this was not so. Both Planta and Hamilton, for
example, expressed opinions on the political instructions the Admiralty requested from the
Foreign Office for vessels serving on the west coast of South America. Minute, Hamilton, and
minute (partially erased), Planta, on J. W. Croker to Hamilton, Admiralty Office, 1 Aug. 1817,
F.O. 72/207 ff. 86–89.

and Burges were the undersecretaries "there was little union between them, and their business was distinct." Canning, as secretary of state, also stressed the separate nature of the work of the two undersecretaries.[31]

Until late in Castlereagh's secretaryship the junior undersecretary usually was the more important. Burges, on one occasion when he had to be away from the office because of his son's death, even felt it necessary to assure Grenville that Aust was "very capable of discharging the business of the office."[32] George Canning by virtue of his own abilities and his connection with Pitt was more active in foreign affairs than Hammond. The most influential of the junior undersecretaries was Edward Cooke. Castlereagh brought Cooke to the Foreign Office with him in 1812. The son of the Dean of Ely, educated at Eton and Kings College, Cambridge, Cooke had been in Ireland as undersecretary in the Civil Department (1796–1801) and had been one of Castlereagh's "ardent assistants in the struggle" which led to the passage of the Act of Union.[33] He had twice served as undersecretary for War and the Colonies under Castlereagh (1804–1806; 1807–1809) and was a man of immense experience.[34] He was not an administrator, and never had been, but he was "a shrewd, outspoken man"[35] and proved to be an indispensable assistant to Castlereagh at the peace negotiations in 1814 and 1815. He offered his opinions freely and frequently, not only to Castlereagh but also to Liverpool. He did not hesitate to criticise when he disagreed with Castlereagh on matters of policy, as he did on the question of Poland.[36] He also had no qualms about offering his approval of his superior's work. He once wrote to Castlereagh after reading the protocols of the Allied Powers in 1814, that "the line

31. Memoirs, Taylor, *Taylor Papers*, p. 17; W. Wellesley-Pole to Charles Bagot, House of Commons, 8 Aug. 1807, Captain Josceline Bagot (ed.), *George Canning and His Friends* (2 vols.; London, 1909), vol. 1, 238–41. By 1861 both undersecretaries read every dispatch and every draft in each division. Evidence by E. Hammond, Q. 7, 15 Apr. 1861, "Report From the Select Committee appointed to inquire . . . into the Diplomatic Service. . . ," *P.P., 1861*, vol. 6, Command 459, p. 1. This practice apparently began in 1849. Minute, Palmerston, 24 June 1849, F.O. 366/280 ff. 47–48.

32. Burges to Grenville, Dartmouth Street, 15 Sept. 1791, Grenville MSS.

33. Bartlett, *Castlereagh*, p. 13.

34. *Annual Biography and Obituary* (21 vols.; London, 1817–1837), vol. 5, 283–85.

35. Marquess of Cornwallis to Major General Ross, Phoenix Park, 25 Dec. 1800, Charles Ross (ed.), *Correspondence of Charles, First Marquess of Cornwallis* (3 vols.; London, 1859), vol. 3, 315; Stratford Canning's memoirs, Poole, *Life of Stratford Canning*, vol. 1, 244.

36. Webster, *For. Pol. Castlereagh*, vol. 1, 330 and note; Liverpool to Bathurst, Bath, 6 Jan. 1815, Private, *H. M. C. Bathurst*, pp. 321–22.

which you have so unvariably [sic] pursued and so successfully maintained, makes me perfectly satisfied as to the part you took . . ." in negotiating them.[37] Unfortunately his health gave way during the Congress of Vienna and he had to retire to Italy to recuperate.[38] He left office in 1817. Nobody could replace him in Castlereagh's confidence, and none of his successors of the following thirty years ever played the role he did in the formation of policy.

After Cooke's retirement the senior undersecretary gradually came to dominate his colleague. Part of this trend was the natural result of one man's remaining through several changes of ministries. But a more important factor was the increasing responsibility for official arrangements that fell to the senior undersecretary.

In the eighteenth century either undersecretary was likely to be concerned with the many personnel and administrative problems of the office. In fact, the junior undersecretary occasionally even took a lead in these questions, and frequently interceded on behalf of office personnel with the secretary of state.[39] George Hammond of necessity inherited this role because of the frequent changes in the other undersecretaryship between 1801 and 1809.[40] Because Cooke lacked interest in administrative questions and was more concerned with matters of policy, William Hamilton performed most of these duties. Hamilton and Castlereagh got along quite well, and Castlereagh allowed him to make final decisions on many financial and relatively unimportant patronage questions.[41]

Planta extended this authority because he was responsible for managing the office and enjoyed the confidence of Canning to a degree that none of his colleagues did. Planta was the first clerk after Aust to work his way through the ranks of the office to the undersecretaryship. He possessed the confidence of both Canning and Castlereagh and worked as well with one as with the other, much to the indignation of Mrs. Arbuthnot, who called him the "*ame damnée* [*sic*]" of the Foreign Office.[42] He was "an excellent man of business,"

---

37. London, 19 Feb. 1814, Londonderry, *Castlereagh Corresp.*, vol. 9, 280.

38. Lord Apsley to Bathurst, Vienna, 2 Jan. [1815], *H. M. C. Bathurst*, p. 319.

39. Burges to Grenville, White Hall, 14 Sept. 1792, Grenville MSS.

40. Minute, Harrowby, 25 Aug. 1804, F.O. 83/13. In addition to Hammond, nine men, eight of whom were junior undersecretaries, served during these years.

41. Webster, *For. Pol. Castlereagh*, vol. 1, 44–45; Minutes, Castlereagh and Hamilton, on Lushington to Hamilton, Treasury Chambers, 3 Aug. 1816, and P. Stuart to Castlereagh, London, No. 316 High Holborn, Sept. 1816, F.O. 27/149.

42. 11 Nov. 1824, Bamford and Wellington, *Journal of Mrs. Arbuthnot*, vol. 1, 355.

prematurely gray and very fat—"a fit type of the prosperity of his country and its venerable Institutions."[43] Canning frequently left Planta in charge of the Foreign Office and gave him the discretion to decide which items to send to and which to withhold from Liverpool and the king.[44] Whereas Cooke ventured opinions, Planta in times of urgency occasionally instructed ministers abroad in particular lines of policy which he knew Canning would have followed had he been in town. Canning apparently always issued the necessary formal instructions on his return to the office.[45] Other undersecretaries occasionally signed dispatches on behalf of the secretary of state when these dispatches dealt with questions that would not admit of delay and had to be sent abroad before the secretary could return to London to sign them. But it appears that on these occasions the dispatches were written at the express direction of the secretary of state and not on the authority of the undersecretary.[46]

Canning at one time thought seriously of having the senior undersecretary work solely with interdepartmental correspondence and establishment problems, but this program was never implemented. He usually consulted Planta, however, on all matters relating to the establishment.[47]

Backhouse in 1832 assured the senior undersecretary's ascendancy in questions affecting the establishment. The clerks petitioned him to intercede with Palmerston to secure them extra money for doing extraordinary duty. Backhouse forwarded their "memorial" to Palmerston with the note that "the paper is sent to *me*, as *Senior* Under Secretary through whose hands it has been usual for the Clerks to transmit their Representations to the Secretary of State." Shee, on the contrary, thought that the clerks under his supervision should have submitted their petition through him. Backhouse was willing on this occasion to work with Shee on the matter, but Shee

43. Stratford Canning's memoirs, Poole, *Life of Stratford Canning*, vol. 1, 196; Stratford Canning to Bagot, 19 Sept. 1823, quoted in Bagot, *Canning and Friends*, vol. 2, 200.

44. Minute, Planta, Foreign Office, 3 Nov. 1823, Canning MSS Bundle 136.

45. Planta to Sir William A'Court, Foreign Office, 14 Oct. 1823, Private, and 17 Oct. 1823, Private, Add. MS 41544 ff. 181–84, 192.

46. For example, Fox-Strangways, Drafts to George Villiers, Foreign Office, 24 Aug. 1837, Nos. 111, 112, 113, F.O. 72/476. Palmerston initialled each of these drafts when he returned to the office.

47. Canning to Lord George Bentinck, Foreign Office, 3 Apr. 1824, Draft, Canning MSS Bundle 79; Planta to Sir Stratford Canning, Fairlight, 23 July 1833, Poole, *Life of Stratford Canning*, vol. 2, 21–22; Minutes, Planta and Canning, on "Memorandum respecting Diplomatic Salaries, F.O., 1824," F.O. 366/525.

refused to have anything to do with the petition since it was submitted only to Backhouse.[48] Thereafter Shee and his successors usually played a secondary role in questions affecting the establishment.[49]

Backhouse occasionally offered an opinion to Palmerston.[50] He also appears to have been the first undersecretary to issue letters written on his own initiative but ostensibly under the direction of the secretary of state. In 1833, for example, on the representation of Prince Talleyrand, the French ambassador, Backhouse wrote a formal letter in Palmerston's name but without his knowledge, requesting the safe conduct of a Dutch vessel under French contract to proceed without being disturbed through the embargo against Holland to dispose of a cargo of flax at Elsinor. Palmerston apparently disapproved of the specific action,[51] but there is no record that he forbade the practice in the future.

The senior undersecretary exclusively performed one other duty. In 1825 Canning discontinued the practice of having either undersecretary attend to the secret service payments of the department. After that year and at least until the 1870s, the senior undersecretary alone was responsible for the foreign secret service accounts.[52] Because of his strategic location Backhouse from time to time also summoned cabinets for various ministers as other undersecretaries in the past had done.[53] Presumably, however, either undersecretary could issue these summonses.

The ascendancy of the permanent undersecretary over his col-

48. Minute, Backhouse to Palmerston, 28 June 1832; Minute, Backhouse to Shee, 28 June 1832, with Shee's minute 28 June, F.O. 366/313.

49. Charles K. Webster, "Lord Palmerston at Work, 1830–1841," *Politica*, 1 (Aug. 1934), 137, maintained that both undersecretaries were active in establishment questions. They certainly were involved in organizational matters affecting their own work. Strangways in 1838 participated fully with Backhouse in determining the arrangement of the new divisions. Disagreement between Addington and Canning in 1844 on reform of the slave trade department, which Canning directed, forestalled any changes in that branch at that time. Minute, Addington, F.O., 10 Mar. 1847, on Addington to Aberdeen, F.O., 1844, F.O. 366/313. But the senior undersecretary was the only one involved in decisions on matters of a general nature if both men were in town.

50. Minute, Backhouse to Palmerston, 27 Oct. 1835, Palmerston Papers GC/GA/5.

51. Minute, Backhouse, 19 Mar. 1833, and Draft ("I am directed by Visct. Palmerston. . . .") to the Council Office, F.O., 11 Jan. 1833, F.O. 24/475.

52. Draft, E. Hammond to Lord Granville, F.O., 9 Oct. 1870, Barnes MSS.

53. Backhouse fortunately preserved some of his instructions to summon cabinets. Minutes, Lord Melbourne, 30 Sept. 1834; Lord John Russell, Sunday [no year]; and Sir Robert Peel, received 16 Dec. 1834, Backhouse Papers; Pitt to Grenville, Hollwood, 6 Oct., [1798], *H. M. C. Fortescue*, vol. 4, 337.

league in departmental questions was firmly established by 1841. The comparative role of the permanent official in matters of policy remained less significant during the 1840s because Lord Canning was a capable and vigorous junior undersecretary and his new colleague, Henry Unwin Addington, was a rather humdrum official whose career was "completely devoid of any sign of brilliance or originality."[54]

There has been some doubt, however, in light of Addington's quarrel in 1848 with the chief clerk, George Lenox-Conyngham, whether this ascendancy extended to the permanent undersecretary's relations with those senior officials in the department who also had some responsibility for the internal arrangements of the Foreign Office.[55] The dispute in 1848 apparently arose over the measures Addington ordered taken to protect the Foreign Office from the possible violence of the Chartist mob when presenting its petition to Parliament. Conyngham disagreed with some of Addington's details and refused to implement them on the grounds that Addington, despite his right to the general superintendance of the office, had no power to order specific actions without the prior instructions of the secretary of state. The general authority of the permanent undersecretary was not challenged, and Conyngham labelled as "preposterous" the notion that it was.[56]

This incident apparently resulted more from a clash of personalities than from a lack of precision on the authority of the permanent undersecretary. Prior to 1845 there is no indication that any clerk ever refused to implement the decision of either undersecretary on any matter. Conyngham, however, was known for his brashness and his ill-temper and Addington's customary abruptness with his subordinates did nothing to minimize the occasional disagreements he had with them. Conyngham and Addington had in fact had several unpleasant experiences. The most serious of these occurred in 1846 when Aberdeen, largely at Conyngham's instiga-

54. Bradford Perkins (ed.), *Youthful America: Selections from Henry Unwin Addington's "Residence in the United States of America, 1822, 23, 24, 25"* ("University of California Publications in History"; Berkeley, 1960), pp. 4–6.

55. Valerie Cromwell, "An Incident in the Development of the Permanent Under Secretaryship at the Foreign Office," *Bulletin of the Institute of Historical Research*, 33 (May, 1960), 99–113.

56. Memorandum, Conyngham, Foreign Office, 17 Apr. 1848, ibid., p. 112.

tion, prohibited smoking in the office.[57] Shortly afterwards Conyngham returned to the office one evening to find it "in a disgusting condition from the smell of Tobacco." He was for calling in each clerk until the "delinquent" had been found and then for giving the guilty clerk a severe reprimand.[58] Addington's reply was curt:

Half the philosophy of life consists of knowing when to shut one's eyes, and when to keep them, or one of them, open.

It is a very good thing sometimes to take the bull by the horns; but it is generally wiser to get out of his way.

When an abuse has become an [sic] use by prescription, it is not quite fair, nor is it wise, to up with the club and knock it down.

Smoking at F.O. is in this category; and we must deal gently with those who have had their long allowed enjoyment suddenly cut off, and who shew some temper at the prohibition. . . .

I am always for mild means in attaining a desired end, unless compelled to resort to the strong hand by perservering resistance.

Do thee likewise.[59]

The events of 1848, though more serious in nature, followed a general pattern of conflict between Conyngham and Addington. The result of the dispute reconfirmed (it did not establish) the absolute authority of the permanent undersecretary over the senior personnel of the office.

Though the undersecretaries had little influence on policy, they were rarely without opinions and frequently they disagreed with decisions of the secretary of state. Only one actually resigned over a question of policy. Fitzharris, who had the unpleasant task in the summer of 1807 of assuring the Danish minister of Britain's perpetual friendship while the British fleet was bombarding the Danish fleet in the harbor at Copenhagen, resigned shortly thereafter. His resignation, however, probably reflected more a dislike for his role

57. Minute, Addington to the Chief Clerk, F.O., 25 Mar. 1846; order by Lenox-Conyngham, F.O., 26 Mar. 1846; and minute ("A good deed done on a good day"), Conyngham, n.d., F.O. 366/280 ff. 171, 175, 176.
58. Minute, Conyngham, F.O., 8 Apr. 1846, F.O. 366/280 ff. 185–88.
59. Addington to Conyngham, F.O., 9 Apr. 1846, Private, F.O. 366/280 ff. 181–83.

on this occasion than a disagreement over the necessity of the action.[60] Most of the undersecretaries complained in private to their friends when some aspect of policy disturbed them. William Fraser lamented the supposed abandonment of the "three Articles of Political Faith, the Barrier Treaty, the King of the Romans, & the Balance of Power," which had been the cornerstones of British foreign policy when he began his career.[61] Charles Arbuthnot, one of Hawkesbury's undersecretaries, was less specific in his complaint. He said that Henry Addington directed "the most inefficient Cabinet that ever cursed a Country."[62] George Canning was less inhibited than most. He wrote not only his colleague, Hammond, but even Pitt that he decidedly disagreed with Grenville's and Pitt's decision to allow Lord Malmesbury virtually no discretion in the negotiations with France at Lisle in 1797.[63]

One undersecretary was openly hostile to the ministries he served. Lord Howard de Walden, the son of Canning's friend Charles Ellis,[64] complained about and criticized both Goderich's and Wellington's Turkish and Greek policies. He told William Huskisson, a Canningite and a cabinet minister, that the decision to allow any except Egyptian and Turkish vessels, regardless of their cargo, to sail through the allied blockade of Greece, was "worse than nugatory" and "will satisfy no one." Later he wrote Granville that Wellington was "so obstinate" about refusing to grant Greek independence that unless Granville could persuade the French government to "*press* the question of an ultimatum to the Turks with the declaration of acknowledgment of the independence of Greece immediately on its rejection . . . ," Metternich would trample "under foot" Canning's treaty of July 1827, which provided for a semi-autonomous Greek state, self-governing but under the suzerainty of the sultan.[65] How-

60. Third Earl of Malmesbury, *Memoirs of an Ex-Minister: An Autobiography* (2 vols.; 3d ed.; London, 1884), vol. 1, 2; Fitzharris's Journal, Malmesbury, *Series of Letters*, vol. 2, 25. In connection with the question of resignations over policy disputes, see Webster, *For. Pol. Castlereagh*, vol. 1, 330 and note, on Cooke's resignation.

61. Fraser to Keith, St. James's, 7 Nov. 1783, Add. MS 35530 ff. 158–59.

62. Arbuthnot to Arthur Paget, Downing Street, 12 Mar. 1804, Add. MS 48402 no folio.

63. Canning to Hammond, Charles Street, Tuesday, 8 Nov. 1796, 1 P.M., P.R.O. 30/29/8/1 ff. 60–61; Canning to Pitt, Spring Garden, Sunday, 10 Sept. 1797, Secret, P.R.O. 30/8/120 ff. 126–37.

64. *The Complete Peerage*, vol. 6, 592–93.

65. Howard to Huskisson, F.O., 4 Oct. 1827, Most Private, Add. MS 38751 ff. 120–23; Howard to Granville, F.O., 6 Apr. [1828], Most Confidential, P.R.O. 30/29/14/5 ff. 207–8. On the Greek question, 1823–1828, see R. W. Seton-Watson, *Britain in Europe, 1789–1914* (Cambridge, 1937), pp. 98–129.

ard was totally identified with the Canningites and Wellington's close allies in the cabinet knew of his hostility.[66] He resigned with the rest of the Canningites in May 1828.

All of the undersecretaries faithfully implemented the policies of their principals, even though they might not have agreed with them. Only James Bland Burges appears to have conceived it his duty, however, to enter warmly into matters passing through his department. "It is neither my disposition," he wrote Lord Auckland,

> nor would it be my duty, merely and coldly to discharge the important functions entrusted to me. I feel it impossible to avoid becoming warm upon a great national business passing thro' my hands, and, tho' perhaps I might avoid censure, & might even be supposed to have done my duty, by acting as others have done in the exact & literal observance of the orders I receive, I think it not blamable in me to go sometimes much further, and, by every proper exertion, to forward, to supplement and to vindicate the measures in which I naturally feel myself a kind of party.[67]

The secretaries of state in theory enjoyed unlimited discretion in appointing their undersecretaries. It was not even necessary to make a formal appointment. Leeds simply sent Dudley Ryder "a letter of Introduction to Mr. Sneyd, The Chief Clerk, directing him to inform the Gentlemen of the Office of your appointment, & to furnish you with the keys of the office Boxes."[68] Undersecretaries were selected, however, for a variety of reasons. Some secretaries, particularly Fox and Castlereagh, chose political friends and allies. Richard Brinsley Sheridan and St. Andrew St. John were both among Fox's circle of friends in Parliament.[69] Cooke had been with Castlereagh since they had served together in Ireland in the 1790s. The Duke of Leeds and Lord Grenville had to accept undersecretaries who owed their allegiance and their appointment to Pitt's influence more than to any other. Pitt in 1789 wished Dudley Ryder to succeed Fraser. Leeds protested that one undersecretary always came from the

66. 6 Feb. 1828, Colchester, *Ellenborough Diary*, vol. 1, 19–20.
67. Burges to Auckland, White Hall, 7 June 1791, Private, Add. MS 34431 ff. 337–38.
68. Leeds to Ryder, St. James's Square, 24 Aug. 1789, Harrowby MSS vol. 8, ff. 119–20.
69. W. A. Darlington, *Sheridan, 1751–1816* (London, 1951), passim; Sir Lewis Namier and John Brooke, *The History of Parliament: The House of Commons, 1754–1790* (3 vols.; London, 1964), vol. 3, 401.

office (an assertion of doubtful truth), but Ryder and not the duke's candidate was appointed.[70] Pitt proposed Canning to Grenville and appears to have insisted on his appointment. Grenville delayed until such time as he could first replace one of his undersecretaries with George Hammond, a man more personally associated with him than Canning, Burges, or Aust could be.[71]

The secretaries of state in the nineteenth century sometimes selected an undersecretary because of his political connections. Relatives of cabinet colleagues frequently were chosen. William Hamilton was Bathurst's nominee and a relation of Lord Harrowby, the president of the Council. William Fox-Strangways, who served under Palmerston, was another Lord President's (Lord Lansdowne) brother-in-law.[72] The most conspicuous appointment of this class was Lord Francis Conyngham. George Canning appointed him in 1823 (after failing four times to get other men) at the suggestion of King George IV, who enjoyed the company of Conyngham's mother. The appointment caused quite a stir in society and some of Canning's enemies saw it as an attempt to get "a regular spy" into the king's Household.[73] Canning was certainly pleased that he could gratify the king, but he accepted George's recommendation only after his own candidates had all turned him down. The king, too, was scrupulously fair in the arrangement, as he did not propose Conyngham until Canning knew for certain that no one else wished the post.[74]

On rare occasions the secretaries of state were really free to choose their undersecretaries without reference to political considerations. In these instances they sometimes chose relatives or close personal

70. Leeds to Ryder, North Mims, 15 Aug. 1789, Harrowby MSS vol. 8, ff. 117–18; Leeds to Pitt, Whitehall, 27 July 1789, Private, Copy, Add. MS 28064, ff. 180–81; Leeds to Postmaster General, Whitehall, 24 Aug. 1789, Copy, F.O. 366/669, vol. 2, 238.

71. Canning to Lord Boringdon, 9 Oct. 1795, Stapleton, *Canning and His Times*, pp. 34–35; Canning to [?], 24 Oct. 1795, Aspinall, *Later Corresp. Geo. III*, vol. 2, 433 n. 1; Canning to John Sneyd, Wootton, 17 Dec. 1795, Bagot, *Canning and Friends*, vol. 1, 52–53; Grenville to Hammond, Downing Street, 9 Dec. 1794, Private, *H. M. C. Fortescue*, vol 2, 651.

72. Hamilton's mother was a sister of Lady Harrowby; see article on Hamilton, *D.N.B.*, vol. 8, 1118–119. Lansdowne to Palmerston, Aug. 1832, Palmerston Papers GC/LA/43/1.

73. Mrs. Arbuthnot's Journal, 8 Sept. 1823, Bamford and Wellington, *Journal of Mrs. Arbuthnot*, vol. 1, 256. Aspinall, *Diary of Hobhouse*, p. 98, says Canning considered only three men before Conyngham. In fact he sought Lord Binning, John William Ward, Frederick Lamb, and William Noel-Hill. The letters of these men in 1822 are in Canning MSS passim.

74. Canning to Lord Boringdon, G.L., 28 Dec. 1824, Private, Add. MS 48221 ff. 115–18; Canning to George IV, Foreign Office, 19 Dec. 1822, and George IV's reply, n.d., Aspinall, *Letters of George IV*, vol. 2, 547–48.

friends to serve with them. William Eliot, Harrowby's undersecretary, was also his brother-in-law. Culling Charles Smith was Wellesley's brother-in-law.[75] Canning's daughter, Harriet, had no sooner married the Marquess of Clanricarde than Canning appointed him undersecretary.[76] Palmerston selected Sir George Shee, a friend from their college days at St. John's College, Cambridge, as his first undersecretary.[77]

Because the undersecretaries were selected for such a variety of reasons, it is difficult to generalize about them. They possessed, however, certain common characteristics. They were recruited overwhelmingly from the ruling class. Twenty-two of the thirty-seven undersecretaries who served from 1782–1846 were peers, sons of peers, baronets, or members of the landed gentry. Six had fathers with a professional background (i.e., men in military, legal, or civil service careers), and the fathers of two were clergymen. Only two came from merchant families while the heritage of four is uncertain.

They ranged in age on appointment from Clanwilliam and St. John, who were twenty-three, to Addington, who was fifty-two, and Cooke, who was fifty-seven. Of the other thirty-three, however, twenty-one were between twenty-five and thirty-five years of age. All but six served in other places under government than the Foreign Office sometime in their careers.[78] Only five, however, were of sufficient energy and ability to attain cabinet rank. Three of these men (Dudley Ryder [later Earl of Harrowby], George Canning, and Lord Leveson [later Earl Granville], served as foreign secretary.[79]

The duties of the undersecretaries were more clerical than might have been expected in the case of officials of their rank. Their

75. Harrowby MSS vol. 3 index; Bamford and Wellington, *Journal of Mrs. Arbuthnot*, vol. 1, 142 n.1.
76. Canning to Granville, Seaford, 13 Oct. 1825, Private & Confidential, P.R.O. 30/29/8/8 ff. 1001–4.
77. Frederick Boase, *Modern English Biography* (6 vols.; Truro, 1892–1921), vol. 3, 533.
78. The undersecretaryship did not automatically entitle a person to diplomatic or other government service, though most often such arrangements were made for retiring undersecretaries if they wished other employment. Canning to Bagot, Foreign Office, 8 Aug. 1807, 6 p.m., Private, Bagot, *Canning and Friends*, vol. 1, 242–43; Same to Granville, F.O., 25 Sept. 1822, private & confidential, P.R.O. 30/29/8/6 ff. 741–42.
79. Lord Canning and the Marquess of Clanricarde were the others who held cabinet positions. Both held the relatively unimportant position of postmaster general. Clanricarde was also for a brief unhappy period Lord Privy Seal. Canning, by far the more able, was Governor General of India during the Mutiny.

principal duty was to supervise the work of the clerks and to distribute the business of the office.[80] But the private papers of every secretary of state contain numerous letters copied by their undersecretaries. Nor did the undersecretaries consider it below their dignity to sit with their clerks and write dispatches.[81] They frequently made a précis of important papers to save their principals the trouble of reading numerous enclosures that sometimes accompanied dispatches. They did not always prepare these précis as willingly as they performed other tasks. Backhouse, after summarizing one series of particularly long enclosures, suggested that Palmerston think seriously about expanding the staff at the Washington mission so that papers could be classified by officials of lesser importance than himself.[82] When secretaries of state were out of town, the undersecretaries sent extracts of all official papers received in their absence if for one reason or another the originals were delayed in London or by the monarch.[83] Burges even kept a diary which he transmitted occasionally to Grenville to keep him informed of "such things as are connected with public business." Probably all of the undersecretaries kept daily records of their appointments similar to those of Backhouse.[84]

One of the responsibilities of the undersecretaries was to meet with representatives of foreign powers and with government officials when the secretary of state was unable to see them. Planta, for example, continued to hold interviews with heads of missions when Canning was out of town.[85] Palmerston frequently employed Backhouse to explain questions of detail to the law officers of the Crown and to give information to other important persons.[86] It was also

80. Memo on the F.O., June 1828, F.O. 366/386.
81. Burges to Auckland, White Hall, 13 Apr. 1790, Private, Add. MS 34430 ff. 356–57; Canning to Granville, Spring Gardens, Sunday night, 14 Jan. 1798, Private, P.R.O. 30/29/8/1 ff. 76–77.
82. Minute, Planta, F.O., 29 Oct. 1823, Canning MSS Bundle 136; Minute, Backhouse, 16 Feb. 1838 on minute, Palmerston, 15 Feb. 1838, F.O. 96/19.
83. This arrangement was more necessary in the eighteenth than in the nineteenth century. Memoranda, 30 Dec. 1782–29 Jan. 1783, in Fraser's hand, Lucas L 29/595.
84. Burges to Grenville, Downing Street, 23 Dec. 1793, ½ past 9 p.m., Grenville MSS; in the Backhouse Papers there are fragments of his journal.
85. Minute, Planta, Foreign Office, 30 Oct. 1823, Private, Canning MSS Bundle 136; Planta to Liverpool, F.O., 25 Oct. 1826, o'C. p.m., Private & Most Confidential, Add. MS 38302 ff. 87–91.
86. Minute, Palmerston, on minute, Backhouse, 25 June 1832, F.O. 96/17; Minute, Backhouse, on "Memorandum on the subject of Mr. Robinson's intended Motion, respecting Tonnage Duty paid in French Ports," F.O., 18 Aug. 1831, F.O. 27/441.

convenient to send an undersecretary to meet delegations from powers not recognized by Britain or persons from areas controlled by other states. On one of these occasions Hamilton, whom Bathurst sent to meet a delegation of Tyrolean deputies, "repeated to them more than once" "that the confidential Conversation I had been instructed to hold with them was [not] tantamount to an engagement on the part of Govt. to comply with their Wishes." Government was not committed to any course of policy or to recognition by these meetings, but benefitted from an exchange of opinions.[87]

Occasionally undersecretaries were employed on special missions. In 1796, when Pitt's ministry tried to make some arrangements with the German powers to secure a peace with France, Grenville employed George Hammond, who had served in the diplomatic service prior to his appointment as undersecretary, on extraordinary missions to Berlin and Vienna.[88] Backhouse went to Portsmouth to meet the Spanish Infant Don Carlos in 1834 in an unsuccessful effort to extract from him a promise to stay out of Peninsular affairs in return for a guaranteed annual income.[89] Cooke acted as an unofficial British representative at the Holy See while he recuperated from the rigors of the Congress of Vienna and urged Castlereagh to establish permanent relations with the Vatican.[90]

Both undersecretaries worked at the office every weekday afternoon and most evenings. They alternated attending on Sundays, one working the afternoon, the other the evening hours. In addition, one undersecretary was always available should dispatches arrive in London during the night or before office hours in the morning.[91] Backhouse and Shee appear to be the first men to have made an arrangement for the undersecretaries to alternate working evenings, though in times of great activity both men stayed late. Backhouse and Strangways modified this arrangement later in the

87. Hamilton to Bathurst, 42 Castle Street, Leicester Fields, 5 Nov. 1809, B.M. Loan 57/4/342; Minute, Canning, on Chevalier W. Floyd to [Canning], No. 35 Windmill St., Tottenham Court Road, 9 Dec. 1808, F.O. 83/15; "Minute of a Conversation held unofficially by Mr. Planta with M: de Zea, Vice President of the Republick of Colombia," 24 June 1820, F.O. 72/241 ff. 300–1.
88. Miscellaneous papers, 1796–1797, *H. M. C. Fortescue*, vol. 3, 227–38, 310–13, 315.
89. Palmerston to Backhouse, Foreign Office, 13 June 1834, No. 1, and Backhouse to Palmerston, Portsmouth, 15 June 1834, No. 1, Copy, F.O. 323/6.
90. Cooke to Castlereagh, Rome, 13 Apr. 1815, Londonderry, *Castlereagh Corresp.*, vol. 10, 308–11.
91. Burges to Auckland, White Hall, 9 Oct. 1792, Private, Add. MS 34445 f. 48.

1830s. Palmerston said they "are very much like the Two Figures in the weather House & rusticate & labour alternately. . . ."[92] Only once were both undersecretaries simultaneously away from London for any extended period of time. In 1841 Backhouse was in the country recuperating from a severe illness and Leveson was electioneering.[93] This constant attendance was very fatiguing and several undersecretaries (Fraser, Hammond, Cooke, Hamilton, and Backhouse) retired in poor health.

Under these circumstances it is scarcely surprising that few of these men sat in the House of Commons after they were appointed undersecretary. Most of those undersecretaries who were also members of the House of Commons served before 1808.[94] Because they were appointed by the secretary of state, the undersecretaries were not affected by the act of 1707 which required that all members of the House of Commons accepting positions of profit under the Crown resign their seat on appointment and stand at a bye-election if they wished to remain in Parliament. After 1742, however, no two undersecretaries serving in the same department could sit in Parliament simultaneously. Ryder was thus forced to resign shortly after taking office as both he and Burges were MPs.[95] After the creation of the third department of state in 1794 contemporaries assumed that only two undersecretaries could sit in Parliament, though a strict interpretation of the act of 1742 would have permitted one undersecretary from each department to be a member. It was not until much later in the nineteenth century that there were more than two undersecretaries of state in the House of Commons.[96]

Undersecretaries who were members of Parliament were not

92. Minute, Backhouse to Palmerston, 14 Nov. 1832, and minute, Palmerston, 15 Nov., F.O. 366/390; Palmerston to Granville, F.O., 22 Nov. 1839, P.R.O. 30/29/14/6 ff. 198–99.
93. Palmerston to Queen Victoria, May 1841, Connell, *Regina vs. Palmerston*, pp. 30–31.
94. Sheridan, St. John, Burges, Ryder, Canning, Frere, Eliot, Hervey, Walpole, Ward, Fitzharris, and Bagot. Namier and Brooke, *History of Parliament*, vols. 2–3 passim.; Gerrit P. Judd, IV, *Members of Parliament, 1734–1832* ("Yale Historical Publications," Miscellany 61; New Haven, 1955), passim.
95. Draft, Ryder to Leeds, Whitehall, 20 Jan. 1790, Harrowby MSS vol. 8, f. 205; George III was never happy about Ryder's appointment since he felt that the sons of peers should learn the habits of business as junior lords of the Admiralty. Burges's account of Leeds's audience with the king, 1789, Hutton, *Burges*, pp. 132–33.
96. Parry, "Undersecretaries of State," pp. 310–12, maintains that the act of 1742 was misinterpreted as a result of Bagot's resignation in 1808. As early as 1806, however, the Grenville ministry decided that no more than two undersecretaries could sit in the Commons at the same time. W. Windham to Grenville, [Pall Mall], 17 Apr. 1806, *H. M. C. Fortescue*, vol. 8, 103.

always assured a seat at general elections. Burges, who sat for Helston where the Duke of Leeds had some election patronage. nonetheless lost his seat in the election of 1790.[97] George Walpole, Howick's undersecretary, stood for Dungarvon (Ireland) in the election in the autumn of 1806. He was only belatedly given the lukewarm assistance of the Irish Government, which had intended to support another man before Walpole declared his candidacy.[98]

With such men as Pitt, Castlereagh, Canning, and Palmerston in the House of Commons, ministries needed no second spokesman for foreign policy. The secretaries of state after 1807 were more in need of administrative assistance. When Canning offered the undersecretaryship to Bagot in 1807 it was on the understanding that Bagot would have little time for attending the House of Commons. Bagot was not required to resign his seat, though clearly it was Canning's intention that he do so as soon as he felt at home in the Foreign Office.[99] By 1822, because of the growth in the volume of business, Canning made it a condition that John William Ward resign his seat if he accepted the undersecretaryship.[100]

Only three members of the House of Commons served as undersecretary after Bagot resigned in 1808. One of them, Viscount Fordwich, resigned after only four days' service because Melbourne's ministry was sacked the day he was appointed. His appointment was delayed, however, because there were already two undersecretaries in the Commons when Palmerston nominated him to succeed Shee.[101] It is possible that he was appointed after Palmerston knew that he was going out and therefore was certain that the other two undersecretaries in the Commons would also be replaced, thus leaving a vacancy for Fordwich to fill. Two other undersecretaries, Viscount Mahon and Lord Leveson, also sat in the Commons. Each of them served such short appointments and under such influential principals (Wellington and Palmerston) that they had little opportunity to make their mark in the House or in the office.

97. Namier and Brooke, *History of Parliament*, vol. 1, 229–30; vol. 2, 141.
98. W. Elliot to Grenville, Dublin Castle, 31 Oct. and 23 Nov. 1806, Private, *H. M. C. Fortescue*, vol. 8, 415–40.
99. W. Wellesley-Pole to Bagot, House of Commons, 8 Aug. 1807, Bagot, *Canning and Friends*, vol. 1, 238–41.
100. Canning to Ward, Gloucester Lodge, 29 Sept. 1822, Private & Confidential, Copy, Canning MSS Bundle 66.
101. Byng to Granville, 28 Oct. 1834, P.R.O. 30/29/7/13 ff. 977–80.

The undersecretaries in the 1780s each received a salary of £500 a year from the Civil List. They also shared a quarter of the Foreign Office share in the fees of the secretary of state's office.[102] There is no evidence of widespread jobbing by the undersecretaries in the Foreign Office, which probably reflects the short terms they served rather than any scrupulous philosophy on their part. William Fraser, the only one among them who served any length of time, was an exception to this pattern. As sole undersecretary from 1784 to 1789 he received the salary and emoluments of the vacant undersecretaryship. He also collected quite an impressive array of sinecures or near sinecures during his twenty-four years of service. On 23 July 1770, he was appointed Gazette Writer (£270) for life. He also held after 1773 the sinecure post of Translator of the German Language (£300) for life. By 1784, in addition to the revenue from these places, a salary of £1,000, and fees totalling £855, he received funds from gratuities (£199); from the Irish Concordatum Fund (£100); for his clerkship of the Signet (£218); as Patent Kings Waiter (£95); a pension (£145); and for secret and confidential service (£300). The Privy Seal was also in commission in 1784 and as one of the three joint commissioners Fraser was paid £318. His total revenues were £3,800; his taxes £95.[103]

Most of the undersecretaries were not as fortunate as Fraser. The usual amount of salary and emoluments appears to have been nearly £1,000.[104] In 1795, when the fees of the secretaries of state were pooled to make a fee fund for each of the departments of state, both undersecretaries received a salary of £1,500. Ministers decided at the same time that all but a third of the salary of a vacant undersecretaryship was to be a saving to the public,[105] though in practice this money was usually portioned amongst the clerks of the office.[106] Between 1795 and 1822 the base salary remained £1,500. In 1822

102. Nelson, The Home Office, p. 40. Occasionally the salary was considerably in arrears. Fraser to Keith, St. James's, 30 Sept. 1783, Add. MS 35530 f. 49.

103. Phyllis Margaret Handover, A History of the London Gazette, 1665–1965 (London, 1965), pp. 58, 62; Earl of Suffolk to Lord North, n.d., Calendar H.O. Paps., vol. 4, 867; "An Account of the Salaries, Fees, Gratuities, Perquisites, & Emoluments . . . for one Year ending 31st December, 1784. . . ," F.O. 95/591; Fraser to Keith, St. James's, 5 Mar. 1784, Add. MS 35531 f. 144.

104. Memorandum on F.O. Salaries, n.d. [ca. 1794], Grenville MSS.

105. Order in Council, "For Regulating the Proper Establishment of the Foreign Office," St. James's, 27 Feb. 1795, F.O. 366/542.

106. See below, chapter 6. Palmerston gave Backhouse half the salary of the vacant undersecretaryship in 1835. Minute, Palmerston, 11 Sept. 1835, on Minute, Backhouse, 10 Sept. 1835, F.O. 366/313.

Canning succeeded in raising it to £2,000, where it remained until 1830. Amidst the rigors of the retrenchments introduced by Grey's government, the salary of the junior undersecretaryship was reduced once again to £1,500.[107]

After 1799 the undersecretaries with three or more years service received an annual augmentation in salary of £500, less any revenue they received from other government sources.[108] This arrangement lasted until 1817, when a select committee of the House of Commons found the period of qualification too short. Thereafter seven years of service was required for an undersecretary to receive the additional £500. This provision, however, did not apply to any undersecretary appointed before 24 July 1817, and Planta, appointed 5 July 1817, received his augmentation in 1820.[109]

There were several other perquisites and gratuities enjoyed by the undersecretaries. From 1778 until 1832 they shared £100 from the Concordatum Fund or Civil List of Ireland *for the dispatch of business relating to Ireland.*[110] Until 1840 they retained franking privileges to all parts of the kingdom.[111] In the 1790s they divided a third of the profits of the *London Gazette*.[112] They shared in the chancery presents given to the establishment of the Foreign Office by foreign sovereigns on the ratification of treaties with other powers, though occasionally they received separate gifts. After 1831, when Palmerston abolished presents, Shee and Backhouse shared £750 a year in compensation.[113] The Post Office gave each undersecretary a New Year's gift of £2.12.6.[114] From 1826 the senior undersecretary received a secret service allowance of £500 for auditing and making disbursements from the secret service accounts.[115] Both men had the privilege of riding on horseback through the Royal Parks in the

107. Salary Books, F.O. 366/380–382. Compare these figures with the salary of the first secretary of the Admiralty, which was £3,200 "with one of the best houses in London. . . ." J. W. Croker to Lord Goderich, 11 Aug. 1827, Jennings, *Croker Corresp.*, vol. 1, 390.

108. Order in Council, 23 Jan. 1799, F.O. 366/542 ff. 18–19.

109. Order in Council, Carlton House, 24 July 1817, F.O. 366/542 ff. 39–40.

110. Minute, Backhouse to Chief Clerk, 16 Jan. 1832, with minutes, Sir Charles Flint, attached, and Treasury to Shee, 11 June 1832, F.O. 366/387.

111. Backhouse to [Rebecca Backhouse], London, 8 Jan. 1840, Backhouse Papers.

112. Ch[arles] Graves to ?, The King's Printing Office, 13 May 1797, F.O. 95/591.

113. Sir Charles Whitworth to Burges, St. Petersburgh, 12 May 1795, Extract, and Burges and Aust to Grenville, Downing Street, 23 July 1794, Grenville MSS; Minute, Backhouse, 23 July 1831, Secret, Palmerston Papers GC/BA/1/1–2.

114. Minute on Castlereagh to Lords of the Treasury, F.O., 3 July 1817, Copy, F.O. 366/672 f. 143; "New Years Gifts from Post Office," 1820–1836, F.O. 366/555.

115. Thomas Staveley to Backhouse, Foreign Office, 17 Nov. 1841, Secret & Confidential, Backhouse Papers.

Whitehall area.[116] They also received momentoes of special occasions. Frederick Byng, a senior clerk, wrote Lord Granville, the ambassador in Paris, at the coronation of Charles X of France, respecting the coronation medals: "it would not be amiss if you were to recollect the accustomed influence & the usual greediness of all underlings of every description & sort & more particularly those with whom Yr. Ex. may have to transact business. It would therefore be taken as a pleasing recollection of Yr. Ex's if you sent one to each of the Foreign Under Secretaries."[117]

Prior to 1817 there were no funds reserved for pensions of undersecretaries of state. Every undersecretary, however, received some consideration when he retired, except perhaps St. John and Sheridan, who served only for very short periods. Sometimes undersecretaries received other places under government. Grenville secured Edward Fisher a place "in the Revenue" in 1801.[118] George Aust worked at the Ordnance as Commissary General of the Musters and Secretary to Chelsea Hospital until 1818, "'having declined a Pension, as I was not worn out'" in 1796, when he retired.[119] George Walpole became Comptroller of Cash in the Excise Office in 1807 when Grenville's ministry resigned.[120]

It was a common practice for secretaries of state to provide for their undersecretaries in case a change of government should leave them without provision or place. Just before going out in 1801, Grenville secured pensions of £600 for both Hammond and Fisher.[121] Pitt promised Robert Ward a pension if he resigned his Welsh judgeship to serve as Mulgrave's undersecretary. Pitt died without fulfilling his promise, but Mulgrave redeemed it by securing a pension of £1,000 for Colonel Thomas Welsh in trust for Mrs. Ward. Since Ward served only a year, Fox and Grenville, who succeeded Mulgrave and Pitt, thought the grant highly improper, though apparently not illegal.[122] All of these pensions were reduced

116. Mount Charles to Field Officer in waiting, Foreign Office, 22 Jan. 1825, F.O. 83/41.

117. 4 Aug. 1825, P.R.O. 30/29/7/12 ff. 704–7.

118. Grenville to Mr. Chamberlayne, 31 Mar. 1801, Copy, Grenville MSS.

119. Aust to Liverpool, Parliament Street, 19 June 1818, Private, Add. MS 38272 ff. 163–64.

120. *Gents. Mag.* (1835), pt. 1, 547–48.

121. Order in Council, St. James's, 11 Feb. 1801, F.O. 366/542 f. 21.

122. Edmund Phipps (ed.), *Memoirs of the Political and Literary Life of Robert Plummer Ward* (2 vols.; London, 1850), vol. 1, 175–76; Order in Council, Queen's Palace, 1 Feb. 1806, F.O.

by the amount of the salary the undersecretary might later receive while employed by government.

The last instance of a secretary of state's providing for his undersecretary when he first appointed him occurred when Canning appointed Backhouse in 1827. Because Backhouse was so closely associated with him, Canning though it wise to secure provision for him outside the Foreign Office. He therefore appointed Backhouse Receiver General of the Excise, a position requiring "only occasional personal Attendance at the office at early hours," but with a salary of £1,500.[123] The remaining £500 of his salary as undersecretary of state was paid at the Foreign Office. This arrangement continued until Backhouse retired in 1842, though after October 1837 he received £1,000 from the Foreign Office.[124]

Difficult situations occasionally arose when a secretary of state wished to replace one undersecretary with another man. Between 1782 and 1846 there were five such instances. Four of these cases involved Grenville. Aust resigned in 1796 with little fuss, though he extracted from Pitt a reversionary pension for Mrs. Aust.[125] Burges, on the other hand, put up stiff resistance to his dismissal. As early as August 1794, Grenville had decided to replace him and even offered him the mission at Copenhagen or in Switzerland at that time. Mrs. Burges, however, was adamantly opposed to these arrangements and Burges declined both appointments as "contrary to my inclinations."[126] Grenville then told him that he would have to accept a privy councillorship and a pension of £1,000 or be turned out.[127] The crisis in Holland in October, however, delayed any final arrangements, as with the exception of Grenville Burges was the only person in the Foreign Office who could write French well.[128] It was over a year later when Burges resigned. By October 1795 Grenville

---

366/542 ff. 27–28; Fox to Grenville, Arlington Street, 27 Feb. 1806, *H. M. C. Fortescue*, vol. 8, 42.

123. Memorandum by Backhouse, Foreign Office, Nov. 1837, Backhouse Papers.

124. A. G. Spearman to Strangways, Treasury Chambers, 26 Feb. 1838, Copy in "Sequel of the Correspondence . . . for an augmentation of . . . Emoluments . . . ," Jan. & Feb. 1838, Backhouse Papers.

125. Canning to ?, 24 Dec. [1795], Aspinall, *Later Corresp. Geo. III*, vol. 2, 433–34.

126. Grenville to Burges, St. James's Square, 19 Aug. 1794, Hutton, *Burges*, pp. 262–63 note; Mrs. Burges to Burges, 21 Aug. 1794, ibid., pp. 263–65; Burges to Grenville, Downing Street, 21 Aug. 1794, ½ past 8 p.m., Grenville MSS.

127. Burges to Mrs. Burges, 23 Aug. 1794, quoted in Hutton, *Burges*, pp. 266–67.

128. Same to Same, 14 Oct. 1794, ibid., p. 271.

had found a replacement and Burges retired as Sir James, first Bart., with a pension and the sinecure office of Knight Marshal of the Royal Household with the remainder to his son.[129]

When an undersecretary was appointed through the influence of or by a secretary's colleague or friend, it was a common practice to consult his patron before dismissing him. Grenville appointed John Hookham Frere to replace Canning in 1799 largely on Canning's recommendation. Frere, however, proved to be impossibly dilatory.[130] Once Grenville decided to replace him he consulted Canning who broke the news to his friend before Grenville said anything to him.[131] Grenville let Frere down gently by appointing him minister to Portugal "as being in the full intimate confidence of Government, and able, on every occasion that may arise, to speak with perfect knowledge of our sentiments, and to impress the Portuguese Government with the persuasion that he does so speak."[132]

Fox replaced Hammond in 1806 only after consulting Grenville. Hammond already had a pension of £600 but was entitled to £600 more as a result of his service in the diplomatic corps. This sum was quickly granted, in the form of pensions of £150 for each of his four children.[133]

The other case of a secretary's replacing an undersecretary occurred in 1840, when Palmerston wished to put Leveson in Strangways's place. Strangways's brother-in-law, Lord Lansdowne, was in the cabinet with Palmerston. His protests and those of other ministers, however, failed to change Palmerston's decision and Strangways was forced to accept the Frankfort mission which at first he had declined.[134]

129. Aspinall, *Later Corresp. Geo. III*, vol. 2, 412–13, n. 1, says his total income from these sources was about £1,600.

130. So dilatory, in fact, that Frere "was a by-word amongst his acquaintance[s] for never doing to-day what could possibly be deferred until to-morrow. . . ." Festing, *Frere*, p. 15; George Rose to the Bishop of Lincoln, 30 July [1800], Aspinall, *Later Corresp. Geo. III*, vol. 3, 362 n. 3.

131. Canning to Grenville, Hollwood, 14 July 1800, Private, *H. M. C. Fortescue*, vol. 6, 268–69.

132. Grenville to Frere, Cleveland Row, 13 Aug. 1800, Copy, ibid., vol. 2, 293–94.

133. Fox to Grenville, Arlington Street, 6 Feb. 1806, ibid., vol. 8, 16; Grenville to George III, Camelford House, 20 Feb. 1806, Copy, ibid., 39; Draft Memorandum, G. Hammond, in W. A. Hammond to Chancellor of the Exchequer, Whitechurch, Reading, 1 Dec. 1837, Private, Copy, Barnes MSS.

134. Lord Lansdowne to Lord John Russell, n.d., in Melbourne to Palmerston, Downing Street, 17 Feb. 1840, Palmerston Papers GC/ME/354/1–2; Russell to Melbourne, 16 Feb. 1840, ibid., GC/ME/352/2; Greville, as usual, has the whole tale. Saturday, 21 Feb. 1840, Strachey & Fulford, *Greville Memoirs*, vol. 4, 247–48.

After 1817 pensions of undersecretaries were regulated by Acts of
Parliament. The first of these acts, passed in July, 1817, provided for
six pensions of £1,000 each for those undersecretaries of state with
ten years or more service. Second secretaries of the Admiralty and
Clerks of the Ordinaries were also covered by the Act, and after
1825, secretaries to the India Board.[135] Unless one of these six
pensions was vacant there was no provision that could be made for
the retirement of an undersecretary since the general Superannuation Act of 1822 specifically excluded them from its provisions.[136]

Of the undersecretaries who served between 1817 and 1846, only
Hamilton, Planta, and Backhouse served long enough to qualify for
a pension. Planta and Hamilton had no difficulty securing theirs,
though Hamilton had to wait six months before one was available.[137]
Backhouse, who was ill and wished to retire in July 1841, had some
difficulty because he also wished to retain his place at the Excise. The
Treasury objected to this arrangement[138] and since Backhouse
could not afford to retire on his pension alone, Aberdeen decided to
"struggle on as we are, [rather] than to propose to him to retire
without any provision."[139] Eventually, Henry Goulburn, the chancellor of the Exchequer, secured Backhouse £500 on the superannuation list of the Board of Excise and he retired in April 1842.[140]

The practice of giving undersecretaries of state honors either
during or after their service, which has apparently become standard
procedure in the twentieth century, was an innovation of the last half
of the nineteenth century. Addington was the first undersecretary to
be made a Privy Councillor on retirement. His successor, Edmund
Hammond, was made a P.C. in 1866, and created Baron Hammond
when he retired in 1874.[141]

The undersecretaryship of state was an ideal position for those
men who wished to become involved in government without too
much responsibility. It was also a flexible enough institution so that

135. 57 Geo. III, c. 65, 7 July 1817; 6 Geo. IV, c. 90, 5 July 1825.
136. 3 Geo. IV, c. 113, 5 Aug. 1822.
137. George Harrison to Planta, Treasury Chambers, Sat. Morning, 31 Jan. 1823,
Confidential, F.O. 83/10; Canning to George IV, Downing Street, 12 July 1827, Aspinall,
Letters of George IV, vol. 3, 267–68.
138. Minute, F[rancis] B[aring], 27 Aug. 1841, Copy, Add. MS 43061 ff. 360–61.
139. Aberdeen to Peel, F.O., 23 Dec. 1841, Add. MS 40453 ff. 67–68.
140. Goulburn to Addington, Downing Street, 21 May 1842, Private, Copy, Backhouse
Papers.
141. Boase, *Modern English Biography*, vol. 1, 21; Henry E. Chetwynd-Stapleton, "Two
Undersecretaries," p. 4, in Barnes MSS.

those few men who were capable and energetic and who served awhile in the office could mold it to suit their interests and abilities. It was not, however, a perch from which the most energetic and capable leaders of the country could be assured of advancement into the policy-making levels of government. Some of the undersecretaries, of course, eventually were important men. But their importance arose solely from their connections or their parliamentary skill. Nor was an undersecretary assured of a high diplomatic position. Though several served abroad after leaving the Foreign Office, only Charles Bagot can be said to have been a first-rate diplomatist. More often than not the undersecretaryship was an interlude (sometimes pleasant, sometimes rushed, always interesting) in mediocre careers. William Lamb, later Lord Melbourne, described the position perfectly when he wrote, "it is one of the pleasantest places under government."[142]

142. To J. W. Ward, Panshangar, 28 Sept. 1822, Dudley, *Letters to Llandaff*, pp. 262–63.

CHAPTER VI

THE FOREIGN OFFICE
ESTABLISHMENT: 1782–1821

Though it does not deal with perhaps so complex a subject as the origins of political parties or of the cabinet, historical writing on the origins of the modern civil service has not been without controversy.[1] Since the pioneer study of Emmeline Cohen,[2] however, there has been general agreement that the critical years were those after 1782 and before the Northcote-Trevelyan Report of 1854. More recent scholarship[3] agrees with this general interpretation but takes issue with the causes of bureaucratic modernization.

English bureaucracy in the eighteenth century was particularized into a "departmental service" in which rules and regulations affecting government offices and the personnel in them were drafted and directed by the various department heads with little or no attempt at interdepartmental coordination.[4] Cohen held the view that in the years after 1780 the financial problems of the government led to the investigation of departmental activities which in due course overturned many of the abuses of the unreformed service. Departmental reorganization was stimulated by the findings of "an important series of Commissions of Inquiry into the administration of public business,"[5] and resulted in increasingly greater efficiency in the bureaucracy. This efficiency was promoted by the abolition of sinecures and by "doing away with many ancient formalities which had

1. See for example G. E. Aylmer, "Place Bills and the Separation of Powers: Some Seventeenth Century Origins of the 'Non-Political' Civil Service," *Transactions of the Royal Historical Society*, 5th ser., 15 (1965), 45–69.
2. *The Growth of the British Civil Service, 1780–1939* (London, 1941).
3. Henry Parris, "The Origins of the Permanent Civil Service, 1780–1839," *Public Administration*, 46 (Summer, 1968), 143–66; Parris, *Constitutional Bureaucracy*.
4. Parris, *Constitutional Bureaucracy*, pp. 21–28.
5. Cohen, *The Civil Service*, p. 20.

outlived their purpose and hampered the prompt execution of public business."[6] Cohen was aware of the politics involved in these changes, but political considerations were seen as being of secondary importance to economic and financial ones.[7]

Parris, on the other hand, argued that political considerations were at the root of administrative reform. What was involved was "the separation of the administrative sphere from the political sphere. . . . Two factors were at work: the drive to reduce 'the influence of the Crown' and the growing demands of political life itself, which made it increasingly difficult for men to combine political with administrative roles."[8] Financial changes which occurred were the means of reforming administrative practice and of making it more systematic. But it was the political forces in the state not the financial crisis of the late eighteenth century which stimulated the reform.

Both Parris and Cohen agreed that the Foreign Office was not among the innovating departments, though the roles of individual foreign secretaries, notably Palmerston, were important in the process of modernization.[9] But how wedded to tradition was the Foreign Office? Did it, in fact, stand out as the exception to the growth of constitutional bureaucracy in the years after 1782? Was its history, as has been claimed, a "study in resistance"?[10] Certainly in the late nineteenth century it was one of the departments least affected by the reforms wrought in the civil service by Parliament and the bureaucratic reformers between the 1850s and the 1870s.[11] In 1898 "the forces of inertia and the sensibilities of its members continued to exercise great influence. From the angle of vision of

6. Ibid., p. 21.

7. Ibid., pp. 22–71.

8. Parris, *Constitutional Bureaucracy*, p. 33.

9. Ibid., pp. 107–10; Cohen, *The Civil Service*, p. 23, which is the only reference to the F.O.

10. Valerie Cromwell and Zara Steiner, "The Foreign Office before 1914: A study in resistance," in *Studies in the Growth of Nineteenth-Century Government*, ed. Gillian Sutherland (Totowa, N.J., 1972), pp. 167–94.

11. Ibid., passim. It is now possible to study the process of reform in one of the major departments, the Colonial Office, which is the only department till now that has been exhaustively studied for the nineteenth century. D. M. Young, *The Colonial Office in the Early Nineteenth Century* ("Imperial Studies," No. 22; London, 1961); John W. Cell, *British Colonial Administration in the Mid-Nineteenth Century: The Policy-Making Process* (New Haven, 1970); Brian L. Blakeley, *The Colonial Office 1868–1892* ("Duke Historical Publications"; Durham, N.C., 1972); Robert V. Kubicek, *The Administration of Imperialism: Joseph Chamberlain at the Colonial Office* ("Duke University Commonwealth Studies Center," No. 37; Durham, N.C., 1969).

Whitehall, Salisbury was in every sense Palmerston's successor."[12]

But was Palmerston Fox's? A satisfactory answer to this question requires a precise definition of the modern civil service. The term "civil service" implies fulltime salaried officers, systematic recruitment, the existence of clear lines of authority, "uniform rules on such questions as superannuation," and some degree of interdepartmental exchange of personnel.[13] None of these practices existed in the eighteenth century; all of them were adopted in the Foreign Office between 1782 and 1841. There can be no doubt that in the broader sense the Foreign Office shared in the benefits of the emergence of a constitutional bureaucracy and that Palmerston was not master of the same sort of institution that Fox had directed.[14]

Nevertheless, despite this conformity to the generalizations of Cohen and Parris, the changes that took place were to some degree unique. The political forces in the state had only a marginal impact on the Foreign Office, and then only indirectly through the pressures of other departments to force the office to conform to what were becoming standard procedures in the bureaucracy.[15] The best example of this process occurred in 1822 when the Treasury succeeded in securing the incorporation of the personnel in the Foreign Office under the provisions of the Superannuation Act. Financial considerations also played a minor role in modernization. Yet on balance the Foreign Office remained relatively impervious to these changes. Successful resistance to these pressures reflected the fact that in many respects the department was in a unique position. The responsibility for directing foreign affairs was only gradually being yielded by the crown, and what the monarch lay down the ministers, not the community through its elected representatives in Parliament, took up. Formulation of foreign policy was an executive, not a legislative responsibility, and the relative independence of the ministers in determining policy served to give the Foreign Office a degree of immunity from the reform movement in the bureaucracy. There were significant changes in the department after 1782 and especially

12. Steiner, *The Foreign Office*, p. 10.

13. Parris, *Constitutional Bureaucracy*, pp. 22–23.

14. Charles R. Middleton, "The Emergence of Constitutional Bureaucracy in the British Foreign Office, 1782–1841," *Public Administration*, 54 (Winter, 1975), 365–81.

15. The most important departmental studies for this period are Roseveare, *The Treasury*, pp. 118–26, 152–68; Nelson, *The Home Office*, pp. 26–64; Young, *The Colonial Office*, pp. 1–146; Roger Prouty, *The Transformation of the Board of Trade 1830–1855* (London, 1957), pp. 99–111.

after 1822. But the reforms instituted at the Foreign Office were almost always the direct result of pressures within the department and only marginally related to external events.

When Charles James Fox received the seals for the Department of State for Foreign Affairs on 27 March 1782, he inherited from Viscount Stormont, the last of the secretaries in the old Northern Department, a staff which had not changed appreciably in size or organization for a quarter of a century.[16] In addition to the executive officers of the department—the principal secretary and two undersecretaries of state—there were eight clerks in the Foreign Office in 1782.[17] Fox's successors during the following forty years gradually increased the size and differentiated the organization of the office. But throughout the period the department remained an uncomplicated, compact organization easily controlled by the secretary of state.[18]

In 1782 there were three classes of clerks: a chief, or first clerk; senior clerks; and junior clerks. There had been a chief clerk in the secretary's office since 1723,[19] and invariably (with one exception between 1782 and 1846), the situation was filled by the clerk who possessed the most seniority at the time it fell vacant. Jeremy Sneyd, the chief clerk in 1782, had been employed in the office since his appointment under the influence of the Duke of Bedford in December 1750.[20] His position was one of immense prestige without corresponding responsibility, for by 1782 the duties of the chief clerk were becoming divorced from the political work of the office. Although everyone in the department worked in preparing the dispatches, especially in periods of great urgency when Sneyd's duties included supervising the work of the other clerks, his principal responsibility was not administrative. As the financial officer he

16. See Thomson, *Secretaries of State*, esp. pp. 128–29 for the best general account of the organization of the departments of state prior to 1782.

17. *The Royal Kalendar* (London, 1782), p. 110. The most complete listing of the staff of the office from 1782 to 1795 is to be found in the *R.K.*

18. Compare the smallness of the British department with the large size of the French, which in the 1780s numbered 70 men or more. Alfred Cobban, *Ambassadors and Secret Agents: The Diplomacy of the First Earl of Malmesbury at the Hague* (London, 1954), p. 17. The complexity of the French Foreign Office also is an interesting contrast to the simple organization of the British department. "Organization of the French Ministry for foreign Affairs, received May 21, 1810," F.O. 27/80.

19. Thomson, *Secretaries of State*, pp. 128–29.

20. Aldworth to Postmaster General, Whitehall, 4 Dec. 1750, Copy, S.P. 44/136 f. 113; Thomson, *Secretaries of State*, Appendix XI, p. 179.

kept the accounts, paid the bills,[21] and was responsible for collecting the fees charged by the principal and undersecretaries for signing warrants, securing commissions for diplomatists and consular officers, and for other services. He was also employed in preparing commissions and other documents on the appointment of officials to the foreign and consular services.[22]

The duties of the chief clerk were not completely divorced from the political business of the office until after Sneyd retired in 1792 and was succeeded by Thomas Bidwell, Sr. In 1795 Lord Grenville, the foreign secretary, and the other secretaries of state proposed that the fees of their offices be pooled, with a third of the revenue alloted to each department to pay the respective establishments. The recommendation reflected the need to insure a more equitable distribution of the fees collected by the secretaries of state after the creation of the third secretaryship in 1794.[23] The plan, implemented by order in council on 27 February 1795, established a fee fund in each office, superintended by the chief clerk, who received the revenues from the fees and paid the salaries of the office personnel. Detailed accounts were kept by the chief clerk, and were attested at the end of each fiscal year before a baron of the Exchequer.[24] Bidwell was also given the responsibility of paying the messengers employed by the Foreign Office, a task which previously had been handled by the Lord Chamberlain's Department, but which in 1795 fell onto the secretaries' shoulders when the superintendence of the messenger's corps was transferred to the offices of state.[25] The chief clerk under the system thus established collected

21. Carmarthen to the Lords of the Treasury, St. James's, 5 Aug. 1784, Copy, F.O. 366/425 f. 255.

22. Jeremy Sneyd to Anthony Merry, Whitehall, 31 July 1787, Extract, F.O. 72/155 ff. 254–55.

23. The lion's share of fees was always collected in the Home Office. In 1800, for example, fees collected totaled H.O. £6,130.9.8; F.O. £427.5.2.; W.O. £378.0.9. "Statement of Fees received in the Three Secretaries of State's Offices to 10 October, 1800," F.O. 366/387.

24. Duke of Portland, Grenville, and Henry Dundas to the Lord President of the Council, Whitehall, 23 Feb. 1795, Copy, F.O. 366/542; Order in Council, St. James's, 27 Feb. 1795, "For Regulating the Proper Establishment of the Foreign Office," ibid. No security was required until an act of Parliament in 1810, when all those holding positions entrusted with public money were given one month in which to post bond "for the due Performance of the Trust reposed in" them. 15 June 1810, 50 Geo. III, c. 85. Thomas Bidwell, Jr., who became chief clerk in 1824, was not required to put up security because he had been employed for over twenty years. "Return of all Persons in the Foreign Department who hold Public Money in their Hands. . . ," F.O., 30 Apr. 1829 [1830?], F.O., 366/366 ff. 134–35.

25. Grenville to the Lords of the Treasury, Downing Street, 1 May 1795, Copy, F.O. 366/427 f. 138.

the fees and deposited them in a personal account from which he made the disbursements of the department. This practice appears to have worked well, for when Bidwell died suddenly in September 1817, his successor, Stephen Rolleston, had no difficulty in obtaining the balances that Bidwell's executors possessed.[26] Payments for stationery, coal, and other incidental expenses were made out of a contingent fund, supplied to the chief clerk out of monies received from the Treasury on the request of the secretary of state.[27] An unforeseen result of the reform, however, was that these duties, which required a considerable amount of bookkeeping, effectively excluded the most experienced clerk on the establishment from participating in the political work of the department.

For a time, from 1804 to 1817, there were two chief clerks. Bidwell retained his duties as financial officer while his colleague, Stephen Rolleston, was concerned more with the political work of the office. The two men must have made quite a pair. Bidwell, an aloof man, treated his subordinates with disdain, and preferred to pass his days superintending his accounts,[28] which he kept with utmost efficiency. Rolleston, on the other hand, was an amiable, kind, and conciliatory gentleman, and a friend of those who worked with him.[29] He owed his advancement to hard work and his assumption of additional authority as an assistant to the undersecretaries. His duties as chief clerk were not different from those he performed as first senior clerk, but the title (and eventually a raise in salary to Bidwell's level) was given to him as a reward for his efficiency.[30]

The chief clerk was the only clerk in the department who received no salary prior to 1795. Instead he received a percentage of the fees collected from diplomatists and others who secured from the sec-

26. Sir John Anthony Cecil Tilley and Sir Stephen Gaselee, *The Foreign Office* (2d ed.; London, 1933), p. 67; Minute by Castlereagh, F.O., 28 Oct. 1817, Copy, F.O. 366/672 f. 147.

27. Grenville to the Lords of the Treasury, Downing Street, 24 Feb. 1795, Copy, F.O. 366/427 f. 126.

28. V. Wheeler-Holohan, *History of the King's Messengers* (London, 1935), pp. 40–45; J. W. Hay to Lord Harrowby, Downing Street, Monday, 23 July 1804, Harrowby MSS vol. 11 ff. 15–16.

29. *Gents. Mag* (1828), pt. 2, 476; S. Rolleston to the Duke of Leeds, Downing Street, 8 Nov. 1794, Add. MS 38067 f. 132.

30. Lord Hawkesbury to the Lord President of the Council, Downing Street, 13 June 1801, Copy, F.O. 366/671 f. 184; Establishment of the Secretary of State's Office for Foreign Affairs [1804], Harrowby MSS vol. 33 f. 259; Order in Council, St. James's, 19 Feb. 1806, F.O. 366/671 ff. 289–300. Rolleston's raise was from £650 to £1,250. Minute, T. Bidwell, Downing Street, 10 Feb. 1807, Copy, F.O. 366/428.

retaries of state warrants, commissions, or other documents. Sneyd averaged £566 per annum in fees and gratuities for the four year period from 1785 through 1788.[31] This income was supplemented by payments received from the Post Office, the East India Company, franking newspapers to Ireland, and miscellaneous other sources[32] so that his average income was between £1,000 and £1,100. In 1795 Bidwell was given a salary of £1,000 which remained the base pay of the chief clerk until after 1846.[33] The share of the fees granted to the chief clerk was thereafter paid into the fee fund, save those fees he collected for passing appointments of diplomatists through the Privy Seal Office. He continued to receive them "during good behavior" until 1834.[34]

The duties of the senior and junior class clerks were confined to preparing the political and interdepartmental correspondence of the office.[35] For the majority the day consisted of nothing but copying dispatches, entering in the registers a record of this correspondence, and making fair drafts and copies of all important papers. The first senior clerk, under the direction of the undersecretaries, was responsible for distributing the business of the office. He also prepared the drafts of circulars to consuls, ambassadors, and ministers. Rolleston, who became a senior clerk in 1794, continued to exercise these duties after he became second chief clerk. Secretaries regarded it a "breach of official duty" for a clerk, whatever his rank, to refuse to carry out any assignment Rolleston gave him. Rolleston's discretion in distributing tasks, however, was limited by the guidelines established by the secretary of state. Three senior clerks and the first junior clerk were responsible for ciphering and deciphering dispatches. The two with the longest service were employed exclusively in periods of great activity putting dispatches

31. "An Account of the Monies Paid to the Secretary of State, Under Secretaries, and the Chief Clerk in the Office for Foreign Affairs on Account of Fees and Gratuities in the Years 1785, 6, 7, & 8," Grenville MSS.
32. "An Account of the Salaries, Fees, Gratuities, Perquisites & Emoluments . . . for one year ending 31 December, 1784. . . ," F.O. 95/591.
33. Establishment of the Secretary of State's Office for Foreign Affairs, Apr. 1795, F.O. 366/380.
34. "First Report of the Committee appointed by the Treasury to inquire into the Fees and Emoluments of Public Offices, 23 March, 1837", *P.P., 1837*, vol. 44, Command 162, p. 166.
35. The details of the duties of the office personnel are taken from "Arrangement of Business in the Foreign Department," signed Grenville, 1 Apr. 1799, Grenville MSS, and "Arrangement of Business in the Foreign Department, 19 Feb. 1806," F.O. 366/671 ff. 292–96.

into cipher. The junior clerks maintained the registers "in a fair and correct manner," and prepared extracts of all correspondence. Everyone, from Rolleston to the most junior clerk, was expected to work at the general duty of the office preparing for signature dispatches and letters of reference to other government departments.

By twentieth-century standards the work of the clerks was not onerous. The hours of attendance were short: eleven to four daily and on foreign post nights (usually twice a week) from eight until the business was completed. Other evenings the two junior clerks with the least seniority of those not absent on leave were "to attend in constant rotation one each night."[36] Many clerks probably regarded these hours as the maximum amount of time they would have to put in at the office. Sir Herbert Taylor, who had begun his career in the Foreign Office, recalled many idle hours and infrequent evening attendance.[37]

After 1782 there was an appreciable increase in the business of the office. The old Northern Department had rarely had as much to do as the Southern Department,[38] and when the whole of the foreign correspondence was thrown onto the shoulders of the establishment they reacted with predictable discomfort. "The hurry in which I continually live," wrote William Fraser, the undersecretary, "is not to be disscribed [sic], & the Confinement of the Office far exceeds what I have ever known. I live in Hopes of better Times." The clerks complained to the Marquess of Carmarthen, the secretary of state, that the volume of their work had doubled.[39] Absenteeism apparently became a serious problem, for in the 1790s George Canning, one of the undersecretaries, began to invite the clerks to dinner on evenings they had to work late. Lord Grenville required all the junior clerks to sign in and out at precise times, and he, as well as his successors, required them to secure the permission of the undersecretary before they left the office in the afternoon.[40] The king, too,

36. Minute, Burges, Whitehall, 28 Sept. 1789, F.O. 366/669, vol 2, 250.
37. Taylor, *Taylor Papers*, pp. 17–18.
38. Sir George Cornewall Lewis, Bart., *Essays on the Administrations of Great Britain from 1783 to 1830*, ed. Sir Edmund Head, Bart. (London, 1864), p. 31.
39. Fraser to Keith, St. James's, 13 May 1783, Add. MS 35528 f. 246; Aust, Bidwell et al. to the Marquess of Carmarthen, 16 Nov. 1787, Add. MS 28062 ff. 444–45.
40. Canning to Lord Granville Leveson-Gower, Charles Street, 16 Aug. 1796, P.R.O. 30/29/8/1 ff. 45–56; "Arrangement of Business in the Foreign Department," signed Grenville, 1 Apr. 1799, Grenville MSS; George Jackson to his mother, 23 July 1805, Jackson, *Letters of George Jackson*, vol. 1, 307.

complained that the public offices, including the Foreign Office, "instead of being in full vigour by nine in the morning . . . seldom are attended even by the clerks untill [sic] noon."[41]

The clerks generally worked hard when there was business to be transacted. Prior to 1795 they were not well paid for their labor. Fraser, replying to a complaint of William Eden, the minister in France, about the expenses of his post, grudgingly admitted that it was "a melancholy Consideration that in every Branch of this Department the Reward is not proportioned to the Labour."[42] Probably one explanation of the low salaries is that the secretaries of state were reluctant to grant too large a proportion of their fees to the clerks. A secretary's desire to retain as much of this revenue for his own use and the fact that supplementary income was available to the clerks did not encourage successive heads of the department to revise the salary scale. As a result, the two senior clerks in the office in 1785, Bryan Broughton and George Aust, were paid a mere £165 per annum while their juniors received sums ranging from £60 to £100. Even with supplementary gratuities from the Post Office as compensation for their loss of franking privileges, Aust and Broughton received only £380 while Francis Moore, the junior clerk on the establishment, had a meager £80.[43] It is scarcely surprising that Herbert Taylor's father continued his son's allowance of £150 a year when he was first employed in the Foreign Office.[44] Doubtless other fathers did the same if they were able.

The clerks under these circumstances naturally sought and relied on supplementary sources of income. Some supplementary revenue came from the office itself. The largest single source in this category was the Post Office grants paid under the authority of acts of Parliament. Prior to 1765 every clerk in the offices of the secretaries of state had enjoyed the privilege of franking letters and newspapers to all parts of the kingdom. When the right to frank letters was withdrawn in 1765, the clerks succeeded, after a great deal of effort, in securing compensation of £500 per annum for each department.

41. George III to Harrowby, Windsor, 27 May 1804, Queen's Lodge, Windsor Castle, Great Britain, Historical Manuscripts Commission, *Report on . . . the Manuscripts of Sir Archibald Edmonstone of Duntreath, Baronet* ("HMC Various Collections," vol. 5; London, 1909), pp. 180–81.
42. Fraser to Eden, Whitehall, 9 Apr. 1787, Add. MS 34424 f. 295.
43. Establishment from Michaelmas 1785, signed Carmarthen, St. James's, 21 Oct. 1785, F.O. 366/699, vol. 2, 132.
44. Taylor, *Taylor Papers*, p. 17.

The Southern and Northern Departments after 1782 shared the £500 granted to the Colonial Office, which was abolished in that year. An additional parliamentary grant of 1784 compensated the clerks for the loss of the privilege of franking letters and packets to Ireland and supplemented these revenues. Each clerk received funds from at least one of these grants.[45]

A second way in which the department contributed to the income of the clerks was in additional payments for special services. Not every clerk received money in this manner, and those who did were paid various amounts according to the duties they performed. James Manby, for example, received in 1784 £1 per diem for his services as secretary to the commissioner for settling a commercial treaty with Spain.[46] George Aust, on the other hand, prior to 1789 received £150 every four years for preparing ciphers for the diplomatic corps. In 1789 this occasional allowance was made a permanent charge on the secret service account "in Consideration of other extraordinary Services, for which no Recompence has hitherto been made him, such as Translation, arranging State Papers etc. etc."[47]

Many clerks, in order to supplement their official earnings, held places that were completely unassociated with their departmental duties. Some, in fact, did not always pay due regard to where their first obligation lay. George Aust, who failed to secure a place as a Commissioner of Bankruptcy in 1783, told the Earl of Hardwicke, through whose influence he sought the appointment, that he had "now sufficient Leisure to attend to the Duties of the Employment, without neglecting the office to the degree some of his more fortunate Fellow-Clerks do, to whom *every* Employment seems compatible with it."[48] The worst offender was the first senior clerk, Bryan Broughton. In addition to a salary and revenues from the Post Office grants totalling £410, he received a pension of £97, was a clerk in the Treasury (£500), agent for Grenada (£172.12), joint receiver

45. Thomson, *Secretaries of State*, pp. 138–39; 3 Geo. III, c. 35; Carmarthen, to the Postmaster General, St. James's, 25 Mar. 1784, Copy F.O. 366/669, vol. 2, 77–78; "Distribution of £250 per Annum additional Post Office allowance from 25 March 1782 and of £500 per Annum from the same Revenue from 5 July 1784." ibid., 131.

46. "An Account of the Salaries, Fees, Gratuities, Perquisites & Emoluments . . . for one Year ending 31st December 1784. . . ," F.O. 95/591.

47. Memorandum, Aust, 5 Aug. 1789, Grenville MSS.

48. Aust to Hardwicke, 15 July 1783, Add. MS 35620 ff. 285–86.

general of the house duty for London and Middlesex (£240), and registrar of seizures (£250).[49]

Broughton's case was a peculiar one since he apparently regarded his clerkship as a sinecure. His fellow clerks succeeded in having his salary diminished in 1776, but his rank in the office was not affected[50] until 1785 when Carmarthen refused to consider his claims to any future vacancy and ordered that every clerk on constant duty would have precedence over him. Before Carmarthen finally required his resignation in 1788, however, Broughton had even had his share of the Post Office grants given to the other clerks. Yet he succeeded in securing a clerkship for his brother so that his removal should not "under these Circumstances [carry] with it a degree of Severity & Disgrace, which, as I am conscious of not deserving it, I am sure Your Lordship does not mean to inflict."[51] This system of paying personnel, in addition to leading to a wide variety of abuses, did nothing to encourage efficiency and permanency within the department. Parliamentary commissions established to enquire into public offices in the 1780s were aware of these conditions. They recommended in their first report that the fees of government offices be funded to pay salaries of the personnel, that a graduated salary scale be established for each office, and that all salaries be paid net and quarterly.[52] It was not until 1795, however, that these recommendations were implemented in the Foreign Office. The reason for doing so then was to insure permanency and trust in those who held clerkships. Salaries of clerks were upgraded and placed on a graduated scale of from £80 for the ninth junior clerk (a position that previously was an unpaid one) to £650 for the first senior clerk. Clerks were allowed to retain places outside the de-

49. "An Account of the Salaries, Fees, Gratuities, Perquisites & Emoluments . . . for one Year ending 31st December 1784. . . ," F.O. 95/591.

50. William Eden to Bryan Broughton, St. James's, 7 Oct. 1776, Copy, F.O. 366/669, vol. 1, 13–14.

51. Memorandum, Carmarthen, St. James's, 13 Dec. 1785, F.O. 366/669, vol. 1, 66; Memorandum, Carmarthen, "Revival of former Regulations respecting Mr. Broughton," Whitehall, 1 May 1787, ibid., 69–70; Broughton to Carmarthen, Rome, 19 Jan. 1788, Add. MS 28063 ff. 31–32.

52. Cohen, *Civil Service*, pp. 36–41; "First Report of the Commissioners appointed . . . to enquire into the Fees, Gratuities, Perquisites, and Emoluments, which are or have been lately received in the General Public Offices . . . ," 11 Apr. 1786, *P.P., 1806*, vol. 7, Command 309 pp. 3ff.

partment that did "not interfere with their official attendance," so that "a means might be afforded to them of acquiring some provision for their families."[53]

The salaries paid by the Foreign Office after 1795 were designed to remunerate clerks for handling the general business of the department. That they were not yet adequate is demonstrated by the fact that some clerks still lived in the office to make ends meet.[54] Extra responsibility, however, continued to earn clerks additional income, and as business increased, extraordinary payments became more frequent. Bidwell after 1801 received £150 a year for checking messengers' accounts; in 1813 the number of papers prepared for Parliament was so great that Castlereagh awarded the chief clerks £50 and everyone else £25; Henry Rolleston, a senior clerk, was granted an annuity of £150 for preparing treaties and diplomatic commissions for signature, and received a further £100 in July 1815 for the extraordinary amount of work that he performed during and after the Congress of Vienna.[55] One curious practice was the payment of the salary of a vacant undersecretaryship or secretaryship to the clerks. Thus, when there was only one undersecretary from 11 November to 13 December 1809, one-third of the salary of the post went to the second undersecretary, William Hamilton, and the four most junior clerks shared the other two-thirds. In a similar situation after Lord Wellesley's resignation in 1812 there were nine days before Castlereagh received the seals. The seven clerks with the greatest seniority (excluding Bidwell Sr. and Rolleston Sr.) shared the secretary's salary for that period.[56]

New sources of income for all the clerks also appeared after 1795. When the clerks in the Home Office received in 1798 £5 in lieu of each *Gazette* they had previously received gratis, the clerks in the Foreign Office petitioned for a similar provision and each man received slightly more than £75 per annum under the new ar-

53. Portland, Grenville, and Dundas to the Lord President of the Council, Whitehall, 23 Feb. 1795, Copy, F.O. 366/542; Establishment of the Secretary of State's Office for Foreign Affairs, Apr. 1795, F.O. 366/380.

54. Charles Warren to Canning, F.O., 9 Dec. 1807, F.O. 83/14. See Hertslet, *Recollections*, pp. 23–24, for amusing tales of the resident clerks and the "Nursery."

55. Unsigned minute, S. Rolleston, 1801, F.O. 366/313; Memorandum, Castlereagh to T. Bidwell, Sr., F.O., 31 Mar. 1813, F.O. 366/672 f. 54; Castlereagh to Lords of the Treasury, F.O., 10 Oct. 1813, Copy, ibid., ff. 68–69.

56. Memorandum, Wellesley to T. Bidwell, Sr., F.O., 13 Jan. 1810, ibid., f. 1; Memorandum, Castlereagh to T. Bidwell, Sr., F.O., 29 Apr. 1812, ibid., f. 42.

rangement. Lord Hawkesbury in 1801 granted compensation to the clerks in lieu of the printed parliamentary votes that clerks had previously received. Payments from this fund varied according to the rank of the clerk,[57] and were justified on the grounds that government was saved the cost of printing the *Gazettes* and the votes.

The base pay of the clerks remained the same from 1795 to the reforms of 1822. Long before that time, however, it was inadequate to meet the rising cost of living that resulted from the wars with France. The clerks "continually renewed" without success their petition for relief, though Viscount Howick was favorably inclined to their claims before he went out of office in 1807.[58] Their grievances, repeated to George Canning in 1808, were not centered on the basic salaries but on the fact that augmentation of income through promotion to a more lucrative clerkship was so insignificant that by the time a man received a promotion the increase in salary was inadequate for him to maintain his proper station in society. In addition "to these Circumstances are added the Nature and Length of Our Services, the Advancement which has taken place in almost every other Public Office, . . . the Hopes so long and so repeatedly held out to us of a similar Indulgence, and above all, the Report given in by the Committee of the House of Commons, which clearly admits the Principle, that Remuneration to Public Officers should be proportioned to their length of Service. . . ."[59] Grenville, moreover, had introduced the principle of augmentation for length of service into the office in 1801 when he secured for Bidwell, the chief clerk, an extra £250 per annum for having served five years as chief clerk and as a just reward for "long labourious Service in the inferior branches of the Office. . . ."[60]

Canning, who always took a particular interest in the problems and welfare of the establishment, had little trouble securing the

57. Clerks in the Office to George Hammond, Downing Street, 21 July 1798, F.O. 366/671 f. 67; Memorandum, Hammond to T. Bidwell, Sr., Downing Street, 23 July 1798, ibid., f. 68; Allowances for "Votes," 1801 to 1806, F.O. 366/387.

58. Copy of memorandum sent to the House of Commons with the account of the establishment, 12 Mar. 1807, F.O. 366/671 f. 316.

59. C. R. Broughton, T. Bidwell, Jr., et al. to George Canning, Foreign Office, 6 Dec. 1808, Canning MSS Bundle 58a.

60. Portland, Grenville, and Dundas to the Lord President, Downing Street, 17 Feb. 1801, Copy, F.O. 366/671 ff. 163–64. In 1814 the chief clerk received another augmentation of £250 for twenty years service in the department. "Draft of proposed letter to the Lord President of the Council," July 1814, F.O. 366/542 ff. 35–36.

augmentation solicited. The principle of giving "special Augmentation to several of the Clerks, in proportion to the length of their respective Services" was introduced in the Foreign Office in April 1809. All but the chief clerk benefitted from the measure. Clerks with five years service received a salary increment of £80 a year; those with ten years an extra £200; those with fifteen and twenty years, £300 and £400 respectively.[61] Canning abolished at the same time some of the more questionable extraordinary payments. Thomas Bidwell, Jr., for example, had to relinquish "an allowance of £100 for summoning the Peers—which of course is a perfect sinecure—the remnant of Lord Grenville's and Lord Hawkesbury's time, but quite unjustifiable and unaccountable at present. I certainly intended to abolish this article when I gave the augmentation allowance. . . .If it be Bidwell, he gets £300 addition and may well give up £200 [sic]. If he had rather not, I cannot help it—he may choose."[62]

Canning, however, did not tamper with two important sources of extra income because they were inextricably wed to the diplomatic system of the country and Europe. They were the practice of exchanging chancery presents on the signing of treaties with foreign powers,[63] and the Foreign Office agencies.

It was the general practice of European princes in the eighteenth century to reward plenipotentiaries of other states for their efforts in securing treaties of defensive alliance, commerce, or marriage. Prior to the last decade of the century, however, there was no convention making the practice mandatory, and there were instances, such as on the signing of the marriage treaty of the Prince of Wales in 1736, when no presents were exchanged.[64] The clerks and undersecretaries of the respective foreign departments of signatory powers

61. Order in Council, Queen's Palace, 10 May 1809, Copy, Add. MS 38255 ff. 29–30. The date on which a clerk was entitled to receive an augmentation was calculated from the time he first entered the office, either as a junior clerk on the establishment or as a supernumerary clerk paid from the contingent fund. Minute, Castlereagh, F.O., 30 Oct. 1813, F.O. 366/672 ff. 60–61. Service in another department, even if that office had a similar program for augmentation, however, was not counted in determining the length of service. Minute, William Hamilton, on Hamilton to George Harrison, (Treasury), Foreign Office, 8 Dec. 1821, Draft, F.O. 95/591.

62. Canning to Charles Bagot, Bruton Street, Thursday morning, 6 July 1809, Bagot, *Canning and Friends*, vol. 1, 312.

63. For a complete discussion of these presents and their abolition see Charles R. Middleton, "Retrenchment and Reform: The Case of the Diplomatic Presents, 1782–1832," *The Rocky Mountain Social Science Journal*, 11 (Oct., 1974), 62–73.

64. George III to Grenville, Windsor, 16 Dec. 1794, *H. M. C. Fortescue*, vol. 2, 652–53.

were usually entitled to a chancery present as compensation for the additional and tedious labor of reading, translating, and copying treaties. Again there were exceptions. No presents were given on the exchange of the treaties of peace with France, Spain, and Holland in 1783.[65] The sums paid were reciprocal and fluctuated widely, ranging from £200 paid to the chancery of the landgrave of Hesse-Cassel on the conclusion of a treaty of alliance in 1787, to £3,779 given to the Prussian chancery in 1788 on the signature of a treaty of defensive alliance.[66] During Lord Grenville's secretaryship (1791-1801) the system was rigidly defined and presents were not only expected but demanded. Five hundred pounds was the usual chancery payment, each court paying its own foreign office to avoid delays and difficulties in exchange rates.[67]

Treaty presents were an uncertain and fluctuating source of income. Yet British and continental statesmen so firmly regarded them as "an acknowledged part of the pecuniary profits of the Employé's [sic] in their respective Offices" that they alone of the presents habitually exchanged were continued from 1814 to 1816, when 45 treaties of one sort or another were negotiated.[68] Each clerk and undersecretary received a share of the chancery present, though when the undersecretaries were given separate gifts, as occasionally happened, the clerks received the whole. The usual proportion was three-quarters to the undersecretaries and one-quarter to the clerks.[69] Amongst the clerks the sum received varied with the chief clerk receiving the lion's share and his juniors portioning out the remainder according to seniority. Eventually the establishment became too large for all to share in these monies, and some of the junior clerks in 1814 and 1815 received no treaty money.[70]

65. William Fraser to William Eden, Whitehall, 21 Jan. 1787, Private, Add. MS 34423 ff. 340-41.

66. Carmarthen to Lords of Treasury, Whitehall, 29 Oct. 1787, and 13 Aug. 1788, F.O. 366/426 ff. 29, 123.

67. Grenville to Lords of Treasury, Whitehall, ibid., passim; Grenville to George III, Dropmore, 15 Dec. [1794], 11 p.m., Aspinall, *Later Corresp. Geo. III*, vol. 2, 282-83; James Bland Burges to Sir William Hamilton, White Hall, 21 June 1793, Private, G. Willis Autograph Collection, London County Record Office Q/WIL/77.

68. On the ratification of treaties with minor German princes, even chancery presents were not exchanged. Extract of Memorandum annexed to Return "Presents from Foreign Sovereigns" laid before the House of Commons, 1 Apr. 1816, F.O. 366/555.

69. George Hammond to William Hamilton, Speen Hill, Newbury, 16 Sept. 1810, F.O. 83/12.

70. Unsigned minute on Memorandum Castlereagh to T. Bidwell, Sr., F.O., 1 July 1816, Copy, F.O. 366/672 f. 120.

There was one other way in which the negotiation of treaties was lucrative to clerks. Francis Moore, assistant secretary to the Marquess of Cornwallis, ambassador to France in 1802, and Joseph Planta, Castlereagh's chief of chancellery in 1814, were paid £547 and £500 respectively for bringing to England treaties that had been signed with France.[71] Both men were clerks temporarily serving abroad. Small wonder that when Castlereagh went to Aix-la-Chapelle in 1818 Woodbine Parish, who had secured a position in his entourage, could write: "there are plenty of other applicants to join the party. . . ."[72]

Entrenched activities and revenues were always difficult to reform. Nothing was done to abolish the practice of giving presents because it was tied to a general European system and was besides not particularly noxious. The system of agents, on the other hand, was seen as a source of evil and caused alarm, anger, and consternation on the part of many members of Parliament and Treasury officials for nearly a century. Agents received "by virtue of letters of attorney" all salaries and other public money paid to ministers and consuls abroad. They either deposited the balance after taxes into the minister's account or made disbursements directly on his behalf.[73] They also performed other special services as requested, such as procuring newspapers, books, and other items necessary for the minister's comfort or amusement.[74] Charles Broughton was able to secure partially free mail for his clients by having all correspondence to them directed through the undersecretary of state, who had a franking privilege, and Henry Rolleston, whose father was entitled to frank letters as chief clerk, promised his employers free postage to *and* from all parts of the kingdom.[75] The secretaries of state approved of the system so long as it did not interfere with the duties of

71. George Pellew, *The Life and Correspondence of the Right Hon. Henry Addington, First Viscount Sidmouth* (3 vols.; London, 1847), vol. 2, 1; "Report from the Committee appointed to consider the Charge upon His Majesty's Civil List Revenue, 8 July 1803," *P.P., 1802–1803*, vol. 5, Command 147, p. 366; Bathurst to Lords of the Treasury, Draft, F.O., 4 June 1814, F.O. 366/555; Messengers in the eighteenth century were paid £30 to perform the same service. Holohan, *King's Messengers*, p. 218.

72. Parish to W. Parish, Sr., Foreign Office, 31 July 1818, Shuttleworth, *Woodbine Parish*, p. 198.

73. Memorandum by William Hamilton, F.O., 15 June 1815, Copy, F.O. 366/375 f. 6.

74. Charles Arbuthnot to Charles R. Broughton, Vienna, 9 Dec. 1804, Arbuthnot Papers, Duke University Library.

75. Broughton to Arthur Paget, Downing Street, 21 Sept. 1798, Add. MS 48402 no folio; H. Rolleston to William A'Court, Foreign Office, 23 Nov. 1815, Add. MS 41537 ff. 109–10.

the office, and Grenville even took an active part in securing agencies for his protégé, Charles Goddard.[76] The only change in the agency system in the eighteenth century was Grenville's prohibiting the chief clerk from acting as an agent after 1795, when that gentleman became responsible for the public funds of the office.[77]

It is doubtful that there would have been any reform of the agency system, despite a vigorous condemnation of it by a committee of the House of Commons in 1786,[78] had not one man overextended his activities to the point of financial collapse. Charles Rivington Broughton came to the Foreign Office in 1788 as part of the arrangements arising out of his brother's resignation. He was a hardworking man who by 1803 had become first senior clerk.[79] Like his brother, however, he was arrogant and self-seeking, and bragged on at least one occasion "that my acceptances are held in equal Estimation at the Bank with those of the first Merchantile Houses in London and *are as readily discounted.*"[80] Through sustained effort he managed to secure the agencies of the majority of the ministers and consuls serving abroad. He was particularly successful in his approaches to the more important (and better-paid) diplomatists such as Lord Granville, Sir Arthur Paget, and Sir Charles Stuart.

Broughton, as others before him, acted in effect as banker to the diplomatists. He received their drafts, paid their accounts and expenses in England, and collected their salaries and the money for extraordinary disbursements from the Treasury.[81] The difficulty with this system was that the Civil List, from which the diplomatic corps was paid, was continually short of funds. The Treasury as a result fell further and further behind in payment of these salaries, and was so habitually in arrears that Broughton complained that

76. Portland, Grenville, and Dundas to the Lord President of the Council, Whitehall, 23 Feb. 1795, Copy, F.O. 366/542; Grenville to the duke of Leeds, St. James's Square, 31 Dec. 1791, Grenville MSS.

77. Minute, T. Bidwell, Sr., Downing Street, [Aug.], 1799, F.O. 95/9. Sneyd had retained his agencies after he became chief clerk. Sneyd to Keith, Whitehall, 20 May 1791, Add. MS 35544 f. 36.

78. Extract from the First report on Fees, Gratuities, &c. of Public Offices, 11 Apr. 1786, F.O. 366/375 f. 1.

79. *Royal Kalendar, 1804*, p. 132.

80. Broughton to Lord Granville Leveson-Gower, Downing Street, 30 July 1805, P.R.O. 30/29/6/6 ff. 1051–54.

81. George Canning was an exception to the usual practice, employing Broughton only as an auditor of his accounts. Canning to Broughton, Claremont, Thursday morning, 3 Nov. 1814, Private, Canning Papers.

"notwithstanding the positive assurance that no Branch of it [the Civil List] shall be permitted to fall two Quarters into arrear, . . . there is no dependance to be placed on the assurances I receive on that head."[82]

As the Civil List fell into debt, so too did Broughton. At least one ambassador, Charles Arbuthnot, gave him the title to the Embassy plate as security against financial collapse.[83] Most accounts fell considerably into arrears without such security. Lord Granville in 1805 was £4,000 overdrawn and Sir Arthur Paget in 1806 drew for £10,500 more than Broughton had received from the Treasury.[84] Only careful management of his funds and temporary stratagems kept Broughton's enterprise afloat. As early as 1809 there was a minor crisis. "I have for *the present* driven the Wolf from my door; but he will soon shew his voracious Jaws again and Lord knows how I am to appease him—to satisfy him is quite out of the Question—until you can afford me efficient aid."[85] The crisis passed, however, and Broughton, undaunted and uninstructed, even sought additional agencies, such as the one for the colony of New South Wales, which fell vacant in 1812.[86]

Broughton's finances completely collapsed in 1815: "so considerable have been my advances to various Characters in the highest Diplomatick and other Situations and so difficult have I found it to get even the Interest on my Money from a great part of them, that I found it absolutely indispensable to apply to the chancellor of the Exchequer for the Aid of the Crown to get in my Debts." Nicholas Vansittart, the chancellor, was alarmed by Broughton's situation, which was complicated by the large sum that he owed to the Crown as a Receiver General of Land, Assessed, and Property Taxes. Much to Broughton's surprise, Vansittart ordered his estate and all his revenues seized until his debt to the Crown was liquidated.[87]

---

82. Broughton to Granville, Downing Street, 21 Jan. 1806, P.R.O. 30/29/6/6 ff. 1055–56.

83. Arbuthnot to Broughton, Trieste, 24 May 1805, Private, Arbuthnot Papers.

84. Broughton to Granville, Downing Street, 30 July 1805, P.R.O. 30/29/6/6 ff. 1051–54; Broughton to Sir Arthur Paget, Downing Street, 9 Aug. 1806, Add. MS 48402 no folio.

85. Broughton to Paget, 9 Jan. 1809, Add MS 48402 no folio.

86. Earl of Moira to Col. MacMahon, Hocherill, 20 Mar. 1812, Aspinall, *Letters of George IV*, vol. 1, 48.

87. Broughton to George Canning, Foreign Office, 18 Dec. 1815, Copy, Add. MS 38740 ff. 266–67. This money included some that had been issued to Broughton on behalf of ambassadors. Sir Charles Stuart never recovered his losses. Stuart to Planta, London, 9 Jan. 1827, F.O. 97/175.

Castlereagh, the secretary of state, immediately issued stringent regulations which restricted the financial activities of agents to keeping records for diplomatists, and prohibited an agent's engaging in any way in the financial concerns of his clients.[88]

Jobbing reflected, among other things, a search for security. In the eighteenth century, with the exception of officers of the excise and customs, public servants were not entitled to pensions, though most departments, and certainly the Foreign Ofice, made provisions for retiring personnel. But even those who recognized the need for a system of superannuation preferred to award pensions according to merit and not by any fixed regulation.[89] In practice in the Foreign Office no officer retiring from the king's service was refused a pension, and most received lucrative awards. Two senior clerks, William Money and John Jenkins, for example, were forced to retire for reasons of health in 1793 and 1794 respectively. Both received grants, which were paid out of the contingent fund, equal to their annual salary and emoluments.[90] The department also willingly accepted the responsibility of supporting dependent relatives of deceased clerks, whether the clerk at his death was still working at the office or was himself retired on a pension. John Hinchliffe's father was paid £100 a year after his son's death in 1799, while Canning gave Elizabeth and Sarah Hay, the maiden sisters of James Hay, who died seven months after retiring, £175 per annum each.[91]

The whole question of superannuation came under the consideration of the House of Commons and the Treasury in 1809. The discussion led the following year to the passage of a comprehensive scheme covering every government department. In the Foreign Office pensions afterwards were paid out of the fee fund (a practice that had become routine after the reform of 1795), with deficiencies of the fund made up out of the Civil List revenues. The new scale provided for pensions ranging from one-third to the whole of a

88. See appendix III.

89. Cohen, *The Civil Service*, p. 29; Portland, Grenville, and Dundas to the Lord President of the Council, Whitehall, 23 Feb. 1795, Copy, F.O. 366/542.

90. Grenville to Lords of the Treasury, Downing Street, 31 Oct. and 5 Nov. 1794, Copy, F.O. 366/427 ff. 107–9.

91. Salary Book, 1799, F.O. 366/380; Memorial of Misses Elizabeth and Sarah Hay, At Mrs. Beckford's, Clifton Down, Bristol, 4 Apr. 1807, Copy, F.O. 366/671 ff. 329–35; Minute, Canning, Downing Street, 7 July 1807, ibid., f. 335. Elizabeth Hay died in 1822 and Canning increased Sarah's pension by £25. Canning to Lords of the Treasury, Foreign Office, 13 Mar. 1823, Copy, F.O. 366/429 ff. 246–47.

clerk's salary, depending on his age on retirement and on the length of his service.[92] Little discretion was left to secretaries of state in recommending persons for pensions. The Treasury in at least one instance, however, refused to grant a clerk in the Foreign Office the pension to which he was entitled under a strict interpretation of the act on the grounds that only "under circumstances of a very special nature" were clerks allowed the amount stipulated by Parliament.[93] Of course after 1810 it was exceedingly difficult to make provision for dependent relatives of deceased clerks.

There were in the Foreign Office by 1822 other officials who performed miscellaneous duties, public and private, for the department and for the secretary of state. Few of them were paid officials on the regular establishment in 1782. Most of their positions were additions made by Lord Grenville to meet specific requirements of the department. The two most important men of this group were the private secretary and the précis writer, who were paid from the office funds after 1795.

The private secretary was the confidential assistant of the secretary of state. As a rule he was a personal friend of the secretary, and entered and left the office with him. Usually these men were inexperienced in official life, though some, such as John Forbes, Wellesley's private secretary, had served in a similar capacity with other government officials.[94] Carmarthen, Grenville, and Hawkesbury secured clerkships for their private secretary, an arrangement Hawkesbury recommended to Lord Harrowby as giving security to the private secretary in case his patron went out of office unexpectedly. Harrowby, however, filled the vacant clerkship he found on entering the office with another gentleman, and was forced when he retired suddenly in 1805 to secure a position as a supernumerary clerk for his private secretary, Charles Woodcock.[95] Those private secretaries who held clerkships did not receive the salary of their clerkship, though they were kept on the establishment and retained

92. "Third Report from Committee upon Public Offices, 1809," *P.P., 1809*, vol. 3, Command 97, p. 99; George Harrison to George Hammond, Treasury Chambers, 12 Sept. 1809, F.O. 83/16; 50 Geo. III, c. 117, 21 June 1810.

93. Stephen Lushington to Joseph Planta, Treasury Chambers, 27 July 1818, Copy, F.O. 366/672 f. 150.

94. Wellesley to Spencer Perceval, Apsley House, 20 Feb. 1810, Private, Holland (Perceval) Papers Bundle I/17.

95. Hawkesbury to Harrowby, Apsley House, 13 May 1804, Harrowby MSS vol. 11, ff. 1–2; George Hammond to Harrowby, Downing Street, 12 Jan. 1805, ibid., vol. 10, f. 210.

their rank in the office. An exception to this rule was Joseph Planta, who received the salary of all three posts of private secretary (£300), précis writer (£300), and clerk (£310) which he held concurrently from July 1814 until his promotion to undersecretary in July 1817.[96]

The duties of the private secretary were primarily to handle the unofficial and semi-official correspondence of his principal. Since he made copies of all the secretary's private correspondence with diplomatists he was usually well-informed. It was only natural, therefore, for the private secretary to work on the official business of the office in times of great activity. Canning, in fact, employed James Ross as an assistant to the undersecretaries for such a length of time in 1808 and 1809 that he earned £600 as compensation for his extra labor.[97]

Like the private secretary the précis writer was closely identified with the secretary of state, though perhaps not to the same degree.[98] Stratford Canning, who began his brilliant career as his cousin's précis writer, recorded his impressions of his official duties:

> They were more interesting than onerous, more instructive than brilliant. They consisted principally in making summaries of the official correspondence carried on between the secretary of state and the diplomatic agents employed under his direction abroad. I had also to assist occasionally in writing out fair the drafts of instructions from the same source. The confidential nature of these duties gave a precarious character to my position. A change of ministry was sure to be as fatal to the précis-writer as to the minister himself; but this air of fellowship with a great man made up, as some might think, for the uncertainty of the tenure.[99]

Before there was a précis writership, a junior clerk in the office was responsible for the secretary's précis books.[100] Grenville appears to have been the first secretary to appoint a précis writer per se, and

---

96. Minute, Grenville, 24 Feb. 1796, F.O. 366/670 f. 371; Establishment of the Secretary of State's Office, 1814–1817, F.O. 366/380 passim.

97. Malmesbury's diary, Sunday, 29 Mar. 1807, Malmesbury, *Diaries*, vol. 4, 379–80; Minute, Canning, F.O., 19 Sept. 1809, F.O. 366/671 f. 387.

98. Canning to Bathurst, Gloucester Lodge, 31 Jan. 1810, Private & Secret, B.M. Loan 57/4/375.

99. Memoirs, 1807–1809, Poole, *Life of Stratford Canning*, vol. 1, 29–30.

100. Fraser to Lord Grantham, St. James's, 6 Apr. 1783, Lucas L 30/14/149.

his nominee, Charles Arbuthnot, came to the post so long after Grenville had become secretary that the assistance of a junior clerk was still necessary for him to catch up on all previous correspondence.[101] After the post was recognized as part of the establishment in 1795, three men (Brook Taylor, William Hamilton, and Joseph Planta) held it and the private secretaryship conjointly. Most of these men worked steadily. Only one, William Hamilton, appears to have been unable to perform his duties as précis writer and private secretary. Lord Mulgrave, his principal, was still attempting to have a précis book prepared four years after he retired from the Foreign Office.[102]

One branch of the office destined to play an increasingly important role in the conduct of foreign affairs in the nineteenth century did not appear until 1801. The creation of the Librarian's Department just prior to his retirement was in fact Grenville's greatest administrative contribution to the Foreign Office. In the eighteenth century officials did not regard state papers as the priceless objects they later became, and made only an imperfect effort to preserve them in any systematic and secure fashion.[103] It was not unusual, for example, for the Foreign Office (particularly when there were voluminous enclosures), to send off dispatches to ministers abroad without keeping copies of them.[104] Long before 1782 the offices of Keeper of State Papers and Collector and Transmitter of State Papers had become virtual sinecures. Despite this fact the secretaries of state managed in 1795 to secure their retention on the grounds that they were "the only means which the Secretaries of State have of rewarding officers for diligence and long services."[105]

Grenville appointed Charles Goddard Collector and Transmitter of State Papers in 1795. Goddard had been a clerk in the Home Office while Grenville was home secretary and served as his private secretary in the Foreign Office from 1795 to 1796. Though he occasionally prepared memoranda for the ministers, he later took

101. Burges to Grenville, White Hall, 2 Oct. 1793, Grenville MSS.

102. Mulgrave to Wellesley, Harley Street, 16 Aug. 1810, Add. MS 37310 ff. 17–18.

103. Sketch of the Origin and present Situation of the State Paper Office, [1799], F.O. 95/635.

104. Fraser to William Eden, Whitehall, 2 Nov. 1787, Add. MS 34427 ff. 43–44.

105. Thomas Astle to Grenville, Battersea Rise, 17 Mar. 1789, Grenville MSS; Portland, Grenville, and Dundas to the Lord President of the Council, Whitehall, 23 Feb. 1795, Copy, F.O. 366/542.

holy orders and held the post as a sinecure until his death in 1848.[106] Between 1795 and 1801, then, no one in the office paid much attention to the preservation of papers in a systematic manner.

Henry Dundas's nominee, John Bruce, was the Keeper of the State Papers. Dundas and later Portland employed him regularly to do research in the archives and to prepare memoranda on military and colonial questions for the cabinet. Dundas eventually came to feel that the position should be upgraded in salary and that Bruce should be given a larger staff to help him organize the papers and prepare any memoranda ministers required. Grenville opposed the idea,[107] but Dundas enlisted the aid of Portland, who as secretary in the Home Office shared with Grenville the patronage of the Paper Office. The State Paper Office was enlarged in 1800 to three clerks and Bruce's salary was raised from £163 to £500 a year.[108] All correspondence was kept under Bruce's superintendence. He was employed preparing reports to "facilitate public Business to his immediate Superiours and prevent those delays, [which] . . . have frequently retarded the dispatch of Affairs, and often frustrated the measures intended to be carried into effect, with Foreign Courts, or in the British Dependencies."[109]

Probably it was the need to refer continually to the correspondence and the inconvenience of having dispatches stored elsewhere than in the Foreign Office that led to Grenville's determination to establish his own indigenous paper office, though his dislike of Bruce and his disapproval of Bruce's appointment may have contributed to the decision as well. Beginning in January 1801 all the foreign correspondence subsequent to 1780 was "*probed out from very obscure places*" and taken to the office.[110] The first librarian, Richard Ancell, formerly a clerk in the Paper Office, received a salary of £200. When he retired in 1810 on a pension equal

106. Nelson, *The Home Office*, pp. 165–66; *Gents. Mag.*, (1848), pt. 1, 555; Grenville to George III, Cleveland Row, 2 Oct. 1800, 3 p.m., Aspinall, *Later Corresp. Geo. III*, vol. 3, 420.

107. Dundas to Grenville, Walmer Castle, 10 Aug. [1798], (1799?), *H. M. C. Fortescue*, vol. 4, 277–79.

108. Dundas to Portland, Downing Street, 24 July 1799, Copy, and Portland to Lords of the Treasury, Whitehall, 12 Aug. 1799, Copy, F.O. 92/635. For a complete study of the Paper Office during this period see Nelson, *The Home Office*, pp. 142–45.

109. Plan of Regulations for the State Paper Office, Mr. Bruce, 6 Mar. 1799, P.R.O. 30/8/231 ff. 72–77.

110. Unsigned minute on "Account of Correspondence in the Foreign Department, Taken by Mr. Ancell in the Month of March 1802," F.O. 95/635.

to his salary he had organized the correspondence into a systematic collection.[111]

Ancell's successor was Lewis Hertslet, whose family controlled the Library for the whole of the nineteenth century. Hertslet served as Ancell's assistant from 5 February 1801. He was the son of a Swiss immigrant, Lewis Hiertzelet, a king's messenger. He probably received little, if any, formal education for he entered the office as a lad of fourteen. He had a natural talent for organization which was trained under Ancell's steady, if unimaginative guidance "in the Good Old Path."[112] He brought with him as his assistant his younger brother James.

One of the most interesting facets of Hertslet's character was his ability to acquire benefits. Scarcely a year after his promotion he persuaded Wellesley to extend the principle of augmentation to the post he held, and he was no less energetic in securing the same benefit for his brother.[113] Castlereagh, in 1815, increased his salary to £300, and by 1821, with ten years service, he was earning £700 a year, £500 more than Ancell who had served nearly an equal length of time when he retired in 1810.[114] Hertslet was always a diligent and imaginative subordinate, which explains his success.

Hertslet's registry, which was so efficient that it was copied by many foreign powers, was basically an index of all dispatches received and sent, together with a brief description of their contents. In addition he made an attempt to list all people mentioned in them. The Hertslets spent the years prior to 1822 organizing the system; after that time they manipulated it more and more to their own and their country's benefit. Thus began the "Hertslet tradition," a tradition of routine and efficiency based on a system of registration and indexing that enabled other branches of the office to operate smoothly.[115]

111. Memorial of Richard Ancell, n.d., Copy, F.O. 366/672 ff. 2–3; Minute, Wellesley, F.O., 5 Jan. 1810, ibid., f. 4.

112. Ancell to Corps of King's Messengers, Downing Street, 23 May 1810, Holohan, *The King's Messengers*, pp. 221–22; Shirley Hall, "Sir Edward Hertslet and His work as Librarian and Keeper of the Papers of the Foreign Office from 1857–1896" (M.A. thesis, University of London, 1958), pp. 2–3.

113. Wellesley to Lords of the Treasury, F.O., 20 Dec. 1811, Copy, F.O. 366/672 f. 30; Stephen Lushington to Hamilton, Treasury Chambers, 1 Feb. 1816, Copy, ibid., f. 113.

114. Castlereagh to Lords of the Treasury, F.O., 19 May 1815, Copy, ibid., f. 98; Hall, "Edward Hertslet," p. 25.

115. Hall, "Edward Hertslet," pp. 5–6.

One position attached to the Foreign Office, that of Translator of the German Language, was subject to fluctuating fortunes. William Fraser, the undersecretary, held the post as a sinecure in the last quarter of the eighteenth century.[116] In 1795 all three secretaries were of opinion that it should be abolished, which it was, though Fraser succeeded in 1797 in getting his salary continued until his death.[117] When the translatorship lapsed, Hawkesbury, according to the arrangements of 1795, refused to refill it. Fox later decided to make it a working position. At the instance of the chief clerks, Bidwell and Rolleston, he appointed their sons Thomas Bidwell, Jr., and Henry Rolleston to the post along with Christian Ruperti, who had in fact done all the work as Fraser's agent. Each man was paid £100 a year, but Ruperti did what little work there was. Canning made the salary augmentations of 1809 contingent on the termination of Fox's "arrangement (which I considered as a very improper one) by which it [the translatorship] was divided into three Sinecures of £100 a year each. . . ."[118] The clerks' increasing fluency in languages made a translator of German or French unnecessary and probably influenced Canning's decision to abolish the position.

Canning created the post of Translator of the Spanish, Portuguese, Italian, and Danish Languages in 1808 to provide means of reading the increasing number of letters received at the office from refugees of these countries. Canning also wished to employ officially John Christian Hüttner who was engaged in translating the appeals sent to the European peoples to resist French aggression.[119] Hüttner held the post until his death in 1847.[120]

There is little evidence to suggest that the Foreign Office, as it evolved between 1782 and 1821 could not have continued to function with reasonable efficiency long after the latter date. The reforms of 1822 were sparked not by a desire to create a more efficient

116. Nelson, *The Home Office*, p. 146.
117. George Canning to Charles Long, Downing Street, 12 June 1797, Copy, F.O. 366/427; Order in Council, St. James's, 21 June 1797, Copy, F.O. 366/671 ff. 20–21.
118. Hawkesbury to Harrowby, Apsley House, 13 May 1804, Harrowby MSS vol. 11, ff. 1–2; Minute, T. Bidwell, Sr., Downing Street, 10 Feb. 1807, Copy, F.O. 366/428; G. C. Ruperti to [Canning], Foreign Office, 29 Sept. 1809, with minute, Canning, 2 Oct. 1809, F.O. 95/99.
119. *D.N.B.*, vol. 10, 350–51.
120. Canning to Lord President of the Council, F.O., 10 Jan. 1809, Copy, F.O. 366/671 f. 358; Salary List for 1847, F.O. 366/383. From 1824 to 1829 there was also an assistant translator, Charles Masterton. Masterton to Palmerston, Foreign Office, 6 Sept. 1834, F.O. 83/60.

system of administration (though that was one of the results) but rather received their impetus from the need for retrenchment in face of Britain's poor economic situation after the peace of 1815.

CHAPTER VII

THE FOREIGN OFFICE
ESTABLISHMENT: 1821–1846

The significant developments in the emergence of constitutional
bureaucracy at the Foreign Office occurred in the quarter century
after the accession of George IV. There was in the early 1820s
considerable activity in the bureaucracy. The Colonial Office, a
department very similar to the Foreign Office in origin, organization, and responsibility, was remodelled extensively between December 1821 and July 1825,[1] and in this period it became the first
department in which "the political heads . . . openly admitted their
inability to handle personally the volume of regular business."[2] This
was also the period of increasing Treasury attempts at interference
in the affairs of other departments.[3]

In the Foreign Office, Londonderry, then after his death in August
1822, Canning ordered a series of administrative reforms which,
when coupled with the reforms made by Palmerston in the 1830s,
established the internal organization of the department for the
remainder of the nineteenth century. Between 1821 and 1841 the
clerks were regraded into four classes and began to assume responsibility for the efficient conduct of affairs within the office. The
establishment was reorganized into political divisions each headed
by a senior clerk. Separate departments for consular and slave trade
affairs were created. Equally important were financial reforms
which eliminated the system of jobbing that was a legacy of the
previous century. The pace of reform was leisurely and the changes
instituted reflected the specific needs of the department. The initial
reorganization was stimulated, however, by external events, not by
internal necessities.

1. Young, *The Colonial Office*, chapter 2.
2. Ibid., p. 3.
3. Roseveare, *The Treasury*, pp. 133–50 discusses the growth of Treasury "control" in light
of political pressures from Parliament.

There was considerable alarm in the office about these measures. "We are in the Agony of most iniquitous, most partial, & most invidious Reductions," wrote William Hamilton, the undersecretary, in 1821. His colleague, Joseph Planta, was even more distressed. "We have had that unhappy question in our office," he told Bagot. The "reduction of our poor clerks of which only a few years ago I was one, while we *political* gentlemen keep the whole of our emoluments, has been a bitter pill to me."[4] Doubtless there were many others who were displeased by the prospect of reform in the winter of 1821–1822. The Foreign Office had remained for forty years an expanding department, employing more and more men and paying them higher and higher salaries. Even immediately following the war, when the Treasury ordered a reduction in the bureaucracy, Castlereagh had succeeded in defending the size of his establishment.[5] But by 1821 the country was again in a major recession and retrenchment was the order of the day, even for the king.[6] Those who had been in the office for most of their adult life must have been incredulous when they discovered they too were faced with reductions in income on the same scale as every other department and that seemingly there was no way to avoid them.

Parliament, assisted by the Treasury, was the driving force behind the movement towards retrenchment in 1821. Early in the summer both Houses passed resolutions calling for "a minute Enquiry into the several Departments of the Civil Government, as well with a view to reducing the Number of Persons employed in those Departments . . . as with reference to the increased Salaries granted to Individuals since the Year 1797."[7] The Treasury was the first to comply with the address, ordering a reorganization in departments immediately under its supervision, such as the Excise and Customs. But since the secretaries of state were virtually autonomous in matters of this nature the scheme instituted by the Treasury was only recommended to them.[8] Londonderry, as Castlereagh had become on

4. Hamilton to A'Court, F.O., 30 Nov. 1821, Add. MS 41523 f. 288; Planta to Bagot, 20 Jan. 1822, Private, Bagot, *Canning and Friends*, vol. 2, 123.
5. Treasury circular, 3 Aug. 1816, Copy, F.O. 366/672 ff. 125–26; Hamilton to S. R. Lushington, F.O., 10 Aug. 1816, Copy, ibid., f. 127. The Colonial Office, however, was reduced in 1816 to nine clerks, a librarian, and a translator. Young, *The Colonial Office*, p. 37.
6. Londonderry to Bathurst, Pavillion, Sunday, n.d., *H. M. C. Bathurst*, p. 529.
7. 2 *Hansard's*, vol. 5, 1345–1445, 1464–74.
8. S. R. Lushington to various Government Offices, 13 Aug. 1821, and 15 Jan. 1822, Copies, T. 27/81 ff. 181, 520, 522.

succeeding his father to the family peerage, had to grapple with the problem of reducing his establishment.

The first principle of the Treasury's reorganization was a return to the size of the establishment of 1797, unless "adequate cause continued to exist which rendered some alteration necessary."[9] There was "adequate cause" for no reduction in the Foreign Office. The greatest administrative problem with which Londonderry had to contend in fact was the increase in volume of business without a corresponding increase in permanent staff. There are no figures available for the numbers of dispatches handled during the period immediately prior to the reforms, but the resumption of regular diplomatic relations with most of Europe in 1814 and 1815, and the various postwar negotiations and settlements must have doubled or trebled the volume of business transacted in the concluding five years of the war. Yet Canning in 1809 was the last man to add to the permanent establishment.[10]

Various expedients were subsequently tried to cope with increasing business. The most important was the employment of supernumerary clerks, who were paid from the contingent fund and who in theory had no claim to promotion.[11] In practice, however, they were placed on the regular establishment as soon as there was a vacancy. George Lenox-Conyngham and Thomas Staveley, for example, were advanced respectively in 1817 on Planta's promotion to undersecretary in July and after Bidwell's death in September. The supernumeraries by 1819 had become a distinct class limited to three clerks. Joseph Cade was in May 1819 unofficially attached to the undersecretary until such time as there should be a vacancy as third supernumerary clerk.[12] Certainly Londonderry could not easily dismiss any of these men. Their assistance was indispensable and their rank had acquired a permanency it previously lacked.

There was also a special problem which made reductions difficult. The establishment was continually below strength as a result of the practice of attaching clerks to missions abroad. Charles Bankhead spent three and a half of the eleven and a half years he was officially employed at the Foreign Office as an attaché to various missions.

9. Extract of Treasury Minute, 10 Aug. 1821, Copy, F.O. 366/672 f. 219.
10. Order in Council, Queen's Palace, 11 Jan. 1809, F.O. 366/542 f. 29.
11. Castlereagh to Lords of the Treasury, F.O., 3 Apr. 1819, Copy, F.O. 366/ 672 ff. 170–71.
12. Minute, Planta to S. Rolleston, F.O., 3 May 1819, Copy, F.O. 366/672 f. 175.

William Turner served abroad seven of his sixteen years as a clerk. Many others were abroad for shorter periods.[13]

Londonderry's plan of reorganization submitted to the Treasury in January 1822 contained no reduction in the size of his regular establishment. The clerks, in addition to a chief clerk, were organized into grades: four first class or senior clerks; four second class clerks; six third class or junior clerks; and the three supernumeraries, who were brought onto the establishment as a distinct class that Canning later called "assistant junior clerks."[14] The Treasury objected to the last provision on the grounds that it was too expensive, but acquiesced in the arrangement when Planta explained that Londonderry was not certain that these men would be replaced after they were promoted to the third class.[15]

A second principle of retrenchment recommended by the Treasury was the reduction of offices no longer needed for the efficient functioning of a department. In a sense at least one such position did exist in the Foreign Office. The entering and dispatch clerk, Richard Bartlett, performed duties that naturally belonged to the registry. Londonderry therefore abolished the position, appointed Bartlett consul at Corunna with a pension of £150 a year to insure that he took no loss in salary as a result of the change, and gave his duties along with £100 per annum to the sublibrarian, James Hertslet. The government saved £250 a year by this complex arrangement.[16]

The third principle of the Treasury was the most difficult for the Foreign Office to accept. Regardless of whether or not reductions were made on the basis of the first two recommendations, salary levels were to be reduced to the levels of 1797. There were two reasons why Londonderry and later Canning refused to implement this recommendation. First, with respect to the office as a whole, the

13. Statement of Services, Charles Bankhead, 19 May 1828, F.O. 366/560; William Turner's employment record, F.O. 366/329 f. 132.

14. Scale of the Establishment of the Office of His Majesty's Principal Secretary of State for Foreign Affairs [from] 5 Jan. 1822, approved by George Canning, F.O. 366/542 f. 41; Lenox-Conyngham and Edward Scheener, who properly belonged on the third class, were placed on the second class as supernumeraries as a reward for their labors. There were to be no additions to that class until both men had succeeded to it. Londonderry to Lords of the Treasury, Foreign Office, 5 June 1822, Copy, F.O. 95/591.

15. Lushington to Hamilton, Treasury Chambers, 9 Jan. 1822, Copy, F.O. 366/672 ff. 229–30; Planta to Lushington, F.O., 14 Jan. 1822, Copy, ibid., ff. 231–34.

16. Memorial of Richard Bartlett, Foreign Office, 3 Jan. 1822, F.O. 72/263 ff. 7–10; Bartlett to Hamilton and Planta, Foreign Office, 4 Jan. 1822, ibid., ff. 11–13; Londonderry to Lords of the Treasury, Foreign Office, 20 Feb. 1822, Copy, F.O. 366/370 ff. 25–27.

basis of the proposed organization changed the nature of payment. A system of ungraded positions, which was essentially what existed prior to 1822, worked on the basis of an increase in salary with each step a clerk made in the establishment. For example, after 1795 the first senior clerk was paid £650, the second senior clerk £480, and the first junior clerk £300. Londonderry's proposals of January 1822 provided that all clerks in the same class be paid the same base pay regardless of seniority. This fact alone made it impossible to reimpose the salary scale of 1797.

There was special ground for protesting the Treasury's suggestion that junior or third class clerks receive £100 a year as their counterparts at the Treasury did. Planta was quick to point out the fact that junior clerks, save only the most junior of them, were always paid more than £100, even in 1797. He defended a £150 minimum salary because the Foreign Office could not be compared with the other government departments in the nature of employment and in the numbers and advantages derived from the length and the strenuous nature of service. The necessity of having clerks in whom the secretary had absolute trust and confidence made higher wages essential.[17] This was the first statement of that sense of superiority which set the Foreign Office apart in the minds of its establishment as a distinct and aristocratic branch of the government, deserving of and demanding special respect and treatment.

The salary arrangements were finally settled only after Canning came to office in August 1822, though they were made retroactive to January.[18] Canning also changed the principle on which augmentations were calculated. The Treasury, in fact, had been dissatisfied for some time with the arrangements of 1809 and in 1821 actually suspended payment of augmentation in offices under its control while the whole system was studied. Augmentations were still paid at the Foreign Office because Londonderry did not have the authority to override the order-in-council that granted them.[19] Londonderry and then Canning reviewed the basis on which these payments were

17. Planta to Lushington, Foreign Office, 14 Jan. 1822, Copy, F.O. 366/672 ff. 231–34. The senior grades of the office were paid the same rates as senior grades at the Treasury. Nicholas Vansittart, speech on 11 Mar. 1822, 2 *Hansard's*, vol. 6, 1019–20.

18. There are miscellaneous drafts of the establishment in the Canning MSS Bundle 136, which leave little doubt that Canning finished the task begun by Londonderry.

19. Harrison to Planta, Treasury Chambers, 14 Apr. 1821, Copy, and Planta to Harrison, Foreign Office, 14 Apr. 1821, Copy, F.O. 366/429 ff. 148–49.

calculated, and the latter's new arrangement provided for each clerk on the regular establishment to receive an augmentation for each year that he served in a particular class of the office. Each class from the chief clerkship to the assistant junior clerks was given a minimum and a maximum salary. A clerk entering one class received the minimum pay for that class plus annual augmentations for each year he served in the class until his salary was equal to the maximum allowed.[20]

It so happened that twelve of the nineteen clerks in 1822 received salaries and emoluments greater in amount than they were entitled to receive under the new arrangement. There were two ways in which these excesses were reduced. The first was by Londonderry's decision that after those who earned an allowance for special services retired, the men who succeeded them to these extra duties were not to be paid that allowance. He also ordered that no future appointees receive allowances for votes and *Gazettes*, nor were those on the establishment to continue receiving them once their salaries equalled the amount to which they were entitled under the new arrangements.[21] These provisions were painful to the clerks but they were equitable since the salary scales of 1822 were as a rule more generous both in terms of augmentation and maximum salary in each class than the arrangements of 1795 and 1809 had permitted.

The second method of reducing exorbitant salaries resulted from the revision of the superannuation scheme. By 1821, when the finances of the country were in poor condition, the noncontributory superannuation plan introduced in 1810 was no longer practical. The Treasury recommended that each public servant pay 5 percent of his salary into a superannuation fund administered by Whitehall. Those who were paid a higher salary than they were entitled to receive under the provisions of the reorganization were to pay an additional 10 percent on the surplus earned until their salary equalled the rates established in 1822.

The method of determining pensions was also revised. Pensions were graduated on a scale of one-third of a candidate's salary for a

20. See appendix IV. This was the same system Vansittart introduced into the Treasury. Speech on 11 Mar. 1823, 2 *Hansard's*, vol. 6, 1019–20.
21. Future Establishment of the Office of His Majesty's Principal Secretary of State for Foreign Affairs, 5 Jan. 1822, signed Londonderry, F.O. 366/366 ff. 21–22.

man with ten to fifteen years service increasing by increments of
one-twelfth for each five years service thereafter until a clerk with
fifty or more years service received a pension equivalent to his salary.
Half the pension was paid from the superannuation fund, the other
half from the contingent funds of the office in which the pensioner
had served. These provisions were enacted by Parliament in July
1822 and applied specifically to the Foreign Office by an order-in-
council in August.[22]

The reorganization of 1822, essentially a fiscal one, had three
important consequences. First, though orders-in-council applied
the reforms to the Foreign Office, they were essentially those
suggested by the Treasury. The Treasury also gave formal approval
to Londonderry's and Canning's proposals before they were implemented. The reorganization thus marked a small beginning towards Treasury control of the bureaucracy. Second, the general
principles of contributory superannuation were recognized in law.
Canning, who opposed the act of 1822 on the grounds that it was a
"breach of faith" with government employees, succeeded in abolishing the contributory scheme in 1824 when the country was enjoying
a period of prosperity.[23] The Treasury, however, reintroduced the
system in 1829, when all new appointees but no former personnel
began to pay the 5 percent surcharge.[24]

One aspect of superannuation remained uncertain after 1822.
Planta, reared in the old school, maintained that "The Doctrine and
Practice as to the foreign office is decidedly that no Person has a right
to a Pension;—the act only enables H. My. to give such Pension
should he choose so to do."[25] The Treasury's interpretation of the
act of 1822 that pensions were a matter of right was enacted specifically only in 1835. From that time candidates were entitled to a
pension equivalent to two-thirds of the amounts established in 1822.
The secretary of state could secure more than this amount for those
whose services were exceptional by attesting to the fact in a special

22. Extract of Treasury Minute, 10 Aug. 1821, Copy, part II: Superannuation, F.O.
366/672 ff. 222–27; Treasury Minute: Reduction and Superannuation, Treasury Chambers, 8
Jan. 1822, Copy, ibid., ff. 237–48; 3 Geo. IV c. 113; Order-in-Council, Carlton House, 5 Aug.
1822, Copy, F.O. 366/672 ff. 271–73.
23. Canning's speech, 26 July 1822, 2 *Hansard's*, vol. 7, 1845–46; Canning to George IV,
Foreign Office, 18 June 1824, ½ past 2 a.m., Aspinall, *Letters of George IV*, vol. 3, 79–80.
24. J. Stewart to Backhouse, Treasury Chambers, 11 Aug. 1829, Circular, Copy, F.O.
96/115.
25. Minute, Planta, N. Burlt. St., 16 June 1823, Add. MS 38295 f. 1.

letter to the Treasury. They thereby regained a measure of discretion in awarding these grants.[26]

The third and most important result of the reform of 1822 was a strengthening of the principle Grenville first imperfectly established in 1795 that the salary of the clerks should be adequate reward for their labors.[27] Some sources of supplementary income Londonderry abolished immediately. None were to survive Palmerston's secretaryships of the 1830s. Most gradually eroded away. The insignificant ones disappeared as soon as they were discovered. The Treasury eliminated one in 1823 when they refused to sanction the clerk's receiving the £525 salary of the vacant secretaryship of state between Londonderry's death and Canning's appointment because "such a measure would establish a precedent of a very inconvenient description with regard to all the Departments of Government."[28] In 1834 Palmerston abolished the last remaining franking privilege of the clerks, the right to frank newspapers in England, Wales, and Scotland, and noted "I was not aware than any such Privilege Existed in F.O."[29]

Two important sources of supplementary income were more difficult to eliminate. The first of these, the chancery presents, was not challenged until the Whigs came to power in November 1830. Prior to that time statesmen, no matter how dissatisfied with the practice, hesitated to abolish it. The Earl of Liverpool, who found them particularly offensive, told Castlereagh that "Presents are always reciprocal & it would be difficult for one Court to abolish them unless there was a general agreement upon the Subject."[30] The Whigs returned to office, however, pledged to retrenchment. Palmerston naturally singled out the presents as an expenditure which "It may not be easy to justify to the economical Spirit of the present times . . . as clearly and essentially necessary for the public ser-

26. Harrison to S. Rolleston, Treasury Chambers, 20 Oct. 1822, Private, Copy, F.O. 366/672 f. 289; 4 & 5 William IV c. 24.

27. Some clerks still found it difficult to live in London without support from their family. See E. Hammond's evidence, 15 Apr. 1861, Q. 135, "Report from the Select Committee appointed to inquire into the . . . diplomatic service . . . ," P.P., 1861, vol. 6, Command 459, p. 13.

28. Harrison to Planta, Treasury Chambers, 27 Jan. 1823, Copy, F.O. 366/429 ff. 227–29. Palmerston also refused in 1835 to parcel out the salary of the vacant undersecretaryship. Minute, Palmerston, on minute, Backhouse, 10 Sept. 1835, F.O. 366/313.

29. Minute, Palmerston, on Duke of Richmond to Palmerston, London, 30 Mar. 1834, F.O. 366/418.

30. Liverpool to Castlereagh, Fife House, 27 July, 1815, Draft, Add. MS 38261 ff. 250–51.

vice. . . ." He ordered them abolished, in true Palmerstonian fashion, without previous explanations or even communication with other powers.[31] The twelve clerks with the greatest seniority, who by 1830 alone shared the presents, received compensation of £500 portioned out according to rank.[32]

No one in 1831 protested this arrangement. George Lenox-Conyngham, who was abroad in 1831, however, sought to alter it in 1834 when he moved up to the first class. "The only arrangement," he wrote, "which I conceive would be just in principle and equally fair to all parties, would be to allow each of the 12 Clerks to enjoy the portion of compensation allotted by the regulation of 1831 to the position in the office to which he may succeed by rotation in the same manner as he would, under the old system have shared the Chancery presents."[33] Backhouse supported this request but Palmerston, though he agreed to submit it to the Treasury, was unfavorable towards the proposal on the grounds that if it were granted every clerk on the establishment in 1831 would be able to claim that he should share in the spoils as soon as he advanced to one of the select twelve positions. Conyngham subsequently dropped the matter because of Palmerston's coolness towards the plan.[34] Each clerk continued to receive the compensation allotted to him in 1831 regardless of promotion until he left the office. Ironically Conyngham was the last of the twelve to retire.

The most difficult source of extraordinary income to abolish was that of occasional payments for additional labor. The reason was the sheer overwhelming growth in the volume of business after 1822. Between 1829 and 1832 alone the political correspondence of the office increased by two thousand pieces. The consular business rose from slightly over four thousand to well over seven thousand pieces during the twenty year period from 1826 to 1846.[35] Everyone com-

31. Aspinall, *Three Early Diaries*, p. xxiii; Memorandum: "Diplomatic Presents," Dec. 1830, Copy, Palmerston Papers, "Presents," unnumbered: Minute, Lenox-Conyngham, on Backhouse's "Memorandum upon the decision of H. M. Govt. with respect to the discontinuance of Diplomatick presents," 12 Jan. 1831, F.O. 366/555.

32. "Memo: Proportionate Share of Chancery Presents [1834]," F.O. 95/522; "An Account of Chancery Presents from 1793 to 1830 (both inclusive)," F.O. 366/366 f. 172.

33. Conyngham to Palmerston, F.O., 30 Aug. 1834, Draft, F.O. 95/522.

34. Minutes, Backhouse, 6 Sept. 1834, Copy, and Palmerston, 7 Sept. 1834, Copy; Conyngham to Palmerston, 9 Sept. 1834, Copy, F.O. 95/522.

35. Chart on office business, 1829–1832, F.O. 83/55; miscellaneous memoranda, undated and unsigned, F.O. 83/583.

plained. Canning wrote to John Hookham Frere, a retired under-secretary, that the "same office in 1808–9 was nothing in point of work, compared with what it is now . . ." and told Liverpool that "the F.O. has nearly broken down under the work, and Planta himself is crying out with over-labour."[36] Fifteen years later Palmerston, one of the hardest working secretaries of the nineteenth century, wrote to Lord Granville, ambassador at Paris: "I have never been more harrassed & hunted by Papers, Interviews &c than this year. The number of Despatches received & Sent from the office in the last 12 months is more than double the number recd. & sent out in 12 months Ten years ago, and Three Times what it was Fifteen years before that."[37]

Office hours, which remained officially twelve to five after 1822,[38] were in fact nonexistent. "We have been working like niggers, half past ten at night at the F.O. not uncommon, sometimes until day-light," was one clerk's lament.[39] Nor were holidays and weekends sacred. Lord Dudley was pleased that he could let everyone save himself get away from the "work shop" on Christmas Day 1827. Planta rejoiced in 1824 when the Post Office rearranged the packet schedule to France ("This will give us a *whole* Holiday on Sunday"), and Lord Canning was pleased on a similar occasion in 1843 to get half a holiday on Saturday.[40] Clerks began to carry work home. George Backhouse apologized to his father in 1843 that he had "been too busy all this week to write to you much, having been more than once this week at work, not at the office, though with a Col-league, after midnight correcting Press[es] &c." Holidays were inter-rupted when a senior official's expertise was needed, and if anyone dared let a matter await that official's return, secretaries were apt to question why the papers were not sent to him in the country.[41]

The great increase in business was the result of many factors. Two

36. Canning to Frere, Bath, 8 Jan. 1825, Festing, *Frere*, p. 264; Same to Liverpool, Seaford, 14 Oct. 1825, Stapleton, *Corresp. of Canning*, vol. 1, 301–2.

37. Palmerston to Granville, C. T., 22 June 1840, P.R.O. 30/29/425.

38. Memorandum, Planta and Lord Francis Conyngham, F.O., 4 June 1823, F.O. 366/390; Minute, J. Backhouse, [1840], Draft, F.O. 366/386.

39. A. Turner to G. C. Backhouse, F.O., 7 July 1840, Backhouse Papers.

40. Dudley to Granville, Arlington St., 25 Dec. 1827, P.R.O. 30/29/14/4 ff. 83–84; Minute, Planta, on Freeling to Planta, General Post Office, 19 Nov. 1824, F.O. 27/326; Lord Canning to Howard de Walden, F.O., 16 Sept. 1843, Private, Add. MS 45176 ff. 215–19.

41. G. C. Backhouse to J. Backhouse, F.O., Friday, 3 Feb. 1843, Backhouse Papers; Bandinel to Hamilton, Hastings, Wednesday, 12 Nov. [1821], F.O. 83/35; Minute, Palmerston, 18 Nov. 1838, F.O. 84/265.

features of British diplomacy after 1815 were important causes of the trend. The recognition of the Spanish American states increased the work load by 50 percent.[42] Much of the increase reflected the unsettled state of affairs in Europe between 1815 and 1840 and Britain's active interest in questions that in the eighteenth century, if they were not of less importance to her, at least were beyond her power to influence. As a result more dispatches had to be sent in copy to missions all over Europe as it became essential for every diplomatist to be aware of his country's position on every issue.[43]

Administrative difficulties also played a role in the increase. George IV's dilatory habits of business forced Canning to have all incoming dispatches copied before they were sent to the king, "who will not speedily return them."[44] Palmerston, who dealt more with routine matters than any of his predecessors, at the same time generated more work. The number of dispatches sent in the first two years of his secretaryship nearly doubled that of Aberdeen's last two years. Small wonder that when he was ill everyone in the service surmised that the pressures of the office temporarily slackened.[45]

Londonderry in the reforms of 1822 had specifically disapproved of extra allowances. Canning, therefore, tried to meet the growth of the volume of business by additions to the establishment. In 1824 he advanced the three supernumerary clerks to the third class and appointed three men to fill their places. Three years later, when the establishment was again inadequate, Canning secured four additional clerks by expanding the second class from four to seven men and by creating a fourth class of eight men from the supernumeraries and new appointees.[46]

Canning apparently only once resorted to extraordinary payments, and that was for preparing papers for Parliament in 1823 before he began adding to the staff.[47] Aberdeen, whose secretary-

42. Canning to Liverpool, Seaford, 14 Oct. 1825, Stapleton, *Corresp. of Canning*, vol. 1, 301–2.
43. Chart in F.O. 83/55.
44. Canning to Liverpool, F.O., 1 Apr. 1828 [1823?], Stapleton, *Corresp. of Canning*, vol. 2, 26.
45. Chart in F.O. 83/55; Edmund Hammond to George Hammond, Madrid, 29 Apr. 1833, No. 21, F.O. 391/28. Canning was also a taskmaster. Planta to Stratford Canning, F.O., 14 Feb. 1826, Private, F.O. 352/13 (Part 1)/1.
46. Canning to Lords of the Treasury, F.O., 14 Apr. 1824, and 30 Dec. 1826, extracts, F.O. 366/386.
47. Minute, Canning to S. Rolleston, F.O., 23 July 1823, F.O. 366/313.

ship coincided with a worsening economic situation in the late 1820s, could not add to the establishment. Nor could he resist the demands of his undersecretaries that the clerks be rewarded for their long hours preparing the voluminous Greek papers for Parliament, though he insisted that only those who really had performed extraordinary duty should share in the award.[48]

Aberdeen made matters worse in 1830 by abolishing two junior clerkships as part of his policy of retrenchment.[49] Subsequently, when Palmerston regularly employed the clerks during the Belgian crisis for eight hours a day, as well as late into the night and on Sundays, and then abolished chancery presents at the same time the whole office was in an uproar.[50] Palmerston agreed in this instance to grant special compensation on the grounds that their work "unquestionably has been far greater than that commonly required in other Departments."[51] He did not, however, continue the practice and in 1835 told Backhouse, "I have an insurmountable objection to Special allowances. . . .It is a bad Principle to overburthen one Person & then to increase the charge on the Public as a Counterbalance for the increased Burthen thrown on a particular Individual. This is a false Doctrine of Equilibrium."[52] Thereafter secretaries returned to the practice of employing supernumeraries.

The organization of the establishment after 1822 became more complex as the volume of business increased with Britain's expanded role in international affairs. The practice of dividing the world into two spheres, each the particular concern of one undersecretary, continued.[53] But the clerks gradually began to work exclusively with one undersecretary and then only on certain countries within his division so that by the 1830s the scope of their duties was rigidly and narrowly defined.[54] The juniors continued to be mere amanuenses, employed in the manual duties of the office while they

48. Memorandum, J. Backhouse, and Lord Dunglas to Aberdeen, July 1830, with minute, Aberdeen, ibid.

49. Draft to Treasury, F.O., Mar. 1830, F.O. 366/553.

50. Memorial of the Clerks, F.O., 27 June 1832, F.O. 366/313.

51. Minute, Palmerston, 28 Aug. 1832, ibid.

52. Minute, Palmerston to Backhouse, 26 May 1835, ibid.

53. See chapter 5 and appendix II for a discussion of the divisions of the office directed by the undersecretaries.

54. Establishment of the Foreign Office as divided into Departments, 27 July 1839, F.O. 366/386. In the Colonial Office "Individual clerks had . . . , possibly from the beginning, been associated with specific colonies . . . ." Young, *The Colonial Office*, p. 54.

gained experience.[55] But the senior class and eventually some of the second class began to play a more imaginative and responsible role in the business of the office.

By comparison the Colonial Office was more advanced in practice. Early in the 1820s the "senior clerks were allowed considerable initiative in the preparation of dispatches. . . . It is probable that at this time they made oral inquiries at other departments on their own initiative. . . ," and they frequently acted as departmental agents in interdepartmental discussions.[56] There is no indication in the records that the Foreign Office consciously modeled its practices after those of the Colonial Office, though it is difficult to believe the clerks were unaware of the differences that existed. The cause of this trend was, in fact, the same thing that encouraged initiative in the Colonial Office: the increasing inability of the secretary of state to do everything. The process was retarded in the Foreign Office only because Canning and Palmerston were not Bathurst and Glenelg.

The chief clerk continued after 1822 to administer financial concerns. He also passed all warrants and commissions through the Privy Seal Office, was responsible for all correspondence with the Treasury relating to financial matters, and prepared the estimates the department submitted annually to Parliament.[57] Responsibility again joined prestige.

Rolleston and his successors were assisted by Henry Dundas Scott, who was not a clerk on the establishment until 1822, though he first came to the office in 1814. After the reforms of 1822 he was given the special position of "clerk attached to the Chief Clerk's Department," and paid from the Fee Fund. As a result of this arrangement, however, he received no automatic advancement when there were vacancies. Canning in 1823 awarded him the pay and augmentation of the junior clerks, and in 1827 agreed to his being paid in the same manner as the second class clerks.[58] Scott, who retired in 1866, kept the books and did all the work connected with the issuing of passports. After forty years service Aberdeen gave him an augmen-

55. Minute, J. Backhouse, on "Draft to Under Secretary of State, Colonial Department," Foreign Office, 26 Oct. 1827, Slave Trade, F.O. 84/75.
56. Young, *The Colonial Office*, p. 56.
57. Memorandum on the F.O., June 1828, F.O. 366/386; Memorandum, Thomas Bidwell, F.O., 23 Aug. 1836, ibid.
58. Minute, Londonderry to Rolleston, F.O., 21 Sept. 1821; Minute, Canning, 30 Sept. 1823; Canning to T. Bidwell, F.O., 28 Apr. 1827, F.O. 366/313.

tation of £100 a year in lieu of promotion to a salary scale equivalent to the senior class.[59] He was the type of dedicated public servant that leaves no lasting monument but does the routine work so well that his superiors are free to handle more important affairs.

Some of the bitterest quarrelling among the staff concerned the chief clerkship. One of the last official duties William Hamilton performed before he retired in 1822 was to explain to Charles Broughton, who as first senior clerk expected to become chief clerk, that his financial affairs left Londonderry little choice but to pass him by when Rolleston retired, as Londonderry could not justify such an appointment in Parliament.[60] Broughton protested, and even devised a plan whereby the chief clerk would do all the bookkeeping while an accountant would handle the funds of the office. Canning, however, who was secretary when Rolleston retired in 1824, felt the same objections to Broughton that Londonderry had, and refused to promote him.[61] It was a misfortune that Broughton's plan was shelved, since it included a proposal to reintegrate the chief clerkship into the political business of the office. Broughton chose to retire rather than be passed over, and Canning gave him a pension of £800 out of the superannuation fund with an additional £200 on the secret service account, the latter going in reversion to his widow.[62]

Rolleston's successor, Thomas Bidwell, had none of his father's work habits. He was careless[63] and tended to be crotchety. In the 1830s he was ill and spent a good deal of time away from the office. Others in the department filled his shoes and he hung on long enough to retire in 1841 on full pension after fifty years service.[64]

Bidwell's inefficiency led to Palmerston's decision in 1838 to abolish his place after his retirement. The undersecretaries, John Backhouse and William Fox-Strangways, fought against this decision and were joined by some of the senior clerks. The most articu-

59. H. D. Scott's memorandum, Foreign Office, 6 Nov. 1826, and minute, Addington, F.O., 15 Dec. 1845, ibid.

60. Memorandum, Hamilton to Planta, Foreign Office, 29 Jan. 1822, Private and Secret, F.O. 366/553.

61. Broughton to Backhouse, Blackheath, Monday, 22 Dec. 1823, and 24 Dec. 1823, ibid.

62. Broughton to Backhouse, 24 Jan. 1824, and minute, Canning, 23 Jan. 1824, Canning MSS Bundle 136.

63. Miscellaneous memoranda and minutes by Bidwell, Backhouse, and Palmerston in F.O. 95/591 indicate Bidwell's lack of care in preparing estimates.

64. Draft to Lords of the Treasury, F.O., 27 July 1841, F.O. 366/553.

late of them was the third senior clerk, George Lenox-Conyngham, a tall, stout, peglegged Irishman, wounded in a hunting accident in his youth. He had a vile temper, but was one of the most capable men in the department,[65] and knew it. Conyngham's defense of the chief clerkship, though partially marred by his insistence that the good of the service and not merely his personal prospects motivated his protest, gave the best reasons for its retention. The chief clerk and his subordinates, he argued, should be "fixtures" of a separate and distinct department:

> for a long performance of the duties of a Chief Clerk must naturally have a tendency to unfit any man for the due discharges of the active, laborious, and heterogeneous everyday business that is connected with the Diplomatick Correspondence of the Foreign Office. The Chief Clerk should therefore be, what he has always been, the Chef du Bureau,— the man who by station, good conduct, and efficiency combined may have attained to this last step of preferment in a Clerk's career:—and his Subordinates should all be *Extra* Clerks,—that is to say, clerks exclusively attached to his Department . . . for it would never answer that the mechanical execution of the business of the Chief Clerkship should be entrusted to raw youths newly appointed to the office, entirely ignorant of official habits, unimpressed with the necessity of accuracy and regularity in the keeping of accounts, and, most probably (when the academical education of these times is considered), not only totally unacquainted with bookkeeping, but even with the common rules of arithmetick.[66]

Palmerston eventually gave way, but only after a year of hard work by the undersecretaries and clerks to drive the "prejudice" out of his mind.[67]

Conyngham had his sights set on the chief clerkship before he

65. Hertslet, *Recollections*, p. 143; John Burke, *A Genealogical and Heraldic Dictionary of the Landed Gentry of Great Britain and Ireland* (3 vols.; London, 1848–49), vol. 1, 253; Tilley and Gaselee, *The Foreign Office*, p. 63; Algernon Cecil. "The Foreign Office," p. 588.

66. "Remarks on Lord Palmerston's minute of 28 April, 1839, on the subject of the internal economy and arrangements of the Foreign Office, by Mr. Conyngham, third Senior Clerk," F.O., 30 May 1839, F.O. 95/591. From 1849 two clerks with skills in accounting were attached to the Chief Clerk's Department. Tilley and Gaselee, *The Foreign Office*, pp. 68–69.

67. J. Backhouse to his father, Brussels, 12 July 1839, Backhouse Papers.

vigorously defended it. He went so far as to suggest to John Bidwell and James Bandinel, the first and second senior clerks, that the three of them meet beforehand to determine who would be the successor to Thomas Bidwell. He suggested that Thomas Ward, a second class clerk, "be taken into our Consultations; . . . I shall be ready to abide, if Arbitration become[s] necessary, by whatever Ward may decide to be fair and just towards us three Individually, and the office generally." Bidwell and Bandinel disdained to reply, however, so he decided to consult his own interests exclusively when the time came.[68] One wonders how Palmerston would have reacted had he heard of such an arrangement.

When Thomas Bidwell announced his intention to retire in 1841, Backhouse immediately called John Bidwell and Bandinel into his room and told them that if they declined the succession it would go by default to Conyngham.[69] Bidwell's and Bandinel's objections to the chief clerkship were twofold. First, they held more responsible and interesting positions as senior clerks. More important, their salary and special allowances were greater than they could earn as chief clerk. Not wishing the appointment for themselves, they resolved to resist Conyngham's success by a personal appeal to Palmerston. Backhouse found Bidwell, particularly,

> in a great state of agitation; all of which I ascertained by a searching cross questioning, turned on his determination to get rid of the office of Chief Clerk if possible, lest it should be held by Conyngham, over his & Bandinel's Heads. In short that it was his & Bandinel's object to persuade Ld. P. that a Chief Clerk was not necessary!—& thus to add additional Labour & an additional grievance to that of the old incompetent Clerk his Relation, to Ld. Leveson & me; to spoil the Establishment; & to rob all the Colleagues below them of a most important advantage now obtained for them as some compensation for all their hardships & some remuneration adequate to their meritorious labours.

68. Conyngham to J. Bidwell, F.O., 25 Apr. 1839, Copy, F.O. 95/591.
69. Backhouse fortunately recorded the events in a letter to his son, a junior clerk temporarily attached abroad. J. Backhouse to G. C. Backhouse, Foreign Office, 27 July 1841, Backhouse Papers.

Backhouse, exhausted from overwork, remembered the uphill battle to retain the post, a battle presumably won in 1839 but renewed off and on over the following two years. He was disgusted and indignant at "the discovery of his [Bidwell's] most wicked plan, founded only on motives of selfishness & malice—like the Dog in the manger in Esop's [sic] Tales,—neither capable to take the office himself nor able to bear to see another & worthier person appointed to it." Backhouse defeated the scheme easily by arranging for Conyngham and Thomas Staveley, another senior clerk, to attend the interview Bidwell and Bandinel had with Palmerston. Backhouse and Leveson also talked with Palmerston both before and after the clerks did. Conyngham was promoted, transferring his duties as head of the Treaty Department to the Chief Clerk.[70]

Between 1822 and 1840 the four senior clerks assumed responsibility for particular branches of the office which grew up during that period. All of these departments, save one, actually originated in the postwar years, but they were not formally established until 1824 and 1825. The first to appear was the Treaty and Royal Letter Department. The fourth senior clerk directed this branch merely because, in 1825, when Canning created it, Henry Rolleston, the clerk who had for a decade been preparing treaties for ratification, happened to be fourth senior clerk.

"Experience, minute accuracy, & an extensive knowledge of Precedents" were the essential qualities the head of the Treaty Department had to possess.[71] The department prepared, under his supervision, the ratifications of all treaties and the copies of them laid before Parliament. Most of the monarch's official personal correspondence with foreign sovereigns passed through it and many of the formal letters were drafted and written fair by Rolleston and his assistant.[72] The fourth senior clerk also had the responsibility of drafting and writing the instructions and commissions of di-

70. Anderson, "Edmund Hammond," p. 43.

71. Minute, J. Backhouse, on "Mr. Conyngham's Recommendation of Mr. Bergne," Mar. 1840, F.O. 366/313.

72. Memorandum to Lords Dudley and Aberdeen, 1828, F.O. 366/386; Draft, His Majesty to the Ottoman Emperor, 5 July 1834, F.O. 96/2. After 1840 the Prince Consort's official correspondence also passed through the department, though Conyngham and Bergne both protested that the consorts of kings never had that privilege. Minutes, Conyngham, F.O., 27 Apr. 1841, and Bergne, 11 Mar. 1840, F.O. 95/714.

plomatists.[73] Rolleston and his successor, Conyngham, both of whom received an annuity of £150 for their additional responsibility, were able men and theirs was one of the best administered branches of the office.

The head of the department assumed increased responsibility after Conyngham succeeded Rolleston in 1834. Wellington gave the additional labor of transacting all the commercial and political business with China to the Treaty Department in 1835, rather than assigning it to one of the overworked political divisions of the office.[74] He did so possibly because of the fluctuating nature of the Treaty Department's work load. Palmerston came to rely on Conyngham's judgment to a greater degree than he had on Rolleston's, and treaties proposed and drafted by other government offices first had to clear the Treaty Department before they received the secretary of state's sanction.[75] Conyngham's efficiency in transacting these affairs and Palmerston's desire to give the chief clerk more work led to the merging of the Treaty Department with the chief clerkship in 1841 when the China business devolved upon the Turkish Department in the political section of the office.[76]

One assistant clerk, John Brodribb Bergne, was attached to the Treaty Department. Rolleston personally first employed him as a clerk in 1814 to help prepare the massive treaties of that and the following year.[77] Bergne remained a special assistant to Rolleston until 1824 when Canning placed his salary on the contingent account. Not until 1841, however, was he placed on the regular establishment as "clerk attached to the Treaty Department."[78] His position between these years was similar to that of James Murray in the Chief Clerk's Department (though Murray was on the establishment), as Bergne received a salary and augmentation equal to the third class after 1827 and to the second class after 1829.[79]

73. Draft to Henry Rolleston, Foreign Office, 2 Dec. 1826, F.O. 84/62.
74. "Report of Mr. Lenox-Conyngham, Fourth Senior Clerk in the Foreign Office. . . ," F.O., 24 Aug. 1836, F.O. 95/591; unsigned minute, Foreign Office, Jan. 1835, F.O. 366/313.
75. Minutes, Palmerston and Conyngham, on "Oyster Fishery, Draft of Convention . . . In Letter from the Board of Trade," 20 Dec. 1838, F.O. 97/189.
76. Anderson, "Edmund Hammond," p. 43.
77. Minute, Thomas Staveley, F.O., 10 June 1829, Private, F.O. 366/313.
78. Canning to Lords of the Treasury, F.O., 10 Feb. 1824, and Conyngham to Backhouse, F.O., Sunday, 22 Mar. 1840, ibid.
79. Canning to T. Bidwell, F.O., 28 Apr. 1827, and Minute, Aberdeen, F.O., 10 July 1829, ibid.

Bergne was an interesting character. A charter member of the Numismatic Society and its Treasurer from 1843 to 1857, he wrote numerous articles for the *Numismatic Journal*. He owed his success in the office to his "neat and distinct penmanship" which was so remarkable that Canning employed him exclusively in preparing documents for the lithographic press installed in the Foreign Office in 1824. He also registered all letters of recommendation from the secretary of state to diplomatists, for which he was paid £50 a year.[80] In 1834 he applied for Rolleston's position as head of the Treaty Department because he felt that his experience entitled him to the post and because the duties of the department required special skills in penmanship and knowledge of precedents which it would be impossible to maintain if there was a new chief for the branch every time the fourth senior clerkship changed hands. Backhouse, however, felt that the Treaty Department, on grounds of expediency and justice to the claims of others, ought to be directed by a senior clerk.[81] Bergne continued to work as Conyngham's assistant until 1849 when the branch was reconstructed as a separate department. In 1854 he became its head and when he died of heart failure nearly twenty years later he was widely respected for his expertise.[82]

The first senior clerk, John Bidwell, was Superintendent of the Consular Department from 1825 until his retirement in 1851.[83] He was the nephew and cousin of the chief clerk Bidwells. Of all the clerks in the office between 1782 and 1846 he was one of the most capable, and had it been the practice to promote clerks to the undersecretaryship at that time, he undoubtedly would have succeeded Planta in 1827. He was a formidable-looking gentleman, bald, possessed of a long straight nose, and mutton chop whiskers. The water colors of Turkish villages, people, and Court preserved in his papers are a testimony to his skill as an artist.[84]

80. Boase, *Modern English Biography*, vol. 1, 253; Canning to Lords of the Treasury, F.O., 10 Feb. 1824, F.O. 366/313; Minute, J. Backhouse, on "Mr. Conyngham's Recommendation of Mr. Bergne," Mar. 1840, ibid.; Bergne to Planta, F.O., 22 Dec. 1825, ibid.

81. Bergne to Backhouse, Foreign Office, 21 May 1834, and Backhouse to Bergne, F.O., 23 May 1834, Copy, ibid.

82. Tilley and Gaselee, *The Foreign Office*, p. 68; *Foreign Office List*, 1856; *The Times* (London), 22 Jan. 1873, p. 9.

83. Temperley said Backhouse held the post in 1825, which is an understandable error since both he and Bidwell initialled their minutes "J.B." See Temperley, *For. Pol. Canning*, pp. 261–62.

84. A lithographic portrait is also in his papers, Add. MS 41315 f. 5.

The Consular Act of 1825, which reorganized the consular service and attempted to make it a more respectable and responsive branch of government, necessitated Bidwell's appointment. Though other clerks had for some time been working with consular affairs (notably Bandinel),[85] Canning chose Bidwell to direct the Consular Department because it was the most important of all the departments headed by senior clerks. Bidwell was assisted by a clerk on the regular establishment, a distinction not given to his colleagues and one that emphasized the permanency and importance of the Consular Department. When the volume of consular business increased to such a level that he needed additional assistance, Canning also appointed an extra clerk, Sydney Smith Saunders.[86] Bidwell received an extra £500 a year for his additional responsibility while his assistant, John Jackson, was paid £100 extra.[87]

Jackson retired in ill health in 1830 amid the rigors of the retrenchment that Aberdeen was forced to implement in the Foreign Office. His successor, James Murray, also a junior clerk, was given no special allowance, though it was supposed to be some consolation that his new duties "will bring you, as Mr. J. Bidwell's representative, into almost constant communication with both the Under Secretaries."[88] Murray eventually received a special allowance in 1835, but only after threatening to quit his "laborious & irksome" assignment and return to general duty. By that time Saunders had accepted a consulship and it had become the practice of the office to place all new clerks under Bidwell's direction until they settled into the routine of the office, after which time they were transferred to one of the political divisions. Since in practice this arrangement meant that Murray had to work with and train inexperienced help ("a task I can assure you of no very pleasant kind"),[89] he deserved the additional allowance.

85. Minute, Clanwilliam, on J. W. Croker to Clanwilliam, Admiralty Office, 14 Sept. 1820, F.O. 72/242 ff. 145–56; Minute, Hamilton, on Thomas Lack to Hamilton, Office of the Committee of the Privy Council for Trade, Whitehall, 10 Nov. 1819, F.O. 72/232 ff. 136–37.

86. Memo on the F.O., June 1828, F.O. 366/386.

87. Canning to Lords of the Treasury, F.O., 25 Nov. 1825, Draft, ibid.; Minute, Planta to T. Bidwell, F.O., 5 Apr. 1826, F.O. 366/313.

88. J. Backhouse to Murray, F.O., 27 Sept. 1830, F.O. 366/313.

89. J. Backhouse to Wellington, Foreign Office, 1 Mar. 1835, Wellington Papers; Memorandum, Murray, "Application either to be removed . . . or to receive some additional remuneration. . . ," 27 May 1835, F.O. 366/313; Minute, Palmerston, 21 Feb. 1836, ibid.; Murray to Backhouse, 1 Oct. 1835, ibid.

The principal duty Bidwell performed was procuring and digesting commercial and manufacturing statistics and information about the various countries in which Britain maintained consuls. This was a tedious job, and as Parliament, the Treasury, and the Board of Trade began to demand more and more data, it became one of great magnitude. Bidwell ran the department as a semi-autonomous satrapy. Prior to 1835, when a postal convention with France required that all official mail be directed to the secretary of state, consuls directed to Bidwell personally.[90] His opinion was decisive on where consulships should be established. In 1843, for example, Aberdeen considered creating a consulship at Geneva, but Bidwell reported that there was no reason to have one there, and his opinion prevailed.[91]

As first senior clerk Bidwell also had other duties. He maintained his predecessors' responsibility for general supervision of the office. All the circulars to diplomatists and consuls originated from his pen, and he had custody of the ciphers and deciphers which he occasionally had to replace. In addition to these duties, Bidwell was expected to pick up any slack in the Chief Clerk's Department,[92] and as his cousin's health deteriorated in the 1830s it was he who took over his duties. After Bidwell's retirement the supervision of consular affairs passed to the undersecretaries. Murray in 1858 became the first assistant undersecretary appointed in the Foreign Office and had special responsibility for the consular service.[93]

The largest branch directed by the senior clerks was the Slave Trade Department. James Bandinel, the second senior clerk, assumed this responsibility in 1824.[94] Britain was the leading power in the crusade to suppress the slave trade, which proved to be one of the most expensive and protracted policies ever undertaken by any country. As the task grew Bandinel's department rose from, "in point of importance and business, a mere nullity, a Dept. of secondary consideration . . . welded on, as it were, to . . . a body of higher quality and nature," to one of the busiest and largest branches of the

90. Draft to Consuls by James Murray, F.O., 8 Dec. 1836, Separate, F.O., 83/95.
91. Unsigned minute, J. Bidwell, F.O., [July 1843], Add. MS 43241 ff. 114-15; Aberdeen to the Duchess of Gordon, F.O., 1 Aug. 1843, Copy, ibid., f. 116.
92. Memorandum of the F.O., June 1828, F.O. 366/386.
93. *Records of the Foreign Office*, p. 6; Tilley and Gaselee, *The Foreign Office*, p. 109.
94. He received £1,000 for his services connected with the slave trade from 1819 to 1824, and an annuity of £200 for the future. Planta to Bandinel, F.O., 4 Dec. 1824, Draft, F.O. 83/40.

office.[95] Bandinel's duties throughout this transformation were both administrative and financial. He directed all the slave trade correspondence with foreign powers and with the commissions created under international conventions to suppress it. He also received the annual grants voted by Parliament to defray the costs of these commissions and paid the salaries and expenses of all British officials employed on them.[96]

The slave trade correspondence was never prepared in the political divisions of the office. It formed a separate series of numbered dispatches which were written fair by Bandinel and his staff. Canning, when he established the department in 1824, did not expect Britain's encountering the difficulties she later did in suppressing the slave trade. Consequently, as it was to be only a temporary branch of the office, he did not place the clerks attached to the department on the regular establishment. Bandinel's first assistant, Charles Pettingal, was appointed in 1825. He was paid from extra funds voted annually by Parliament,[97] as were the other clerks that served in the branch before 1841. In that year the salaries of the four clerks attached to the department were transferred to the Fee Fund, an arrangement "more proper, and more in conformity with the general principle upon which Estimates for Parliament are framed. . . ."[98] The clerks were not placed on the regular establishment, however, but retained a separate hierarchy unaffected by promotions elsewhere in the office.

Bandinel, as paymaster for the commissioners abroad, received the annual grant of Parliament to defray their expenses. These grants averaged between £20,000 and £30,000 a year, for which "No pecuniary Security is required. The Stake held by the individual in his Situation in the Office together with the Check over the receipts and payments, have been held to be sufficient security." Bandinel also paid contingent expenses as well as salaries and up to 1842 the pensions of these personnel.[99] Because he acted in effect as agent to

95. Addington to Aberdeen, F.O., 1844, F.O. 366/313.
96. Memorandum on the F.O., June 1828, F.O. 366/386.
97. "Slave Trade Commissions, Jan. 1828," F.O. 96/28.
98. Palmerston, Draft to the Treasury, Foreign Office, 9 Aug. 1841, F.O. 366/386.
99. Memorandum in Letter to Treasury, 19 June 1827, F.O. 84/74; C. E. Trevelyan to Addington, Treasury Chambers, 2 Aug. 1843, F.O. 84/489; "Return of all Persons in the Foreign Department who hold Public Money in their Hands. . . ," F.O., 30 Apr. 1829 [1830?], F.O. 366/366 ff. 134–35.

the commissioners, he collected 1 percent agency fee on their salaries, an arrangement that the Treasury knew nothing of until they decided to assume responsibility for paying the commissioners themselves.[100]

This lax system of control was challenged only once when the Treasury in 1829 tried to get Bandinel to agree to let the governors of the colonies in which the commissions sat pay and charge their contingent expenses. Backhouse, however, refused to consider the proposal lest "we allow the insertion of the small end of a wedge,"[101] and the matter dropped. Henry Goulburn, Peel's chancellor of the Exchequer, finally placed the slave trade commissioners on the same footing as the diplomatic service in 1843, not because he feared abuses, but because he wished to assert greater Treasury control of expenditure.[102]

The Slave Trade Department was the most specialized of the branches. Clerks with many years experience were often appointed judges and arbitrators on the mixed commission courts.[103] Bandinel became the greatest expert on the slave trade that the office ever produced. He was diligent but not brilliant. Lord Leveson, who served as Palmerston's undersecretary and worked closely with Bandinel, told his father that Bandinel "who I believe knows as much about his department the Slave Trade, as one can know on such a subject, expresses himself very awkwardly. It is disagreeable to me to correct as if he was a schoolboy all his sentences. . . ."[104]

Bandinel's expertise was recognized beyond the office. Thomas Fowell Buxton invited him to the first gathering of the Foreign Anti-Slavery Society, which he attended with Palmerston's permission after the undersecretary had expressed hopes that he "might gain some information useful to his department by attending this matter."[105] He was the only person in the Foreign Office who had

100. Memorandum by Trevelyan, Treasury, 22 Nov. 1843, F.O. 84/489.

101. J. Stewart to Backhouse, Treasury Chambers, 5 May 1829, with Bandinel's minute, 25 May, F.O. 84/97.

102. Trevelyan to Addington, Treasury Chambers, 2 Aug. 1843, F.O. 84/489.

103. Minute on J. H. Frere to Aberdeen, Malta, 15 Aug. 1843, Private, Add. MS 43239 ff. 302–4; Draft to Chief Clerk, Foreign Office, 28 July 1843, F.O. 84/500.

104. Leveson to Granville, F.O., 20 Mar. 1840, Lord Edmond Fitzmaurice, *The Life of Granville George Leveson-Gower, Second Earl Granville* (2 vols.; London, 1905), vol. 1, 29.

105. Buxton to Bandinel, London, 20 June 1839, and minutes, Strangways and Palmerston, 21 June 1839, F.O. 84/305.

any knowledge of Africa, and explorers met with him to seek his advice and help in furthering their projects. Palmerston, too, consulted him about Britain's previous policy with regard to French expansion in Africa when the French began to make excursions in the area of the River Gambia in the 1830s.[106] Bandinel reached the pinnacle of his career during Aberdeen's second secretaryship when he published a history of the slave trade, and when Aberdeen appointed him to the commission established to revise the cruising instructions of the British fleets for suppressing it.[107]

Bandinel's experience gave him a voice in policy that no other clerk and perhaps few undersecretaries in his time enjoyed. As early as 1822 he began to take an active part in questions relating to the slave trade.[108] Canning had great respect for his judgment. In 1826 his argument that "we have never admitted, and have never thought, that the carrying of Slaves to the Cape de Verds could be legal, until the King's advocate gave his opinion to that effect in March last," induced Canning to resubmit the whole question to the King's Advocate with his opinion that Bandinel's and not the Advocate's position was correct.[109] Palmerston realized the importance of his expertise and consulted with him frequently during the negotiations of the five major powers on a slave trade treaty in 1839.[110] In Aberdeen's second secretaryship Bandinel's influence reached its greatest point and his rejection in 1843 of a Brazilian project for a treaty to suppress the slave trade led Aberdeen to conclude that perhaps Britain should suppress the trade "as we think proper," which Aberdeen's Act in 1845 was designed to accomplish.[111]

Bandinel retired in 1845 under peculiar circumstances. Peel's

106. John Davidson to Bandinel, 1 St. James's Street, 15 July 1835, Bandinel Family Papers; Minutes, Palmerston and not signed, on "Question as to the reimbursement of the Expenses incurred by the French Govt. in furnishing assistance to the Govt. of Bathurst in the Gambia, memorandum," [Dec. 1833], F.O. 27/477; Bandinel to J. Bidwell, received 17 Aug. 1836, F.O. 27/496.

107. *Some Account of the Trade in Slaves. . .* (London, 1842); Aberdeen to Lushington, Bandinel, Denman and Rotheray, Foreign Office, 14 Dec. 1842, Draft, Slave Trade, F.O. 84/446.

108. Minute by Bandinel, unsigned, "Address of the House of Commons to His Majesty on the Slave Trade," 27 June 1822, F.O. 84/19.

109. Memorandum, Private, Portuguese, Foreign Office, 4 Sept. 1826, with minute, Canning, F.O. 84/61.

110. Minute, Palmerston, on Bandinel to J. Bidwell, Lyme, 26 Aug. 1841, Copy, F.O. 84/389.

111. Memorandum on the Brazilian project on the slave trade, F.O., 3 Feb. 1843, and Minute, Aberdeen, n.d., F.O. 96/29; 8 & 9 Victoria, c. 122, 8 Aug. 1845.

government, wracked with dissent over the question of the repeal of the corn laws, resigned on 9 December. On the tenth Bandinel applied for his pension, which Aberdeen granted immediately.[112] The probable reason for this flurry of activity was Bandinel's great antipathy towards Palmerston, Aberdeen's likely successor, who on several occasions in the 1830s had been extremely critical of Bandinel's work. On one instance Palmerston returned a draft prepared by Bandinel with the comment "I wish I was not compelled to waste, in putting these Drafts into Such Shape as to be producible to Parliament, that Time which I could employ far more usefully for the public Service." What disturbed Bandinel so on this particular occasion was that he had come into the office because there was a shortage of help and had spent the whole day preparing the dispatch on his own initiative, telling two confused officials what duties they were expected to perform on the mixed commission to which they were attached. Bandinel's anger is reflected by his comment, "To be kept *for the hereafter*," and by the fact that this is one of the few rough drafts that have been preserved.[113] It is probable that he wished to retire while Aberdeen was secretary so that he would receive the maximum allowance under the law, lest Aberdeen's successor still be in office when he had completed fifty years of service in April 1849.

The least important officially and the most interesting personally of the senior clerks was the third among them, Frederick Gerald "Poodle" Byng, who owed his sobriquet to his kinky hair.[114] Byng was a dandy who moved in London society as few of his contemporaries and none of his colleagues could. He also was an egotist ("Brighton is quite full but of Persons even *I* am not acquainted with," he told Lord Granville in 1832), and it was perhaps this quality which led Countess Granville to call him "a hard, selfish, ill-tempered, presumptuous animal" whose only saving grace was his "instinct about his puppies."[115] His great shortcoming was his laziness and his

112. Aberdeen to Bandinel, Foreign Office, 12 Dec. 1845, and Addington to Bandinel, 13 Dec. 1845, Bandinel Family Papers.

113. Minutes, Palmerston, n.d., and Bandinel, 14 Dec. 1836, on Draft to E. W. H. Schenley and Dr. R. R. Madden, Foreign Office, Dec. 1836, F.O. 96/28.

114. T. B. Macaulay to Hannah M. Macaulay, London, 25 Sept. 1832, Sir George Otto Trevelyan, Bart., *The Life and Letters of Lord Macaulay* (2 vols.; London, 1932), vol. 1, 255.

115. Byng to Granville, F.O., 17 Aug. 1832, P.R.O. 30/29/7/13 ff. 893–96; Lady Granville to Lady G. Morpeth, Wherstead, Jan. 1822, and The Hague, 18 Apr. 1824, Leveson-Gower, *Letters of Countess Granville*, vol. 1, 221–22, 279.

lack of enthusiasm for the routine of official life, especially when there were interesting things going on elsewhere: "I must creep out to the Levee today & the Drawing Room tomorrow—as I am on Duty."[116]

Byng alone of the senior clerks in 1824 did not merit the direction of a special branch of the office. Canning offered him a consulship which he declined as being inadequate to his needs. Canning, probably to avoid intraoffice turmoil, then created a special branch to occupy his energies auditing the contingent accounts of diplomatists and consuls.[117] Only after "Mr. Auditor General Byng," as John Bidwell facetiously called him,[118] performed this task admirably for nearly two years, however, did he receive the customary annuity of £150.[119] He was despite, or perhaps because of, his failings the perfect man for the job. His limited concentration and ability were not too strained by the routine nature of it and his social position enabled him to chastise any diplomatist when he found errors in an account. Even Lord Granville, the senior serving diplomat, was not spared: "I recur again to the House Expenses. You must give the office a resumée of all the different charges—& in English too—the Clerks of the Treasury & the Country gentlemen cannot understand French figures & such words as 'Devis'. I conclude the whole bundle will be sent back to you that you may return us something to forward to the Treasury."[120]

Byng's habits of business deteriorated once the novelty of his post wore off, however, and by 1832 he was looking towards quitting as soon as "I can persuade them that the saving would enable them to give me a tolerable retirement."[121] He got his wish in 1839 when his duties were transferred to the chief clerk, where they properly belonged.[122] Conyngham succeeded him as third senior clerk, keeping the Treaty and China Departments in his hands. Byng continued to grace the Court and society for another thirty-two years, during

116. Byng to Granville, 27 May 1836, P.R.O. 30/29/7/13 ff. 1143–46.
117. Howard de Walden to Granville, Foreign Office, 23 Mar. 1824, P.R.O. 30/29/6/7 ff. 1255–59; Byng to Same, F.O., 1 Jan. 1826, P.R.O. 30/29/7/12 ff. 719–24.
118. Bidwell to Planta, 24 Sept. 1826, F.O. 366/292.
119. Planta to Canning, N. B. St., 26 Dec. 1826, ½ p. 10, and Canning to Lords of Treasury, F.O., 30 Dec. 1826, F.O. 366/386.
120. Byng to Granville, F.O., 14 Mar. 1826, Private, P.R.O. 30/29/7/12 ff. 729–32.
121. Byng to Granville, F.O., 23 Oct. 1832, P.R.O. 30/29/7/13 ff. 903–6.
122. Unsigned minute, Apr. 1839, F.O. 366/98.

which time he received £827 a year in superannuation payments.[123]

During the 1820s and 1830s the five clerks with the greatest seniority assumed responsibility for branches of the office completely divorced from political correspondence and concerns. The political divisions which arose in this period were headed by second-class clerks, designated in the 1820s "private secretary to the undersecretaries of state," and after 1830 "Clerks Assistant." Each of these men received an annuity of £150 in addition to his salary.

Stephen Rolleston as first senior clerk and later as second chief clerk, had had special responsibility for assisting the undersecretaries in directing the preparation of the political business of the office. When he became sole chief clerk he had little if any time to perform these duties. The undersecretaries at first employed the two most junior third-class clerks, Thomas Staveley and Woodbine Parish, to distribute the business as directed.[124] Each man worked with one undersecretary. Canning assigned a third assistant, Conyngham, to the third undersecretary appointed in 1824, and when the volume of business increased dramatically in the next decade, Palmerston created a fourth clerk assistantship in 1836. By the late 1820s new appointees were invariably of the second class, to which Staveley had advanced by that time. They were appointed not according to seniority but at the discretion of the undersecretaries who selected the most capable men of that class, Thomas Lawrence Ward, Richard Charles Mellish, and Edmund Hammond.[125]

Each clerk assistant headed one division of an undersecretary's department. They exercised little if any influence over policy, though drafts they prepared were frequently accepted by the secretary of state with little or no alteration.[126] Their daily involvement with a few countries, however, gave them the opportunity of developing expert opinions on certain aspects of foreign affairs and paved the way for increased responsibility later in the century.

The great shortcoming of the organization of the office was that the political divisions were headed by men of inferior rank, while the

123. Pennington to Fox-Strangways, Treasury Chambers, 22 Apr. 1839, F.O. 366/553.
124. Minute, Planta to Rolleston, F.O., 25 July 1820, F.O. 366/313; Shuttleworth, *Woodbine Parish*, pp. 229–30.
125. F.O. Salary books, F.O. 366/380–383 passim.
126. For example, unsigned minute, E. Hammond, "On the Draft to the Portendick Merchants, submitted for Lord Palmerston's approval," and minute, Palmerston, 16 Oct. 1835, F.O. 96/18.

abilities and experience of the senior clerks were employed in matters of secondary importance. Palmerston first recognized this situation in 1834 when Conyngham succeeded to the fourth senior clerkship. He proposed that Conyngham, who was a clerk assistant, assume Rolleston's duties and keep his own. King William IV sacked the Whig ministry on the day Conyngham protested this decision, and Wellington refused to uphold it because, in his opinion, no senior clerk should "be employed in a Duty in which one of his Rank in the Office ought not to be employed."[127] After his return to the office Palmerston remained dissatisfied with the practice of employing second-class clerks to perform duties "which are in their nature sufficiently important and confidential to be assigned to the five persons of longest standing and of the highest rate of Salary." He appointed a second class clerk to the fourth clerk assistantship he created in 1836, but ordered a thorough study of the duties of the chief and senior clerks with the clear intention of reforming the system as then established.[128]

Only three years later, however, was there any significant attempt to place the position on a more practical footing. The impetus for the reforms of 1839 to 1841 came initially from two factors unrelated to the responsibilities of the clerks. The volume of business rose from 7,300 pieces in 1829 to 16,400 in 1838, while the size of the staff decreased by two. The clerks were particularly dissatisfied under these circumstances with the slow rate of promotion from class to class. In 1839 there was a log jamb in the second and third classes, where the five senior members of the second and the two clerks on the third class with the most tenure had served in their respective classes from nine to thirteen years. Some reshuffling of the size of the classes was imperative.[129]

Because of the expense involved in reorganizations Palmerston's original proposal was designed to meet these problems only partially. It provided for the addition of two clerks by expanding the second class from seven to ten men, the third class from six to seven, and by decreasing the fourth class from six to four clerks. Francis

127. Conyngham to Palmerston, F.O., 17 Nov. 1834, Copy, F.O. 366/313; Memorandum by the Duke of Wellington on "Mr. Conyngham's Case," 10 Jan. 1835, Wellington MSS, Duke University Library.
128. Copy of minute by Palmerston, 26 Apr. 1836, F.O. 95/591.
129. Backhouse to Palmerston, [1839], fragment, Palmerston Papers, GC/BA/18.

Baring, the chancellor of the Exchequer, agreed to the addition of two clerks, but adamantly refused to approve an alteration in the size of the classes until he could study the proposal. Baring feared that by granting Palmerston's request too precipitously the Home and Colonial Office clerks might be "at once *roused* into demands for similar alterations producing considerable increase to the public expenditure."[130]

Baring took the opportunity of the delay resulting from this study to raise an issue that for some time had been a point of contention between the Foreign Office and the Treasury. Backhouse wrote John Bidwell in December 1839 in a state of agitation: "Refresh your memory by a glance at the inclosed papers & then let me talk with you on the Chancer of the Exchr's present *declared intention to force the Secy of State to abolish these agencies as the condition of his (Mr. Baring's) assenting to* ANY *of our proposed alterations in the Establishment* of the office."[131] Baring's attack was unjust. The agency system had functioned well after Castlereagh's reform of 1816. The Treasury and a select committee of the House of Commons had attacked it in 1836–1837, but their arguments and opinions had not forced Palmerston to abolish it.[132] The Colonial Office, however, had put an end to its agency system after 1837,[133] and the Foreign Office was left exposed as the only department still permitting the practice.

Backhouse, who perhaps more than any other undersecretary shared the clerk's antipathy towards any Treasury incursions into matters which in their minds were the sole responsibility of the secretary of state, had several meetings with Baring early in 1840 to discuss his objections. Baring dropped the matter of the agencies reluctantly and only after Backhouse finally convinced him that the organization of the office was a distinct question from the expediency of maintaining the agency system, and that as the practice cost the public nothing, it was not a proper matter for Treasury interference. Backhouse secured the proposed alteration in the size

130. Palmerston to Lords of the Treasury, Foreign Office, 27 July 1839, Draft, F.O. 366/386; Thomas Spring Rice to Palmerston, Downing Street, 2 Aug. 1839, Confidential, Palmerston Papers, GC/MO/125.
131. Backhouse to J. Bidwell, H.P., 23 Dec. 1839, Confidential, F.O. 366/375 f. 59.
132. Various minutes and memoranda by office personnel in F.O. 366/375 ff. 16–45; "First Report of the Committee . . . to enquire into the Fees and Emoluments of Public Offices," 23 Mar. 1837, *P. P. 1837*, vol. 44, Command 162, pp. 258–59.
133. Hammond's memorandum on F.O. Agencies, Jan. 1840, F.O. 366/375 ff. 61–63.

of the second class by showing Baring that with only four senior class clerks in an establishment of twenty-five, the Foreign Office still had a disproportionate number of junior clerks as compared to the Home and Colonial Offices.[134] Baring's acquiescence in the face of Backhouse's persistence reflected the imperfect control the Treasury had over the establishment, especially when the secretary of state chose to exert his authority, or, since Palmerston was indifferent on the agency question, had it exerted for him.

The second stage of the reorganization was more important than the first, though achieved with considerably less difficulty. Thomas Bidwell's retirement in 1841 paved the way for a complete reorganization of the senior class, as Conyngham, the new chief clerk, retained responsibility for the Treaty Department.[135] Thomas Staveley, the fourth senior clerk, had retained his clerk assistantship on his promotion from the second class in 1839. He became third senior clerk. Palmerston extended this breach in the system established by Canning. He promoted the heads of the political divisions to the senior class, and expanded the class to six men. The second class was reduced to eight clerks. The first and second senior clerks continued to direct consular and slave trade affairs, while the third through the sixth were clerks assistant, though the title was abolished. The clerks assistant, however, were not prohibited from succeeding to the supervision of the departments headed by Bidwell and Bandinel in 1841. Staveley eventually succeeded to both their positions. All extraordinary allowances (save Bidwell's) were abolished, and salaries were raised to a maximum of £1,000.[136] The reforms of 1839–1841 had important and far-reaching consequences. The efficiency and the tradition of the office came to depend largely on the senior clerks[137] and these men eventually exercised an influence over policy far beyond that of their predecessors.

134. Memorandum, Backhouse, "New Classification of the Clerks," 6 Jan. 1840, with minutes in red ink, Backhouse, 13 Mar. 1840, F.O. 366/375 ff. 65–67; J. Backhouse, Draft to the Chancellor of the Exchequer, F.O., 26 Feb. 1840, F.O. 366/375 ff. 74–78. Agencies were abolished in 1870. Cecil, "The Foreign Office," p. 593.

135. Minute, Backhouse, on First Draft to Treasury, F.O., 27 July 1841, F.O. 366/553.

136. Palmerston to Lords of the Treasury, Foreign Office, Draft, 9 Aug. 1841, F.O. 366/386; Order-in-Council, Windsor, 21 Aug. 1841, F.O. 366/542 f. 78.

137. Testimony of Lord Wodehouse, Q. 701, 29 Apr. 1861, "Report from the Select Committee appointed to enquire . . . into the diplomatic service. . . ," P. P., 1861, vol. 6, Command 459, pp. 78–79.

Edmund Hammond, R. C. Mellish, and T. L. Ward were the three clerks who advanced to the senior class in 1841. Ward was the first clerk of the second class and his promotion was expected. Mellish and Hammond, however, were the third and the fifth clerks of their class. Their advancement brought forth protests from Edward McMahon and Hugo St. John Mildmay, the second and fourth clerks of the second class. They claimed that Palmerston had violated the principle of promotion on the basis of seniority which had always been followed by his predecessors.[138] The fact of the system could not be disputed. Despite the Treasury's maxim laid down in 1822 that vacancies in superior classes should be filled by "the fittest Individual" who possessed seniority enough to qualify for them,[139] no secretary of state in the history of the Foreign Office had ever promoted clerks on any basis other than seniority. The exceptions, Bidwell's and Conyngham's appointments to the chief clerkship in 1824 and 1841, were both peculiar cases which proved the rule. Palmerston was opposed to this system, which he labeled "the Prescriptive Right of Idleness and Dulness [sic] to succeed Hackney Coachlike from Bottom to Top of an Office by Dint of more living."[140] The principle he laid down in 1841, followed thereafter, was that "in Promoting from one Class to another my Rule has been and will be to select the Individuals whom I may think the best qualified without Reference to Seniority." In practice this rule was applied only to the senior classes, and no clerk of adequate abilities for a vacancy was ever passed over in order to promote a man of superior qualifications.[141]

There was little change in the functions of the private secretary and the précis writer between 1821 and 1846. These men continued to be regarded as the secretary of state's personal assistants and sometimes were the only friends he had in the office.[142] They always came and went with their principal, though one man, Digby Cayley

138. Mildmay to Palmerston, Foreign Office, 28 July 1841, and McMahon to Same, Foreign Office, 23 July 1841, Palmerston Papers, PAT/M/117/1-3 and PAT/M/29.

139. Treasury minute, "Reduction and Superannuation," Treasury Chambers, 8 Jan. 1822, Copy, F.O. 366/672 ff. 237-48.

140. Palmerston to Lord John Russell, Windsor, 20 Oct. 1839, P.R.O. 30/22/3D ff. 83-85.

141. Minute, Palmerston, on McMahon to Palmerston, Foreign Office, 23 July 1841, Palmerston Papers, PAT/M/29; Lord Wodehouse's testimony, Q. 869, 29 Apr. 1861, "Report from the Select Committee appointed to inquire into the Diplomatic service. . . ," *P. P., 1861*, vol. 6, Command 459, p. 94.

142. Dudley to Harrowby, F.O., 22 Oct. 1827, Harrowby MSS vol. 14, ff. 232-33.

Wrangham, served first as Dudley's and then as Aberdeen's private secretary. They were chosen for their loyalty to the person of the secretary, not to the department. Both Canning and Aberdeen, however, refused to regard the hostile politics of the family of their précis writer and private secretary as reason to dismiss them or to accept their resignations. As long as they remained personally loyal and performed their duties, they were free to retain their position.[143] Some of them were given a clerkship as security for the future, though none collected a salary for it while they were employed as the confidential assistant of the secretary. The practice of exclusively employing clerks on the establishment in these positions[144] was a later development. Palmerston certainly was opposed to it,[145] and it is likely that his predecessors and immediate successor shared his view since they did not alter his practice.

The private secretary, contrary to the practice of the first quarter of the nineteenth century, did not play an important role in policy or administration during this period. Canning attempted to maintain a rigid distinction between his private and his official correspondence, and insisted that the undersecretaries of state, not the private secretary, deal with the latter.[146] Palmerston's private secretaries were too young and inexperienced to assume much initiative. Only after the private secretary was invariably chosen from the clerks with many years experience in the office did he begin to have an important share in questions of internal organization or national policy.[147]

The Librarian's Department, like every other branch after 1821, was overwhelmed by the great volume of business. Hertslet's practice of registering every piece of correspondence became an unmanageable task as the business increased, especially since he tried not only to keep abreast of the current correspondence, but also attempted to catch up on previous years as well. Canning attached a

143. Greville's memoirs, 4 Nov. 1822, London, Strachey and Fulford, *Greville Memoirs*, vol. 1, 135–36; Aberdeen to the Duke of Richmond, F.O., 23 Jan. 1846, Copy, Add. MS 43245, f. 232.
144. Evidence of Hammond, Q. 144, 15 Apr. 1861, "Report from the Select Committee appointed to inquire into the diplomatic service...," *P. P., 1861*, vol. 6, Command 459, p. 14.
145. Palmerston to William Temple, Foreign Office, 7 May 1833, Bulwer, *Life of Palmerston*, vol. 2, 160–61.
146. Minute, Canning, on H. Bristow to Canning, 33 Craven Street, Strand, 22 Apr. 1824, F.O. 72/296 f. 245.
147. Jones, *The Nineteenth-Century Foreign Office*, p. 15; Zara Steiner, "Last Years of the Old Foreign Office," p. 61.

clerk to the department in 1826. When the clerk died thirteen years later he was not replaced. Hertslet employed instead one of his sons as an unofficial unpaid assistant from 1839 to 1841.[148] The Librarian's Department benefitted from the reorganization of 1841 when Palmerston appointed two clerks to assist Hertslet and his brother. A third clerk added in 1842 and a fourth clerk appointed in 1844 enabled Hertslet to keep pace with the growth of the correspondence. Despite the fact that the Librarian's Department was usually behind in preparing the registers, Hertslet made certain that the files of those countries of greatest concern at any particular moment were current. During the first two years of Aberdeen's second secretaryship, for example, the French, American, and Spanish correspondence was brought up to date at the expense of the rest of the registers.[149]

The Librarian assumed new duties after 1822. The most arduous of these responsibilities was the superintendence of the corps of king's messengers. Hertslet in 1810 had inherited from his predecessor the private agency of the corps. His duties were similar to those of the other agents in the office, but instead of receiving a percentage of a messenger's salary he was paid a fixed rate of eight guineas a year by each man.[150]

The messengers corps by 1824 was inefficient to a degree that was unparalleled in the public departments. Each of the messengers was employed on both home and foreign service, and if a journey of an arduous nature was proposed, it was as likely as not to be turned down. There were many decrepit messengers who were too old to employ on any but the simplest of journeys, but who were kept on because there were no adequate retirement provisions.[151] Hertslet's initiative sparked a reform of the corps. The messengers were divided into home and foreign services. They were to serve on a rotating basis, and if a messenger refused to go on a journey for any reason but illness, he was dismissed.[152] Hertslet was placed in charge

148. Hertslet to Palmerston, Foreign Office, 17 May 1841, Palmerston Papers, PAT/H/50.
149. "List of Registers, and Dates to which they are registered," signed Edward Hertslet, Foreign Office, 29 July 1843, F.O. 83/241.
150. Richard Ancell to Corps of King's Messengers, Downing Street, 22 May 1810, Holohan, The King's Messengers, pp. 221–22, 225.
151. Unsigned minute, L. Hertslet, 3 Mar. 1824, F.O. 96/117.
152. "Plan agreed upon by the Under Secretaries, Messrs. Hobhouse, Planta, & Wilmot-Horton, at the Home Department," 3 Apr. 1824, ibid.

of the corps and received payments from all three offices of state to manage it. As superintendent of the messengers he acted as their public agent, securing their pay from the chief clerk of the three offices. He was also responsible for all assignments given to messengers and for their being on duty at the proper times. His brother assumed the private agency.[153] These arrangements finally were abolished in 1854 when the chief clerk took responsibility for the messenger corps.[154]

The second additional responsibility Hertslet assumed was the preparation of the *British and Foreign State Papers*. He first thought of this work in 1822, when he planned a small publication merely for the use of the office.[155] Encouraged by Planta and Canning, however, he produced the first volume in 1825. For each subsequent volume he received a grant of £150 paid out of the secret service fund.[156] It is probable that government at least shared the cost of printing before 1830, as most government offices and all cabinet ministers received a copy of the work gratis before that year. Newly appointed ministers were given a complete set. The *State Papers* became a commercial enterprise in 1830 when the rigors of the retrenchment cut into all such "superfluous" programs.[157] Hertslet, however, continued to receive his secret service grant as compensation for his work on them.

After 1822 Hertslet amassed considerable extraordinary and ordinary revenue for his labors, which, to be fair, were also considerable. Palmerston in 1837 raised his salary from £700 to £800, the maximum salary of the senior clerks "with which class Mr. Hertslet's Rank in the office will henceforward be assimilated."[158] This decision had unfortunate consequences in 1843 when Hertslet tried to have it applied to the arrangements of 1841 which raised the senior clerks to £1,000. In seeking his raise in salary Hertslet enlisted the support of Backhouse, since it was he who had encouraged Pal-

153. L. Hertslet to Viscount Canning, F.O., 23 Jan. 1844, Copy, F.O. 351/10 ff. 216–21; Memorandum "respecting The Queen's Messengers and their Private Agent," 26 Aug. 1846, F.O. 96/117.

154. Lord Clarendon to the Lords of the Treasury, F.O., 10 Aug. 1855, Draft, F.O. 366/553.

155. Fragment of memo, L. Hertslet, unsigned, F.O., Jan. 1822, F.O. 83/181.

156. Minute, Hertslet, on draft memorandum, Foreign Office, 5 Mar. 1825, ibid.

157. Distribution of the State Papers, Dec. 1831, ibid.; Backhouse to George Elliot (Admiralty), Foreign Office, 11 Feb. 1832, Adm. 1/4248.

158. Minute, Palmerston, Foreign Office, 22 July 1837, Copy, Backhouse Papers.

merston to grant the increase of 1837.[159] Backhouse, who had retired, was astonished when he calculated Hertslet's average income for the eighteen years after 1825. Hertslet received as superintendent of the messengers and from the secret service fund an average of "£679.10 leaving, in addition to his Salary of £800 as Librarian, his total Emoluments only £20.10 short of those of the Junior Undersecretary of State; viz £1,500 a year!"[160] Backhouse related the results of his calculations to Henry Unwin Addington, his successor. Addington, who sarcastically referred to Hertslet as "that modest and unassuming official," resolved to bring him "to his bearings" in "the remarkably impolitic proceeding into which he has now thought proper to plunge, guided by his selflove and ill-temper."[161] For the first and only time in his career Hertslet was decidedly rebuked.

Lewis Hertslet retired in 1857 "nearly worn out" after fifty-six years service.[162] The Librarian's Department grew under his direction from an auxiliary branch to one of the most important divisions of the office. His meticulous care and intricate system of registering and filing the official correspondence insured subsequent librarians an influential role in policy. His son and successor, Edward, continued the work of his father, expanded the role of the Librarian, and prepared most, if not all, historical memoranda in the latter part of the nineteenth century.[163]

There was one person, the decipherer, who was associated with the Foreign Office but never officially attached to it. The Willis family appears to have held the position as a matter of right from 1710 or 1711.[164] They were employed in breaking the code of foreign diplomats, whose letters they came by with the aid of the secret department of the Post Office.[165] As they were paid from the secret service fund, their names never appeared on the official

159. Hertslet to Backhouse, Foreign Office, 11 Dec. 1843, ibid.
160. Minute, Backhouse, on "Comparative Statemt annexed to Mr. Hertslet's further memorandum respecting his Income and services, January, 1837," ibid.
161. Addington to Backhouse, F.O., 14 Dec. 1843, Private, and Estcourt Telbury, 3 Jan. 1844, Private, ibid.
162. L. Hertslet to Clarendon, Claygate Esher, 14 Nov. 1857, F.O. 366/553.
163. Hall, "Edward Hertslet," passim.
164. Memorandum, Addington, "Office of Secret Service Decypherer, Messrs Willes & Lovel," F.O., 7 Oct. 1844, Secret, Add. MS 40551 ff. 400–3.
165. See Kenneth Ellis, The Post Office in the Eighteenth Century: A Study in Administrative History (London, 1958), pp. 127–31 for a discussion of these activities.

establishment lists. They rarely worked in the office, and it was not until 1838 that they were prohibited from taking papers into the country.[166] Early in the nineteenth century they apparently received an allotment paid at fixed intervals. After 1827 this was certainly the case. Lord Dudley, in what Addington termed a "lax and doubtful arrangement," granted the chief decipherer £1,400 with the provision that he could pay an assistant up to £400.[167] By the 1840s the office had become a virtual sinecure as the diplomatic services of Europe rarely used the post and always sent important dispatches by courier. Aberdeen abolished the position in 1844 and gave the decipherer, Francis Willis, and his nephew and assistant, John Lovell, secret service pensions of £700 and £200 respectively.[168]

When Palmerston returned to the Foreign Office in July 1846 the establishment was organized efficiently and rationally. Most of the practices that had characterized the office in the eighteenth century did not survive the reforms of Londonderry, Canning, Aberdeen, and Palmerston. All of these reforms, though undertaken in the milieu of general administrative reorganization, reflected primarily the desire of the men in the Foreign Office to make the department a more efficient institution. Two of the reforms particularly made this efficiency possible. First was the fact that the clerks were paid adequate salaries for their labors, and the extraordinary and irregular emoluments had been abolished. More important, they were organized into political divisions so that when the volume of business increased sufficiently to warrant the hiring of additional personnel, the essential organization of the office, though perhaps not the precise division of responsibility, could remain unaltered. The significance of these reforms and their success in transforming the antiquated personalized bureau of the eighteenth century into a modern administrative department received eloquent testimony from the greatest taskmaster of all the secretaries of state, Viscount Palmerston:

> Some answer or acknowledgement ought always to be Sent to Every application, when it is received, in order to Shew that due

166. J. Backhouse to Francis Willis, Foreign Office, 24 May 1838, Secret, Add. MS 45520 ff. 49–50.

167. Planta to Backhouse, Paris, 12 Aug. 1844, Private, By Bag, Backhouse Papers; Addington's memorandum, 7 Oct. 1844, Secret, Add. MS 40551 ff. 400–3.

168. Addington to Backhouse, 78 Eaton Place, 25 Nov. 1843, Private, Backhouse Papers;

attention is paid in the office to communications made to it. When Parties who apply are allowed to remain for many weeks without any Reply they naturally go about Saying how idle and inattentive the Foreign Office is . . . & the office thus gets a Character the very reverse of what it deserves.[169]

The Foreign Office performed its duties efficiently and competently. Any other interpretation for the years up to 1850 cannot be supported by the evidence.

Addington to Francis Willis, Foreign Office, 31 Aug. 1844, Private & Secret, Add. MS 45520 ff. 53–54.
    169. Minute, 2 Nov. 1836, F.O. 96/18.

CHAPTER VIII

THE DIPLOMATIC SERVICE:
1812–1850

Professor D. B. Horn's exhaustive studies of the British diplomatic service in the century following the accession of William III[1] form a convenient background for tracing the development of the service in the first half of the nineteenth century. After the reign of George III the organization of the diplomatic service remained essentially unchanged until the second half of the nineteenth century. There were five ranks of diplomatists. Ambassadors, the most important, were appointed infrequently and only the mission at Paris regularly was headed by a diplomatist of this rank. Increasingly during the eighteenth century men with the title of envoy extraordinary and minister plenipotentiary were employed at the lesser courts of Europe. The third class of diplomatists, the minister plenipotentiary, was accredited to the smallest of the foreign courts. Secretaries of embassy, first appointed occasionally in the reign of William III, invariably accompanied ambassadors in the reign of George III. The secretaries were given the additional title of minister plenipotentiary so that they could conduct the business of the embassy in the absence or illness of the ambassador.[2] Also in the reign of George III secretaries of legation were assigned occasionally to

1. *The British Diplomatic Service; Great Britain and Europe in the Eighteenth Century*; "Rank and Emolument in the British Diplomatic Service, 1689–1789," *Transactions of the Royal Historical Society*, 5th ser., 9 (1959), 19–49. There is no comparable study of the service in the nineteenth century, though some of the problems are discussed in Jones, *The Nineteenth-Century Foreign Office*, chapter 8. This chapter is intended to give only a brief account of the more important aspects of the service prior to the era of reform.

2. At St. Petersburg the secretary remained as envoy and transacted the routine business of the embassy when the ambassador accompanied the court to Moscow. Charlotte Ann Albania Disbrowe, *Old Days in Diplomacy: Recollections of a Closed Century* (London, 1903), p. 72. Foreign powers were not always pleased with this arrangement. In Spain the government "maliciously observed" "that they appeared to have been invested with that character, and sent hither, only for the purpose of obtaining a valuable present in diamonds." St. Helens to Grenville, Aranjuez, 15 June 1791, *H. M. C. Fortescue*, vol. 2, 99.

the more important courts to which envoys were accredited.[3] Emoluments, with the possible exception of the embassy at Constantinople,[4] remained poor, dependent on the court not the rank to which a diplomatist was assigned, and were irregularly paid. Serving in the diplomatic corps more often than not was expensive and this fact explains in great part why the diplomatic service remained until the twentieth century an almost exclusive preserve of the aristocracy and landed gentry.[5]

There were, despite the great similarities between the diplomatic organizations before and after 1789, several important differences. The most obvious change was the increase in the size of the service. Between 1815 and 1860 the number of missions rose from twenty to thirty-seven, most but not all located in South America. A more significant change was the growing professionalism in the service, a factor which had been as conspicuously absent from the diplomatic corps of the eighteenth century (with a few notable exceptions such as Auckland and Malmesbury) as it had been a hallmark of the Jacobean diplomatic service. Of 119 heads of missions who served between 1812 and 1860 over half (sixty-two) had worked their way up from the lowest position in the service, the unpaid attaché. Perhaps more important, only nineteen had no diplomatic experience prior to their appointment.[6] The period between 1782 and 1860 was a transitional period containing elements of both the unreformed diplomatic service of the eighteenth century and the reformed diplomatic service that arose as a result of the recommendations in 1861 of a select committee of the House of Commons.

French conquests of the European continent and the establish-

3. Fraser to Keith, St. James's, 11 Nov. 1785, Add. MS 35535 ff. 240–41. In the absence of the envoy the secretary of legation held the rank of chargé d'affaires. F.O. 366/329 passim.

4. Corruption was a way of life in the Ottoman Empire and British diplomatists shared fully in the spoils. A. C. Wood, "The English Embassy at Constantinople, 1660–1762," *English Historical Review*, 40 (1925), 533–61. Charles Arbuthnot, appointed Ambassador to Constantinople in 1804, felt "from events now in contemplation I may expect presents which may come very opportunely to our aid." Arbuthnot to Broughton, Vienna, 9 Dec. 1804, Arbuthnot Papers. Arbuthnot, however, eventually "uniformly rejected" "this species of emolument." Same to Same, Langley, 31 Aug. 1807, ibid.

5. There were exceptions, especially in the lower ranks of the service, where positions were occasionally filled by men with little if any social or political status.

6. Maurice Lee, Jr., "The Jacobean Diplomatic Service," *The American Historical Review*, 72 (July, 1967), 1264–82; S. T. Bindoff, "The Unreformed Diplomatic Service," *Transactions of the Royal Historical Society*, 4th ser., 18 (1935), 143–44; Phyllis S. Lachs, *The Diplomatic Corps under Charles II and James II* (New Brunswick, New Jersey, 1965).

ment of French satellite governments in these territories reduced the number of British missions to six by 1812 when Castlereagh became foreign secretary.[7] As the allies liberated the continent, Castlereagh appointed ministers to the sovereigns restored to their thrones and when peace was secured in 1815 he reorganized the diplomatic service. The missions were graded into classes in a descending order of importance and the rank of minister plenipotentiary was no longer employed. There were slightly more ambassadors than had been appointed in the eighteenth century, a fact that reflected Britain's increased importance in international affairs and the increased diplomatic significance of some of the other powers. The Whigs in the 1830s made a few slight alterations in the system, the most important of which was to revive the rank of minister plenipotentiary.[8]

The rank of a minister accredited to a foreign power was based on several considerations, foremost among them the military and political importance of that power. For that reason the British government invariably sent an ambassador to France. Palmerston considered Paris "the pivot of my foreign policy,"[9] and Castlereagh selected Wellington as first British ambassador to France after the defeat of Napoleon because of "the authority . . . your name and services would give, through this Court to our general politics on the Continent."[10] A second consideration was the importance attached to the security or the affairs of a foreign power. There was usually an ambassador at The Hague in the eighteenth century and invariably so from 1815 to 1831 when the Netherlands was a buffer state between France and Germany. Canning regarded the position as the best appointment in the service and one that should always be filled by a personal friend of the secretary of state.[11] After the revolution of 1830, however, Belgium became a separate kingdom and Palmerston could think of "really no adequate reason" for maintaining an embassy to the truncated Kingdom of the Netherlands.[12] The

7. Webster, *For. Pol. Castlereagh*, vol. 1, 44–46.
8. See appendix V.
9. Palmerston to William Temple, Foreign Office, 27 June 1834, Bulwer, *Life of Palmerston*, vol. 2, 195–96.
10. Castlereagh to Wellington, Paris, 13 Apr. 1814, Londonderry, *Castlereagh Corresp.*, vol. 9, 461.
11. Canning to Liverpool, Ickworth, 27 Oct. 1824, Stapleton, *Corresp. of Canning*, vol. 1, 182–87.
12. To Grey, Stanhope Street, 27 Nov. 1831, Copy, Palmerston Papers GC/GR/2360/13.

third factor in determining the rank of a diplomatist was the rank of the minister accredited to the Court at St. James by the power to which he was being sent. Sir James Harris in 1784, though he received the allowances of an ambassador, was accredited to The Hague as a minister plenipotentiary because Pitt and Carmarthen refused to send a higher ranking mission than the Dutch government sent to London.[13] This rule was so inflexible that the king of the Netherlands in 1823 forced the resignation of Lord Clancarty when he threatened to replace the Dutch embassy in London with a mission.[14]

There were two significant changes in the subordinate ranks of the service after 1815. Secretaries of legation, appointed only to the more important missions in the eighteenth century and then with considerable opposition from some heads of missions,[15] were invariably appointed to all missions after 1815. The increase in the volume of business transacted by the missions made a second person indispensable, and Castlereagh seems to have desired to eliminate the use of private secretaries as assistants at these places.[16] Although the secretary of legation was empowered to direct affairs when his principal was not at the mission, his primary duties were to copy dispatches and keep the records of the mission.[17]

The increase in the volume of diplomatic correspondence also led to the appointment of attachés after 1815. Prior to 1815 attachés had been only infrequently included among mission personnel.[18] Ministers usually were accompanied by friends or sons of friends and relatives who had no official capacity though they did from time to time help with the business of the mission. To a degree this system continued in the 1820s. Unpaid attachés frequently owed their appointments to the minister who employed them and when they

13. Sir J. Harris's Account of his Nomination to Holland, 1784, Malmesbury, *Diaries*, vol. 2, 68–73.

14. George IV to Clancarty, 24 Sept. 1823, Copy, Aspinall, *Letters of George IV*, vol. 3, 22–23; Clancarty to George IV, Brussels, 3 Oct. 1823, *W.N.D.*, vol. 2, 144–45.

15. Charles Whitworth to Grenville, St. Petersburg, 7 Nov. 1791, Private, *H. M. C. Fortescue*, vol. 2, 226.

16. Hamilton to Arbuthnot, F.O., 12 July 1817, Draft, F.O. 366/525. The first appointments of secretaries of legation were also designed to reduce the use of private secretaries who had no official title in the service and were severely handicapped in executing certain functions as a result. Unsigned memorandum, 1786–1787, ibid.

17. Palmerston to Addington, Foreign Office, 18 Jan. 1833, Copy, Circular, F.O. 528/26.

18. "Assistant Secretaries or Paid Attachés to Missions previously to 1816," F.O. 366/525.

wished to move to other missions they applied (if they applied at all) to the minister, not to the secretary of state, for permission to do so.[19] Castlereagh, despite Clancarty's desire that these appointments be made in London, did not attempt to alter this system.[20] Canning, however, in 1825 instituted a regulation that no person could in the future be attached to a mission without the written approval of the secretary of state.[21] The secretaries remained reluctant to send an unpaid attaché to any minister without his previous consent "because they become when not wanted encumbering Idlers in Time present, and troublesome & hopeless Suitors in Time Future."[22] Most of the unpaid attachés were in the service merely to learn something of foreign affairs; few intended to make diplomacy a career. The authority of the secretary of state over their activities remained as a result tenuous as was shown in 1834 when two men resigned when ordered to return to their posts.[23] The rate of "wastage" among attachés was consequently high.

During this period there were also a number of paid attachés in the service. These men usually were career diplomatists and because the government paid their salaries, however meager, they were more amenable to direction from home. From 1816 all the embassies had one or more paid attachés,[24] and after the late 1820s many missions also had one. Palmerston, in an effort to screen applicants, employed all paid attachés in the Foreign Office for three to six months before sending them to their posts.[25] This procedure taught them the forms of diplomatic correspondence, prepared them for the type and quality of work (mostly copying)[26] expected of them at the missions, and enabled the Foreign Office to put some sort of common system of work habits into the service.

19. Mr. Eliot to Clancarty, 28 May 1822, and Clancarty to Londonderry, Garbally, 3 June 1822, Londonderry, *Castlereagh Corresp.*, vol. 12, 474–75.

20. Clancarty to Castlereagh, Frankfort sur Maine, 13 Dec. 1815, ibid., vol. 11, 98–99; Hamilton to Robert Gordon, F. Office, 13 May 1815, Add. MS 43217 f. 245.

21. Minute, Planta, F.O., 27 Oct. 1825, Canning MSS Bundle 136.

22. Aberdeen to Wellington, Foreign Office, 23 July 1829, Copy, Add. MS 43057 ff. 200–1; Minute, Palmerston, 16 June [1836], on Memorandum, Fox-Strangways, 16 June 1836, F.O. 366/526.

23. Minute, Backhouse, 4 Feb. 1834, F.O. 96/17.

24. Extract of a Letter from the Foreign Office to the Treasury, 19 Feb. 1821, F.O. 366/525.

25. Minute, Palmerston, 29 Nov. 1837, F.O. 366/505; Minute, Palmerston, 2 Oct. 1838, and Minute, Backhouse, 8 Jan. 1838, F.O. 96/19.

26. On rare occasions attachés were left as chargé d'affaires at a mission. F.O. 366/329 f. 100. Palmerston, however, did not approve of the practice and discouraged it. Minute, Palmerston, 18 Mar. 1839, F.O. 96/20.

It was impossible for there to be a sense of professionalism in the diplomatic service so long as there was no routine by which junior members advanced from grade to grade according to some fixed criteria. Most of the foreign secretaries who served in the first half of the nineteenth century recognized the need for such a system. Hawkesbury, for example, sought to promote men "to the higher Situations according to their Talents & length of Service," and felt that all save the most important posts should be filled by the promotion of junior diplomatic personnel.[27] Yet despite the prevalence of this attitude promotions never were made on the basis of strict seniority. Canning made promotions on the basis of comparing the qualifications of everyone in the service and Aberdeen told one applicant in 1844 that he made promotions only "with due regard to the claims of all who are engaged in the Diplomatic profession, [and] I cannot admit that any calculation of comparative length of service should fetter my discretion in making such appoint[men]ts as appear to me, on the whole, to be desirable & expedient."[28]

In addition to the fact that missions and embassies were graded by class there was a hierarchy of positions in the lower grades of the service. Presuming an individual were to begin his career as an unpaid attaché he would serve successively as paid attaché, secretary of legation, secretary of embassy, head of a mission, and head of an embassy. With the exception of the major ambassadorial positions, entrance into the service was always at the attaché level except in the immediate post-war period when there were suddenly so many positions to fill. Most often an unpaid attachéship was all an applicant could hope to receive, though men with connections could secure for their sons appointments as a paid attaché.[29] There were a few exceptions made to this practice, such as when Sir George Shee became minister at Würtemberg in 1836 after serving as Palmerston's undersecretary and when John Ralph Milbanke and Francis George Molyneux became secretary of legation at Frankfort in 1826 and 1835 respectively after serving as clerks in the Foreign

27. Hawkesbury to Addington, Coombe Wood, 12 Jan. 1804, Copy, Add. MS 38240 ff. 79–80.
28. Canning to Bagot, Fairlight, 12 July 1826, Private, Bagot, *Canning and Friends*, vol. 2, 353; Aberdeen to H. Wellesley, Argyll House, 9 Mar. 1844, Private, Copy, Add. MS 43242 f. 200.
29. William IV to Palmerston, St. James's, 5 July 1831, and Windsor Castle, 12 July 1831, Palmerston Papers RC/A/40–41.

Office.[30] Within the ranks as head of missions there were certain positions regarded as steps to embassies. Washington, Berlin, and Naples were in this category.[31] Few career diplomatists, however, became ambassadors and those who did generally began their careers in one of the important missions.

Special missions sometimes were sent to particular courts. Most of these missions were either congratulatory on the accession of a new sovereign or missions of condolence on the death of a monarch. Great care was taken to divest them of all political overtones,[32] though Wellington's mission to congratulate Czar Nicholas I on his accession in 1825 was political in nature. Most British foreign secretaries preferred not to send special missions to deal with substantive questions, though there was a greater reliance on them before 1815 than afterwards. When they did employ them the regularly accredited minister invariably received the special envoy coldly. Sir Morton Eden seriously considered resigning when Francis James Jackson was sent to Vienna in 1795 to see if Austria would surrender the Low Countries to the French in a peace settlement.[33] Jackson himself was sullen during the whole of Lord Harrowby's stay at Berlin while he tried to enlist Prussian aid in the struggle against France in 1805.[34] Palmerston, though he occasionally resorted to special missions, recognized that they undermined the influence of the regularly accredited minister without giving the special envoy any influence beyond that the resident minister possessed. He also opposed them because he was afraid that in case of a dispute between the two ministers nothing would be done until they referred to London for instructions, and because he did not think that as a rule the special envoy could familiarize himself sufficiently with the politics of a given court to be of any real use in resolving disputes.[35]

The emoluments of the foreign service in every grade were in-

30. F.O. 366/329 ff. 93, 95.

31. Memorandum, Backhouse, 25 Feb. 1835, Wellington Papers; Berghersh to Aberdeen, Hill Street, 25 Aug. 1830, F.O. 366/770.

32. Liverpool to Canning, Fife House, 21 Sept. 1824, Yonge, *Liverpool*, vol. 3, 292–94.

33. Eden to Auckland, Vienna, Sunday, 8 Nov. 1795, Robert John Eden 3d Baron Auckland (ed.), *The Journal and Correspondence of William, Lord Auckland* (4 vols.; London, 1861–1862), vol. 3, 320–23.

34. F. J. Jackson to his mother, Berlin, 15 Dec. 1805, Jackson, *Letters of George Jackson*, vol. 1, 380–81.

35. Palmerston to Russell, C. T., 6 Nov. 1840, Palmerston Papers GC/RU/964/1.

adequate. After 1815 the salaries paid to ministers in each class were the same, though the Whigs created a range in salary scales for the classes they introduced in 1831.[36] Perhaps the greatest injustice was the method of paying diplomatists. Prior to 1831 the expenses of the diplomatic corps were met from the funds of the third class of the king's Civil List. Because George III's Civil List was continually in arrears[37] delays of up to a year in issuing salaries were not uncommon.[38] Only the charges of the South American missions were not provided for in the Civil List of George IV. They were paid out of public revenues.[39] The Whigs transferred all of the expenses of the diplomatic service to the Consolidated Fund in 1831.[40] This reform did not appreciably diminish the delay in paying foreign service personnel because the system of life certificates required that before a minister's salary could be issued from the Exchequer a sworn statement signed by him and dated the quarter day on which salaries were to be paid had to be presented by the Foreign Office. In 1816 the Treasury abolished the practice of waiting until all life certificates had been received before issuing any salaries since this system penalized diplomatists stationed close to England.[41] After 1827 life certificates were prepared in the Foreign Office and sent to the Treasury as soon as a minister reported he was alive. By 1836, however, they were sent only once a week, "in consequence of the temptation which exists to make the Lists long & few instead of frequent & short."[42]

The reform of 1815 abolished fees charged on the appointment of diplomatists and the taxes levied against their salaries. For some unknown reason, however, the Treasury insisted that the taxes be

36. See appendix V.
37. E. A. Reitan, "The Civil List in Eighteenth Century British Politics: Parliamentary Supremacy versus the Independence of the Crown," *Historical Journal*, 9 (1966), 318–37.
38. Sneyd to Keith, St. James, 15 Mar. 1774, Add. MS 35507 f. 20; "Query submitted for the Consideration of Mr. Canning," 29 Oct. 1822, F.O. 366/525.
39. Draft to Treasury, F.O., 1828, F.O. 366/525.
40. Wellington's ministry was planning to make the same change in 1830 when they went out of office. 5 Oct. 1830, Colchester, *Ellenborough Diary*, vol. 2, 383. This change in the mode of payment included the paid attachés, who prior to 1831 were paid from the contingent funds of the missions to which they were assigned. 3&4 William IV c. 116, 16 Aug. 1832; Backhouse to Heytesbury, Foreign Office, 4 May 1831, Copy, Circular, Add. MS 41561 f. 180.
41. Lushington to Hamilton, Treasury Chambers, 27 June 1816, Copy, F.O. 366/387.
42. "Regulations respecting Life Certificates of Ministers and Consuls," Nov. 1827, F.O. 366/525; Minute, Backhouse, 31 Mar. 1836, FQ.O. 366/526.

deducted and reimbursed in one payment to the chief clerk of the
Foreign Office after all salaries had been paid, a practice that continued until 1828 when all salaries were issued net.[43]

The ministers complained frequently and bitterly against these
delays in receiving their salaries. They also complained about the
similar tardiness in issuing money to cover the operating expenses of
the missions.[44] All ministers had to borrow or expend their own
money on the public service until they could be reimbursed by the
Treasury.[45] Charles Arbuthnot, for example, received only in 1812
the final charges he made for his expenses at Constantinople from
1805 to 1807.[46] Most diplomatists did not have to wait so long but
they all protested against what Granville termed "the sic volo, sic
jubeo System of the holders of the public Purse."[47]

When a diplomatist was appointed he received a sum of money
known as the outfit which was equal to approximately one-third of
his salary. This money, given to all diplomatists except the attachés, was used to defray any expenses they incurred in securing
necessary items for their mission. Prior to the 1820s the heads of
missions also received an allowance for plate and the king's portrait,
both of which they retained on retiring from the service. The retrenchments of the 1820s, however, led to reforms in this practice
and thereafter a set of plate and the sovereign's portrait remained
part of the property of the mission.[48] Only at Constantinople and
Paris were successive ambassadors provided with lodgings in the
same building. At all other missions and embassies house allowances
were provided instead, a practice not too different from that of the

43. Unsigned memorandum dated "pre 1824," F.O. 366/387; Henry Rolleston to A'Court,
Foreign Office, 30 Nov. 1816, Add. MS 41517 ff. 317–18; Draft to Treasury, F.O., 1828, F.O.
366/525.

44. Addington to Dunglas, Frankfort, 5 Oct. 1828, F.O. 366/101 saying "I am not a
grasping man, though a poor one." Memorandum, Lord Strangford, "on the termination of
his salary," [May. 1827], F.O. 366/525.

45. Granville tried to charge the interest on his loans to his extraordinary account because it
was unjust for him to have to pay £5 a year "merely because the money he is *already obliged* to
advance is not punctually repaid him." When the Treasury refused to accept this reasoning he
gave up in disgust. Ashburnham to Byng, Paris, 25 Nov. 1833, and Paris, 20 Dec. 1833, F.O.
366/96.

46. F. J. Jackson to G. Jackson, 12 Feb. 1812, Lady Jackson (ed.), *The Bath Archives: A Further
Selection from the Diaries and Letters of Sir George Jackson, 1809–1816* (2 vols.; London, 1873), vol.
1, 326.

47. Granville to Byng, Paris, 7 Dec. 1833, Private, F.O. 366/96.

48. Backhouse to Sir Henry Wheatley, Foreign Office, 26 May 1831, Add. MS 40862 ff.
270–71.

French foreign service which maintained an embassy building only at St. Petersburg.[49] Probably the main reason permanent lodgings were not supplied for every mission was the expense of maintaining the buildings in Paris, which despite extensive repairs in the 1820s and 1830s, was still "so bad that it was impossible to live in it" in 1841.[50]

The system of presents from which the personnel of the Foreign Office benefitted also was a minor source of income for foreign ministers who received, in addition to presents on the signature of treaties, gratuities from foreign sovereigns when they completed their assignments at foreign courts. Usually these presents were gold snuff boxes or portraits of the foreign sovereign framed in precious stones. If a minister had particularly displeased a foreign power he might receive no gift or a gift designed to show displeasure. When Lord Henry Spencer left Stockholm in 1794, for example, instead of the king's picture he received a very lewd painting which he left behind to be returned by his successor.[51] Such instances were rare.

Palmerston abolished the presents given in the foreign service in 1830 at the same time he prohibited them at the Foreign Office.[52] The only exception made was for Stratford Canning at Constantinople who was given permission to dispense presents if he thought he could further British policy by doing so.[53] Even in the rest of the service the regulation was not at first strictly enforced. Backhouse wrote George Chad, the minister at Berlin, that as long as a gift was stated to be "a *special* personal one," he could accept it.[54] The King of Sweden presented Lady Disbrowe, wife of the British minister, with a "pink porphyry vase" when her husband's mission ended in 1833.[55] In the same year, however, Stratford Canning sold a diamond snuff box given to him by the sultan and applied the proceeds to the expenses of his mission when he returned home.[56] By the closing years of William IV's reign the practice was not tolerated in any form.

49. Count de Vaudreuil to Backhouse, 25 June 1830, 4 p.m., Private, F.O. 366/525.
50. 1 Nov. 1841, Colonel Frederick Arthur Wellesley (ed.), *The Diary and Correspondence of Henry Wellesley, First Lord Cowley, 1790–1846* (London, 1928), p. 211.
51. Spencer to Auckland, Copenhagen, 23 Dec. 1794, Auckland, *Corresp.*, vol. 3, 276–78.
52. Memorandum on Diplomatic Presents, Dec. 1830, Copy, Palmerston Papers.
53. Draft to Stratford Canning, F.O., Nov. 1831, Separate & Secret, F.O. 366/555.
54. 20 Nov. 1832, F.O., Confidential, ibid.
55. Disbrowe, *Recollections*, p. 203.
56. Draft to the Treasury, F.O., 13 Sept. 1833, F.O. 366/292.

There were no funds provided for diplomatic pensions in the eighteenth century. Most heads of missions who served with moderate distinction, however, received pensions from Civil List revenues. Auckland retired with £2,000 in 1793 and Grenville gave Joseph Ewart £1,000 in 1791.[57] Ewart's widow and children also received small pensions after his death in 1792.[58] Secretaries were not so fortunate. Castlereagh granted George Jackson a pension of £300 in 1812 four years after he had completed his service in Spain while Charles Oakley, who retired in 1810 from his position as secretary of legation in Washington, had to wait until 1813 for his pension.[59]

The same Act of Parliament that in 1810 provided for a regular system of superannuation in government departments contained provisions for diplomatic pensions. No diplomatist was eligible for a pension during the ten years after his first appointment. Those whose total service was at least three years in these ten were eligible for a pension of up to £2,000.[60] Since pensions were paid from the third class of the Civil List, the numbers that could be granted were in fact limited by the amount of funds available. Occasionally the Treasury scraped together the money for pensions only by enforcing measures of rigid economy in other branches of the service. When Lord Cathcart retired in 1821, the funds for his pension were provided out of the savings which resulted from the termination of the embassy at Madrid and the mission at Lisbon.[61] Diplomatists receiving a pension had it suspended whenever they reentered the active service of the Crown in any capacity. Stratford Canning also surrendered his pension when he returned to the House of Commons in 1831.[62]

Because of the shortage of funds, pensions were unofficially restricted to those diplomatists who had inadequate private sources of

57. Auckland to Morton Eden, Beckenham, 1 Nov. 1791, Auckland, *Corresp.*, vol. 2, 393–95; see also ibid., vol. 3, 387 n.

58. Grenville to Ewart, Weymouth, 20 Sept. 1791, Private, Copy, and Grenville to Mrs. Ewart, Whitehall, 17 Feb. 1792, Private, Copy, *H. M. C. Fortescue*, vol. 2, 195–96, 256.

59. George Jackson to his mother, Stephen's Hotel, 16 Dec. 1812, and 28 Feb. 1813, Jackson, *Bath Archives*, vol. 1, 444; vol. 2, 19.

60. 50 George III c. 117, section 13, 21 June 1810.

61. Arbuthnot to Liverpool, Woodford, Sunday, 9 Dec. 1821, Private, Liverpool Scrapbook, f. 28, Duke University Library.

62. Planta to the Treasury, F.O., 4 Apr. 1825, Draft, F.O. 366/525; Poole, *Stratford Canning*, vol. 2, 49. Pitt told William Eden, however, that there was nothing "inconsistent" in a diplomatist in receipt of a pension sitting in the House of Commons. Pitt to Eden, Downing Street, Wednesday, 8 June 1788, Private, Eden Papers, Duke University Library.

income. Canning objected in 1823 to giving a pension to Lord Londonderry, Castlereagh's half-brother, because "giving a Pension to a person of his fortune I should think [would be] fatal to the system. . . ."[63] Londonderry protested but Liverpool agreed with Canning about the "*absolute Impossibility* of granting the Diplomatick or any other pension" to him.[64] When the system of granting pensions was reorganized in 1829 applications such as his were officially discouraged as being "improper charges" on the public revenue.[65]

The regulations introduced in 1829 were made more stringent than those established in 1810 in an effort to contain the expanding charge for pensions which accompanied the increase in the size of the service.[66] Diplomatists were to be eligible for pensions fifteen years instead of ten after their first appointment at a rank of secretary of legation or higher. Pensions were regulated strictly according to the rank the applicant had attained. The total length of service he had to perform before he could qualify for a pension of the appropriate class was increased to five years in every rank below ambassador, in which class three years service qualified a diplomatist for a pension.[67] The Whigs maintained this system when they transferred the expense of the diplomatic service to the public revenue. But they limited the amount of new pensions granted in any one year to £2,000 until the total charge of the service was reduced to £180,000 per annum.[68]

The men who served in the British diplomatic service between 1782 and 1860 were for the most part of mediocre but adequate ability. In the eighteenth century employment abroad was regarded as a distant second best to employment at home. Economic retrenchment enhanced the importance of foreign assignments somewhat, Fraser said, "as the Reductions of Civil Offices has made them more valuable."[69] But men of first-rate ability generally still

63. Canning to Liverpool, G. L., 2 June 1823, Secret and Confidential, Draft, Canning MSS Bundle 70.

64. Londonderry to Planta, Paris, 10 June 1823, Copy, Canning MSS Bundle 136; Liverpool to Canning, F.H., 2 June 1823, Secret, ibid., Bundle 70.

65. Draft Circular to His Majesty's Ministers Abroad, F.O., 1829, F.O. 366/525.

66. "Third Report of the Select Committee . . . [on] Public Income and Expenditure. . . ," *P. P., 1828*, vol. 5, Command 480, p. 479.

67. Draft circular to His Majesty's Ministers Abroad, F.O., 1829, F.O. 366/525. Pension scales were as follows: ambassadors: £2,000; envoys extraordinary and ministers plenipotentiary to the major courts: £1,500; to the minor courts; £1,000; all other personnel: £800.

68. 3 & 4 William IV c. 116, 16 Aug. 1832. In 1832 the charge was £203,510.

69. To Keith, St. James's, 23 May 1783, Add. MS 35528 ff. 272–73.

preferred to make a career in Parliament, the law, or some other branch of service in England.

The senior diplomatists in the early nineteenth century—men such as Granville, Cowley, Stratford Canning, Bagot, and Stuart de Rothsay—were all subordinate figures. It is significant that Bagot, an excellent foreign minister, was only an undersecretary in England. The few diplomatists with imagination and ability such as Auckland, Clarendon, and Minto, served abroad only briefly before returning to hold ministerial positions in London. The worst among them clung to their posts long after they were effective and expected to receive appointments abroad when the party they supported was in power. Lord Stuart de Rothsay was one of this class. While ambassador to Paris from 1828 to 1830 he sent home dispatches that were "seldom very clear or of much importance."[70] Wellington told Aberdeen to give Stuart "a little Warning respecting the mode in which he transacts Business; that is to say [about our] not being certain whether what he communicates to the French Minister is understood by Him, or that he understands correctly what is communicated to him by the French Minister for the Information of His Govt."[71] Yet in 1841 Aberdeen sent Stuart to St. Petersburg, the second embassy in the service, where he remained until Peel forced his resignation in 1843 because he was "utterly unfit" for the position.[72] Lord Cowley, ambassador at Paris from 1841 to 1846, was not replaced despite his age and deafness probably because he was Wellington's brother. Peel merely lamented his being there and Victoria urged Aberdeen to send an efficient secretary to Paris, "as Lord Cowley is rather infirm."[73]

The vast majority of diplomatists performed their duties tolerably well. They were certainly generally better qualified than many of their predecessors of the eighteenth century.[74] Most of them were intensely patriotic, and a few overzealous in their activities.[75] None of their principals, however, complained about the quality of the

---

70. Wellington to Aberdeen, Stratfield Saye, 6 Dec. 1828, *W.N.D.*, vol. 5, 312–13.
71. 21 July 1829, Walmer Castle, Add. MS 43057 ff. 192–93.
72. Peel to Aberdeen, Whitehall, 11 Oct. [1843], Add. MS 43063 ff. 22–23.
73. Peel to Aberdeen, Drayton Manor, 28 Dec. [1842], Add. MS 43062 ff. 285–86; Victoria to Aberdeen, Windsor Castle, 9 Oct. 1843, Add. MS 43043 ff. 181–84.
74. There were, of course, exceptions. Few diplomatists of the nineteenth century, for example, were as able as the first Earl of Malmesbury.
75. Edmund B. D'Auvergne, *Envoys Extraordinary* (London, 1937), pp. 5–8.

service as a whole and most secretaries probably would have agreed
with Palmerston who described them as "independent & honourable
men, who look to the approbation of their own Sovereign as their
only reward, & who are not swayed by the expectation of presents &
stars from the Sovereigns of the Continent. . . . If our Diplomatists
were all men of slender capacity, & of timid & subservient characters, we should probably hear them highly praised at Vienna, Berlin,
& Petersburgh; but perhaps His Majesty's service would not be so
well performed."[76]

There were no established criteria for the selection of a diplomatist. Lord Auckland thought he ought to be conversant in
French, have a general knowledge of history, and have a specific
understanding of the affairs and institutions of the country in which
he was stationed.[77] But this was an ideal, not a practical program,
and many diplomatists learned their history and geography as well
as their French only after they were employed abroad. During the
1830s Palmerston tried to assure that the attachés at the German
courts could read German script,[78] and in the two decades preceding the reforms of 1861 there was an attempt to send oriental
scholars from Oxford and Cambridge to Constantinople where they
could replace the dragomans, Turkish subjects who acted as translators for the embassy.[79] Neither of these programs was successful,[80]
and until the Civil Service examinations were instituted in the 1850s
there were no qualities on which to base the selection of one candidate over another.

Despite the fact that the diplomatic service expanded greatly after
the peace with France in 1815, the amount of patronage available to
the foreign secretary was limited when compared with the number
of applicants. Every secretary of state was as beseiged as Palmerston,
who complained of being "torn to pieces by Earls and Dukes . . . for
paid attachéships & secretaryships of Legation for their sons and

76. Palmerston to Taylor, Stanhope Street, 30 Oct. 1833, Palmerston Papers RC/CC/
10/1-3.
77. Auckland to John Hatsell, Palace Yard, 20 Feb. 1796, Auckland, Corresp., vol. 3,
329-31.
78. Minute, Palmerston, 17 Mar. 1839, F.O. 366/526.
79. These oriental attachés were paid £250 and were selected on a competitive basis.
Edward Barrington De Fonblanque, Lives of the Lords Strangford (London, 1877), p. 254.
80. Testimony of E. Hammond, Q. 154, 15 Apr. 1861, "Report from the Select Committee
appointed to enquire . . . into the diplomatic service. . . ," P.P., 1861, vol. 6, Command 459,
p. 15.

nephews."[81] As the number of applicants increased their political affiliation assumed a significance far beyond that of appointees prior to 1815. Mulgrave, for example, in 1805 offered Lord Minto the embassy at St. Petersburg despite his open opposition to Pitt's government in Parliament.[82] Palmerston in 1831, however, wished to know what line Stratford Canning would take in the House of Commons before offering him the same embassy.[83] Though there were never any wholesale changes of diplomatic personnel on a change of ministries in London, the ambassadors at Paris, Vienna, and St. Petersburg were invariably replaced on these occasions.[84] The senior diplomatists who were appointed to these embassies, in fact, came to be regarded as attached to one party or the other, though Cowley as late as 1831 hoped that since his only career was the foreign service he might not be replaced by Grey's government.[85]

The secretary of state enjoyed the bulk of the patronage of the diplomatic service. While Castlereagh attended the allied conferences in 1814 Liverpool ordered that no appointments be made "except in cases of absolute necessity where Publick Inconvenience would arise from Delay."[86] These appointments, such as William A'Court's to Sicily, were always made subject to Castlereagh's eventual approval.[87] Peel felt that only the secretary of state had a sufficient enough knowledge of candidates and the various missions to decide on all appointments of the second rank or below.[88] All foreign secretaries considered their close personal friends and their relations for high diplomatic positions so long as they were otherwise qualified. Canning admitted, however, that although he was "at liberty to appoint friends of my own, occasionally, without reference to other claims—yet I do think that two at a time, or even two in unbroken succession, without an intervening nomination of

81. To Taylor, Stanhope Street, 27 July 1835, Private, Palmerston Papers RC/CC/17.
82. Minto to Lady Minto, Pall Mall, 2 Sept. 1805, Lady Minto (ed.), *Life and Letters of Sir Gilbert Elliott, Earl of Minto* (3 vols.; London, 1874), vol. 3, 368.
83. Palmerston to Granville, Foreign Office, 13 May 1831, Confidential, P.R.O. 30/29/404.
84. Melbourne to Victoria, Woburn Abbey, 12 Sept. 1841, Benson and Esher, *Q.V.L.*, vol. 1, 408–9.
85. Cowley to Wellington, Vienna, 23 May 1831, *W.N.D.*, vol. 7, 441.
86. Minute, Liverpool, on R. Sheppel Craven to Hamilton, Albany, Tuesday, 8 Feb. 1814, F.O. 83/25.
87. Hamilton to Castlereagh, Foreign Office, 8 Feb. 1814, Londonderry, *Castlereagh Corresp.*, vol. 9, 254.
88. Peel to Wellington, Whitehall, 22 Dec. 1834, Confidential, Wellington Papers.

routine, would have been most inexpedient both for myself and the appointees."[89]

The prime minister, because he was responsible for the general patronage dispensed by his ministry, was always consulted about diplomatic appointments. Usually he was interested only in influencing the nominations to the major embassies, since the political situation of his ministry had to be considered in making such decisions. Wellington recognized this fact when in 1834 he suggested to Peel that Stuart be sent to Vienna as "He has been and is still very active in our Elections."[90] Peel, in reply, insisted that Sir Robert Gordon, Aberdeen's brother and a retired ambassador, be employed "in some important Station."[91] When Peel was unable to give Stratford Canning a place at his ministry in 1841, he secured Canning's appointment to the embassy at Constantinople "on the ground of political disappointment."[92] The premier's wishes, however, were not always decisive. Palmerston, for example, refused to appoint Robert Adair to the embassy at Vienna in 1831 and told Grey, who had strongly urged him to do so, that Adair would not be an "active & Energetic ambassador." Palmerston's selection, however, was Frederick Lamb, "the best man we have in our Diplomatic List" and one whose "Family & Connections . . . are not Such as to excite Surprize that he Should be employed under your administration."[93]

The prime minister retained absolute control over one aspect of patronage, the awarding of honors. Although diplomatists were frequently knighted or created peers when they retired from the service, few were so distinguished while they were on active duty. Palmerston, on one of these instances, secured from Melbourne a step in the peerage for Lord Ponsonby because of his "Courage, Firmness, & ability" as ambassador to Constantinople.[94] Another practice related to granting honors was that of creating ministers privy councillors in an effort to give them added influence abroad. Even this practice was severely curtailed after 1815. Palmerston told

89. Canning to Morley, G. L., 23 Sept. 1823, Add. MS 48221 ff. 146–49.
90. "Memn. for Sir Robert Peel," 21 Dec. 1834, Copy, Wellington Papers.
91. Peel to Wellington, Whitehall, 22 Dec. 1834, Confidential, ibid.
92. Peel to Lord Stanley, 21 Sept. 1841, Charles Stuart Parker (ed.), *Sir Robert Peel, From His Private Papers* (3 vols.; London, 1890–1899), vol. 2, 485.
93. Palmerston to Grey, Stanhope Street, 16 Jan. 1831, Draft, Palmerston Papers GC/GR/2346/1–2.
94. Palmerston to Melbourne, Stanhope Street, 19 July 1836, Copy, Palmerston Papers GC/ME/524.

Howard de Walden in 1838 that although admission to the "Privy Council . . . in former Times was a matter of Course," both he and Melbourne felt that there were too many missions to continue the practice.[95]

The monarch also exercised an influence on the selection of foreign ministers. The fact that the secretary of state had to secure formal approval before he announced any appointment from the meanest paid attaché to the most important ambassador,[96] gave the sovereign an opportunity to object if he wished to do so. George III and George IV took an active part in selecting diplomatists. Ministers frequently chose individuals known to have ties with the court.[97] Canning told Frere to try his best to impress George III, "as it gives you an existence independent of the favour of Ministers."[98] Once Canning became secretary of state, however, he objected to the notion of an ambassador's holding his position because of the will of the king alone, maintaining in 1826, for example, that the Duke of Devonshire's appointment as ambassador extraordinary to the coronation of Emperor Nicholas I of Russia was in no way "a *personal* nomination of the King." "For though I had no doubt that the Duke of Devonshire's appointment would be most agreeable to His Majesty . . . I do assure you, *upon my honour*, that the original suggestion of the D. of D's name was from me to the King; *not* from His Majesty to me."[99] George IV nevertheless did exercise real influence over appointments. He insisted on the selection of Lord Stuart as ambassador to Paris in 1828 and though Aberdeen was "much annoyed" and Ellenborough said that "This will not do," Wellington and they acquiesced because it was not "worth while to make a quarrel about it."[100]

The personal wishes of William IV also influenced the disposal of diplomatic patronage. Lord Marcus Hill and John Bligh owed their promotions to the secretaryships of embassy at Constantinople and The Hague respectively in 1830 in part to the king's interest in their

95. 20 Sept. 1838, Windsor, Add. MS 45176 ff. 121–22.

96. F.O. 366/505 passim contains many instances of royal approval of diplomatic appointments at all levels.

97. F. J. Jackson to G. Jackson, Bulstrode Street, 19 Feb. 1811, and G. Jackson Diary, 22 Mar. 1811, Jackson, *Bath Archives*, vol. 1, 213, 228.

98. [Apr. 1802], Festing, *Frere*, p. 72.

99. Canning to Granville, F.O., 7 Apr. 1826, No. 17, Private & Confidential, P.R.O. 30/29/8/10 ff. 1190–93.

100. 13 and 15 June 1828, Colchester, *Ellenborough Diary*, vol. 1, 145, 148.

affairs.[101] Wellington nominated Sir Charles Bagot ambassador to St. Petersburg in 1831 after William's strong expression of hope that "something may arise to employ ... this wretched well-disposed Gentleman."[102]

Victoria's approval of diplomatic appointments was nearly always granted as a matter of course.[103] She occasionally developed strong dislikes of particular ministers but her disapproval of their conduct in no way endangered their position in the service. In 1842 she thought the dispatches of Sir Edward Disbrowe, minister at The Hague, showed a "decided unfairness towards Belgium." When she tried to get him removed "quietly" to some other mission,[104] however, Aberdeen merely agreed to see what he could arrange and promised in the meantime to send a "private admonition" to Disbrowe,[105] who eventually remained at his post another nine years.

Appointments to missions requiring persons with technical or other special experience occasionally were made by the head of other government departments or interested individuals. Palmerston left to the Board of Trade the nomination of one commissioner in the mission sent to France in 1839 to negotiate a commercial treaty.[106] The abolitionists at the request of the Foreign Office frequently submitted names of persons acceptable to them to serve on the commissions for suppressing the slave trade, though their nominees were not always selected because the governors of the colonies in which these bodies sat by law shared in this patronage.[107]

101. Taylor to Aberdeen, Brighton, 1 Sept. 1830, Private, and Aberdeen to William IV, F.O., 7 Sept. 1830, Add. MS 43040 ff. 114–15, 126–27.

102. William IV to Wellington, Pavillion Brighton, 14 Jan. 1835, Most *private* and *confidential*, and Wellington to Emperor Nicholas I, London, 6 Apr. 1835, draft, Wellington Papers.

103. For example, Victoria to Aberdeen, Buckingham Palace, 21 May 1846, Add. MS 43046 ff. 39–40, approving a promotion for J. H. Howard and then asking who he was.

104. Victoria to Peel, Claremont, 16 July 1842, Benson and Esher, *Q.V.L.*, vol. 1, 512–13.

105. Aberdeen to Victoria, F.O., 26 July 1842, Copy, Add. MS 43042 ff. 82–83. The queen was certainly being overly sensitive in this instance. Disbrowe's dispatches for the most part are inoffensive reports concerning the events in the Belgian-Dutch negotiations on some disputes between the two countries. The strongest anti-Belgian statement occurred in reference to outside interference in these negotiations. "Although the general tenour of these Communications are far from agreeable to this court, it is probable that they will have the effect of inducing the King of the Netherlands to make further concessions if possible, whilst the knowledge of their tenour will probably augment the pretensions of The Belgians." Disbrowe to Aberdeen, The Hague, 4 July 1842, No. 79, F.O. 37/236.

106. Minute, Palmerston, 22 Nov. 1839, F.O. 27/596.

107. Macaulay to Planta, 26 Birchin Lane, 25 Aug. 1818, Private, F.O. 83/30; Minute, Planta, on Same to Same, 16 Mansion House Palace, 21 Aug. 1823, Private, F.O. 84/27; Sir J. Copley to Planta, Serjeant's Inn, 24 Sept. 1825, F.O. 84/46.

Before the diplomatic service was reorganized and expanded in 1815 the heads of missions exercised an influence over the secretary of state's appointments. The Duke of Manchester, in asking for a secretary for his embassy to Paris in 1783, insisted "That he may neither be a Scotchman nor have any Scotch Connection."[108] When the Duke of Dorset temporarily left his embassy in Paris to return to England on private business in September 1788, he was determined to secure the removal of his secretary, Daniel Hailes. Carmarthen agreed with his request and Hailes became minister to Poland in November of the same year.[109] Grantham, in appointing Viscount Mount Stewart to the Spanish embassy, suggested an individual for his secretary but added that "being particularly desirous that every Circumstance of your Lordship's Mission should be perfectly agreeable to yourself I assure you of my Acquiescence in your View on this occasion."[110] After 1815, when there was a recognizable hierarchy of positions and many career diplomatists, the heads of missions except in the cases of unpaid attachés apparently had little influence over the selection of their subordinates.

It was a standard practice in European diplomacy in the early part of the nineteenth century to submit the name of a head of mission informally to the sovereign to whom he was to be accredited to see if there were any objections to the appointment. Sometimes the name of a potential nominee was sent abroad before the minister himself was notified of his selection. Lord Cowley's appointment to Paris in 1834 was handled in this fashion.[111] The king was usually consulted before a name was unofficially transmitted to a foreign government, though Palmerston proposed Durham's appointment at St. Petersburg in 1835 to William IV only after Nicholas had said he would be pleased to receive him.[112] The foreign sovereign in effect had a veto over any British appointment since he could refuse to receive at court any minister whom he considered *persona non grata*. Emperor Nicholas I declined to accept the appointment of Stratford

108. Portland to Fox, Chiswick, Sunday Even., 31 Aug. 1783, Add. MS 47561 ff. 59–60.
109. Dorset to William Eden, Paris, 15 Aug. 1788, Auckland, *Corresp.*, vol. 2, 228; D. B. Horn (ed.), *British Diplomatic Representatives, 1689–1789* ("The Camden Society, 3d Series," vol. 46; London, 1932), p. 95.
110. Grantham to Mount Stewart, Whitehall, 20 Jan. 1783, Add. MS 36806 ff. 3–4.
111. Wellington to Peel, Apethorpe, 2 Jan. 1834 [1835], Add. MS 40310 ff. 8–9.
112. Palmerston to Melbourne, Stanhope Street, 29 June 1835, Draft, Palmerston Papers GC/ME/511/1–4.

Canning as ambassador to St. Petersburg in 1832 despite the fact that it had already been officially announced and Palmerston was forced to withdraw the nomination.[113] Though they could exercise a similar veto, British ministers were extremely reluctant to do so. In 1835 when Wellington learned that the French government intended to send General Sebastiani to London as ambassador and had announced his appointment without consulting the British government, he said that "However inconvenient His presence here may be, I don't think that we could have a quarrel or even a Coolness in order to avoid it. . . ."[114] Such references were usually made as a matter of form and the instances were rare when a country failed to adhere to the procedure.

Parliament had little influence over the appointment of diplomatic personnel and rarely took an interest in the patronage dispensed by the ministers so long as appointments were not blatantly inappropriate. One such instance occurred in 1835 when Lord Londonderry's appointment as ambassador to St. Petersburg raised such a storm in the House of Commons that Peel's government was faced with a censure motion. Londonderry, whose activities with respect to his pension in the 1820s and his political ultraconservatism caused the uproar, voluntarily resigned in order to prevent the defeat of the government on the issue.[115] This affair was extremely unusual and occurred only because many members of both parties had little doubt that Londonderry's record made him peculiarly unfit for the position.

Most of Britain's diplomatic policies were implemented by diplomatists abroad, not by the secretary of state in London. The most important reason for conducting business in this manner, which Lord Auckland called "the English plan," was the necessity of having detailed records of all diplomatic transactions.[116] Occasionally ministers preferred not to deal with representatives of foreign powers in London for personal or political reasons. Carmarthen refused to send his communications to Russia through M. Simolin, the

113. Franklin A. Walker, "The Rejection of Stratford Canning by Nicholas I," *Bulletin of the Institute of Historical Research*, 40 (May, 1967), 50–64.

114. Wellington to Peel, Apethorpe, 2 Jan. 1834 [1835], Add. MS 40310 ff. 8–9.

115. Londonderry to Peel, 16 Mar. 1835, Confidential, Parker, *Peel*, vol. 2, 269–70; 13 and 16 Mar. 1835, 3 *Hansard's*, vol. 26, 938–90, 1018–31.

116. Auckland to Morton Eden, Beckenham, 1 Nov. 1791, Auckland, *Corresp.*, vol. 2, 393–95.

Russian ambassador, because he regarded him "as unworthy to confidence."[117] The Lievens were such intriguers against Wellington's ministry that he and Aberdeen resolved "to listen to Lieven but answer through Lord Heytesbury; . . . [so that] the Emperor [of Russia] will discover the inconvenience of trusting His Relations with England to such Persons."[118] Only Castlereagh and Canning seem to have transacted business regularly with representatives of foreign powers in London. Castlereagh did so because he preferred working that way. Canning probably conducted affairs personally because he did not have diplomatists of his own selection and persuasion abroad. As a result of the insecurity of his position, however, Canning always contrived to secure a record of these meetings and refused all interviews without assurances that he would receive one.[119]

Communications with foreign capitals were extremely poor.[120] Though messengers were occasionally employed on a regular basis to and from various posts, much of the correspondence of the foreign service prior to the 1820s was sent by the regular post in cipher. It was as a result regularly subjected to "the fiery ordeal of some Imp"[121] who was employed to break the diplomatic codes in one or another continental post office. Messengers were so infrequently sent, and then with only the most important of communications, that the arrival of one in a foreign capital created quite a sensation. The reorganization of the messenger corps in 1824 permitted the secretary of state to station them on a rotating basis for short periods of time at certain courts such as Paris, Vienna, or St. Petersburg where three or four men were able to provide safe and more or less regular communication between London and the British missions in those and intermediary capitals.[122] Diplomatists at the minor courts in the 1820s, however, still were required to use the common post and ciphers because of the expense of the mes-

117. Diary, 1784, Browning, *Leeds Political Memoranda*, pp. 103–4.
118. Wellington to Aberdeen, Stratfield Saye, 8 Nov. 1829, Add. MS 43058 ff. 75–80.
119. Canning to Granville, F.O., 4 Mar. 1825, Private, No. 37, and G. L., 8 Apr. 1825, Private Political, No. 47, P.R.O. 30/29/8/7 ff. 835–40, 876–77.
120. K. L. Ellis, "British Communications and Diplomacy in the Eighteenth Century," *Bulletin of the Institute of Historical Research*, 31 (Nov., 1958), 159–67.
121. St. Helens to Paget, St. Petersburg, 16 Mar. 1802, Paget, *Paget Papers*, vol. 2, 45.
122. Stratford Canning to Planta, Constantinople, 13 June 1826, F.O. 366/490; Backhouse to Stuart, F.O., 12 May 1829, Copy, ibid.; Memorandum, Herstlet, "Communication by Messenger with St. Petersburgh by Hamburgh," Dec. 1835, F.O. 366/491.

senger corps.[123] Palmerston eventually provided for messengers to pass through every mission, including "a messenger every month to sweep up and down Italy,"[124] and by 1844 so much of the correspondence of every major power was transmitted by messenger that the position of decipherer of intercepted letters at the Foreign Office was abolished as an unnecessary luxury. During the 1850s and 1860s the telegraph came into increasing use.

Poor roads, bad weather at sea and on land, and the delays caused by the dispatches having to pass through several foreign post offices frequently left diplomatists without instructions. Lord Clancarty complained about the "irregular and ill-administered post," and joined Lord Cathcart and others in urging Castlereagh (without effect) to establish a regular messenger service for their courts.[125] Francis James Jackson at Washington regularly employed his secretary of legation as a courier, [126] and Lord Cathcart on at least one occasion sent "despatches by a gentleman in merchantile business, to whom I have given a courier's passport, to enable him to proceed with more expedition on his own concerns—Mr. Littlewood Andrew."[127] Only the increased employment of messengers eliminated the complaints against the irregularity of communications between London and British missions.

A second cause of complaint was the dearth of correspondence sent by the Foreign Office to the missions abroad. Auckland regularly received copies of dispatches sent to other ministers only as a result of the kindness of Burges, who, "as I never let matters of this nature get into the office," was "obliged to employ one confidential person to transcribe them . . . " at his own house.[128] Other ministers were not so fortunate. Arthur Paget complained about being kept "totally uninformed" and Jackson urged Arbuthnot when he became undersecretary in 1803 "in remembrance of your old Colleagues [to] endeavour to obtain for them a portion of the Atten-

123. Temperley, *For. Pol. Canning*, p. 267.

124. Palmerston to William Temple, Foreign Office, 5 Mar. 1836, Bulwer, *Life of Palmerston*, vol. 3, 8.

125. Clancarty to Castlereagh, Frankfort sur Maine, 1 Jan. 1816, Londonderry, *Castlereagh Corresp.*, vol. 11, 117; Cathcart to Castlereagh, St. Petersburg, 28/16 Dec. 1815, ibid., vol. 11, 102–3.

126. Jackson, *Bath Archives*, vol. 1, passim.

127. Cathcart to Castlereagh, St. Petersburg, 26 Sept. 1816, Londonderry, *Castlereagh Corresp.*, vol. 11, 297.

128. Burges to Auckland, White Hall, 20 July 1790, Private, Add. MS 34432 ff. 139–40.

tion" his principals showed to Parliament.[129] Lord Henry Spencer at age twenty-one was appointed minister to Sweden but received no instructions so that "at present I have nothing to do but to eat and drink, and I am not authorized to ask the Regent what o'clock it is." Auckland, to whom he complained, suggested that he order "a good supply of papers, as you will very seldom hear from the office. . . ."[130] Ministers were instructed to correspond with one another to keep themselves informed of events.[131] But it is impossible to see how they could have benefitted much from pooling their ignorance.

Canning in 1808 ordered that each mission be written at least once a week, "if it be merely to acknowledge their dispatches or to say that none have arrived. This will be sure to remind one if there is anything to say."[132] This regulation was only imperfectly enforced until Canning's second secretaryship when he began to send copies of papers abroad as a matter of course. Palmerston extended this practice until Granville in Paris received copies of every substantive dispatch "unless I give a Special Direction to the Contrary."[133] The regular departure and arrival of messengers usually insured a steady flow of information, though in 1835 the mission at Madrid for over two months received nothing from London.[134]

Diplomatic instructions and the reports of diplomatists were sent in numbered dispatches. In the eighteenth century dispatches had occasionally been addressed to the undersecretaries,[135] but in the nineteenth century they were always directed to the secretary of state.[136] Because dispatches were public papers instructions were given that they be intelligible, to the point, and legibly written. This was the ideal; the execution was somewhat less than perfect. Clarity

129. Paget to Malmesbury, Berlin, 4 Oct. 1794 [Lemon juice], Paget, *Paget Papers*, I, 53–55; Jackson to Arbuthnot, Berlin, 30 Aug. 1803, Copy, F.O. 353/88.

130. Spencer to Auckland, Hague, 23 July 1793 and Hamborough [sic], 6 Aug. 1793, Auckland, *Corresp.*, vol. 3, 82–83, 103; Auckland to Spencer, Beckenham, 25 July 1793, ibid., 83–84.

131. Paget to Whitworth, Palermo, 10 May 1800, Paget, *Paget Papers*, vol. 1, 201.

132. Canning to Bagot, Bruton Street, 30 Sept. 1808, Secret, Bagot, *Canning and Friends*, vol. 1, 276–77.

133. Minutes, Palmerston, 8 Sept. 1835, and 13 Nov. 1835, on unsigned minute, E. Hammond, n.d., F.O. 96/18.

134. Unsigned minute, E. Hammond, F.O., 19 Oct. 1835, ibid.

135. For example, Francis Wilson to Burges, F.O. 26/15 passim.

136. Planta to A'Court, Foreign Office, 19 Sept. 1823, Private, Add. MS 41544 f. 129.

was not one of the strong points of dispatches written by English diplomatists. "I wish you would require your foreign ministers to write *English*," Peel wrote to Aberdeen in 1842. "I read some dispatches yesterday from Lord Stuart—and I think from Mr. Mandeville or Mr. Hamilton or I believe both—which are too slovenly [written] for endurance."[137] Palmerston, whose own dispatches were models of style and logic, was exasperated by the dispatches he received: "I Should like to give Some of our Diplomatists a Hint also to write their Despatches to this office in English, & not to Slide into Such Gallicisms as 'Reclamation' for Complaint or Remonstrance and 'abounding in a Person's Sense' for agreeing with what they Say; and other Similar Departures from the English Language."[138]

Too frequently dispatches were rambling discourses which contained little useful information. George III longed for the days "when foreign ministers thought the matter of their dispatches and not the length of them their true merit."[139] Dudley complained in 1828 that Frederick Lamb "is gone into opposition—and writes short pamphlets against the govt. which he is pleased to transmit to me under the whimsical title of 'Dispatches.'"[140] Palmerston authorized Granville to open and read Addington's dispatches when they passed through Paris, "and if you would abridge as well as read them I Should forgive you."[141] Both George III and George IV remarked on the paucity of intelligence contained in the verbiage of reports sent by their English as opposed to their Hanoverian diplomatic service.[142] And despite the Foreign Office regulation that separate dispatches be sent for each subject reported by a diplo-

137. 16 Nov. [1842], Drayton Manor, Add. MS 43062 ff. 186–91.

138. Minute, Palmerston, 23 May 1831, F.O. 96/17.

139. George III to Grenville, Windsor, 5 Apr. 1796, *H. M. C. Fortescue*, vol. 3, 186. Ministers were dependent on dispatches for information and despite the complaints usually accepted without question the material contained in them. To what extent ministerial opinions were influenced by other factors, the degree of selectivity of information included in these documents, and the process of evaluation by the secretaries of state cannot be readily determined until specific missions and individual diplomatists have been studied. The passages in the text indicate, however, that the secretaries of state were concerned with issues involving the quality and reliability of information they received.

140. Dudley to Granville, F.O., Friday, 28 May 1828, P.R.O. 30/29/14/4 ff. 163–64.

141. Palmerston to Granville, F.O., 22 May 1831, P.R.O. 30/29/404.

142. George III to Grenville, Windsor, 23 Dec. 1797, *H. M. C. Fortescue*, vol. 3, 405–6; Canning to Granville, Seaford, 13 Oct. 1825, Private & Confidential, No. 80, P.R.O. 30/29/8/8 ff. 995–98.

matist, some men had to be reprimanded and warned not to mix "heterogenous matters."[143]

Dispatches were to be written in a round legible script in black ink so that they were easy to read and would be lasting records to which successive foreign secretaries could refer. Palmerston, whose own handwriting was one of the most legible of all English statesmen and who rarely wrote with anything but the blackest of inks, rigidly enforced this regulation. In 1835 he instructed the undersecretary to tell Sir Robert Porter to write his dispatches in a larger hand since "Life is not long enough to Spell out these Small cramped Hands."[144] George Dawkins received on one occasion "a Specimen of the large Round office Hand for his Sedulous Imitation; and he Should have a Hint that Ink ought to be Black."[145] When the diplomatists resisted reform and continued to write their dispatches in a "Pale liquid," he returned their "Invisible Ink Despatches" to them to be recopied.[146]

The official dispatches were supplemented by private correspondence between the secretary of state (and occasionally between the premier)[147] and the heads of missions abroad. Prior to Canning's secretaryship in the 1820s private letters were of two sorts. The first, more formal, frequently was written on the same paper as dispatches and was distinguishable from them only by the heading "Private" and by being unnumbered. These letters commonly were filed in the Foreign Office.[148] The second type of private letter, employed only to a limited extent before 1822, but very common afterwards, was more informal in tone and usually remained the personal property of the secretary of state.[149] The private letters of Canning, Palmerston, and Aberdeen were all of the second category. Canning and Palmerston conducted an extensive private correspondence with their subordinates, the volume of which depended on the importance of the court and the personal relationship be-

143. Canning to Frere, Pay Office, 17 Jan. 1801, 10 p.m., Festing, *Frere*, pp. 36–38; Planta to James Henderson, Foreign Office, 31 Aug. 1824, F.O. 357/2.
144. Minute, Palmerston, 17 Sept. 1835, F.O. 96/18.
145. Minute, Palmerston, 13 Jan. 1831, F.O. 96/17.
146. Minutes, Palmerston, 14 Aug. 1837, and 26 Apr. 1837, F.O. 96/19.
147. Pitt, for example, encouraged the diplomatists to correspond with him though he was one of the worst correspondents ever to serve as head of a ministry. Pitt to Granville, Downing Street, 21 Jan. 1805, P.R.O. 30/29/384A.
148. For example, St. Helens to Grenville in 1794, F.O. 37/55.
149. Webster, *For. Pol. Castlereagh*, vol. 2, 35–36.

tween the secretary and the minister. For these reasons both men corresponded most extensively with Granville at Paris.

The employment of private letters in the eighteenth century had been designed primarily to enable the secretaries of state to withhold information from the king and their colleagues.[150] This was less true of the practice after 1782 when the prime minister, the undersecretaries, and the king frequently read private letters addressed to the secretary.[151] The secretary, however, retained his discretion over which of these letters he wished his colleagues or sovereign to see,[152] and when Canning submitted them to George IV he did so in part to gain credit at the court for himself and his diplomatists.[153]

The great increase in the use of private letters in the 1820s and the 1830s reflected in part the increasing inability of ministers to resist parliamentary pressure for printed papers.[154] But it would be incorrect to assume that the private correspondence of the secretary of state was employed as a substitute for the official instructions contained in public dispatches. Official dispatches formed an accurate record of the foreign policy of any ministry, though they did not reveal all the motives that influenced policy. Ministers were conscious of the importance of dispatches as records of their successes and failures, though only occasionally did they send "ostensible" dispatches to fill gaps in their correspondence. Aberdeen, for example, in 1829 wrote Wellington that "in consequence of the acknowledgement of Don Miguel by the King of Spain, we shall probably be accused of being the authors of the measure; and at all events we shall be questioned upon the subject. With a view of putting something on record, I inclose the draft of a despatch, which, if you approve, I propose to send to Mr. Bosanquet" at Madrid.[155]

150. Pares, *George III and Politicians*, pp. 201–2.
151. Grenville to Auckland, Whitehall, 17 June 1791, Private, Copy, *H. M. C. Fortescue*, vol. 2, 101; Howard de Walden to A'Court, F.O., 12 Jan. 1828, Private & Confidential, Add. MS 41556 ff. 220–22; William IV to Palmerston, Windsor Castle, 7 Oct. 1832, Palmerston Papers RC/A/156/1.
152. Wellington to Aberdeen, Walmer Castle, 16 Aug. 1830, Add. MS 43059 ff. 50–53.
153. Canning to Granville, F.O., 21 Jan. 1825, No. 21, Private, P.R.O. 30/29/8/6 ff. 777–78; Same to Same, F.O., Sunday Night, 13 Nov. 1825, Secret as well as Most Private & Confidential, P.R.O. 30/29/8/9 ff. 1047–50.
154. Webster, *For. Pol. Palmerston*, vol. 1, 60–63.
155. Aberdeen to Wellington, Foreign Office, 18 Oct. 1829, Copy, Add. MS 43058 ff. 61–62. The draft began "As it is probable that the recognition of Don Miguel as King of

The secretaries of state corresponded privately with the members of the diplomatic service for a variety of reasons. Perhaps the most important motive was to enable the secretary or diplomatist "to discuss more freely and confidentially the subjects on which I write officially."[156] Private letters, because they were less formal than dispatches, could deal with shades of opinions or questions not considered proper subjects for dispatches. Fox told Malmesbury in 1783 that his "public letter will hardly be sufficient to give you an idea of the extreme anxiety of the Court of France about this Turkish business, and of the pains they have taken to persuade us to act in concert with them."[157] Grey felt a private letter, not a public dispatch, should be employed to enter "minutely into what is passing internally in another Country."[158] Secretaries discussed internal and external political events in their letters to foreign ministers to keep them informed and to enable them to take these events into account during their own transactions.[159] Unofficial communications of foreign powers, rumors, and speculative reports of diplomatists also were properly subjects of private correspondence, not public dispatches.[160]

Occasionally, when there were delays in preparing official dispatches, private letters were employed to instruct diplomatists in particular courses of action. The undersecretaries wrote some of these letters at the direction of the secretary of state, though the secretaries also wrote some. Usually they dealt with some important issue (such as the Austrian capitulation to France in 1799 or the state of Cuba in 1825) on which it was absolutely essential for the diplomatist to have something to guide his action while the cabinet was settling on a precise course of policy, while the secretary of state was

---

Portugal will not be longer deferred by Spain. . . ," Draft to Mr. Bosanquet, Foreign Office, 18 Oct. 1829, No. 20, F.O. 72/352.

156. Grenville to Ewart, Whitehall, 26 July 1791, Private, *H. M. C. Fortescue,* vol. 2, 142; Castlereagh to Clancarty, Foreign Office, 31 Jan. 1816, and J. James to Castlereagh, The Hague, 10 Feb. 1816, Londonderry, *Castlereagh Corresp.,* vol. 11, 164–65.

157. 27 July 1783, St. James's, Malmesbury, *Diaries,* vol. 2, 50–52.

158. Grey to Palmerston, Downing Street, 18 Nov. 1832, Palmerston Papers GC/GR/2173.

159. Canning to Wellington, Gloucester Lodge, 24 Oct. 1822, *W.N.D.,* vol. 1, 413.

160. Abercrombie to Fox-Strangways, Parma, 9 June 1836, Private, Palmerston Papers GC/AB/56; F. J. Jackson to Hawkesbury, Berlin, 3 Dec. 1802, Private, Copy, and Berlin, 14 Apr. 1804, Private, Copy, F.O. 353/88.

dealing with other important questions, or until he recovered from an illness sufficiently to prepare formal instructions.[161]

Sometimes questions of a delicate nature were discussed initially in private correspondence. Canning, for example, told Granville in 1826 to ask the French government how much longer French troops were to be stationed in Spain and on what grounds they remained there. "If you get a satisfactory answer to this inquiry I will convert this Letter into a despatch. If not, it is better that no such despatch should appear on the records of your Embassy until we have weighed well . . . the course which will be fit to be pursued—& the time to be chosen for entering upon it."[162] When Palmerston in 1834 wrote to Sir Charles Vaughan, the minister to Washington, instructing him to offer his good offices in settling a Franco-American dispute,[163] he employed a private letter, which, though "it contained Some Suggestions intended to be useful, . . . out of Deference to the Two Governments concerned, I did not think it advisable to give a formal & official Character."[164]

The effectiveness of Foreign Office control over the activities of agents abroad cannot be fully explored until specific studies of individual missions and diplomatists have been made. In the broadest sense it can be argued that policy was directed from Whitehall. Every ambassador, those accredited to remote courts as well as those appointed to posts near England, was on his appointment clearly and carefully instructed on the general policy his principals wished pursued. Beyond this generalization statements about the question of Foreign Office control become more difficult to make. Two things seem evident. First, there was no direction or control of policy at remote assignments in the sense that such control existed over the activities of diplomatists at nearby stations. The old problems of distance and poor methods of communication already discussed continued to plague the secretaries of the first half of the nineteenth century the way they had troubled secretaries in the past.

161. Frere to Minto, London, 23 July 1799, Copy, *H. M. C. Fortescue*, vol. 5, 176–77; Canning to Granville, F.O., 21 June 1825, Private Political, No. 58, P.R.O. 30/29/8/8 ff. 923–26; Aberdeen to Stratford Canning, Foreign Office, 20 Sept. 1828, Private, F.O. 352/20 (Part 2)/9; Addington to Cowley, Foreign Office, 4 Feb. 1843, Copy, F.O. 27/663.
162. 24 Jan. 1826, F.O., Private, P.R.O. 30/29/8/9 ff. 1106–11; the letter was later converted to a dispatch. Same to Same, F.O., 31 Jan. 1826, Private, No. 6, ibid., ff. 1126–27.
163. 12 Nov. 1834, F.O., Private, Copy, Palmerston Papers GC/VA/100.
164. Palmerston to Wellington, Broadlands, 20 Jan. 1835, F.O. 5/305 ff. 87–88.

These problems could not be easily overcome without technological changes. At the courts nearer to London, however, more careful attention to business was sufficient to give the secretaries more control over the activities of diplomatic personnel. This was important because of the relatively greater significance of western European states in British foreign policy as compared to the importance attached to relations with more remote countries, Russia excepted.

More important, there was the fact that the individual diplomatist lacked the perspective of his superiors and therefore was not always capable of assessing to the fullest extent the impact of every situation. Ignorance of the complexities of specific events more than the inability to appreciate the interests of the country was responsible for this circumstance. Diplomatists rarely returned to London on leave though Palmerston felt that ideally they ought occasionally to come home for extensive consultations.[165] The Whigs after 1830, because of their weakness in the House of Lords, usually tried to get the peers who were serving at missions abroad to return for the initial session of each new parliament so that they might take their seats and leave their proxies in the hands of the government. Political conditions abroad, however, frequently prevented some of these men from leaving their posts,[166] while others were too far from home to make the journey feasible. As a result of these two factors, diplomatists had to rely heavily on correspondence for their information, general as well as specific, and they were frequently unable as a result to form valuable judgments on any but the most specific issues involving their own assignment. In times of crisis, moreover, the secretary of state was more apt than not to assume personal control over events and even to work to the relative exclusion of his diplomatic personnel.[167]

Nevertheless, some diplomatists exercised more discretion in the conduct of affairs than others. None perhaps went so far as Lord Malmesbury who said that he enjoyed great latitude and scope of action and knew better than his superiors from his own experience what powers he had and when he could exercise them at any court to

165. Palmerston to Villiers, F.O., 14 July 1836, Copy, Palmerston Papers GC/CL/269/1–3.
166. Melbourne to Palmerston, Panshanger, 25 Dec. 1835, Private, Palmerston Papers GC/ME/59.
167. Granville to Leveson, Paris, 8 Mar. 1841, Private, P.R.O. 30/29/18 Bundle 2 No. 18.

which he was accredited.[168] Ambassadors stationed at the more remote courts were encouraged to exercise greater discretion than those nearer to London. Hawkesbury felt that the distance to Russia was so great that the ambassador there had to be given "that Confidence which will enable him to act as Events may render necessary, without referring home upon every occasion. . . ."[169] Canning urged Sir Arthur Paget when appointing him ambassador at Constantinople "to adapt the general spirit of your instruction as nearly as possible to whatever circumstances may occur."[170] Palmerston thought it unwise to send specific instructions to the Persian mission as "the Events upon which you found such Instructions are five or six months old when the Instructions are received, and new Circumstances may have quite altered the Case."[171] Yet even at the missions closer to England the secretary of state sometimes left to the discretion of the minister how and when he would implement his instructions.[172]

The British diplomatic service during the first half of the nineteenth century, despite the need for reform, adequately performed the duties required of it. Those reforms instituted served to make it a more professional service than it had been in the eighteenth century. They also brought it more under the direct control of the secretary of state. It remained, however, closed to all but the well-to-do and the politically influential. This is perhaps as it should have been given the social and political conditions of England and Europe at the time. Certainly the limited and haphazard method of recruitment meant that the abilities of the men in the service varied considerably. But the great majority were capable of executing their assignments with reasonable proficiency, and since this was usually all that was expected of them, the service and the system adequately met the needs of the country.

168. Malmesbury, *Diaries*, vol. 4, 417.

169. Hawkesbury to Harrowby, Coombe Wood, 5 Oct. 1804, Harrowby MSS vol. 11, ff. 3–4.

170. Canning to Paget, Foreign Office, 26 May 1807, Private, Paget, *Paget Papers*, vol. 2, 295–98.

171. Palmerston to Russell, Windsor, 1 Oct. 1838, Rollo Russell (ed.), *The Early Correspondence of Lord John Russell* (2 vols.; London, 1913), vol. 2, 223–26.

172. Minute, Palmerston, on William Rothery to Palmerston, Hotel de Douvres, Rue de la Paix, 10 Aug. 1840, F.O. 27/643.

Chapter IX

THE CONSULAR SERVICE

Despite Britain's growing commercial and industrial preeminence in the nineteenth century successive foreign secretaries paid little attention to the consular service, which remained until 1943, when it was merged with the diplomatic service, the "step-child" of the Foreign Office.[1] Canning instituted reforms that brought it more closely under the direction of the Foreign Office and his creation of a Consular Department headed by the first senior clerk seemed to reflect the growing importance the government attached to commercial affairs. But these measures, though they made the consular service more respectable and led to an increase in applications for consular appointments, enhanced the importance of the service only to a small degree. It was clearly an auxilliary branch of the Foreign Office whose officials did little more than gather commercial information for the Treasury and the Board of Trade. The consuls remained, therefore, social outcasts in the network of officialdom supervised by the Foreign Office. "Their crowning misfortune," it has been observed,

> which they themselves, with social pretentions of their own, were slow to recognize, was their subordination to a Department . . . where social distinctions and snobberies were really important. The consul was ill-regarded by his social superiors, and it was from among his social superiors that his official superiors were drawn.[2]

There was prior to 1826 no consular service in the same way there was a diplomatic service, and it can be argued that even after 1826 there was no true service because it was not until 1903 that "systema-

1. Bishop, *British Foreign Relations*, p. 208; Steiner, "Last Years of the Foreign Office," pp. 70, 85.
2. D. C. M. Platt, *The Cinderella Service: British Consuls since 1825* (London, 1971), p. 1.

tic recruitment, control, transfer and promotion" were introduced.[3]
Before 1826 there were merely consuls resident in numerous
foreign ports and even many among these consuls scattered throughout the world were not all under the supervision of the Foreign Office. The consuls in the Levant until 1825 were appointed
and paid by the Levant Company with which they corresponded.[4]
The Colonial Office was responsible for the activities of the consuls
on the Barbary Coast until 1837.[5] Even the consuls appointed by the
foreign secretary were poorly and irregularly directed until 1815
when Castlereagh had a uniform set of consular instructions prepared. Alexander Cockburn, for a time consul general for the Circle
of Lower Saxony, complained in 1809 that the Foreign Office sent
consuls abroad "like lost sheep in the Wilderness, without any sort of
instructions or any information respecting their duty, in consequence of which they have been obliged to follow the steps of their
Predecessors, and are generally considered by Merchants as doing
more injury than service to the Trade which they are intended to
protect. . . ."[6]

There were other factors that distinguished the consular establishment from the diplomatic service. There were in use the titles of
consul general, consul, and vice-consul.[7] But though the vice-
consuls were unquestionably deputies of consuls, there was little
distinction between the duties and authority of consuls and consuls
general. Nor was there much communication between them. John
Hunter, consul general in Spain, in reporting the number of consuls
in that country in 1810 said that there was a "Mr. Tupper at Valencia,
who I have heard acts there, but I know not by what Commission."[8]
The foreign secretary appointed the consuls and consuls general,
but consuls appointed vice-consuls at their own convenience subject
only to the pro forma confirmation of the Foreign Office.[9]

3. Ibid., p. 5.
4. Extract of Treasury Minute, 23 Aug. 1825, Copy, F.O. 366/348 ff. 25–33. On the
Levant service see Platt, *The Cinderella Service*, pp. 125–79.
5. Unsigned minute, 1 May 1837, F.O. 366/462.
6. Memorandum, Cockburn, 4 Nov. 1809, F.O. 83/16, copy in F.O. 95/592 without date
or other identifying mark.
7. The Whigs abolished in 1831 the appointment of consuls general at all places save
Constantinople where there were embassies or missions. Draft to British Consuls in France,
F.O., 28 Dec. 1831, Circular, F.O. 27/437.
8. "List of the Gentlemen employed as Consuls in the ports of Spain," London, 2 May
1810, F.O. 72/102 ff. 284–85.
9. Croker to James Murray, 15 Sept. 1819, Jennings, *Croker Papers*, vol. 1, 144–45.

Many consuls enjoyed salaries on the king's Civil List. Most received revenues from a combination of their salary and the fees levied on British trade in the ports at which they resided. Though every consul collected these fees, Stephen Lushington, secretary to the Treasury, told Planta in 1818 that he did not think "that British Consuls have any legal authority to demand fees. . . ."[10] Because of the lack of direction from the Foreign Office or the Treasury the rates levied against British commerce as well as the services for which fees were collected varied greatly throughout the service. So, too, did the revenues of consuls. Francis Keinitz, consul at Liebau, received no salary and in 1821 his fees totalled only £14.7.2.[11] On the other extreme, Joseph Charles Mellish, agent and consul for the Circle of Lower Saxony and the free cities of Hamburg, Bremen, and Lubeck received between 1815 and 1823 a Civil List salary of £480 a year and fees ranging from £1,200 to £1,800.[12]

Most consular officials were merchants. James Bandinel said that they were "the head, acknowledged by their Government, of the merchants of their Country resident in their Consulate."[13] Apparently the heads of certain merchant houses were traditionally appointed consuls at some of the ports. When consul Murray at Madeira moved to Lisbon in 1799, for example, Lord Loughborough asked that Murray's partner, Joseph Pringle, be appointed his successor because "it would be a very sensible mortification to be deprived of the sort of consequence which is attached to it, and to see it transferred to any house of more modern establishment; for I believe this house has been settled in Madeira for almost a century."[14]

Not everyone approved of the selection of merchants to fill these positions, and for an obvious reason. Lord St. Helens, minister at St. Petersburg in 1802, told Hawkesbury that "Cases must continually arise where a Merchant so employed would find his private Interests to be in direct opposition to his Consular Duty—An observation which I believe to be generally true" throughout the service.[15] Little was done prior to 1825 to alter the practice of appointing merchants,

10. 14 May 1814, Treasury Chambers, Private, F.O. 27/197.
11. F.O. 366/247 f. 2.
12. Ibid., f. 32.
13. Memorandum on Consuls [1823–1825?], F.O. 95/592.
14. To Grenville, Tunbridge Wells, 12 Aug. 1799, *H. M. C. Fortescue*, vol. 5, 278.
15. 8 Jan. 1802, St. Petersburg, Private, F.O. 83/11.

in great part because the expense of the service and the uncertainty of financial rewards made it an unattractive alternative to other employment. Another factor that made it difficult to recruit other than merchants into the service was the fact that the consular service never benefitted from reforms instituted in other branches of the government service. For example, the fees collected on consular appointments, always more exorbitant than those collected on diplomatic appointments,[16] were still collected after those levied against the personnel of the diplomatic service were abolished. There were no provisions for pensions, though occasionally consuls and their dependents received allowances from the Civil List when they retired.[17] When travel expenses were granted to consuls the sum was strictly regulated and for no reason were they allowed to charge more than their original allowance.[18] The Foreign Office reimbursed consuls any money they expended on forwarding diplomatic mail, but each consul was responsible for meeting the expenses of his consulate without any government assistance.[19] The worst feature of the service in so far as recruitment went was the lack of opportunity for promotion. Although an occasional consular officer (Anthony Merry, for example) was elevated to the diplomatic service, most foreign secretaries had a decided prejudice against such promotions. When Grenville appointed Frere to Lisbon in 1800 he said that "many considerations" made it "impossible" for Arbuthnot to become minister after serving as consul general there.[20] Canning objected in 1825 to the promotion of consular personnel to the diplomatic service as being "unjust" to the lower ranks of the diplomatic service.[21]

16. £12.15.0 for the commission, £110.2.6 for gratuities (£86 to the undersecretaries, £23.12.0 to the chief clerk, 10/6 to the office keepers; all after 1795 paid to the fee fund of the office), 12/6 stamp duty, and 10/6 to have their name put in the *Gazette*. This is to be compared with the £102.17.0 charged on the appointment of an ambassador and the £72.7.6 collected from each envoy appointed. "William England, Esq.; Fees on his appointment as His Majesty's Consul at Malta," 16 June 1794; fees of Robert Liston as ambassador to Constantinople, Sept. 1793; and fees of Lord Henry Spencer as envoy to Sweden, 6 July 1793, F.O. 366/387.
17. An account of pensions paid, 1792–1821, F.O. 366/350; Grenville to Lords of Treasury, Downing Street, 5 Nov. 1798, Copy, F.O. 366/427.
18. Carmarthen to Lords of Treasury, St. James's, 11 July 1785, Copy, F.O. 366/425 ff. 304–5; Fraser to George Rose with margin minute, Whitehall, 6 Apr. 1787, Copy, F.O. 366/426 f. 52.
19. Fraser to Thomas Steele, St. James's, 24 Aug. 1785, Copy, F.O. 366/425 f. 317.
20. Grenville to Frere, Cleveland Row, 13 Aug. 1800, Copy, *H. M. C. Fortescue*, vol. 6, 293–94.
21. To George IV, Eastham, 9 Dec. 1825, Stapleton, *Corresp. of Canning*, vol. 1, 341–45.

Castlereagh made the first tenuous reforms in the consular service. Instructions prepared under his direction in 1815 were issued to every consul and consul general and to all new appointees thereafter. These instructions, eleven in number, stressed the duty of the consul to promote British trade in his area and gave him responsibility "by every fair & proper means" to do so. He was also to safeguard the interests and rights of all British subjects and to report regularly to the consul general in the country to which he was assigned all trade information and to the British minister there all other matters affecting Britain's national intereests.[22] Other instructions required him to be vigilant against the slave trade (number 3), to protect the subjects of the Ionian Islands (number 4), to give physical aid and other assistance to British vessels and their crews (numbers 5, 6, 7, 9, 10), and to provide reports on the nature of all trade and tariffs at his port (numbers 8, 11). These measures went a short way towards establishing the direct supervision of the Foreign Office over the service and towards creating a standardized system of action and reporting within the service. The consuls general were recognized as the superior commercial agents and the diplomatists as the superior political agents of the consuls in every country.[23]

Canning's reforms of the service were more significant. There were two goals that he hoped to achieve in his Consular Act of 1825. The more important object was to promote British trade by reducing as much as possible the charges and the irregular practices of the consular service. The second object was to establish a paid, professional service whose sole interest and business was to protect and promote British trade.[24] The act, which went into effect on 1 January 1826,[25] established a scale of fees for the consular service and provided for a system of fines to be levied against any consul who collected more than the act authorized. Fees were charged only for services performed and were not based on the value of a cargo or the tonnage of a vessel calling at a particular port. The act also au-

22. F.O. 366/247 ff. 113–14, Instructions numbered 1 and 2. Instructions 3–11 at ff. 114–17.

23. The consul general at Odessa corresponded with the embassies at St. Petersburg and Constantinople. Draft to Earl of Durham, F.O., 7 Apr. 1837, No. 73, F.O. 65/231.

24. "Memorandum, for the consideration of Mr. Huskisson in regard to the new Consular Bill," F.O., Jan. 1824, F.O. 95/592.

25. 6 George IV c. 87, 5 July 1825.

thorized the king by order-in-council to establish salaries for the service, extended the provisions of the Superannuation Act of 1822 to consuls, and provided for the appointment of a chaplain at every port where a consul resided. These chaplains were paid partly from public funds and partly from funds raised by the merchants at the port. They were usually appointed by the bishop of London who had at any rate to approve all nominees of the merchants.[26] The Act recognized the authority of the consuls to serve as notaries, which they had been doing semi-officially for some time.[27] There was no provision for the elimination of fees and though Canning made some attempt before the act was passed to have them abolished they remained in effect until 1837.[28]

Perhaps the most important decision Canning made was to prohibit consuls from participating directly or indirectly in the trade of the port at which they served. The salaries of the service were raised to more respectable levels and every consul received some payment from government. This system was short-lived as the Whigs, in an effort to curtail government expenditure, reduced in 1832 most consular salaries and as compensation relaxed the ban on trading with the exception of certain consulships with political or other official duties.[29]

From 1826 to 1837 the appointments of consuls were antedated so that they could use the additional salary they received as an outfit. Palmerston abolished this "objectionable" practice and established a sliding scale for outfits proportionate to the distance the consul had to travel to his post. Appointees already resident at the port to which they were assigned received no outfit.[30] Also after 1837 the Foreign Office began to reimburse consuls for the cost of their postage and

26. Aberdeen to the Bishop of London, F.O., 26 Aug. 1829, Draft, F.O. 27/401; minute, Palmerston, on Benjamin Churchill to [Bidwell?], Honfleur France, 2 Sept. 1834, F.O. 27/493.
27. Unsigned minute, Castlereagh, on Croker to Planta, Admiralty Office, 26 Aug. 1819, F.O. 27/220.
28. Planta to Clerk of the Council in Waiting, F.O., 6 Mar. 1824, Draft, F.O. 366/387; "First Report of the Committee . . . to enquire into the Fees and Emoluments of Public Offices," 23 Mar. 1837, *P.P., 1837*, vol. 44, Command 162, p. 165.
29. "Memorandum on Consular Arrangements by Mr. Poulett Thomson," 1832, No. 3 F.O. 95/592. See appendixes VI and VII for the organization of the service in 1828 and for which consuls were not allowed to trade.
30. "Extract of Lord Palmerston's Letter to the Lords Commissioners of H. M. Treasury," 16 Oct. 1837, F.O. 366/350.

for the other expenses of their consulates.[31] The payment of their salaries was subject to the same inconvenient delay as the payments of the salaries of diplomatists, though since consuls were regularly collecting fees and had considerably fewer expenses than diplomatic personnel they did not complain very frequently about it.

After 1826 the consular service became a more respectable as well as a more profitable vocation. Backhouse regarded consulships as promotions from clerkships at the Foreign Office[32] and an increasing number of clerks were appointed consuls or consuls general during the period following Canning's reforms. Peers and other influential persons began to solicit consulships for their friends and relations and Aberdeen told Peel in 1841 that his list of candidates was "numerous beyond all precedent."[33] Merchants continued to receive most consular appointments once Palmerston removed the ban on trading. There was a vacancy at Leghorn in 1843 for which Aberdeen "had about fifty Candidates, military, naval, legal, and diplomatic of all Sorts [but] I appointed a Resident Merchant whose reputation led me to believe that the interests of British Commerce could best be entrusted to Him."[34] Palmerston, unlike his predecessors, regulated the conduct of the merchant-consuls by prohibiting them, on pain of dismissal, from "ostentatiously" dating their letters concerning their private or commercial transactions "from the *Consulate* which is an office for Public Business and not a merchant's Counting House."[35] The general effect of these changes was to make the service more professional and more respectable. After the 1830s there was less toleration of the Beau Brummel type of consular appointment. Backhouse, for example, complained to Aberdeen as soon as he had come into office in 1841 of Palmerston's appointment of a Mr. Hart, the Jewish keeper of a low class gaming house in London, as consul at Leipzig. This "flagitious & disgraceful step" "and the miscreant's conduct in every part, official & private has provoked from the publick authorities of Prussia and Saxony, serious & repeated Remonstrances to the British Govt., to which Ld.

31. Form #17 to Consuls, F.O., May 1837, ibid.
32. Unsigned minute, Backhouse, on unsigned memorandum, J. Bidwell, 24 Feb. 1829, F.O. 95/592.
33. Grey to Palmerston, 1 May 1834, Private, Palmerston Papers GC/GR/2303; Aberdeen to Peel, F.O., 18 Oct. 1841, Copy, Add. MS 43061 ff. 291–92.
34. Aberdeen to Lord Douglas, F.O., 23 Dec. 1843, Copy, Add. MS 43242 f. 26.
35. Minute, Palmerston, 26 Sept. 1833, F.O. 27/475.

Palmerston to their great surprise, & to our deep mortification, has uniformly refused to listen!"[36] Most consuls fortunately were of a better class than consul Hart.

The secretary of state almost exclusively enjoyed the patronage of the consular service, though his appointments were subject to royal approval.[37] Before 1823 some effort was made to attend to the wishes of the patrons of consuls who were to be removed from their posts for being incompetent.[38] Canning, however, made it clear that their tenure depended upon their "publick service" and not on their "private connections & support."[39] Because it was impossible for him to know the qualifications of all applicants for consulships, Palmerston consulted Backhouse on consular appointments and in 1835 he sent Adolphus Turner, a clerk at the Foreign Office, to Jersey to see whether or not there were any respectable merchants to fill the vice-consulship at Granville.[40]

The House of Commons had little influence over the consular service and with the exception of an occasional debate[41] little notice of it was taken in Parliament. Those few attempts by members to establish commissions for enquiring into consular affairs were uniformly resisted by the Foreign Office. John Bidwell, head of the Consular Department in the office, objected to such enquiries because they infringed on the prerogative of the crown and he was afraid they would establish an inconvenient precedent for enquiries into the diplomatic service. Wellington and his undersecretary, Viscount Mahon, felt that the House had a sufficient check on the service by the annual vote of supplies and that the organization and patronage of the service were not valid subjects of enquiry by a committee of the House.[42]

36. 4 Oct. 1841, Frankfort, Confidential as to the first point, Add. MS 43238 ff. 18–23.
37. Wellington to Aberdeen, Walmer Castle, 29 July 1829, Add. MS 43057 ff. 231–32; Minute, Palmerston, 21 Mar. 1839, F.O. 366/502.
38. Unsigned minute, Bandinel, with minutes, Hamilton and Castlereagh; Bandinel to Col. James Wood, Foreign Office, 17 Jan. 1818; Col. Wood to Hamilton, Littleton, 21 Jan. 1818, F.O. 27/197.
39. Planta to James Henderson, Foreign Office, 6 Oct. 1823, F.O. 357/1.
40. Minutes, Palmerston and Backhouse, 11 Aug. 1833, F.O. 96/17; Adolphus Turner to James Murray, Jersey, 25 July 1835, F.O. 27/510.
41. Hesketh Fleetwood's Motion of 26 June 1834, to establish a select committee to enquire into all aspects of the service, 3 Hansard's, vol. 24, 883–91; Benjamin Disraeli's motion to have the diplomatic and consular services merged into a single foreign service, 8 Mar. 1842, ibid., vol. 61, 219–81.
42. Mahon's "Memorandum on Mr. Hesketh Fleetwood's letter," 4 Mar. 1835, and Mahon to Peel, Foreign Office, 5 Mar. 1835, Add. MS 40416 ff. 154–59.

Although the duties of consuls were primarily commercial in nature, they performed other services for the government. The consuls at the ports on the French and Netherlands coasts corresponded with the Treasury in an effort to prevent smuggling in the English Channel.[43] The consul at Calais received £200 a year to forward dispatches to all parts of the continent.[44] Several consuls acted as agents for Lloyds, and though they were restricted from corresponding with the company on political subjects,[45] it is difficult to see how the government could have effectively enforced this regulation. Many consuls in France were employed to gather intelligence. The consuls at Nice and Brest reported regularly on all French naval activity.[46] The consul at Marseilles after 1828 made four trips a year to Toulon, where there was no British consul, to secure accurate information about French naval movements and armaments and then reported personally to the ambassador in Paris so that there would be no written record of his activities.[47] One consul, Captain Barnes at Mortaix, was prohibited from gathering intelligence because he had been employed by Sir Charles Stuart, the ambassador in Paris, as an agent prior to being appointed to the consulship.[48]

Few consuls had political duties and the Foreign Office always strongly disapproved their assuming any. Consul Fagan at Naples in 1814 was reprimanded for "running about Italy, giving himself the airs of a Minister, and . . . [for being] absurd enough to demand a formal audience of Murat, presenting himself to him as British Consul-General at Naples."[49] Backhouse in 1832 cautioned consul Frederick Chatfield in Poland to avoid expressions "which might be construed as identifying him with local feelings & opinions" about

43. Lushington to Hamilton, 8 Feb. 1817, F.O. 27/172.
44. Unsigned minute, Planta, on Richard Martin to Lord Francis Conyngham, 19 Feb. 1824, F.O. 27/324.
45. Unsigned Memorandum, J. Bidwell, [October, 1832], F.O. 27/449.
46. Aust to Grenville, Whitehall, 14 Sept. 1791, Grenville MSS; Croker to Wellington, London, 14 Nov. 1828, W.N.D., vol. 5, 248–49.
47. Croker to Dudley, Admiralty, 2 May 1828, Confidential & Secret, with unsigned minute, J. Bidwell, F.O. 27/385.
48. Unsigned minute, Hamilton, on Stuart to Hamilton, Paris, 20 Nov. 1818, Private, F.O. 97/163.
49. A'Court to Hamilton, Palermo, 7 Sept. 1814, Copy, and A'Court to Castlereagh, Palermo, 8 Oct. 1814, Londonderry, Castlereagh Corresp., vol. 10, 109, 154–55.

Russian measures in that country.[50] The only exceptions to this rule were the consuls general in Peru, Chile, and occasionally in other South American countries. These men were also given the rank of chargé d'affaires since the "Chief Business of whoever resides there will be Commercial rather than political, & a Minister would not do the former, but a Consul general might perform the latter."[51]

The consular service in the first half of the nineteenth century remained an auxiliary branch of government. Consuls exercised little initiative but they were excellent sources of information about the commercial and industrial affairs of other states. There was little glamor in being a consul, but there was also little work at any but the most important ports. Few men of great ability, therefore, could be found among the consuls, most of whom performed their duties tolerably well but with little imagination and less enthusiasm.[52]

50. Backhouse to Heytesbury, Foreign Office, 19 June 1832, Private, Add. MS 41563 f. 217.

51. Minute, Palmerston, 27 Aug. 1831, F.O. 96/17.

52. The important changes in the service were made only gradually in the nineteenth century and the most significant reforms were those that took place after 1900. Platt, *The Cinderella Service*, pp. 16–124.

CHAPTER X

CONCLUSION

The years between the loss of the continental colonies in North America in 1782 and the repeal of the Corn Laws in 1846 were eventful ones in British history. The Napoleonic wars and the resulting realignment of power in Europe in and of themselves perhaps would have had a significant impact upon British foreign policy and the manner in which it was conducted. Containment of France, the growing power of Russia in the east, the emergence of new states in the Americas (to mention only a few of the new features of diplomacy after 1815) clearly presented new problems and new opportunities for British statesmen. As it was, however, other factors were of equal and perhaps even greater importance to the changes which took place.

These were eventful years in domestic history for Britain as well. Changing demographic and economic patterns began to transform British society. The pressure for change in both the political and social structure increased with the passage of time. The new groups, capitalists and proletariat alike, sought a fuller role in the political process. The old order responded slowly to this pressure, but it did begin the accommodation of the new interests which in the course of the century after 1815 led to a more democratic and representative government. In the process the traditional institutions of British society and politics were also remodeled.

Yet, too often it is forgotten that changes in these institutions were already underway by the late eighteenth century. The Yorkshire Association and the economical reform program of the Rockingham Whigs were reflections of the demands by certain portions of the traditional groups for fundamental change in the old order. The forces of change were also evident in the evolution and development of traditional institutions such as the cabinet in the eighteenth century. The process of the gradual modification of these institutions prior to 1800 was accelerated and redirected to a great extent after 1815 in response to the new pressures brought forth by industrialization. No part of the traditional structure was totally immune to change. In the end, because of the impact of these forces on the political structure as a whole, they fully influenced both decisions and the manner in which foreign policy was conducted.

Much, of course, remained the same. Most important was the fact that those who formulated policy and those who carried out their decisions retained their separate and distinct identities. The conduct of foreign policy was too intimately tied to the prerogative for the monarch immediately to yield the power of decision-making to nameless civil servants in Whitehall. Yet concessions had to be made to the politicians. William III had been the last king for whom foreign policy was the policy of the king rather than of the nation. By the reign of George III initiative had already passed to the ministers. George III still played an active role which his successors did not even approximate. Yet even in the 1780s and the 1790s the king was not responsible for the initiation of policy. His objection to proposed courses of action could not be overlooked. But he could be overridden if the ministers were determined and united in what they wished to do.

Circumstances and time conspired to diminish the royal role in the ensuing reigns. George IV was too indolent to maintain the vigilance necessary for the king to be sufficiently informed to cooperate effectively with ministers. William IV worked hard but at best he could only hope to check the process of dissolution in the royal role in decision-making which had begun in his brother's reign. William more actively expressed his opinions than his brother had. On occasion he may even have influenced decisions in point of some detail or another. Beyond the occasional incident, however, he could not hope to force major changes of policy. Victoria's youth and attendant inexperience at the outset of her reign completed the process. British policy was solely that of the ministers after 1837. The queen's role closely approximated that predicated for a constitutional monarch by Bagehot at mid-century: "To state the matter shortly, the sovereign has . . . three rights—the right to be consulted, the right to encourage, the right to warn."[1]

---

1. Quoted in Hanham, *Nineteenth-Century Constitution*, p. 32.

None of these developments would have been possible had not the politicians been better organized and more cohesive than their predecessors in the eighteenth century. The importance of the emergence of political parties at the turn of the nineteenth century should not be underestimated. It helped to create political cohesiveness that transcended personal ambition and forged unity based in part on shared ideas about policies. It also created a focal point for promoting alternative policies advocated by different groups within the political community. The cabinet, already a formalized institution in the executive government, could and did become a place where policies of those in office could be debated and decided outside the closet.

These changes are not apparent at first glance. The historian reading through the papers of cabinet ministers is struck with the inefficiency of deliberation which was characteristic of the period down to 1830. But the events of the 1830s made more clear the political divisions that had been emerging prior to that time. They also reinforced party development[2] and encouraged ministers to think in terms of their responsibility to the electorate for their decisions. Under the circumstances the monarch could only yield with greater frequency to ministerial decisions. Ministers in turn could only assume that theirs was increasingly the determining factor in policy-making.

In practice not all in the cabinet were equally involved in determining foreign policy. The creation of the foreign secretaryship, whatever the intent of Fox and his colleagues in 1782, had the effect of giving the foreign secretary considerable initiative in the cabinet on matters affecting his own department. This authority was usually shared with the prime minister. Indeed, strong prime ministers such as the younger Pitt and a generation later Peel had a more significant impact on policy than Grenville and Aberdeen did as foreign secretaries in the same ministries. Nonetheless, these cases were the exceptional ones. Circumstances placed powerful politicians in the Foreign Office and these men in turn were able effectively to dominate decision-making. Castlereagh, Canning, and Palmerston shared a view that they were *primus inter pares* in the cabinet on questions of foreign policy. Their grasp of issues, forcefulness in

2. Gash, *Politics in the Age of Peel,* passim.

debate, and political abilities elevated the role of foreign secretary within the ministries of the early nineteenth century. As the cabinet asserted its role in determining policy at the expense of the monarch, so too did the foreign secretaries assert their superiority on these matters over the other members of the cabinet.

One advantage the foreign secretary had over his colleagues was his responsibility to conduct policy on a daily basis. This duty enabled him to be better informed than other cabinet members. It offered opportunity for subtle influence over the precise manner of carrying out general cabinet decisions. It also gave him power to set the tone of foreign policy generally, and specifically how it was perceived by representatives of other states. Increasingly, however, this responsibility to oversee the daily implementation of policy became as onerous as it was advantageous. Other factors were impinging on the secretary of state's time, forcing him to delegate some of his authority.

The growth of the volume of business diminished the secretary's ability to supervise in a detailed fashion the daily operation of the bureaucracy. Equally important were the other political and parliamentary obligations required of successive secretaries of state. These duties were concomitant on the rise of party. The necessity of political management limited the time available for routine administrative matters. These duties fell to the undersecretaries who at first assumed them and retained the quasi-political status they had enjoyed in the eighteenth century. This was a false position in the political world as it was being transformed. By the 1820s it was becoming clear that as the foreign secretary was required to perform regularly purely political responsibilities, his deputies were less important in that arena. The vacuum was in administration. Here expertise was required both in the absence of the secretary and to provide administrative continuity when there was a change in ministries. The creation of the permanent undersecretaryship in the person of John Backhouse, who at any rate was unsuited to play a political role, was perhaps the most significant development in administration during this period.[3]

There were other important administrative developments as well.

3. Middleton, "John Backhouse and the Origins of the Permanent Undersecretaryship for Foreign Affairs," gives the details of the story.

As foreign affairs became more complex the bureaucracy grew. The personalized department of 1782 required few rules and regulations. The work was routine. It entailed little responsibility and less opportunity for initiative. With growth and complexity came specialization. So too came the need to regulate the structure of the department and to specify duties in a more precise form within that structure. The undersecretaries assumed more general supervisory roles. To the senior members of the establishment, who had at any rate through long service acquired considerable knowledge about departmental procedures, developed specific supervisory tasks. Sub-departments for consular and slave trade affairs, among other specialties, emerged. Political divisions headed by clerks assistant, men of the second class, enabled the undersecretaries to delegate specific clerical duties in the 1820s. By 1846 these men had all progressed to the first class to which their successors inevitably belonged. They were not only senior in years of service. They were also experienced in the affairs of certain countries and were seen as experts on these matters even if they were not yet systematically encouraged to recommend policy.

These important changes took place against the backdrop of other developments. Salaries were upgraded and regularized. Extraordinary payments, carryovers from the days of sinecures and jobbing, ceased. A pension scheme was implemented. The office established a tradition of excellence and hard work reinforced by an *esprit de corps* which emphasized that clerks were always gentlemen if not usually scholars. The result of these and other reforms was the creation of a constitutional bureaucracy[4] in all its dimensions.

Despite these developments in Whitehall the foreign and consular services remained relatively intact as they had existed in the eighteenth century. Attachés, it is true, by the 1830s were trained for brief periods before they were sent out on foreign assignments. This reform to a limited degree helped to instill in the foreign service some of the notions of efficiency which were standard in Whitehall. A few clerks became consuls during this period, which portended a notion of professionalism in that service in the next century. But these were minor changes. The diplomatic service remained the preserve of the aristocracy. Breeding and gentility counted more

4. Parris, *Constitutional Bureaucracy*, chapter 1, deals with the emergence of the modern civil service between 1780 and 1830.

than education and ability, at least on initial appointments if not ultimate advancement. On the other hand consular affairs were too often entrusted to whoever could be found to manage them. It was indicative of the low status of this service that John Bidwell, a clerk, managed consular affairs with little supervision from the undersecretaries, to say nothing of the secretary of state. Fundamental changes in the overseas services would have to await developments later in the nineteenth and early in the twentieth centuries.

Nearly a quarter of a century ago Richard Pares, in his Ford Lectures at Oxford, spoke of a prevailing amateurism in eighteenth-century politics.[5] This ideal transcended the realm of politics into that of administration as well. The history of the administration of British foreign policy between 1782 and 1846 is the account of how this tradition was replaced gradually but assuredly by another ideal, one more congenial to the modern industrial-administrative state. By 1846 in the cabinet, at the Foreign Office, and even to a limited degree in the diplomatic and consular services, there was no place for the amateur. There were standards of professionalism to which all were accountable, if in different ways. The days of the amateur were over.

5. Pares, *George III and Politicians*, pp. 1–30.

Appendix I

The Personnel of the Foreign Office, 1782–1846

I have attempted to compile as complete a biography as possible for each of the men listed below. Exceptions have been made for those individuals whose careers are discussed in the *D.N.B.* In these cases I have merely given the nature of their employment at the F.O. and appended a note referring the reader to the appropriate volume and page of the *D.N.B.* where additional information may be found. References to the *D.N.B.* refer to the edition of 1908 and supplements. Each individual is listed as he appears in the salary books of the office (F.O. 366/380—383) but all of his subsequent honors and titles are given in parentheses. Superscript numbers, i.e., the number 1, are repeated in the text to avoid repetition and confusion in the notes. In such cases they always refer to the first citation.

1. Abercromby, (Sir) Ralph (2d Baron Dunfermline). (1803–68).
   B. 6 Apr. 1803 to James Abercromby, later speaker of the House of Commons 1835–39 and 1st Baron,[1] by Mary Anne, dau. of Egerton Leigh of High Leigh co. Chester,[2] ed. Eton c. 1814–18,[2] matric. Feb. 1821 Peterhouse Cambridge,[3] m. 1838 Mary Eliza, dau. of Gilbert, 2d Earl of Minto.[2] Attaché at Frankfort 1821, The Hague 1824, Paris 1824,[4] secretary to the plenipotentiaries negotiating with the United States Dec. 1826–5 July 1827, Précis Writer at F.O. 5 July 1827–12 Aug. 1828, secretary to Lord Strangford's special mission to Brazil 12 Aug. 1825–5 Feb. 1830,[5] secretary to special mission to Brussels 1830, Resident at Florence 1835, Minister Plenipotentiary (Min. P.) Germanic Confederation 1839, Envoy Extraordinary (E.E.) and Min. P. Turin 1840, and the Hague 1851.[4] Ret. 1858 on accession to Peerage,[6] and d. 12 July 1868. Lady Granville said he was ". . . a very amiable quiet, gentlemanlike creature, with lots of tact, and a good deal of intelligent conversation," though susceptible to impatience when he was not promoted rapidly enough in the service.[7]

   1. Strachey and Fulford, *Greville Memoirs*, vol. 1, 175 n. 2.
   2. G. E. C., *Complete Peerage*, vol. 4, 534.

3. J. A. Venn (ed.), *Alumni Cantabrigienses: Part II, 1772–1900* (6 vols.; Cambridge, 1940), vol. 1, 3.

4. *F. O. List*, 1853, p. 30

5. F. O. 366/559.

6. Gower, *Letters of Countess Granville*, vol. 1, 247 n. 1.

7. To Lady G. Morpeth, Calais, 26 Feb. 1824, and to Lady Carlisle, Paris, Oct. 1826, ibid., pp. 257, 398–99.

2. Aberdeen, 4th Earl of. See Hamilton-Gordon, George (no. 88).

3. Adams, William Pitt. (1804–52).

B. 11 Dec. 1804 to William Dacres Adams, Secretary to William Pitt and clerk in the Home Office[1] by Elizabeth dau. of Mayow Wynall-Mayow of Sydenham Kent, ed. Westminister 1817–20 and Oriel Oxford 1823–26, m. 1847 Georgina Emily dau. of Robert Lukin, a nephew of William Wyndham.[2] Clerk 2 Apr. 1826–16 Nov. 1834, special mission to The Hague on business connected with American boundary discussions 10 Mar. 1830–Apr. 1830, then attached to Washington with his clerk's salary 29 June 1830–16 Nov. 1834,[3] Sec. of Legation Bogota 1834 and Mexico 1841,[2] Consul General in Peru 1842[4] until he was assassinated there on 1 Sept. 1852.[5]

1. Nelson, *Home Office*, p. 161.

2. G. F. Russell Barker and Alan H. Stenning (eds.), *The Record of Old Westminsters* (2 vols.; London, 1928), vol. 1, 5.

3. F. O. 366/329 f. 4.

4. Boase, *Mod. Eng. Biog.*, vol. 1, 20.

5. William Pitt Adams, *Papers Relating to the Death and Funeral of the Late William Pitt Adams, Esq.* (London, 1853).

4. Addington, (Rt. Hon.) Henry Unwin. (1790–1870).[1]

Permanent Undersecretary 5 Apr. 1842–9 Apr. 1854.

1. *D.N.B.*, vol. 1, 121.

5. Alston, (Sir) Francis Beilbey. (1820–1906).

B. 1820 to Rowland Alston, M.P. for Hertfordshire, ed. Eton, m. 1862 a daughter of Bridges Taylor (see no. 196).[1] Supernumerary clerk 15 Dec. 1839, clerk 5 Jan. 1840 to retirement as Chief Clerk[2] 1 Dec. 1890. Compensation allowance of £794.2.0 p.a. on abolition of F.O. agencies in 1870.[3] J. P. for Middlesex, served in Hertfordshire militia,[4] K.C.M.G. 1886,[5] d. 24 Aug. 1906.

1. *The Times* (London), 25 Aug. 1906, p. 4.

2. Tilley and Gaselee, *Foreign Office*, p. 213.

3. "Superannuations in Public Offices," *P.P. 1871*, vol. 37, Command 155, p. 444.

4. *F.O. List*, 1907, p. 397.

5. Boase, *Mod. Eng. Biog.*, vol. 4, 106 under Edward Gardiner Alston.

6. Ancell, Richard. (c. 1755–1844).

B. c. 1755 to Thomas Ancell, deputy Chamber Keeper in the F. O.[1] Clerk in State Paper Office Nov. 1776–5 Feb. 1801 when he became the first Librarian and Keeper of the Papers at the F.O.[2] until retirement with £200 pension on 5 Jan. 1810.[3] d. at Gifford Lodge, Twickenham Green 18 Jan. 1844.[4]

1. Nelson, *Home Office*, pp. 150–51 & n. 58.
2. Memorial of Richard Ancell [c. 1810], Copy, F.O. 366/672 ff. 2–3.
3. Memo. by Wellesley, F.O., 5 Jan. 1810, ibid., f.4.
4. *Gents. Mag.* (1844), pt. 1, 444.

7. Ancram, Earl of. See Kerr, John William Robert (no. 118).

8. Antrobus, Gibbs Crawfurd. (1793–1861).

B. 27 May 1793 to John Antrobus by Anne, dau. of Gibbs Crawfurd, M.P. for Queenborough, ed. Eton, St. Johns Cambridge (M.A. 1821),[1] m. 1st. June, dau. of Sir Thomas Coutts Trotter, Bart.,[2] and 2d. 1832 Charlotte, dau. of Sir E. Crofton, Bart.[1] Supernumerary clerk w/o pay June–Nov. 1814, attached to Castlereagh's special mission at Vienna Nov. 1814–July 1815, attaché Switzerland July 1815,[3] Sec. of Legation U.S.A. 18 June 1816, Turin 8 Feb. 1823, Two Sicilies 1 Oct. 1824–May 1826. M.P. for Aldborough Yorks 1820–26 and for Plympton Devon 1826–32.[4] J.P. and High Sheriff of Cheshire, resided Eaton Hall co. Cheshire,[2] d. 21 May 1861.

1. *Gents. Mag.* (1861), pt. 2, 94–95.
2. Edward Walford, *The County Families of the United Kingdom* (London, 1875), p. 23.
3. Antrobus to Backhouse, 3 Sept. 1828, F.O. 366/560.
4. Boase, *Mod. Eng. Biog.*, vol. 1, 76.

9. Arbuthnot, (Rt. Hon.) Charles. (1767–1850).[1]

Précis Writer 1793–95, undersecretary 5 Aug. 1803–5 Apr. 1804.
1. *D.N.B.*, vol. 1, 533.

10. Ashburnham, Hon. Charles. (1803–48).

B. 23 Mar. 1803 to George, 3d Earl of Ashburnham by Charlotte Percy, sister of George, 5th Duke of Northumberland,[1] ed. Westminster 1811, 1815–18, Trinity Cambridge 1820–24 (M.A.), m. 1832 Sarah Joanna, dau. of William Murray of Jamaica.[2] Précis Writer 12 Aug. 1828–17 Aug. 1829, Sec. of Legation Mexico 1835–41,[3] and of Embassy Constantinople 1848.[2] Lady Granville said he was ". . . rheumatic, languid, and upon my woord I doont kno-o-ow *genre*, which is not useful or efficient, but he seems sensible and gentlemanlike."[4] d. 22 Dec. 1848.

1. *Burke's Peerage*, 60th ed., p. 70.
2. Barker and Stenning, *Old Westminsters*, vol. 1, 28.
3. S. T. Bindoff, E. F. Malcolm Smith, and C. K. Webster (eds.), *British Diplomatic Representatives, 1789–1852* ("The Camden Society, 3d Series," vol. 50; London, 1934), p. 77.
4. To Lady Carlisle, Gower, *Letters of Countess Granville*, II, 74.

11. Aust, George A. (d. 1829).

Raised in Bath,[1] relation of Thomas Percy, Bishop of Dromore (1782–1811),[2] m. 1st 1786 Sarah, widow of William Murray,[3] 2nd Jane———, and 3rd Catharine———, who survived him. Clerk c. Sept. 1763, sr. clerk 1782,[4] 1784 to 1789 acted as assistant undersecretary,[5] undersecretary 1790–5 Jan. 1796. Removed from office in order to find a place for George Canning, though Pitt subsequently provided for him.[6] Muster Master General 1796–May 1817.[7] Agent to Cambridgeshire militia which was supported by the Earls of Hardwicke, 20 Apr. 1778–5 Feb. 1799.[8] d. 1829.

1. Aust to Hardwicke, St. James's, 5 June 1784, Add. MS 35622 ff. 247–49.
2. Same, Dromore House, 24 Sept. 1805, Private, Add. MS 35762 ff. 89–90.
3. For whom see *D.N.B.*, vol. 1, 730.
4. *Royal Kalendar*, 1782, p. 110.
5. Case of Mr. Aust, Delivered to Lord Grenville, 27 Mar. 1795, Eg. MS 3505 Bundle 4.
6. Hinde, *Canning*, p. 41.
7. Catherine Aust to Palmerston, Wooland Blandford, Dorset, 14 Aug. [1835], F.O. 83/62.
8. Aust to Hardwicke, St. James's, 20 Apr. 1778, Add. MS 35659 f. 279 and Same, Horse Guards, 5 Feb. 1799, Add. MS 35671 f. 71.

12. Backhouse, George Canning. (c. 1818–55).

B. c. 1818 to John Backhouse (see no. 13), ed. Harrow and Christ Church Oxford,[1] m. 1851 Grace Margaret, dau. of John Mullins Sandham, Esq. of Hans Place Chelsea.[2] Clerk 5 Apr. 1838–15 Dec. 1852, attached with clerk's pay to Frankfort in 1841,[3] Commissary Judge on Slave Trade Commission at Havana 16 Dec. 1852 to his assassination 30 Aug. 1855. Civil List pension of £100 granted to his widow 15 Nov. 1856.[4]

1. Foster, *Alumni Oxon.*, vol. 1, 44.
2. *Gents. Mag.* (1851), pt. 1, 659.
3. Palmerston to Fox-Strangways, Foreign Office, 17 July 1841, Copy, Backhouse MSS.
4. Boase, *Mod. Eng. Biog.*, vol. 1, 119.

13. Backhouse, John. (1784–1845).

B. 14 Oct. 1784 to John Backhouse of Wavertree, Lancs., prominent Liverpool merchant,[1] ed. Carmel School, Westmoreland, and Foundation School of Clitheroe, m. 1810 Catharine, dau. of Thomas Nicholson of Stockport.[2] Partner in father's business, secretary of Liverpool Office in London 1812, private sec. to Canning at Board of Control 1816[1] and at F.O. Sept. 1822–Jan. 1823, Commissioner of Excise 1824, Receiver General of Excise 1827,[2] permanent undersecretary at F.O. 5 Apr. 1827–5 Apr. 1842, ret. ill-health. Backhouse was a close friend of John Murray, the publisher. He wrote in popular periodicals and ed. *Narrative of the American Sailor Robert Adams's residence in the Interior of Africa, at Timbuctoo.*[2] d. 13 Nov. 1845.

1. MS biographical sketch, Backhouse MSS.
2. *Gents. Mag.* (1846), pt. 1, 95–97.

14. Bagot, (Sir) Charles. (1781–1843).[1]

Undersecretary 18 Aug. 1807–10 Oct. 1809.

1. *D.N.B.*, vol. 23 (Supp.), 98.

15. Bandinel, James. (1783–1849).[1]

B. 1783 to Rev. Dr. James Bandinel, rector of Netherbury,[2] brother of Rev. Bulkeley Bandinel, Librarian of Bodleian Library,[3] m. c. 1813 Marianne Eliza, dau. of Rev. Robert Hunter, rector of Burton Bradstock, Dorset.[4] Clerk 5 Apr. 1799, private sec. to Pierrepont (see no. 156) on special mission to king of Sweden 1807,[5] senior clerk 5 Jan. 1822, head of Slave Trade Dept. 1824, ret. ill-health 12 Dec. 1845 with pension £1,159.18.6.[6] Bandinel was the recognized expert on slave trade and African affairs at the F.O. and frequently consulted with representatives of the Treasury and Colonial Office on African policy.[7] He believed in temperance, drank no wine at the end of his life, and actively supported public charities in London. d. 6 July 1849 of cholera contracted at Salisbury while attending a meeting of the Archeological Society of Salisbury.[8]

1. *D.N.B.*, vol. 1, 1035 has a very incomplete and inaccurate sketch.
2. For whom see *Gents. Mag.* (1804), pt. 2, 804.
3. For whom see Strachey and Fulford, *Greville Memoirs*, vol. 1, 246 n. 1.
4. Bandinel Papers, *passim.*; *Gents. Mag.* (1781), p. 353.
5. Minute, Canning to Bidwell, Downing Street, 26 May 1807, F.O. 366/671 f. 326.
6. "Superannuations in Public Offices," *P.P., 1846*, vol. 25, Command 146, p. 568.
7. Bandinel to Aberdeen, Foreign Office, 23 Nov. 1843, Private, Draft, Bandinel Papers.
8. *Gents Mag.* (1849), pt. 2, 327.

16. Bankhead, Charles. (c. 1797–1870).

B. c. 1797, probably son of Dr. Charles Bankhead, personal physician to Castlereagh.[1] Clerk 5 July 1814–5 Jan. 1826 during which time he was (with his clerk's pay) attached to The Hague Oct. 1817–May 1818, to St. Petersburg June 1820–Dec. 1822 and Dec. 1824–June 1825,[2] Sec. of Legation Washington 1826, Sec. of Embassy Constantinople 1838, Min. P. Mexico 1843, ret. 6 Apr. 1851.[3] d. 11 Mar. 1870.

1. For whom see Hobhouse diary, Mon. 12 Aug. 1822, Aspinall, *Diary of Hobhouse*, pp. 88–90.
2. "Statement of Services . . . Charles Bankhead," 12 May 1828, F.O. 366/560.
3. F.O. List, 1854, p. 52.

17. Bartlett, Richard. (d. 1849).

Entering and dispatch clerk 4 June 1806–5 Jan. 1822,[1] pension of £150 in addition to salary as consul Coruna 1822–30,[2] consul Teneriffe 1830 to d. there 3 Aug. 1849.[3]

1. Londonderry to Lords of Treas., Foreign Office, 20 Feb. 1822, Copy, F.O. 366/370 ff. 25–27.
2. "List of consuls," *P.P., 1835*, vol. 15, in Command 499, p. 278.
3. F.O. 366/462.

18. Bathurst, Henry, 3d. Earl Bathurst. (1762–1834).[1]
Secretary of State 11 Oct. 1809–6 Dec. 1809.
    1. *D.N.B.*, vol. 1, 1328.

19. Bentinck, Lord George. (1802–48).[1]
Private secretary 10 Oct. 1822–5 Apr. 1824.
    1. *D.N.B.*, vol. 2, 297.

20. Bergne, John Brodribb. (1800–73).[1]
Clerk in Treaty Dept. 5 Jan. 1817, attached to Chief Clerk's Dept. 21 Aug. 1841–30 June 1854, superintendant of Treaty Dept. 1 July 1854–1 Dec. 1870, compensation allowance £127.7.10 p.a. on abolition of F.O. agencies in 1870,[2] and served in F.O. to d. of heart disease, 16 Jan. 1873.[3] Member of commission to revise slave trade instructions 1865.[4] For the last twenty years of his service he was regarded as the leading office expert on treaties. He was very popular and as a tribute to his skill and popularity both Lord Granville, the secretary of state, and Edmund Hammond, the permanent undersecretary, attended his funeral.[3]
    1. *D.N.B.*, vol. 2, 336.
    2. "Superannuations in Public Offices," *P.P., 1871*, vol. 37, Command 155, p. 444.
    3. *The Times*, 22 Jan. 1873, p. 6.
    4. Boase, *Mod. Eng. Biog.*, vol. 1, 253.

21. Bidwell, John. (c. 1782–1853).
Nephew of Thomas Bidwell (see no. 23). Supernumerary clerk 5 July 1798, clerk 5 Jan. 1799, attached with clerk's pay to Sir Robert Adair's mission to Constantinople 1808–09,[1] and to Sir Charles Stuart's mission to Prussia 1813–14,[2] senior clerk 5 July 1818, superintendant of the Consular Dept. 1825, ret. 30 Sept. 1851 with pension £1494.[3] Bidwell was among the most able of the clerks in the office and was generally regarded by his peers as well as by the political heads of the department as being the most reliable and useful assistant when the undersecretaries were unavailable,[4] though in his last years in the office he was less forceful than he previously had been and the impatient juniors felt he was merely serving time so that he would be able to retire on full salary after fifty years' service.[5] He was an able painter in the medium of water colors.[1] d. at his residence in Park Place,[6] 31 Oct. 1853.
    1. Add. MS 41315, passim.
    2. Bidwell to Col. Howe, Göttingen, 16 Nov. 1813, Add. MS 20111 f. 211, and Same, Langues, 29 Jan. 1814, Add. MS 20192 f. 22.
    3. "Superannuations in Public Offices," *P.P., 1854*, vol. 39, Command 125, p. 659.
    4. Byng to Granville, 18 Nov. 1834, P.R.O. 30/29/7/13 ff. 990–93.
    5. Staveley to Lenox-Conyngham, 4 Jan. 1848, Private, F.O. 366/386.
    6. *The Times*, 1 Nov. 1853, p. 10.

22. Bidwell, John Jr. (c. 1825–73).

Son of John Bidwell (see no. 21). Clerk 5 Jan. 1842, attached to Washington with clerk's pay 26 Dec. 1843–Apr. 1846, attached to Clarendon's special mission to Paris Feb.-Apr. 1856, private sec. to Malmesbury while he was foreign secretary 1852 and 1858–59, attached to Malmesbury on Queen Victoria's trip to Potsdam 1858,[1] compensation allowance £794.2.0 p.a. on abolition of F.O. agencies in 1870,[2] which ceased on ret. as 2d senior clerk, ill-health, 6 June 1871 with pension £500.[3] Served as a liason between Disraeli and John Earle, an attaché at Paris, on Earle's efforts to provide Disraeli in 1857–58 with material to attack Palmerston's foreign policy.[4] Ensign, 2d Derbyshire Militia (the Chatsworth Rifles) 15 Aug. 1856,[1] d. at Llangattock, S. Wales, 22 Aug. 1873.[5]

1. *F.O. List*, 1874, p. 202.
2. "Superannuations in Public Offices," *P.P., 1871*, vol. 37, Command 155, p. 444.
3. "Superannuations in Public Offices," *P.P., 1873*, vol. 39, Command 129, p. 536.
4. Blake, *Disraeli*, pp. 370–71.
5. *The Times*, 26 Aug. 1873, p. 1.

23. Bidwell, Thomas. (c. 1744–1817).

Clerk c. 1765, senior clerk 1788, chief clerk 1792 until d. at Cheltenham 28 Sept. 1817.[1] Appointed Supt. of St. James's and Hyde Parks by the Duke of Grafton, and during his tenure he carried out an extensive program of planting.[2] Bidwell took a long time to rise to a position of responsibility in the F.O.,[3] and perhaps for this reason once he was given some authority he acted in a condescending manner to those whom he regarded as his juniors. He was involved in at least one law suit against a messenger whom he apparently accused of insolence—a suit which he lost—and on one occasion he was indiscreet enough to tell some messengers that if the Lord Chamberlain's Office could not pay them it was because the Lord Chamberlain, Lord Salisbury, had been appropriating funds for private uses. He later apologized to Salisbury for this statement after failing to persuade him that he never made it.[4]

1. *The Times*, 1 Oct. 1817, p. 3.
2. *Gents. Mag.* (1817), pt. 2, 473.
3. Memorial of T. Bidwell to Lord Stormont (c. 1780), Tilley and Gaselee, *Foreign Office*, pp. 22–25.
4. Holohan, *King's Messengers*, pp. 40–45.

24. Bidwell, Thomas Jr. (1775–1852).

B. 1775 to Thomas Bidwell (see no. 23), matric. Westminster 1786, m. 1805 Mary Anne, dau. of Shelford Bidwell of Thetford, Norfolk.[1] Clerk 20 Oct. 1790, assistant précis writer 1793,[2] private secretary to Lord St. Helens's Mission to St. Petersburg 1801,[3] senior clerk 5 Jan. 1806, Joint Translator of German Language 7 Feb. 1806–5 Apr. 1809, chief clerk 5 Jan. 1824, ret. ill-health 5 Apr. 1841 with pension £1396.[4] Deputy clerk of the signet after c. 1815.[5] Bidwell was always far from being as able as his cousin John (see no. 21) and George Jackson thought him "somewhat of a blockhead" even as a young man.[6] d. at his residence in Gloucester Place, Portman Square, 1 May 1852.[7]

1. Barker and Stenning, *Old Westminsters*, vol. 1, 87.
2. Burges to Grenville, Whitehall, 2 Oct. 1793, Grenville MSS.
3. Hawkesbury to Bidwell, Downing Street, 8 May 1801, F.O. 366/671 f. 181.
4. "Superannuations in Public Offices," *P.P., 1852–53*, vol. 57, Command 277, p. 620.
5. "Account of Fees . . . in the Signet Office," 31 Mar. 1815–31 Mar. 1816, F.O. 366/387.
6. Jackson, *Bath Archives*, vol. 1, 444.
7. *The Annual Register* (1852), p. 276.

25. Blackburn, John Edward. (c. 1818–55).

B. c. 1818 to E. B. Blackburn, later Chief Justice in the Mauritius 1825–35,[1] by Eliza Maria, dau. of John Edward Madocks of Glenywen, Denbighshire.[2] Clerk 1834, attached to Naples with clerk's pay 1836–37,[3] ret. ill-health 1851 with pension £140.[4] d. at Paris 27 Jan. 1855.[5]

1. *Gents. Mag.* (1855), pt. 1, 334.
2. *Burke's Landed Gentry* (1848), vol. 2, 821.
3. *F.O. List*, 1854, p. 52.
4. "Superannuations in Public Offices," *P.P., 1852*, vol. 28, Command 197, p. 924.
5. *Ann. Reg.* (1855), p. 248.

26. Bouverie, (Rt. Hon.) Edward Pleydell. (1818–89).[1]

Private secretary 6 Jan. 1840–5 Apr. 1840, précis writer 5 Apr. 1840–19 June 1840.

1. *D.N.B.*, vol. 15, 1309.

27. Broughton, Bryan. (d. 1825).

Son of Rev. Thomas Broughton, secretary to S.P.C.K. 1743–77, mother's maiden name was Capel.[1] Clerk 16 July 1762, senior clerk 1782, resigned 19 Jan. 1788.[2] Clerk in the Treasury 1766–1806,[3] pension of £100 granted on retirement.[4] Resided at Barnes, Surrey and d. 16 Jan. 1825 at the home of his brother-in-law, the Rev. Dr. Gaskin, Rector of Stoke Newington.[5]

1. *Notes and Queries*, ser. 6, vol. 3, 288; *D.N.B.*, vol. 2, 1372.
2. Broughton to Carmarthen, Rome, 19 Jan. 1788, Add. MS 28063 ff. 31–32.
3. *Royal Kalendar* (1767 and 1807).
4. "Accounts relating to Pensions," *P.P., 1820*, vol. 9, Command 140, p. 325.
5. *Gents. Mag.* (1825), pt. 1, 188.

28. Broughton, Charles Rivington. (c. 1764–1831).

B. c. 1764, brother of Bryan (see no. 27), matric. St. Paul's 1775.[1] Clerk 22 Apr. 1788, senior clerk 5 Jan. 1803, ret. 5 Jan. 1824 with pension £800.[2] Receiver General of Land, Assessed, and Property Taxes c. 1804,[3] associated with the Trustees of the Church Building Fund at Calais.[4] Broughton was an ambitious and able man, and before his financial difficulties in 1815 he was regarded as "a sober, careful, trusty person. . . ."[5] d. 14 Nov. 1831.

1. Rev. Robert Barlow Gardiner (ed.), *The Admission Registers of St. Paul's School, from 1748 to 1876* (London, 1884), p. 159.
2. "Superannuations in Public Offices," *P.P., 1825*, vol. 19, Command 203, p. 264.
3. Hammond, Arbuthnot, and Bidwell to Winter, Downing Street, 19 Mar. 1804, Copy, F.O. 366/671 ff. 240–41.
4. Broughton to the Bishop of London, 21 Downing Street, 5 May 1827, F.O. 27/373.
5. Goddard to Grenville, Paris, 11 Aug. 1806, *H.M.C. Fortescue*, vol. 8, 269.

29.   Browne, John Henry Temple.

Clerk attached to Slave Trade Dept. 6 June 1834–8 Apr. 1835, 13 Dec. 1837–11 Sept. 1840. A dilatory individual who did little work while employed at the F.O. and who Bandinel said was "confident in his negligence" despite official reprimands.[1] Palmerston apparently took a special interest in him. He tried to get him a position in a merchant's house in Dunkirk in 1835 when he was "in much Distress,"[2] then reappointed him in 1837, and finally appointed him vice-consul at Cette, France in 1841, a situation Browne later resigned without having left England.[3] Browne was a chronic debtor and had to be given advances on his salary to keep him out of prison.[4]

1. Bandinel to Mahon, Foreign Office, 7 Apr. 1835, Copy, Wellington Papers.
2. Minute, Palmerston, 27 May 1835, F.O. 27/510.
3. Browne to Canning, St. Albans Hotel, 28 July 1842, F.O. 27/658.
4. Browne to Bandinel, 1 Upper Baker Street, Lloyd Square, 20 July 1839, Private with enclosed Minute, Browne, n.d.; Minutes, Strangways, 31 July 1839, Palmerston, 1 Aug. 1839, and Bandinel, 3 Aug. 1839; Statement from Court for Relief of Insolvent Debtors, 2 Nov. 1839, and minute, Palmerston, n.d., F.O. 84/305.

30.   Bruce, Hon. James. (1769–98).

B. 23 Mar. 1769 to Charles, 5th Earl of Elgin, by Martha, dau. of Thomas White, Esq., Banker of London,[1] ed. Westminster 1778–8?, Christ Church, Oxford 1786, B.A. 1790, M.A. 1793, admitted Lincoln's Inn 1790.[2] Served with his brother, the 7th earl of Elgin, in Belgium 1793–94, acting occasionally as chargé d'affaires while Elgin was at allied headquarters,[3] M.P. Marlborough 1796–97,[2] res. to become précis writer[4] 10 Oct. 1797–5 July 1798. Drowned in the Don, near Barnesby Down while attempting to ford the stream on horseback,[2] d. unm.[1] 10 July 1798.

1. *Burke's Peerage*, 6oth ed., p. 518.
2. Barker and Stenning, *Old Westminsters*, vol. 1, 132.
3. Bindoff et al., *Br. Dip. Reps.*, p. 136.
4. Unsigned memo, [Oct. 1797], F.O. 366/671 f. 45.

31.   Bruce, W. Stewart Crawford. (1801–78).

B. 20 Jan. 1801 to Rev. Sir Henry Hervey Aston Bruce, 1st. Bart of Down Hill, by Latitia, dau. of Rev. Dr. Henry Barnard,[1] matric. Trinity College Dublin 1818, B.A. 1822, M.A. 1839,[2] matric. Downing College, Cambridge

1823,[3] m. 1828 Helen Baillie, dau. of William Alves, Esq. of Enham Place, Hants.[1] Clerk 5 July 1826–26 July 1827, attaché Florence 26 July 1827.[4] d. 18 Feb. 1878.

1. *Burke's Peerage*, 60th ed., p. 209.
2. George Damas Burtchaell and Thomas Ulick Sadleir (eds.), *Alumni Dublinenses* (new ed.; Dublin, 1935), p. 107.
3. Venn, *Alumni Cantab.*, vol. 1, 422.
4. Bruce's memo in Burghersh, separate dispatch, 3 Apr. 1828, F.O. 366/560.

32. Burges, (Sir) James Bland (1st. Bart.). (1752–1824).[1]
Undersecretary 22 Aug. 1789–10 Oct. 1795.

1. *D.N.B.*, vol. 3, 305.

33. Bury, Richard. (c. 1824–81).
B. c. 1824, possibly 3d son of Phineas Bury of Little Island, co. Limerick, by Jane, dau. of Boyle Aldworth of Newmarket, co. Cork.[1] Clerk attached to Treaty Dept. 23 Dec. 1844–22 Feb. 1874, ret. ill-health, with pension £233.6.8.[2] d. 15 Dec. 1881.

1. *Burke's Landed Gentry of Ireland*, 4th ed., p. 128.
2. "Superannuations in Public Offices," *P.P., 1874*, vol. 35, Command 71, p. 536.

34. Byng Hon. Frederick Gerald "Poodle". (1784–1871).
B. 1784 to John, 5th Viscount Torrington, diplomatist, by Bridget, dau. of Commodore Arthur Forrest,[1] ed. Westminster,[2] m. Catherine Neville.[1] Page of Honour to the Prince of Wales 1791, clerk in War Office (c. 1790s),[3] clerk in F.O. 23 Jan. 1801, senior clerk 5 Jan. 1824, auditor of diplomatic accounts 1826, ret. "impaired eyesight" 5 Apr. 1839 with pension £827.[4] Lt. of 27th Light Dragoons 1799, of 53d Foot 1801, half-pay 1802, ensign in St. George's Voluntary Infantry 1803,[5] Chamberlain to the king and queen of the Sandwich Islands on their visit to London 1824,[6] Gentleman Usher to the Privy Council 1831–71,[7] Church Warden of St. James's Parish 1836,[8] Commissioner for Enquiry into Sheffield Market 1849,[9] Queen's (Westminster) Volunteer Rifles 1859.[5] Byng was not a very active or useful clerk,[10] but he was well-known in society and, despite Lady Granville's evaluation of him as "hard, selfish, ill-tempered, [and] presumptuous,"[11] seems to have been generally well-liked. Along with Lansdowne, Palmerston, and Lord John Russell he was one of the last men to appear in society (Bowood House 1850) in a blue coat and brass buttons.[12] He was one of the few men at the F.O. who was fluent in Spanish.[13] d. 5 June 1871.

1. *Burke's Peerage*, 60th ed., p. 1440.
2. Barker and Stenning, *Old Westminsters*, vol. 1, 153.
3. Hertslet, *Recollections*, pp. 138–40.
4. *F.O. List*, 1863, p. 169.
5. *Ann. Reg.*, (1871), p. 153.
6. Bamford and Wellington, *Journal of Mrs. Arbuthnot*, vol. 1, 315–16.
7. Ibid., p. 316, n. 1.

8. Byng to Granville, 5 Apr. 1836, P.R.O. 30/19/7/13 ff. 1106–9.

9. Boase, *Mod. Eng. Biog.*, vol. 1, 505.

10. Palmerston to Granville, F.O., 14 June 1836, P.R.O. 30/29/421.

11. To Lady G. Morpeth, Wherstead, Jan. 1822, Gower, *Letters of Countess Granville*, vol. 1, 221–22.

12. Strachey and Fulford, *Greville Memoirs*, vol. 1, 67 n. 2.

13. Minute, Byng, 20 Jan. 1838, F.O. 84/244.

35. Cade, Joseph. (c. 1800–60).

Clerk 3 May 1819–10 Oct. 1823 when appointed paid attaché to Commission (after 1837 mission) to Colombia,[1] consul at Panama 21 Oct. 1838[2] – 1 Sept. 1841,[1] ret. ill-health[2] with pension £450.[3] d. 22 Aug. 1860.

1. *F.O. List*, 1854, p. 53; F.O. 366/329 f. 28.

2. F.O. 366/462.

3. "Superannuations in Public Offices," *P.P., 1861*, vol. 35, Command 121, p. 401.

36. Campbell, John Frederick Vaughan (2d Earl Cawdor). (1817–98).

B. 11 June 1817 to John Frederick, 2d Baron Cawdor, lord lieut. Carmarthenshire, by Elizabeth, dau. of Thomas, 2d Marquess of Bath,[1] ed. Eton, Christ Church, Oxford B.A. 1838, M.A. 1840, m. 1842 Sarah Mary, maid of honour to the queen 1837–42, dau. of Gen. Hon. Frederick Compton Cavendish.[2] Assistant précis writer 1842. Cons. M.P. for Pembrokeshire 1841–59, private sec. to Duke of Buccleuch, Lord Privy Seal, 1841–42, deputy lieut. Carmarthenshire and Nairnshire 1852–61, 2d Earl 1860, lord lieut. and Custos Rotulorum Carmarthenshire 1861.[3] d. 29 Mar. 1898.

1. *Burke's Peerage*, 60th ed., p. 284.

2. G.E.C., *Complete Peerage*, vol. 3, 124.

3. *F.O. List*, 1898, p. 83.

37. Canning, Charles John, Viscount (later Earl) Canning. (1812–62).[1]

Undersecretary 3 Sept. 1841–26 Feb. 1846.

1. *D.N.B.*, vol. 3, 866.

38. Canning, Rt. Hon. George. (1770–1827).[1]

Undersecretary 5 Jan. 1796–5 Apr. 1799, secretary of state 25 Mar. 1807–10 Oct. 1809, 16 Sept. 1822–30 Apr. 1827.

1. *D.N.B.*, vol. 3, 872.

39. Canning, Stratford (Viscount Stradford de Redcliffe). (1786–1880).[1]

Précis writer 5 July 1807–5 Jan. 1809.

1. *D.N.B.*, vol. 3, 883.

40. Carmarthen, Marquess of, and 5th Duke of Leeds. See Osborne, Francis Godolphin (no. 146).

41. Carter, Richard.
    Clerk 1770–c. 1785.

42. Cartwright, (Sir) Thomas. (1795–1850).[1]
    Unpaid attaché Vienna 24 Apr. 1815–5 July 1817,[2] précis writer 5 July 1817–5 Jan. 1821. In addition to the diplomatic positions he held which are listed in the *D.N.B.*, Cartwright also served in 1830 as a special observer in Belgium and as a joint commissioner of the Conference of London to the provisional government in Brussels until Ponsonby arrived to begin his mission.[3] He m. 1824 Elizabeth Augusta, dau. of Bavarian Count Sandizell. He was an enthusiast of cattle breeding which he promoted on his estates.[4] d. 17 Apr. 1850.
    1. *D.N.B.*, vol. 3, 1141.
    2. F.O. 366/329 f. 31.
    3. Bindoff et al., *Br. Dip. Reps.*, p. 137.
    4. *Gents. Mag.* (1850), pt. 2, 91.

43. Casamajor, Justinian. (c. 1761–1821).
    B. c. 1761 to Justinian Casamajor of Antigua West Indies, ed. Harrow, Trinity College, Cambridge, B.A. 1793, M.A. 1797, admitted Lincoln's Inn 1786 [96?].[1] Clerk 18 Aug. 1797–5 Apr. 1799, sec. of Legation and chargé d'affaires Berlin 1801–02,[2] slave trade commissioner at Havana 1818.[3] d. 12 Aug. 1821.
    1. Venn, *Alumni Cantab.*, vol. 1, 534.
    2. Bindoff et al., *Br. Dip. Reps.*, p. 99.
    3. Casamajor to Hamilton, no. 15 Henrietta Street, Cavendish Square, 21 Jan. 1819, F.O. 72/229 ff. 58–59.

44. Castlereagh, Viscount, and 2d Marquess of Londonderry. See Stewart, Robert (no. 190).

45. Clanricarde, 1st Marquess of. See de Burgh, Ulick John (no. 54).

46. Clanwilliam, 3d Earl (I.), (1st Baron, U.K.). See Meade, Richard Charles Francis Christian. (no. 134).

47. Cockburn, Alexander. (1776–1852).
    B. 20 Aug. 1776 to Sir James Cockburn, 6th Bart., by Miss Ayscough, dau. of the Dean of Bristol and niece of George, Lord Lyttleton,[1] m. Yolande, dau. of Viscount de Vignier, by whom he had Sir Alexander, 10th Bart., Lord Chief Justice of the Court of Common Pleas and of the Court of

Queen's Bench.[2] Clerk 5 Jan. 1794–5 Jan. 1799, Agent and Consul General Lower Saxony 5 Jan. 1799–10 Oct. 1807, ret. with pension £600, special mission to the Hans Towns[3] and to the Russian military commander at Hamburg Apr.–July 1813[4] after which his pension was increased to £1000, E. E. Hans Towns & Circle of Lower Saxony 1815, E. E. & Min. P. Würtemberg 1820, ret. 1823 with pension £1700, E. E. & Min. P. Colombia 1826–27.[3] Cockburn, who was the brother of Admiral Sir George C., was displaced in 1827 because he had "expended 11,000£ of the public money, and then declined going to Bogota,"[5] though he did go to other parts of South America.[6] By 1830 he managed to repay the public money he had spent on his travels,[7] but despite his efforts and the assistance of his brother he continually failed to secure another appointment.[8] d. 14 Oct. 1852.

1. *Burke's Peerage*, 8th ed. (1845).
2. Boase, *Mod. Eng. Biog.*, vol. 1, 661–62; *D.N.B.*, vol. 4, 633 for Sir Alexander.
3. F.O. 366/329.
4. Bindoff et al., *Br. Dip. Reps.*, p. 67.
5. 6 Aug. 1828, Colchester, *Ellenborough Diary*, vol. 1, 191.
6. 16 Aug. 1828, ibid., 197.
7. Aberdeen to Sir George Cockburn, Foreign Office, 16 Jan. 1830, Private, draft, Add. MS 43234 ff. 194–95.
8. Sir Herbert Taylor to A. Cockburn, Brighton, 23 Nov. 1835, Copy, Palmerston Papers RC/C/207/2; Peel to Aberdeen, Whitehall, 14 Dec. 1841, Add. MS 43061 ff. 350–52.

48. Coles, Augustus Leopold. (c. 1815–69).

B. c. 1815 to George Coles of Tiverton, ed. Blundell's School 10 Aug. 1826–29 June 1835.[1] Clerk 10 Oct. 1835, senior clerk 1854,[2] ret. 9 Oct. 1866 with compensation allowance £503.15.0 on abolition of his senior clerkship.[3] d. at his residence Moore Park Road, Fulham, 6 May 1869.[4]

1. Arthur Fisher (ed.), *The Register of Blundell's School* (Exeter, 1904), p. 119.
2. *F.O. List*, 1869, p. 75.
3. "Superannuations in Public Offices," *P.P.*, *1867*, vol. 40, Command 155, p. 573.
4. *The Times*, 12 May 1869, p. 1.

49. Conyngham, Lord Francis, Earl Mount Charles (2d Marquess of Conyngham). (1797–1876).

B. 11 June 1797 to Henry, 1st Marquess of Conyngham, by Elizabeth, dau. of Joseph Denison, Esq.,[1] matric. Eton 1811,[2] m. 1824 Lady Jane Paget, dau. of Henry, 1st Marquess of Anglesey.[1] Attaché Paris 1816–18, attached to Castlereagh's mission to Aix-la-Chapelle 1818,[3] M.P. Westbury 1818–20, co. Donegal 1825–31,[4] Master of the Robes 1820,[5] undersecretary 5 Jan. 1823–5 Apr. 1825, succeeded his brother as Lord Mount Charles 1824, Lord of the Treasury 1826–30,[4] succeeded as 2d Marquess 1832,[1] Postmaster General 1834–35, Lord Chamberlain 1835–39,[4] Lord Lieut. co. Meath.[1] Conyngham's mother was in 1819 the reputed mistress of the Prince of Wales[6] and later became the leading lady at the court in

George IV's reign. She was unpopular with the Ultras and the Tories as was her son, whom Mrs. Arbuthnot labeled "a regular spy" for the government at the Court.[7] Planta, who supervised Conyngham's work at Aix in 1818, said that "He writes a very good hand, has a good knowledge of Business, is intelligent, and of a thoroughly amiable disposition. . . ."[3] d. 17 July 1876.

1. *Burke's Peerage*, 60th ed., p. 343.
2. Stapylton, *Eton Lists*, p. 70.
3. Planta to A'Court, Aix-la-Chapelle, 4 Nov. 1818, Private, Add. MS 41519 ff. 141–42.
4. Strachey and Fulford, *Greville Memoirs*, vol. 1, 122 n. 2.
5. 16 Apr. 1820, Diary, Jennings, *Croker Corresp.*, vol. 1, 173.
6. Aspinall, *Later Corresp. Geo. III*, vol. 3, 467 n. 14.
7. Bamford and Wellington, *Journal of Mrs. Arbuthnot*, vol. 1, 263.

50. Cooke, Edward. (1755–1820).[1]
Undersecretary 28 Feb. 1812–5 July 1817.
1. *D.N.B.*, vol. 4, 1004.

51. Cowper, Hon. Charles Spencer. (1816–79).
B. 9 June 1816 to Peter, 5th Earl Cowper, by Emily Lamb, later Lady Palmerston, dau. of Peniston, 1st Viscount Melbourne,[1] matric. Eton 1829,[2] m. 1st 1853 Lady Harriet Anne, Dowager Countess D'Orsay, dau. of Charles, Earl of Blessington, and 2d 1871 Jessie Mary, dau. of Col. Clinton McLean, U.S.A.[3] Clerk 14 Nov. 1834, private secretary retaining his clerkship w/o pay 11 May 1835, Sec. of Legation Stockholm retaining his clerkship w/o pay (which he res. 5 Jan. 1840) 22 Nov. 1839–11 Sept. 1843.[4] Cowper inherited in 1843 the estates of John Motteaux, Esq., of Bechampwell & Sandringham and in 1846 became J.P. and High Sheriff of Norfolk.[3] d. 30 Mar. 1879.

1. *Burke's Peerage*, 60th ed., p. 356.
2. H. E. C. Stapylton (ed.), *The Eton School Lists from 1791 to 1850* (2d ed.; London, 1864), p. 141.
3. Walford, *County Families*, p. 236.
4. *F.O. List*, 1854, p. 54.

52. Cowper, George Augustus Frederick, Viscount (6th Earl Cowper). (1806–56).
B. 26 June 1806, eldest brother of Charles Spencer Cowper (see no. 51), matric. Eton 1820,[1] m. 1833 Anne Florence, Baroness Lucas, dau. of Thomas, Earl de Grey.[2] M.P. for Canterbury 1830–34,[3] undersecretary 13–17 Nov. 1834, succeeded as 6th Earl 1837, Lord Lieut. of Kent 1846–57.[3] d. 15 Apr. 1856.

1. Stapylton, *Eton Lists*, p. 103.
2. *Burke's Peerage*, 60th ed., p. 356.
3. Boase, *Mod. Eng. Biog.*, vol. 1, 738.

53. Dawkins, Clinton George Augustus. (1808–71).

B. 1808 to H. Dawkins, Esq., M.P., of Over Norton, Chipping Norton co. Oxford, ed. Harrow 1821–25,[1] m. 1850 Marianne, dau. of James Roberts, Esq.[2] Clerk and précis writer 27 Aug. 1829, res. as précis writer 5 Apr. 1830, private secretary retaining clerkship w/o pay (which he res. 25 June 1846) 3 Sept. 1841–5 July 1846, Consul-General Lombardy 26 June 1846–26 Oct. 1852 when post abolished,[3] ret. on compensation allowance £600,[4] served as private secretary to Aberdeen while Aberdeen was prime minister 1852–54.[3] Dawkins was a close friend of Joseph Planta (see no. 157) and Henry Parish (see no. 149) who described him as "a very quick, clever person."[5] Lord Leveson, when considering the appointment of a second paid attaché at Paris, told Lord Granville that he was "a clever nice fellow—a great friend of the Rivers—and I think will be very useful."[6] d. 13 Oct. 1871.

1. M. G. Dauglish and P. K. Stephenson (eds.), *The Harrow School Register, 1800–1911* (London, 1911), p. 99.
2. *Burke's Landed Gentry*, 8th ed., p. 483.
3. *F.O. List*, 1854, p. 54.
4. "Superannuations in Public Offices," *P.P., 1872*, vol. 36, Command 141, p. 418.
5. H. H. Parish to Stratford Canning, F.O., 20 Sept. 1828, Confidential, F.O. 352/22/2.
6. F.O., 29 May 1840, P.R.O. 30/29/6/4/ ff. 722–23.

54. de Burgh, Ulick John, 1st Marquess of Clanricarde. (1802–74).[1]

B. 20 Dec. 1802 to Gen. John, 13th Earl of Clanricarde, by Elizabeth, dau. of Sir Thomas Burke, Bart. of Marble Hill co. Galway,[1] succeeded as 14th Earl 1808, matric. Eton 1814,[2] Christ Church, Oxford 1820,[3] m. 1825 Harriet, dau. of Rt. Hon. George Canning[1] (see no. 38). Undersecretary 5 Jan. 1826–12 Aug. 1827. Cr. Marquess 1825,[4] cr. Baron Somerhill (U.K.) 1826, P.C. 1830,[5] K.P. 1831, Ambassador St. Petersburg 1838–41, Postmaster General 1846–52, Lord Privy Seal 1858,[4] Lord Lieut. co. Galway.[5] Lady Granville described him as "immensely rich, quite good-looking enough, clever and very gentlemanlike," whose "only flaw is said to be his fondness for low company. . . ."[6] d. 10 Apr. 1874.

1. *Burke's Peerage*, 60th ed., p. 309.
2. Stapylton, *Eton Lists*, p. 84.
3. George Foster (ed.), *Alumni Oxonienses: The Members of the University of Oxford, 1715–1886* (4 vols.; London, 1882), vol. 1, 193 under John Ulyses de Burgh.
4. Strachey and Fulford, *Greville Memoirs*, vol. 1, 161, n. 1.
5. Boase, *Mod., Eng. Biog.*, vol. 1, 621–22.
6. To Lady G. Morpeth, Paris, 17 Jan. 1825 and 7 Feb. 1825, Gower, *Letters of Countess Granville*, vol. 1, 337–42.

55. Douglas, Andrew Snape. (1788–1869).

B. 6 Jan. 1788 to Sir Andrew Snape Douglas, R.N., by Anne Burgess of New York,[1] matric. Eton 1802.[2] Assistant private sec. Mar.–May 1807,[3] sec. to earl of Pembroke on his special embassy to Vienna May–Nov. 1807, asst.

précis writer Nov. 1807–5 Jan. 1809, Sec. of Legation Sicily 1809–11 and 1813–24, Sec. of Embassy The Hague 1824–5 Jan. 1829, ret. with pension £800.[4] At his death at his residence, 24 Bolton, S. Kensington, on 19 Nov. 1869 Douglas was the senior diplomatist on the retirement list.[5]

1. *Burke's Peerage*, 8th ed., p. 476.
2. Stapylton, *Eton Lists*, p. 41.
3. Douglas to Backhouse, Brussels, 28 Apr. 1828, F.O. 366/560.
4. F.O. 366/329 f. 44.
5. *The Times*, 22 Nov. 1869, p. 1.

56. Dowling, Daniel Morton. (B. c. 1823).

B. c. 1823 to Daniel Dowling, matric. Trinity, Dublin 1840.[1] Clerk attached to the Slave Trade Dept. 21 Aug. 1841–20 Nov. 1845. Dowling was in severe financial difficulties in 1845 and was unable to come to the office because his creditors "have been watching in the Street for me and all my hopes of settling everything satisfactorily depend in great measure in my not being in actual restraint from them."[2] He continued, however, to receive his pay despite his absence.[3]

1. Burtchaell and Sadleir, *Alumni Dublinenses*, p. 241.
2. Dowling to Bandinel, 9 New Palace Yard, 20 May 1845, Private, F.O. 84/816.
3. Minute, Bandinel, on Dowling to Bandinel, 9 New Palace Yard, 4 July 1845, ibid.

57. Dudley, 1st Earl of. See Ward, John William Henry. (no. 211).

58. Dunglas, Lord (11th Earl of Home). See Home, Cospatrick Alexander. (no. 104).

59. Edwardes, Hon. Richard. (1807–66).

B. 25 Oct. 1807 to William, 2d Baron Kensington, by Dorothy, dau. of Richard Thomas, Esq.,[1] ed. Rugby, St. John's Cambridge,[2] m. 1st 1846 Emma, dau. of George Roope, 2d 1864, Rosa, dau. of T. Cadell and widow of Hugh William Burgess.[3] Supernumerary clerk c. autumn 1826, clerk 5 Jan. 1827–17 Aug. 1832 when Byng reported that he had been "obliged to resign his Clerkship in this office."[4] Attaché St. Petersburg and private sec. to Lord Clanricarde (see no. 54) 1838–Aug. 1841[5] when Palmerston appointed him paid attaché at Berlin. Aberdeen, however, canceled that appointment in Oct. 1841 and returned Edwardes to St. Petersburg as first paid attaché,[6] where he remained until appointed paid attaché Paris 1847, Sec. of Legation Frankfurt 1851, Sec. of Legation Madrid 1859, Chargé d'Affaires and Consul General Venezuela 1864,[5] appointed Min. P. Argentina 10 Aug. 1865, but d. 23 Mar. 1866 before he could leave England to assume his duties.[7]

1. *Burke's Peerage*, 60th ed., p. 817.
2. Venn, *Alumni Cantab.*, vol. 2, 389.
3. *Gents. Mag.* (1866), pt. 1, 757.
4. To Granville, 24 Aug. 1832, P.R.O. 30/29/7/13 ff. 897–902.

ADMINISTRATION OF BRITISH FOREIGN POLICY

5. *F.O. List*, July 1866, p. 177.
6. F.O. 366/330 f. 1.
7. Boase, *Mod. Eng. Biog.*, vol. 1, 964.

60. Eliot, Hon. William (2d Earl of St. Germans). (1767–1845).

B. 1 Apr. 1767 3d son of Edward, 1st Baron Eliot, by Catherine, dau. of Edward Elliston, Esq. of Gestinghorse co. Essex,[1] ed. Pembroke, Cambridge, M.A. 1786, m. 1st 1797 Georgiana Augusta, dau. of Granville, 1st Marquess of Stafford, 2d 1808 Letitia, dau. of Sir William A'Court, Bart., and sister of William, 1st Baron Heytesbury, diplomatist, 3d 1812 Charlotte, dau. of Lt. Gen. John Robinson of Denston Hall co. Suffolk, and 4th Susan, dau. of Sir John Mordaunt, 7th Bart.[2] M.P. for St. Germans 1791–1802, for Liskeard 1802–23 when he succeeded his brother as 2d Earl, Sec. of Legation Berlin 1791 (Chargé d'Affaires 1793), Min. P. *ad int.* The Hague 1793–94, special mission to Brunswick 1794, Lord of the Admiralty 1800–04,[3] undersecretary 5 Apr. 1804–5 Jan. 1805,[4] Lord of the Treasury 1807–12.[3] d. 19 Jan. 1845.

1. *Burke's Peerage*, 20th ed., p. 1271.
2. G.E.C., *Complete Peerage*, vol. 11, 310–11.
3. Aspinall, *Later Corresp. Geo. III*, vol. 1, 574 n. 2.
4. Harrowby to Post Office, Downing Street, 5 June 1804, and Mulgrave to Same, Downing Street, 25 Jan. 1805, F.O. 366/671 ff. 252, 265.

61. Elliot, (Sir) Henry George. (1817–1907).[1]

Précis writer 19 June 1840–3 Sept. 1841.

1. *D.N.B.*, 2d Supp., vol. 1, 620.

62. Ellis, Charles Augustus, 6th Baron Howard de Walden (2d Baron Seaford). (1799–1868).[1]

Précis writer 10 Oct. 1822–5 July 1824, undersecretary 5 July 1824–30 May 1828.

1. *D.N.B.*, vol. 6, 691.

63. Fisher, Edward. (d. 1805).

Son of John Fisher of Malshanger and Tangley co. Hants.,[1] ed. probably at Eton 1779–80,[2] attached to Thomas Grenville's mission to Berlin 1799,[3] undersecretary 10 Oct. 1800–23 Feb. 1801 when he ret. on pension £600.[4] Grenville secured him a place worth £150 in the customs in Mar. 1801[5] which he surrendered in Aug. 1801 to Addington for the agency of Upper Canada which had a revenue of between £300 and £400.[6] Fisher was a Commissioner of the Excise at his d. at Malshanger,[7] unm.,[1] on 5 Mar. 1805,[4] after which his estates were sold by Trustees.[1]

1. *Victoria History of Hampshire*, vol. 4, 225, 336.
2. Richard Arthur Austin Leigh (ed.), *The Eton College Register, 1753–1790* (Eton, 1921), p. 193.

3. T. Grenville to Lord Grenville, Taplow, 26 Aug. 1800, *H.M.C. Fortescue*, vol. 6, 307–8.
4. F.O. 366/380.
5. Lord Grenville to Mr. Chamberlayne, 31 Mar. 1801, Copy, Grenville MSS.
6. Fisher to Lord Grenville, Pall Mall, 21 Aug. 1801, *H.M.C. Fortescue*, vol. 7, 43.
7. *Gents. Mag.* (1805) pt. 1, 291.

64. Fitzharris, Viscount (2d Earl of Malmesbury). See Harris, James Edward. (no. 91).

65. Flint, (Sir) Charles William. (c. 1777–1834).

B. in Scotland c. 1777, ed. Edinburgh.[1] Clerk c. 1793 when his principal responsibility was to assist Stephen Rolleston (see no. 164) in his duties as assistant Gazette Writer.[2] In May 1795 Grenville sent him as Sec. to the special mission to Switzerland, whence he accompanied William Wickham in June 1795 to the headquarters of the prince of Conde where he was involved in the negotiations to bring Conde's army into British pay.[3] Superintendent of Aliens in the H.O. 2 July 1798 (though at least temporarily his clerkship in the F.O. remained in abeyance[4]) where he was responsible during the wars with France for dealing with the emigrés and for assisting their correspondence with friends and relatives in France.[3] His services were much appreciated by the French royal family and Charles X later gave him the Legion of Honor,[5] though the British government refused to grant him a baronetage in 1826 as the French king requested because Flint's position in the government was not important enough to warrant such an honor which Canning said was to be given to "Country Gentlemen & to first-rate merchants; & to be useable as a reward upon retirement for civil services of the second Class."[6] Sec. of Legation to Wickham's special mission to Austrian Headquarters 1800–01,[7] appointed undersecretary for Ireland resident in Britain 1801,[8] knighted for standing proxy for Sir Henry Wellesley in May 1812 at the installation of the Bath.[9] Flint was described after his death as "an affectionate husband and father, and a most amiable, friendly, and worthy man."[8] d. at Bolton Street, London, 19 Jan. 1834.[9]

1. Nelson, *Home Office*, p. 126 n. 27.
2. Unsigned memo [probably by Flint, c. 1828], F.O. 366/413.
3. "A short narrative, showing the nature of the Services rendered by Sir Charles William Flint to the late Prince of Conde, and to the Royal cause of France, during a succession of years from 1795 to 1814," No. 17 Great Queen Street, Westminster, 5 Aug. 1826, F.O. 27/359.
4. Minute, Grenville, Downing Street, 2 July 1798, F.O. 366/671 ff. 64–65.
5. Canning to Liverpool, F.O., 21 July 1826, Copy, Canning MSS Bundle 72.
6. Canning to Granville, F.O., 3 Jan. 1826, Private, No. 3, P.R.O. 30/29/8/9 ff. 1079–80.
7. Wickham to Grenville, Vienna, 3 Jan. 1801, Private and Confidential, *H.M.C. Fortescue*, vol. 6, 419.
8. *Ann. Biog. and Obit.* (1835), vol. 19, 416.
9. *Gents. Mag.* (1834), pt. 1, 228.

66. Forbes, John.

Served as private secretary to Wellington and Dundas[1] and was in the Irish Office c. 1809[2] before becoming Wellesley's (see no. 217) private sec. at F.O. 5 Jan. 1810–5 Apr. 1812.

    1. Wellesley to Perceval, Apsley House, 20 Feb. 1810, Private, Holland (Perceval) Papers, Bundle 1, 17.

    2. Forbes to Wellesley, Irish Office, 3 Apr. 1809, Private, Add. MS 37309 ff. 283–84.

67. Fordwich, George Augustus Frederick Cowper, Viscount (6th Earl Cowper). See Cowper, George Augustus Frederick. (no. 52).

68. Forster, Henry Francis. (1808–63).

Supernumerary clerk 11 Jan 1828, clerk 27 Aug. 1829 to his death at his residence 124 Pall Mall[1] 1 Aug. 1863.

    1. *The Times*, 4 Aug. 1863, p. 1.

69. Fox, Charles James. (1749–1806).[1]

Secretary of state 27 Mar.–4 July 1782, 2 Apr.–19 Dec. 1783, 7 Feb.–23 Sept. 1806.

    1. *D.N.B.*, vol. 7, 353.

70. Fox-Strangways, Hon. William Thomas Horner (4th Earl of Ilchester). (1795–1865).

B. 7 May 1795 to Henry, 2d Earl of Ilchester, by Julianna, dau. of the Hon. and Very Rev. William Digby, Dean of Durham,[1] matric. Westminster 1807,[2] ed. Christ Church, Oxford, B.A. 1816, M.A. 1820,[3] m. 1857 Sophia Penelope, dau. of Sir Robert Sheffield, Bart.[2] Attaché St. Petersburg 1816, Constantinople 1820, Naples 1822, The Hague 1824, Sec. of Legation Florence 1825, Naples 1828, Turin 1832, Sec. of Embassy Vienna 1832,[3] undersecretary 15 Aug. 1835–6 Mar. 1840, E. E. and Min.P. Frankfort 17 Mar. 1840–Jan. 1849.[3] Lady Granville said that "He gains upon being known; he has such valuable and general information, is so entirely free from anything like pedantry or conceit, and appears so thoroughly amiable and good, that he rises every day in our estimation . . . . He is the reverse of the proverb 'all is not gold that glitters.'"[4] d. 10 Jan. 1865.

    1. *Burke's Peerage*, 60th ed., p. 787.

    2. Barker and Stenning, *Old Westminsters*, vol. 2, 891.

    3. Boase, *Mod. Eng. Biog.*, vol. 2, 5.

    4. To Lady G. Morpeth, The Hague, 2 May 1824, Gower, *Letters of Countess Granville*, vol. 1, 286–87.

71. Franklin, George Fairfax.

Clerk in Consular Dept. 5 Apr. 1835 where he previously (from 6 Jan. 1827) had been a supernumerary clerk w/o pay. Res. 19 July 1837.[1]

    1. "Persons in Public Offices receiving Superannuations," *P.P., 1835*, vol. 37, Command 594, p. 510; *Records of the Foreign Office*, p. 152.

72. Fraser, John Henry David. (1803–67).

B. 27 Dec. 1803 to Henry David Fraser by Mary Christina, dau. of John Forbes of Skellater, Aberdeenshire.[1] Clerk 5 Apr.–Aug. 1826 when he was attached to Gordon's mission to Brazil.[2] d. 18 Apr. 1867.

1. *Burke's Peerage*, 23d ed., p. 933.
2. Gordon to Backhouse, Rio de Janeiro, 7 July 1828, F.O. 366/560.

73. Fraser, William. (1727–1802).

Fraser was travelling with Lord Holderness in 1751 when Holderness was appointed secretary of state.[1] He was appointed clerk 31 July 1751[2] and became undersecretary in 1759, but was removed by Bute 25 Mar. 1761. In May 1761, however, he was appointed Commissary with the Allied Army where he served at the headquarters of Duke Ferdinand of Brunswick. He became Commissary General in 1762, a post he held until the end of the war when in Sept. 1763 he went to Dublin as a private sec. to the Earl of Northumberland, then Lord Lieut. of Ireland.[1] Grafton appointed him undersecretary in the Northern Dept. 23 July 1765,[3] and he served at various times between then and 1782 in both departments of state,[4] remaining in the F.O. as undersecretary from 1782 until he ret. Aug. 1789. Appointed Gazette Writer for life 23 July 1776,[5] appointed Translator of the German Language for life 6 Oct. 1773,[6] and was Clerk of the Signet from 1782 to his death.[7] Horace Walpole called Fraser "punctuality and care itself,"[8] and George III, who commanded Fraser in Dec. 1783 to collect the seals from Portland's ministry, "was pleased to make several remarks on the various troublesome and disagreeable scenes to which I had for so many years been witness, and ended with the most gracious approbation of my conduct with this expression—that it had always afforded him great satisfaction during the various changes, that he had been able to preserve one honest man."[1] d. in London after a long illness 11 Dec. 1802.[9]

1. Biographical Fragment, printed in *Notes and Queries*, ser. 4, vol. 2, 436–37.
2. Holderness to Postmaster General, Whitehall, 31 July 1751, S.P. 44/136 f. 180.
3. Grafton to Postmaster General, 23 July 1765, *Calendar of Home Office Papers*, vol. 1, 579.
4. Ibid., vols. 1–3, passim.
5. Handover, *History of the London Gazette*, p. 58.
6. Earl of Suffolk to Lord North, n.d., *Calendar of Home Office Papers*, vol. 4, 867; Canning to Long, Downing Street, 12 June 1797, Copy, F.O. 366/427.
7. Nelson, *Home Office*, p. 154 n. 71.
8. To Rev. William Mason, Middleton Park, 9 Sept. 1772, W. S. Lewis (ed.), *The Yale Edition of Horace Walpole's Correspondence* (34 vols.; New Haven, 1937–65), vol. 28, 44.
9. *The Times*, 15 Dec. 1802, p. 4.

74. Frere, George. (1810–78).

B. 22 Feb. 1810 to George Frere of Twynford House, Herts., by Elizabeth Raper, dau. of William Grant, M.D. of London and Rothiemurchus, Inverness,[1] matric. Charterhouse 1820,[2] m. 1842 Margaret Anne, dau. of Edgar Corrie of Arlington Manor, Berks.[1] Clerk in Slave Trade

Dept. 5 Dec. 1826, Sec. in charge at Switzerland while the Sec. of Legation there was absent 1835–36, sec. to commission to revise slave trade instructions 1842,[3] res. clerkship 20 Nov. 1842 and appointed on 24 Jan. 1843, partly through the influence of his uncle, John Hookham Frere[4] (see no. 75), Slave Trade Commissioner at the Cape of Good Hope under the provisions of the Anglo-Portuguese Treaty of 1842. Appointed Judge in the U.S.–U.K. Mixed Court for Suppressing the Slave Trade created after the Anglo-American Treaty of 1862, Oct. 1862–Sept. 1867[3] when he ret. with pension £900.[5] Frere was temporarily employed in the Librarian's Dept. 30 June 1868–29 June 1874, and from 1 Aug. 1876 to his death at his residence 15 Great College Street, Westminster, 26 Oct. 1878.[6]

1. *Burke's Landed Gentry*, 18th ed., vol. 2, 227.
2. William D. Parish (ed.), *List of Carthusians 1800–1879* (Lewes, 1879), p. 90.
3. *F.O. List*, 1879, p. 214.
4. J. H. Frere to Aberdeen, Malta, 15 Aug. 1832, Private, with minute on docket, 12 Nov. 1842, Add. MS 43239 ff. 302–4.
5. "Superannuations in Public Office," *P.P., 1878–79*, vol. 42, Command 122, p. 794.
6. *The Times*, 28 Oct. 1878, p. 1.

75. Frere, John Hookham. (1769–1846).[1]

Undersecretary 5 Apr. 1799–10 Oct. 1800.

1. *D.N.B.*, vol. 7, 708.

76. Gifford, Hon. Edward Scott. (1825–72).

B. 26 May 1825 to Sir Robert Gifford, 1st Baron Gifford, Attorney General, Lord Chief Justice of the Court of Common Pleas, and Master of the Rolls, by Harriet Maria, dau. of Rev. Edward Drewe, rector of Willand.[1] Clerk 5 Feb. 1846, sec. to Earl Cowper's special mission to Copenhagen to invest King Christian IX with the Garter 1865, senior clerk 1 Jan. 1868[2] until he d. unm.[1] 26 May 1872.

1. *Burke's Peerage*, 6oth ed., p. 618.
2. *F.O. List*, July 1872, p. 203.

77. Goddard, Charles. (c. 1769–1848).

B. c. 1769 to Charles Goddard of Westminster, matric. Christ Church, Oxford 1787, M.A. 1821, B.D. and D.D. 1821,[1] m. 1812,[2] clerk in Home Office Aug. 1789 where he served as Grenville's (see no. 81) private sec. and précis writer,[3] précis writer in F.O. 8 June 1791 when Grenville went to that dept.,[4] acted as agent to Sir Morton Eden 1792,[5] private sec. c. 1793–24 Feb. 1796,[6] appointed Collector and Transmitter of State Papers by Letters Patent 10 Oct. 1795 and retained the position to his death,[7] Consul General Lisbon 21 Dec. 1796–31 Oct. 1799,[3] ret. with pension £850.[8] Agent for Upper Canada and deputy for St. James's (?) Park until 1799.[3] Goddard was imprisoned by Napoleon's government in 1806 but managed to secure an appointment from Grenville as Sec. of Legation in Paris which enabled him to leave France on parole.[9] He was Archdeacon of Lincoln 1818[10]— 1844, sub-dean 1844 to his death, rector of St. James's, Garlick Hill, London 1821–36, rector of Ibstock 1836 to his death, chaplain to the Bishop of Rochester.[3] Goddard's career was enhanced by his attachment to the Grenvilles whose influence with Pitt's old master, Bishop Pretyman of Lincoln, was decisive in securing his initial ecclesiastical appointments.[8] d. 21 Jan. 1848.

1. Foster, *Alumni Oxon.*, vol. 2, 531.
2. Nelson, *Home Office*, p. 165.
3. Ibid., pp. 18, 365–66 where the biographical sketch is not entirely accurate.
4. Buckingham to Grenville, [Stowe], 26 June 1791, *H.M.C. Fortescue*, vol. 2, 109.
5. M. Eden to Grenville, Berlin, 4 Sept. 1792, Private, ibid., vol. 2, 309.
6. Minute, Grenville, Downing Street, 24 Feb. 1796, F.O. 366/670 f. 371.
7. Marginal note on unsigned minute, Downing Street, 22 Oct. 1795, ibid., f. 353.
8. *Gents. Mag.* (1848), pt. 1,555.
9. Lauderdale to Grenville, Paris, 11 Aug. 1806 11 o'clock at night, Most private, and Grenville to Lauderdale, Downing Street, 14 Aug. 1806, Private, *H.M.C. Fortescue*, vol. 8, 277–78.
10. Bishop of Lincoln to Grenville, Great George Street, 11 June 1818, ibid., vol. 10, 438.

78. Graham, David. (1785–1824).

B. 28 Jan. 1785 to Robert Graham, 12th Laird of Fintry, by Margaret Elizabeth, dau. of Thomas Mylne of Mylnefield.[1] Clerk 18 Oct. 1805–5 July 1817, ret. because of an "infirm state of mind,"[2] with pension £190.[3] d. 11 Sept. 1824.

1. *Burke's Commoners* (1848), vol. 1, 492.
2. Castlereagh to the Treasury, F.O., 21 July 1817, Copy, F.O. 366/672 f. 141.
3. "An Account of all Pensions . . . for the Year 1819," *P.P., 1820*, vol. 11, Command 11, p. 296.

79. Grantham, 2d Baron. See Robinson, Thomas. (no. 162).

80. Green, Alfred Schrimshire (c. 1825–75).

B. c. 1825 to Vice Admiral Sir Andrew Pellatt Green, K.C.H.,[1] naval aide de camp of William IV (1837) and Victoria (1841).[2] Clerk attached to Librarian's Dept. 19 Dec. 1844, Sub-librarian 17 Jan. 1859[3] to his death 4 Oct. 1875.

1. *The Times*, 8 Oct. 1875, p. 1.
2. Boase, *Mod. Eng. Biog.*, vol. 1, 1222.
3. *F.O. List*, 1876, p. 214.

81. Grenville, William Wyndham Grenville, 1st Baron Grenville. (1759–1834).[1]

Secretary of State 8 June 1791–20 Feb. 1801.

1. *D.N.B.*, vol. 8, 576.

82. Greville, Algernon Frederick. (1798–1864).[1]
Private secretary 17 Nov. 1834–17 Apr. 1835.
1. *D.N.B.*, vol. 8, 600.

83. Greville, Henry William. (1801–72).[1]
Précis writer 17Nov. 1834–7 Apr. 1835.
1. *D.N.B.*, vol. 8, 606.

84. Grey, Charles, Viscount Howick (2d Earl Grey). (1764–1845).[1]
Secretary of state 24 Sept. 1806–5 Apr. 1807.
1. *D.N.B.*, vol. 8, 616.

85. Hamilton, William John. (1805–67).[1]
Précis writer 5 Apr. 1830–21 Nov. 1830.
1. *D.N.B.*, vol. 8, 1118.

86. Hamilton, William Richard. (1777–1859).[1]
Précis writer 5 Apr. 1804–6 Mar. 1806, private sec. 5 Apr.–5 July 1804, undersecretary 10 Oct. 1809, leave of absence 14 Apr. 1820–29 July 1821, ret. 29 Jan. 1822.
1. *D.N.B.*, vol. 8, 1118.

87. Hamilton-Gordon, (Gen. Sir) Alexander. (1817–90).
B. 11 Dec. 1817 to George, 4th Earl of Aberdeen (see no. 88), by Harriet, dau. of Hon. John Douglas,[1] ed. Harrow,[2] Trinity College, Cambridge,[3] m. 1852 Charlotte Amelia Mary, dau. of Sir John Herschal, 1st Bart.[2] Précis writer 25 Nov. 1843–6 Feb. 1846, Lieut. Col. in Grenadier Guards, Equerry to Prince Albert,[4] fought with distinction in the allied victory in the Crimean War at the Battle of Alma 1854, held various posts in the Queen's Body Guards, M.P. for E. Aberdeenshire 1875–85, J.P. for Middlesex.[3] d. 19 May 1890.
1. *Burke's Peerage*, 60th ed., p. 9.
2. Walford, *County Families*, p. 2.
3. *The Times*, 20 May 1890, p. 8.
4. *F.O. List*, 1854, p. 55.

88. Hamilton-Gordon, George, 4th Earl of Aberdeen. (1784–1860).[1]
Secretary of State 2 June 1828–21 Nov. 1830, and 2 Sept. 1841–July 1846.
1. *D.N.B.*, vol. 8, 200.

89. Hammond, Edmund (1st Baron Hammond). (1802–90).[1]
Clerk 5 Apr. 1824, senior clerk 21 Aug. 1841, permanent undersecretary 1854–73.
1. *D.N.B.*, vol. 8, 1124.

90. Hammond, George. (1763–1853).[1]
Undersecretary 11 Oct. 1795–20 Feb. 1806, 5 Apr. 1807–11 Nov. 1809.
1. *D.N.B.*, vol. 8, 1125.

91. Harris, James Edward, Viscount Fitzharris (2d Earl of Malmesbury). (1778–1841).
B. 19 Aug. 1778 to James Harris, later 1st Earl of Malmesbury, diplomatist, by Harriet Mary, dau. of Sir George Amyand, Bart.,[1] ed. Eton, matric. Christ Church, Oxford 1796, M. A. 1798, m. 1806 Harriet Susan, dau. of Francis Bateman Dashwood of co. Lincoln.[2] Secretary to the Board of Trade 1801, M.P. for Helston 1802–04, for Horsham 1804–07, for Heytesbury 1807–12, for Wilton 1816–20, Lord of the Treasury 1804–06.[2] Accepted the undersecretaryship 25 Mar. 1807 (effective 5 Apr.) "thinking that confinement with business was better than confinement and *no* business, which would have been the case at the Treasury,"[3] but res. 18 Aug. 1807 "quite worn down by the fatigue and attendance at the Foreign Office."[4] On leaving the F.O. he became Governor of the Isle of Wight,[5] a position he held until 10 Sept. 1841 when the office was abolished.[4]
1. *Burke's Peerage*, 6oth ed., p. 965.
2. G.E.C., *Complete Peerage*, vol. 8, 361–62.
3. Diary 25 Mar. 1807, Malmesbury, *Diaries*, vol. 4, 337.
4. Ibid., pp. 389–90 & n.
5. Malmesbury, *Series of Letters*, vol. 2, 39 n.

92. Harrowby, 1st Earl of. See Ryder, Dudley. (no. 167).

93. Hawkesbury, Baron (2d Earl of Liverpool). See Jenkinson, Robert Banks. (no. 116).

94. Hay, James William. (c. 1760–1806).
Clerk 17 Oct. 1788, secretary of Lord Hertford's special mission to Baden, Hesse-Cassel, and Hesse Darmstadt 1793,[1] senior clerk 1803,[2] ret. ill-health 5 July 1805 with pension £500.[1] Hay was responsible for summoning the peers in the 1780s and the 1790s, a duty he alternated with a clerk in the Home Office.[3] He was secretary to the Board for American Claims with a salary of £500 1802–04.[4] After his death which his maiden sisters said was the result of illness caused by overwork, Canning granted each of his sisters a pension of £75 p.a.[5] Burges said that Hay "both in manners and connections is much superior to the rest of these [clerks] we have here."[6] d. 18 Jan. 1806.
1. Order-in-Council, Queen's Palace, 27 June 1805, F.O. 366/542; Bindoff et al., *Br. Dip. Reps.*, pp. 19, 69, 71.
2. *Royal Kalendar*, 1804, p. 132.
3. Hay to Harrowby, Downing Street, Monday, 23 July 1804, Harrowby MSS, vol. 11, ff. 15–16.

4. Hay to Harrowby, Downing Street, 14 June 1804, and Same, Downing Street, 20 June 1804, ibid., ff. 9–14.

5. Memorial of Misses Elizabeth & Sarah Hay, at Mrs. Beckford's, Clifton Down, Bristol, 4 Apr. 1807, Copy, with minute, Canning, Downing Street, 7 July 1807, F.O. 366/671 ff. 329–35.

6. To Grenville, Whitehall, Friday Evening, 6 Jan. 1792 but really 1793, Grenville MSS.

95. Hertslet, (Sir) Edward. (1824–1902).[1]

Employed without pay in Librarian's Dept. from Mar. 1840,[2] clerk attached to Librarian's Dept. 8 Jan. 1842, Sub-librarian 1 Apr. 1855, Librarian and Keeper of the Papers 20 Nov. 1857 to his ret. 3 Feb. 1894, though he continued to discharge the duties of the office until 2 Feb. 1896.[3] He "not only possessed a more intimate knowledge than perhaps any other man living of the literature of diplomacy, but his long experience and judgment lent more than a technical value to the advice he was constantly called upon to give. . . ."[4]

1. *D.N.B.*, 2d Supp., vol. 2, 258.
2. Lewis Hertslet to Palmerston, Foreign Office, 17 May 1841, Palmerston Papers PAT/H/51.
3. *F.O. List*, 1902, p. 139.
4. *The Times*, 5 Aug. 1902, p. 5.

96. Hertslet, James. (c. 1794–1862).

B. c. 1794 to Jean Louis Pierre Hiertzelet (later Anglicized), a Swiss immigrant and king's messenger, by Hannah Caldecourt or Caldecott.[1] Sub-librarian 5 Jan. 1811 until retirement, entering and dispatch clerk with allowance of £100 p.a. from 5 Jan. 1822,[2] ret. ill-health 1 Apr. 1855 with pension £537.10.0.[3] Hertslet was the younger brother of Lewis H. (see no. 97), and uncle of Sir Edward H. (see no. 95). He d. at his home in Brighton 20 Feb. 1862.[4]

1. *Notes and Queries*, ser. 10, vol. 7, 492.
2. Londonderry to Treasury, Foreign Office, 20 Feb. 1822, Copy, F.O. 366/370 ff. 25–27.
3. "Superannuations in Public Offices," *P.P., 1856*, vol. 48, Command 112, p. 531.
4. *Gents Mag.* (1862), pt. 1, 516.

97. Hertslet, Lewis. (1787–1870).[1]

B. 25 Nov. 1787, elder brother of James H. (see no. 96) and father of Sir Edward H. (see no. 95), m. 1st Hannah Harriet, dau. of George Cooke of Westminster,[2] 2d Mary Spencer, dau. of William Wainewright of Westminster.[3] Deputy Librarian w/o pay 5 Feb. 1801, granted annual allowance of £50 in Oct. 1809,[4] Librarian and Keeper of the Papers 5 Jan. 1810[5] to retirement, Superintendent of Messengers 1824–54 when the position was abolished[6] and Hertslet was given, effective 1 Jan. 1856, a compensation allowance of £200 p.a.[7] Ret. ill-health 20 Nov. 1857 on pension £800[8] and d. 15 or 16 Mar. 1870.[9]

1. *D.N.B.*, vol. 9, 726.
2. See their son Lewis Cooke Hertslet in Barker and Stenning, *Old Westminsters*, vol. 1, 451.
3. *Notes and Queries*, ser. 10, vol. 7, 492.

4. Minute, Bathurst, F.O., 9 Nov. 1809, F.O. 366/671 f. 396.
5. Minute, Wellesley, F.O., 6 Jan. 1810, F.O. 366/672 f. 5.
6. Boase, *Mod. Eng. Biog.*, vol. 1, 1450.
7. Trevelyan to Hammond, Treasury Chambers, 11 Oct. 1855, and Same to Wodehouse, Treasury Chambers, 11 Dec. 1855, F.O. 366/533.
8. "Superannuations in Public Offices," *P.P., 1857–58*, vol. 34, Command 169, p. 438.
9. *The Times*, 17 Mar. 1870, p. 7 says he died the 16th; Boase, *Mod. Eng. Biog.*, vol. 1, 1450 says he died the 15th.

98. Hervey, Frederick William, Lord Hervey (5th Earl and 1st Marquess of Bristol). (1769–1859).

B. 2 June 1769, the 2d and only surviving son of Rt. Rev. Frederick Augustus Hervey, Bishop of Derry and 4th Earl of Bristol, by Elizabeth, dau. of Sir Jermyn Davers, Bart.,[1] ed. St. John's, Cambridge, M.A. 1798, LL.D. 1811,[2] where he was at the top of his class in every subject.[3] m. 1798 Elizabeth Charlotte Upton, dau. of Clotworthy, 1st Baron Templetown.[1] M.P. for Bury St. Edmunds 1796–1803,[4] appointed undersecretary 23 Feb. 1801 by his brother-in-law Lord Hawkesbury (see no. 116) and ret. 5 Aug. 1803 after succeeding as 5th Earl on 8 July 1803.[1] F.R.S. 1805, cr. Marquess of Bristol 1826.[2] Spent his later years in Brighton where he was a popular figure because of his "philanthropy and charitable works."[5] d. 15 Feb. 1859.

1. *Burke's Peerage*, 60th ed., p. 193.
2. Boase, *Mod. Eng. Biog.*, vol. 1, 403.
3. Brian Fothergill, *The Mitred Earl: An Eighteenth Century Eccentric* (London, 1974), p. 143.
4. G.E.C., *Complete Peerage*, vol. 2, 328–29.
5. Fothergill, *Mitred Earl*, p. 144.

99. Hervey, Lord William. (1805–50).

B. 27 Sept. 1805, third son of the 1st Marquess of Bristol (see no. 98),[1] matric. Eton 1817, matric. Trinity College, Cambridge 1822, M.A. 1825,[2] m. 1844 Cecelia Mary, dau. of Vice Admiral Sir T. F. Fremantle.[3] Clerk 5 Jan. 1825–5 Jan. 1828, paid attaché Vienna 5 Jan. 1828,[4] Sec. of Legation Spain 1830–39, Sec. of Embassy France 1843–50.[5] Aberdeen, who appointed Hervey to his posts in Madrid and Paris, found him "rather clever, but odd, as all Herveys are,"[6] d. May 1850.

1. *Burke's Peerage*, 60th ed., p. 193.
2. Stapylton, *Eton Lists*, p. 93; Venn, *Alumni Cantab.*, vol. 3, 344.
3. *Gents. Mag.* (1850), pt. 1, 683.
4. Hervey's memo in Cowley to Dudley, Vienna, 5 Apr. 1828, F.O. 366/560.
5. Bindoff et al, *Br. Dip. Reps.*, pp. 54, 145.
6. Aberdeen to Peel, Haddo House, 10 Oct. 1843, Add. MS 40453 ff. 470–71.

100. Hill, Lord Arthur Marcus Cecil (Baron Sandys). (1798–1863).

B. 28 Jan. 1798 to Arthur, 2d Marquess of Downshire, by Mary, Baroness Sandys, dau. of William Trumbell, Esq., of East Hampstead Park, Berks.,[1] matric. Eton 1811,[2] ed. Edinburgh, D.C.L. Oxford 1834, m. 1857 Louisa, dau. of Joseph Blake, the brother of Admiral Blake.[3] Attached to

Madrid 1817–21, précis writer 29 Jan.–10 Oct. 1822, attached to Wellington's special embassy to Verona 1822–23, attaché Paris 1823, Sec. of Legation Florence 1824, Sec. to Lord Stuart's special embassy to Rio de Janeiro and Lisbon 1825–26, Sec. to Lord Hertford's special mission to invest the Emperor Nicholas with the Garter June–Aug. 1827, appointed Sec. of Embassy Constantinople 1830 but never went to his post.[4] M.P. for Newry 1832–35,[3] for Evesham 1837–52.[5] Hill was successively comptroller and treasurer of the Royal Household during the Whig ministries of 1841 and 1846–52.[5] d. 10 Apr. 1863.

1. *Burke's Peerage*, 60th ed., p. 464.
2. Stapylton, *Eton Lists*, p. 68.
3. *Gents. Mag.* (1863), pt. 1, 673.
4. F.O. 366/329 f. 74.
5. *F.O. List*, 1859, p. 80.

101. Hinchliffe, John. (d. 1799).

Appointed clerk after 27 Mar. but before 16 July 1782,[1] appointed to assist Arbuthnot (see no. 9) in 1793, but refused "to abide by the arrangement which had been settled, and says he prefers being left in the Class of unappropriated Clerks," to which he was returned.[2] Senior clerk 1794–his ret. ill-health 5 Jan. 1799[3] with pension £500,[4] and with a pension of £100 to his father.[5] d. c. July–Dec. 1799.[6]

1. F.O. 366/669, vol. 2, 5.
2. Burges to Grenville, Whitehall, 2 Oct. 1793, Grenville MSS.
3. Grenville to the Lord President, Downing Street, 7 Jan. 1799, F.O. 366/671 ff. 91–92.
4. Order-in-Council, 8 Jan. 1799, referred to in red ink marginal note, F.O. 366/380.
5. Minute, Grenville, Downing Street, 23 Jan. 1799, F.O. 366/671 f. 96.
6. F.O. 366/380 shows that Hinchliffe was not paid his pension after July 1799. His father's pension began 5 Jan. 1799 and ended 5 Apr. 1801., ibid.

102. Hole, John Boger. (c. 1822–92).

B. c. 1822 to Francis Hole, Esq., of Collipriest Cottage, Tiverton,[1] by Jane, dau. of John Boger of Smytham, Little Torrington, co. Devon,[2] ed. Blundell's 14 Aug. 1832–29 June 1838.[1] Supernumerary clerk 16 Aug. 1841, clerk 21 Aug. 1841, senior clerk 1865,[3] ret. on the reorganization of the establishment 18 Feb. 1872 with a compensation allowance £566.13.4 p.a.[4] d. 29 July 1892 at Standerwick Court, Frome, where he was a J.P.[5]

1. Fisher, *Blundell's Register*, p. 130.
2. *Notes and Queries*, vol. 163, 29.
3. *F.O. List*, 1892, p. 126.
4. "Superannuations in Public Offices," *P.P.*, *1873*, vol. 39, Command 129, p. 536.
5. *The Times*, 4 Aug. 1892, p. 1.

103. Holland, John.

Served as Embellisher to both offices of State after 1774.[1] His principal duty was to embellish the king's letters to Eastern Princes, for which he was paid £24 p.a.[2]

1. *Royal Kalendar*, 1775 new ed., p. 107.
2. George Hammond to Lewis Wolfe, Downing Street, 15 July 1800, Copy, F.O. 366/671 f. 144.

104. Home, Cospatrick Alexander, Lord Dunglas (11th Earl of Home). (1799–1881).

B. 27 Oct. 1799 to Alexander, 10th Earl of Home, by Elizabeth, dau. of 3d Duke of Buccleuch and Queensberry,[1] matric. Christ Church, Oxford 1819, m. 1832 Lucy Elizabeth, dau. of Henry, 2d Baron Montagu of Broughton.[2] Attaché St. Petersburg 1822–23,[3] précis writer 5 July 1824–5 July 1827, Sec. of Embassy to Wellington's special embassy to St. Petersburg 1826,[4] undersecretary 20 May 1828–21 Nov. 1830. Ranger of the Ettrick Forest and Captain of the Berwickshire militia c. 1828,[5] succeeded as 11th Earl 1841,[1] Scottish Representative Peer 1842–74,[2] Keeper of the Great Seal of Scotland 1853–58,[6] cr. Baron Douglas (U.K.) 1875.[3] Canning, who first brought Dunglas into the F.O., recommended him to Wellington as "an excellent young man, sufficiently versed in business, clever, but singularly modest and unpretending."[4] d. 4 July 1881.

1. *Burke's Peerage*, 60th ed., p. 765.
2. G.E.C., *Complete Peerage*, vol. 6, 560.
3. Boase, *Mod. Eng. Biog.*, vol. 1, 1519.
4. Canning to Wellington, Foreign Office, 23 Jan. 1826, *W.N.D.*, vol. 3, 71.
5. F.O. 366/366 f. 142.
6. Strachey and Fulford, *Greville Memoirs*, vol. 1, 218 n. 1.

105. Hoppner, Richard Belgrave. (c. 1785–1872).

B. c. 1785 to John Hoppner, R.A.,[1] portrait painter to the Prince of Wales,[2] by Pheobe, dau. of Mrs. Patience Wright,[1] American painter,[3] ed. Eton. 1799–1801,[4] as a child learned to paint and became an able amateur,[1] m. a "Swiss lady."[5] Hoppner grew up in the Royal Household and was on good terms with the Royal family. At age 14 he was sent to Germany to learn the language and was in his later years fond of declaring "that any fool could learn a foreign language in six weeks."[6] Clerk 1 Feb. 1801, private sec. with clerk's pay to John Hookham Frere (see no. 75) at Madrid 1808,[7] Consul General and Chargé d'Affaires ad. int. The Hague 20 May–6 June 1814,[8] res. Clerkship 5 July 1814, Consul General Venice where he met and began corresponding with Byron 4 Oct. 1814 to his retirement 5 Apr. 1825[9] with pension £650.[10] Palmerston brought him out of retirement in 1831 and appointed him Acting Consul General in charge of affairs at Lisbon[8] where he served until 1833 when Palmerston decided to replace him for being "rather Indiscreet lately & since villa Flors [sic] arrival at Lisbon, hoisting Donna Marias Flag upon his House & writing to Parker to urge him to land the Marines; I wish therefore upon all accounts to give him an honourable Retirement & to carry the Consular arrangement into Effect—we ought to have a Steady man there."[11] Hoppner was one of the most able linguists in the F.O., reading Spanish fluently[12] and translating from the German in 1813 *Voyages around the World, in the Years 1803,4,5, and 6; by the command of His Imperial Majesty Alexander I in the ships Nadeshda and Neva, under the orders of Captain A.J. Von Krusnestem.*[13] After his retirement in 1833 Hoppner resided at Grenoble and Versailles, moving to Turin in 1869 or 1870[5] after his wife's death.[6] He was appointed British chaplain at Baden Baden by the Bishop of London 8 Feb. 1869.[9] d. at Turin 6 Aug. 1872.[14]

1. *Notes and Queries*, ser. 4, vol. 11, 505.
2. For John Hoppner see *D.N.B.*, vol. 9, 1236.
3. For whom see *D.N.B.*, vol. 21, 1036.
4. Stapylton, *Eton Lists*, p. 32.
5. *Notes and Queries*, ser. 7, vol. 9, 35–36.
6. "Notes taken from Mama's Anecdotes and from Uncle Belgrave's Letters, John Hoppner R.A.," n.d., Add. MS 38510 ff. 237–99.
7. Canning to Frere, Foreign Office, 7 Oct. 1808, Add. MS 38833 ff. 254–55.
8. Bindoff et al., *Br. Dip. Reps.*, p. 179.
9. *F.O. List*, 1873, p. 202.
10. "Superannuations in Public Offices," *P.P.*, *1873*, vol. 39. Command 129, p. 598.
11. Minute, Palmerston, 11 Aug. 1833, F.O. 96/17.
12. Unsigned minute, Canning, on W. Deane to R. F. Tauberman, Monte Video, 2 May 1807, F.O. 72/69 f. 119.
13. *Notes and Queries*, ser. 7, vol. 10, 230.
14. *The Times*, 13 Aug. 1872, p. 1.

106. Howard, James Kenneth. (1814–82).

B. 5 Mar. 1814 to Thomas, 16th Earl of Suffolk, by Elizabeth Jane Dutton, dau. of James, 1st Lord Sherborne,[1] ed. Charterhouse,[2] m. 1845 Louisa, dau. of Henry, 3d Marquess of Lansdowne.[1] Précis writer 27 Apr. 1838–5 Jan. 1840, private sec. 5 Jan. 1840–24 Aug. 1841. M.P. for Malmesbury, 1841–52,[3] private sec. to Palmerston when Palmerston was Home Secretary 1854, Commissioner of Woods and Forests 1855–82.[4] J.P. for co. Hants.[2] d. 7 Jan. 1882.

1. *Burke's Peerage*, 6oth ed., p. 1399.
3. Walford, *County Families*, p. 511.
3. Boase, *Mod. Eng. Biog.*, vol. 1, 1552.
4. Strachey and Fulford, *Greville Memoirs*, vol. 7, 98 n. 2.

107. Howard de Walden, 6th Baron (2d Baron Seaford). See Ellis, Charles Augustus. (no. 62).

108. Howick, Viscount (2d Earl Grey). See Grey, Charles. (no. 84).

109. Huskisson, William Milbanke. (c. 1816–49).

B. c. 1816 to Captain Thomas Huskisson, R.N.,[1] by Elizabeth, dau. of

Francis Wedge of Aqualate Park, Staffs.[2] Huskisson, who was a nephew of
Rt. Hon. William Huskisson, was appointed clerk 17 Nov. 1834 and served
until his death at Greenwich[3] 13 Jan. 1849.

1. William R. O'Byrne, *A Naval Biographical Dictionary* (2 vols.; London, 1849), vol. 1, 558.
2. *D.N.B.*, vol. 10, 323.
3. *Gents. Mag.* (1849), pt. 1, 327.

110. Hüttner, John Christian. (c. 1764–1847).[1]

Translator of the Spanish, Portuguese, Italian, and Danish Languages
10 Oct. 1808–28 May 1847. Hüttner was ed. at the University of Leipzig,[2]
wrote about foreign affairs in the periodicals,[3] and was generally regarded
as "a very able scholar" of "placid and curteous temper. . . ."[2] He was a
member of the Lutheran Church, was m. twice,[2] and d. 24 May 1847 at his
residence 11 Fludyer Street, Westminster, of "apoplexy of the heart"[4]
caused by his being run over by a cab a fortnight before. He was buried at
Kensal Green.[2]

1. *D.N.B.*, vol. 10, 350.
2. *Gents. Mag.* (1847), pt. 2, 99–100.
3. *Ann. Reg.*1847, pp. 233–34.
4. *The Times* (Supplement), 29 May 1847, p. 1.

111. Irving, Francis. (c. 1827–96).

Clerk attached to the Librarian's Dept. 7 May 1845, assistant in the
Treaty Dept. 11 Mar. 1873, ret. 8 July 1882.[1] d. at Tunbridge Wells 18 Sept.
1896.[2]

1. *F.O. List*, 1897, p. 234.
2. *The Times*, 21 Sept. 1896, p. 1.

112. Jackson, Francis James (1770–1814).[1]

Clerk 1786–88. Jackson, whom Carmarthen described as a "very deserving young man," was ed. at the University of Erlangen where he studied
with professor Berger and where he became fluent in French and German.[2] He brought to England the Treaty of Defensive Alliance with the
Dutch (1788),[3] and after a career in the diplomatic service[1] he received a
pension of £1700 on 10 Oct. 1806.[4] After his death 5 Aug. 1814 his widow
was granted a pension of £600.[5]

1. *D.N.B.*, vol. 10, 527.
2. Carmarthen to Joseph Ewart, Whitehall, 2 Jan. 1789, Private, Copy, Add. MS 28064
ff. 1–2.
3. Carmarthen to Treasury, Whitehall, 25 Apr. 1783, Copy, F.O. 366/426 ff. 110–11.
4. F.O. 366/460.
5. Minute on Petition of Elizabeth Charlotte Jackson, Brighthelmstone, 16 Aug. 1814, F.O.
83/25.

113. Jackson, John. (c. 1780–1844).

Clerk 4 June 1806, assistant in Consular Dept. 1826–5 July 1830 when he was ret. because of poor eyesight[1] on the reduction of the establishment.[2] He received a compensation allowance of £520 p.a.[3] until he d. at Brighton 2 Dec. 1844.[4] He resided at Hans Place, Chelsea.[4]

    1. Draft to Treasury, F.O., Mar. 1830, F.O. 366/553.
    2. Backhouse to Goulburn, F.O., 26 Apr. 1830, ibid.
    3. "Superannuations in Public Offices," *P.P.*, *1845*, vol. 28, Command 149, p. 594.
    4. *Gents. Mag.* (1845), pt. 1, 110.

114. Jenkins, John Warham. (d. 1800).

Clerk 1770, senior clerk 1789,[1] ret. because of old age and poor health with a pension equal to his salary of £480[2] 29 Sept. 1794. d. at Margate after three days' illness 30 Aug. 1800.[3]

    1. *Royal Kalender*, 1790 new ed., p. 104.
    2. Grenville to Treasury, Downing Street, 5 Nov. 1794, Copy, F.O. 366/427 ff. 108–09.
    3. *Gents. Mag.* (1800), pt. 2, 905.

115. Jenkinson, Charles Cecil Cope (3d Earl of Liverpool). (1784–1851).[1]

Précis writer 5 Apr. 1803–5 Apr. 1804.

    1. *D.N.B.*, vol. 10, 747.

116. Jenkinson, Robert Banks, Baron Hawkesbury (2d Earl of Liverpool). (1770–1828).[1]

Secretary of state 20 Feb. 1801–11 May 1804.

    1. *D.N.B.*, vol. 10, 748.

117. Johnson, William.

Clerk attached to Slave Trade Dept. 25 Jan. 1837–12 Feb. 1838 when he went to Canada[1] possibly on some sort of government commission.[2] Solicited but failed to secure employment at the F.O. in 1839.[3]

    1. Johnson to Fox-Strangways, F.O., 19 Feb. 1838, F.O. 84/261.
    2. Minute, Palmerston, 14 Mar. 1838, ibid.
    3. Johnson to Bandinel, Bawn, Longford, 17 Aug. 1839, Private, and Bandinel to Johnson, Foreign Office, 30 Aug. 1839, Copy, F.O. 84/305.

118. Kerr, John William Robert, Earl of Ancram. (7th Marquess of Lothian). (1794–1841).

B. 1 Feb. 1794 to William, 6th Marquess of Lothian by Henrietta dau. of John 2d Earl of Buckinghamshire,[1] matric. Christ Church Oxford 1813,[2] m. 1831 Cecil Chetwynd, dau. of Charles 2d Earl Talbot.[1] Private Sec. 5 July 1819–5 Jan. 1820,[3] M.P. for Huntingdon 1820–24, Lord Lieut. Roxburghshire and 7th Marquess 1824.[1] d. 14 Nov. 1841.

    1. G.E.C., *Complete Peerage*, vol. 8, 155.
    2. Foster, *Alumni Oxon.*, vol. 2, 790.
    3. F.O. 366/380.

119. Kuper, Henry George. (1804–1856).

B. 1804 to Rev. William Kuper, D.D., Chaplain to Queen Adelaide,[1] his mother was Wilhelmina Kuper,[2] brother of Admiral Sir Augustus Leopold Kuper,[3] matric. Merton, Oxford 1825,[4] m. 1847 Mary, dau. of W.H. Driffield of Thealby, co. Lancs.[2] Clerk 5 July 1826–5 Jan. 1827, attached to the mission at Frankfort as German Translator 5 Jan. 1827,[5] paid attaché Germanic Confederation 1838–43,[6] Consul in Denmark resident in Elsinore 5 Mar. 1844,[7] Consul at Baltimore, Md., c. 1851–7 Dec. 1856 when he d. of suffocation when the rooming house in which he resided was destroyed by fire.[8] Backhouse thought that Kuper was one of the most underrated men in the diplomatic service, and severely criticized Palmerston for refusing to promote him despite the support he had received from the Duchess of Kent and others.[9]

1. O'Byrne, *Naval Biog. Dict.*, vol. 1, 623.
2. *Notes and Queries*, ser. 7, vol. 8, 493.
3. For whom see *D.N.B.*, vol. 11, 345.
4. Foster, *Alumni Oxon.*, vol. 2, 807.
5. F.O. 366/559.
6. Bindoff et al., *Br. Dip. Reps.*, 59–60.
7. *Gents. Mag.* (1844), pt. 1, 415.
8. *The Baltimore Sun*, 8 Dec. 1856, p. 1.
9. Backhouse to Aberdeen, Pyremont, 18 Sept. 1841, No. 2, Add. MS 43237 ff. 342–47.

120. Lamb, Thomas Davis. (1775–1818).

B. Aug. 1775 to Thomas Phillips Lamb, M.P. for Rye, Sussex, by Elizabeth Dorothy, dau. of D. Davis, ed. Westminster 1788–93, matric. Christ Church, Oxford 1793.[1] At Westminster he became a close friend of Robert Southey who called him one of his "two most intimate associates."[2] Private sec. 20 Feb. 1801–5 July 1802 when he res. to become M.P. for Rye to Oct. 1806. Private sec. to Liverpool when Liverpool was prime minister, d. unm.[1] 13 May 1818.

1. Barker and Stenning, *Old Westminsters*, vol. 2, 550.
2. Rev. Charles Cuthbert Southey (ed.), *Life and Correspondence of Robert Southey* (6 vols., London, 1849–50), vol. 1, 154.

121. Le Mesurier, John James. (1807–1834).

Baptised 30 Aug. 1807,[1] son of Rev. Thomas Le Mesurier, rector of Haughton-le-Skerne, co. Durham,[2] by Margaret, dau. of Rev. Dr. James Bandinel,[3] nephew of James Bandinel (see no. 15),[4] Foundation Scholar Charterhouse 11 Jan. 1819–1823, and received a grant to qualify him in foreign languages for public office 15 May 1824.[1] Clerk attached to Slave Trade Dept. 19 Apr. 1827. He became very ill in 1832[4] and sometime in 1833 was appointed attaché to Buenos Ayres where he hoped the warmer climate would aid in his recovery so that he could return to the F.O. where his clerkship remained in abeyance. When he failed to improve he set out to try the climate at Madeira and d. aboard ship 1 Mar. 1834.[5]

1. Marsh and Arthur, *Alumni Carthusiani*, p. 211.
2. For whom see Foster, *Alumni Oxon.*, vol. 3, 947.
3. *Gents. Mag.* (1800), pt. 2, 900.
4. Le Mesurier to Bandinel, 5 Craven Street, Strand, 1 Apr. 1832, F.O. 84/132.
5. Bandinel to Shee, F.O., 6 June 1834, F.O. 84/162.

122. Lenox-Conyngham, George William. (c. 1796–1866).

B. c. 1796 to George Lenox-Conyngham of Spring Hill, co. Londonderry, by Olivia, dau. of William Irvine of Castle Irvine, co. Fermanagh, half brother of William L-C. of Spring Hill, magistrate and deputy lieut. for co. Tyrone and co. Londonderry, m. Elizabeth, dau. of Robert Holmes, barrister at law in Dublin.[1] Supernumerary clerk 5 July 1812, clerk 5 July 1817, senior clerk 16 May 1834, chief clerk 5 Apr 1841 to his death 26 Nov. 1866. Conyngham, who lived at 69 Eaton Place, S.W. London,[2] had one leg amputated as a young man after he shot himself accidentally while getting into his carriage. He was "a very tall, stout, and heavy man," and was particularly formidable when changes in the humidity left his leg in great pain.[3] He was "a very able man and a most excellent public servant; he was always at the office, early and late, summer and winter, year after year."[4] Yet because his temper was short he had few intimates among his peers. He was continually provoking incidents with the undersecretaries,[5] and Edmund Hammond, who in many respects was like Conyngham, on one occasion purposely spoke well of Sir George Shee, the undersecretary (see no. 177), so that Conyngham would "go back to England with a favourable impression of that person, as I think that is the only chance of peace being maintained."[6]

1. *Burke's Landed Gentry of Ireland*, 4th ed., p. 176.
2. Dauglish and Stephenson, *Harrow Register*, p. 219 for his son.
3. Hertslet, *Recollections*, p. 143.
4. Tilley and Gaselee, *Foreign Office*, p. 63.
5. See for example Cromwell, "Incident at the F.O."
6. E. Hammond To T. Staveley, Napoli, 4 Jan. 1832, Barnes MSS.

123. Leveson, Lord (2d Earl Granville). See Leveson-Gower, Granville George. (no. 124).

124. Leveson-Gower, Granville George, Lord Leveson (2d Earl Granville). (1815–91).[1]

Undersecretary 6 Mar. 1840–3 Sept. 1841, secretary of state 1851–52, 1870–74, 1880–85.

1. *D.N.B.*, vol. 11, 1029.

125. Liddell, Henry Thomas. (c. 1798–1887).

Assistant sec. to the Levant Company before becoming clerk 5 Jan. 1824, asst. private sec. 5 Apr. 1824 while retaining clerkship,[1] res. 5 Jan. 1826 to become Consul at Göttenburg 3 June 1826–1 Jan. 1847,[2] ret. on pension £240 which lapsed in 1873 because he failed to claim it.[3] Howard de Walden called him "the finicking Tommy Liddell."[1] d. at The Abbey, Winchester, 8 Nov. 1887.[4]

1. Howard de Walden to Granville, Foreign Office, 3 May 1824, private, P.R.O. 30/29/6/7 ff. 1271–76.
2. *F.O. List*, 1854, p. 57.
3. "Superannuations in Public Offices," *P.P., 1874*, vol. 25, Command 71, p. 596.
4. *The Times*, 14 Nov. 1857, p. 1.

126. Lovell, John Harvey.

Son of Peter Harvey Lovell, esq., of Cole Park, Wilts.[1] Assistant decypherer 1827–44. Lovell was the nephew of Francis Willis (see no. 222)[2] and m. 1843 Emma, dau. of Christopher Bethell-Codrington, Esq., of Dodington Park, co. Gloucester.[3]

1. *Gents. Mag.* (1843), pt. 2, 428.
2. Memorandum, Addington, "Office of Secret Service Decypherer, Messrs. Willes & Lovell," Secret, F.O., 7 Oct. 1844, Add. MS 40551 ff. 400–3. Ellis, *The Post Office*, p. 131 errs in saying that Willes's assistant was Rev. William Willes Lovell.
3. *Burke's Peerage*, 6oth ed., p. 329.

127. Lowth, George Thomas. (1807–93).

B. 25 June 1807 to Rev. Robert Lowth of Hipton, Hants., Grove House, Chiswick,[1] and Prebend. of Winchester,[2] ed. Eton, matric. Magdelene Cambridge July 1824.[2] Clerk 5 Jan. 1826, leave of absence to recover his health Feb. 1837,[3] ret. ill-health 5 Apr. 1838 with pension £78.[4] He was J.P. and D.L. on his death at Kenegie, Ascot, 31 Dec. 1893.[1]

1. *The Times*, 4 Jan. 1894, p. 1.
2. Venn, *Alumni Cantab.*, vol. 4, 222.
3. Draft to Treasury, F.O., 28 Apr. 1838, F.O. 366/553.
4. "Superannuations in Public Offices," *P.P., 1839*, vol. 30, Command 151, p. 668.

128. McMahon, Edward. (c. 1803–74).

Clerk 14 July 1818, attached (retaining clerkship) to Legation at Stockholm 18 Mar. 1826–27 May 1828,[1] ret. impaired health 5 Jan. 1846[2] with pension £350 and a secret service allowance of £100 which was transferred to the consolidated fund in 1872.[3] d. 20 Aug. 1874.

1. *F.O. List*, 1875, p. 206.
2. "Superannuations in Public Offices," *P.P., 1847*, vol. 34, Command 222, p. 431.
3. "Superannuations in Public Offices," *P.P., 1873*, vol. 39, Command 129, p. 136.

129. Maddison, George. (1747–83).

B. 1747, bap. 2 Mar. 1748, to John Maddison of Hole House, Allensford, by Elizabeth, dau. of Thomas Todd of Bridge End, Frasterley.[1] Clerk in the Secret Dept. of the Post Office by 1763,[1] Sec. to Sir Joseph Yorke in the United Provinces 1773–80,[2] undersecretary 17 July 1782–15 Apr. 1783, appointed Sec. to the Duke of Manchester's extraordinary embassy to Spain 15 Apr. 1783,[3] Sec. of Embassy Paris 1783 where he d. 27 Aug. 1783 "supposed to have been accidentally poisoned."[4]

1. Ellis, *Post Office*, pp. 88, 94, 143.
2. Horn, *Br. Dip. Reps.*, pp. 26, 166.
3. Fox to Lord Chamberlain, St. James's, 15 Apr. 1783, F.O. 366/669, vol. 2, 37.
4. *Gents. Mag.* (1783), pt. 2, 805.

130. Mahon, Viscount (5th Earl Stanhope). See Stanhope, Philip Henry. (no. 186).

131. Manby, James. (1755–1786).

B. Amersham Bucks., bap. 30 May 1755, son of Edward Manby, Surgeon and his wife Judith, brother of John M., vicar of Lancaster 1806–44 and chaplain to the Duke of Sussex, King's Scholar at Eton 1767–71.[1] Manby, who had traveled in Italy and Spain and could translate Italian,[2] was appointed clerk 15 Aug. 1780, sec. (retaining clerkship) to the commission established in 1786 to deal with all matters of commerce between England and Spain after the American War for Independence with an allowance of £1 per diem,[3] and d. at Eton 4 Aug. 1786.[4]

1. Leigh, *Eton Register*, p. 352.
2. Aust to Hardwicke, Tuesday, 9 Jan. 1781, Add. MS 35617 ff. 166–67.
3. Carmarthen to Treasury, Whitehall, 8 Dec. 1786, Copy, F.O. 366/426 ff. 37–38.
4. *Gents. Mag.* (1786), pt. 2, 715.

132. Mann, Lucius Edward. (d. 1878).

Son of James Mann, Esq., of Hallow Park near Worcester, matric. St. Catherine's, Cambridge 1840, m. 1850 Charlotte, dau. of Captain Cockshutt Heathcote.[1] Clerk in the Librarian's Dept., c. 1843, when he was granted extraordinary leave of absence "for the temporary purpose of enabling him to complete his Education by keeping his Terms at the University of Cambridge."[2] d. 7 Dec. 1878.[1]

1. Venn, *Alumni Cantab.*, vol. 4, 309.
2. Draft letter of L. Hertslet, Foreign Office, 20 Feb. 1843, F.O. 83/241.

133. Masterton, Charles.

Clerk attached to Translator of Spanish, Portuguese, Italian, and Danish Languages 23 Oct. 1823[1]–1829. Consul in Bolivia March 1835,[2] replaced in Jan. 1847.[3] Masterton was a minor dramatist. He published three tragedies, *The Seducer* (1811), *Beativoglio* (1824), and *The Stern Resolve* (1837) as well as two dramatic romances, *The Wreck* (1824) and *The Blighted Love* (1832).[4] It is not likely that any of these was ever performed.

1. Planta to Canning, F.O., 23 Oct. 1823, *Secret and Confidential*, Canning MSS Bundle 136.
2. "Return of Consuls," *P.P., 1846*, vol. 44, Command 746, p. 119.
3. "List of Consuls," *P.P., 1847–48*, vol. 39, Command 989, p. 315.

4. Allardyce Nicholl, *A History of English Drama, 1660–1900* (2d ed.; 6 vols.; Cambridge, 1965–67), vol. 4, 353.

134. Meade, Richard Charles Francis Christian, 3d Earl (I), (1st Baron, U.K.) Clanwilliam. (1795–1879).[1]

Private Secretary 5 July 1817–5 July 1819, 5 Jan. 1820–29 Jan. 1822, acting undersecretary 29 Jan. 1822–5 Jan. 1823.

1. *D.N.B.*, vol. 13, 187.

135. Mellish, Richard Charles. (c. 1800–65).

B. c. 1800 to Joseph Charles Mellish, diplomatist[1] and friend of Canning,[2] by a German lady "of high blood & low fortune,"[3] ed. St. John's, Hamburg,[4] Trinity College Cambridge 1821–25 (B.A.).[5] Clerk 10 Oct. 1823, attached (retaining clerkship w/o pay) to embassy at Constantinople Mar. 1828–Mar. 1830[6] where he acquired such "a strong taste for Turkish & Russian Questions" that on his return to the F.O. he drafted for Palmerston "a Minute on the present state of the Russo-Turkish Question, as it effects Great Britain, in which there is considerable merit. . . ."[7] Mellish as a resident clerk in the 1830s occupied two rooms on the second floor of the F.O. and was responsible for receiving and sending to the undersecretaries dispatches that arrived out of office hours.[8] Senior clerk 21 Aug. 1841, sec. to earl of Wilton's special mission to Saxony Sept. 1842,[9] ret. poor health[10] 31 Dec. 1854 with pension £700, which was more than a full allowance for his years of service because of his excellence.[11] Mellish was a distant relative of Queen Adelaide[12] who supported his unsuccessful effort to become sec. of Embassy at Constantinople in 1834.[13] He was also a favorite of William IV and the FitzClarences.[14] K.H. 1832,[12] Gentleman Usher to Queen Adelaide 1834–49.[9] Like many others in the F.O. he resided in Eaton Place (#26).[10] Canning said he was "clever & well educated,"[3] and Leveson, who as undersecretary was his immediate superior, found him "more clever [than Ward, the other clerk assistant in Leveson's division (see no. 213)] but not so sensible I should think, or with so agreeable a manner."[15] d. 29 Dec. 1865.

1. For whom see Bindoff et al., *Br. Dip. Reps.*, pp. 68, 130.
2. Canning to Harrowby, South Hill, 2 Nov. 1804, Harrowby MSS vol. 9, ff. 159–60.
3. Canning to Liverpool, Paris, 5 Oct. 1826, Private & Confidential, Add. MS 38193 ff. 257–60.
4. Venn, *Alumni Cantab.*, vol. 4, 387.
5. J. C. Mellish to Canning, Hamburg, 5 July 1821, Canning MSS Bundle 145.
6. Boase, *Mod. Eng. Biog.*, vol. 2, 836.
7. Minute, Backhouse, 23 Nov. 1833, F.O. 96/17.
8. "A Return of All the House and Apartments . . . ," F.O., 25 Feb. 1831, F.O. 366/366 f. 161.
9. *F.O. List*, Jan. 1866, p. 177.
10. Mellish to Clarendon, 26 Eaton Place, 14 Dec. 1854, F.O. 366/553.
11. Treasury Minute, 26 Jan. 1855, ibid.

12. Strachey and Fulford, *Greville Memoirs*, vol. 2, 351 n. 1.
13. H. Taylor to Palmerston, Windsor Castle, 2 Apr. 1834, Private, Palmerston Papers RC/C/143.
14. Same to Same, Windsor Castle, 7 Apr. 1832, ibid., RC/C/31.
15. To Granville, Foreign Office, 10 Mar. 1840, P.R.O. 30/29/6/4 ff. 705–6.

136. Milbanke (-Huskisson), (Sir) John Ralph (8th Bart.). (1800–68).

B. 5 Nov. 1800 to Sir John Peniston Milbanke, 7th Bart., by Eleanor, dau. of Julines Hering, Esq., of Jamaica,[1] m. 1843 Emily, dau. of John Mansfield of Digswell House, Herts.[2] Clerk 10 Oct. 1823–5 July 1826, Sec. of Legation Frankfort Sept. 1826, Sec. of Embassy St. Petersburg Oct. 1835, Vienna Oct. 1838, E.E. and Min.P. Munich Nov. 1843, succeeded to Baronetcy 27 July 1850, E.E. and Min. P. The Hague Oct. 1862, ret. 29 Sept. 1867.[3] Milbanke's aunt was the wife of Rt. Hon. William Huskisson whose estates he inherited on her death.[2] By Royal License dated 5 Jan. 1866 he had his legal name changed to Milbanke-Huskisson in accordance with her will.[3] d. 30 Dec. 1868.

1. *Burke's Peerage*, 60th ed., p. 1008.
2. *The Times*, 4 Jan. 1869, p. 3.
3. Boase, *Mod. Eng. Biog.*, vol. 2, 870.

137. Mildmay, Hugo Cornwall St. John. (1807–49).

B. 13 May 1807 to Sir Henry Paulet St. John Mildmay, 3d Bart., M.P., by Jane, dau. of Carew Mildmay, Esq., of Shawford House, Herts.[1] Clerk 5 Jan. 1824, attached (retaining clerkship) to Embassy at Vienna where he served as Chargé d'Affaires 1838,[2] Sec. (retaining his clerkship) to Lord Ashburton's special mission to the U.S.A. 1841,[3] res. clerkship 8 Mar. 1844 to become Sec. of Legation Naples,[3] though there is no record of his having gone to his post.[4] d. unm.[1] 28 Jan. 1849.

1. *Burke's Peerage*, 60th ed., p. 1010.
2. Bindoff et al., *Br. Dip. Reps.*, p. 17.
3. Minute of Diplomatic Appointments approved by the Queen [27 Nov. 1843], Add. MS 43043 f. 236.
4. Bindoff et al., *Br. Dip. Reps.*, pp. 134–35.

138. Molyneux, Hon. Francis George. (1805–86).

B. 5 Mar. 1805 to William, 2d Earl of Sefton by Maria, dau. of William, 6th Lord Craven,[1] ed. Eton and Trinity College, Cambridge M.A.,[2] m. 1842 Lady Georgiana Ashburnham, dau. of George, 3d Earl of Ashburnham.[3] Clerk 31 Aug. 1827–10 Oct. 1835, Sec. of Legation Frankfort 13 Nov. 1835–47.[4] Aberdeen considered replacing him in 1841 when he failed to resign with the defeat of the Whigs in the election of 1841,[5] but did not do so. At his d. after a long illness at Earls Court, Tunbridge Wells, 24 May 1886,[6] he was J.P. for Kent and Sussex.[2]

1. *Burke's Peerage*, 60th ed., p. 1299.

2. Walford, *County Families*, p. 689.
3. Strachey and Fulford, *Greville Memoirs*, vol. 5, 41 n. 2.
4. *F.O. List*, 1854, p. 59.
5. Aberdeen to Backhouse, F.O., 27 Sept. 1841, Copy, Add. MS 43237 ff. 372–73.
6. *The Times*, 27 May 1886, p. 1.

139. Money, William. (c. 1739–1809).

Secretary to Onslow Burrish at Bavaria and the Circles of the Empire c. 1750–55, Sec. to Robert Keith at Vienna 1755–57, Sec. to Lord Stormont in Poland 1757–61, Chargé d'Affaires Poland 1761–62, Sec. to the Earl of Buckinghamshire at St. Petersburg 1762–65,[1] when he ret. with pension £100.[2] Clerk 15 Aug. 1780,[3] translated German documents for the Treasury 1784–87,[4] senior clerk 1792, ret. 29 Sept. 1794 because of age and ill-health with a pension equal to his salary of £380.[5] d. of apoplexy at his home, Dorsetplace, Stockwell, Surrey, 8 Aug. 1809.[6]

1. Horn, *Br. Dip. Reps.*, passim.
2. The Case of Mr. Money, late Secretary to the Earl of Buckinghamshire, [c. 1787], F.O. 366/313.
3. Stormont to Post Office, St. James's, Copy, 15 Aug. 1780, F.O. 366/669, vol. 1, f. 31.
4. Money to Carmarthen, Whitehall, 14 Apr. 1787, Add. MS 28062 ff. 155–56.
5. Grenville to Treasury, Downing Street, 31 Oct. 1794, Copy, F.O. 366/427 f. 107.
6. *Gents. Mag.* (1809), pt. 2, 789.

140. Moore, Francis. (1767–1854).

B. 1767 to John Moore, M.D., of Dovehill, physician and man of letters, by a dau. of Prof. Simson, a professor of Divinity at Glasgow University, brother of Gen. Sir. John Moore,[1] m. Frances, dau. of Sir William Twysden, 6th Bart. of Royden Hall, East Peckham, co. Kent, and widow of Archibald, 11th Earl of Eglington.[2] Clerk 5 July 1784,[3] private secretary 1784–91,[4] précis writer 1784–91,[5] deputy Gazette Writer 1790–31 Dec. 1796,[6] agent to several diplomatists,[7] one-third share in Rolleston's (see n. 150) army agency profits,[5] official observer of events in France both before and after the recall of Gower 1791–92,[8] senior clerk 5 Jan. 1799, Sec. of Legation (retaining clerkship) to Marquess of Cornwallis at Amiens 1802,[4] received an allowance of £547.11.6 "for bringing over the Definitive Treaty of Peace from Amiens," 1802,[9] ret. 5 Jan. 1803 with pension £800.[10] Deputy Sec. at War 21 Aug. 1803 when his F.O. pension ceased[10] to Dec. 1809,[11] ret. with pension £1800. Thomas Grenville told Lord Grenville that "Moore's retirement is a scandalous job. He retires by his own desire in perfect health with a pension of 1800 *l. per annum* after holding the office of Secretary *six years*."[12] d. on Island of Ischia, 11 Aug. 1854.[13]

1. *D.N.B.*, vol. 13, 810.
2. *Burke's Peerage*, 60th ed., p. 1458.
3. Carmarthen to Post Office, St. James's, 5 July 1784, F.O. 366/669, vol. 2, 87.
4. Hawkesbury to Lord President, Downing Street, 25 Jan. 1803, Copy, F.O. 366/671 ff. 221–22.
5. Moore to Grenville, 9 Jan. 1796 but actually 1797, Grenville MSS.

6. Nelson, *Home Office*, p. 147 n. 36.

7. Rolleston to Grenville, Downing Street, 1 Jan. 1797, Grenville MSS.

8. Moore to Burges, Paris, 4 Aug. 1791, *H.M.C. Fortescue*, vol. 2, 153–54; Burges to Auckland, Whitehall, 17 Aug. 1792, Private, *Auckland Corresp.*, vol. 2, 433.

9. "Report from the Committee on His Majesty's Civil List Revenue," *P.P., 1802–03*, vol. 5, Command 147, p. 366.

10. F.O. 366/380.

11. Ross, *Cornwallis Corresp.*, vol. 3, 383 n. 2.

12. [Cleveland Square, 12 Jan. 1810], *H.M.C. Fortescue*, vol. 10, 5.

13. *Gents. Mag.* (1854), pt. 2, 410.

141. Morier, Greville. (c. 1823–70).

B. c. 1823 to James Justinian Morier, diplomatist and novelist, by Harriet, dau. of William Fulke Greville,[1] ed. Harrow 1834–40, Monitor 1839, Head Boy 1840,[2] Christ Church, Oxford 1840–44 (B.A.).[3] Clerk 26 Aug. 1843, attached (retaining clerkship) to Lord Howden's special mission to the River Plate 25 Mar. 1847 then attached to Legation at Rio de Janeiro to Apr. 1848, senior clerk 1860,[4] ret. ill-health 1 Jan. 1868 with pension £300.[5] d. at Brighton 14 Dec. 1870.[6]

1. *D.N.B.*, vol. 13, 948.
2. Daughlish and Stephenson, *Harrow Register*, p. 154.
3. Foster, *Alumni Oxon.*, vol. 3, 983.
4. *F.O. List*, 1869, p. 138.
5. "Superannuations in Public Offices," *P.P., 1868–69*, vol. 34, Command 112, p. 509.
6. *The Times*, 21 Dec. 1870, p. 1.

142. Mulgrave, 1st Earl of. See Phipps, Henry. (no. 155).

143. Murray, James. (1806–78).

Clerk in the Navy Pay Office 23 Aug. 1823–11 Nov. 1826[1] when he became clerk in the F.O., assistant in the Consular Dept. 1830, worked on the Mercantile Marine Act 1846,[2] appointed in 1858 the first assistant undersecretary at the F.O. with special responsibility for consular affairs,[3] ret. 31 Mar. 1868 with pension £1,375.[4] Murray, who was a F.R.G.S., received a C.B. 7 Aug. 1869[4] and d. at his residence 149 Sloane Street, 19 Feb. 1878.[5]

1. *F.O. List*, 1853, p. 40.
2. *F.O. List*, 1879, p. 215.
3. Tilley and Gaselee, *Foreign Office*, p. 109.
4. Boase, *Mod. Eng. Biog.*, vol. 2, 1047, where his ret. date is given as 4 July.
5. *The Times*, 22 Feb. 1878, p. 1.

144. Noel, Charles Noel (3d Baron Barham and 1st Earl of Gainsborough, 2d creation.). (1781–1866).

B. 2 Oct. 1781 to Sir Gerard Noel Noel, Bart., by Dianna, Baroness Barham, dau. of Charles, 1st Baron Barham,[1] ed. Langley School, Kent, matric. but probably never resided Trinity College Cambridge 1801, matric. Lincoln's Inn 1803,[2] m. 1st 1809 Elizabeth, dau. of Thomas Walman,

Esq., of Poundsford Park, Somersetshire, 2d 1817 Elizabeth, dau. of the Hon. Sir George Grey, Bart., 3d 1820 Arabella, dau. of Sir James Hamlyn-Williams, Bart. of Cloveley, and 4th 1833 Frances, dau. of Robert, 3d Earl of Roden.[1] Clerk 2 July 1798–3 Apr. 1799. Noel was a nominal Whig and supported Grey's government on reform, though usually he refrained from political activity. He supported numerous charitable institutions, was the patron of seven livings, deputy lieut. for Rutlandshire and M.P. Rutlandshire 1812–14.[3] Succeeded as 3d Baron Barham 1823, cr. Earl of Gainsborough 1841.[1] d. 10 June 1866.

1. *Burke's Peerage*, 6oth ed., p. 604.
2. Venn, *Alumni Cantab.*, vol. 4, 557.
3. *Gents. Mag.* (1866), pt. 2, 258–59.

145. Oom, Adolphus Kent. (1807–59).

B. c. Apr. 1807 to Thomas Oom of Bedford Square[1] by Charlotte Augusta Oom the celebrated pianist[2] and later wife of Joseph Planta (see no. 157),[3] matric. Eton 1820.[4] Oom, whom his colleagues affectionately called "Dolphy,"[5] was appointed clerk to the Anglo-Spanish Commission 10 Oct. 1823,[6] clerk in F.O. 5 Apr. 1824, senior clerk 12 Dec. 1845, ret. ill-health[7] 31 Mar. 1859. Oom, who served as joint executor of Planta's estate and papers,[3] resided at no. 1 Duchess Street, Portland Place, London, d. 27 Oct. 1859 at Tunbridge Wells.[8]

1. *Gents. Mag.* (1807), pt. 1, 482.
2. *Gents. Mag.* (1854), pt. 1, 666; *Notes and Queries*, ser. 4, vol. 7, 379.
3. *Gents. Mag.* (1847), pt. 2, 87.
4. Stapylton, *Eton Lists*, p. 106.
5. G. C. Backhouse to J. Backhouse, Foreign Office, 15 Sept. 1838, Backhouse Papers.
6. *F.O. List*, 1853, p. 41.
7. Oom to Malmesbury, London, 31 Mar. 1859, F.O. 366/553.
8. *The Times*, 1 Nov. 1859, p. 1.

146. Osborne, Francis Godolphin, Marquess of Carmarthen and 5th Duke of Leeds. (1751–99).[1]

Secretary of state 23 Dec. 1783–Apr. 1791.

1. *D.N.B.*, vol. 14, 1180.

147. Paget, Augustus Berkeley. (1823–96).[1]

The *D.N.B.* says he was ed. privately but he was actually a Foundation Scholar at Charterhouse.[2] Clerk 21 Aug. 1841–25 June 1846, serving also as précis writer 6 Feb.–25 June 1846.

1. *D.N.B.*, vol. 22 (Supp.), 1111.
2. Boase, *Mod. Eng. Biog.*, vol. 6, 341–42.

148. Palmerston, 3d Viscount. See Temple, Henry John. (no. 200).

149. Parish, Henry Headley. (1801–75).

B. 6 July 1801 to Woodbine Parish, chairman of the Board of Excise in Scotland 1815–23, by Elizabeth, dau. of Rev. Henry Headley, rector of North Walsham co. Norfolk, brother of Sir Woodbine P. (see no. 150),[1] matric. but probably did not reside Caius College, Cambridge 1819[2] m. 1831 Caroline Lateward.[1] Clerk Nov. 1819–Aug. 1820, private sec. to Stratford Canning (see no. 39) at Washington Aug. 1820–Aug. 1823,[3] accompanied Stratford Canning to St. Petersburg in 1825,[4] employed by Backhouse (see no. 13) in very confidential work at the F.O. in 1828.[5] Parish was author of *The Diplomatic History of the Monarchy of Greece* (1838), *British Diplomacy Illustrated by an Old Public Servant* (1838), *England in 1839* (1839), and *The Diplomat Revelation* (1851).[2] d. 29 Mar. 1875.

1. Kay-Shuttleworth, *Life of Woodbine Parish*, passim, and appendix 1.
2. Venn, *Alumni Cantab.*, vol. 5, 21.
3. F.O. 366/559.
4. Lane-Poole, *Life of Stratford Canning*, vol. 1, 354.
5. Parish to S. Canning, F.O., 20 Sept. 1828, Confidential, F.O. 352/22/2.

150. Parish, (Sir) Woodbine. (1796–1882).[1]

Attached to Castlereagh's (see no. 190) special mission at Paris July–Dec. 1815, clerk Jan.–June 1816, attached to special mission for cession of Parga Oct. 1816–Dec. 1817, reappointed clerk Oct. 1817, served as part of the British delegation at Aix-la-Chapelle in 1818, [2] res. to enter diplomatic service Oct. 1823.

1. *D.N.B.*, vol. 15, 213.
2. W. Parish to Backhouse, Buenos Ayres, 25 July 1828, F.O. 366/560.

151. Parnther, Charles Henry. (1813–54).

B. 1 Oct. 1813, son of Robert Parnther, Barrister at law at the Inner Temple,[1] ed. Eton and Trinity College, Cambridge B.A. 1836.[2] Clerk in Slave Trade Dept. 8 Apr. 1835, dismissed sometime in 1836 but reinstated though not immediately after his father wrote in 1937 to Palmerston saying that he regretted his conduct at the F.O.[3] He remained in the office until 10 Sept. 1853, resided at Brompton,[4] and d. 11 Nov. 1854.

1. For whom see Foster, *Alumni Oxon.*, vol. 3, 1071.
2. Venn, *Alumni Cantab.*, vol. 5, 33.
3. Robert Parnther to Palmerston, 5 Grafton Street, 27 Sept. 1837, and Palmerston to R. Parnther, Windsor, 28 Sept. 1837, Copy, Palmerston Papers PAT/P/12/1–2.
4. *Gents. Mag.* (1855), pt. 1, 105.

152. Passmore, Udney. (c. 1793–1864).

Passmore, Planta said, was "some connection of [William] Hamilton's [see no. 86] family" and before coming to the F.O. had served five years as clerk to Mr. Rowcroft, later consul in Chile.[1] Clerk 15 Aug. 1817, served with Antrobus (see no. 8) (retaining his clerkship) while Antrobus was Chargé d'Affaires in Washington 1819–20,[1] res. 15 Apr. 1825 when he became consul at Arequipa, Peru until the post was abolished 1 Apr. 1837[2] when he received a compensation allowance £480.[3] Planta, who strongly supported his unsuccessful application for a consulship in 1823, said that "though his Qualifications are exactly what a Consul should have, they are not such as make him the sort of Person which I should wish always to see in this office," and urged Canning to appoint him quickly "and then give us a real good *Gentleman* to fill his Place in the Office."[1] d. at Pimlico 24 July 1864.[4]

1. Planta to Canning, F.O., 23 Oct. 1823, *Secret and Confidential*, Canning MSS Bundle 136.
2. *F.O. List.*, 1854, p. 60.
3. "Superannuations in Public Offices," *P.P.*, *1865*, vol. 31, Command 162, p. 521.
4. *The Times*, 29 July 1864, p. 1.

153. Pennell, John Croker. (1825–65).

B. 7 May 1825, son of William Pennell of East Moseley, Surrey,[1] Foundation Scholar Charterhouse 1835–43,[2] matric. Queen's, Cambridge 1843,[1] m. a dau. of Sir William Follett.[3] Pennell was appointed clerk 9 Mar. 1844 through the influence of his uncle, John Wilson Croker,[4] attaché (retaining clerkship) Washington 1849–51,[5] senior clerk 1863 until his d. of cancer[3] at Kensington Palace[6] 3 June 1865.

1. Venn, *Alumni Cantab.*, vol. 5, 85.
2. Marsh and Arthur, *Alumni Carthusiani*, p. 231.
3. *The Times*, 7 June 1865, p. 7.
4. W. Pennell to Croker, Portsmouth, 15 Mar. 1844, John Wilson Croker Papers, Duke University Library.
5. *F.O. List*, 1853, p. 41.
6. *Gents. Mag.* (1865), pt. 2, 124.

154. Pettingal, Charles. (1799–1845).

B. 1799, son of Captain Pettingal of Chelsea who served with Wellington in Spain.[1] Clerk in Slave Trade Dept. 22 Nov. 1825–10 Oct. 1843, Arbitrator on Mixed Anglo-Portuguese Commission for Suppressing the Slave Trade established under the Treaty of July 1842 at Boa Vista, Cape Verd Islands 28 Sept. 1843[2] to his d. there of an epidemic fever while in quarantine on a ship travelling from Boa Vista to St. Nicholas 5 Dec. 1845.[3]

1. Thomas Pettingal to Bandinel, Bagshot, 15 Nov. 1825, F.O. 84/46.
2. *Gents. Mag.* (1843), pt. 2, 536.
3. H. W. Macaulay to Aberdeen, Saint Nicholas, Cape Verd Islands, 10 Dec. 1845, No. 183, Extract, Great Britain, *British and Foreign State Papers*, 35 (1846–47), 372–73.

155. Phipps, Henry, 1st Earl of Mulgrave. (1755–1831).[1]

Secretary of state 5 Jan. 1805–Feb. 1806.

1. *D.N.B.*, vol. 15, 1191.

156. Pierrepont, Hon. Henry Manvers. (1780–1851).

B. 18 Mar. 1780 to Charles, 1st Earl Manvers, by Anne Orton, dau of William Mills, Esq., of Richmond, Surrey,[1] ed. Christ Church, Oxford, B.A.

1800, D.C.L. 1834,[2] m. 1818 Sophia, dau. of Henry, 1st Marquess of Exeter.[1] His only dau., Augusta, m. 1844 Lord Charles Wellesley and was the mother of the 3d and 4th Dukes of Wellington.[3] Private sec. 5 July 1802–5 July 1803. E.E. and Min. P. Sweden 20 Apr. 1804–19 Jan. 1807, special mission to Sweden 1 Mar.–13 Nov. 1807,[4] ret. on pension £1200.[5] Canning considered appointing him undersecretary in 1807, "But I doubt his liking it, and *I* should not like to offer and be refused."[6] Pierrepont, who was called "Poggy" by his friends,[7] was made a P.C. 1807.[3] He resided at Conholt Park, Hants.,[1] and was the last surviving member of the Dandy Club[2] when he d. 9 Oct. 1858.

1. *Burke's Peerage*, 6oth ed., p. 972.
2. Boase, *Mod. Eng. Biog.*, vol. 2, 1529.
3. Strachey and Fulford, *Greville Memoirs*, vol. 5, 282 n. 1.
4. Bindoff et al., *Br. Dip. Reps.*, pp. 150–51.
5. F.O. 366/460.
6. Canning to ?, 6 Aug. 1807, Aspinall, *Later Corresp. Geo. III*, vol. 4, 589 n.
7. Wellesley-Pole to Bagot, Savile Row, 6 Mar. 1818, Bagot, *Canning and Friends*, vol. 2, 70.

157. Planta, (Rt. Hon.) Joseph, Jr. (1787–1847).[1]

Clerk 27 Sept. 1802–5 July 1817, précis writer retaining clerkship with pay 5 Jan. 1809–5 July 1817, private sec. retaining clerkship and précis writership with pay 5 July 1814–5 July 1817, undersecretary 5 July 1817–19 Apr. 1827.

1. *D.N.B.*, vol. 15, 1284.

158. Ponsonby, John George Brabazon (5th Earl of Bessborough). (1809–80).

B. 4 Oct. 1809 to John, 4th Earl of Bessborough, Lord Lieut. co. Kilkenny, by Lady Maria Fane, dau. of John, 10th Earl of Westmorland,[1] ed. Charterhouse,[2] m. 1st 1835 Frances, dau. of John, 1st Earl of Durham, 2d 1849 Caroline, dau. of Charles, 5th Duke of Richmond.[1] Attached to Durham's special mission to Russia July–Oct. 1832,[3] précis writer 3 May 1833–17 Nov. 1834. M.P. for Bletchingley 1831, for Higham Ferrars 1831–32, for Derby 1835–47, Lord Lieut. co. Carlow 1838,[2] succeeded as 5th Earl 1847,[1] Master of the Buckhounds in Aberdeen's and Palmerston's administrations,[4] Lord Steward Jan.–July 1866, Dec. 1868–Mar. 1874.[2] d. 28 Jan. 1880.

1. *Burke's Peerage*, 6oth ed., p. 145.
2. Boase, *Mod. Eng. Biog.*, vol. 1, 261.
3. F.O. 366/329 f. 106.
4. Ponsonby, *Ponsonby Family*, p. 151.

159. Ponsonby (-Fane), (Sir) Spencer Cecil Brabazon. (1824–1915).

B. 14 Mar. 1824, brother of John Ponsonby (see no. 158), m. 1847 Louisa, dau. of Henry, 13th Viscount Dillon.[1] Supernumerary clerk 29 Oct.

APPENDIX I 303

1840, clerk 21 Aug. 1841, private sec. 1851–52, 1855–57,[1] res. clerkship 6 Dec. 1857. Comptroller of the Lord Chamberlain's Dept. 1857–1902 where he became in effect permanent undersecretary and attended all Court functions.[2] Gentleman Usher to the Sovereign 1859–1915 and Gentleman Usher to the Sword of State 1901–15, Bath King of Arms 1904–15, Ponsonby was a prominent member of the MCC for seventy-five years.[1] He loved the game and he played sometimes well but always with enthusiasm.[2] d. 1 Dec. 1915, the last survivor of those who served in the F.O. before 1846.

    1. Ponsonby, *Ponsonby Family*, pp. 159–63.
    2. *The Times*, 3 Dec. 1915, p. 11.

160. Quick, William Fortescue. (c. 1802–44).

B. c. 1802 son of William Quick of Tiverton, ed. Blundell's 2 Apr. 1813–29 Sept. 1817.[1] Quick was apparently one of Palmerson's constituents at Tiverton. Palmerston secured him a place in the Customs in 1836,[2] and when he later complained that after four years' service his prospects remained "truly deplorable" Palmerston appointed him clerk in the Librarian's Dept. 21 Aug. 1841[3] where he served until 19 Aug. 1844, when he died.[4]

    1. Fisher, *Blundell's Register*, p. 84.
    2. Quick to Palmerston, No. 6 Astle Street, Hoxton, 8 Aug. 1836 with minute, Palmerston, 8 Aug. 1836, Palmerston Papers PAT/Q/4.
    3. Same to [S. Cowper?], No. 2 Seymour Place, York Street, Walmouth Road, 26 June 1841 with unsigned minute, Lenox-Conyngham, 14 Aug. 1841, ibid., PAT/Q/7.
    4. *Records of the Foreign Office*, p. 153.

161. Robinson, Henry Stirling. (1807–33).

B. 27 July 1807 to Sir George Abercrombie Robinson, 1st Bart., military auditor general in Bengal and a Director of the East India Company, by Margaret, dau. of Thomas, 14th Earl of Suffolk and Berkshire.[1] Clerk 5 July 1826–27 Aug. 1829. d. unm. 1833.[1]

    1. *Burke's Peerage*, 23rd ed., p. 907.

162. Robinson, Thomas, 2d Baron Grantham. (1738–86).[1]

Secretary of state 17 July 1782–2 Apr. 1783.
    1. *D.N.B.*, vol. 17, 51.

163. Rolleston, Henry John. (1787–1834).

B. 18 Sept. 1787 to Stephen Rolleston (see no. 164), by Margaret Rolleston, Foundation Scholar Charterhouse 1799–1801 when he finished his education abroad.[1] Clerk 1 Feb. 1801, joint Translator of the German Language 7 Feb. 1806[2] –5 Apr. 1809,[3] senior clerk 5 Jan. 1824, Head of the Treaty Dept. 1825 to his d. at his residence in Hans Place, Chelsea 16 May 1834.[4]

    1. March and Arthur, *Alumni Carthusiana*, p. 184.

2. Minute, Fox, Downing Street, 7 Feb. 1806, F.O. 366/671 f. 303.
3. F.O. 366/380.
4. *Gents. Mag.* (1834), pt. 2, 108.

164. Rolleston, Stephen. (d. 1828).

Possibly the eldest son of Rev. Stephen Rolleston of Bridgepark, co. Cork, Rector of Knockmorne, by Eleanor Parr.[1] Clerk 31 July 1783, senior clerk 1794, deputy Gazette Writer 30 Jan. 1797,[2] Army agent for fencibles and some militia units by 1797,[3] Gazette Writer by letters patent 12 Dec. 1802[2] to his death, second chief clerk 10 Aug. 1804, assistant to the undersecretaries 1804–09,[4] declined appointment as undersecretary in 1806,[5] sole chief clerk 28 Sept. 1817–5 Jan. 1824 when he ret. with pension £1509.[6] Rolleston, who was noted for his "amiable qualities, and his kind and conciliatory disposition," d. in Brighton 19 Nov. 1828.[7]

1. *Burke's Landed Gentry of Ireland*, 4th ed., p. 609.
2. Minute, Rolleston, n.d., F.O. 366/413.
3. Moore to Grenville, 9 Jan. 1796 but really 1797, Grenville MSS.
4. "Establishment of the Secretary of State's Office for Foreign Affairs," a copy c. 1804 in Harrowby MSS vol. 33, f. 259, and a copy c. 1809 in F.O. 366/671.
5. Aspinall, *Later Corres. Geo. III*, vol. 4, 398 n. 1.
6. "Superannuations in Public Offices," *P.P., 1825*, vol. 19, Command 203, p. 264.
7. *Gents. Mag.* (1828), pt. 2, 476.

165. Ross, James Tyrell. (c. 1764–1830).

Private sec. to the Earl of Malmesbury on his special mission to Berlin 1793–94,[1] attached to Malmesbury's special missions to France 1796 and 1797,[2] granted pension £230 on 17 Nov. 1797, increased to £393 8 Dec. 1807.[3] Private sec. in F.O. 15 Apr. 1807–10 Oct. 1809. Planta said he was "an excellent person, and has worked very hard in his time. . . ."[4] d. at Avon Cottage, near Ringwood, 19 Feb. 1830.[5]

1. Diary, Thurs. 14 Nov. 1793, Malmesbury, *Diaries*, vol. 3, 5–6.
2. Ross to Malmesbury, Fludyer Street, 4 Nov. 1807, Malmesbury, *Series of Letters*, vol. 2, 61.
3. "Accounts Relating to Pensions," *P.P., 1820*, vol. 11, Command 140, p. 331.
4. Planta to Frederick Robinson, Foreign Office, 26 Mar. 1823, Private, Add. MS 38293 ff. 200–1.
5. *Gents. Mag.* (1830), pt. 1, 188.

166. Ruperti, G. Christian.

Younger son of the Master of the Mines and of the Mint in Hartz, Lower Saxony, studied to be a clergyman at the University of Helmstaat where he became c. 1781 the tutor of the sons of a Mr. Drake, an Englishman residing in Brunswick and married to a dau. of the Minister of the Interior of Brunswick. The Prince of Wales was his patron in England after he came to England in 1789 in the party of Sir Luke Stapleton, Bart., with whom he toured the continent of Europe. In 1789 he met C. R. Broughton (see no. 28) and William Fraser (see no. 73)[1] who employed him as his deputy Translator of the German Language since Fraser knew no German. After

Fraser's death in 1802 Ruperti continued to perform the duties of the Translator and from 5 Jan. 1806–5 Apr. 1809 when the post was abolished he was a joint Translator with H. Rolleston (see no. 163) and T. Bidwell Jr. (see no. 24), though he apparently did all the work.[2]

1. Broughton, memo, [Jan., 1810], F.O. 83/17.
2. Ruperti to Wellesley, F.O., 17 Jan. 1810, ibid.

167. Ryder, Dudley, 1st Earl of Harrowby. (1762–1847).[1]

Undersecretary 24 Aug. 1789–20 Feb. 1790, secretary of state 14 May 1804–5 Jan. 1805.

1. *D.N.B.*, vol. 17, 531.

168. Ryder, Hon. Frederick Dudley. (1806–82).

B. 11 July 1806 to Dudley, 1st Earl of Harrowby (see no. 167), by Susan, dau. of Granville, 1st Marquess of Stafford,[1] ed. Charterhouse,[2] Trinity College, Cambridge M.A. 1827,[3] m. 1839 Marian Charlotte Emily, dau. of Thomas Cockayne of Ickleford House, near Hitchin, Herts.[4] Clerk 5 Jan. 1827–29 Oct. 1834 when he was probably forced to resign.[5] d. at Ickleford House, Hitchin, 19 Nov. 1882.

1. *Burke's Peerage*, 6oth ed., p. 706.
2. *The Times*, 21 Nov. 1882, p. 1.
3. Venn, *Alumni Cantab.*, vol. 5, 394.
4. Walford, *County Families*, p. 851 under her name.
5. See Byng to Granville, 24 Aug. 1832, P.R.O. 30/29/7/13 ff. 897–902 announcing the forced resignation of Richard Edwardes (see no. 59) and stating that "Fredk. Ryder will follow soon."

169. Sasse, Frederick Richard. (c. 1816–79).

Sec. of the Mixed British and French Fishery Regulations Commission Aug. 1841–Sept. 1843,[1] clerk attached to the Librarian's Dept. 10 Nov. 1844 to his d. at his residence 19 Fawcett Street, South Kensington,[2] 4 June 1879.

1. *F.O. List*, 1853, p. 42.
2. *The Times*, 7 June 1879, p. 1.

170. Saunders, (Sir) Sydney Smith. (c. 1804–84).

B. c. 1804 to William Saunders of Wandsworth[1] by a dau. of Stephen Rolleston (see no. 164).[2] Clerk in Consular Dept. 5 July 1826–18 Apr. 1835. Consul in Albania 18 Apr. 1835,[1] Consul at Alexandria 1859,[3] Consul-Gen. Ionian Islands 1864–1870[1] when the office was abolished and he ret. on a pension £833.6.8.[4] By Letters Patent Knight of the Greek Royal Order of the Redeemer[1] 10 May 1873.[3] d. at his residence Gatestone, Upper Norwood 15 Apr. 1884.[5]

1. Boase, *Mod. Eng. Biog.*, vol. 3, 420.
2. Saunders to Palmerston, Foreign Office, 21 Feb. 1832, Palmerston Papers PAT/S/11/1–2.

3. *F.O. List*, 1885, pp. 214–15.
4. "Superannuations in Public Office," *P.P.*, *1871*, vol. 37, Command 155, p. 508.
5. *The Times*, 17 Apr. 1884, p. 6.

171. Scheener, Edward S. (c. 1791–1853).

B. c. 1791, a natural son of Edward, Duke of Kent, 4th son of George III,[1] m. Harriet, dau. of David Boyne.[2] Clerk in Council Office 6 Sept. 1806[3] to appointment as clerk in F.O. 5 Aug. 1809, private sec. to the Duke of Clarence (retaining clerkship) at Boulogne and Paris 1814.[4] The expense of Scheener's service abroad was the source of a long and unpleasant solicitation on his part from 1821 to 1823 to be reimbursed for his financial losses.[5] At the outset of his appeal Scheener was described as "a very efficient Clerk,"[4] but when his persistent efforts to secure a favorable review of his case despite previous Treasury and F.O. rejections culminated in a law suit against Planta, Canning suspended him from attendance at the office.[6] He apparently later dropped the suit when Canning threatened to dismiss him.[7] In 1826, however, he had another dispute with his superiors[8] and though he continued to receive his salary he was suspended from attendance at the office[9] until he was ret. 5 July 1830 with compensation allowance £272.10.0 on the retrenchment of the second class clerkships.[10] d. 31 Jan. 1853.

1. Duke of Clarence to Lord F. Conynham, Bushy House, 12 Aug. 1823, Add. MS 41315 f. 139.
2. *Gents. Mag.* (1852), pt. 1, 315.
3. "Memorandum as to Mr. Scheener's Claim . . . ," F.O. 95/591.
4. Minute, Planta and Hamilton, F.O., 28 Nov. 1821, ibid.
5. Temperley, *For. Pol. Canning*, pp. 262–63, gives a sketchy account of the affair. The papers are all in F.O. 95/591.
6. Backhouse to Scheener, Foreign Office, 8 Feb. 1823, Copy, F.O. 95/591.
7. Draft to Treasury, Foreign Office, Aug. 1823, ibid.
8. Scheener's accounts of the incident are in Edward Scheener, *Memoir of an Employé Most Respectfully Addressed to the King* (London, 1830), and Edward Scheener, *Statement of Facts Most Respectfully Submitted to His Majesty's Ministers 3d Nov. 1830* (London, 1830).
9. Draft to Treasury, F.O., Mar. 1830, F.O. 366/553.
10. "Superannuations in Public Offices," *P.P.*, *1854*, vol. 39, Command 125, p. 659.

172. Scott, Charles. (1811–41).

B. 1811 to Sir Walter Scott, Bart., man of letters, by Margaret Charlotte, dau. of John Carpenter of Edinburgh, ed. Brasenose, Oxford B.A. 1827, M.A. 1834.[1] Scott was appointed clerk 5 Jan. 1828 through the patronage of the king whose admiration of his father was as genuine as it was great.[2] Scott was still a clerk when he d. unm.[3] while temporarily serving as attaché in Tehran in 1841.[1] He was remembered as a man "of a reserved and diffident temper and disposition, but possessed of considerable intelligence and a fund of quiet humour, which he delighted to exercise among his friends."[4]

1. Foster, *Alumni Oxon.*, vol. 4, 1263.

2. Sir Walter Scott to Knighton, Edinburgh, 15 Nov. 1827, Knighton, *Memoirs*, vol. 1, 387–89, describing his son as being "of excellent disposition, clever and steady, well-informed, and of a good person and address . . . ," and as "the nearest object of my heart"; Fulford, *George the Fourth*, p. 256.
3. *Burke's Peerage*, 8th ed., p. 879.
4. *Gents. Mag.* (1842), pt. 1, 230–31.

173. Scott, Henry Charles. (d. 1857).

Clerk attached to the Treaty Dept. 2 Nov. 1842–10 Dec. 1853.

174. Scott, Henry Dundas. (c. 1797–1866).

Clerk attached to Chief Clerk's Dept. 5 July 1814–18 June 1866 when he ret. ill-health on pension £645.[1] d. at his residence 10 Eccleston Street, Chester Square, London 30 Oct. 1866.[2]

1. "Superannuations in Public Office," *P.P., 1867–68*, vol. 41, Command 177, p. 483.
2. *The Times*, 1 Nov. 1866, p. 1.

175. Seale, Robert Bewick. (1815–81).

B. 12 Feb. 1815 to Sir John Henry Seale, 1st Bart. of Dartmouth, M.P., by Paulina Elizabeth, dau. of Sir Paul Jodrell,[1] admitted to Middle Temple 1835, ed. Trinity Hall, Cambridge B.A. 1839.[2] Seale worked in the London Custom House[3] before becoming clerk attached to the Slave Trade Dept. 21 Aug. 1841 until he was dismissed 23 Oct. 1844.[4] His father was a loyal Whig M.P. and his appointment as clerk in the F.O. was a political favor.[5] Seale declined Melbourne's offer of a position in the Treasury because his father preferred having him at the F.O.[6] d. unm. 1881.

1. *Burke's Peerage*, 60th ed., p. 1296.
2. Venn, *Alumni Cantab.*, vol. 5, 453.
3. Sir John Seale to Palmerston, Mount Boone, 12 Aug. 1841, Palmerston Papers PAT/S/30.
4. *Records of the Foreign Office*, p. 154.
5. Seale to Palmerston, Mount Boone, 6 Aug. 1841, Private, ibid., PAT/S/29/1.
6. Same to Same, Brooks's, 17 Aug. [1841], Most Private, ibid., PAT/S/31.

176. Seymour, (Sir) George Hamilton. (1797–1880).[1]

Précis writer 5 Jan. 1821–29 Jan. 1822, private sec. 29 Jan.–10 Oct. 1822.
1. *D.N.B.*, vol. 17, 1259.

177. Shee, Sir George, 2d Bart. (1784–1870).

B. 14 June 1784 to Sir George Shee, 1st Bart., Irish borough monger, politician, and undersecretary in the H.O. 1800–03, in W.O. 1806–07, by Elizabeth Maria, dau. of James Crisp, Esq.,[1] ed. Sandy Mount near Dublin, St. John's, Cambridge B.A. 1806, M.A. 1811,[2] m. 1st 1808 Jane, dau. of William Young of Hexton House, Herts., 2d 1841 Sarah, dau. of Henry Bowett of Denton, co. Norfolk.[3] While at Cambridge Shee met and became friends with Palmerston (see no. 200).[4] Succeeded as 2d Bart. 3 Feb. 1825,[5] High Sheriff of co. Galway,[6] undersecretary 26 Nov. 1830–14 Nov. 1834.

Shee was appointed E.E. and Min. P. to Berlin in 1834 but did not go to his post before the Whigs were dismissed from office.[7] E.E. and Min. P. Würtemberg 1836–44, Min. P. Baden 1841–44.[8] d. at his residence in Grosvenor Place 25 Jan. 1870.[3]

1. Ross, *Cornwallis Corresp.*, vol. 3, 108 n. 5.
2. Venn, *Alumni Cantab.*, vol. 5, 485.
3. *The Times*, 28 Jan. 1870, p. 10.
4. Their extant correspondence for 1806–34 is in Palmerston Papers GC/SH/72–100.
5. Boase, *Mod. Eng. Biog.*, vol. 3, 533.
6. Case of Sir George Shee, Baronet, Dublin, 9 Sept. 1828, Add. MS 40335 ff. 183–84.
7. William IV to Wellington, Pavillion, Brighton, 28 Nov. 1834, Wellington Papers.
8. Bindoff et al, *Br. Dip. Reps.*, pp. 19, 197.

178. Sheridan, Richard Brinsley. (1751–1816).[1]

Undersecretary 22 Mar.–4 July 1782.

1. *D.N.B.*, vol. 18, 78.

179. Skelton, George. (c. 1830–65).

Clerk attached to Slave Trade Dept. 28 Feb. 1845–1 Dec. 1856, Arbitrator on various mixed commission courts established at Sierra Leone for the suppression of the slave trade 1856–59, Judge at Sierra Leone on these courts 1859–62, Judge of Mixed U.S.-U.K. Court at Sierra Leone 1862[1] to his d. there of fever on 22 May 1865 after nine days' illness.[2]

1. *F.O. List*, Jan. 1866, p. 178.
2. William Smith to Earl Russell, Sierra Leone, 20 June 1865, *Br. and For. St. Paps.*, vol. 56 (1865–66), 1193.

180. Smith, Culling Charles. (1775–1853).

B. 1775 to Charles Smith, Gov. of Madras,[1] by Xavier Charlotte, dau. of James Francis Law, commander-in-chief of the troops of the French East India Company,[2] ed. possibly Harrow May 1792–1793,[3] matric. Christ Church, Oxford 1793,[4] m. 1799[2] Anne, dau. of Garret, 1st Earl of Mornington.[5] Undersecretary 12 Nov. 1809–18 Feb. 1812, agent for Sir Henry Wellesley (see no. 216) while Wellesley was in Spain.[6] Commissioner of Customs 1827–53, a position he secured from Liverpool on the patronage of the Duke of Wellington and which Liverpool said was "one of the best offices I ever had to dispose of."[7] Smith tried unsuccessfully in 1827 to resign his place in favor of an appointment as Comptroller of Army Accounts because "there is attached to the office, of Receiver General, the necessity of giving high securities, which at this moment embarrasses me very painfully, because it interferes with certain family arrangements I am called upon to make."[8] d. at the house of his son-in-law the Duke of Beaufort, in Arlington Street, 26 May 1853.[2]

1. Strachey and Fulford, *Greville Memoirs*, vol. 1, 61 n. 1.
2. *Gents. Mag.* (1853), pt. 2, 93.
3. W. T. J. Gun (ed.), *The Harrow School Register, 1571–1800* (London, 1934), p. 129.

4. Foster, *Alumni Oxon.*, vol. 4, 1311.
5. *Burke's Peerage*, 6oth ed., p. 1510.
6. Smith to Hamilton, 36 Upper Brook Street, 16 Feb. 1814, F.O. 72/166 ff. 146–47.
7. To Arbuthnot, Fife House, 8 Sept. 1826, Yonge, *Liverpool*, vol. 3, 392.
8. Smith to Liverpool, Receiver General's Office Customs, 27 Sept. 1826, Private, and Liverpool to Smith, Walmer Castle, 30 Sept. 1826, Copy, Liverpool Scrapbook, f. 50.

181. Smith, Lt. Col. (Sir) George.

Private sec. 5 Jan. 1805–7 Feb. 1806, col. of the 82d Foot 1799, knighted 9 Dec. 1807 while serving as A.D.C. to the king.[1] Later served as military liaison officer between Spanish and British Generals in Spain in 1808.[2]

1. Aspinall, *Later Corresp. Geo. III*, vol. 4, 301 n. 2.
2. Mulgrave to George III, Admiralty, 7 July 1808, ibid., vol. 5, 100 and n. 1.

182. Smythe, George Sydney (7th Viscount Strangford). (1818–57).[1]

Undersecretary 26 Feb.–25 June 1846.

1. *D.N.B.*, vol. 18, 601.

183. Sneyd, Jeremy.

B. in Ireland, from a prominent Staffordshire family, recommended to the Duke of Bedford by Sir Richard Boxley,[1] appointed clerk 4 Dec. 1750,[2] chief clerk 1781,[3] ret. 18 Apr. 1792.[4] Agent for Sir Robert M. Keith 1769–92.[5]

1. Thomson, *Secretaries of State*, appendix XI, p. 179.
2. Aldworth to Post Office, Whitehall, 4 Dec. 1750, S.P. 44/136 f. 113.
3. *Royal Kalendar*, 1782, p. 110.
4. Grenville to Post Office, Whitehall, 18 Apr. 1792, Copy, F.O. 366/670 ff. 125–26.
5. Add. MSS 35503–35544 passim.

184. Somerville, (Sir) William Meredyth (3d Bart. and 1st Baron Meredyth).

Clerk 1 Sept.–Nov. 1826, unpaid attaché Berlin Nov. 1826,[2] paid attaché Berlin 6 Nov. 1829–19 Dec. 1832.[3]

1. *D.N.B.*, vol. 18, 666.
2. Somerville's memo in Brook Taylor to Backhouse, 5 Apr. 1828, F.O. 366/560.
3. *F.O. List*, 1854, p. 61.

185. Spring-Rice, Hon. Charles William. (1819–70).

B. 10 Jan. 1819 to Thomas, 1st Baron Monteagle, by Lady Theodosia Pery, dau. of Edmond, 1st Earl of Limerick,[1] ed. privately, matric. Trinity College, Cambridge 1837, M.A. 1840,[2] m. 1855 Elizabeth Margaret, dau. of William Marshall, Esq. M.P., of Halsteads and Petterdale Hall, co. Cumberland.[1] Supernumerary clerk 15 Dec. 1839, clerk 5 Jan. 1840, attached to Clarendon's mission to Paris 1856, senior clerk 1857, Supt. of Commercial and Consular Dept. 1866,[3] assistant undersecretary with special responsibility for consular affairs 31 Mar. 1868. Spring-Rice was interested in the reform of the F.O. but died before his ideas could make an impact on official practices.[4] d. at Folkstone 13 July 1870.[5]

1. *Burke's Peerage*, 38th ed., p. 824.
2. Venn, *Alumni Cantab.*, vol. 5, 611.
3. *F.O. List*, Jan. 1871, p. 199.
4. Tilley and Gaselee, *Foreign Office*, p. 109.
5. *The Times*, 18 July 1870, p. 1.

186. Stanhope, Philip Henry, Viscount Mahon (5th Earl Stanhope). (1805–75).[1]

Undersecretary 15 Dec. 1834–17 Apr. 1835. Declined to resume the undersecretaryship in 1841,[2] and refused the mission at Madrid in 1843 because of the illness of his mother and the advice of his doctors that the climate would be harmful to his children.[3] Lord Macaulay thought him "a violent Tory, but a very agreeable companion, and a very good scholar."[4]

1. *D.N.B.*, vol. 18, 927.
2. Philip Henry, 5th Earl Stanhope, *Notes of Conversations with the Duke of Wellington, 1831–1851* (London, 1888), p. 267.
3. Mahon to Aberdeen, Grosvenor Place, 18 Aug. 1843, Add MS 43241 ff. 175–76.
4. T. B. Macaulay to Hannah More Macaulay, London, 30 May 1831, Trevelyan, *Macaulay*, vol. 1, 192.

187. Stapleton, Augustus Granville. (1801–80).[1]

Clerk 10 Oct. 1823–31 Aug. 1827, private sec. retaining clerkship with pay 5 Apr. 1824–31 Aug. 1827.

1. *D.N.B.*, vol. 13, 981.

188. Staveley, Thomas. (1792–1862).

Clerk in the Navy Office for eight months in 1812,[1] supernumerary clerk in F.O. 5 July 1814, served in Paris as sec. to Mixed Commission appointed under additional Articles of the Treaty of Peace with France 1814,[2] clerk 28 Sept. 1817, senior clerk 5 Apr. 1839, Supt. of Slave Trade Dept. 12 Dec. 1845, Supt. of Consular Dept. 1 Oct. 1851[1] to his ret. ill-health[3] 12 Mar. 1857[1] as first senior clerk with a pension, the highest allowed by law for civil servants of his experience,[4] £933.10.10.[5] Staveley was for some years before his death a member of the Council of the Royal Geographical Society.[6] d. suddenly at Southborough, near Tunbridge Wells, 8 Dec. 1862.[7]

1. Printed "Draft Particulars required . . . in reference to each Person recommended for a Superannuation Allowance," Thomas Staveley, 13 Mar. 1857, F.O. 366/553.
2. *F.O. List*, 1853, p. 43.
3. Staveley to Clarendon, Brighton, 1 Dec. 1856, F.O. 366/553.
4. Trevelyan to Hammond, Treasury Chambers, 3 Apr. 1857, ibid.
5. "Superannuations in Public Offices," *P.P., 1857–58*, vol. 34, Command 169, p. 431.
6. *F.O. List*, 1863, p. 165.
7. *Gents. Mag.* (1863), pt. 1, 133.

189. Staveley, Thomas George. (1825–87).

Son of Thomas Staveley (see no. 188), clerk 26 Aug. 1843, senior clerk 1860,[1] received a compensation allowance £487 p.a. on the abolition of F.O. agencies in 1870,[2] ret. 1 May 1885. d. at 6 York Terrace, Sidmouth, South Devon, 29 Dec. 1887.[3]

1. *F.O. List*, 1888, p. 219.
2. "Superannuations in Public Offices," *P.P.*, *1871*, vol. 37, Command 155, p. 444.
3. *The Times*, 31 Dec. 1887, p. 1.

190. Stewart, Robert, Viscount Castlereagh and 2d Marquess of Londonderry. (1769–1822).[1]

Secretary of state 4 Mar. 1812–12 Aug. 1822.

1. *D.N.B.*, vol. 18, 1233.

191. St. John, St. Andrew (13th Baron St. John). (1759–1817).

B. 22 Aug. 1759, second son of John, 11th Baron St. John, by Susanna Louisa, dau. of Peter Simond, Esq.,[1] London merchant,[2] ed. Easton School near Stamford,[3] Lincoln's Inn 1773, called to the bar 1782,[2] matric. St. John's, Cambridge 1776,[3] m. 1807 Louisa, dau. of Sir Charles William Rouse-Boughton, Bart., M.P.[1] St. John, who was a Foxite M.P. for co. Bedford 1780–1806,[2] was undersecretary 2 Apr.–19 Dec. 1783. He was part of the committee managing the trial of Warren Hastings in 1787,[2] succeeded his brother as 13th Baron 1805,[1] became a Privy Councillor 12 Feb. 1806, Capt. of the Gentlemen Pensioners 1806–07.[2] d. 15 Oct. 1817.

1. *Burke's Peerage*, 6oth ed., p. 1273.
2. Namier and Brooke, *History of Parlt.*, vol. 3, 401.
3. Venn, *Alumni Cantab.*, vol. 5, 400.

192. Stopford (-Sackville), William Bruce. (1806–72).

B. 1 Apr. 1806 to Rev. Richard Bruce Stopford, Canon of Windsor, Prebendary of Hereford, and later chaplain to Queen Victoria, by Eleanor, dau. of Thomas, 1st Lord Lilford, m. 1837 Caroline Harriet, dau. of Hon. George Germain and niece and representative of Charles, 2d Viscount Sackville and 5th and last Duke of Dorset.[1] Clerk 5 Jan. 1826, resident clerk with Mellish (see no. 135) at F.O. in 1830s,[2] ret. 6 Aug. 1843. Stopford later acquired Drayton House, Thrapston, co. Northampton, which had been the seat of the 1st Viscount Sackville.[1] He assumed the additional name of Sackville in 1870.[3] d. at 7 Grosvenor Gardens, London, 29 May 1872.[4]

1. *Burke's Peerage*, 6oth ed., p. 360.
2. "A Return of all the Houses and Apartments . . . ," F.O., 25 Feb. 1831, F.O. 366/366 f. 161.
3. *Burke's Peerage*, 99th ed., pp. 486–87.
4. *The Times*, 31 May 1872, p. 1.

193. Sulivan, Stephen Henry. (1812–57).

B. c. Nov. 1812[1] to Lawrence Sulivan, Deputy Secretary at War and Commissioner of the Royal Military Asylum, by Elizabeth, dau. of Henry, 2d Viscount Palmerston,[2] ed. privately and St. John's, Cambridge.[3] Clerk 17 Aug. 1832–16 Nov. 1834, précis writer (retaining clerkship w/o pay) 16 Nov. 1832–3 May 1833, private sec. (retaining clerkship w/o pay) 3 May 1833–16 Nov. 1834. Paid attaché The Hague 16 Nov. 1834, Lisbon 1835, Sec. of Legation Lisbon 1836, Turin 1837, Munich 1839, Commissioner at Naples with Sir Woodbine Parish (see no. 150) to liquidate claims arising out of the sulphur monopoly 1840–41, Sec. of Legation Munich 1841, Consul-Gen. and Chargé d'Affaires Chili 1849,[4] Consul-Gen. and Chargé d'Affaires Peru 17 Jan. 1853 to his assassination there 11 Aug. 1857.[5] Palmerston, who was Sulivan's uncle, said that he "does his duty extremely well, and shews much industry and intelligence."[6]

1. *Gent's Mag.* (1812), pt. 2, 492.
2. *Burke's Peerage*, 23d ed., p. 833.
3. Venn, *Alumni Cantab.*, vol. 6, 80.
4. *F.O. List*, Jan. 1858, p. 96.
5. Boase, *Mod. Eng. Biog.*, vol. 3, 822; *Gents. Mag.* (1857), pt. 2, 567 gives his d. as 13 Aug.
6. To William Temple, Foreign Office, 25 June 1833, Dalling and Bulwer, *Life of Palmerston*, vol. 2, 164.

194. Synge, William Webb Follett. (1826–91).[1]

Clerk 26 June 1846–27 Dec. 1861.

1. *D.N.B.*, vol. 19, 283.

195. Talbot, Robert.

Private sec. 12 Dec. 1806–5 Apr. 1807.

196. Taylor, Bridges. (1815–96).

B. 1815 to Edward Taylor, M.P., of Bifrons, Kent, elder brother of Sir Herbert T. (see no. 198), Sir Brook T. (see no. 197), and William Watkinson T. (see no. 199), by Louisa, dau. of Rev. J. C. Beckingham.[1] Deputy Clerk of the Signet for his uncle Sir Brook T., clerk in Audit Office 1832–34, clerk in F.O. 29 Oct. 1834, attaché in Hanover (retaining clerkship) 1838, précis writer (retaining clerkship w/o pay) Mar.—Dec. 1852,[2] res. from F.O. and became Consul at Elsinore 14 Dec. 1852[3] –Apr. 1871[4] when the office was abolished and he received a compensation allowance £466.13.4[5] which was augmented in 1875 by an additional allowance of £19.6.0 p.a.[6] d. at his residence 6 Montpelier Square 20 Dec. 1896.[7]

1. *Burke's Landed Gentry*, vol. 2, 1363.
2. *F.O. List*, 1853, p. 44.
3. F.O. 366/462.

4. *F.O. List*, 1897, p. 235.
5. "Superannuations in Public Offices," *P.P., 1872*, vol. 36, Command 141, p. 418.
6. "Superannuations in Public Offices," *P.P., 1876*, vol. 42, Command 136, p. 462.
7. *The Times*, 22 Dec. 1896, p. 1, which adds "New Zealand papers please copy."

197. Taylor, (Rt. Hon. Sir) Brook. (1776–1846).

B. 30 Dec. 1776 to Rev. Edward Taylor of Bifrons, Kent, rector of Patrixbourne,[1] by Margaret, dau. of Thomas Payler of Ileden, Kent,[2] brother of Sir Herbert T. (see no. 198) and twin of William Watkinson T. (see no. 199). Clerk Dec. 1793–5 July 1798, private sec. 5 Jan. 1796 (retaining clerkship w/o pay[3])–20 Feb. 1801, précis writer (retaining private secretaryship with pay) 5 July 1798–20 Feb. 1801. Clerk of the Signet worth £270 p.a. Jan. 1801[4] to his death, Min. P. Cologne 1801–06, Hesse-Cassel 1801–06,[5] ret. on pension £1,200[6] which was in abeyance temporarily while he was E.E. and Min. P. *ad. int.* Denmark 1807,[5] and then resumed[6] until he undertook a special mission to the Hague 1814, E.E. and Min. P. Würtemberg 1814, Munich 1820, Berlin 1828[5] to his ret. with pension £1,500 on 1 Nov. 1830.[6] After his retirement Taylor briefly headed an unofficial mission to Rome 1831.[5] Grenville told Fox he was "a very discreet, prudent, and excellent young man, and I can with great confidence recommend him to your protection."[7] d. unm. at his residence in Eaton Place 15 Oct. 1846.[1]

1. *Gents. Mag.* (1847), pt. 1, 82.
2. *D.N.B.*, vol. 9, 413.
3. Minute, Grenville, Downing Street, 24 Feb. 1796, F.O. 366/670 f. 371.
4. F.O. 366/366 f. 33.
5. Bindoff et al., *Br. Dip. Reps.*, passim.
6. F.O. 366/460.
7. Downing Street, 6 Mar. 1806, *H.M.C.Fortescue*, vol. 8, 49.

198. Taylor, (Rt. Hon. Sir) Herbert. (1775–1839).[1]

Clerk 2 Aug. 1792–Dec. 1793.

1. *D.N.B.*, vol. 19, 413.

199. Taylor, William Watkinson. (1776–97).

B. 30 Dec. 1776, twin of Sir Brook T. (see no. 197), clerk Dec. 1793–5 July 1797 when he drowned in the Thames near Richmond Bridge when the boat in which he and his brothers Herbert and Brook were sailing capsized.[1]

1. Taylor, *Taylor Papers*, pp. 45, 51.

200. Temple, Henry John, 3d Viscount Palmerston. (1784–1865).[1]

Secretary of state 21 Nov. 1830–16 Nov. 1834, 18 Apr. 1835–1 Sept. 1841, 6 July 1846–Dec. 1851.

1. *D.N.B.*, vol. 19, 496.

201. Temple, Hon. (Sir) William. (1788–1856).

B. 19 June 1788 to Henry, 2d Viscount Palmerston, by Mary, dau. of Benjamin Thomas Mee of Bath,[1] ed. Harrow, St. John's, Cambridge, M.A. 1808,[2] brother of 3d Viscount Palmerston (see no. 200). Attaché The Hague Jan.–Sept. 1814, Sec. of Legation Stockholm 1814, Frankfort 1817, Berlin 1823, Sec. of Embassy St. Petersburg 1828,[3] précis writer 21 Nov. 1830–16 Sept. 1832,[4] Min. P. Dresden Sept.–Nov. 1832, E.E. and Min. P. Naples Nov. 1832 to his d. 24 Aug. 1856.[3] Temple, who d. unm.,[1] was made K.C.B. 1851[5] and left a valuable collection of classical antiquities to the British Museum.[3]

    1. G.E.C., *Complete Peerage*, vol. 10, 297 note e.
    2. Venn, *Alumni Cantab.*, vol. 6, 137.
    3. Boase, *Mod. Eng. Biog.*, vol. 3, 909.
    4. Bindoff et al., *Br. Dip. Reps.*, p. 115, says that he remained in St. Petersburg from 1828–33.
    5. Strachey and Fulford, *Greville Memoirs*, vol. 6, 44 n. 1.

202. Trotter, John Bernard. (1775–1818).[1]

Private sec. 7 Feb.–12 Dec. 1806, serving also with the salary of both offices as précis writer 6 Mar. 1806–12 Dec. 1806, and retaining précis writership to 5 July 1807. Fox's most recent biographer, after reading Trotter's account of Fox's visit to Paris in 1802, concludes that he "was by temperament something of a prig. . . ."[2]

    1. *D.N.B.*, vol. 19, 1181.
    2. Derry, *Fox*, p. 393.

203. Turner, Adolphus. (1805–49).

B. 1805, son of Sir Hilgrove Turner of Gorray Lodge Jersey,[1] ed. Charterhouse.[2] Clerk 5 Apr. 1824–5 Apr. 1843. Consul-Gen. and Chargé d'Affaires Uruguay 1 July 1843[3] –1846 when he ret. with pension £675.[4] d. at Geneva 9 Aug. 1849.[1]

    1. *Gents. Mag.* (1849), pt. 2, 558.
    2. Parish, *List of Carthusians*, p. 236.
    3. F.O. 366/462.
    4. "Superannuations in Public Offices," *P.P., 1847–48*, vol. 39, Command 203, p. 621. F.O. 366/462 lists his pension as £700.

204. Turner, William. (1792–1867).[1]

Clerk 10 Oct. 1808–5 Apr. 1824 during which time he retained his clerkship with pay while serving as attaché Constaninople Apr. 1812–Apr. 1817, Madrid Jan.–Apr. 1823, Lisbon Aug. 1823–Nov. 1824, and sec. to the commission of British Claims in Spain 1823–24[2] and 1826.[3] Planta, who used Turner as a messenger on one occasion, told A'Court that "He speaks and understands the Spanish Language:—you will find he *rides*, and is moreover well acquainted with travelling and much used to it."[4]

    1. *D.N.B.*, vol. 19, 1295.

2. F.O. 366/329 f. 132.
3. *F.O. List*, July, 1867, p. 188.
4. Foreign Office, 17 Jan. 1823, Private, Add. MS 41542 ff. 115–16.

205. Vaughan, (Sir) Charles Richard. (1774–1849).[1]
Private sec. 10 Oct. 1809–5 Jan. 1810.

1. *D.N.B.*, vol. 20, 161.

206. Vincent, Sir Francis, 9th Bart. (1780–1809).

B. 23 July 1780 to Sir Francis Vincent, 8th Bart.,[1] diplomatist,[2] by Mary, dau. of Richard Mullman Trench Chiswell, Esq., M.P.,[1] matric. Pembroke, Cambridge 1797, M.A. 1798,[3] called to the bar 18 June 1804,[4] m. 1802 Jane, dau. of Hon. Edward Bouverie.[1] Undersecretary 20 Feb. 1806–5 Apr. 1807. Trotter (see no. 202), who served with him, recalled him as being "a very assiduous and very respectable young man," though "always in a hurry."[5] d. of a cold 17 Jan. 1809 at Lord Spencer's estate in Sussex.[6]

1. *Burke's Peerage*, 60th ed., p. 1474.
2. For whom see Bindoff et al., *Br. Dip. Reps.*, p. 193.
3. Venn, *Alumni Cantab.*, vol. 6, 292.
4. Lincoln's Inn, London, *Records of the Honourable Society of Lincoln's Inn: The Black Books, 1422–1845* (4 vols.: London, 1897–1902), vol. 4, 243.
5. Trotter, *Memoirs of Fox*, p. 373.
6. *Gents. Mag.* (1809), pt. 1, 94.

207. Walmisley, Arthur. (1819–1910).

B. 4 Feb. 1819, son of Thomas Forbes Walmisley, a composer of religious music and organist of St. Martins-in-the-Fields 1814–54,[1] grandson of Edward W., Chief Clerk of the Parliament Office, House of Lords.[2] Employed five years at the House of Lords[1] before becoming supernumerary clerk attached to Librarian's Dept. 9 Aug. 1845, put on the regular establishment 1 July 1858,[3] sub-librarian 1875,[1] ret. 1 July 1888. d. at his residence in Brixton 14 Dec. 1910.[2]

1. Boase, *Mod. Eng. Biog.*, vol. 3, 1171–72.
2. *The Times*, 16 Dec. 1910, p. 13.
3. F.O. Salary Books. *The Times* says in his obituary that the date was 1854.

208. Walpole, Gen. George. (1758–1835).[1]
Undersecretary 7 Feb. 1806–5 Apr. 1807.

1. *D.N.B.*, vol. 20, 620.

209. Walpole, Col. the Hon. John. (1787–1859).

B. 17. Nov. 1787 to Horatio, 2d Earl of Orford (2d creation), by Sophia, dau. of Charles Churchill, Esq.,[1] matric. Eton 1802.[2] Served with the Guards in the Peninsula, severely wounded at the Siege of Burgos, M.P. for King's Lynn 1827–31.[3] Private sec. 25 Nov. 1830–5 Apr. 1833. Consul-Gen. Chile 3 Aug. 1833, Consul-Gen. and Plenipotentiary Chile 7 July 1837, Consul-Gen. and Chargé d'Affaires Chile 24 May 1841[4]–1 Mar.

1849[3] when he ret. on pension £426.[5] d. unm.[1] at Sydenham, Kent, 10 Dec. 1859.[6]

1. *Burke's Peerage*, 60th ed., p. 1120.
2. Stapylton, *Eton Lists*, p. 40.
3. *F.O. List*, 1854, p. 62.
4. Bindoff et al., *Br. Dip. Reps.*, p. 33.
5. "Superannuations in Public Offices," *P.P.*, *1860*, vol. 40, Command 180, p. 577. F.O. 366/462 gives his pension as £425.
6. *Gents. Mag.* (1860), pt. 1, 195.

210. Ward, Edward Michael. (1789–1832).

B. 5 Feb. 1789 to Rt. Hon. Robert Ward, 3d son of 1st Viscount Bangor, by Sophia Francis, dau. of Richard Chapel Whaley of co. Wicklow,[1] matric. Peterhouse, Cambridge 1797, M.A. 1810,[2] m. 1815 Lady Matilda Charlotte Stewart, dau. of Robert, 1st Marquess of Londonderry.[1] Private sec. 10 Oct. 1812–5 July 1814. Sec. of Legation Stuttgart 5 July 1814–24 Oct. 1815, Lisbon 15 Feb. 1816–5 July 1824,[3] Lt. Col. of South Downshire Militia May 1816,[4] Sec. of Embassy St. Petersburg June 1824, Vienna July 1826, Min. P. Saxony July 1828 to his d. there 12 Sept. 1832.[3]

1. *Burke's Peerage*, 23d ed., p. 60.
2. Venn, *Alumni Cantab.*, vol. 6, 342.
3. F.O. 366/329 f. 142.
4. F.O. 366/366 f. 33.

211. Ward, John William Henry, 1st Earl of Dudley. (1781–1833).[1]

Secretary of State 30 Apr. 1827–30 May 1828.

1. *D.N.B.*, vol. 20, 781.

212. Ward, Robert Plumer. (1765–1846).[1]

Undersecretary 5 Jan. 1805–7 Feb. 1806.

1. *D.N.B.*, vol. 20, 788.

213. Ward, Thomas Lawrence. (1799–1866).

B. 1799 to Rt. Hon. Robert Ward, 3d son of 1st Viscount Bangor, by Louisa Jane, dau. of Rev. Dr. Abraham Symes, Ward was half-brother of Edward Michael W. (see no. 210).[1] matric. Trinity College, Oxford 1816.[2] Clerk 19 Nov. 1817, attached (retaining clerkship) to Castlereagh's special mission to Aix-la-Chapelle 1818,[3] Capt. in Royal South Downshire Militia 20 Apr. 1819,[4] attached (retaining clerkship) Berlin 1823–24, to Adair's special mission to Brussels 1831, to Durham's extraordinary embassy to St. Petersburg 1832,[5] senior clerk 5 Apr. 1841, Supt. of Slave Trade Dept. 1851, Supt. of Consular Dept. 1857[5] to his ret. as 1st senior clerk ill-health 31 Dec. 1859 with pension £860,[6] which was more than clerks with his experience would normally expect to receive and was granted as a mark of special approbation of his services.[7] Leveson said Ward was "an excellent man" as head of one of the political divisions in the office.[8] d. unm.[1] 17 July 1866.

1. *Burke's Peerage*, 6oth ed., p. 98.
2. Foster, *Alumni Oxon.*, vol. 4, 1499.
3. Kay-Shuttleworth, *Woodbine Parish*, pp. 198, 224.
4. F.O. 366/366 f. 32.
5. *F.O. List*, July, 1867, p. 188.
6. "Superannuations in Public Offices," *P.P., 1861*, vol. 35, Command 121, p. 409.
7. Treasury Minute, 8 Dec. 1859, copy, F.O. 366/553.
8. To Granville, Foreign Office, 10 Mar. 1840, P.R.O. 30/29/6/4 ff. 705–6.

214. Warren, Charles.

Clerk 20 Oct. 1790,[1] resident clerk in F.O. from appointment to c. 1805,[2] granted leave of absence with pay to go to America on his private affairs 8 Sept. 1804,[3] senior clerk 5 Jan. 1806, granted one year's leave of absence to go to a warmer climate 8 Dec. 1814,[4] ret. ill-health 5 July 1818 with pension £500.[5]

1. Leeds to Post Office, Whitehall, 20 Oct. 1790, Copy, F.O. 366/670 f. 61.
2. Warren to ?, F.O., 9 Dec. 1807, F.O. 83/14.
3. Harrowby to Bidwell, Downing Street, 8 Sept. 1804, F.O. 366/671 f. 256.
4. Minute, Bathurst, F.O., 8 Dec. 1814, F.O. 366/672 f. 90.
5. "An Account of all Pensions . . . for the year 1819," *P.P., 1820*, vol. 11, Command 11, p. 296.

215. Wellesley, Arthur, 1st Duke of Wellington. (1769–1852).[1]
Secretary of State 15 Nov. 1834–18 Apr. 1835.

1. *D.N.B.*, vol. 20, 1081.

216. Wellesley, (Sir) Henry, (1st Baron Cowley). (1773–1847).[1]
Précis writer 5 Apr. 1795–10 Oct. 1797.

1. *D.N.B.*, vol. 20, 1116.

217. Wellesley, Richard Colley, 1st Marquess Wellesley. (1760–1842).[1]
Secretary of state 6 Dec. 1809–18 Feb. 1812.

1. *D.N.B.*, vol. 20, 1122.

218. Wellesley, Richard Gerald. (1822–61).

B. 18 Nov. 1822,[1] son of Richard Wellesley who was an illegitimate son of Richard, 1st Marquess Wellesley (see no. 217),[2] matric. Eton 1802.[3] Supernumerary clerk 5 Apr. 1839, clerk 22 Nov. 1839 to ret. 21 Aug. 1860 as 3d senior clerk with pension £280.[4] d. of consumption at Malta 18 May 1861.[3]

1. Richard Wellesley to H. D. Scott, Linden Lodge, Linden Grove, Bayswater, 20 Aug. 1860, F.O. 366/553.
2. *Gents. Mag.* (1861), pt. 1, 710.
3. Stapylton, *Eton Lists*, p. 158.
4. "Superannuations in Public Offices," *P.P., 1861*, vol. 35, Command 121, p. 409.

219. Wellington, Arthur Wellesley, 1st Duke of. See Wellesley, Arthur. (no. 215).

220. Werry, Francis Peter.

Possibly the son of Francis Werry, Esq., consul at Smyrna for 32 years, by Elizabeth Werry (d. 7 Jan. 1846).[1] Clerk Jan. 1811–July 1812, attaché St. Petersburg July 1812, attaché Congress of Vienna Aug. 1814, Sec. of Legation Dresden May 1816–Apr. 1824 when he ret. on pension £436.[2]

    1. *Gents. Mag.* (1846), pt. 1, 447.
    2. "Return of Persons Receiving Pensions for Diplomatic Service," *P.P., 1833*, vol. 33, Command 756, p. 400. Werry is not listed in Bindoff et. al, *Br. Dip. Reps.*, p. 125 which does not give a sec. of legation at Dresden 1816–24.

221. Wesley, (Sir) Henry (1st Baron Cowley). See Wellesley, (Sir) Henry. (no. 216).

222. Willis, Sir Francis. (1735–1827).

B. 1735 to Dr. Edward Willis, Bishop of Bath and Wells (1743–73),[1] by Jane, dau. of Henry White, ed. Westminster.[2] Unpaid clerk in Decyphering Branch of P.O. 1758, paid clerk 1764–72, undersecretary of state 1772–75, Decypherer 1775–1827, knighted 1784.[2] d. at his residence in Charles Street, Berkeley Square 30 Oct. 1827.[1]

    1. *Gents. Mag.* (1827), pt. 2, 474.
    2. Ellis, *Post Office*, pp. 129–30.

223. Willis, Francis. (1778–1847).

B. 1778 son of Rev. William Willis, archdeacon of Wells, Willis was nephew of Sir Francis W. (see no. 222),[1] m. 1814 Caroline, dau. of Sir Thomas Whichcote, Bart.[2] Decypherer 30 Oct. 1827–7 Oct. 1844,[3] though he performed the duties of the office for some years before 1827 as deputy to his uncle.[1] Ret. on pension £700, payable out of the secret service account.[3] d. 26 Dec. 1847 at his residence Hangar Hill House, near Ealing, buried at St. Marylebone.[4]

    1. Ellis, *Post Office*, pp. 130–31.
    2. *Gents. Mag.* (1847), pt. 2, 220. She d. 17 June 1847 aet. 55.
    3. Memorandum, Addington, "Office of Secret Service Decypherer, Messrs. Willes & Lovell," F.O., 7 Oct. 1844, Secret, Add. MS 40551 ff. 400–3.
    4. *Gents. Mag.* (1848), pt. 1, 220.

224. Wilson, Robert. (d. 1839).

Clerk attached to Librarian's Dept. 1826 to his d. Aug. 1839.

225. Woodcock, Charles. (d. 1852).

Matric. Eton 1793,[1] private sec. 5 July 1804–5 Jan. 1805, appointed supernumerary clerk with a salary of £150 paid out of the contingent fund of the F.O. on 5 Jan. 1805,[2] but was never placed on the regular establishment. Later served in East Indian Company Service.[1]

1. Stapylton, *Eton Lists*, p. 14.
2. Hammond to Harrowby, Downing Street, 12 Jan. 1805, Harrowby MSS vol. 10, f. 210.

226. Woodford, John William Gordon. (c. 1827–89).

Clerk 12 Dec. 1845, private sec. (retaining clerkship) to Earl of Cowley at Paris Feb.–May 1852, senior clerk 1866[1] to his ret. ill-health 1 May 1877 with pension £490.10.0.[2] After his ret. he was employed temporarily as an extra foreign service messenger 1877–88.[1] d. 27 May 1889.

1. *F.O. List*, 1889, p. 213.
2. "Superannuations in Public Offices," *P.P.*, *1878*, vol. 46, Command 125, p. 321.

227. Wrangham, Digby Cayley. (1805–65).

B. 1805 to Francis Wrangham, Archdeacon of Cleveland and the East Riding of Yorkshire, a second-rate versifyer, historian, and linguist, by Dorothy Cayley, an heiress of £700 p.a.,[1] ed. Brasenose, Oxford, double first 1826, B.A. 1826, M.A. 1829,[2] m. Amelia, dau. of Walter Ramsden Fawkes, M.P., of Farnley Hall, Yorks.[3] Clerk 5 Jan. 1827, private sec. (retaining clerkship with pay) 31 Aug. 1827–21 Nov. 1830, res. clerkship 25 Apr. 1831. M.P. Sudbury, Suffolk 1831–32, barrister G.I. 1831,[2] during the 1830s his health failed[4] but he recovered sufficiently to become a Serjeant-at-Law 1840[2] and to conduct almost all the contested election cases of 1841–42 for the Tories.[5] Granted a patent of precedence 1843, Queen's Serjeant 1858.[2] d. 10 Mar. 1865.

1. Michael Sadler, *Archdeacon Francis Wrangham*, *1769–1842* ("Supplement to the Biographical Society's Transactions No. 12"; Oxford, 1937), passim.
2. Boase, *Mod. Eng. Biog.*, vol. 3, 1507.
3. Barker and Stenning, *Old Westminsters*, vol. 2, 1024, under his son Walter Francis.
4. Wrangham to Peel, 9 King's Bench Walk, Temple, 13 Sept. 1841, Private, Add. MS 40488 ff. 351–54.
5. Same to Aberdeen, Shanklin, I. of Wight, 19 Oct. 1842, Private, Add. MS 40453 ff. 216–17.

228. Wylde, William Henry. (1819–1909).

B. 11 Apr. 1819, son of Col. (later Gen.) Wylde of the Royal Artillery,[1] m. 1846 Elizabeth Mary, dau. of Richard Massy.[2] Wylde was with his father on the North Coast of Spain in 1835 while Col. Wylde was corresponding officer attached to the British Auxillary Legion under the command of Major General Evans.[1] Extra copyist in Slave Trade Dept. 13 Dec. 1837, clerk attached to Slave Trade Dept. 14 Mar. 1838, attached (retaining clerkship) to his father who was reporting military events in Portugal Oct. 1846–Aug. 1847, member of the commission in London to revise the slave trade instructions 1865, Supt. of Commercial and Consular Dept. 1869 before which time he had been transferred to the regular establishment,[3] chairman of the Commission of Inquiry into Consular Establishments 1872,[2] member of Commission on Coolie Immigration to Réunion in Paris 1880, C.M.G. 1880.[3] Ret. old age 30 Mar. 1880 as 1st senior clerk with pension £833.6.8.[4] d. at his residence in Collingham Place, S.W. London, 2 Mar. 1909, buried in Chiswick churchyard.[2]

1. *F.O. List*, 1853, p. 46.
2. *The Times*, 4 Mar. 1909, p. 13.
3. *F.O. List*, 1910, p. 419.
4. "Superannuations in Public Offices," *P.P., 1881*, vol. 57, Command 149, p. 576.

229. Wynn, (Sir) Henry Watkin Williams. (1783–1856).[1]

Clerk 5 Jan. 1796, précis writer (retaining clerkship) 20 Feb. 1801–5 Apr. 1803 when he also res. his clerkship.

1. *D.N.B.*, vol. 21, 1171.

230. Wynne, Thomas E.

Clerk 21 Apr. 1796 to his resignation 17 Feb. 1802.[1]

1. *Records of the Foreign Office*, p. 155.

Appendix II

Office Divisions Directed by the Undersecretaries of State

It is very difficult to trace with precision every fluctuation of the countries in each division directed by the undersecretaries of state. Draft circulars were habitually sent to the British missions each time an undersecretaryship changed hands. Yet frequently for unknown reasons they were not sent to some of those courts under the direction of the new officer. Private letters served to supplement and even to replace these more formal communications. Prior to 1822 the records are very scanty and this fact contributes to the difficulty of tracing changes in these divisions. Because there are virtually no minutes on dispatches it is also impossible to trace these changes through the files of political correspondence.

The first record is for 1794, when the responsibilities of the undersecretaries were:

Aust: *South*—Italian Courts, Austria, the German Electors (save Saxony), France, Spain, Portugal, Turkey.

Burges: *North*—Saxony, U.S.A., Sweden, Russia, Prussia, Holland, Denmark.[1]

These assignments were much the same in 1807.[2] In 1817 Planta succeeded Cooke in the Northern Division, which included Russia, the Netherlands, Sweden, U.S.A., Turkey, Saxony, Hanse Towns, and the consuls in these countries.[3] Planta was also made responsible for Prussia.[4]

The undersecretary at the head of the Southern Division between 1820 and 1831 directed slave trade correspondence.[5] Planta switched to the Southern Division in 1823. Thereafter the senior undersecretary always

1. Aust to Sir William Hamilton, Downing Street, 14 Jan. 1794, Add. MS 41199 ff. 154–55.
2. Canning to Bagot, Foreign Office, 8 Aug. 1807, 6 p.m., Private, Bagot, *Canning and Friends*, vol. 1, 242–43.
3. Draft circular, Planta, F.O., 5 Aug. 1817, F.O. 83/81.
4. Planta to Sir George Rose, Foreign Office, 14 Aug. 1817, Private, Add. MS 42781 ff. 99–100.
5. Minutes on S. R. Lushington to Planta, Treasury Chambers, 6 Dec. 1820, F.O. 84/7.

directed French affairs. Since these changes were made several months after Lord Francis Conyngham became undersecretary it is probable that Canning wished to have Planta's judgment and experience applied to those courts where the most important foreign activity at that time was taking place.

> Conyngham: *North*—Germanic Confederation, Würtemberg, Bavaria, Turkey, Russia, Netherlands, Sweden, Denmark, Saxony, U.S.A., Prussia.
>
> Planta: *South*—Sardinia, other Italian Courts, Switzerland, France, Austria, Spain, Portugal, Sicily.[6]

In January 1824, Austria, Naples, Florence, and Turin were transferred to the North; U.S.A. and Netherlands were transferred to the South.[7] These changes again reflected in part the political situation at that time.

The third undersecretary, Lord Howard de Walden, was appointed in 1824. He took the Netherlands and Portugal from the South and Sweden, Denmark, and all of Germany save Prussia from the North. He added Brazil, a new state, to his responsibilities. He also took the consuls of these countries.[8] When Lord Mount Charles retired in April 1825 there was a redistribution of diplomatic and consular business.[9]

> Planta: *South*—U.S.A., Netherlands, Austria, the Italian Courts, Switzerland, France, Spain, Turkey, Russia, Prussia.
>
> Howard: *North*—Portugal, Brazil, Sweden, Denmark, the minor German States, the South American States.

Canning again appointed a third undersecretary in January 1826. The Marquess of Clanricarde took the German Courts, the Italian Courts, Switzerland and on February 24, Prussia.[10]

When John Backhouse entered the F.O. in April 1827, succeeding Planta, he directed only the U.S.A., Brazil, Mexico, Colombia, and Argentina. Howard and Clanricarde must have directed between them the Netherlands, Austria, Spain, Turkey, France, and Russia, the remaining countries in Planta's division.[11]

On Clanricarde's resignation in August 1827, the work of the office again fell onto two undersecretaries. There was a general redistribution at this time. Backhouse retained the Americas, North and South, and added

---

6. Draft Circular, Conyngham, F.O., 4 Aug. 1823, F.O. 83/82; Planta to Sir William A'Court, Foreign Office, 19 Sept. 1823, Private, Add. MS 41544 f. 129.

7. Draft to His Majesty's Ambassador/Minister, Foreign Office, 8 Dec. 1823, F.O. 83/82.

8. Circulars signed by Howard, Foreign Office, 28 May and 31 May 1824, ibid.

9. Draft Circular, Planta, Foreign Office, 7 Nov. 1825, ibid.

10. Draft Circular, Clanricarde, Foreign Office, 1 Jan. 1826, ibid.

11. Draft Circular, Backhouse, Foreign Office, 30 Apr. 1827, F.O. 83/83.

Russia, Prussia, Denmark and Sweden. Though Howard's division included some countries inherited from Clanricarde, others must have been under his own direction since Planta's resignation. He had after August 1827, Austria, France, Turkey, Portugal, Spain, Sicily, the Italian States, the minor German Courts, and Switzerland.[12] Dunglas replaced Howard in June 1828, and assumed the same responsibilities with two important exceptions: France and Spain were transferred to Backhouse's division.[13]

In 1831 Palmerston divided the work of the office again. This arrangement survived until 1838. Backhouse, with the assistance of Thomas Staveley and (after 1836) Edmund Hammond, managed one division (18,026 pieces). In 1837 Staveley, assisted by four clerks, supervised France, Spain, the United States, Mexico, Guatemala, and interdepartmental correspondence (8767 pieces). William Fox-Strangways, who inherited Sir George Shee's, Viscount Fordwich's, and Viscount Mahon's responsibilities (11,511 pieces), had the assistance of Thomas L. Ward and Richard C. Mellish. Ward and four other clerks were concerned with Austria, Portugal, Brazil, Buenos Ayres and Monte Video, New Granada, and Venezuela (4825 pieces). Three clerks assisted Mellish with the business of Holland, Belgium, Sweden, Denmark, Bavaria, Naples, Sardinia, Switzerland, Saxony, Tuscany, and Würtemberg (6686 pieces). There was by 1838 an obvious need for reforming these arrangements to make the volume of business under the direction of each undersecretary more equal. The changes were as follows:

Staveley: *The French Department*—dropped Mexico and Guatemala.
Hammond: *The Russian and Turkish Department*—dropped Prussia.
Ward: *The South European and South American Department*—assumed responsibility for Mexico and Guatemala, Saxony, Naples, and Switzerland.
Mellish: *The North European Department*—assumed responsibility for Prussia, dropped Saxony, Naples and Switzerland.

The junior undersecretary directed slave trade affairs and the China business Conyngham, the third senior clerk, was supervising. Both undersecretaries continued to supervise the consular business of the countries in their divisions.[14]

Leveson's division was slightly smaller than Strangways's had been after 1838. More important, however, by 1840 the two most important courts

12. Draft Circulars, Backhouse and Howard, Foreign Office, 22 Aug. 1827, ibid.
13. Draft, Backhouse to Granville (Paris) and Bosanquet (Madrid), F.O., 10 June 1828, ibid.
14. Backhouse's "Memo No. 2 on the change . . . in the Two Divisions of the Under Secretaries of State, 1838.", F.O. 366/386.

(Austria and Prussia) had been transferred to the permanent undersecretary. None of the major powers came under the supervision of the junior undersecretary.[15]

There were fluctuations in the countries within the divisions from time to time, as questions of policy made it necessary to join some states together that had previously not been under the direction of one undersecretary. Sometime after 1841, therefore, Texas and Mexico were added to Staveley's responsibilities for the United States, and once Greece became a serious concern of France and Britain the correspondence with that country was also transferred to his department.[16]

15. Leveson to Granville, F.O., 3 Apr. 1840, P.R.O. 30/29/6/4 ff. 717–18. I have found no evidence to support the contention that Aberdeen in 1828 decided to give the permanent undersecretary the most important countries in Europe. See Cromwell, "Incident," p. 103.

16. "Memorandum showing the state of the business in Mr. Staveley's division of Mr. Addington's Department on the 19th of December 1845," F.O. 83/98.

Appendix III

"Regulations for Agents to Foreign Ministers, Foreign Office, March 1, 1816."[1]

"1. Each Agent to be appointed by the Minister, at his own choice, in [i.e., from the clerks in] the Office.

2. No Agent to be allowed to make any advances of money, upon salary or allowances, to such Foreign Minister, or to act as his Banker.

3. Each Foreign Minister to report to the Secretary of State what Banker he employs; and the Agent to pay to such Banker the balance of this salary and other allowances, as soon as received.[2]

4. The Foreign Minister to draw no bills whatsoever upon his Agent.

5. Extra allowances, according to practice, or for special service, to be issued 'to the Minister or his Assigns,' and immediately made over by the Agent to the Banker.

6. The Agent not to be allowed to deduct more than one per cent upon the salaries and outfit of the Ambassadors and Envoys, for the service rendered to them, and to charge no percentage upon the extra disbursements.

7. Accounts of the extra disbursements of Ministers, accompanied by proper explanations, and supported by Vouchers, to be sent in to the Secretary of State, at the expiration of each quarter."

1. F.O. 83/27. Transcripts of Crown—Copyright records in the Public Record Office appear by permission of H.M. Stationery Office.
2. Henry Rolleston refused even to receive the money, preferring to send the bankers of diplomatists to the Treasury to collect it when it was ready. Hamilton to Sir William A'Court, Chelsea, 22 Oct. 1819, Add. MS 41520 ff. 122–23.

Appendix IV

"Scale of the Establishment of the Office of His Majesty's Principal Secretary of State for Foreign Affairs, [from] January 5, 1822. 'Approved: George Canning.'"[1]

Position	Base Pay	Annual Augmentation	Maximum Pay
Secretary of State	£6,000		£6,000
Under Secretaries ea.	2,000		2,000
Chief Clerk	1,000	£50	1,250
1st Senior Clerk	700	20	900
2nd–4th Senior Clerks	600	20	800
Second Class Clerks	350	15	545
Junior Clerks	150	10	300
Assistant Junior Clerks	100	10	150
Clerk Attached to the Chief Clerk's Dept.	150	10	300
Librarian and Keeper of the Papers	350	15	545
Sub-Librarian	150	10	350
Private Secretary	300		300
Précis Writer	300		300
Translator	300		300
Collector and Transmitter of State Papers	500	"To be abolished on a Vacancy"	500

Special Allowances totalled: £650.
House Keeper, Office Keepers, Door Porters and a Printer: £544.12.0.
Total Minimum Charge: £19,394.12.0; Total Maximum Charge: £22,709.12.0."

1. F.O. 366/542 f. 41.

Appendix V

The Emoluments of the Foreign Service

A. "Estimate of Ordinary Allowances and Pensions to Foreign Ministers and Consuls," [1815].[1]

1st Class: Ambassadors at Paris, St. Petersburg, Vienna, Madrid, and the Netherlands. Salary: £11,000; Outfit: £4,000; House allowance (except at Paris): £1,000. Secretary of Embassy with a salary of £1,000 and an outfit of £400.

2nd Class: Ambassador at Constantinople. Salary: £8,000; Outfit: £3,000. Secretary of Embassy with a salary of £1,000 and an outfit of £300. Oriental Secretary with a salary of £1,000.

3d Class: Envoy Extraordinary and Minister Plenipotentiary at Berlin. Salary: £7,000; Outfit: £2,500; House allowance: £500. Secretary of Legation with a salary of £700 and an outfit of £250.

4th Class: E.E. and Min. P. at Lisbon, Naples, and Washington. Salary: £5,500; Outfit: £2,000; House allowance: £500. Secretary of Legation with a salary of £550 and an outfit of £200.[2]

5th Class: E.E. and Min. P. at Stockholm, Munich, Copenhagen, and Turin. Salary: £4,500; Outfit: £2,000; House allowance: £400. Secretary of Legation with a salary of £500 and an outfit of £200.

6th Class: E.E. at Würtemberg, Tuscany, Switzerland, and Saxony. Salary: £3,600; Outfit: £1,500; House allowance: £300. Secretary of Legation with a salary of £500 and an outfit of £200.

7th Class: E.E. at Hamburg. Salary: £2,800; Outfit: £1,000; House allowance: £300. Secretary of Legation with a salary of £300 and an outfit of £100.

Wellington's government proposed reductions in the establishment in 1830, but were defeated in the House of Commons before they could

1. F.O. 366/525.
2. After 1820 Frankfort was placed in this class. Castlereagh to Lords of Treasury, F.O., 9 Sept. 1820, Copy, ibid.

implement their program. Lord Althorp, Grey's chancellor of the Exchequer, first proposed slashing Aberdeen's estimates for some missions and reducing the rank of accredited British representatives at these courts. Palmerston successfully defeated this plan and secured cabinet approval of his own scheme, which was slightly less expensive than Aberdeen's.[3]

B. "Lord Althorp's Scheme of the Reductions in Diplomatic Salaries & Allowances," December, 1830.[4]

Court	Salary and Rent 1829	Aberdeen's proposal	Althorp's proposal	(rank proposed)
Paris	£11,000	£11,000	£11,000	
St. Petersburg	12,000	12,000	12,000	
Vienna	12,000	9,900	9,900	
Netherlands	12,000	8,800	1,825	(chargé d'affaires)
Portugal	8,800	7,000	1,825	(chargé d'affaires)
Spain	8,000	6,500	1,460	(chargé d'affaires)
Naples	6,000	4,900	500	(Sec. of Legation)
Brazil	5,500	4,500	4,500	
Sweden	4,900	4,000	1,095	(chargé d'affaires)
Denmark	4,900	4,000	1,095	(chargé d'affaires)
Bavaria	4,900	4,000	500	(Sec. of Legation)
Sardinia	4,900	4,100	2,700	(Minister Plenip.)
Würtemberg	3,300	2,300	500	(Sec. of Legation)
Saxony	2,900	2,300	730	(chargé d'affaires)
Frankfort	2,900	2,900	1,095	(chargé d'affaires)
Tuscany	3,900	2,300	400	(Sec. of Legation)
Switzerland	2,900	2,250	400	(Sec. of Legation)
Greece	2,900	2,200	730	(chargé d'affaires)
Mexico	5,500	4,000	4,000	
Colombia	5,500	4,000	4,000	
Buenos Ayres	3,300	3,300	3,300	

3. Palmerston to Grey, Stanhope Street, 27 Nov. 1831, Copy, Palmerston Papers GC/GR/2360/1–3.
4. F.O. 366/526.

C. "Estimate of the sum required for . . . His Majesty's Diplomatic Service abroad," [1831].[5]

1st Class:	Salary
A. Ambassadors at Paris and St. Petersburg.	£10,000
Secretaries of Embassy.	1,000
Paid Attaché.	400
B. Ambassador at Vienna.	9,000
Secretary of Embassy.	900
Paid Attaché.	250
C. Ambassador at Constantinople.	6,500
Secretary of Embassy	800
Paid Attaché.	250

2nd Class:	Salary
E.E. and Min. P. at Madrid, Berlin, Washington, Naples, Lisbon, Brazil, Brussels and The Hague.	(Salary range*)3,600 to 6,000
Secretaries of Legation	(Salary range*) 500 to 550
Paid Attachés at Madrid and Berlin.	250
Paid Attaché at Washington.	200

3d Class:	Salary
E.E. at Stockholm, Copenhagen, Munich, and Turin.	(Salary range*)3,000 to 3,600
Secretaries of Legation	500

4th Class:	Salary
A. Min. P. at German Diet, Würtemberg, Saxony, Tuscany, and Switzerland.	(Salary range*) 2,000 to 2,600
Secretaries of Legation	400
B. Minister Resident in Greece.	2,000
Secretary of Legation.	400
C. Min. P. at Mexico City, Colombia, and Buenos Ayres	(Salary range*)3,000 to 3,600
Secretaries of Legation.	(Salary range*) 500 to 600
D. Agent in Albania	1,000

*Salary dependent on the court to which the diplomatist was assigned.

5. Ibid.

Appendix VI

List of His Majesty's Consuls General and Consuls, August, 1828[1]

Country	Consuls General	Consuls	Vice-Consuls
Russia	Odessa; St. Petersburg	Archangel; Riga; Libau	Taganrog
Sweden		Stockholm; Gottenburg	
Norway		Christiana	
Denmark		Elsinore	
Prussia		Königsberg; Mench; Danzig	Pillau
German States	Hamburg		Hamburg; Bremen; Lubeck; Auschaven
Holland		Amsterdam; Rotterdam; Antwerp; Ostend	
France	Paris	Calais; Boulogne; Havre; Caen; Brest; Nantes; La Rochelle; Bordeaux; Bayonne; Marseilles; Corsica	
Spain	Madrid	Bilbao; Corunna; Cadiz; Adra; Malaga; Almeria; Barcelona; Mahon; Canary Islands	San Lucan; Oratava
Portugal	Lisbon; Madeira	Oporto	Lisbon; Madeira
Cape Verd Is.		Island chain	
Italy	Naples	Genoa; Nice; Cagliari; Leghorn; Ancona	Naples; Gallipoli; Otrano
Sicily	Palermo	Messina	Palermo
Austria	Venice	Trieste; Fiume; Ragusa	
United States	Washington	New York; Philadelphia; Charleston; New Orleans; Boston; Baltimore; Pensacola; Norfolk; Savannah; Portsmouth; Wilmington, Del.; New London; Newport	
Brazil	Rio	Maranham; Pernambuco; Bahia	
Mexico	Mexico City		San Blas; Veracruz; Tampico

1. F.O. 366/348 ff. 95–99.

Colombia	Bogota		Carthagena; Panama; La Guarya; Maracaibo; Puerto Cabello; Guayaquil
Buenos Ayres	Buenos Ayres	Monte Video	Buenos Ayres
Guatemala		Guatemala City	
Chile	Valparaiso	Concepcion; Coquinbo	Valparaiso
Peru	Lima	Arequipa	Lima (2)
Haiti			Port au Prince (2)
Sandwich Islands		Island chain	
Turkey[2]	Constantinople	Andrianople; Caena; Beyrout; Smyrna	Salonica; Smyrna; Scio; Milo
Egypt[3]	Cairo	Alexandria	Rosetta; Damietta
Albania	Prevesa		

2. Also on the consular establishment in Turkey were consular agents at Bucharest and the Dardanelles; agents at Cyprus and Scanderoon; chancellors at Constantinople and Smyrna; a physician at Constantinople; a surgeon at Smyrna; a chaplain at Smyrna; and four dragomans at Smyrna.

3. The establishment in Egypt also included a chancellor at Alexandria; an interpreter at Cairo; two dragomans at Alexandria; and a troop of janassaries at Alexandria.

Appendix VII

Consuls Prohibited from Trading after 1832[1]

1. Political Agents: Warsaw; Danzig; Hamburg*; Paris**; Bayonne; Corsica; Madrid**; Venice*; Constantinople*; Smyrna; Albania; Moldavia; Servia; Walachia; Damascus; Cairo; Alexandria; Barbary States***; New York.
2. Responsible for British mail packets: Gottenburg, Sweden; Ostend; Calais; Boulogne.
3. Miscellaneous:
   a. Cape Verd Islands: watched activities of slave traders.
   b. Carthagena, Spain: naval depot, consul not allowed to trade so that he would be free from local influence.
   c. Elsinor, Denmark: acted as intermediary between British masters and Danish officials who collected dues of ships passing through the sound.
   d. Granville, Jersey: created in 1835 to protect Jersey Island fishermen.
   e. All the principal consuls in South America: to keep them from becoming involved in speculative ventures.
4. No reason given: Leipzig; Brest.

1. "List of Her Majesty's Consuls Abroad: Distinguishing those who are Restricted from Trading, and Those who are not," 1838, F.O. 366/350.
   *Consul General.
   **Consular Assistant.
   ***All Vice-Consuls, save the one at Bona Algiers, prohibited from trading.

Appendix VIII

The Foreign Secret Service

Mention of the foreign secret service evokes images of British spies infesting the capitals of Europe gathering intelligence. To be sure the government employed secret service funds to support such activities. Secret service money, for example, financed the attempt to rescue political prisoners from Neapolitan prisons,[1] was employed in struggles for influence over the affairs of other states,[2] and could be traced to efforts to bribe foreign legislators into approving commercial treaties between their states and Britain.[3] But from the evidence in British archives, which is admittedly scant, it seems that charges for these activities formed only a small fraction of the total secret service expenditure. Ellenborough said that "Five-sixths of the Foreign Secret Service money" was pledged to "permanent old charges,"[4] and though this percentage was perhaps a slight exaggeration it is certain that vast amounts of this money went for such expenses.[5] Aberdeen suspected that fully half the charge in 1844 "really has nothing whatever secret about it,"[6] though he was not unduly upset about this circumstance: "for although there are many charges upon it which ought not to be there, they at least always remain secret."[7]

1. G. B. Henderson, "Lord Palmerston and the Secret Service Fund," *English Historical Review*, 53 (July, 1938), 485–87.
2. Cobban, *Secret Agents*, especially pp. 110–21.
3. Palmerston to Granville, F.O., 19 Feb. 1833, Secret, P.R.O. 30/29/415.
4. 31 Oct. 1830, Colchester, *Ellenborough Diary*, vol. 2, 408–9.
5. The secret service accounts of Dudley, Aberdeen, and Wellington show how the sums were spent:

	Dudley	*Aberdeen*	*Wellington*
Issued:	£54,661. 3. 8	£106,507.10. 9	£12,114.10. 4
Spent by undersecretary:	38,217.13. 1	79,188.18. 8	10,792.18. 4
Spent by diplomatists:	4,931. 4.10	11,172. 1. 9	118.19. 0
Returned to Treasury:	10,000. 0. 0	15,000. 0. 0	nil
Balance paid successor:	1,507.10. 9	1,133. 5. 4	1,202. 2. 6
Stamp duty:	4.15. 0	13. 5. 0	10. 0

"The Sole and Final Accounts of. . ." Dudley, Aberdeen, and Wellington, A.O. 2/13 ff. 25–28; A.O. 2/15 ff. 23–27; A.O. 2/29 ff. 285–87. Accounts of earlier Secretaries of State are given in Alfred Cobban, "British Secret Service in France, 1784–1792," *English Historical Review*, 69 (Apr., 1954), 233–36.
6. Aberdeen to Peel, Argyll House, 27 Mar. [1844], Add. MS 40454 ff. 149–50.
7. Aberdeen to Peel, Blair Castle, 28 Sept. 1844, Add. MS 40550 ff. 343–44.

The routine nature of secret service expenditure has been clouded by the fact that a few well-documented cases of activities financed by these accounts have dominated recent historiography on the subject. William Eden, for example, had an extensive and effective network of paid informers employed by the mission of Franklin, Deane, and Lee to France in 1777. From these informers he knew a good deal if not all of the details of Franco-American relations, and at least on one occasion managed to secure the original dispatches the commissioners sent home. Yet Eden's expenditure of secret service money was not totally beneficial to the British cause. The contacts established between his agents and British officials in London were known by the commissioners, who, when approached about reconciliation late in 1777, used the British terms and their known authenticity to convince Vergennes, the French foreign minister, of the necessity of signing a treaty with the colonies irrespective of what Spain did.[8] British secret service funds produced even less success when employed by William Wickham to finance the counterrevolution in France during the 1790s.[9]

With the exception of conclusions drawn from these and similar instances, it is difficult to generalize about foreign secret service expenditures. Prior to 1824 both undersecretaries were active in the expenditure of secret service money. Canning, however, made these duties the exclusive responsibility of the permanent undersecretary.[10] Between 1797 and 1824 there was also a secret service clerk, Charles Broughton, who prepared all the warrants and collected the money from the Exchequer.[11] The sums expended were large—sometimes well in excess of £40,000 a year—and the records of where the money was expended had to have been voluminous. Apparently, however, all have been destroyed or lost. The fact that most of the charges were permanent ones meant that the records had to pass from one ministry to the next.[12] Hence the eventual employment of the permanent undersecretary in keeping the accounts. George Hammond, who while undersecretary worked extensively with these funds, kept no papers on secret service expenditure after his retirement. He said that Canning

8. Samual Flagg Bemis, "British Secret Service and the French-American Alliance," *American Historical Review*, 29 (Apr., 1924), 474–95.

9. Harvey Mitchell, *The Underground War Against Revolutionary France: The Missions of William Wickham 1794–1800* (Oxford, 1965).

10. Temperley, *For. Pol. Canning*, p. 269.

11. Draft, Hamilton to George Harrison (Treasury), 5 Mar. 1810, F.O. 83/17; Additional Memorandum respecting Mr. Broughton, [1824], F.O. 366/553.

12. These permanent charges were always accepted without question by each new ministry. Canning said that it was "not the practice of the office to go back into the grants of ones Predecessors, as the List . . . of Secret Pensions abundantly testifies; and the Oath taken on quitting the office is (as I have always thought) to be considered as a sufficient guarantee that the grants have been made on a just ground of publick service." To Wellesley, Hinchley, 10 Nov. 1811, Private & Secret, Add. MS 37296 ff. 36–37.

retained the documents, though Liverpool received all the vouchers.[13] If Canning did keep any secret service papers they have since disappeared. It is probable that he eventually passed them on to his successor as other secretaries invariably did. Palmerston, for example, told Backhouse in 1844 that he had "no Papers of any Kind connected with Secret Service money. . . ."[14]

A second factor that helps to explain the scarcity of records was the periodic revision of the lists to remove the names of all those who through death, termination of service, or any other reason were no longer in receipt of secret service money. Doubtless the old records were destroyed once a new list had been completed. Probably for this reason Backhouse in 1834 could not provide Palmerston with "a statement of the Total amount voted for F.O. Secret Service in Each year from 1815 downwards & the Distribution of that Sum into its Several Heads of Drawn by ministers abroad, Home expense, & pensions." Backhouse did have this information for the period after 1831, but could provide only the total sums voted by Parliament for secret service prior to that year.[15]

The Civil List Act of 1782 held the secretaries of state, their undersecretaries, and the personnel of the diplomatic service responsible for their dispersal of foreign secret service money.[16] They could fulfill their legal responsibilities in two ways. Receipts were submitted to the Exchequer for all expenditures actually made abroad and whoever expended the money had to swear before a baron of the Exchequer that he spent the sum in question on a secret service. As a rule only small sums were expended in this manner. Most diplomatists, particularly after 1815, spent little by way of secret service. Ambassadors actually spent only £9,500 of £126,100 issued to Palmerston for secret service between November 1830 and November 1834.[17] The proportion was, of course, considerably larger during the wars with France. Grenville authorized William Wickham, for example, to spend in 1795 £30,000 in Switzerland to promote the French Royalist cause.[18] Before the war with France Malmesbury lavishly spent secret service money in a successful effort to secure British influence in Holland.[19] On the other

13. Hammond to C. C. Smith, Dennington, Newbury, 26 May 1811, Private, F.O. 27/87; Same to Hamilton, Broadstairs, 29 Aug. 1821, Private, F.O. 27/263.
14. 24 May 1844, C. T., Backhouse Papers.
15. Minute, Backhouse, on minute, Palmerston, 2 Feb. 1834, F.O. 96/17.
16. 22 Geo. III c. 82.
17. "The Account of the Right Honourable Henry John Viscount Palmerston. . . ," A.O. 2/29 ff. 159–63.
18. C. Goddard to W. Wickham, Dover Street, 10 Mar. 1795, Copy, *H. M. C. Fortescue*, vol. 3, 33–34.
19. Cobban, *Secret Agents*, passim. In 1787 £70,000 was allotted "to the Stadholder's party in the United Provinces. . . ." George III to Pitt, 26 May 1787, Stanhope, *Pitt*, vol. 1, Appendix, xxi.

hand, Sir Robert Keith said in 1792 that he "never charged a *single shilling* for Secret Service . . ." during his twenty-five year career.[20]

Most of the secret service money was paid in England, either directly by the secretary of state and his undersecretary, or through agents of persons receiving secret service monies for services abroad. Such expenditures were considered accounted for merely by the oath sworn before the baron of the Exchequer. Receipts were still taken when the money was issued but they were not given in at the Exchequer.

These were not very strict regulations over what was in fact considerable government spending. Grenville, for example, between June 1791 and February 1797 spent £320,417 on various secret services.[21] Yet the secret service accounts remained, as Canning said, "the only fund which has not been pried into" by Parliament.[22] The Commissioners for Auditing the Public Accounts in 1802 attempted to judge whether or not every charge was a legitimate one. But the law officers of the Crown decided that the Act of 1782 provided a sufficient safeguard to public funds[23] and thereafter no other department of government attempted to procure detailed explanations of these expenditures.

There are many scattered references to secret service expenditures. It is possible here to give only an indication of the variety of charges on the secret service account and to give some of the most interesting examples of the uses of this fund. There appear to have been six broad categories of foreign secret service expenditure. The most important, though not always the largest, was the sum expended for securing intelligence or for distributing British propaganda on the continent. Other charges were for pensions, foreign and domestic; salaries and allowances of British officials abroad; rewards for services performed for government in England; funds to support continental refugees; and miscellaneous expenses. Representative examples from each class include the following:

Intelligence Services: Between 1778 and 1782 M. Friquetti, Sardinian Consul General at Amsterdam received £200 p.a. to send intelligence from Holland, especially about naval activity at his port.[24] From 1789 to 1792 M. Sundersberg was given £200 plus a pension of £100 to provide regular

20. Keith to Grenville, 15 Feb. 1792, Keith, *Memoirs*, vol. 2, 475.

21. "Account of all Monies issued to the Right Honourable Lord Grenville for Foreign Secret Service. . . ," Exchequer, 21 Aug. 1797, F.O. 83/6.

22. Canning to Portland, Claremount, 7 Nov. 1808, Private & Secret, copy, Canning MSS Bundle 32.

23. Hammond to Grenville, Eastbourn[e], 1 Aug. 1802, *H. M. C. Fortescue*, vol. 7, 103–4; Extract of opinion of Spencer Perceval and Thomas Manners Sutton, Lincoln's Inn, 21 Sept. 1802, F.O. 83/13, copy in *H. M. C. Fortescue*, vol. 7, p. 125.

24. Memorandum, [26 August, 1782?], Lucas L 29/579.

and frequent means of communication between The Hague and Brussels.[25] An agent was employed during the 1790s in the Hanoverian Post Office at Nienberg to open foreign correspondence.[26] William Windham in 1798 expended about £20,000 "for services connected with the Royalists in France. . . ."[27] Friedrich von Gentz from 1800 to at least 1809 received occasional payments for writing anti-French propaganda tracts for distribution on the continent.[28] Pitt in 1805 spent £5,000 for intelligence concerning French designs on Ireland.[29] Captain George Cockburn R. N. in 1810 was given £800 and jewels valued at £7,417 to expend in his attempt to rescue King Ferdinand VII of Spain from France and to return him to Madrid.[30] Sir Charles Stuart, ambassador in France, spent £350 in 1819 for the surveys taken by Napoleon in preparation for the maritime defence of the Adriatic and Illurian provinces.[31] James Regnier from 1800 to 1805 published with secret service funds the *Courier de Londres* and from 1806 to 1815 the *Courier d'Angleterre*, both of which were distributed exclusively abroad.[32] Secret service money in the 1830s was the main financial support of the Lisbon Mail published by Señor Rosas.[33]

Pensions: Until 1810 £600 a year was paid to Mr. Forth "for services . . . performed during Lord Stormont's embassy in France" (1772–1778).[34] Major Russillion, a Swiss who, from 1795 until 1804 when he was captured by the French, acted as intermediary between the Swiss Cantons and the British government, received £200 annually after 1814.[35] Charles Broughton, clerk at the Foreign Office, received £200 with a reversion to

25. Burges to Auckland, White Hall, 3 July 1792, Private, Add. MS 34443 ff. 248–49.

26. The agent was Mr. Bodes. Hammond to Grenville, Hamburgh, 8 Aug. 1796, Private, *H. M. C. Fortescue*, vol. 3, 233.

27. "Memorandum of Conversation between Mr. Pitt, Mr. Windham, and Lord Grenville," 19 Jan. 1798, Add. MS 37846 f. 61.

28. Carysfort to Hawkesbury, Berlin, 3 Oct. 1801, Separate, Cypher, Copy, F.O. 353/25. With respect to Gentz Canning wrote: "He is and always has been in good political principles: & has this certain recommendation & guarantee for his security, that he would be infallibly shot if Buonaparte should catch him." To Bathurst, Gloucester Lodge, 12 Oct. 1809, Private & Secret, B.M. Loan 57/4/332.

29. Receipts 5 July 1805 and 22 Aug. 1805, Harrowby MSS vol. 33, ff. 264, 265.

30. Draft to Cockburn, Foreign Office, 2 Feb. 1810, Secret, No. 1 and "G. Cockburn, Capt., R.N., H.M. Ship Implacable in Cowsand Bay, 2 March, 1810, Official," Add. MS 37291 ff. 214–15, 235–36.

31. Unsigned minute, Castlereagh, on Stuart to Hamilton, Paris, 12 Apr. 1819, Private, F.O. 97/164.

32. Memorial of James Regnier, Manchester, 15 June 1819, F.O. 27/219.

33. Palmerston to Howard de Walden, Stanhope Street, 16 Oct. 1838, Add. MS 45176 ff. 123–24.

34. Hammond to ?, Southampton, 4 Mar. 1810, fragment, F.O. 27/80.

35. Sir Charles Flint to C. Sullin, Irish Office, 15 July 1814, Private, and unsigned minute, S. Rolleston, on Russillion to Ld. L[iverpool?], Londres, le 12 Juillet, 1814, F.O. 27/107.

his widow when he retired in 1824.[36] The ambassador at The Hague regularly paid the Princess of Stalberg £400 a year during the 1820s.[37]

Salaries and allowances of personnel abroad: Phineas Bond, American loyalist and consul and commissary at Philadelphia after 1786, received his salary from secret service accounts.[38] David Urquhart was sent in the 1830s to the Levant on a mission of "Commercial Investigation, with certain allowances that were to be paid to him out of Secret Service Money."[39] British officers stationed in Persia and Turkey during the 1830s as advisors to local forces were paid from secret service funds.[40]

Services performed in England: In 1789 Carmarthen gave George Aust, a clerk in the Foreign Office, £200 p.a. for preparing ciphers, "and in Consideration of other extraordinary Services . . . such as Translation, arranging State Papers etc. etc. . . ."[41] Henry Darlot, Deputy Comptroller of the Foreign Post Office, was given £40 a year while he held that position,[42] presumably for opening intercepted letters. Clerks in the office also received allowances from secret service funds. James Bandinel in 1827 received £150 for a memoir on the Albreda question; Edmund Hammond prepared a précis on Greek affairs in 1830 and was paid £150 for his efforts; and Richard Mellish in 1832 earned £100 for a précis on Belgian affairs.[43]

Continental refugees: Fox made regular disbursements to French royalists. The sums ranged from between two to eight shillings a day to £20 a month.[44] Canning between June 1824 and August 1825 paid £5,191.3.0 for the relief of Spanish refugees.[45]

Miscellaneous charges: The Cardinal of York, the last surviving member of the line of Stuart kings, received after 1799 £4,000 a year from the secret service fund.[46] The children of the Duchess of Brunswick were supported by secret service grants rather than other funds because ministers "thought that these Princes might be the objects of greater Jealousy & oppression, upon the Continent, if they were notoriously supported by the British Government, and also that they would have less chance of obtaining any

36. Minute, Canning, G.L., 23 Jan. 1824, Canning MSS Bundle 136.
37. Bagot to Shee, The Hague, 25 Sept. 1831, Private, Palmerston Papers GC/BA/97.
38. Carmarthen to Pitt, St. James's, 8 Apr. 1786, Private, P.R.O. 30/8/151 ff. 47–48.
39. Palmerston to Wellington, Broadlands, 21 Jan. 1835, Private, Wellington Papers.
40. Palmerston to H. Taylor, Stanhope Street, 29 May 1836, Confidential, Palmerston Papers RC/CC/21/1–2.
41. Memorandum, Aust, 5 Aug. 1789, Grenville MSS.
42. Receipt signed by Darlot, Foreign Post Office, 17 Jan. 1804, Add. MS 38358 f. 19.
43. Minute, Backhouse, 27 Aug. 1832, F.O. 366/313.
44. Miscellaneous receipts in Add. MSS 51462–51465.
45. Unsigned memorandum, F. Conyngham, "*Note* of the Sums paid by the foreign office for Relief of Spanish Refugees," F.O., 7 Mar. 1827, F.O. 360/2.
46. Grenville to Minto, Windsor, 27 Nov. 1799, Secret, draft, Aspinall, *Later Corresp. Geo. III*, vol. 3, 299 n. 1.

relief from their late Father's Dominions."⁴⁷ £2,000 secret service money was employed to support the Duke of Orlean's attempt in 1808 to rescue his mother from Spain and take her to Malta.⁴⁸ Woodbine Parish, consul general at Buenos Ayres, paid the captain of a merchant vessel £30 in 1829 to quarter British marines called in to protect the British mission during some local unrest.⁴⁹ Aberdeen authorized Lord Cowley, ambassador at Paris, to advance £200 to a debt-ridden Englishman so that he could return to England and resume his profession. The amount was to be repaid to government.⁵⁰

47. Perceval to Wellesley, Downing Street, 8 Dec. 1809, Private, Add. MS 37295 ff. 199–200.
48. Canning to Portland, Claremount, 7 Nov. 1808, Private & Secret, copy, Canning MSS Bundle 32.
49. Minute, Backhouse ?, on Parish to Aberdeen, Buenos Ayres, 25 July 1829, F.O. 366/77.
50. Addington to Cowley, Foreign Office, 21 Mar. 1845, Private, F.O. 519/65.

Select Bibliography

Manuscript Sources

The manuscript sources consulted for this study are listed below. In every case the complete collection of each set of papers has been listed rather than the specific volumes in which relevant material was found. This information is contained in the footnotes throughout the text.

British Museum:

Add. MSS 28040–28095; Eg. MSS 3498–3505. Leeds Papers.

Add. MS 33099. Correspondence of Thomas Robinson, Baron Grantham, and his family with the Earl of Chichester and members of his family.

Add. MSS 34412–34471. Auckland Papers.

Add. MSS 35349–36278. Hardwicke Papers.

Add. MS 36806. Official and private letters to Lord Mountstuart as Ambassador to Spain, 28 January 1783 to 15 December 1784.

Add. MSS 37274–37318. Wellesley Papers.

Add. MSS 37842–37935. Windham Papers.

Add. MSS 38190–38489; 38564–38581. Liverpool Papers.

Add. MSS 38734–38770. Huskisson Papers.

Add. MSS 40181–40617. Peel Papers.

Add. MSS 40862–40877. Ripon Papers.

Add. MSS 41197–41200. Sir William Hamilton Papers.

Add. MSS 41312–41319. Ellis Papers. (Add. MS 41315 letters and correspondence of John Bidwell).

Add. MSS 41511–41566. Heytesbury Papers.

Add. MSS 42772–42846. Rose Papers.

Add. MSS 43039–43358. Aberdeen Papers.

Add. MS 45176. Howard de Walden Papers.

Add. MSS 45518–45523. Willes Papers.

Add. MSS 46914–46915. Broughton Papers. (Supplement).

Add. MSS 47559–47601. Papers of and Relating to Charles James Fox the statesman.

Add. MSS 48218–48301. Morley Papers.

Add. MSS 48383–48416. Paget Papers.

Add. MSS 49173–49195. Perceval Papers.
Add. MSS 51318–52254. Holland House Papers.
B.M. Loan 57. Bathurst Papers.

Public Record Office: Departmental Records:

F.O. 5. United States, General Correspondence, 2d Series.
F.O. 22. Denmark, General Correspondence.
F.O. 26. Flanders, General Correspondence.
F.O. 27. France, General Correspondence.
F.O. 37. Holland, General Correspondence.
F.O. 64. Prussia, General Correspondence.
F.O. 65. Russia, General Correspondence.
F.O. 67. Sardinia, General Correspondence.
F.O. 72. Spain, General Correspondence.
F.O. 78. Turkey, General Correspondence.
F.O. 83. Great Britain and General Correspondence.
F.O. 84. Slave Trade Correspondence.
F.O. 92. Continent Treaty Papers.
F.O. 95. Miscellaneous, First Series.
F.O. 96. Miscellaneous, Second Series.
F.O. 97. Supplement to General Correspondence.
F.O. 366. Chief Clerk's Department, Correspondence.
S.P. 44. Domestic Entry Books and other records of the Secretaries of State
    prior to 1782.
A.O. 2. Audit Office, Declared Accounts.
T. 27. Treasury Out Letters, General.
Adm. 1. Admiralty In Letters.

Public Record Office: Collections of Private Papers:

F.O. 323/6 Papers of Backhouse's Mission to Don Carlos in June 1834.
F.O. 334. Henry Pierrepont Papers.
F.O. 351. Hertslet Papers.
F.O. 352. Stratford Canning Papers.
F.O. 353. Jackson Papers.
F.O. 355. Arthur Aston Papers.
F.O. 357. Henderson Papers.
F.O. 360. Howard de Walden Papers.
F.O. 391. Edmund Hammond Papers.
F.O. 519. Cowley Papers.
F.O. 528. Hervey Papers.
P.R.O. 30/8. Chatham Papers.

P.R.O. 30/22. Lord John Russell, first Earl Russell Papers.
P.R.O. 30/29. Granville Papers.
P.R.O. 30/58. Dacres Adams Papers.

Duke University Library:

Charles Arbuthnot Papers.
John Backhouse Papers.
Bandinel Family Papers.
George Canning Papers.
John Wilson Croker Papers.
Sir John Easthope Papers.
William Eden, First Baron Auckland Papers.
Robert Banks Jenkinson, Second Earl of Liverpool Scrapbook.
Arthur Wellesley, First Duke of Wellington MSS.

Other Collections of Private Papers:

Barnes MSS. The Papers of George Hammond and Edmund, Lord Hammond, in the possession of Colonel A. C. Barnes, D.S.O., O.B.E., Foxholme, Surrey.
Canning MSS. The Papers of George Canning, Archives Department, Leeds Public Libraries.
Grenville MSS. Microfilm and Notes in possession of the estate of the late Professor W. B. Hamilton, Duke University.
Hammond Papers. Letters from eminent Statesmen to George Hammond, c. 1795 to 1829, M581, British Library of Political and Economic Science, London.
Harrowby MSS. Manuscripts of the Ryder Family in possession of the Right Honourable, the Earl of Harrowby, Sandon Hall, Staffordshire.
Holland (Perceval) Papers. The Papers of Spencer Perceval in the possession of David Holland, Librarian, The Library, House of Commons, Westminster.
Lucas Collection. Includes the papers of Thomas Robinson, second Baron Grantham. Bedfordshire Record Office, Bedford.
Palmerston Papers. The papers of Henry John Temple, 3d Viscount Palmerston, owned by the Trustees of the Broadlands Archives and on temporary deposit for cataloguing at the National Register of Archives, London.
Wellington Papers. The papers of Arthur Wellesley, first Duke of Wellington from 1832 to 1852, in possession of His Grace the Duke of Wellington and on temporary deposit for cataloguing at the National Register of Archives, London.

G. Willis Autograph Collection. Collection of Letters from miscellaneous British statesmen, politicians, and other eminent figures of the eighteenth to the twentieth centuries. London County Record Office, County Hall.

PRINTED SOURCES

Adams, Ephraim Douglass. *The Influence of Grenville on Pitt's Foreign Policy, 1787–1798.* "Carnegie Institute of Washington, No. 13." Washington, D.C., 1904.

Adams, William Pitt. *Papers Relating to the Death and Funeral of the Late William Pitt Adams, Esq.* London, 1853.

Allen, W. Gore. *King William IV.* London, 1960.

Anderson, Mary Adeline. "Edmund Hammond, Permanent Under Secretary of State for Foreign Affairs, 1854–1873." Ph.D. dissertation, University of London, 1955.

Annual Biography and Obituary. 21 vols. London, 1817–1837.

The Annual Register.

Ashley, Evelyn. *The Life and Correspondence of Henry John Temple, Viscount Palmerston.* 2 vols. London, 1879.

Ashton-Gwatkin, Frank T. *The British Foreign Service.* Syracuse, N.Y., 1950.

Aspinall, Arthur. "The Cabinet Council, 1783–1835," *Proceedings of the British Academy*, London, 38 (1952), 145–252.

———. "Canning's Return to Office in September, 1822," *English Historical Review*, 78 (July, 1963), 531–45.

———. *Politics and the Press c. 1780–1850.* London, 1949.

——— (ed.). *The Diary of Henry Hobhouse, 1820–1827.* London, 1947.

———. *The Formation of Canning's Ministry, February to August, 1827.* "The Camden Society, 3d Series," vol. 59. London, 1937.

———. *The Later Correspondence of George III.* 5 vols. Cambridge, 1962–1970.

———. *Letters of King George IV, 1812–1830.* 3 vols. London, 1938.

———. *Three Early Nineteenth Century Diaries.* London, 1952.

——— and E. Anthony Smith (eds.). *English Historical Documents 1783–1832.* London, 1959.

Auckland, Robert John Eden 3d Baron (ed.). *The Journal and Correspondence of William, Lord Auckland.* 4 vols. London, 1861–1862.

Aylmer, G.E. "Place Bills and the Separation of Powers: Some Seventeenth Century Origins of the 'Non-Political' Civil Service," *Transactions of the Royal Historical Society*, 5th ser., 15 (1965), 45–69.

———. "Problems of Method in the Study of Administrative History,"

Annali della Fondazione Italiana per la Storia Amministrativa, 1 (1958), 20–26.

Bagot, Captain Josceline (ed.). *George Canning and His Friends*. 2 vols. London, 1923.

Balfour, Lady Francis. *The Life of George, Fourth Earl of Aberdeen*. 2 vols. London, 1923.

The Baltimore Sun (1856).

Bamford, Francis and the Duke of Wellington (eds.). *The Journal of Mrs. Arbuthnot, 1820–1832*. 2 vols. London, 1950.

Bandinel, James. *Some Account of the Trade in Slaves from Africa as connected with Europe and America; From the Introduction of the Trade into Modern Europe down to the Present Time; Especially with Reference to the Efforts Made by the British Government for its Extinction*. London, 1842.

Barker, G. F. Russell and Alan H. Stenning (eds.). *The Record of Old Westminsters*. 2 vols. London, 1928.

Barnes, Donald Grove. *George III and William Pitt, 1783–1806*. Reprint. New York, 1965.

Bartlett, C. J. *Castlereagh*. New York, 1966.

———. "Statecraft, Power and Influence." In *Britain Pre-Eminent: Studies of British World Influence in the Nineteenth Century*, ed. C. J. Bartlett, pp. 172–93. London, 1969.

——— (ed.). *Britain Pre-Eminent: Studies of British World Influence in the Nineteenth Century*. London, 1969.

Bell, Herbert C. F. *Lord Palmerston*. 2 vols. London, 1936.

Bemis, Samuel Flagg. "British Secret Service and the French-American Alliance," *American Historical Review*, 29 (Apr., 1924), 474–95.

Benjamin, Lewis Saul (ed.). *The Windham Papers*. 2 vols. London, 1913.

Benson, Arthur Christopher and Viscount Esher (eds.). *The Letters of Queen Victoria, 1837–1861*. 3 vols. New York, 1907.

Bindoff, S. T. "Unreformed Diplomatic Service," *Transactions of the Royal Historical Society*, 4th ser., 18 (1935), 143–72.

———, E. F. Malcolm Smith, and C. K. Webster (eds.). *British Diplomatic Representatives, 1789–1852*. "The Camden Society, 3d Series," vol. 50. London, 1934.

Bishop, Donald G. *The Administration of British Foreign Relations*. Syracuse, N.Y., 1961.

Blake, Robert. *Disraeli*. London, 1966.

Blakeley, Brian L. *The Colonial Office 1868–1892*. "Duke Historical Publications." Durham, N.C., 1972.

Boase, Frederic. *Modern English Biography*. 6 vols. Truro, 1892–1921.

Bourne, Kenneth. *The Foreign Policy of Victorian England 1830–1902*. London, 1970.

Brock, William Ranulf. *Lord Liverpool and Liberal Toryism, 1820–1827.* 2d ed. London, 1967.

Brooke, John. *King George III.* New York, 1972.

Browning, Oscar (ed.). *The Political Memoranda of The Duke of Leeds.* "The Camden Society, New Series," vol. 35. London, 1884.

Bryant, Arthur. *The Age of Elegance, 1812–1822.* London, 1950.

Burke's Commoners.

Burke's Landed Gentry of Great Britain and Ireland.

Burke's Landed Gentry of Ireland.

Burke's Peerage and Baronetage.

Burtchaell, George Dames and Thomas Ulick Sadleir (eds.). *Alumni Dublinenses.* New ed. Dublin, 1935.

Butterfield, Herbert. *George III and the Historians.* London, 1957.

Cecil, Algernon. *British Foreign Secretaries, 1807–1916.* London, 1927.

———. "The Foreign Office," *Cambridge History of British Foreign Policy,* ed. Sir. Adolphus W. Ward and G. P. Gooch, vol. 3, 538–630. 3 vols. Cambridge, 1922–1923.

Cell, John W. *British Colonial Administration in the Mid-Nineteenth Century: The Policy-Making Process.* New Haven, 1970.

Christie, Ian R. "The Cabinet in the Reign of George III, to 1790," pp. 55–108 in *Myth and Reality in Late Eighteenth-Century British Politics and Other Papers,* ed. Ian R. Christie. Berkeley, 1970.

Cobban, Alfred. *Ambassadors and Secret Agents: The Diplomacy of the First Earl of Malmesbury at The Hague.* London, 1954.

———. "British Secret Service in France, 1784–1792," *English Historical Review,* 69 (Apr., 1954), 226–61.

Cohen, Emmeline W. *The Growth of the British Civil Service, 1780–1939.* London, 1941.

Colchester, Lord (ed.). *A Political Diary 1828–1830 by Edward Law, Lord Ellenborough.* 2 vols. London, 1881.

The Complete Peerage of England Scotland Ireland Great Britain and the United Kingdom, Extant Extinct or Dormant by GEC. New ed. 13 vols. London, 1910–1940.

Connell, Brian (ed.). *Regina vs. Palmerston: The Correspondence Between Queen Victoria and Her Foreign and Prime Minister, 1837–1865.* London, 1962.

Cromwell, Valerie. "An Incident in the Development of the Permanent Under Secretaryship at the Foreign Office," *Bulletin of the Institute of Historical Research,* 33 (May, 1960), 99–113.

———. "The Private Member of the House of Commons and Foreign Policy in the Nineteenth Century," *Liber Memorialis Sir Maurice Powicke: Studies Presented to the International Commission for the History of Representative and Parliamentary Institutions,* 27 (Louvain, 1965), 193–218.

—— and Zara Steiner. "The Foreign Office before 1914; A study in resistance," pp. 167–94 in *Studies in the Growth of Nineteenth-Century Government*, ed. Gillian Sutherland. Totowa, N.J., 1972.

Dalling and Bulwer, Sir Henry Lytton, Lord. *The Life of Henry John Temple, Viscount Palmerston.* Vol. 3 ed. Evelyn Ashley. 3 vols. London, 1870–1874.

Darlington, W. A. *Sheridan, 1751–1816.* London, 1951.

Dauglish, M. G. and P. K. Stephenson (eds.). *The Harrow School Register, 1800–1911.* London, 1911.

D'Auvergne, Edmund B. *Envoys Extraordinary.* London, 1937.

De Fonblanque, Edward Barrington. *Lives of the Lords Strangford.* London, 1877.

Derry, John W. *Charles James Fox.* New York, 1972.

The Dictionary of National Biography. 24 vols. London, 1921–1927.

Disbrowe, Charlotte Anne Albania. *Old Days in Diplomacy: Recollections of a Closed Century.* London, 1903.

Dobreé, Bonamy (ed.). *The Letters of King George III.* London, 1935.

Dudley, Earl of. *Letters of The Earl of Dudley to the Bishop of Llandaff.* London, 1840.

Ehrman, John. *The British Government and Commercial Negotiations with Europe, 1783–1793.* Cambridge, 1962.

——. *The Younger Pitt: The Years of Acclaim.* London, 1969.

Elliot, Sir Henry G. *Some Revolutions and other Diplomatic Experiences.* Ed. by his daughter. London, 1922.

Ellis, K. L. "British Communications and Diplomacy in the Eighteenth Century," *Bulletin of the Institute of Historical Research,* 31 (Nov., 1958), 159–67.

——. *The Post Office in the Eighteenth Century: A Study in Administrative History.* London, 1958.

Evans, Florence M. Greir. *The Principal Secretary of State.* "Publications of the University of Manchester, Historical Series," vol. 43. Manchester, 1923.

Festing, Gabrielle. *John Hookham Frere and His Friends.* London, 1899.

Fisher, Arthur (ed.). *The Register of Blundell's School.* Exeter, 1904.

Fitzmaurice, Lord Edmond. *The Life of Granville George Leveson-Gower, Second Earl Granville.* 2 vols. London, 1905.

Fortescue, J. W. *British Statesmen of the Great War, 1793–1814.* Oxford, 1911.

—— (ed.). *The Correspondence of King George The Third, 1760–1783.* 6 vols. London, 1928.

Foster, Joseph (ed.). *Alumni Oxonienses: The Members of the University of Oxford, 1715–1886.* 4 vols. London, 1888.

Fothergill, Brian. *Mitred Earl: An Eighteenth Century Eccentric.* London, 1974.

Fulford, Roger. *George the Fourth*. London, 1935.

Gardiner, Rev. Robert Barlow (ed.). *The Admission Registers of St. Paul's School, from 1748–1876*. London, 1884.

Gash, Norman. *Politics in the Age of Peel*. London, 1953.

The Gentleman's Magazine.

Ginter, Donald. *Whig Organization in the General Election of 1790*. Berkeley, 1967.

Gooch, G. P. (ed.). *The Later Correspondence of Lord John Russell, 1840–1878*. 2 vols. London, 1925.

Great Britain. *Hansard's Parliamentary Debates*.

———. *Parliamentary Papers*.

———. Foreign Office. *British and Foreign State Papers*.

———. *Foreign Office Lists*.

———. Historical Manuscripts Commission. *Report on the Manuscripts of Earl Bathurst preserved at Cirencester Park*. London, 1923.

———. *Report on the Manuscripts of J. B. Fortescue, Esq., Preserved at Dropmore*. 10 vols. London, 1892–1927.

———. *Report on . . . the Manuscripts of Sir Archibald Edmonstone of Duntreath, Baronet*. "H.M.C. Various Collections," vol. 5. London, 1909.

———. Public Record Office. *Calendar of Home Office Papers, George III*. 4 vols. London, 1878–1899.

Grey, Henry, Earl. (ed.). *The Correspondence of the Late Earl Grey with His Majesty King William IV and with Sir Herbert Taylor from November 1830 to June 1832*. 2 vols. London, 1867.

Guedalla, Philip. *Palmerston*. New York, 1927.

Gun, W. T. J. (ed.). *The Harrow School Register, 1571–1800*. London, 1934.

Hall, Shirley. "Sir Edward Hertslet and His Work as Librarian and Keeper of the Papers of the Foreign Office from 1857–1896." M.A. Thesis, University of London, 1958.

Hamilton, W. B. "Constitutional and Political Reflections on the Dismissal of Lord Grenville's Ministry," *Report of the Annual Meeting of the Canadian Historical Association*, 49 (1964), 89–104.

Handover, Phyllis Margaret. *A History of the London Gazette, 1665–1965*. London, 1965.

Hanham, H. J. *The Nineteenth-Century Constitution 1815–1914: Documents and Commentary*. Cambridge, 1969.

Harcourt, Leveson Vernon (ed.). *Diaries and Correspondence of George Rose*. 2 vols. London, 1860.

Henderson, G. B. "Lord Palmerston and the Secret Service Fund," *English Historical Review*, 53 (July, 1938), 485–87.

Hertslet, Sir Edward. *Recollections of the Old Foreign Office*. London, 1901.

Hibbert, Christopher. *George IV, Prince of Wales, 1762–1811.* New York, 1972.
———. *George IV, Regent and King, 1811–1830.* London, 1973.
Himmelfarb, Gertrude. "The Writing of Social History: Recent Studies of 19th Century England," *The Journal of British Studies,* 11 (Nov., 1971) 149–70.
Hinde, Wendy. *George Canning.* London, 1973.
Holmes, Geoffrey. *British Politics in the Age of Anne.* London, 1967.
Horn, D. B. *The British Diplomatic Service, 1689–1789.* Oxford, 1961.
———. *Great Britain and Europe in the Eighteenth Century.* Oxford, 1967.
———. "Rank and Emolument in the British Diplomatic Service, 1689–1789," *Transactions of the Royal Historical Society,* 5th ser., 9 (1959), 19–49.
———. "The Machinery for the Conduct of British Foreign Policy in the Eighteenth Century," *Journal of the Society of Archivists,* 3 (July 8, 1966), 299–40.
——— (ed.). *British Diplomatic Representatives, 1689–1789.* "The Camden Society, 3d Series," vol. 46. London, 1932.
Hutton, James (ed.). *Selections from the Letters of Sir James Bland Burges, Bart.* London, 1885.
Jackson, Lady (ed.). *The Bath Archives: A Further Selection from the Diaries and Letters of Sir George Jackson . . . 1809–1816.* 2 vols. London, 1873.
———. *The Diaries and Letters of Sir George Jackson.* 2 vols. London, 1872.
Jennings, Louis J. (ed.). *The Correspondence and Diaries of John Wilson Croker.* 3 vols. London, 1884.
Joll, James (ed.). *Britain and Europe Pitt to Churchill, 1793–1940.* "The British Political Tradition," ed. Alan Bullock and F. W. Dakin, Book 3. London, 1961.
Jones, J. R. *Britain and Europe in the Seventeenth Century.* New York, 1966.
Jones, Ray. *The Nineteenth-Century Foreign Office: An Administrative History.* "L.S.E. Research Monographs, 9." London, 1971.
Jones-Parry, E. "Undersecretaries of State for Foreign Affairs, 1782–1855," *English Historical Review,* 49 (Apr., 1934), 308–20.
——— (ed.). *The Correspondence of Lord Aberdeen and Princess Lieven, 1832–1854.* "The Camden Society, 3d Series," vols. 60, 62. London, 1938–1939.
Judd, Gerrit P. IV. *Members of Parliament, 1734–1832.* "Yale Historical Publications," Miscellany No. 61. New Haven, 1955.
Kaufman, W. W. *British Policy and the Independence of Latin America.* "Yale Historical Publications," Miscellany No. 52. New Haven, 1951.
Kay-Shuttleworth, Nina L. *A Life of Sir Woodbine Parish.* London, 1910.
Keith, Sir Robert Murray. *Memoirs and Correspondence of Sir Robert Murray Keith.* 2 vols. London, 1849.

Klein, Ira. "The Anglo-Russian Convention and the Problem of Central Asia, 1907–1914," *The Journal of British Studies*, 11 (Nov., 1971), 126–47.

Knighton, Lady D. *Memoirs of Sir William Knighton*. 2 vols. London, 1838.

Kriegel, Abraham D. "The Politics of the Whigs in Opposition, 1834–1835," *The Journal of British Studies*, 7 (May, 1968), 65–91.

Kubicek, Robert V. *The Administration of Imperialism: Joseph Chamberlain at the Colonial Office*. "Duke University Commonwealth Studies Center," No. 37. Durham, N.C., 1969.

Lachs, Phyllis S. *The Diplomatic Corps under Charles II and James II*. New Brunswick, N.J., 1965.

Lane-Poole, Stanley. *The Life of the Right Honourable Stratford Canning, Viscount Stratford de Redcliffe*. 2 vols. London, 1888.

Lascelles, Edward Charles Ponsonby. *The Life of Charles James Fox*. Reprint. New York, 1970.

Lee, Maurice J. "The Jacobean Diplomatic Service," *The American Historical Review*, 72 (July, 1957), 1264–82.

Leigh, Richard Arthur Austin. *The Eton College Register, 1753–1790*. Eton, 1921.

Leveson-Gower, F. (ed.). *Letters of Harriet Countess Granville, 1810–1845*. 2 vols. London, 1894.

Lewis, Sir George Cornewall, Bart. *Essays on the Administration of Great Britain from 1783–1830*, ed. Sir Maurice Head, Bart. London, 1864.

Lewis, W. S. (ed.). *The Yale Edition of Horace Walpole's Correspondence*. 34 vols. New Haven, 1937–1965.

Lincoln's Inn, London. *Records of the Honourable Society of Lincoln's Inn. The Black Books, 1422–1845*. 4 vols. London, 1897–1902.

Londonderry, Charles William Stewart Vane, Marquess of (ed.). *Correspondence, Despatches, and other Papers of Viscount Castlereagh*. 12 vols. London, 1848–1853.

Lynch, John. "British Policy and Spanish America, 1783–1808," *Journal of Latin American Studies*, 1 (May, 1969), 1–30.

Macalpine, Ida and Richard Hunter. *George III and the Mad-Business*. New York, 1969.

MacDonagh, O.O.G.M. "The Nineteenth-Century Revolution in Government: A Reappraisal," *Historical Journal*, 1 (1958), 52–67.

Malmesbury, Third Earl of. *Memoirs of an Ex-Minister: An Autobiography*. 2 vols. 3d ed. London, 1884.

——— (ed.) *Diaries and Correspondence of James Harris, first Earl of Malmesbury*. 4 vols. London, 1844.

———. *A Series of Letters of the First Earl of Malmesbury*. 2 vols. London, 1870.

Martin, Kingsley. *The Crown and the Establishment*. London, 1962.

Melville, Lewis (ed.). *The Huskisson Papers*. London, 1931.

Middleton, Charles R. "The Emergence of Constitutional Bureaucracy in the British Foreign Office, 1782–1846," *Public Administration*, 54 (Winter, 1975), 365–81.

—————. "The Formation of Canning's Ministry and the Evolution of the British Cabinet, February to August 1827," *Canadian Journal of History*, 10 (Apr., 1975), 17–34.

—————. "John Backhouse and the Origins of the Permanent Undersecretaryship for Foreign Affairs: 1828–1842," *The Journal of British Studies*, 13 (May, 1974), 24–45.

—————. "Retrenchment and Reform: The Case of the British Diplomatic Presents, 1782–1832," *The Rocky Mountain Social Science Journal*, 11 (Oct., 1974), 61–73.

Minto, Lady (ed.). *Life and Letters of Sir Gilbert Elliot, Earl of Minto.* 3 vols. London, 1874.

Mitchell, Harvey. *The Underground War against Revolutionary France. The Missions of William Wickham, 1794–1800.* Oxford, 1965.

Namier, Lewis. *Crossroads of Power: Essays on Eighteenth-Century England.* London, 1962.

—————. *England in the Age of the American Revolution.* 2d ed. New York, 1961.

————— and John Brooke. *The History of Parliament: The House of Commons, 1754–1790.* 3 vols. London, 1964.

Nelson, Ronald Roy. *The Home Office 1782–1801.* Durham, N.C., 1969.

Nicholl, Allardyce. *A History of English Drama, 1660–1900.* 2d ed. 6 vols. Cambridge, 1965–1967.

Nightingale, Robert T. "Personnel of the British Foreign Office and Diplomatic Service, 1851–1929," *American Political Science Review*, 24 (May, 1930), 310–31.

O'Byrne, William R. *A Naval Biographical Dictionary.* 2 vols. London, 1849.

Paget, Sir Augustus B. (ed.). *The Paget Papers: Diplomatic and other Correspondence of the Right Hon. Sir Arthur Paget, G.C.B., 1794–1807.* 2 vols. London, 1896.

Pares, Richard. *King George III and the Politicians.* Oxford, 1953.

Parker, Charles Stuart (ed.). *Sir Robert Peel, from His Private Papers.* 3 vols. London, 1890–1899.

Parish, William D. (ed.). *List of Carthusians 1800–1870.* Lewes, 1879.

Parris, Henry. *Constitutional Bureaucracy.* "Minerva Series of Student Handbooks," No. 23. London, 1969.

—————. "The Nineteenth-Century Revolution in Government: A Reappraisal Reappraised," *Historical Journal*, 3 (1960), 17–37.

—————. "The Origins of the Permanent Civil Service, 1780–1830," *Public Administration*, 46 (Summer, 1968), 143–66.

Peel, George (ed.). *The Private Letters of Sir Robert Peel.* London, 1920.

Pellew, George. *The Life and Correspondence of the Right Honble. Henry Ad-*

dington, First Viscount Sidmouth. 3 vols. London, 1847.

Perkins, Bradford (ed.). *Youthful America: Selections from Henry Unwin Addington's "Residence in the United States of America, 1822, 23, 24, 25."* "University of California Publications in History," vol. 65. Berkeley, 1960.

Phipps, Edmund (ed.). *Memoirs of the Political and Literary Life of Robert Plummer Ward.* 2 vols. London, 1850.

Platt, D. C. M. *The Cinderella Service: British Consuls since 1825.* London, 1971.

———. *Finance, Trade, and Politics in British Foreign Policy, 1815–1914.* Oxford, 1968.

Plumb, J. H. "The Organization of the Cabinet in the Reign of Queen Anne," *Transactions of the Royal Historical Society*, 5th ser., 7 (1957), 137–57.

Ponsonby, Major General Sir John. *The Ponsonby Family.* London, 1929.

Prouty, Roger. *The Transformation of the Board of Trade 1830–1855.* London, 1957.

The Records of the Foreign Office 1782–1939. "Public Record Office Handbooks, No. 13." London, 1969.

Reich, Jerome. "The Slave Trade at the Congress of Vienna—A Study in English Public Opinion," *Journal of Negro History*, 53 (Apr., 1968), 129–43.

Reitan, E. A. "The Civil List in Eighteenth-Century British Politics: Parliamentary Supremacy versus the Independence of the Crown," *Historical Journal*, 9 (1966), 318–37.

Ridley, Jasper. *Lord Palmerston.* New York, 1971.

Roberts, Michael. *The Whig Party, 1807–1812.* London, 1939.

Rolo, P. J. V. *George Canning: Three Biographical Sketches.* London, 1965.

Romilly, S. H. *Letters to 'Ivy' From the First Earl of Dudley.* London, 1905.

Roseveare, Henry. *The Treasury: The Evolution of a British Institution.* New York, 1970.

Ross, Charles (ed.). *Correspondence of Charles, First Marquis Cornwallis.* 3 vols. London, 1859.

The Royal Kalendar.

Russell, Lord John (ed.). *Memorials and Correspondence of Charles James Fox.* 4 vols. London, 1853–1857.

Sadler, Michael. *Archdeacon Francis Wrangham, 1769–1842.* "Supplement to the Bibliographical Society's Transactions No. 12." Oxford, 1937.

Sanders, Lloyd G. (ed.). *The Melbourne Papers.* London, 1889.

Scheener, Edward. *Memoir of an Employe Most Respectfully Addressed to the King.* London, 1830.

———. *Statement of Facts Most Respectfully Submitted to His Majesty's Ministers 3rd Nov. 1830.* London, 1830.

Seton-Watson, R. W. *Britain in Europe, 1789–1914.* Cambridge, 1937.

Sherwig, John M. *Guineas and Gunpowder: British Foreign Aid in the Wars with France, 1793–1815*. Cambridge, Mass., 1969.

Southey, Rev. Charles Cuthbert (ed.). *Life and Correspondence of Robert Southey*. 6 vols. London, 1849–1850.

Southgate, Donald. *'The Most English Minister . . .': The Policies and Politics of Palmerston*. New York, 1966.

Stanhope, Philip Henry 5th Earl. *Life of the Right Honourable William Pitt*. 4 vols. London, 1861–1862.

———. *Notes of Conversations with the Duke of Wellington, 1831–1851*. London, 1888.

Stapleton, Augustus Granville. *George Canning and His Times*. London, 1859.

Stapleton, Edward J. (ed.). *Some Official Correspondence of George Canning*. 2 vols. London, 1887.

Stapylton, H. E. C. (ed.). *The Eton School Lists from 1791 to 1850*. 2d ed. London, 1864.

Steiner, Zara. *The Foreign Office and Foreign Policy 1898–1914*. Cambridge, 1969.

Strachey, Lytton and Roger Fulford (eds.). *The Greville Memoirs, 1814–1860*. 8 vols. London, 1938.

Taylor, Alan J.P. *The Trouble Makers: Dissent Over Foreign Policy, 1792–1939*. London, 1957.

Taylor, Ernest (ed.). *The Taylor Papers*. London, 1913.

Temperley, Harold. *The Foreign Policy of Canning 1822–1827*. 2d ed. London, 1966.

——— and Lillian M. Penson. *A Century of Diplomatic Blue Books, 1814–1914*. Cambridge, 1938.

Thomson, Mark Alméras. *The Secretaries of State, 1681–1782*. Oxford, 1932.

Tilley, Sir John Anthony Cecil and Sir Stephen Gaselee. *The Foreign Office*. 2d ed. London, 1933.

The Times (London).

Trevelyan, George Macaulay. *Lord Grey of the Reform Bill*. 2d ed. London, 1929.

Trollope, Anthony. *The Three Clerks: A Novel*. London, 1858.

Trotter, John Bernard. *Memoirs of the Latter Years of the Right Honourable Charles James Fox*. London, 1811.

Venn, J. A. (Compiler). *Alumni Cantabrigienses: Part II, 1772–1900*. 6 vols. Cambridge, 1940.

The Victoria History of the County of Hampshire.

Walford, Edward. *The County Families of the United Kingdom*. London, 1875.

Walker, Franklin A. "The Rejection of Stratford Canning by Nicholas I," *Bulletin of the Institute of Historical Research*, 40 (May, 1967), 50–64.

Ward, Adolphus William. *Great Britain and Hanover*. Oxford, 1899.

Webster, C.K. *The Foreign Policy of Castlereagh, 1812–1822*. 2 vols. Vol. 2, 2d ed. London, 1931–1934.

———. *The Foreign Policy of Palmerston, 1830–1841*. 2 vols. London, 1951.

———. "Lord Palmerston at Work, 1830–1841," *Politica*, 1 (Aug., 1934), 129–44.

——— (ed.). *Some Letters of the Duke of Wellington to his Brother William Wellesley-Pole*. "The Camden Society, 3d Series," vol. 79. London, 1948.

Wellesley, Frederick Arthur (ed.). *The Diary and Correspondence of Henry Wellesley First Lord Cowley, 1790–1846*. London, 1928.

Wellington, Duke of (ed.). *Despatches, Correspondence, and Memoranda of Field Marshal Arthur Duke of Wellington, 1819–1832*. 8 vols. London, 1867–1880.

———. *Supplementary Despatches, Correspondence, and Memoranda of Field Marshal Arthur Duke of Wellington*. 15 vols. London, 1858–1872.

Wheatley, Henry Benjamin (ed.). *The Historical and Posthumous Memoirs of Sir Nathanial Wraxall*. 5 vols. London, 1884.

Wheeler-Holohan, V. *History of the King's Messengers*. London, 1935

Wickwire, Franklin B. "The King's Friends, Civil Servants or Politicians," *The American Historical Review*, 71 (Oct., 1965), 18–42.

Williams, Basil. "The Foreign Office Under the First Two Georges," *Blackwood's Magazine*, 81 (Jan., 1907), 92–105.

Williams, E. T. "The Cabinet in the Eighteenth Century," in *The Making of English History*, ed. Robert Livingston Schuyler and Herman Ausubel, pp. 378–91. New York, 1952.

Wood, A. C. "The English Embassy at Constantinople 1660–1762," *English Historical Review*, 40 (1925), 533–61.

Woodham-Smith, Cecil. *Queen Victoria: Her Life and Times*, vol. 1, *1819–1861*. London, 1972.

Yonge, Charles Duke. *Life and Administration of Robert Banks Jenkinson, 2d Earl of Liverpool*. 3 vols. London, 1868.

Young. D. M. *The Colonial Office in the Early Nineteenth Century*. "Imperial Studies," No. 22. London, 1961.

Ziegler, Philip. *King William the Fourth*. New York, 1973.

INDEX

Abercromby, Ralph, biog., 260–61
Aberdeen, Earl of. *See* Hamilton-Gordon
A'Court, Sir William (1st Baron Heytesbury), 45, 80; as diplomatist, 228, 234
Adair, Robert, as diplomatist, 229
Adams, William Pitt, biog., 261
Addington, Henry (1st Viscount Sidmouth), 49, 58, 77, 109, 110; ministry of, 55, 136
Addington, Henry Unwin, 14, 212; biog., 261; as diplomatist, 237; as undersecretary, 127n, 133n, 134–35, 139, 149, 211
Adelaide, Queen, 295
Admiralty, 105, 120; relations with F.O., 8, 129; secretaries of, 142n, 145n, 149
Adrianople, Treaty of (1829), 80
Africa, 8, 200
Aix-la-Chapelle, Congress of (1818), 166
Albert, Prince, 16, 193n; foreign policy and, 94
Alexander I, Emperor, 32
Alston, Francis Beilbey, biog., 261
Althorp, Viscount. *See* Spencer
America, United States of, 10, 209, 254; British relations with, 30, 38–39, 74n, 75, 241; mission of Franklin, Deane, and Lee from, 334
American secretaryship: office of, 160; responsibilities of, 10, 10n
Amiens, Treaty of (1802), 24, 297
Ancell, Richard, 173–74; biog., 261–62
Ancram, Earl of. *See* Kerr
Andrew, Littlewood, 235
Anne, Queen, reign of, 20, 42–43
Antrobus, Gibbs Crawfurd, biog., 262
Arbuthnot, Charles, 120; biog., 262; as consul general, 247; as diplomatist, 168, 215n, 222; as précis writer, 172; as undersecretary, 136, 235–36
Arbuthnot, Harriett, 131, 273
Army, foreign policy and, 25
Ashburnham, Charles, biog., 262
Auckland, Baron. *See* Eden
Aust, George, 16–17; biog., 263; as senior clerk, 124, 159, 160, 338; as undersecretary, 126–27, 127n, 129–30, 138, 146, 147, 320
Austria, 90, 240; British relations with, 27–29, 32, 34, 61, 74, 76, 89, 220

Backhouse, George Canning, 186, 192n; biog., 263

Backhouse, John, 53, 85, 115n, 119, 185, 186, 188, 195n, 223, 250–51, 252; biog., 263; permanent undersecretaryship and, 128–29, 132–33, 257; secret service and, 335; as undersecretary, 124, 127, 127n, 133, 133n, 140, 141–42, 144n, 145, 147, 149, 190–93, 199, 205–6, 210–11, 322–23
Bagot, Sir Charles, 110, 178; biog., 264; as diplomatist, 150, 226, 231; as undersecretary, 142n, 143
Baltic, British interests in, 35–36
Bandinel, James, 16, 116, 196, 246, 268, 338; biog., 264; chief clerkship and, 192–93; as senior clerk, 197–201, 206
Bankhead, Charles, 179; biog., 264
Baring, Francis, 204–6
Barnes, Captain, 252
Bartlett, Richard, 180; biog., 264
Bathurst, Henry (3d Earl Bathurst): biog., 265; as colonial secretary, 189; F.O. undersecretaryship and, 138, 141; as foreign secretary, 106; in inner cabinet, 48, 82, 109, 127
Bavaria, 74
Belgium, 29, 45, 51, 89, 93, 188, 216; British relations with, 33, 231, 231n
Bentham, Jeremy, 13
Bentinck, Lord George, 116; biog., 265
Beresford, William Carr (1st Viscount Beresford), 55
Bergne, John Brodribb, 193, 194–95; biog., 265
Berlin, Congress of (1878), 3
Bidwell, John, 202, 205; biog., 265; chief clerkship and, 192–93; as senior clerk, 195–97, 206, 251
Bidwell, John Jr., 17; biog., 266
Bidwell, Thomas, 116, 162, 175, 179, 195; biog., 266; as chief clerk, 155–57, 162, 163
Bidwell, Thomas Jr., 164, 195, 207; biog., 266–67; as chief clerk, 155n, 190, 192, 206; as Translator of the German Language, 175
Binning, Lord. *See* Hamilton
Blackburn, John Edward, biog., 267
Bligh, John, as diplomatist, 230–31
Board of Control, 128, 149. *See also* East India Company; India
Board of Trade: consular service and, 244;

diplomatic service and, 231; F.O. relations with, 197
Bond, Phineas, 338
Bosanquet, George, 239
Bouverie, Edward Pleydell, biog., 267
British foreign policy, vii, 97, 122, 153–54, 187; principles of, 20–41, 242
Broughton, Bryan: biog., 267; as senior clerk, 159, 160–61
Broughton, Charles Rivington, 337–38; biog., 267–68; chief clerkship and, 190; F.O. agencies of, 166–69; secret service account and, 334
Browne, John Henry Temple, 16n; biog., 268
Bruce, James, biog., 268
Bruce, John, 173
Bruce, W. Stewart Crawfurd, biog., 268–69
Brunswick, Duchess of, 338–39
Burges, Sir James Bland Bart., 101, 283; biog., 269; as undersecretary, 100, 123n, 125, 130, 137, 138, 140, 142–43, 147–48, 235, 320
Burke, Edmund, economical reforms of, 6
Bury, Richard, biog., 269
Bute, Earl of. See Stuart
Buxton, Thomas Fowell, 199
Byng, Frederick Gerald: biog., 269–70; as senior clerk, 146, 201–3

Cabinet, 100; foreign policy and, 3–5, 44–65, 74–75, 79–81, 87–88, 91, 98, 101, 112–13, 114, 151, 239, 240, 255–57, 259; general development of, vii, 4, 42–44, 46n, 59, 67, 68–69; minutes of, 56–58, 73, 75; summoning of, 133
Cade, Joseph, 179; biog., 270
Campbell, John Frederick Vaughan, biog., 270
Canning, Charles John (1st Viscount Canning), 186; biog., 270; as cabinet minister, 139n; as undersecretary, 125, 133n, 134
Canning, George, 45, 52–53, 55, 58, 63, 79–82, 116, 120, 123, 126, 128n, 140, 143, 186, 195, 210, 277, 287, 295; biog., 270; consular service and, 244, 247, 248–49, 250, 251; diplomatic service and, 216, 218, 219, 225, 228–29, 230, 234, 236, 238–39, 241, 243; as diplomatist, 167n; F.O. reforms and, 11, 163–64, 171, 175, 177, 179–83, 187, 189, 190, 193, 194, 196, 198, 202, 203, 206, 208–9, 212, 244, 322; F.O. undersecretaryship and, 124–25, 125n, 127, 128, 130, 131–32, 133, 138, 138n, 139, 145, 147, 302; foreign policy of, 26, 27–28, 29, 32, 33,
34, 35, 37, 78, 136, 200; as foreign secretary, 97, 97n, 98, 105–6, 109–11, 112–13, 115, 169, 187n, 189, 256; in inner cabinet, 48–49; secret service and, 334–35, 335n, 336, 337n, 338; as undersecretary, 130, 136, 138, 139, 142n, 148, 158, 263
Canning, Harriet, 139, 274
Canning, Stratford (1st Viscount Stratford de Redcliffe), 107; biog., 270; as diplomatist, 223, 224, 226, 228, 229, 232–33; as précis writer, 171
Carlos, Don, 57, 141
Carmarthen, Marquess of. See Osborne
Carter, Richard, 271
Cartwright, Thomas, biog., 271
Casamajor, Justinian, biog., 271
Castlereagh, Viscount. See Stewart
Cathcart, William Schaw (1st Earl Cathcart), as diplomatist, 224, 235
Cavendish, William Spencer (6th Duke of Devonshire), as diplomatist, 230
Cavendish-Bentinck, Lord George. See Bentinck
Cavendish-Bentinck, Henry (3d Duke of Portland), 17, 97, 102, 173; ministry of (1783), 23, 279
Cavendish-Bentinck, William Henry (4th Duke of Portland), 116
Cecil, James (1st Marquess of Salisbury), 266
Chad, George, 223
Charles X, King, 146, 277
Chatfield, Frederick, 252
Chatham, Earl of. See Pitt
Chaumont, Treaty of (1814), 25
Chelsea Hospital, 146
China, 194, 202, 323
Civil List, 102, 144, 167–68, 169, 221, 224, 246; Act (1782), 335, 336. See also Irish Concordatum Fund
Civil service: examinations in, 227; reform of, viii, 4, 10, 12–13, 13n, 151–53, 177. See also Foreign Office
Clancarty, Viscount. See Trench
Clanricarde, Marquess of. See de Burgh
Clanwilliam, Earl of. See Meade
Clarendon, Earl of. See Villiers
Cockburn, Alexander: biog., 271–72; as consul, 245
Cockburn, Admiral Sir George, 55–56, 272, 337
Coles, Augustus Leopold, biog., 272
Colonial Office: clerks in, 205, 206; consuls and, 245; history of, 152n, 177, 178n, 188n, 205; F.O. relations with, 8, 189, 264

Commerce: foreign policy and, 18, 21, 37–39, 100, 102, 231; secret service money and, 333, 338. *See also* Consular service

Commons, House of, 82, 95, 99, 105, 108–9, 110, 111, 112, 115, 118, 119, 120 145, 163; diplomatists in, 224, 224n, 228, reform of diplomatic service and, 215. *See also* Parliament

Congress system, 26–29, 107

Consular offices abroad, 330–31; on Barbary Coast, 245; at Calais, 252; at Circle of Lower Saxony, 246; at Constantinople, 245n; on French and Netherlands coasts, 252; at Geneva, 197; at Granville (Jersey), 251; at Leghorn, 250; at Leipzig, 250–51; at Liebau, 246; at Lisbon, 247; at Madeira, 246; at Marseilles, 252; at Naples, 252; at Nice and Brest, 252; at Odessa, 248n; in Poland, 252; in South America, 253; at Valencia, 245

Consular service, 3, 18, 45, 323; chaplains in, 249; circulars to, 157; Consular Act (1825) and, 196, 248–49; consuls prohibited from trading in, 332; duties of, 248, 251–53; fees charged on appointment to, 155, 247, 247n; F.O. clerks appointed to, 14, 180, 202, 250; history of, 244–45, 253n; merchants in, 246–47, 250; professionalism in, 250–51, 253, 258–59; ranks in, 245; reforms in, 248–49; salaries and emoluments in, 246, 249–50, 252. *See also* Appendix I, passim.; Bidwell, John; Consular offices abroad; Foreign Office, consular affairs in; Foreign Office, consular department in; Monarchy; Secretary of state

Constitutional bureaucracy. *See* Civil service

Conyngham, Lord Francis (Earl Mount Charles): biog., 272–73; as undersecretary, 124–25, 125n, 138, 322

Cooke, Edward: biog., 273; as undersecretary, 123–24, 125, 130–31, 132, 139, 141, 142

Corn Laws, repeal of, 254

Cornwallis, Charles (1st Marquess of Cornwallis), 166

Corsica, 102

Cowley, Baron. *See* Wellesley

Cowper, Charles Spencer, biog., 273

Cowper, George Augustus Frederick (Viscount Fordwich): biog., 273; as undersecretary, 143, 323

Crimean War, 25, 29, 37

Croker, John Wilson, 106, 301

Cuba, 240

Cumberland, Ernest Augustus 1st Duke of, 83

Darlot, Henry, 338

Dawkins, Clinton George Augustus: biog., 274; as diplomatist, 238

de Burgh, Ulick John (3d Marquess of Clanricarde): biog., 274, as cabinet minister, 139n; as undersecretary, 125, 126, 139, 322–23

Denmark, 55; British relations with, 24, 35–36, 60, 77, 135

Derby, Earl of. *See* Stanley

Devonshire, Duke of. *See* Cavendish

Diplomatic Service, 3, 18, 106, 199, 202; appointments in, 115, 227–33; cabinet deliberations and, 56; circulars and dispatches in, 157, 172, 187, 235–38, 238n; compared with consular service, 244–45; in eighteenth century, 8, 214–15, 226; expense of, 159, 215, 250; fees charged on appointment to, 155, 156, 157, 221–22, 247; F.O. clerks attached to, 179–80, 258; Jacobean, 215; private correspondence of diplomatists in, 109, 109n, 238–41; professionalism in, 215, 215n, 219–20, 258–59; qualities of personnel in, 225–27; ranks in, 214–20; representatives of foreign powers in London and, 98, 102, 105, 112, 140–41, 211–12, 233–34; salaries and emoluments in, 215, 218, 220–23, 250, 327–29; secret service and, 335–39; size of, 215–16; special missions in, 220; volume of business in, 217. *See also* Appendix I, passim.; Commons, House of; Foreign Office, agencies in; Missions abroad; Monarchy; Presents; Secretary of state; Superannuation

Disbrowe, Lady Edward, 223

Disbrowe, Sir Edward, 223; as diplomatist, 231, 231n

Disraeli, Benjamin, 3, 17, 59n, 251n, 266

Dorset, Duke of. *See* Sackville

Douglas, Andrew Snape, biog., 274–75

Dowling, Daniel Morton, biog., 275

Dundas, Henry (1st Viscount Melville), 52, 55, 64, 100, 117, 173, 278; in inner cabinet, 47, 102

Dundas, Robert (2d Viscount Melville), 117

Dudley, Earl of. *See* Ward

Dunglas, Lord. *See* Home

Durham, Earl of. *See* Lambton

Earle, Ralph, 17, 266

East India Company, 102–3, 157, 319. *See also* Board of Control; India

Eden, William (1st Baron Auckland), 137, 159; as diplomatist, 215, 220, 224, 224n, 226, 227, 233, 235, 236; secret service and, 334

Edwardes, Richard, biog., 275–76

Eldon, Earl of. See Scott

Eliot, William: biog., 276; as undersecretary, 139, 142n

Ellenborough, Earl of. See Law

Elliot, Sir Gilbert (1st Earl of Minto), as diplomatist, 228

Elliot, Gilbert (2d Earl of Minto), as diplomatist, 226

Elliot, Henry George, biog., 276

Ellis, Charles, 136

Ellis, Charles Augustus (6th Baron Howard de Walden), 52, 114, 293; biog., 276; as diplomatist, 230; as undersecretary, 124–25, 136–37, 322–23

Esterhazy, Prince, 82

Ewart, Joseph, 224

Excise Office, 146, 149; Receivers General in, 147

Fagan, Mr. Consul, 252

Fane, John (10th Earl of Westmorland), 58

Ferdinand VII, King, 337

Fisher, Edward: biog., 276–77; as undersecretary, 146

Fitzharris, Viscount. See Harris

Fitzherbert, Alleyne (1st Baron St. Helens), 246

Fitzroy, Augustus Henry (3d Duke of Grafton), 60, 126

Flanders, 45

Fleetwood, Hesketh, 251n

Flint, Charles William, biog., 277

Florence, 102

Forbes, John, 170; biog., 278

Fordwich, Viscount. See Cowper

Foreign Office: accommodations in, 15, 110, 295; agencies in, 164, 166–69, 198–99, 205–6, 206n, 209, 210, 325; cabinet room in, 52–53, 53n; chief clerks department in, 134–35, 154–57, 163n, 167, 189–93, 194, 197, 210, 222; clerks assistant in, 120, 203–7, 258; consular affairs in, 129, 185; consular department in, 177, 195–97, 206, 244, 258; decypherer in, 211–12, 235; duties of clerks in, 54, 86–87, 156, 157–59, 171, 177, 188–89, 197, 203–7, 212; history of, 3, 10, 154n; librarians department in, 172–74, 208–11; lithographic press in, 195; locations of, 17–18; précis writers in, 119, 170, 171–72, 207–8; private sec-

retaries in, 119, 170–71, 207–8; qualities of clerks in, 15–17; reforms in, viii, 11–15, 14n, 102–4, 106, 115–17, 144–46, 151–54, 155–56, 177–86, 189, 203–7, 257–58; relations of clerks with secretaries of state in, 100, 101, 104–5, 107, 110, 115, 118–19, 200–1; salaries and emoluments of clerks in, 103, 144, 156–57, 159–69, 177–78, 180–82, 184–86, 194, 195, 196, 202, 203, 206, 326; slave trade department in, 133n, 177, 197–201, 206, 258; supernumerary clerks in, 179, 187; treaty department in, 193–95, 202, 206; volume of business in, 110–11, 118–19, 125, 158, 162, 179, 185–89, 204, 208, 257, 323. See also Appendix I, passim.; Civil service; Consular service; Diplomatic service; Presents; Secretary of state; Superannuation; Undersecretaries

Foreign Office List, undersecretaryship and, 127

Foreign secretaryship. See Secretary of state

Forster, Henry Francis, biog., 278

Fox, Charles James, 4, 10, 17, 45, 50, 77, 102, 105, 116, 126, 153; biog., 278; diplomatic service and, 240; F.O. reforms and, 175, 256; F.O. undersecretaryship and, 127, 137, 146, 148; as foreign secretary, 98–99, 154; secret service and, 338

Fox, Elizabeth (Lady Holland), 50

Fox, Henry Richard Vassal (3d Baron Holland), 53, 58; cabinet influence of, 50–51, 61

Fox's India Bill (1783), 99

Fox-Strangways, Thomas, 119; biog., 278; as undersecretary, 125, 129, 133n, 138, 141–42, 148, 190, 323

France, 50, 58, 64–65, 68, 89–90, 97, 159, 165, 209, 334; British relations with, 23–24, 27, 29–30, 32–33, 34, 37–39, 54–55, 61–62, 73, 74–75, 76, 85, 86, 88, 93–94, 136, 166, 197, 227, 231, 240, 241, 254; Foreign Office of, 154n; foreign service of, 223; July monarchy of, 32; naval activity of, 252; revolutionary and Napoleonic wars with, vii, 6, 20–21, 24–26, 101–2, 112, 163, 175, 215–16, 220, 335; rivalry in Africa with, 8, 200; royalist refugees from, 337, 338; slave trade and, 49, 51

Frankfort, Diet of (1832), 90–91

Franklin, George Fairfax, biog., 278

Fraser, John Henry David, biog., 279

Fraser, William, 23, 99, 158, 159, 225; biog., 279; as Translator of the German Language, 175; as undersecretary, 124,

125–26, 126n, 136, 137, 142, 144
Frederick, Prince of Wales, 164
Frere, George, biog., 279–80
Frere, John Hookham, 186; biog., 280; as
  diplomatist, 230, 247; as undersecretary,
  142n, 148, 148n
Friquetti, M., 336

Gascoyne-Cecil, Robert Arthur Talbot (3d
  Marquess of Salisbury), 96, 153
George I, King, court of, 66n
George III, King, 5–6, 10, 23, 54–55, 56,
  80, 84, 88, 94, 99, 105, 106, 112, 158–59,
  214, 221; diplomatic service and, 230,
  237; as Elector of Hanover, 76; F.O.
  undersecretaryship and, 142n, 279;
  foreign policy and, 72–74, 75–76, 255;
  personality of, 71–72, 72n; relations of
  ministers with, 66, 66n, 67–69, 74–75, 77
George IV, King, 5–6, 55, 57, 88, 89, 91,
  94, 109, 116, 177, 178, 221, 272–73; diplomatic service and, 230, 237, 239; F.O.
  undersecretaryship and, 139; foreign policy and, 77–79, 255; as King of Hanover,
  76, 79; personality of, 77, 77n, 81–82,
  187; relations of ministers with, 69–70,
  79–81, 82–83
German Language, Translators of, 144, 175
Gifford Edward Scott, biog., 280
Gladstone, William E., 59n
Glenelg, Baron. See Grant
Goddard, Charles: attachment to Lord
  Grenville of, 172–73; biog., 280–81; F.O.
  agencies of, 167
Goderich, Viscount. See Robinson
Gordon, Sir Robert, as diplomatist, 229
Goulburn, Henry, 117, 149, 199
Government departments: influence on
  foreign policy of, 8. See also Admiralty;
  Colonial Office; Home Office; Law Of-
  ficers; Treasury
Grafton, Duke of. See Fitzroy
Graham, David, biog., 281
Graham, Sir James, 5
Grant, Charles (1st Baron Glenelg), 189
Grantham, Baron. See Robinson.
Granville, Earl. See Leveson-Gower
Greece, 93, 188; British cabinet and, 44, 51,
  56, 114; British interest in, 36, 82–83,
  136; George IV on, 81, 82
Green, Alfred Schrimshire, biog., 281
Grenada, 160
Grenville, Thomas, 297
Grenville, William Wyndham (1st Baron
  Grenville), 17, 24, 51, 52, 54, 55, 56, 58,
  60, 64, 73, 74, 76, 100, 116, 117, 123n,

130, 136, 140, 313; biog., 281; consular
  service and, 247; F.O. reforms and,
  102–4, 155, 158, 163, 164, 165, 167, 170,
  171–73, 184; F.O. undersecretaryship
  and, 125, 137–38, 141, 146, 147–48;
  foreign policy of, 101–2; as foreign secretary, 101–4, 106n, 111, 256; in inner
  cabinet, 47–48, 102; ministry of, 142n; se-
  ret service and, 335, 336
Greville, Algernon Frederick, biog., 282
Greville, Henry William, biog., 282
Grey, Charles (Viscount Howick and 2d Earl
  Grey), 36, 45, 51–52, 59, 63–64, 85,
  86–87, 89, 103, 116, 127, 143; biog., 282;
  diplomatic service and, 229, 240; F.O. reforms and, 163; as foreign secretary, 105;
  ministry of, 9, 50, 90, 98, 120, 145, 228,
  328

Hailes, Daniel, as diplomatist, 232
Hamilton, Hamilton Charles James, as diplomatist, 237
Hamilton, Thomas (Lord Binning), F.O.
  undersecretaryship and, 138n
Hamilton, William John, biog., 282
Hamilton, William Richard, 300; biog., 282;
  as private secretary and précis writer,
  172; as undersecretary, 127, 129n, 131,
  141, 142, 149, 162, 178, 190
Hamilton-Gordon, Alexander, biog., 282
Hamilton-Gordon, George (4th Earl of
  Aberdeen), 15, 17–18, 45, 49, 50, 51, 53,
  62, 63, 64, 70–71, 80, 81, 81n, 84, 91–92,
  120, 125, 128, 128n, 134, 187, 200, 201,
  208, 209, 229, 274, 285; biog., 282; consular service and, 197, 250; diplomatic
  service and, 219, 226, 230, 231, 234, 237,
  238, 239, 328; F.O. reforms and, 115–17,
  187–88, 189–90, 196, 212, 324n; F.O.
  undersecretaryship and, 149; foreign policy of, 28–29, 30, 32, 33–34, 37, 38,
  82–83; as foreign secretary, 104, 114–15,
  256; secret service and, 333, 333n, 339
Hammond, Edmund (1st Baron Hammond), 15, 119n, 203, 292, 338; biog.,
  282; as senior clerk, 207, 323; as undersecretary, 149, 265
Hammond, George: biog., 283; secret service and, 334–35; as undersecretary, 127,
  127n, 130, 131, 131n, 136, 138, 141, 142,
  146, 148
Hanover, 55, 109; British agent in, 337;
  diplomatic service of, 237; German Office
  in London of, 76. See also George III;
  George IV; William IV
Hardwicke, Earl of. See Yorke

Harley, Robert (1st Earl of Oxford), 42
Harris, Sir James (1st Earl of Malmesbury), 23, 55, 58, 77, 136; as diplomatist, 215, 217, 226n, 240, 243, 335
Harris, James Edward (Viscount Fitzharris), 110; biog., 283; as undersecretary 135–36, 142n
Harrowby, Earl of. *See* Ryder
Hart, Mr. Consul, 250–51
Hawkesbury, Baron. *See* Jenkinson
Hay, Elizabeth and Sarah, 169
Hay, William, 169; biog., 283–84
Hertslet, Sir Edward, 211; biog., 284
Hertslet, James, 174, 180, 209, 210; biog., 284
Hertslet, Lewis: biog., 284–85; *British and Foreign State Papers* and, 210; as F.O. Librarian, 174, 208–11
Hervey, Frederick William (Lord Hervey): biog., 285; as undersecretary, 142n
Hervey, Lord William, biog., 285
Hesse-Cassel, 165
Heytesbury, Baron. *See* A'Court
Hiertzelet, Lewis, as King's messenger, 174
Hill, Lord Arthur Marcus Cecil: biog., 285–86; as diplomatist, 230–31
Hinchliffe, John, 169; biog., 286
Hobhouse, Henry, 117
Hole, John Boger, biog., 286
Holland, Baron. *See* Fox
Holland, John, biog., 286–87
Home, Cospatrick Alexander (Lord Dunglas): biog., 287; as undersecretary, 128n, 323
Home Office, 10, 97, 102, 103n, 116–17, 172, 173, 277, 283; clerks in, 162, 205, 206
Hoppner, Richard Belgrave, biog., 287–88
Howard, J.H., as diplomatist, 231n
Howard, James Kenneth, biog., 288
Howard de Walden, Baron. *See* Ellis
Howick, Viscount. *See* Grey
Hunter, John, 245
Huskisson, William, 52, 104, 136, 289, 296
Huskisson, William Milbanke, biog., 288–89
Hüttner, John Christian, 175; biog., 289

India, 128; mutiny (1859), 139n. *See also* Board of Control; East India Company
Ionian Islands, 35; consuls and, 248
Ireland: Act of Union with, 130; franking privileges to, 157, 160
Irish Concordatum Fund, 102, 144, 145. *See also* Civil List
Irving, Francis, biog., 289

Jackson, Francis James: biog., 289; as diplomatist, 220, 235–36
Jackson, George, 267; as diplomatist, 224
Jackson, John, 196; biog., 289–90
Jenkins, John Warham, 169; biog., 290
Jenkinson, Sir Charles (1st Earl of Liverpool), 105n
Jenkinson, Charles Cecil Cope, biog., 290
Jenkinson, Robert Banks (Baron Hawkesbury and 2d Earl of Liverpool), 32, 33, 34, 54, 55, 58, 63, 100, 108, 109, 113, 117, 121, 128, 130, 132, 136, 186, 308; biog., 290; consular service and, 246; diplomatic service and, 219, 228, 243; F.O. reforms and, 163, 164, 170, 175, 184; as foreign secretary, 104–5, 105n; in inner cabinet, 47–48; ministry of, 28, 48, 57–58, 80–81, 108; secret service and, 335
Johnson, William, biog., 290

Keinitz, Francis, 246
Keith, Sir Robert Murray, 336
Kerr, John William Robert (Earl of Ancram), biog., 290
Knighton, Sir William, 81, 88n
Kuper, Henry George, biog., 291

Lamb, Frederick: as diplomatist, 229, 237; F.O. undersecretaryship and, 138n
Lamb, Thomas Davis, biog., 291
Lamb, William (2d Viscount Melbourne), 64, 64n, 98, 307; diplomatic service and, 229, 230; F.O. undersecretaryship and, 150; ministry of, 30, 50, 61–62, 97, 120, 143
Lambton, John (1st Earl of Durham), 64; as diplomatist, 232
Lansdowne, Marquess of. *See* Petty-Fitzmaurice
Latin America, 63, 125, 221; British interest in, 28, 38–39, 215, 254; British relations with various states of, 57, 58, 78–79, 80–81, 113, 121, 187
Law, Edward (1st Earl of Ellenborough), 45, 50, 53, 230, 333
Law Officers of the Crown: F.O. relations with, 140, 200; secret service and, 336
Lawrence, Sir Thomas, 100
Leeds, Duke of. *See* Osborne
Le Mesurier, John James, biog., 291–92
Lennox, Charles (3d Duke of Richmond), 60
Lenox-Conyngham, George William, 179, 180n, 203, 204, 207; biog., 292; as chief clerk, 134–35, 193–95, 206; as senior clerk, 185, 191–93, 193n, 202, 323

Leopold I, King, 81, 81n, 82–83, 93
Levant. *See* Turkey
Levant Company, 245
Leveson-Gower, Granville (1st Marquess of Stafford), 60
Leveson-Gower, Granville (1st Earl Granville), 44, 54, 81, 100, 110, 146, 167, 186, 201; as diplomatist, 168, 202, 222, 222n, 226, 236, 237, 239, 241, 274
Leveson-Gower, Granville George (Lord Leveson), 295, 316–17; biog., 292; as foreign secretary, 265; as undersecretary, 139, 143, 148, 192–93, 199, 274, 323–24
Leveson-Gower, Henrietta (Countess Granville), 114, 201, 261, 262, 269, 274, 278
Liddell, Henry Thomas, biog., 292–93
Lieven, Prince and Princess, 82, 234
Liverpool, Earls of. *See* Jenkinson
Liverpool Office, in London, 128
Lloyd's insurance company, 252
London Conference (1830), 29, 45
London Gazette, 103, 145, 162–63, 182; Gazette Writer and Gazette Printer in office of, 117, 144
Londonderry, Marquesses of. *See* Stewart
Lord Chamberlain's Department, 155, 266
Lords, House of, 43n, 101, 115, 242. *See also* Parliament
Loughborough, Baron. *See* Wedderburn
Lovell, John Hervey, 212; biog., 293
Low Countries. *See* Belgium; Netherlands
Lowth, George Thomas, biog., 293
Lushington, Stephen, 246
Lyons, Edmund, 45

Macaulay, Thomas Babington (1st Baron Macaulay), 310
McMahon, Edward, 15, 207; biog., 293
Maddison, George, biog., 293–94
Mahon, Viscount. *See* Stanhope
Malmesbury, Earl of. *See* Harris
Manby, James, 15, 160; biog., 294
Manchester, Duke of. *See* Montagu
Mandeville, John Henry, as diplomatist, 237
Mann, Lucius Edward, biog., 294
Masterton, Charles, 175n; biog., 294–95
Meade, Richard Charles (3d Earl of Clanwilliam): biog., 295; as undersecretary, 127n, 139
Mecklenburgh, Prince Charles of, 83
Mecklenburgh-Strelitz, Grand Duke of, 83
Mehemet Ali, 36–37, 61
Melbourne, Viscount. *See* Lamb
Mellish, Joseph Charles, 246
Mellish, Richard Charles, 15–16, 203, 338; biog., 295–96; as senior clerk, 207, 323

Melville, Viscounts. *See* Dundas
Merry, Anthony, 247
Messenger corps: duties of, 53, 116, 209–10, 234–35, 236; supervision of, 155, 162, 209, 211
Metternich, Prince, 27, 29, 30, 34, 82, 89, 90, 108, 123, 136
Miguel, Don, 239
Milbanke, John Ralph: biog., 296; as diplomatist, 219
Mildmay, Hugo Cornwall St. John, 207; biog., 296
Minto, Earls of. *See* Elliot
Missions abroad: F.O. control over, 241–43; F.O. divisions supervising, 321–24; at Berlin, 220; at Constantinople, 215n, 222, 223, 227, 227n, 243, 248n; at Frankfort, 148, 219; at The Hague, 216–17; at Lisbon, 224, 247; at Madrid, 214n, 224, 236; at Naples, 220; at Paris, 214, 216, 222–23, 228, 234, 236, 238–39, 252; in Persia, 243; at St. Petersburg, 214n, 226, 228, 234, 248n; at Vienna, 228, 234; at Washington D.C., 140, 220. *See also* Diplomatic service
Molyneux, Francis George: biog., 296–97; as diplomatist, 219
Monarchy: foreign policy and, 3, 5–7, 45, 66–95, 101, 153–54, 239; "influence of the Crown" and, 152, 255–56, 257; patronage in consular service and, 251; patronage in diplomatic service and, 230–31, 232
Money, William, 15, 169; biog., 297
Montagu, George (4th Duke of Manchester), as diplomatist, 232
Moore, Francis, 16, 159, 166; biog., 297–98
Morier, Greville, biog., 298
Mount Charles, Lord. *See* Conyngham
Mount Stewart (also Mount Stuart), Viscount. *See* Stuart
Mulgrave, Earl of. *See* Phipps
Municipal Corporations Act (1835), 4
Münster, Count, 79
Murat, 252
Murray, Mr. Consul, 246
Murray, David (7th Viscount Stormont), 56, 102, 154; as diplomatist, 337
Murray, James, 194, 196; as assistant undersecretary, 107; biog., 298

Naples, 27
Napoleon I, Emperor, 97, 216, 337
Navarino Bay, defeat at, 114
Navy, foreign policy and, 22, 25, 37
Netherlands, 51, 74, 165, 220; British rela-

tions with, 24, 32–33, 77, 88, 133, 147, 216–17, 231n, 335; King of, 89, 217
New South Wales, colony of, 168
Nicholas I, Emperor, 35, 64, 90, 220, 230, 232–33, 234
Noel, Charles Noel, biog., 298–99
Noel-Hill, William: F.O. undersecretaryship and, 138n
Northcote-Trevelyan Report, 151
Northern Department, 8, 11, 98, 126, 129, 154, 158, 160

Oakley, Charles, 224
Oom, Adolphus Kent, biog., 299
Orleans, Duke of, 339
Osborne, Francis Godolphin (Marquess of Carmarthen and 5th Duke of Leeds), 17, 35, 45, 46–47, 59n, 60, 101, 143, 158, 161; biog., 299; diplomatic service and, 217, 232, 233–34; F.O. reform and, 170; F.O. undersecretaryship and, 124, 125, 126, 137–38; as foreign secretary, 99–100; secret service and, 338

Paget, Sir Arthur, as diplomatist, 167, 168, 235, 243
Paget, Augustus Berkeley, biog., 299
Palmerston, Viscount. See Temple
Parish, Henry Headley, 274; biog., 300
Parish, Sir Woodbine, 166, 203, 339; biog., 300
Parliament, 6, 43, 46–47, 128, 152, 153, 159, 189, 190, 193, 197, 198, 201, 226, 228, 236; Chartist petition and (1848), 134; civil service reform and, 151–52, 161–62, 166, 167, 169–70, 177n, 178, 183, 205; consular service and, 251; diplomatic service and, 233, 251; F.O. undersecretaries in, 137, 142–43; foreign policy and, 7–8, 59–60, 62, 87, 111–13, 115, 120, 162, 187–88; printed votes of, 163, 182; secret service and, 335, 336; selection of ministers and, 69–71
Parnther, Charles Henry, biog., 300
Passmore, Udney, 14; biog., 300–1
Patent Office, 103
Peel, Sir Robert (2d Bart.), 30, 32, 45, 49, 50, 51, 52, 59, 62, 65, 86, 117, 120, 199, 250; diplomatic service and, 226, 228, 229, 237; foreign policy and, 115, 256; ministry of (1834–35), 97–98, 121–22, 233; ministry of (1841–46), viii, 44, 200–1
Pennell, John Croker, biog., 301
Perceval, Spencer, 63, 106, 127
Pettingal, Charles, 116, 198; biog., 301
Petty-Fitzmaurice, Henry (3d Marquess of

Lansdowne), 51, 54, 61, 138, 148, 269
Petty-Fitzmaurice, William (2d Earl of Shelburne), ministry of, 46
Phipps, Henry (1st Earl of Mulgrave), 54, 105, 116, 172; biog., 301; diplomatic service and, 228; F.O. undersecretaryship and, 146; as foreign secretary, 100–1
Pierrepont, Henry Manvers, biog., 301–2
Pitt, William (1st Earl of Chatham), 9
Pitt, William, 17, 45, 51, 55, 59, 60, 64, 75–76, 97, 99, 104, 105, 111, 136, 143; diplomatic service and, 217, 224n, 238n; F.O. undersecretaryship and, 125, 130, 137–38, 146, 147, 263; foreign policy and, 100, 101–2, 256; in inner cabinet, 47, 102; ministry of (1783–1801), 23, 44, 54, 65, 69, 80, 141; ministry of (1803–5), 228; secret service and, 337
Planta, Joseph, 14, 52, 128, 166, 180, 181, 183, 186, 195, 246, 273, 274, 300–1, 304, 306; biog., 302; as private secretary and précis writer, 171, 172; as undersecretary, 124, 127, 127n, 129n, 131–32, 140, 145, 149, 178, 179, 210, 321–22, 323
Poland, 64, 130
Political parties, development of, vii, 6–7, 66, 69, 95, 151, 256, 257
Ponsonby, John (1st Viscount Ponsonby), as diplomatist, 229
Ponsonby, John George Brabazon, biog., 302
Ponsonby, Spencer Cecil Brabazon, 120n; biog., 302–3
Porter, Sir Robert, as diplomatist, 238
Portland, Dukes of. See Cavendish-Bentinck
Portugal, 102, 148; British relations with, 30, 37–38, 38n, 39–40, 55, 57, 64
Post Office, 103, 145, 157, 159, 161, 211
Pozzo di Borgo, Count, 90
Presents: ratification of treaties and, 103, 145, 164–66, 184–85, 188, 214n, 223
Prime minister: foreign policy and, 44, 46, 52, 59, 63–65, 65n, 128, 239, 256; general authority of, 66; patronage in diplomatic service and, 229–30
Pringle, Joseph, 246
Privy Seal Office, 157, 189
Prussia, 60, 74, 90, 165; British relations with, 24, 27, 29, 32, 33–34, 47, 61, 83, 101, 220; King of, 83

Quick, William F., 120n; biog., 303

Reform Act (1832), 4, 6–7, 70, 120
Regnier, James, 337
Richmond, Duke of. See Lennox

Robinson, Frederick John (1st Viscount
Goderich), 136; ministry of, 55
Robinson, Henry Stirling, biog., 303
Robinson, Thomas (2d Baron Grantham),
23; biog., 303; diplomatic service and,
232; as foreign secretary, 99
Rockingham, Marquess of. See Watson-
Wentworth
Rolleston, Henry John, 117, 166, 204, 325n;
biog., 303–4; as senior clerk, 162, 193–
94; as Translator of the German Lan-
guage, 175
Rolleston, Stephen, 16, 162, 175; biog., 304,
as chief clerk, 156, 166, 189, 190; as
senior clerk, 157–58, 203
Rosas, Señor, 337
Rose, George, 105
Ross, James Tyrell, 171; biog., 304
Ruperti, Christian, 175; biog., 304–5
Russell, John (4th Duke of Bedford), 154
Russell, Lord John, 53, 61–62, 92, 269;
ministry of (1846–52), viii
Russia, 39, 55, 89, 90; British relations with,
27, 29, 32, 34–37, 54, 61, 86, 252, 254;
Ochakov crisis and, 24, 34–35, 59–60,
100
Russillion, Major, 337
Ryder, Dudley (1st Earl of Harrowby), 116,
127; biog., 305; cabinet influence of, 44,
49–50; as diplomatist, 220; F.O. reforms
and, 170; F.O. undersecretaryship and,
138; as foreign secretary, 100, 101, 105;
as undersecretary, 137–38, 139, 142,
142n
Ryder, Frederick Dudley, biog., 305

Sackville, John Frederick (3d Duke of Dor-
set), as diplomatist, 232
Salisbury, Marquesses of. See Cecil;
Gascoyne-Cecil
Sasse, Frederick Richard, biog., 305
Saunders, Sydney Smith, 196; biog., 305–6
Scheener, Edward, 180n; biog., 306
Scott, Charles, 116; biog., 306–7
Scott, Henry Charles, 307
Scott, Henry Dundas, 189–90; biog., 307
Scott, John (1st Earl of Eldon), 58
Scott, Sir Walter, 116, 307n
Seale, Robert Bewick, 120n; biog., 307
Sebastiani, General, 233
Secret service: general account of, 333–39;
payment of F.O. personnel from accounts
of, 160, 190, 210, 211–12; payments for,
133, 160, 190; in wars with France, 102
Secretary of state: F.O. patronage of, 115–
17, 119–20, 131, 137–39; history of posi-

tion of, viii, 3, 8–9, 96–99, 102–4;
influence in cabinet of, 44, 45, 63–65,
256–57; patronage in consular service of,
251; patronage in diplomatic service of,
227–32; salary and emoluments of,
102–4, 162. See also individual secretaries
of state
Settlement, Act of (1701), 19
Seymour, George Hamilton, biog., 307
Shee, Sir George, 292; biog., 307–8; as diplomatist, 219; as undersecretary, 123n,
132–33, 139, 141, 143, 145, 323
Shelburne, Earl of. See Petty-Fitzmaurice
Sheridan, Richard Brinsley: biog., 308; as
undersecretary, 137, 142n, 146
Sicily, 100
Sidmouth, Viscount. See Addington
Simolin, Monsieur, 233–34
Skelton, George, biog., 308
Slave trade, 5, 28, 30, 39–40, 323; Aber-
deen's Act (1845) and, 200; abolitionists'
relations with F.O. on, 231; consuls and,
248; Five Power Treaty (1841) and, 49.
See also Foreign Office, slave trade de-
partment
Smith, Culling Charles: biog., 308–9; as
undersecretary, 139
Smith, George, biog., 309
Smythe, George Sydney, biog., 309
Sneyd, Jeremy: biog., 309; as chief clerk,
137, 154–55, 157
Somerville, William Meredyth, biog., 309
Southern Department, 8, 11, 126, 129, 158,
160
Spain, 21n, 27, 85, 93–94, 106, 165, 209;
British relations with, 30, 37–38, 38n,
39–40, 57, 87, 160, 241
Spanish succession, war of, 42
Spencer, Lord Henry, as diplomatist, 223,
236
Spencer, John Charles (Viscount Althorp),
328
Spring-Rice, Charles William, biog., 309–10
Stafford, Marquess of. See Leveson-Gower
Stalberg, Princess of, 338
Stanhope, Philip Henry (Viscount Mahon):
biog., 310; as undersecretary, 143, 251,
323
Stanley, Edward Geoffrey (14th Earl of
Derby), 59n
Stapleton, Augustus Granville, biog., 310
State Paper Office: Collector and Transmit-
ter of State Papers in, 117, 172; Keeper
of State Papers in, 117, 172–73; patron-
age in, 173
Staveley, Thomas, 179, 203; biog., 310; as

senior clerk, 193, 206, 323, 324
Staveley, Thomas George, biog., 311
Stewart, Charles William (Baron Stewart &
3rd Marquess of Londonderry), 56; as
diplomatist, 225, 233
Stewart, Robert (Viscount Castlereagh and
2d Marquess of Londonderry), 56, 82,
106, 110, 123, 125, 128, 141, 143, 166,
184, 225; biog., 311; consular service and,
245, 248; diplomatic service and, 216,
217–18, 224–25, 228, 234, 235; F.O. reforms and, 162, 169, 174, 177–83, 187,
190, 205, 212; F.O. undersecretaryship
and, 130–31, 137; foreign policy of, 22,
25–27, 31–32, 33, 34, 35, 78; as foreign
secretary, 97, 106–9, 112, 256; in inner
cabinet, 48
St. Helens, Baron. See Fitzherbert
St. John, St. Andrew: biog., 311; as undersecretary, 126, 137, 139, 142n, 146
Stopford, William Bruce, biog., 311
Stormont, Viscount. See Murray
Stratford de Redcliffe, Viscount. See Can-
ning
Stuart, Sir Charles (1st Baron Stuart de
Rothsay), 167, 168n; as diplomatist, 226,
229, 230, 237, 252, 337
Stuart, Henry Benedict, as Cardinal of
York, 338
Stuart, John (3d Earl of Bute), 71n
Stuart, John (Viscount Mount Stuart [also
Mount Stewart]), as diplomatist, 232
Stuart de Rothsay, Baron. See Stuart
Stuart Kings: foreign policy of, 19; as Pre-
tenders, 20, 338
Sulivan, Stephen Henry, biog., 312
Sundersberg, M., 336–37
Superannuation: Acts of (1810), 169–70,
224; (1817), 149; (1822), 149, 153, 182–
83, 249; consuls and, 247; diplomatists
and, 224–25, 225n; F.O. clerks and,
169–70, 182–84, 190, 200–1, 202–3; un-
dersecretaries and, 146–47, 149; secret
service and, 337–38
Sussex, Augustus Frederick 1st Duke of, 90
Sweden, 55; British relations with, 35–36;
King of, 223
Switzerland, 335
Synge, William Webb Follett, biog., 312

Talbot, Robert, 312
Talleyrand, Prince, 108, 123, 133
Taylor, Bridges, biog., 312–13
Taylor, Sir Brook: biog., 313; as private sec-
retary and précis writer, 172
Taylor, Col. Sir Herbert, 129–30; biog.,

313; as F.O. clerk, 158, 159; as King's
private secretary, 88–89
Taylor, William Watkinson, biog., 313
Temple, Henry John (3d Viscount Palmerston), 4, 9, 12, 17, 44, 45, 46, 47,
50–52, 53–54, 57, 63–64, 64n, 85–86, 89,
90–93, 97, 123, 123n, 128, 140, 142, 143,
153, 186, 187, 199, 208, 219, 268, 269,
312; biog., 313; consular service and, 249,
250–51, 287–88; diplomatic service and,
216, 218, 220, 223, 227–28, 229–30,
232–33, 235, 236, 237, 238–39, 241, 242,
243, 328; F.O. reforms and, 152, 177,
184–85, 185n, 188, 190–93, 194, 203–7,
209, 210–11, 212, 323; F.O. undersecretaryship and, 132–33, 133n, 139, 144n,
145, 148; foreign policy of, 28–31, 32,
34, 35, 36, 37, 39–40, 61–62, 200; as
foreign secretary, 97, 98, 104, 110, 115,
117–20, 189, 256; newspaper press and,
120–21; secret service and, 335
Temple, William: biog., 314
Thurlow, Edward (1st Baron Thurlow),
54, 60
Times (London), 120–21
Treasury, 12n, 103, 156, 160, 166, 167–68,
169; consular service and, 244, 246, 252;
F.O. relations with, 124–25, 149, 153,
170, 177–85, 189, 197, 199, 202, 205–6,
221–22, 222n, 264; supervision of other
departments and, 120, 177, 177n, 207,
224
Trench, Richard le Poer (1st Viscount Clancarty), as diplomatist, 217, 218, 235
Trotter, John Bernard, 99n, 315; biog., 314
Tupper, Mr. Consul, 245
Turkey, 28–29, 56, 58, 83, 89; British rela-
tions with, 35, 36–37, 60–62, 136, 240
Turner, Adolphus, 251; biog., 314
Turner, William, 180; biog., 314–15

Undersecretaries of state: duties of, 52, 72,
91–92, 98, 101, 111, 120, 129–42, 157,
158, 188, 196, 197, 200, 203, 208, 236,
239, 240–41, 258, 321–24, 334–35;
foreign service appointments of, 141,
147–48, 150; other careers of, 139, 139n,
150; pensions and other retirement provisions for, 146–49; permanent undersecretaryship and, 124, 124n, 126–29,
132–35; policy making and, 135–37; position in government of, 9–10, 123–28,
149–50, 162, 257; salary and emoluments
of, 103, 144–46, 164–65, 166, 184n, 211;
social standing of, 139; third undersecretaryship and, 124–25. See also Foreign

Office List; individual undersecretaries of state

Urquhart, David, 338

Vansittart, Nicholas, 168, 182n
Vatican, British relations with, 141
Vaughan, Sir Charles Richard: biog., 315; as diplomatist, 241
Vergennes, Charles Comte de, 334
Verona, Congress of (1822), 109
Victoria, Queen, viii, 5–7, 57, 83, 95, 114; diplomatic service and, 226, 231, 231n; foreign policy and, 93–94, 255; personality of, 92–93; relations of ministers with, 66, 67–68, 70–71, 91–92
Vienna, Congress and Treaty of (1815), 26–27, 30, 107, 141, 162; F.O. staff at peace negotiations of, 16, 130–31
Villiers, George William (4th Earl of Clarendon), 87, 92; as diplomatist, 226
Vincent, Sir Francis: biog., 315; as undersecretary, 127, 127n
von Gentz, Friedrich, 337, 337n

Walmisley, Arthur, biog., 315
Walpole, George: biog., 315; as undersecretary, 142n, 143
Walpole, Horace, 279
Walpole, John, biog., 315–16
War Office, 97, 102, 120
Ward, Edward Michael, biog., 316
Ward, John William (1st Earl of Dudley), 32, 45, 47, 49–50, 51, 52, 81, 116, 128n, 186, 208; biog., 316; diplomatic service and, 237; F.O. reforms and, 212; F.O. undersecretaryship and, 138n, 143; as foreign secretary, 97, 113–14; secret service and, 333n
Ward, Robert Plummer: biog., 316; as undersecretary, 142n, 146
Ward, Thomas Lawrence, 203; biog., 316–17; as senior clerk, 192, 207, 295, 323
Warren, Charles, biog., 317
Watson-Wentworth, Charles (2d Marquess of Rockingham): ministry of (1782), viii, 10, 23; Party of, 254
Webster-Ashburton Treaty (1842), 38
Wedderburn, Alexander (1st Baron Loughborough), 246
Wellesley, Arthur (1st Duke of Wellington), 30, 32, 35, 45, 47, 52, 55, 56, 58, 62, 63, 64, 80, 81, 81n, 82–83, 90, 104, 106, 112–13, 136–37, 143; biog., 317; consular service and, 251; diplomatic service and, 226, 229, 230, 231, 233, 239; as diplomatist, 216, 220; F.O. reforms and, 194, 204; as foreign secretary, 86, 97–98, 111, 121–22; in inner cabinet, 48–49; ministry of, 36, 44, 50, 114, 128–29, 234, 327–28; secret service and, 333n
Wellesley, Henry (1st Baron Cowley), 55, 277, 339; biog., 317; as diplomatist, 226, 228, 232
Wellesley, Richard Colley (1st Marquess Wellesley), 63, 79, 162, 170; biog., 317; F.O. reforms and, 174; F.O. undersecretaryship and, 127, 139; as foreign secretary, 106
Wellesley, Richard Gerald, 15; biog., 317
Wellington, Duke of. See Wellesley
Welsh, Col. Thomas, 146
Werry, Francis Peter, biog., 318
Westmorland, Earl of. See Fane
Wickham, William, 334, 335
William III, King, 19–20, 67, 214
William IV, King, 5–7, 57, 92, 94, 95, 97, 118, 223, 295; diplomatic service and, 230–31, 232; foreign policy and, 84n, 85–90, 255; as King of Hanover, 76, 90–91; personality of, 83–84, 84n; relations of ministers with, 69–70, 84, 84n, 85, 89, 204
Willis, Sir Francis, biog., 318
Willis, Francis, 211–12; biog., 318
Wilson, Robert, 318
Windham, William, 102, 337
Woodcock, Charles, 170; biog., 318–19
Woodford, John William Gordon, biog., 319
Wrangham, Digby Cayley, 207–8; biog., 319
Wylde, William Henry, biog., 319–20
Wynn, Henry Watkin Williams, biog., 320
Wynne, Thomas E., 320

York, Cardinal of. See Stuart
York, Frederick Augustus Duke of, 55, 84
Yorke, Philip (2d Earl of Hardwicke), 160
Yorkshire Association, 254
Yorktown, surrender at, 6, 22